BREAKING THE ACADEMIC MOULD

Breaking the Academic Mould

ECONOMISTS AND AMERICAN HIGHER LEARNING IN THE NINETEENTH CENTURY

Edited by William J. Barber

Contributors

RICHARD P. ADELSTEIN
WILLIAM J. BARBER
MICHAEL D. BORDO and WILLIAM H. PHILLIPS
A. W. COATS
MARY E. COOKINGHAM
JOHN P. HENDERSON
BYRD L. JONES
FRANEK ROZWADOWSKI
STEVEN A. SASS
JOHN K. WHITAKER

 Wesleyan University Press

MIDDLETOWN, CONNECTICUT

Copyright © 1988 by Wesleyan University

Library of Congress Cataloging-in-Publication Data

Breaking the academic mould.

Includes index.
1. Economics—Study and teaching (Higher)—United States—History—19th century. 2. Economists—United States—History—19th century.
I. Barber, William J.
HB74.8.B74 1988   330'.07'1173   87-21023
ISBN 0-8195-5176-7

All inquiries and permissions requests should be addressed to the Publisher, Wesleyan University Press, 110 Mt. Vernon Street, Middletown, Connecticut 06457.

Distributed by Harper & Row Publishers, Keystone Industrial Park, Scranton, Pennsylvania 18512.

Manufactured in the United States of America

First Edition

Contents

Preface   vii

1. Political Economy and the Academic Setting
   before 1900: An Introduction   3
   WILLIAM J. BARBER

2. Early Flowering in the Old Dominion: Political
   Economy at the College of William and Mary and the
   University of Virginia   15
   JOHN K. WHITAKER

3. Faithful Index to the Ambitions and Fortunes of the
   State: The Development of Political Economy at South
   Carolina College   42
   MICHAEL D. BORDO and WILLIAM H. PHILLIPS

4. Political Economy from the Top Down:
   Brown University   72
   WILLIAM J. BARBER

5. A Quest for National Leadership: Institutionalization of
   Economics at Harvard   95
   BYRD L. JONES

6. The Fortunes of Political Economy in an Environment of
   Academic Conservatism: Yale University   132
   WILLIAM J. BARBER

7. From Recitation Room to Research Seminar: Political
   Economy at Columbia University   169
   FRANEK ROZWADOWSKI

8. Political Economy in the Flagship of Postgraduate
Studies: The Johns Hopkins University   203
WILLIAM J. BARBER

9. An Uneasy Relationship: The Business Community
and Academic Economists at the University
of Pennsylvania   225
STEVEN A. SASS

10. Political Economy in an Atmosphere of Academic
Entrepreneurship: The University of Chicago   241
WILLIAM J. BARBER

11. Political Economy in the Far West: The University of
California and Stanford University   266
MARY E. COOKINGHAM

12. Mind and Hand: Economics and Engineering at the
Massachusetts Institute of Technology   290
RICHARD P. ADELSTEIN

13. Political Economy and the Service of the State: The
University of Wisconsin   318
JOHN P. HENDERSON

14. The Educational Revolution and the Professionalization
of American Economics   340
A. W. COATS

Notes   377

Index   453

Contributors   469

Preface

This volume represents the American contribution to a multination project dealing with the institutionalization of political economy in European, North American, and Japanese universities. Scholars from twelve countries have participated in this undertaking, which was organized on the initiative of the Research Centre in Political Economy and Society at King's College, Cambridge, England, and the Institute for the Study of the History of Economic Thought at the University of Florence, Italy. The findings of the national research teams are being published separately. The scholarship on each nation, however, has been enriched by exchanges between colleagues from other participating countries, particularly through discussions at a conference called for this purpose at San Miniato, Italy, in April 1986. All those involved are indebted to our Italian hosts for making arrangements which permitted national delegations to share the preliminary results of their work. Financial support from the William T. Rich Fund of Wesleyan University—which enabled American contributors to meet for planning sessions in Middletown, Connecticut, in July 1985—is also gratefully acknowledged.

There are many other debts to recognize. From his abundant learning, A. W. Coats has generously contributed detailed comments to strengthen every chapter. Among those who have read one or more chapters, the editor is especially grateful to Hugh Hawkins, David Potts, Richard Buel, Robert Wood, Stanley Lebergott, Robert Rosenbaum, Ronald Schatz, and Merton J. Peck. None of the above should be held responsible for any errors that may remain. Special commendation is in order to Frances Warren and Joan Halberg for their dedication and skill in converting draft copy into press-worthy typescript.

William J. Barber

BREAKING THE ACADEMIC MOULD

1

Political Economy and the Academic Setting before 1900: An Introduction

WILLIAM J. BARBER

Economists and their forebears (variously styled as moral philosophers, political scientists, or political economists) played an important role in the shaping of the American academic landscape in the nineteenth century. Some lobbied as faculty members for reforms that would open and widen space for "modern" subjects in the curriculum. As senior academic administrators, some were on the cutting edge of innovation in restructuring established colleges and universities or in designing new ones. Some were caught in fire storms for expressing controversial views, and the ensuing debates contributed to consciousness raising on a national scale about issues of academic freedom.

The case studies in this volume report on the experience of a number of institutions which, at one moment or another, have figured prominently in the annals of American higher education. The focus of attention is on the way the "dangerous science" of economics (as John Maynard Keynes would characterize it) became institutionalized within the educational system. Each institution has a story with its own unique features. Each story, in turn, throws light on some obscure corners in the history of American economic thought and in the history of higher education in the United States.

The approach to these issues in this volume is necessarily selective. Nevertheless, the institutions to which detailed attention is accorded differ in their seniority, in their sponsorship, in their self-defined objectives, and in their regional situations. Collectively, they reflect the pluralism of America.

THE PRE−CIVIL WAR CONTEXT

The first generation of colleges in colonial America borrowed heavily from English models (most particularly from Oxford and Cambridge) in shaping the program of studies and in modes of instruction.[1] Even so, there was something distinctive about academia in the New World. In the standard European pattern, colleges had tended to cluster and to collaborate in forming a university to which degree-awarding authority was assigned. American institutions, on the other hand, were geographically dispersed, and they conjoined the teaching and degree-granting functions. The description of America as "a land of neighborhood colleges" was a coinage of the nineteenth century when their numbers had mushroomed. But the phenomenon to which that phrase draws attention was in evidence before the American Revolution.

Long distances and difficulties in travel in the new continent no doubt contributed to the localism of American colleges. The resource deprivation of most newly founded institutions, in turn, left its mark on their organizational form. In the post-Reformation era, Old World universities had drawn educational "laymen" who represented the interests of church and state into their management. American institutions built on this pattern by vesting ultimate authority not in their faculties but in bodies labeled as the Board of Trustees, the Corporation, or the Fellows.[2] The institution's assets were the property of these entities, and its liabilities were their responsibility. This machinery for the conduct of business had stronger recommendations in America than elsewhere. Fledgling colleges were much in need of patrons and advocates. Survival depended on an ability to form a network of influential champions to push a college's cause, whether it be in campaigning for funding from church groups, legislatures, and affluent citizens or in arguing in the political arena for tax immunities and against the chartering of potential rivals.

In curricular matters, the early American colleges were generally faithful to European models. The handful of colleges founded before the American Revolution typically offered a prescribed menu of studies with emphasis on Latin and Greek, theological and biblical studies, and with some attention to mathematics. In addition, some exposure to moral philosophy was frequently provided in the final year of study for the baccalaureate degree, more often than not through lectures delivered by the college's president. Most instruction was provided by ordained clergymen or by young men oriented toward a career in the church. And, at the time, it seemed altogether proper that things should be done this way. The tender age of students—most of them matriculated at the age of fifteen— was understood as mandating that a college should provide a strict regimen of intellectual and moral discipline. Moreover, the content and style of instruction seemed to be ideally suited to the subsequent careers of college graduates, a substantial fraction of whom were destined for the ministry.

Nor did this pattern change significantly in the first several decades of America's life as an independent nation. New institutions were founded, the majority of them in states that had not earlier had a college on their own turf. Some of the new entrants were brought into being with sponsorship from state governments. Technically, this was a novelty: All of the colonial colleges (save the University of Pennsylvania) had been spawned by religious interests. Even so, the dividing line between church and state institutions remained elusive in the early decades of the nineteenth century. Harvard and Yale—though church-sponsored—were the beneficiaries of tax moneys, appropriations that seemed natural when the governments of Massachusetts and Connecticut were committed to promoting an established church. The University of North Carolina, on the other hand, was set up by civil authorities. But when the state government was dominated by particular religious groups, tests of orthodoxy could be as rigorous there as in colleges that were formally "clerical" in orientation.

Within this framework, there was little scope for absorbing new fields of study—such as political economy—into the instructional program. One might have imagined that Adam Smith's support for the American colonists, articulated in *The Wealth of Nations* in 1776, would have won him an instant audience. Though he had appreciative readers, few of the men of the cloth who presided over the tuition of the collegiate population were among them. Smith was read at the College of William and Mary in the late eighteenth century.[3] Elsewhere, his work made little dent in the traditional curriculum. Not only were the producers of higher learning generally content with the inherited pattern; they also suspected that Smith was unsound on matters of religious doctrine.

The decade of the 1820s witnessed a significant change in the national climate. To borrow an overworked expression from the late 1960s, demand for "relevance" in the educational process gathered momentum. Both clerical dominance and the "dead languages" were under attack. This movement was led by rising sentiment for popular democracy, and it found expression in the creation of colleges by state governments. The flagship institution in this category was the University of Virginia, opened in 1825. Inspired by Thomas Jefferson, it was committed to the promotion of secular knowledge and offered an elective curriculum in which "modern" subjects predominated. Meanwhile, the long-standing colleges in New England were under pressure to reform. In New Hampshire, beginning in 1817, the state legislature attempted to compel Dartmouth College to modernize its curriculum. (Though the politicians did not succeed, the legal battle surrounding this case resulted in a Supreme Court judgment that gave sharper delineation to the "private" and "public" spheres in higher education.) Even in conservative Connecticut, there was ferment for change. Yale responded to it with a resounding apologia for the traditional ordering of prescribed studies, but—at the margin—it made some concessions to new materials (including political economy). By 1830 some instruction in "political economy" was available in virtually all institutions.

What materials could then serve these instructional needs? America had already produced native-soil doctrines in its Franklins, Hamiltons, and Jeffersons. But their commentaries on economic questions—however much they may have infiltrated the public mentality—lacked sufficient system and sweep to satisfy schoolmen. Europe, on the other hand, was well advanced in the production of treatises purporting to provide perspective on the complexities of the economic process. It was understandable that Americans should first look across the Atlantic for inspiration. One of the available options was to import texts from Europe. In some measure, this was done. Prinsep's translation of Jean-Baptiste Say's *Treatise on Political Economy* (which became available in an American edition in 1821) filled part of the gap for more than a decade, as did the edition of McCulloch's essay on political economy prepared by the Reverend John McVickar of Columbia in 1825.

But transplantation of works produced abroad was not held for long to be a satisfactory solution. Classical economics needed to be adapted to American conditions and American audiences. Ricardo was widely acknowledged to be the leading thinker on the subject, but his writings were regarded as too difficult for novices. For Americans, the substance of pure Ricardian teaching was problematic as well. In the first instance, his doctrine of land rent, which presupposed that extension in the margin of cultivation necessarily meant that inferior soils would be brought into tillage, was suspect. This proposition seemed to be out of touch with the realities of America's westward expansion. With a few exceptions (McVickar being one of them), all American writers of note on political economy rejected this component of Ricardian doctrine.

To many, British classical teaching was also objectionable for other reasons. In church-sponsored colleges, the classical treatment of "unproductive labor"—that is, labor engaged in providing services—was inadmissible. This implied that the vocations of ministers and educators made no contribution to the enlargement of the national wealth. Nor were the conclusions of later British classicism concerning the conflicting interests of various social classes acceptable. This line of argument suggested that social friction was inevitable and that economic growth would ultimately be checked. The textbook that found the most favor in the colleges of pre–Civil War America—the Reverend Francis Wayland's *Elements of Political Economy* (first published in 1837)—carefully expunged these features of British political economy. There was to be nothing dismal about the new science in the New World. Fears of the Malthusian population treadmill and of the emergence of a stationary state could be banished, so long as the correct principles of morality were practiced and new knowledge was applied to extend the frontiers of production possibilities. Indeed, political economy could be interpreted as a divinely ordained extension of Christian moral philosophy.

Though textbooks welcomed in New England might convey that the "invisible hand" was really the hand of God, those produced by writers based in some southern colleges could offer a different message. Their numbers were not large, but a few of them made lively contributions to intra-American debates in the 1820s and 1830s. A notable case in point was the work of Thomas Cooper whose *Lectures on the Elements of Political Economy* were published in 1826 while he was president of South Carolina College. Cooper was anything but sympathetic to the clerical tradition: Indeed, he described a "hired and paid priesthood" as a "public nuisance."[4] Through him, the teaching of classical economics was secularized, and it came through as a vigorous defense of free trade. This argument played well in the antiprotectionist South. But there was a southern accent as well in Cooper's ambivalent treatment of an issue over which American political economists—as well as the American populace—were divided. He argued that slave labor was not cost-effective because it was "forced" and thus could not be justified "in point of economy." The survival of the institution of slavery, however, was explained on the basis of soil and climate in the Deep

South, "which incapacitates a white man from laboring in the summer time."[5] Cooper, however, stopped short of an outright defense of slavery. Thomas Roderick Dew, who taught political economy and served as president of the College of William and Mary, took on that assignment.

Product differentiation in the teaching of political economy in southern institutions took other forms as well in the decades preceding the Civil War. In general, institutions in that region were more receptive to intellectual influences from the European continent than was the case in the Northeast. In New England, French economic and social thought in the late eighteenth and early nineteenth centuries tended to be suppressed as the work of godless men. The situation was different in freer-thinking Jeffersonian territory. The doctrines of the French philosophes were compatible with the political ideologies of the American Revolution, and those of the physiocrats reinforced the Jeffersonian vision of the primacy of agriculture.

Even though Americans rang some ingenious changes on imported doctrines, most of what was presented as political economy in pre–Civil War colleges was derived from European thinkers. Beyond the academy, however, an indigenous body of doctrine took shape that contrasted sharply with European classical economics. It reached its fullest expression in Pennsylvania in a school launched by Mathew Carey in the 1820s and carried forward—with a few lapses—into the 1870s by his son, Henry C. Carey. The organizing thread of this doctrine was that a genuinely "national" system of political economy should be built on American soil. Most particularly, the influence of the classical economists in promoting support for free trade was malicious. As a young country, America should think afresh, and it should mould its future on its own terms. Reaching that objective required that domestic industries be sheltered from foreign competition. But the tariff wall, in the view of the Careys, should not be interpreted as of benefit only to the manufacturers it protected. It was instead a boon to the whole country. A prosperous and expanding industrial sector meant more and better jobs for laborers and improved markets for farmers. In short, the economic structure should be seen as an integrated whole in which the interests of the various parts were mutually reinforcing. But, in the Careys' vision, these harmonies would not resonate from the natural order; they needed to be supported by the intervention of government as a tariff maker and as a promoter of improvements in transportation and communication. There was a political constituency for this message in the Middle Atlantic states. And this doctrine became the first distinctively American contribution to European economic debate. Friedrich List—who had been associated with the Careys in the 1820s and early 1830s—exported the conception of a "national system" to Germany.

The Careys met with little success in promoting their brand of economic truth within the halls of academe in pre–Civil War America. It was not, however, for want of trying. Mathew Carey attempted to subsidize a place for a disciple, George Raymond, at the University of Maryland in 1822, but negotiations over this transaction broke down.[6] The Careys were also disappointed when a suitable academic post for List could not be found in the United States. Their indefatigable lobbying did succeed in mobilizing influential business opinion—especially in Pennsylvania—in support of their program. This influence, in turn, ultimately conditioned the University of Pennsylvania to be more receptive to this doctrine. But even there "national economics" did not acquire academic standing until after the Civil War. Elsewhere, its impact on teaching was slight. In the South, protectionist arguments got little hearing. In the Northeast, the virtues of comparative advantage continued to be preached in the standard textbooks. There were, however, a few exceptions: For example, Francis Bowen of Harvard produced a treatise defending protection in 1856. When New Englanders were ready to listen to protectionist arguments, however, they preferred to do so when they were articulated by Yankees, not by Pennsylvanians.

The broad contours of American economic discourse were thus heavily moulded by sectionalism in the years before the Civil War. Meanwhile, the period between 1830 and 1860 witnessed a substantial enlargement in the number of colleges. But the newcomers brought no dramatic innovations in the pattern or content of their curricula. Most of them were clones of institutions established earlier. There was, however, some stirring for change in the programs of the more mature institutions of the first generation. At their peripheries, a number of them made accommodations for applied scientists (who had little taste for the classics) and for students seeking professional training in the law, medicine, and divinity. Such activities were typically segregated administratively and fiscally from the ongoing work of the undergraduate college. Nevertheless, their proximity added weight to those factions seeking more thoroughgoing "modernization."

By one measure, American higher education had moved a long

way by the time the guns fired on Fort Sumter. There were then more than 200 degree-granting colleges in existence, by comparison with nine when the Declaration of Independence was signed. But this appearance of dynamism needs to be tempered by other facts. By 1860 the total student population still did not exceed 17,000, a figure representing only slightly more than 1 percent of the white male population between the ages of fifteen and twenty.[7] In addition, the range of materials provided by the institutions they attended was necessarily constrained by limitations in their scale. In the mid-1850s, only three institutions in the land enrolled more than 300 students: the University of Virginia (with approximately 470), Yale (with about 440), and Harvard (with roughly 340). The majority of them were struggling enterprises with fewer than 100 enrollees.[8]

THE LATE NINETEENTH-CENTURY ENVIRONMENT

The configuration of American higher education was transformed in the last third of the nineteenth century—and with it the hospitality of the educational system to political economy underwent a sea change. Numerous factors fed into this phenomenon: among them, the birth of new institutions fashioned for purposes quite different from those of antebellum colleges, the emergence of new perceptions about the method and substance of political economy itself, and a fresh set of perplexities—shared by the public and the academicians—concerning the way industrial capitalism actually worked. A sense of the dimensions of change can be captured in a few numbers. By the close of the century, about 350 liberal arts colleges were in business with total enrollments of about 82,000. The makeup as well as the size of the college population had altered. Students were older; the typical age of entry had now risen to eighteen, a fact that reflected the enlargement of opportunities for high school education in late nineteenth-century America. But the postbellum clientele of colleges was also different in further respects. Before 1860, only a handful of women were the beneficiaries of higher education; by 1900, their numbers accounted for 24 percent of college enrollments. Even more striking was the transformation that had occurred outside the framework of the traditional colleges. Antebellum higher education had largely been the preserve of those seeking a career in the learned professions. In the later nineteenth century, on the other hand, expansion in the higher education industry was led by technical, professional, and postgraduate schools. By the turn of the century, aggregate enrollments in all categories of postsecondary education approached 300,000.[9]

Behind the scenes, numerous forces converged to produce this change. One of the most significant was a consequence of the passage of the Morrill Act in 1862. This legislation stipulated that funds generated by federal grants of land should be allocated to each state for the purpose of establishing and maintaining institutions offering training in agriculture, the mechanical arts, and the applied sciences. This responded to public sentiment, which had been building in the decade before the Civil War, to make education more "practical." Through its initiative in creating the land-grant college system, the federal government, for the first time, put its weight behind education of a particular type. The ultimate result was a network of institutions that were unambiguously "public" in character.[10]

While the "practical" in higher education was being promoted by government money, private wealth began to underwrite the creation of new institutions designed to stimulate scholarly research. The pioneering educational enterprise with this mandate, the Johns Hopkins University, opened in 1876. This was to be an institution dedicated to the encouragement of research at the postgraduate level. Members of its faculty were expected to produce work that would command respect internationally and to breed a new generation of American scholars whose subsequent professional careers would help to move colleges to genuine university status. Part of the inspiration for Johns Hopkins can be traced to the model of German research universities and to the desire of its founders to provide a domestic alternative to the migration of Americans to Germany for graduate study. But part was linked as well with a larger perception that American scholarship had contributed little or nothing to the world's pool of fundamental knowledge. This was a recurrent theme in the journals of commentary in the mid-1870s when the experience of America's first century as an independent nation was brought under review. Why, it was asked, had the United States, with its abundance of material resources, remained such a cultural backwater? And was it not time to enhance the status of American scholarship? As for American contributions to thinking on political economy, Charles F. Dunbar of Harvard (who then assessed that aspect of the situation) was damning in his indictment. In his reading, American thought to date had been derivative, stagnant, and sterile. Moreover, most of the domestic restatements of imported doctrine were flawed, and challenges to

English classicism (such as those mounted by Henry Carey) were mischievous.[11] Foreign observers tended to echo this appraisal. In Britain, Cliffe Leslie, for example, shared Dunbar's judgment about the quality of American intellectual achievement and advanced a number of possible explanations: among them, a resource environment in which problems of scarcity seemed largely absent; a cultural climate in which the life of action and moneymaking enjoyed prestige, whereas the life of reflection did not; the failure of the United States government to ratify the international copyright convention, which made it cheap to pirate the fruits of the intellectual labors of foreigners.[12]

The Johns Hopkins attempt to address the problem of the intellectual desert was soon to have imitators. In the 1880s and 1890s, most of the first-generation American colleges created or extended programs of postgraduate studies, and many of the newer state institutions did so as well. In addition, private endowments created several new institutions which incorporated features of the Johns Hopkins commitment to research—notably, the University of Chicago (opened in 1892), Leland Stanford Junior University (opened in 1891), and Clark University (opened in 1889). Private money also contributed to breaking the antebellum configuration when Ezra Cornell supplemented land-grant funds to launch an institution that opened in 1868. Practical and liberal learning were to be united there, and undergraduate students were to be accorded a wide choice in their selections of studies.

By the later decades of the nineteenth century, American higher education had become highly differentiated. Students had a wider range of choice among institutions with differing styles: those assigning priority to practical and utilitarian learning, those committed to research and the advancement of knowledge, and those seeking to sustain the cultural values of the classical tradition. New things were being done in new ways, and old things were being done in new depth. Even in some of the older institutions, undergraduates were offered more options in their programs of study. The most celebrated—and the most radical—reform of this type was President Eliot's elective system at Harvard, introduced in the 1870s. Some institutions, on the other hand, tried to fight off the momentum for reform at the undergraduate level—Yale exemplified this reaction—and to hold fast to the time-honored principles of the traditional curriculum.[13] But even they were obliged to make some accommodations. Economists—actual and aspiring—

in these institutions were in the vanguard in pressuring for curricular reforms.

All of these changes enlarged the space for the teaching of political economy at a variety of levels. But what kind of political economy should be taught? In the years following the Civil War, the influence of the clerical tradition could still be found in such native texts as the one published by Arthur L. Perry of Williams College in 1866. It was less detectable in *The Science of Wealth,* published in the same year by Amasa Walker of Amherst College. These works tended to displace the commanding hold of Wayland on collegiate instruction. The issue of the brand of political economy to be promulgated in classrooms was joined in earnest in the 1880s. By then a younger generation of Americans had returned from graduate work in Germany where many of them had absorbed the German historical approach to the discipline with its predispositions toward an activist role for the state. Old-fashioned laissez-faire was now brought under attack on both methodological and moral grounds. The challengers, led by Richard T. Ely, then at Johns Hopkins, pressed for the formation of a national organization of the like-minded (to be known as the American Economic Association) to counteract the influence of the older conservatives. The intellectual battles that ensued generated a new body of home-made instructional materials. The "new view" found expression in Ely's *Problems of Today* (1888) and *An Introduction to Political Economy* (1889), as well as in *Institutes of Economics,* published in 1889 by Elisha Benjamin Andrews of Brown University. Distaste for governmental intervention, on the other hand, ran through the essays of William Graham Sumner of Yale and his *Problems of Political Economy* (1884). Similar doctrine was conveyed by J. Laurence Laughlin (then at Harvard) in his *Elements of Political Economy* (1889) and in his abridgment of John Stuart Mill's *Principles* (1884), from which the original author's judgments about the positive effects of state intervention were systematically purged. Francis Amasa Walker, son of Amasa Walker and president of the Massachusetts Institute of Technology, avoided the extremism of the main contending factions in his *Political Economy* (1883). In his view, there was a place for informed governmental involvement in the economy, but judgments on policy should be made with a respect for facts and not solely on the basis of analytic preconceptions.

But more was at stake in the disputations among American economists in the later years of the nineteenth century than the outcome of *Methodenstreit*. Changes in the character of the economy itself in the Gilded Age threw up an abundance of "real-world" issues that presented interpretive challenges. In the foreground were questions about the implications of industrial concentration, about conflicts between capital and labor, about the rights or wrongs of labor organization, and about the virtues of monometallism versus bimetallism. Could, then, the new "science" provide guidance to legislators and to the citizenry on the disposition of this agenda? In fact, those who professed it in the academy offered few answers in common.

By the turn of the century, economics as a discipline had established a firm beachhead in American colleges and universities (even though their catalogues might still list it under "political science" or "political economy"). It did not follow that the positions of its professors were necessarily secure. The tests of academic acceptability imposed by the clerical tradition were no longer pertinent. But the new-style managements of major colleges and universities in the late nineteenth century set other norms, and not infrequently these norms led to tensions with economists in their employ. Such conflicts, in turn, brought economists to the forefront in the efforts to establish national ground rules for freedom of academic expression. Within the wider academic community, economists—with their propensity to champion unsettling views—were among the most vulnerable to dismissal and had much to gain from the mobilization of collective defenses. At the same time, they were catalysts in the ultimate formation of the Association of American University Professors, an organization that was to render noble service to the entirety of academia in the United States.

In the essays to follow, these themes will be explored in much greater depth. The case of each institution yields fresh insight into the yeast the economists supplied to American higher learning in the nineteenth century.

Early Flowering in the Old Dominion: Political Economy at the College of William and Mary and the University of Virginia

JOHN K. WHITAKER

THE COMMONWEALTH of Virginia played a notable part in the establishment of economics as an academic discipline in the United States during the first half of the nineteenth century.[1] Shortly before the turn of the century, Bishop James Madison introduced the teaching of political economy at the College of William and Mary in Williamsburg, using Adam Smith's *Wealth of Nations* as his text. His was apparently the first course dealing with political economy proper to be taught in the United States. Later, Thomas Jefferson made the subject an integral part of his ambitious plans for the University of Virginia in Charlottesville, founded in 1819. Jefferson himself was not entirely innocent of economics. His polymathic interests extended to the literature of political economy as well as to practical economic issues, and he was responsible for the publication of an English translation of Destutt de Tracy's *Treatise on Political Economy* in 1817. From the mid-1820s to the mid-1840s political economy was taught in the two principal Virginia institutions by two individuals who established themselves as leading southern writers on economic topics: George Tucker at the University of Virginia and Thomas Roderick Dew at the College of William and Mary. (Dew also achieved fame as a defender of slavery.) Unfortunately, Virginia's early prominence in the teaching of political economy was not to be maintained after 1845. Relative

I am indebted to Kurt Schaefer for valuable research assistance and to librarians and archivists at the University of Virginia and the College of William and Mary for advice and assistance. Particular acknowledgment is due to my colleague emeritus Tipton R. Snavely, for his pioneering work on George Tucker and the early teaching of economics at the University of Virginia, on which I have drawn heavily.

economic decline, exacerbated by the Civil War, kept the early blossom from yielding full fruit, and the chronicling of the remainder of the century can be accordingly brief. For the pre-1845 period, which will be the main focus, stress will be placed on the curricular setting within which these early developments arose and on the intertwined and contrasting institutional histories of the College of William and Mary and its younger rival.

THE COLLEGE OF WILLIAM AND MARY UP TO 1812

The College of William and Mary was founded by royal charter in 1693, yielding temporal precedence only to Harvard among the colleges of North America.[2] The charter's objective was to "establish a certain Place of Universal Study, or perpetual College of Divinity, Philosophy, Languages, and other good Arts and sciences, consisting of one President, six Masters or Professors and an hundred Scholars, more or less."[3] The college did not attain its full complement of six professors until 1729. Of these, one taught in the associated Indian school, another headed an associated classical or grammar school for youths, and two were devoted to divinity, although the founders' hopes that the college would fill the commonwealth's need for ministers of the established church was to be only meagerly met. The remaining two professors taught in the "philosophical school" that comprised the undergraduate college proper, one dealing with mathematics and "natural philosophy" and the other with "moral philosophy," including logic, ethics, rhetoric, and belles lettres. This pattern remained essentially undisturbed up to the time of the American Revolution. The student body was never large, rarely equaling the target of 100, especially if the grammar school is excluded.[4] Nevertheless, the college's products comprised a remarkable galaxy of talent, including many of Virginia's revolutionary leaders, not least Thomas Jefferson.[5] The professors were predominantly clergymen, and there was a strong Oxford connection, especially with Queen's College. Among the prerevolutionary professors, three names deserve mention: the Reverend Hugh Jones who left the college in 1721 and in 1724 published in London *The Present State of Virginia,* which discussed issues of commercial policy and argued for restricting the output of tobacco;[6] William Small, Jefferson's revered teacher, a graduate of Aberdeen and an exception to the Oxford-clerical pattern, something of a polymath who returned to Britain in 1764; and the Reverend S. Henley, professor of moral philosophy from 1770, who returned to Britain when revolution threatened and eventually became the first principal of Haileybury College (founded by the East India Company to train young men for its administrative service) and hence Thomas Robert Malthus's superior. However, there is no indication that the interests or teaching of these or any other of the early professors involved economic issues in other than an entirely incidental way.

Revolution and its aftermath inevitably brought changes to a royal foundation with its close connection to the established Church of England. The college lost many of the revenues granted by the crown, although its endowment and original charter were retained. Financial difficulties were to loom large for the next century and were amplified by the permanent shift of the state capital to Richmond in 1780, which left the college in a decaying miasmic backwater. The military campaigns of the revolutionary war also seriously affected the college, which was practically closed for the academic years 1780–82. The college buildings were occupied at various times by British and French troops and suffered considerable dilapidation.

The structure and curriculum of the college were substantially modified in 1779. The change was instigated by Thomas Jefferson, then governor of Virginia, who had been elected to the college's Board of Visitors. Jefferson described the change in his autobiography as involving

abolishing the Grammar school, and the two professorships of Divinity and Oriental Languages [the latter a part of the Divinity School], and substituting a Professorship of Law and Police, one of Anatomy, Medicine Chemistry, and one of Modern Languages; and the charter confining us to six professorships, we added the law of Nature and Nations, and the Fine Arts to the duties of the Moral professor, and Natural history to those of the professor of Mathematics and Natural philosophy.[7]

The institution now referred to itself, rather optimistically, as the College and University of William and Mary. The teaching of medical subjects soon came to an end, but the teaching of law flourished, first under George Wythe, Jefferson's esteemed law tutor, who had previously taught privately in Williamsburg, and after 1789 under St. George Tucker. Undoubtedly, commercial subjects were covered in the law courses,[8] but chief interest in this period focuses upon the teaching of James Madison (1749–1812), an older second cousin of the U.S. president of the same name. Madison, a graduate of the college, had been appointed professor of natural philosophy in 1773 and, having been ordained in England in 1775, was elected president of the college in 1777.[9] In 1784 he began to lecture on moral philosophy, handing over his previous mathematical responsibilities to Robert Anderson, who had served since 1779 as Professor of Moral Philosophy, the Law of Nature and Nations, and Fine Arts. Sometime between 1786 and the turn of the century, Madison—who became Episcopalian bishop of Virginia in 1790 and is usually referred to as Bishop Madison to distinguish him from his more famous kinsman—introduced the regular coverage of political economy into his teaching, using Adam Smith's *Wealth of Nations* as his textbook. The precise date at which this began has been the subject of dispute.[10] Few records survive from this phase of the college's history, but printed "Statutes of the University of William and Mary" of 1792 make it clear that such a development had not been incorporated into the formal description of the curriculum by that date.[11] On the other hand, in 1803, Samuel Miller, obviously quoting or paraphrasing a college document, gave the following description of the courses in the "Moral School."

1. Logic and the Philosophy of the Human Mind. On these subjects, the works of DUNCAN, REID, and Professor [Dugald] STEWART are studied.
2. Rhetoric and Belles Lettres. Here Dr. BLAIR's Lectures are chiefly used.
3. Moral Philosophy. In this Department the author studied is PALEY.
4. Natural Law. RUTHERFORTH and BURLAMAQUI, etc.
5. Law of Nations. VATTEL and MARTENS.
6. Politics. LOCKE, MONTESQUIEU, ROUSSEAU, etc.
7. Political Economy. SMITH's Wealth of Nations.

He added that "there is probably no College in the United States in which political science is studied with so much ardour, and in which it is considered so pre-eminently a favourite subject, as in this."[12] That the study of political economy was already well established by the turn of the century is further suggested by passages from letters written by a student of the college in 1801:

In the Political Course we are advanced as far as Smith. We have read Rousseau. The Bishop has introduced Locke on Government which we have read also. I have also read Paine's *Rights of Man.* . . . These three are celebrated, and, perhaps, the most excellent that have written upon the Science of Politics.

My studies . . . require . . . considerable labour and exertion. Few sciences, if any, are more abstruse are [or?] intricate than that of political economy. Yet the extensive information, the comprehensive and powerful talents of Smith, have thrown upon the subject a light which I believe no other man could have given.[13]

A further slight piece of evidence is the existence of a copy of *The Wealth of Nations* with the inscription "Robert Stanard, Wm. and Mary College, 1798."[14]

In the absence of further documentation, it must remain a matter for speculation as to when *The Wealth of Nations* began to be regularly covered by Bishop Madison in his "political" course. The facts that the first American edition of Smith appeared only in 1789, that the 1792 regulations do not mention political economy, but that the teaching of Smith's work was apparently well established in 1801 make an inception date in the mid-1790s the most likely.

Madison's chief intellectual interest was in "natural philosophy," that is, physical science, and he was an ardent observer of nature.[15] It seems improbable that he had any profundity as a social thinker. The emphasis on providence in his address, "Manifestations of the Beneficence of Divine Providence towards America,"[16] suggests that he was of the general clerical school, seeing a preordained harmony in social arrangements. He did, however, have an enthusiasm for liberty and was thought by some churchmen to be too accommodating in his theology. He seems to have published nothing bearing on his economic views, and no notes on his teaching of political economy have survived. It appears likely that he used Smith as a textbook proper, working steadily through each chapter with the students and explicating and commenting on the text. This certainly was the practice followed by his successor (see the fourth section of this chapter). Given Smith's genius, there are worse ways, even yet, of acquiring economic wisdom. Madison was evidently a gifted and devoted teacher. Bishop William Meade reported that

He was indefatigable in his lectures, and when in good health is known to have been engaged in his lecture-room for four to six hours a day. He first introduced a course of systematic lectures in political economy in the College. In the department of natural philosophy he excelled, his enthusiasm throwing a particular charm over his lectures.[17]

The pains he took are illustrated by the forty pages of questions he had propounded on *The Wealth of Nations* that were recorded in the notebook of a student who attended the college in 1806.[18] We cannot be sure whether Madison continued to teach Smith right up to his sudden death in 1812, but this seems likely. It certainly remained a regular part of the curriculum in 1815.

Although the record is slight, there does seem to be enough clear evidence to justify the belief that Madison was the first person in North America to teach a systematic course based on *The Wealth of Nations,* and probably the first to teach a course that could properly be characterized as dealing with the new science of political economy.[19]

The college prospered modestly under Madison's governance, but enrollments remained small, financial difficulties were ever-present, and the future looked unpromising.[20] Despite these difficulties, William and Mary at the turn of the century was an impressive institution, offering an education second to none in North America and probably superior on average to that then available at Oxford or Cambridge.[21] It had been, and continued to be, an institution where the scions of the gentry—seven-eighths from Virginia and the remainder preponderantly from farther south—were given a liberal education and prepared for participation in public life. The prominent role Virginians took in the Revolution and the first few decades of the new Republic owed a considerable debt to William and Mary. Nevertheless, as the new century opened, the migration of Virginia's youth to the rising northern institutions was increasing, and William and Mary was losing its traditional clientele.[22] To Jefferson, at least, it seemed that a new alternative was needed.

THOMAS JEFFERSON AND THE UNIVERSITY OF VIRGINIA

The importance of universal education free from religious ties and inhibitions and the legitimacy of governmental support for education were among the tenets of Jefferson's views on democracy. They formed an important component of his hopes and plans for his own state.[23] As early as 1779 he drafted an ambitious set of educational bills for the legislature, the General Assembly. These envisaged a locally financed and controlled system of elementary schools, feeding into a system of regional academies, capped by a state university and library. At this time, Jefferson hoped that the reform of William and Mary could provide the new university. The reformed college was to have seven academic professors:

one of moral philosophy, and the laws of nature and of nations, and of the fine arts; one of law and police; one of history, civil and ecclesiastical; one of mathematics; one of anatomy and medicine; one of natural philosophy and natural history; one of the ancient languages, oriental and northern; and one of modern languages.[24]

At this stage there was no explicit mention of political economy, and the extensive brief of the professor of moral philosophy, and so on, left little scope for it. In any case, none of Jefferson's educational bills of 1779 was acted upon. But the internal reforms, already described, which were instigated by Jefferson at William and Mary in the same year, went some considerable way in the direction that his "Bill for amending the Constitution of the College of William and Mary" had indicated, although within the constraint of the existing charter.

Jefferson never departed from the broad objectives of his 1779 bills but eventually became convinced that reform and development of his alma mater would not serve to provide the keystone institution that was to cap the hoped-for educational system. His thoughts turned to a new institution, more centrally located in his own part of the state. In 1800 he wrote to Joseph Priestley, seeking advice.

We have . . . a College (William and Mary) just well enough endowed to draw out the miserable existence to which a miserable constitution has doomed it. It is moreover eccentric in its position, exposed to all bilious diseases as all the lower country is, and therefore abandoned by the public care, as that part of the country itself is in a considerable degree by its inhabitants. We wish to establish in the upper country, and more centrally for the State, an University on a plan so broad and liberal and *modern*, as to be worth patronizing with the public support, and to be a temptation to the youth of other States to come and drink of the cup of knowledge and fraternize with us.[25]

Jefferson indicated a further, and perhaps ultimately decisive, reason for ceasing to pin hopes on William and Mary. Its Episcopalian ties had proved firm and had aroused the suspicions of the Presbyterians and Baptists who were particularly numerous in the western portions of the state (which then included the present West Virginia). They were unlikely to favor promotion of William and Mary at the expense of the Presbyterian foundations, Washington College in Lexington or Hampden-Sydney College in Prince Edward County.[26] A new institution, free of sectarian ties, was called for. On general grounds, too, Jefferson was anxious that higher education remain strictly secular.

Jefferson asked Priestley for advice on the coverage and grouping of subjects, suggesting, in a list that was "imperfect because I make it hastily," "Botany, chemistry, zoology, anatomy, surgery, medicine, natural philosophy, agriculture, mathematics, astronomy, geography, politics, commerce, history, ethics, law, arts, fine arts."[27] The inclusion of "commerce" in this list is the first clear indication of a desire to have economical subjects covered, although there is as yet no emphasis on political economy as an independent subject. Jefferson also hoped to "draw from Europe the first characters in science, by considerable temptations."[28] His ambitions were now expanding to encompass an institution of international stature.

Jefferson's horizons had been widened by his stay in France as U.S. envoy from 1784 to 1789. He had seen European universities at first hand and had come to know various intellectual leaders: Dugald Stewart had become a good friend while staying in Paris, and Jefferson had moved in physiocratic circles, becoming well acquainted with Pierre Samuel Du Pont de Nemours and the Comte Antoine Destutt de Tracy, descendant of an exiled Scottish family. Jefferson was to become a great admirer and promoter of the latter's writings on government and economics.[29]

The scope for attracting "the first characters in science" from a war-torn and politically disturbed Europe had become apparent in 1794, when Jefferson was approached about a possible move to the United States of the entire faculty of the College of Geneva. He strongly supported the move and strove to direct it to his own state, but the proposal came to nothing, the desire to continue instruction in French and the Calvinist affiliation being among the many obstacles.[30]

Between his return from France in 1789 and the end of his second term as U.S. president in 1809, Jefferson was preoccupied with national affairs. Nevertheless, he proceeded, cautiously and intermittently, with educational schemes for his own state. He sought advice on curriculum matters, not only from Priestley but also from Du Pont, who produced in response his ambitious pamphlet *Sur l'éducation nationale dans les Etats-Unis d'Amerique,* with its proposal for a national university in Washington in which a school of social sciences and legislation would train would-be statesmen and administrators in political economy, among other things.[31] Jefferson had asked Du Pont

to state what are the branches of science which in the present state of man, and particularly with us, should be introduced into an academy, and to class them together in such groupes [sic], as you think might be managed by one professor devoting his whole time to it. It is very interesting to us to reduce the important sciences to as few professorships as possible because of the narrowness of our resources.[32]

In 1803 Jefferson asked Professor Pictet of the College of Geneva for a sketch of "the branches of science taught at your college," observing that

I have still had constantly in view to propose to the legislature of Virginia the establishment of one [a college] on as large a scale as our present circumstances would require or bear. But as yet no favorable moment has occurred. In the meantime I am endeavouring to procure materials for a good plan.[33]

An unsuccessful try to establish a university in the central part of the state was made in the legislature in 1805. Jefferson was not directly involved, but the effort bears the stamp of his influence.[34] And doubtless he continued over the years, as the opportunity arose, to mull over his schemes and solicit advice. Nevertheless, after he returned to private life in 1809 he lay low for some years, and it was only gradually and cautiously that he allowed himself to be drawn once more into educational struggles. The opportunity arose early in 1814 when he was co-opted to a committee planning the development of a modest local academy (Albemarle Academy) in his native Albemarle County. He soon discerned wider possibilities. In January 1814 he was writing to Thomas Cooper, whom he much admired and of whom he had observed in 1810 that "the best pieces on political economy which have been written in this country were by Cooper."[35]

I have long had under contemplation and have been collecting materials for the plan of an University in Virginia which should comprehend all the sciences useful to us, and none others. . . . Should it happen it would offer places worthy of you and of which you are worthy.[36]

He urged his fellow board members to enlarge their vision, and in a famous letter to the chairman, his nephew Peter Carr, he sketched ambitious schemes for education at all levels.[37] For the academy itself, he urged adoption of a plan "adapted, in the first instance, to our slender funds, but susceptible of being enlarged, either by their own growth or by accession from other quarters." His goal was "an establishment, either with or without incorporation into that of William and Mary where every branch of science, deemed useful in this day and in our country, should be taught in its highest degree." Chief among the "other quarters" from which funds might be hoped was the commonwealth of Virginia itself. Establishment in 1810 of a Literary Fund, with modest but significant revenues dedicated to it, had opened an obvious avenue for state support of higher education. But such an employment was to face continued opposition from those favoring the fund's use to support elementary education, which Jefferson himself believed should be financed at a local-government level rather than centrally.

The letter to Peter Carr sketched the curriculum for the proposed new university-level institution. The subject of political economy was to be included: "In the Philosophical department, I should distinguish 1. Ideology; 2. Ethics; 3. the Law of Nature and Nations; 4. Government; 5. Political Economy."[38] Jefferson sent a copy of the Carr letter to Cooper, who concurred in including "the theory of government, statistics and political economy," although demurring somewhat on other matters.[39]

There is little reason to think that the inclusion of political economy depended significantly on advice Jefferson had received in consequence of his inquiries to others. By 1814 he was well read in the literature of the subject, being familiar with the economic works of Smith, Turgot, Malthus, Du Pont, and Say.[40] His experience in national affairs had heightened his awareness of practical economic issues and of the importance of a sound understanding of them among both statesmen and electors. He had well-formed views on economic matters, especially on questions concerning banking and the protection of manufactures.[41] If this were not enough, he had already begun in January 1813 the long process of negotiation and supervision that led to the publication in 1817 of Destutt de Tracy's *Treatise on Political Economy*. In that month he had written to the publisher William Duane of Philadelphia describing the French manuscript as

a work of great ability; it may be considered as a review of the principles of the Economists, of Smith, and of Say, or rather an elementary book on the same subject. As Smith has corrected some principles of the economists and Say some of Smith's; so Tracy has done as to the whole. He has in my opinion corrected fundamental errors in all of them, and by simplifying principles has brought the subject within a narrow compass.[42]

Here then was a book he believed tailor-made for college instruction of the science of political economy just as he had believed Tracy's previous *Commentary and Review of Montesquieu's Spirit of the Laws* (which Duane had published in 1811 under Jefferson's supervision) would become the standard text on the science of government.[43]

Jefferson evidently persuaded his coadjutors of Albemarle Academy to expand the scope of the enterprise, and on February 14, 1816, the General Assembly chartered a new institution, called Central College to emphasize its geographical centrality to the state. An appeal for funds having been surprisingly successful, plans for opening the college proceeded. The foundation stone for the first building was laid on October 6, 1817, and the first professorial appointment, that of Thomas Cooper, was confirmed by December 6. Cooper had been offered "the professorship of chemistry etc. . . . adding to it that of law." The emolument per year was to be a salary of $1,000 plus a twenty-dollar fee from each student.[44]

Jefferson's plans, both architectural and academic, were too ambitious to proceed far without state support, and there now began a long struggle to obtain assured financial support from the state and to convert Central College into *the* University of Virginia, with the seal of leadership carried by such a title.[45] Success in the latter goal came in two stages. First, on February 21, 1818, the legislature established a university with an appropriation of $15,000 per year from the Literary Fund, leaving the selection of site and plan of organization to a commission. This commission, which Jefferson chaired, is known as the Rockfish Gap Commission, from its meeting place. It duly opted for the elevation of Central College. The recommendation was accepted by the legislature, although not without controversy, and the University of Virginia at Charlottesville was formally constituted by an act of January 25, 1819. It was to be 1825 before the first students were admitted—Central College never admitted one—all available funds being meanwhile absorbed in creating Jefferson's glorious group of buildings. By 1827 the state had been cajoled, almost blackmailed, into appropriating over $250,000 for this purpose, well beyond the $15,000 per year initially provided.

The Board of Visitors of the new university, essentially reappointed from Central College, included Joseph Cabell and former U.S. president James Madison, but Jefferson was in effective control. Cooper's appointment was reaffirmed but was proving an embarrassment, partly because the date for admitting students kept receding but also because of hostile criticism, especially from the Presbyterians, focusing on Cooper's supposed religious views. Jefferson staunchly supported Cooper, but the other visitors seem to have accepted with relief his decision in 1820 to withdraw. Cooper was to make a significant contribution to the establishment and teaching of political economy as an academic subject in South

Carolina, but he was valued by Jefferson primarily for his abilities in natural science. The teaching of law was added to his responsibilities, but this was meant as a temporary expedient for the infant stage of the institution, when each professor would have to cover a daunting range of subjects. Political economy might have been regarded as a minor appendage to law, but through all the long-drawn-out negotiations there was no mention of the subject.[46]

At an earlier stage, Jefferson had expressed to Cabell the hope that the French economist Jean-Baptiste Say might be attracted to the new institution, but this seems to have been mere wishful thinking, and no negotiations, direct or indirect, were entered into. Say had written in 1814 to Jefferson, with whom he had previously exchanged letters, indicating that he thought of immigrating to the United States, not surprisingly, given the then unsettled state of Europe. He evidently had in mind manufacturing or agricultural possibilities and sought information and advice. Jefferson's long response lauding his native Albemarle County probably never reached Say, and nothing further came of the matter.[47]

The report of the Rockfish Gap Commission, drafted by Jefferson, listed the subjects to be taught in the proposed university, forming them into groups "within the powers of a single professor." The first seven groups covered languages ancient and modern, mathematics, and scientific and medical subjects. The remaining three groups were:

VIII. Government, Political Economy, Law of Nature and Nations, History, being interwoven with Politics and Law.
IX.   Law, municipal.
X.   Ideology, General Grammar, Ethics, Rhetoric, Belles Lettres, and the fine arts.[48]

The 1819 act also listed political economy among the subjects to be taught.[49]

It was not until 1824 that the Board of Visitors formally established the university's curriculum.[50] It was then decided that, owing to financial stringency, only eight rather than ten professorships would be established: ancient languages, modern languages, mathematics, natural philosophy, natural history, anatomy and medicine, moral philosophy, and law. With each professor was to be associated a "school" involving a defined range of subjects. Students were to be free to attend any schools of their choice and would normally be expected to attend three. The timetable was carefully established to preserve this freedom of choice. Successful performance in a school was to be recognized by making the student a graduate of that school.[51] To the Schools of Moral Philosophy and Law, the following subjects were allotted.

In the school of moral philosophy shall be taught mental science generally, including ideology, general grammar, logic and ethics.
In the school of law shall be taught the common and statute law, that of chancery, the laws feudal, civil, mercatorial, maritime and of nature and nations; and also the principles of government and political economy.

The inclusion of political economy under law was perhaps a matter of convenience: Provision was made for "occasional transpositions of a particular branch of science from one school to another in accommodation of the particular qualifications of different professors," and at this stage no professors had been appointed. It was deemed expedient that the professors of both moral philosophy and law should be U.S. citizens, and sound Republican principles were looked for; the contaminating ideas of such men as Alexander Hamilton or John Marshall were to be excluded. Indeed, the textbooks on U.S. government were formally prescribed to insure that harmful principles were not inculcated, the selection being deputed to Jefferson and Madison. On other subjects, Jefferson took the view that choice of texts was "better left to the professors, until occasion of interference shall be given." He had told Destutt de Tracy in 1820 that his two books "certainly shall be the elementary books of the political department in our new University," but there is no record of any attempt to insure this.[52] Indeed, it is a remarkable fact that the 1828 catalogue of the university library does not even list a copy of the *Treatise on Political Economy*.[53] The book appears to have gone out of print rapidly, and Jefferson's call in 1823 for a new edition went unheeded.[54]

The law professorship proved difficult to fill, and it was not until 1826, after a series of unsuccessful offers to others, that John Tayloe Lomax accepted the position. Meanwhile, on March 4, 1825, the visitors had resolved, at Jefferson's nomination, that "George Tucker, Esquire, of Lynchburg, be appointed professor of the school of moral philosophy."[55] He accepted the position after some deliberation. The emoluments seem to have been a salary of $1,500 plus student fees. As events transpired, it was George Tucker (1775–1861), not Lomax, who inaugurated the teaching of political economy at the university in 1826, continuing to teach it until his retirement in 1845.

To legislate that a subject should be taught, even to emphasize the desirability of teaching it, does not insure that it will be taught well. This was especially so at a time when professors were expected to be proficient in a bewildering range of subjects. To Jefferson must be given the credit for placing political economy firmly on the map of knowledge for his new institution. But whether or not the subject would be treated seriously depended almost entirely on the personality and interests of the teacher to whom it was assigned, who would face many competing claims on his time and energies. Virginia was fortunate in finding in Tucker a serious teacher of political economy and a thinker who was to become one of the more significant economic writers in antebellum America.

This was far from predictable in 1824. Indeed, Tucker's appointment must have seemed something of a gamble. He was already turning fifty and had behind him a checkered career as lawyer, agriculturalist, and congressman. Born in Bermuda, a nephew of St. George Tucker of William and Mary and himself once a student there, Tucker had just published a novel and had attained some reputation as an essayist.[56] Jefferson admired his essays—which ranged from belles lettres to politics, including some discussions of population, banking, and national debt—and, perhaps wrongly, deemed him sound politically. But just where Tucker's future interests might lie must have been hard to foretell.

This was only one of many uncertainties facing an enterprise heading into virtually uncharted waters. Despite all Jefferson's care and planning, it nearly foundered at the outset of the voyage on the rocks of indiscipline, as an innocent faculty, and an institution designed for students as intellectually serious and capable as Jefferson himself, came face to face with an actual student body, which was youthful, boisterous, high-spirited, ill prepared, and imbued with southern notions of honor, treating any exercise of authority as a potential insult not to be borne.[57]

GEORGE TUCKER AND THE TEACHING OF POLITICAL ECONOMY AT THE UNIVERSITY OF VIRGINIA, 1826–1845

The circumstances that led George Tucker to begin to teach political economy in the university's second session were described in his autobiography.

The subject of political economy had been assigned to the law professor [Lomax], and understanding from him that he was not particularly desirous of lecturing on it, and that his other duties would be sufficient to occupy the whole of his time, I applied to the Board to assign the subject to the chair of Moral Philosophy which was done; and after a temporary use of Say as a text book I prepared a full course of lectures on the subject, which had always been a favorite one with me.[58]

The catalogue for the session 1832–33 was the first to list the courses, and it describes Tucker's courses in moral philosophy quite fully.

There are two classes in the school. The junior class studies Rhetoric, Belles-Lettres and Logic, the first half of the session, and Belles-Lettres and Ethics the last half. The senior, studies Mental Philosophy, the first part of the session, and Political Economy the last. The examinations are on the Professor's lectures and the following books:—In Rhetoric and Belles-Lettres, Blair, Campbell and Lord Kaim's [sic] Elements; in Ethics, Stewart's Active and Moral Powers; in Metaphysics, Brown, Stewart and Locke; in Political Economy, Say and Adam Smith. In discussing the controverted questions of the last-mentioned science, all the ablest writers, both of Europe and America, are referred to. The students in this school are required to exercise themselves in composition.

Tucker continued to teach political economy until his retirement in 1845. In 1837 he published *The Laws of Wages, Profits, and Rent, Investigated,* his main theoretical contribution, noting in the preface that "the following pages constitute part of a series of lectures on Political Economy, which the author has delivered in the University of Virginia for the past ten years."[59] This book, and his *Theory of Money and Banks Investigated,*[60] which appeared in 1839, were added to the course syllabus in the 1841–42 catalogue.[61]

Fortunately, excellent notes taken by a student on Tucker's lectures for the 1840–41 session have survived, and the character and content of his instruction can best be gleaned by a brief account of these.[62] At this time, the thirty lectures composing the course were spread over the full academic year. The first four lectures dealt with the nature of economics, the general character of the economic evolution of society, and the determinants of wealth and of differences in wealth among countries. "Moral" causes were emphasized, and the advantages of increased population density were stressed. Lecture 5 introduced the effects of land limitations, which lead as population grows to rising rents, deteriorating terms of trade of manufactures against primary products, and ultimately to Malthusian stagnation if the population growth remains uncontrolled. Lecture 6 covered value deftly, integrating satisfactorily the role of demand and emphasizing the impossibility of an absolute measure of value. Lectures 7–10 covered the accumulation of capital, the role of capital in production, and the economic advantages of commerce and other forms of intangible production. Smith's views on the debilitating effects of the division of labor and his distinction between productive and unproductive labor were disputed. Lectures 11 and 12 dealt approvingly with Say's "law of markets." The unlimited nature of wants was emphasized, and Malthus's views on gluts were criticized, as was the argument that spendthrifts encourage trade. Free trade and free markets were recommended on the grounds that men are sufficiently motivated to industry and are the best judges of how to use their own resources. In lecture 13 the errors of the mercantilist system were displayed and Smith's exceptions to free trade were considered, the infant-industry argument being accepted. Lectures 14–17 covered questions of tariff policy. A rather sectional view was taken, with unflattering references to "the Yankees," but false antitariff arguments of "our friends," including one by Dew, were properly criticized. Again, the infant-industry argument was indicated as a legitimate theoretical exception to the "great principle" of free trade but one that it was dangerous to rely on in practice. Tucker stressed that he was not opposed to manufactures but felt they could safely be left to arise naturally. In lecture 18 he observed that it is untrue that reliance on slave labor precludes manufactures. He then began a consideration of violations of the "great principle" of free trade by domestic laws, moving in lecture 19 to a consideration of corn laws and other attempts to protect or stabilize the food supply. Lecture 20 dealt with government production, judged appropriate in certain cases such as armaments, and then with colonies, which were disposed of briefly. Lecture 21 was omitted, or perhaps a slip was made in the numbering, and lecture 22 turned to money, "almost a science itself," referring students to Tucker's book on money and banks. The disadvantages of barter and the monetary advantages of gold and silver were indicated, leading to a consideration of the determinants of the demand for money. Lecture 23 turned to paper money and banks. Lecture 24 returned to basic topics in value theory, demand-supply and production-cost approaches again being reconciled, leading in lecture 25 to a consideration of wage differentials. Lecture 26 covered usury laws, lecture 27 was concerned with the theory of rent, Ricardo's stress on marginal land being criticized, and lecture 28 dealt with Malthus's views, accepted in general but deemed too pessimistic. Lecture 29 considered checks on population growth, with remarkably frank references to prostitution, sexual relations, and abortion. Finally, lecture 30 dealt with the undesirability of sumptuary laws and went on to the use of resources by the government, with some consideration of the appropriate economic functions of government and principles for remunerating government employees.

As a whole, the lectures are highly individual, independent-minded, cogent, and informative, although the organization, which broadly follows Say, might be judged defective. Tucker clearly knew his subject. Some acknowledgment must also be given to the auditor for the quality of the notes, which must have been carefully written up after the lectures. The lectures did not merely replicate Tucker's published texts, although there was of course some overlap, but were supplementary to them.[63] The lecture system, as opposed to the recitation of textbooks, was one of the distinctive features of the university and had been encouraged by Jefferson.[64]

The views presented in the lectures are consistent with, although less comprehensive than, those appearing in Tucker's published works. He was substantially influenced by Say and was a mild critic of Ricardo and Malthus. He emphasized American land abundance and the scale economies due to increased population density as reasons for welcoming rapid population growth in the short term. Nevertheless, he accepted the long-term consequences of the classical model. These were central to his belief that slavery would in due course be extinguished automatically by the slave's subsistence cost rising above his productive contribution through increased land scarcity.[65] The lectures were reticent about slavery. Tucker was clearly no great supporter of the institution, and he became increasingly concerned about the threat it posed to the Union, yet he never felt able to take publicly a clear antislavery stance. It seems unlikely that this was the result of pressures inside the university, which appears to have been a remarkably tolerant and broad-minded institution and was to remain so even in the darkest days of sectional stress. But in the general climate of southern opinion after 1830 it was doubtless safer to avoid broadcasting antislavery views, just as religious doubts were better not aired publicly. Public clamor was easily aroused and likely to be undiscriminating.

It is impossible to ascertain the number of students who attended Tucker's classes in political economy. The minutes of the faculty indicate that in July 1828 twenty-three students were due to be examined in the subject and that for the academic years 1831–32 to 1844–45 a "certificate of proficiency" in political economy was awarded to eight, five, four, three, one, four, three, thirteen, fifteen, five, twelve, three, eleven, and twelve candidates, respectively.[66] Robert Lewis Dabney, who prepared the notes summarized above, received one of the five certificates awarded in 1840–41. It seems probable that class enrollment was typically in the range of eight to twenty students.

THE TEACHING OF POLITICAL ECONOMY AT THE COLLEGE OF WILLIAM AND MARY, 1812–1846

Two years of turmoil followed Bishop Madison's death in 1812, partly because the militia was quartered in the college but largely because of the unpopularity of the new president, the Reverend John Bracken, whose resignation was eventually forced in August 1814.[67] His successor as president was John Augustine Smith (1782–1865), who was at the time teaching medical subjects at the College of Physicians and Surgeons in New York.[68] Smith was also made Professor of Moral and Political Philosophy. He appears to have taught government and political economy over the years until his return in 1826 to the College of Physicians and Surgeons, where he resumed his medical interests. The course of instruction in the College of William and Mary, as recently modified, was described in a "Statement of the Visitors and Governors" of July 4, 1815, as

First year— Rhetorick, Belles Lettres and Moral Philosophy, Chemistry, Mathematics as far as plane geometry.
Second year— Conclude Mathematics, Natural Philosophy, Metaphysics, Natural and National Law.
Third year— Government and Political Economy.[69]

The textbooks used were specified in regulations of 1817 as

First, or Freshman Year.
    Blair's Lectures, Andrew's Logic, Campbell's Philosophy of Rhetoric, Paley's Moral Philosophy, Hutton's Mathematics, Flint's Surveying, and Thompson's Chemistry.
Second, or Junior Year.
    Vattel's Law of Nature and Nations, Stewart's Philosophy of the Human Mind, Viner's Conic Sections and Fluxions, Cavallo's Natural Philosophy.
Third, or Senior Year.
    Keith's Trigonometry, Gregory's Astronomy, Smith's Wealth of Nations.

> A Syllabus of the Lectures on Government has been drawn up by the Professor of that subject for the use of this class.[70]

Evidently the 1815 plan to devote the third year entirely to government and political economy had not been sustained.

As this list indicates, *The Wealth of Nations* continued to be used as the textbook for political economy, and it was as a textbook in the literal sense that John Augustine Smith employed it. Surviving student lecture notes make it clear that he worked through the book chapter by chapter in the traditional style, doubtless with class members called on to summarize and construe successive passages.[71]

Greater interest attaches to the syllabus of lectures on government that Smith published in 1817 under the title *Syllabus of the Lectures delivered to the Senior Students in the College of William and Mary on Government.*[72] This syllabus has some fame as the earliest American textbook on government. Apparently, Smith first taught the course on government, and perhaps also that on political economy, in the academic year 1815–16—there may well not have been a third-year class in 1814–15. Dissatisfied with Rousseau, which had been used previously, he had sought advice on possible texts. On Jefferson's recommendation, the *Review and Commentary upon Montesquieu* by Destutt de Tracy had been adopted, but this was "soon laid aside notwithstanding its merits, so defective was its arrangement." *Faute de mieux*, Smith had then written his own text, despite a diffidence in dealing with matters "to which his attention was very lately turned." He took the view that "from the only political chair in the Union the purest principles of republicanism should undoubtedly be promulgated."[73]

The *Syllabus* includes some interesting notes on usury laws, taken from the author's lectures on political economy, "of all sciences, next morality and government, the most important—and of the whole circle the one with which mankind at large, have the least acquaintance." Smith took an uncomplicatedly free-market view of the matter, asserting the right to free contract and the lack of any essential difference between contracts dealing with vendible commodities and contracts as to the lending of money. A belief that the latter were in need of special regulation was likened to a belief in witchcraft:

while gravitation fixes other mortals to the earth, certain old women, it has been thought, could fly; so, although the ratio of supply to demand, keeps down all other commodities to their just level, money it is supposed, has not only the power, but a propensity to soar beyond this height.[74]

Smith's views on interest rates are coherent and competently expressed, but there is nothing to suggest that he had significant originality as an economic thinker or teacher.

A much more interesting figure is Thomas Roderick Dew (1802–46), who took over the teaching of political economy when Smith left the college in 1826. Dew, an 1820 graduate of the college, was appointed Professor of Political Law in October 1826 with a salary of $1,000.[75] His duties were laid out in the 1830 *Laws and Regulations*.

The Professor of Political Law shall deliver Lectures on Natural and National Law, Political Economy, Metaphysics, Government and History. The Text Book on Natural and National Law shall be Vattel, with reference to Rutherforth's Institutes. In Political Economy—Smith's Wealth of Nations; Metaphysics—Browne abridged; Government—Locke and Rousseau's Social Compact.[76]

At this time, the regular college course for the B.A. had been reduced to two years. Political economy was covered in the "Senior Political" course, which also dealt with "the Philosophy of the Human Mind" and was required for the degree.[77]

Dew became president of the college in 1836, retaining his previous post, and continued to teach political economy until his unexpected death while on a visit to Europe in 1846. He is remembered as an economist primarily for the eloquent attack on protectionism in his *Lectures on the Restrictive System*, published in 1829, and for his defense of slavery, especially his *Review of the Debates in the Virginia Legislature of 1831 and 1832 on the Abolition of Slavery* with its wide-ranging consideration of the historical, political, social, moral, legal, demographic, and economic aspects of slavery and emancipation. His posthumously published *Digest of the Laws, Customs, Manners, and Institutions of the Ancient and Modern Nations*, which was based on his historical lectures, also had considerable merit and was repeatedly republished during the remainder of the century.[78]

Lectures on the Restrictive System is a considerably amplified version of ten lectures given to the Senior Political class at William and Mary. They cover only a portion of the entire course, and "it will be found that frequent reference has been made to others previously delivered."[79] These earlier lectures appear to have been a general review of Smithian economics as qualified by wide reading in the more recent literature, American, British, French, and German (Dew had spent two years in Europe after graduation in 1820). The treatment of value and distribution was essentially Ricardian.[80] The published lectures are an able but not particularly original statement of the case for free trade and against the special protection of manufactures. The infant-industry argument is denied.[81] The lectures show considerable polemic power and an ability to synthesize arguments drawn from a wide variety of sources. They became a popular document among southern opponents of northern protectionism.

Dew's conservative writings on slavery, although perhaps his most influential, seem to have been less closely connected to his college teaching. However, they were added to the list of Senior Political textbooks, which after 1836 had been modified to "Say's Political Economy, Dew's Lectures on the Restrictive System, and on Usury, Dew's Essay on Slavery, and Brown's Philosophy of the human mind."[82] The "Lectures . . . on Usury" mentioned here, fully titled *Essay on the Interest of Money, and the Policy of Laws against Usury,* were published in 1834 and drawn from Dew's college lectures. The published version contained "the substance of two lectures, much enlarged," but indications of the original context were retained:

I have already in former lectures given you an account of the causes which render a circulating medium necessary in the progress of society, and pointed out the circumstances which determine the relative values of the metals and other commodities throughout the civilized world: I have shown you how, by judicious banking, the circulating medium may be economised, and a convertible paper be made to perform the functions of the precious metals, at the same time pointing out the multifarious evils consequent on this system, so great and hitherto so universally attendant on it, as to render it a problematical question whether banks up to the present day, have not generated more mischief than good. In my present lecture[s] I propose to conclude my remarks on the subject of money, by an investigation of the principles which regulate interest, and an examination of the policy of those laws which fix and limit its rate. . . . I need scarcely inform you that my own opinions on this subject are in unison with those entertained by me on other branches of our science, and shall endeavor to prove to you, that with few exceptions, the interest of money ought not to be restrained by law.[83]

Important additional evidence on Dew's teaching of political economy comes from student notes, the most complete and satisfactory set of which relates to the session 1840–41.[84] The notes record forty-six lectures. The first eleven were a general introduction to the subject, rather philosophic and discursive in tone and adopting a promarket and proproperty stance. Lectures 12 and 13 set out the Ricardian theory of rent and distribution, using numerical illustrations. This was the only part of the course focusing on general theoretical issues. Population issues were considered in lectures 14–19, and various topics, including the desirable role of government, in lectures 20–29. Lectures 30–45 were a detailed consideration of money, credit, banking, and U.S. Treasury policies, paying particular attention to recent controversies concerning the U.S. National Bank and the Subtreasury.[85]

The pattern revealed here, and in the *Lectures on the Restrictive System,* suggests that Dew's practice was to conclude his course with an extended discussion of a particular issue of current interest: arguments concerning protectionism in the late 1820s, banking in the early forties, and other issues, such as usury laws, or perhaps slavery, in the interim.

Dew's classes were large, and he was a dedicated, inspiring, and eloquent teacher. In the 1840–41 session the college had 110 students, ninety-four of whom were from Virginia, and fifty-seven of them were taking the Senior Political course, which included political economy. Another seventy-one were taking the Junior Moral course (obviously some of them simultaneously with the Senior Political). Another five students were taking the "Mor. and Pol. A. M. course," a postgraduate course for those having already attained the B.A. degree. By contrast with Dew's total registration of 133, registrations in law were ninety-nine; in science, eighty-six; in mathematics, sixty-eight; and in classics, seventeen. The college was unique in its heavy emphasis on morals, politics, and law. On his method of teaching, Dew noted that

The Professor, at each meeting of the [Moral and Political] classes, is in the habit of explaining the text, and making such additions as he deems necessary, upon all of which the student is rigorously examined; and when the nature of the subject requires it, he delivers independent lectures, upon which the student is likewise examined.

Each class met for three hours a week.[86]

Dew was an influential southern writer whose works helped shape southern attitudes toward emancipation and protectionism.[87] The college prospered modestly under his careful governance, recovering from a serious setback in the mid-1820s when a campaign to shift the college to Richmond, a plan vehemently opposed by Jefferson, was defeated in the legislature. The number of matriculations, which had averaged forty-five in the academic years 1816–19, was down to an average of twenty for the next eight academic years, 1819–27. Thereafter matriculations rose to around fifty and during the years 1836–46 of Dew's Presidency to an average of 101, with a peak of 141 in 1839–40.[88] With no guarantee of an adequate enrollment from one year to the next, finance continued to be a hand-to-mouth matter. But the modest prosperity of the Dew years was not to be maintained.

A SKETCH OF DEVELOPMENTS BETWEEN 1845 AND 1900

When it lost Tucker and Dew in the mid-1840s, Virginia also lost any claims to eminence in economic writing and teaching. No new figures of comparable stature in the subject were to appear during the remainder of the nineteenth century. The teaching of economics continued uninterrupted at the University of Virginia, but the Civil War and its aftermath were to bring hard times to William and Mary. After Dew's death political economy was taught at William and Mary temporarily by the professor of law, Beverley Tucker, a son of St. George Tucker and cousin of George Tucker, well known along with Dew as a defender of states' rights and slavery.[89] The appointment in 1847 of George Frederick Holmes as Professor of History, Political Economy, and Ancient and Modern Languages proved very temporary, as he left within a year for the University of Missouri. His departure was hastened by the personal animosities then racking the college, which were to lead eventually to the forced resignation of the entire faculty.[90] Holmes was succeeded in 1849 by Henry Augustine Washington, a descendant of George Washington's brother Augustine. Washington appears to have been a serious scholar and was asked by Congress to edit and publish the Jefferson papers held by the Library of Congress. His interests seem to have been historical, but his recommendations to the senior class for a "preparatory course of reading" in political economy—"Smith, McCullock [sic], Ricardo and Mills [sic]"—were quite ambitious. One hopes for the students' sake that the errors were the printer's and not Washington's own.[91] When Washington died in 1858 his successor was Robert J. Morrison, about whom little seems to be known except that his interests too appear to have been primarily historical. He died in 1861. Disruption by the Civil War was an almost fatal blow to the struggling college, which was closed for the duration and lost the bulk of both its buildings and its endowment, the latter having been mainly invested in Confederate bonds. Reconstruction did not impinge significantly on its independence, but its recovery was so limping that it lost entirely any claim to be regarded as an institution of the first rank and became little more than a grammar school. Political economy was no longer taught, and teaching was entirely suspended for some years after 1880 when the college was without students. Recovery began only in 1888 under the presidency of Lyon G. Tyler, son of U.S. president John Tyler.[92] In that year a Normal School for Men—one of a series of normal schools established by the state for the training of teachers—was incorporated into the college, which eventually became in 1906 entirely a state institution, ending over 200 years of independence. President Tyler served as Professor of Moral Science, Political Economy, and Civil Government. He taught political economy, suggesting as reference books "Perry's Political Economy; Dew's Restrictive System; Jevons' Political Economy"—a rather odd combination.[93] But he was primarily a historian and genealogist, and his chief claim to remembrance by economists rests on his efforts to uncover the details of Bishop Madison's pioneering teaching of the subject—part of a general stress on past glories designed to promote the prestige and ambition of an institution struggling to find a new role.

When George Tucker retired from the University of Virginia in 1845, the vacant professorship of moral philosophy was first offered to Dew, who declined it. Eventually, William Holmes McGuffey, the author of the famous *Eclectic Readers* that were used in primary schools throughout the nation, was appointed. Dew seems to have been wanted for his scholarly stature rather than his views on slavery, for McGuffey, a northerner, was no admirer of "the peculiar institution." McGuffey taught political economy at the university from 1845 until 1868. In that year the subject was transferred temporarily to the School of History, General Literature, and Rhetoric, where it was taught by George Frederick Holmes, formerly of William and Mary, who had joined the faculty in 1857. When McGuffey died in 1873 the subject reverted to the School of Moral Philosophy, and McGuffey's successor, Noah Knowles Davis, taught it until it was transferred back to Holmes in a reorganization of 1882. With this restructuring, Holmes became Professor of Historical Sciences, including political economy. He taught the latter subject until his death in 1897 at age seventy-seven. It was not until 1906 that a trained specialist in economics, Thomas Walker Page, was appointed—although Richard Heath Dabney, a historian who filled the gap between Holmes and Page, had received some exposure to the teachings of the German historical school when a graduate student in Germany.[94]

McGuffey, a staunch Presbyterian, was more preacher than scholar and published little or nothing except the *Readers*. His course on political economy, of which student notes survive, was undemanding, and his knowledge of the subject does not seem to have been deep. Davis was a respectable philosopher but seems to have had little interest in political economy. His copious writings did not touch the subject. Holmes was by far the most interesting of the three self-taught economists, almost as interesting a social thinker as George Tucker had been, albeit wild. A correspondent and critic of Auguste Comte, Holmes had wide-ranging literary, historical, and sociological interests. He wrote extensively on all kinds of matters, but the only specifically economic topic to attract him was gold. His economic views and teaching were idiosyncratic, and his opinion of the traditional British school of political economy was not high. His ambitions lay rather in a "Science of Society," a blend of history and sociology.

The University of Virginia remained open during the Civil War, and there was a remarkable recovery in enrollments afterward.[95] The Reconstruction era in Virginia was relatively short-lived, and the university was little affected. Control remained in enlightened hands, and there seems to have been no overt intervention or censorship. The remainder of the nineteenth century was characterized by modest development and improvement, building on the antebellum Jeffersonian tradition without sharp change or discontinuity. In the humanities and social sciences, the changes were especially modest, but even in other fields there was nothing to match the veritable explosion of change overtaking higher education outside the South.[96] The reasons for this are not hard to find. Virginia, like the rest of the South, was relatively poor and had suffered much damage in the war. The economic basis for a rapid expansion and improvement of the state's educational system was simply lacking. In any case, the University of Virginia had never enjoyed unalloyed legislative and popular support. It had been suspected at various times of elitism and irreligion, and a long history of student turbulence had not increased its popularity. Its ties to the state were in fact quite weak, and when the time came to expand higher educational opportunities the state preferred to found new institutions. Nor did private donations appear on the scale of those founding Stanford, Chicago, or even Johns Hopkins. There were generous gifts, and they were important in assisting the ongoing steady improvement, but they were not of a magnitude permitting radical change. Last but not least, Jefferson's original design had been remarkably forward-looking, and it was not necessary to deviate very far from it in order to be a modern institution by late nineteenth-century standards. Unlike Harvard or Yale, there was no need to break out of a radically different earlier mould. Yet this advantage imposed its own cost, because continuity preserved vested interests and complacent attitudes, which might have been broken up had radical change been needed but which could threaten future excellence if left undisturbed. By the late nineteenth century the University of Virginia was an institution of high quality, but it was no longer in the van of advancement in higher education. This was certainly so in the field of economics.[97]

CONCLUDING REMARKS

During the first third of the nineteenth century, the teaching of economics took hold in the two Virginia institutions in contrasting ways: backward-looking in the case of William and Mary, and forward-looking in the case of the University of Virginia. William and Mary, a small, struggling institution, harked back to the glories of its past associations with the foundation and early years of the Republic and strove to recapture this aura by emphasizing training for civic and political affairs through the study of law, morals, and politics. Politics had included political economy ever since Bishop Madison's day, and the teaching of this subject attained a peak of success and influence under Thomas Dew. Dew, in his inaugural address as president of the college in 1836, emphasized this reliance on tradition:

The law, political and moral departments of this College have always been upon a high and respectable footing, and moral and political subjects have here always received a due consideration. Hence it is that old William and Mary can boast of so astonishing a number of distinguished statesmen.

He also indicated a darker side to this conservative desire to cling to the past, and a more pressing justification for emphasizing "political" education.

You are generally members of that portion of our confederacy whose domestic institutions have been called in question by the meddling spirit of the age. You are slaveholders, or the sons of slaveholders, and as such your duties and responsibilities are greatly increased. . . . Prepare yourselves then for this important relation, so as to be able to discharge its duties with humanity and wisdom. Then can we exhibit to the world the most convincing evidence of the justice of our cause.[98]

That an institution which had become a center of proslavery sentiment should have difficulty adapting to the postbellum era is hardly surprising.

In contrast to this conservative hankering after old ways and past glories, the University of Virginia was a product of Thomas Jefferson's fertile and forward-looking brain and his expansive desire to found a university that was "broad and liberal and modern," covering "all the sciences useful to us." Jefferson included the new science of political economy among the latter, certainly after 1814. His design was well in advance of its day and was to serve as the blueprint for the institution right through the nineteenth century. As the century progressed, the university fell behind the vanguard of educational advance, largely because of the modesty of the resources available to it. Distinguished scholars and scientists served on its faculty, but the age of academic specialization reached it only in the twentieth century. Throughout the nineteenth century, political economy was taught by individuals with wide-ranging interests and the responsibility for teaching several subjects. Only George Tucker achieved real distinction in this particular branch of his extensive brief, but his successors were eminent men in their own fashion.

In their contrasting ways, both Dew and Tucker were particularly attuned to the ethos of their respective institutions. For Dew, economics was the handmaiden of policy and the commitment to a cause. Tucker's interests were much more scientific and pragmatic, although his skeptical, ironical mind took a lively interest in the affairs of the day—as became an ex-congressman.

Faithful Index to the Ambitions and Fortunes of the State: The Development of Political Economy at South Carolina College

MICHAEL D. BORDO and
WILLIAM H. PHILLIPS

In 1804, PRESIDENT Thomas Jefferson received a letter from Dr. Thomas Cooper, a Pennsylvania politician, lawyer, and chemist with whom he had corresponded since shortly after the presidential elections. Cooper, a disciple of the famous English chemist and Unitarian, Joseph Priestley, did not begin his letter with a discussion of chemistry or religion or of the political and legal intrigues between the Republicans and the Federalists. Rather, his mind was turned to the emerging field of political economy:

We are yet in the infancy of knowledge respecting political economy. Malthus's remarks on the tables of population, his observations on the corn laws and the poor law are just; . . . but his general ideas have been forestalled by Dr. James Steuart, Adam Smith, and Arthur Young; and most of them are found . . . in the treatise of Herenschwand.[1]

These remarks reveal a classic case of the enlightened scholar of the Age of Reason, for whom all branches of knowledge were proper possessions, regardless of where one's own primary scientific interests lay. Nevertheless, this was not just a passing fancy, for in a subsequent letter of 1814 Cooper, then holder of the chair of chemistry at Dickinson College in Carlisle, Pennsylvania, made a

The authors wish to thank Daniel Walker Hollis and the staffs of the South Caroliniana Library and the McKissick Museum of the University of South Carolina for their help in this project. Research assistance was provided by Ivan Marcotte and Earl Shinn. Helpful comments and suggestions were freely given by Lacy Ford and Anna Schwartz. They should not be held responsible for any remaining shortcomings in our analysis.

novel proposal that Jefferson's planned University of Virginia specifically include a political economy course in its curriculum.[2]

Meanwhile, the early 1800s witnessed a growing interest in academic instruction for the prosperous state of South Carolina. In an act of 1801, the legislature allocated $50,000 for buildings and $6,000 per annum for faculty salaries to establish South Carolina College. This funding was sufficient to make Carolina's new college, opened in 1805, one of the more amply supported in the nation, and the new faculty and the leaders of the state were committed to building an educational institution as good as its financing would allow. In 1815, the standing committee of the Board of Trustees made the following recommendation:

That in order to keep pace with the growing knowledge of the world, and to place this institution on a footing with the great and improving colleges of the northern states, it would be advisable to establish new professorships. . . . Professorships for Political Economy, for Elocution and Belles Lettres and others, might be usefully established in succession, according to their order of importance.[3]

Given these convergent interests, it should not have been unexpected that Thomas Cooper would one day introduce political economy into the college's course of study, although he was originally hired by South Carolina in 1819 to teach chemistry. Thus would be initiated a period, however brief, of exemplary achievement in the antebellum development of American economic thought.

This essay surveys this period, analyzes its underlying causes, and chronicles the eventual downfall of the college's heritage in political economy instruction. It will be found that its early flowering can be explained by two distinct processes. First, a unique set of historical circumstances combined to make the state of South Carolina in the early nineteenth century one of the most receptive areas of the United States to a relatively uncensored discussion of the intellectual currents of the day, including debates in political economy. The analogy can be made in some ways to Italy during the Renaissance. Second, a significant proportion of the college's achievement in political economy must be attributed to the two major personalities involved: Thomas Cooper and his successor, Francis Lieber, neither of whom was a native-born American. As is often the case in personnel decisions in modern times, South Carolina hired Cooper and then Lieber uncertain about how significant their contributions to the college would be, and uncertain as well about the precise areas to which they would contribute. The college did not explicitly set out to hire two of the leading political economists in the United States at the time. They hired people who appeared to be good scholars and awaited the results. As in the Renaissance, the intellectual environment of the times was important, but credit for many of the individual accomplishments must still be assigned to the unique abilities of extraordinary people who made the most of favorable circumstances. The intellectual history of South Carolina College is both social history and biography in roughly equal proportions.

THE LAUNCHING OF THE THOMAS COOPER ERA AT SOUTH CAROLINA COLLEGE

Thomas Cooper (1759–1839) was one of that special breed of men who relish their influential friends and seem to relish their influential enemies even more. He managed to accumulate some of both throughout his life. In England as a young man, he was counted among the radical philosophers. He joined Priestley and Jeremy Bentham in praising Rousseau, Locke, Paine, and the French Revolution, while at the same time engaging in written battle with the conservative Edmund Burke. Soon after immigrating to the United States in 1793, Cooper joined the Republicans of Pennsylvania in their contests against the Federalists. Thus began his friendship with Jefferson. He also managed to get himself tried, convicted, and briefly jailed for violations of the Sedition Act, a consequence of many intemperate letters and pamphlets attacking President John Adams. Once Jefferson attained power, Cooper was rewarded with various political positions in Pennsylvania, culminating in a judgeship. However, his faith in democracy waned, and his strongly voiced opinions on the matter led his former political associates in that state to remove him from his judicial post. By the time Cooper made his move to South Carolina, he was already sixty years old.

Cooper arrived in South Carolina when the state was at the apex of its economic importance. The accumulated profits of lowland indigo, rice, and sea-island cotton had made Carolina the wealthiest state in the union. The social life of the planters centered around the active port of Charleston, which proudly claimed to be the true seat of culture in the United States. Meanwhile, economic advance was occurring in the state's once backward up-country. The demand for short-staple cotton generated by the cotton gin had turned the inferior lands of the sand hills and the Piedmont into valuable property. The immigration induced by these developments enlarged the population of the upper part of the state, making it a potent political force. This shift in the population balance had posed severe problems, owing to a legislative apportionment biased toward the low-country districts. But the lauded "Compromise of 1808" had at least partially redressed the problem, and tensions between the two sections seemed to be quickly abating.[4]

Intellectually and religiously, South Carolina was one of the most liberal areas in early nineteenth-century America. This frame of mind had been largely established by the landed aristocracy of the coast and Charleston. Members of the nonevangelistic Anglican church and wealthy enough to cultivate the contemplative, philo-sophic, world view of the gentleman, these low-country planters continued in the tradition of the Virginian founding fathers. Their belief in natural law and the efficacy of reason was supreme. Deism or even outright skepticism regarding matters of religion was openly tolerated and often considered the essence of "modern" thinking. Inland—away from this aristocracy—popular attitudes toward religion and free thought were not so much ones of doubt as of disinterest. The up-country still had too much of the unsettled frontier atmosphere about it to permit the establishment of a strong and stable religious base, and the low-country Anglicans were not of a mood to seek wholesale conversions. Irreligion was a dominant force, although Presbyterians, Methodists, and Baptists were present and determined to spread their message.[5]

The importance of this historical background lies in the perspec-tive it gives to the founding and early operation of South Carolina College. As a wealthy state, the public of South Carolina had the demand for and the ability to support higher learning. Wealthier Carolinians had for some time sent their sons in large numbers to Europe or to the North for education, with apparent appreciation for the fruits of classical learning. Why then was the founding of a local college delayed until the early nineteenth century? Part of the explanation can be traced to the absence of a religious group of sufficient strength and commitment to create a denominational in-stitution. In addition, the era's "limited government" intellectual temper meant that it was necessary to wait until public sentiment was ready to demand a state-sponsored college. But, once the col-lege was established, it was readily supported by the citizenry, both through the provision of state funds and through its willingness to enroll its sons there. To the enlightened leadership of the state, the college was seen as a tool in the service of reason—in addition to or in lieu of religion—which would be passed on to the forthcoming planters, gentlemen, and statesmen of Carolina, thus insuring wise leadership for the future. Finally, the college would spread the culture of the low-country aristocracy to the upper regions of the state through the shared education of their sons. In this way, the low country would protect its political influence even after it had lost numerical superiority in the state's political institutions.[6]

The story of Cooper's arrival at Carolina's college must begin with his aborted appointment to the nascent University of Virginia.[7] Jefferson had opened the possibility of Cooper's appointment there as early as 1814, and in 1819 Cooper was formally offered the professorship of chemistry, mineralogy, and natural philosophy (and temporarily of law), to begin in April 1820 with salary and fees totaling $3,500. However, opposition to Cooper arose over his oft-stated religious views, particularly his Unitarianism and his criticisms of Calvinism. The attacks in Virginia, as would later be the case in South Carolina, were led by the Presbyterians. Although usually smaller in numbers than their Methodist and Baptist cousins, Presbyterians had strength in wealthier households that were sensitive to the importance of religion in higher education.[8] Virginia was at this time undergoing many of the same economic, political, and intellectual developments as South Carolina, including a contest between aristocratic Episcopalianism and growing back-country evangelism. The resulting controversy led the university's Board of Visitors—in October 1819—to delay the onset of Cooper's appointment until building construction was finished.

Cooper was then caught without an appointment for the following year, having left a position in applied chemistry and mineralogy at the University of Pennsylvania and failing to obtain one in chemistry in that university's medical school. Cooper shortly learned of a similar vacancy at South Carolina College, occasioned by the death of its professor of chemistry. Cooper's application was speedily accepted, and he was elected professor of chemistry for one year on December 3, 1819, at a salary of $2,000. Cooper at first hoped that this would be just a temporary stop pending his departure for Charlottesville. But opposition from religious groups in Virginia did not abate, and South Carolina College, apparently quite satisfied with its acquisition, offered in the spring of 1820 to make Cooper's appointment permanent, adding to it a position in geology and mineralogy that raised his salary to $3,000. An agreement was subsequently worked out with Virginia in which Cooper resigned his appointment there in return for an indemnity of $1,500. Although Cooper continued to correspond with Jefferson over the possibility of an eventual move to his university, the position he coveted moved ever farther away.[9]

In South Carolina, Cooper's success was quick in coming. During the preceding few years, the college's reputation had suffered with the prolonged illness of its respected president, Jonathan Maxcy, who had headed the institution since its founding. Cooper was the college's preeminent scholar at the time of Maxcy's death in the summer of 1820 and an obvious candidate to succeed him. The trustees, however, first offered the presidency and membership on the board to the president of the Bank of the State of South Carolina. Perhaps a politically inspired appointment, this invitation was nonetheless declined, and Cooper was unanimously elected president pro tempore in December 1820. The trustees advertised for applications to the permanent post during the following year, but Cooper felt that he had the inside track.[10]

In December 1821, Cooper was elected permanent president of South Carolina College by a vote of ten to nine over fellow faculty member Robert Henry. Although no record of the trustees' assessments of the rival candidates seems to have survived, the narrowness of Cooper's victory may have been the consequence of religious opposition to him in South Carolina. Robert Henry was young and inexperienced, particularly by comparison with Cooper; yet he had been a minister for the French Protestant Church in Charleston and later took pains to point out his disagreements with Cooper's heresies when the Presbyterian clergy mounted a challenge to Cooper's position in 1822 and 1823.[11] In the early 1820s, however, anti-Cooper forces had no major political allies and were eventually defeated. The leadership of the state and the college were pleased with the renown that Cooper brought to the institution. As Cooper stated in a letter to Jefferson, "the favorable opinion of the trustees, even of the calvinistic part of them, is unchanged; on their part, I have nothing to dread; . . . So that my standing here is higher than it ever was among the persons best qualified to judge."[12]

THE DEVELOPMENT OF POLITICAL
ECONOMY INSTRUCTION

In 1823 negotiations began between the Board of Trustees and Cooper that would lead to the initiation of formal instruction in political economy at South Carolina in 1825. What is less certain, however, is the amount of exposure to political economy given to the college's students before that time. Moral philosophy, as the ancestor of most of today's social sciences, was taught in almost every college of the day and was primarily conceived of as a "finishing-off" subject, often presented to the senior class by the college president, its most distinguished or senior scholar. The purpose was to provide the soon-to-be graduates with a generalized humanistic view of the state of knowledge and its application to the human condition. It not only provided basic prescriptions for the proper conduct of one's personal life but also presented the sound doctrine of the day regarding the proper relationship of man to society and thus the correct course of public policy.[13]

South Carolina began instruction in moral philosophy in 1809 with the hiring of the Reverend John Brown, soon followed by the appointment of the Reverend Benjamin R. Montgomery in 1811. Both were Presbyterian ministers of limited education, and there is no conclusive evidence to indicate any political economy content in their courses. In 1818 Robert Henry, Cooper's opponent for the presidency of the college, succeeded to the chair of moral philosophy and logic. A native of Charleston, Henry had nonetheless been educated at Edinburgh where evidently he had obtained some exposure to modern British thought. As a text, he used Paley's *Principles of Moral and Political Philosophy,* a popular course book that ran through fifteen editions from 1785 to 1804. Paley's thought was based on a utilitarian system of philosophy as the ultimate basis for judging human action. In addition, the eleventh chapter out of twelve in the two-volume text (1804 edition) is headed: "Of Population and Provision; and of Agriculture and Commerce, as subservient thereto." This chapter contains some very simple Smithian notions about agriculture, commerce, and taxation, as well as some Malthusian-like discussions about the causes and effects of population growth, particularly with respect to the nation's material wealth.[14] Such a chapter was apparently quite common in the moral philosophy courses of the day, but as is true in modern times, the issue is whether this subject matter was covered by the instructor of the course.[15]

The opportunity to give political economy a status separate from moral philosophy at South Carolina arose in part as a by-product of the necessity to reallocate teaching assignments after the death of President Maxcy. Maxcy had been responsible for instruction in metaphysics. In 1822 it was proposed by the Board of Trustees that Cooper should take this work.[16] One can only imagine the reaction of the local clergy to the prospect that the materialist Cooper would train the state's youth in metaphysics, but, fortunately for them, Cooper was not interested in this arrangement. In the spring of 1823, Cooper presented the following response to the proposal:

The president professes himself qualified and competent to teach metaphysics (having devoted much more time to that unsatisfactory subject than most men; so much so as to be fully persuaded it is not worth the time required to be bestowed upon it). If required to teach it, he will teach it in the best manner he is able. If the trustees on reflection should think it fit to change a course of metaphysics for a course of political economy, the president is of the opinion that it will be a change well suited to the modern views of liberal education, and he will prepare a course accordingly.[17]

The board apparently agreed to Cooper's proposition, for he reported to Jefferson that summer that he had been requested to give lectures on political economy, in effect being given "carte blanche" as to his choice of courses. Henry was subsequently charged to cover metaphysics, a subject for which Cooper had no taste. The launching of his projected course in political economy, however, was delayed until Cooper had persuaded a budget-minded board to hire an additional instructor to relieve him of teaching duties in rhetoric and belles lettres that he had inherited from Maxcy.[18]

In December 1824 Cooper presided over the college's commencement and, in his own words, "delivered an address recommending the study of Political Economy, and the regular appointment of a professor for the purpose—a proposal at that time, new in the United States."[19] At the beginning of classes in the new year, Cooper initiated his lectures in political economy to the senior class of South Carolina College. At first, in 1825, Cooper made use of the elementary *Conversations on Political Economy* by Mrs. Jane Marcet. In 1826 he turned to the *Outlines of Political Economy* (John McVickar's republication of J. R. McCulloch's article in the *Encyclopaedia Britannica,* with critical notes supplied by the editor).[20] By the end of Cooper's second year of instruction, he had developed his lecture notes into one of the first American political economy texts, namely, his *Lectures on the Elements of Political Economy,* which he used in his course for the duration of his tenure at South Carolina College. This text, which eventually went through three editions, was well received in the scholarly and public press. It received favorable reviews in the *Charleston Southern Patriot* and the *Southern Review* (the Charleston journal of Nicholas Cardozo, who was also a noted political economist of the time). It was also praised outside the South in the *American Quarterly Review* and the *North American Review*. Such was the book's reputation that Francis Lieber, a young German immigrant living in Boston who had taken on the enormous task of editing the new *Encyclopaedia Americana,* saw fit to list Cooper's text as one of the principal works on the topic of "political economy."[21]

The work was not widely adopted, however, by other American colleges. One reviewer noted that the quality of the printing "does no credit to the state of the typographical arts in Columbia." Another observed that, although Cooper's position in favor of free trade was correct, he had not listed some common objections to the policy that could easily have been shown to be fallacious—"for the writer of a textbook, this is wrong." Nonetheless, the major obstacle to a wider readership in colleges was Cooper's materialistic philosophy, which could never be fully accepted at the predominantly clerical schools of the day. The 1845 assessment by the renowned English economist McCulloch draws attention to an element of paradox that ran through all of Cooper's activities: "this work, though not written in a very philosophical spirit, is the best of the American works on political economy that we have met with."[22]

THE SUBSTANCE OF COOPER'S ECONOMICS

Cooper's first apparent expression of interest in political economy dated from his 1799 publication, *Political Essays,* in which he wrote of the need for the scattered facts about economic activity to be gathered together so that policy makers could be better informed. His first tract specifically addressing an issue of economic policy was an 1823 pamphlet entitled *On the Proposed Alteration of the Tariff,* in which he initiated the southern economic attack against northern tariff policy. In addition to the *Lectures,* he published *A Manual of Political Economy* (an elementary primer based on the *Lectures*) in 1834 for students in preparatory academies.[23]

To Cooper, political economy was the natural extension of materialistic philosophy to public conduct.[24] He had absorbed the utilitarian credo of the greatest happiness of the greatest number from his study of moral philosophy, political philosophy, and law, and over time he became increasingly convinced that political economy was essential to the conduct of public policy. In his view, no legislator or other public official could do his job properly without exposure to the ideas of Adam Smith, Say, and the classical school.[25] In this way, Cooper fit in well with the teaching philosophy of

South Carolina College, which held that a primary goal of education was to train enlightened statesmen and legislators.

Cooper considered himself—and was considered by others—to be a follower of the modern school of Ricardo, which had built upon and improved Adam Smith.[26] In the introductory chapter to his *Lectures,* Cooper lists the principles of Smith with which he continued to agree: labor as the sole foundation of all value; the role of the mercantile, manufacturing, and agricultural sectors as common creators of utility and value; the propensity to accumulate as the source of permanent wealth; the advantages of division of labor; the fallacy of counting gold and silver as wealth; and the virtues of individual self-interest left unregulated by government. However, according to Cooper, the new principles of Ricardo and his followers had revealed Smith to be mistaken in the following respects: Agriculture is not any more beneficial to society than other pursuits; wealth does not have to be attached to material objects; the value of corn is not fixed; rent does not enter into price; prices do not fluctuate with wages, as changes in wages lead to offsetting changes in profits, the other component in price; value in the long run is determined not by demand and supply but by the cost of bringing the commodity to market, which ultimately depends on the quantity of labor required to produce the good, either directly or indirectly, in the accumulated labor embodied in capital.

Cooper listed and approved of Malthus's elements of population theory while giving qualified assent to Say's assertion that supply creates its own demand.[27] Cooper supplemented Malthusian economics with the following proposition: that as population pressure increased, the resulting growth in human want would induce greater exertion on the part of labor, enabling an enlarged population to feed itself. Therefore, so long as preventive checks or, in America's case, additional land cultivation could forestall disastrous famine, a moderate excess in population was in fact beneficial to productivity and economic growth. Cooper's qualification to Say consisted in asserting that some time must be allowed for demand to accompany increased supply, for if production increased too rapidly temporary gluts could exist. Finally, Cooper differed with some aspects of Ricardian rent and distribution theory. He still preferred the Smithian perspective of rent arising from the bounty of nature (as opposed to its niggardliness), and he neglected the impact of the intensive margin of cultivation. Both of these reinterpretations were likely the result of Cooper's reading of American conditions, which also influenced his distribution theory. Although he agreed with Ricardo that in mature economies growing rents would conflict with the shares remaining for profits and wages, there could be concurrent growth in rents, profits, and wages if ample and increasing investment opportunities were available, as was the case in the United States.

When applying economic reasoning to the practical issues of the day, Cooper was dogmatic in his assertions, yet his strong positions were subject to change with the intellectual mood of his surroundings. As a militant free-trade advocate, Cooper—along with Thomas Dew of William and Mary—became a primary target of the northern protectionist school of Mathew Carey and Friedrich List.[28] During his days in Pennsylvania, however, Cooper had supported protection under certain circumstances: For example, tariffs might usefully dampen the commercial disruptions to which America was vulnerable as a neutral during the Napoleonic era. Advocates of the "American system" later referred to this position to accuse Cooper of opportunism. Yet a review of his economic writings reveals that he had backed laissez-faire principles from the very beginning, and his protectionist episodes seem based on exceptions admitted to by Adam Smith himself. A letter to Jefferson discussing these issues, for example, seems definitely charged with the overhanging fear of imminent warfare with the European sea powers, making heavy reliance on British goods risky in the event of embargoes and blockades.[29]

On the slavery question, Cooper's sentiments varied considerably. As a young radical in England, he had written a pamphlet opposing the slave trade. But, after moving to the United States, his views shifted to considering slavery to be a local issue, best handled in a pragmatic way by the society in question. In this sense, Cooper appears to have gradually adopted the "necessary evil" doctrine that dominated the nation, both North and South, before the late 1820s and 1830s.[30] As tensions rose in the nation over the slavery question, Cooper defended the institution for reasons that were basically sociological and constitutional. It was simply not thinkable in his view for the South to risk the anarchy of a freed slave populace. Moreover, to allow the federal government to force the issue on the South would pave the way for tyrannical absolutism in a formerly democratic society. Cooper never formulated a serious economic defense of slavery; instead, his *Lectures* assumed that slave labor was inherently less efficient than free labor because it was not voluntary and was based on an inferior class of worker, an attitude reflecting the popular prejudices of the day, both North and South. It was unprofitable compared to free white labor, and it was used in the South only because white labor could not tolerate the unhealthy southern geography and climate.

On money and banking issues, Cooper was a quantity theorist, although a rather crude one, as he ignored the factors of velocity and growth of real output. He generalized a connection between excess money balances and inflation to a price–specie flow mechanism of international trade. He approved of note-issuing banks that operated under two conditions: Paper money would be issued only in the conduct of real business transactions, and notes were convertible into coin on demand. He apparently had serious doubts about the efficacy of convertibility in controlling private bank note issue, for he felt that the bankers of the United States had an inherent tendency to overissue their notes, to the detriment of public welfare. He considered the possibility of a government-controlled bank but distrusted such a concentration of power. He concluded that a system of private banking was best but that Congress would have to regulate its note issuance. During the disputes between Andrew Jackson and the Bank of the United States, Cooper consistently sided with Nicholas Biddle, a position at odds with that of many South Carolinian supporters of Jackson.[31] Cooper appears to have eventually decided that it was up to an enlightened individual such as Biddle, who was a personal friend, to resist political expediency and to control the issuance of private bank notes in the public interest.

What conclusions can be drawn about the instruction given to South Carolina's students by Cooper? His own work contained little originality and was quickly forgotten after his death.[32] As was the case throughout his life, it was the forcefulness of Cooper's opinions, not their originality, that pushed them into public view. Yet much the same can be said of every American political economist of his time. The immature scholastic base of the United States necessitated a concentration on understanding and translating European thought, not advancing upon it. Cooper was not aiming for more than this, as he noted in the preface to the *Lectures*. His book was written for his students, with whom he originally had to use a text designed for preparatory academies (Marcet). Although entrance standards were raised under Cooper's presidency, the typical student of South Carolina College was young, undisciplined, and relatively untutored.[33] Little more could be expected from most than that they learn the bare outlines of this complicated subject. For those who wished to go further, Cooper recommended reading

Smith, Say, Malthus, Ricardo, McCulloch, and the elder Mill, and there is no doubt that he induced some of his brighter students to do this.[34]

It would be difficult to argue that any students in the United States in the 1820s had superior opportunities to make the acquaintance of leading European thinkers. As a student of Ricardo's works, Cooper taught principles that were largely neglected in other colleges, where an instructor more interested in history or moral philosophy might have been satisfied with an overview of Adam Smith. In addition, Cooper's materialist nature left him with no qualms about citing directly the great English and French economists whose deistic and rationalistic viewpoints were considered dangerous at many church-sponsored colleges.[35] Finally, contentious though he apparently was, Cooper was regarded as an excellent lecturer and speaker, and his students knew that they were being taught by an extraordinary man.[36] What his scholarship lacked in originality it made up for in activity. He published detailed reviews of the works of the classical economists, was quoted and talked about in the southern and northern press, and cultivated the feeling in the college and the state that they were pioneers in the nation's study of political economy.[37]

THE DEMISE OF COOPER

The end of the Cooper era at South Carolina College was largely a function of the rapid social changes occurring in the South beginning in the 1820s. These changes were particularly significant in South Carolina, which became as a result the recognized leader of southern militancy toward the North down to the Civil War.[38] Although Cooper's views were generally compatible with and in many ways anticipated emerging southern thought, he was not the type of person who flourished in a narrowing intellectual environment that increasingly required strict orthodoxy. Consequently, his few strongly voiced disagreements with public opinion and with certain public officials eventually made his position at the college untenable.

The period prior to the Civil War was the heyday of the southern cotton economy. Ironically for South Carolina, the rapid development of the lower South doomed the state to severe relative, albeit not absolute, decline. The tired cotton lands of Carolina could not compete with the fertile soils of Alabama, Mississippi, Louisiana, and Texas. Short-staple cotton prices fell to levels that remained profitable in the West but brought hardship in the East. Fortunately, sea-island cotton prices stayed high and low-country planters fared better. But Charleston suffered from a technological revolution in transportation with the introduction of the steamboat. Trapped on a river basin that extended only a few miles inland, the proud city steadily lost ground to Savannah, Mobile, New Orleans, and the upriver cities connected by navigable water to these ports. Upland cotton, even that of Carolina, increasingly bypassed Charleston on its way to northern and British markets.

An immediate consequence of this economic dislocation was the reemergence of sectional politics in South Carolina. Whereas northern tariffs had previously been only minor nuisances tolerated in good times, they now appeared as strength-sapping threats to economic survival. Carolina was ready by the early 1830s—independently for the most part from significant support in the rest of the South—to threaten the sanctity of the Union in the name of a state's right to nullify tariff laws passed by the Congress. Although the nullification crisis passed, the "nullifiers" remained and soon found another issue over which to battle for southern rights: slavery. Abolitionism began as a distinctly minority movement in a nation seemingly reconciled to the unfortunate necessity of southern slave labor. In fact, before this era, it had generally been the aristocratic slaveholders of Virginia and South Carolina themselves who had expressed the most dismay over the inconsistency of believing in the "equality of all men" while owning the lives of other human beings. The Old South's economy, however, was no longer vital enough to contemplate the additional disruption of restructuring its mode of production. Moreover, with the decline of the Carolina plantations, the best asset remaining to the planter was his valuable slaves, who could be sold westward at ever-higher prices as the new cotton economy prospered there. The final element that made Carolina the first militant defender of slavery was the frightening reality of slave emancipation in the state with the highest ratio of slaves to whites.[39] South Carolina society increasingly regarded it as crucial to declare slavery not a necessary evil to be eventually dispensed with but, rather, a positive good that must immediately be declared as permanently acceptable, not just where the institution was currently established but also wherever it could be spread.

The rise of Protestant fundamentalism added a further ingredient to the changing social fabric of the South. The Age of Reason was dead and had given way to romanticism and emotionalism.

The sway of the aristocratic lowland planters had sharply diminished. The new wealthy plantation owner grew upland cotton and traced his roots to back-country ancestors. Although he enjoyed putting on the airs of the country gentleman, he had little time to waste on esoteric philosophy and culture. He wanted a simple life with simple values that provided emotional contentment and an identity as one of the common people. Thus, the Presbyterians, Methodists, and Baptists were able to extend their influence beyond the conversion of the white yeoman farmers who had been left behind by the cotton economy, and they became the guiding philosophical force behind the South's new leadership. Accordingly, deism and skepticism fell prey to ever-growing intolerance. In education, the result was a rapid growth in the founding of southern denominational colleges as alternatives to the "godless" colleges of the state, soon followed by increasingly insistent demands that the public colleges begin to reflect more faithfully the religious opinions of the populace.[40]

It was into this economic, political, and religious atmosphere that Cooper emerged once again as the center of controversy in 1827.[41] The occasion was a meeting in Columbia to protest against a proposed increase in the tariff being pushed by northern manufacturing interests. Cooper was one of many state and college notables asked to speak, and Cooper's credentials for the occasion were unquestioned. His pamphlet of 1823 in favor of free trade had given the South its economic justification for calling the current tariff policy unfair. Moreover, Cooper's teachings in political philosophy had increasingly warned of the dangers of a dominant federal government destroying the precious liberties of the states and their people. His influence had so grown that he was now styled the "schoolmaster of states' rights," and his pupils were to rule the state with this philosophy for the next thirty-four years.[42] However, this night Cooper was to take the step that no one of such stature had dared to take in public before:

We shall, before long, be compelled to calculate the value of our union; and to inquire of what use to us is this most unequal alliance? . . . Is it worth our while to continue this union of states, where the north demand to be our masters, and we are required to be their tributaries? . . . The question . . . is fast approaching to the alternative, of submission or separation. . . . Every man who hears me, wish on fair and equal terms to avoid it. But, if the monopolists are bent upon forcing the decision upon us, with themselves be the responsibility.[43]

It is paradoxical that this speech, so in line with the emerging mood of the South, eventually put Cooper's job in jeopardy. Previously, Cooper's opponents in South Carolina were primarily religious ones. Now, however, he had created political enemies at the same time he had created political friends. Cooper's remarks attracted wide notice in the North and precipitated deep controversy in South Carolina. Although practically everyone in the state deeply resented the tariff, the suggestion of disunion was regarded by many as treason or at least as an overly drastic response to the situation. Cooper's statement, in fact, marked the beginning of a severe political split within the state between the secessionists (or "fire-eaters"), on the one hand, and the Unionists, on the other. Cooper, after this speech, generally stayed in the background while Senator John C. Calhoun led the nullification crusade in the state. But all sides knew where he stood, and he became a target of the Unionist politicians.[44]

Cooper's position might nevertheless have been safe had he not stirred up old religious animosities. He was a hero in the nullifiers' camp, and their relative strength was growing with each passing year. In fact, it may have been a false confidence generated by this popularity that led Cooper to write new letters and pamphlets attacking Calvinism and the clergy from 1829 to 1831.[45] The final straw was the revelation that Cooper was delivering a lecture to each senior class exposing the fallacies, as he saw them, of the Pentateuch. This led the clergy to make a renewed attempt to remove Cooper. This time they allied their efforts with his influential Unionist foes. In 1831 Cooper's opponents submitted a motion in the state legislature calling for his dismissal. In what became another test of strength between the secessionists and Unionists, the motion was defeated and a substitute resolution was passed calling for an investigation by the college's Board of Trustees into Cooper's conduct. It was widely known that Cooper would be supported by the trustees, but the forum was used by both the clergy and Cooper to present their cases in full. In December 1832, Cooper was formally acquitted of all charges, and the nullifier and Unionist papers issued the expected reactions to the verdict.

Cooper's victory was a Pyrrhic one. He had won politically, but the controversy had severely damaged the college's reputation with the public, which began to heed the clergy's call for a boycott of the institution. The number of students normally attending the college averaged between 110 and 115. However, enrollment in 1833 was down almost 25 percent from 1831 and by the end of the year was showing no signs of recovering.[46] Cooper resigned the presidency in November in order to return to full-time chemistry instruction, where presumably his social and religious views could be kept away from his students. Thus ended the era of Cooper's political economy instruction at South Carolina College. His departure says much about changes in the state's attitude toward toleration in a period of less than fifteen years. Cooper was an unquestioned champion of southern interests in his views on free trade and states' rights. Although his secessionist spirit was slightly ahead of public opinion, it was nonetheless clear by the time of his departure that the region was moving in this direction. His economic defense of slavery was weak, but his public defense of slavery was strong on political grounds. Only on religious matters was Cooper out of touch with his constituency. He was a relic of a disgraced Age of Reason, and the compatibility of his views with local opinion on political issues was no longer enough. The public was now demanding acceptable opinions in all areas, and a strong individualist such as Cooper could never comply. His successor, Francis Lieber, whose opinions were in fact less representative of the South, survived because he was willing and able to keep his heresies out of the sight of those who had no tolerance for dissent.

THE FRANCIS LIEBER ERA AT SOUTH CAROLINA COLLEGE

Francis Lieber (1800–72) had been born in Prussia during the Napoleonic era. His memories as a young boy included the French occupation of Berlin, which led to a lifelong love of nationalism as the only force to maintain liberty—first in his native Germany and later in his adopted home of America.[47] His youthful idealism led him to fight at the Battle of Waterloo and to join in German student movements, which led to arrests and eventual government banishment from study in German universities. He fled to England in 1826, where he unsuccessfully sought a professorship in German at the proposed University of London. While there, he did meet with the aging Jeremy Bentham and the young John Stuart Mill. He then set off for America, arriving in 1827, where he conceived the project of editing an *Encyclopaedia Americana,* modeled after the *Encyclopaedia Britannica.* The work was a great success, and in the process of arranging for American contributors he became a celebrity in Boston social circles, making the acquaintance of such notables as Henry Clay, Daniel Webster, Henry Wadsworth Longfellow, and Nicholas Biddle. Lieber finished his work by early 1833 and once again had to face the problem of finding suitable employment.

Meanwhile, controversy continued to swirl at South Carolina College. Upon Cooper's resignation of the presidency at the end of 1833, the position was given to the now familiar Robert Henry. As Cooper was now teaching chemistry, it fell upon Henry to instruct the senior class in political economy. No evidence bearing on the content of Henry's teaching has been found. But, given his clerical background and his preference for metaphysics, it is doubtful that his treatment of the subject was much different from that which predominated in New England colleges. The fallout from the Cooper affair, however, was still not over. Opponents of the college railed over Cooper's continued presence as a faculty member and charged that the entire faculty consisted of religious misfits protected by political cronies. Enrollment had now fallen to fifty-two—well under half the college's normal student body—and the trustees in December 1834 called for the resignation of the entire faculty. The college would have to be reconstituted in a manner acceptable to all factions, and that meant that there would be no place for Thomas Cooper.[48]

In the initial attempt at reorganization, the presidency of the college was offered to Benjamin Silliman at Yale, and a new chair of political economy and history was offered to Thomas R. Dew of William and Mary. Both declined, and criticism of the Board of Trustees mounted. The clergy complained that offers were not going to men of suitable piety, and Unionists objected to the invitation to the militantly proslavery Dew as another attempt to stack the college by the secessionists. For a while in early 1835, the complete disbanding of the college appeared a distinct possibility. This outcome, in fact, would probably have been quite acceptable to many of the institution's ecclesiastical critics as it could only enhance the position of denominational schools. But the prospect shook up the state's leadership, both nullifier and Unionist, which alike had shared their education at South Carolina. Friends of the college decided that a compromise had to be found, and the two political factions began to cooperate in a search for suitable faculty.

A major figure in the Unionist camp, Colonel William Drayton (who recently had moved to Philadelphia), was called upon to look for acceptable candidates in the North. On Nicholas Biddle's recommendation, Drayton talked with Lieber, who was actively seeking an academic post. Following their meeting in late January 1835, Drayton reported to the governor of South Carolina that Lieber's "various accomplishments and attainments, both in private life and as a public instructor, in the opinion of the most distinguished literary and scientific gentlemen in the United States, eminently qualify him for the presidency of a college."[49] Lieber was subsequently called to Charleston for an interview and to meet with the state's leaders. Although they found Lieber impressive and suitable for a position, his views, relative youth, and heavy German accent precluded the presidency. The Board of Trustees offered Lieber the professorship of history and political economy at a salary of $2,000 along with a house on the campus.[50] Although Lieber really did not want to leave the culture of the Northeast, he had a family to support and no other employment opportunities. He joined the faculty for the opening of the reorganized college in October 1835.

To the politicians attempting to save the college, Lieber appeared to be an acceptable compromise between the desire for scholars of good reputation and people who could fit in with the state's volatile moods. He was an ardent free trader, which satisfied the nullifiers, and was a nationalist Whig in politics, which mollified the Unionists. Although he was not Calvinist, he rejected outright materialism and displayed a personal piety that satisfied the trustees. Major concerns were Lieber's foreign birth and his attachment to northern culture. Nevertheless, Lieber showed no fondness for socialism and seemed willing to accept slavery as a given in southern life. Only the Presbyterians were dissatisfied, and they claimed in the local press that Lieber was secretly an abolitionist and an atheist. In fact, it was necessary for Lieber and his supporters to respond publicly to these charges before his arrival in South Carolina. He affirmed his faith in a letter to the *Columbia Telescope* in July 1835 and, although avoiding a positive statement in support of slavery, declared that he was not an abolitionist—that is, a person desiring immediate and unconditional emancipation against the wishes of the local electorate.[51]

The first evidence on Lieber's instruction in the political economy course comes from a report submitted to the college president in May 1837. At that time, Lieber was making use of Cooper's text, supplemented by his own lecture notes on taxation, currency, and wages. In November 1840 Lieber reported that he was using Say's *Treatise on Political Economy.* Cooper had died in 1839, and perhaps Lieber no longer felt obliged to use a text that was more

Ricardian than his own opinions.[52] In May 1843 Lieber supplemented his use of Say with his own *Essays on Property and Labour*. The report of November 1847 notes that the Board of Trustees had expanded his course from two hours a week to three and that he was thus able to cover the entire work of Say and had "delivered numerous lectures on such subjects as relate to us in particular as are treated by Mr. Say in a manner that does not agree with that of many other prominent Economists." Earlier, Lieber apparently had covered only books 1 and 3 of Say, omitting the discussion of the distribution of wealth in book 2.[53]

In an assessment of his work in political economy, it is necessary to note that Lieber's paramount intellectual interest was in political philosophy. He wanted to establish political science as a distinct subject in the social sciences. His most quoted works, *Manual of Political Ethics* (1839) and *On Civil Liberty and Self-government* (1853), took as their goal the deductive derivation of an ideal government based on law that protected man's individuality, recognized his property rights, and permitted the maximum latitude to his self-interest. Limited government was necessary for liberty, but so too was it necessary for a government to be strong enough to perform its functions. Lieber saw the secessionist movement in South Carolina as presenting a future as bleak as that of the divided German principalities, each of which was subject to a form of local tyranny. Only a truly national government could guarantee civil liberty to all of its citizens. His view of political economy concentrated on its demonstration of the importance of property rights and free exchange to a well-functioning society. This is aptly demonstrated by the titles of his two major writings in political economy, namely, *Essays on Property and Labour* (1841) and "Notes on Fallacies of American Protectionists" (1869). The latter work was the published version of his many years of lectures on free trade.[54]

Lieber dismissed the labor theory of value in favor of the value theory of Say. In his *Essays on Property and Labour,* he rejected the doctrines of the emerging workers' movements and noted that "a product of our labor is always the joint effect of labor, appropriation, and accumulation of value reinvested in the new product."[55] Capital contributed to value and should receive a return for its efforts. He emphasized the role of the cost of production to value in the long run and of demand to value in the short run. Wages, the return to labor, as in the market for goods, were determined by demand and supply, and just as attempts to regulate demand and supply in markets always failed, so too would policies designed to raise wages above their natural level. Capital was the source of the demand for labor and should be appreciated by workers as necessary to encourage employment. If wages were forced up by combinations of labor, the return to capital would fall, factories would close, and labor's gains would disappear. Ricardian rent discussions were avoided by defining land as capital. The final conclusion of Lieber's theory of distribution was that the inequality of incomes and wealth was natural and necessary to civil liberty. Only under inequality could the possession of individual property have meaning, and it was only the desire to accumulate wealth and property that permitted economies to advance and support civilizations and governments strong enough to protect man's freedom.

Lieber took a great deal of interest in issues of public finance, that is, expenditures and taxation necessary to support his ideal government. His views, however, merely copied those of Adam Smith. His faith in free trade was complete, based on the superiority of free exchange. He continued to hold these opinions strongly, even after the Civil War, when he was a prominent official in the tariff-supporting Radical Republican party of the Reconstruction era. Lieber's letters to his northern friends revealed a strong and growing dislike of slavery. However, he did not publicly declare these feelings until after he left South Carolina for the North, and he mainly sought to use his influence to strengthen the Unionist faction in the state at the expense of the secessionists. An unpublished analysis, undated but evidently written by Lieber while at South Carolina, outlined his economic indictment of slavery.[56] Slavery as an institution was suited only to large farms and so tended to create large accumulations of landed property for the privileged few. This meant that the South could not support a large yeomanry of landed free whites, so that property ownership was limited. As only a society based on the widespread existence of private property could progress and support liberty, the South under slavery was doomed to decay and tyranny.

In 1843 Lieber outlined to the president of the college a teaching philosophy for his lectures:

All that can be effected in a college course of Political Economy is, in my opinion, the clearest possible representation of the elements of the industrial household of mankind, the production, distribution and exchange of values and the nature of property as one of the indispensable requisites of all material and intellectual as well as moral advancement of human society.[57]

In Lieber's mind, this did not mean a simple word-for-word memorization of Say's text, as was apparently quite common with the pedagogy of the time. Lieber's personal annotated copy of the Say text is reported by O'Connor to contain an outline of topics covered by Lieber relative to book 1.[58] Comparison of the outline with Say's text shows that Lieber had his own definite ideas about how to teach political economy. The order of some topics was rearranged, some chapters were skipped, and some topics not covered by Say were inserted. Lieber was a pioneer in the development of the lecture-and-examination method, as opposed to the standard recitation exercises of the day.[59] He used his text as a starting point—or something to disagree with—rather than as the authoritative statement of the subject and always required supplemental readings. Often he would bring in maps, globes, or recent newspaper articles to illustrate his concepts. Should the lazy students become too inattentive, they were always in danger of being called to the front of the room for a blackboard session on the major concepts of the day's lesson.

In part, Lieber's extensive efforts may have been due to his insecurities. South Carolina was his first college teaching assignment, his Prussian accent left him an easy target for teasing, and he knew quite well that he had enemies in the state. Nevertheless, even when his opponents roared the loudest, he always seemed to have the support of his students. The only complaint that might be made of his political economy was its avoidance of serious discussion of the Ricardian system. Nonetheless, as with Cooper, his students were being taught by an active scholar whose work and ideas were known in both sections of the nation. Even if his original writings were in political science, his understanding of political economy was on a par with other American economists, and it is very doubtful that many other students received more vigorous and rigorous instruction in the subject.

For many years, Lieber was able to protect his position at South Carolina College through diplomatic exposure of his free-trade opinions and relative silence, in public, on those issues on which he could not agree with popular opinion. However, the years after 1840 witnessed the spread of sectionalist sentiment and intolerance throughout the entire South. The maturing of the lower South gradually led planters to realize the immensity of their accumulated wealth in slaves and to foresee the severe financial losses to which they would be exposed by any restrictions on the institution's existence. Moreover, southern politicians and the public began to sense the inevitability of minority status in the Union, as population and industrial growth exploded in the North. The North was becoming increasingly hostile to slavery and with each passing year possessed a greater ability, legislatively and militarily, to carry out its wishes. In such an atmosphere, the avoidance of open disagreement was no longer sufficient. The South felt that only unified public support of all aspects of its culture could offer hope of effective resistance to the North. All southerners had to be proslavery, prosecession, and profundamentalist. Even Lieber's support of free trade became largely irrelevant with a Congress, controlled by northern manufacturing interests, that would impose tariffs anyway. It was now only a matter of time before most of the nonconforming elements of southern life would be forced by degrees either to seek refuge in the North or to give up all pretense of exerting effective power or influence.[60]

The chain of events that was to occasion Lieber's departure from South Carolina College began in November 1854 when the college's current president, James Thornwell, announced his resignation, effective in December 1855. Thornwell has become in many ways a symbol to southern historians of what the antebellum South had become. One of the most powerful Presbyterian ministers in the nation, Thornwell publicly declared many aspects of northern life depraved and demonstrated his intolerance for substantial deviations from southern orthodoxy many times over. His presidency of the college had been treated by his ecclesiastical supporters like a sacred mission to convert Cooper's atheist academy into a school for Christian soldiers. Nevertheless, he was now called by his church for higher duties in its administration and, with some reluctance, had given notice of his imminent departure.[61] Thus, one of the most public positions in the state of South Carolina was thrown open to a year-long contest between its various religious and political factions.

By the traditional academic standards for college presidencies, Lieber was now the heir apparent. He was the senior professor in terms of service, and the recent publication of *Civil Liberty* had made him clearly the college's most visible scholar in national intellectual circles.[62] In the eyes of some on the local scene, however, Lieber's candidacy was flawed. From the very beginning of his tenure at South Carolina, he had written often to his influential northern friends, bemoaning the sterility of southern intellectual and cultural life and seeking their good offices to help him obtain a position in the North. Although possibilities at Harvard, Columbia, and Girard College always seemed to elude him, he nonetheless took advantage of practically every summer vacation to travel northward and to carry on his job search in person. He, of course, avoided overt criticisms of the South while in South Carolina. But his constant trips and rumors of various job openings for him elsewhere no doubt offended many of his southern acquaintances. Many of his relationships with fellow faculty members, although publicly cordial, were distant and cool. In 1842 rumors circulated that Lieber's position was to be abolished, and it appears that they were started by some of his own colleagues. One of Lieber's adversaries on the Board of Trustees subsequently moved that he be dismissed, but the matter was referred to a committee that reported unfavorably on the proposal.

Following a political relaxation in Germany, Lieber received a pardon for his youthful radicalism and took an extended leave of absence in 1844 to visit Europe and his homeland. He used the occasion to negotiate with the University of Berlin and with King Frederick over positions in academia, prison reform administration, and U.S.–German diplomacy. As had been the case with his northern job search, any offers he received were at salaries far below his current pay, and so he returned to South Carolina. But his extended absenteeism abroad and the growth of nationalism on the eve of the Mexican War led to another ouster attempt in 1845. This time Lieber's American loyalties were called into question; the trustees, however, voted their confidence in him. A subsequent move to bring the issue before the state legislature failed, and Lieber's post was expanded to cover political philosophy as well as history and political economy. Thereafter, Lieber seemed to become more resigned to his situation in South Carolina, and the state seemed more willing to recognize his value to the college. Lieber began to lose some of his more radical northern abolitionist friends, who lost patience with his attempts to find a reasonable middle ground between the pro- and antislavery positions. He also won approval in the state during the early 1850s with public articles about alternative crops that might pull Carolina out of its cotton-induced depression.[63]

Early in 1855, Lieber's chances for the presidency seemed good. The noncollege candidates put forward by various religious and political factions fell one by one to attacks from their enemies while Lieber's supporters waited for the position to fall upon him by default. At first, Lieber was pessimistic, noting to friends that as soon as it would come time to elect him someone would bring up that he was a foreigner, or that he took so many trips to the North, or that he was mysteriously quiet on slavery. Lieber over time had become more open in publicizing his opposition to southern secession. For a period, he "ghost-wrote" speeches for the state's Unionist politicians. In 1851 he left a pro-Union speech under his own name to be read at a Greenville Fourth of July celebration while he was again visiting Europe. From this moment onward, Lieber was publicly identified with the Unionist faction, with the benefits and costs that this entailed.

Nevertheless, as the election neared in December 1855, Lieber had the apparent support of a majority of the trustees, his fellow faculty members, the editorial press of the up-country, and students of the college. Even Lieber became optimistic and openly campaigned for himself. Then the last-minute strategy of Lieber's opponents was revealed. The retiring President Thornwell wrote to the trustees asking that they vote for a recently hired mathematics professor from Georgia, Charles McCay, on grounds that he was a good member of the Presbyterian church. Shortly thereafter, the state's governor, James H. Adams, a militant secessionist, also threw his support to McCay. The plan of the allied religious and secessionist factions was not to elect McCay, whose record was quite undistinguished, but rather to deadlock the election—a two-thirds majority was required—and then to submit a dark-horse candidate on the grounds that neither Lieber nor McCay could work effectively under the other. Lieber led the balloting during the first few rounds but could not obtain the requisite number of votes. Momentum then swung to McCay, who was eventually elected with exactly two-thirds of the trustees' ballots.

Lieber submitted his resignation the following day, effective at the end of 1856. He immediately renewed his efforts to obtain a northern position, this time emphasizing to the northern press that he had been unseated for suspected antislavery feelings.[64] Meanwhile, once the college began the new year, the unfortunate President McCay faced faculty, students, and religious and political leaders who all thought him incapable of doing his job, whether or not they had supported or opposed him. Lieber's initial lack of success in obtaining a new position, combined with McCay's deepening troubles, gave some brief hope that the board would reverse its decision and ask Lieber to withdraw his resignation. Before its meeting, however, Governor Adams published excerpts from Lieber's *Encyclopaedia Americana* that condemned slavery. The board thereupon accepted Lieber's resignation, and he departed for

New York in December 1856. He joined the faculty of Columbia College in 1857.[65]

The Lieber affair marked South Carolina College's withdrawal from the academic mainstream of America.[66] The disastrous presidency of Charles McCay led to a complete reorganization of the college in 1857, at which time the institution was re-created in the state's image. From this time until well after the Civil War the primary qualification for academic appointment at South Carolina College was strict conformity to southern ideals, to the almost total exclusion of scholarly credentials. The desire of the state to suppress dissent was so great that first preference for positions was given to native South Carolinians (as opposed to just any southerner), and, whenever possible, positions were filled by the graduates of South Carolina College.

The nepotism of the post-Lieber college was immediately evident in the instruction in political economy. Lieber's course was assigned in spring 1857 to R. W. Barnwell, Jr., graduate of the class of 1850 and nephew of a former president of the college. When Barnwell was later reassigned to teach sacred literature, moral philosophy, and criticism, Charles Pelham (graduate of the class of 1838 and previously the instructor of Greek and Roman literature) handled the course in political economy in the fall of 1857. During that term, the college hired a new president, Augustus Longstreet, a Yale-educated Georgia native who had been a fairly successful politician and writer of short stories. Longstreet took over the teaching of political economy and history in the spring of 1858. The college's histories describe Longstreet as an ineffective teacher, and there is no definitive record of the teaching materials he, Barnwell, or Pelham used. There is reason to believe, however, that Say was the school's text in political economy until the Civil War.[67]

THE INSTRUCTION OF POLITICAL ECONOMY AT SOUTH CAROLINA AFTER THE CIVIL WAR

South Carolina College closed in 1861 shortly after hostilities commenced in Charleston harbor. From the time that the college reopened in 1866 until the University of South Carolina's Department of Economics was established in 1910, there was little break from the intellectual stagnation that had set in with Lieber's departure. Some instructors were effective and dedicated teachers, and some were not. But in no sense could the college's postbellum economics teachers be regarded as scholars of accomplishment.

With the Reconstruction after 1865, South Carolina entered a period of profound political uncertainty. The uncertainty turned on which faction—moderate or radical—of the national and local Republican party would dominate and on how much local control would be allowed to the state. Until 1873 republicanism in the state was moderate enough that no major reforms were required at South Carolina College. The school reopened in 1866 and tried as best it could to return to business as usual. The course in political economy at this time was taught by Robert Barnwell (the uncle of the R. W. Barnwell, Jr., mentioned earlier), who had served as president of the college from 1835 to 1841. A South Carolina native and graduate of Harvard, Barnwell had been a prominent state politician and had taught metaphysics and philosophy during his presidency. The college catalogue of 1866 notes that Barnwell used Say as his text and recommended the reading of Wayland's *Elements of Political Economy*. But the Civil War had left an impact on the educational preparation of students. The catalogue for 1869 notes that the more elementary Wayland text was now used, with Say demoted to recommended reading.[68]

In 1873 the renamed University of South Carolina fell under the control of the Radical Republicans, who reorganized the faculty and the school and opened its doors to students of all races.[69] White attendance fell dramatically, as a faculty of Republican appointees sought to teach a largely black student body. All that is known about the instruction of political economy is that the course was assigned to a T. N. Roberts, M.D., who had been brought in by the Republicans in 1872 to teach chemistry. No information has survived on Dr. Roberts, who simply appeared in 1872 and disappeared in 1877 at the end of the Reconstruction era.

Once the retreat of the Republicans was completed, political control of the state was seized by the Bourbon Redeemers, the heirs of the state's antebellum aristocracy. Their goal was to resurrect as much as possible of the earlier order in an environment in which the black population was legally freed. In education, they hoped to restore South Carolina College in its classical form. When the school reopened in 1880, however, it did so as an agricultural and mechanical college. This arrangement was necessary in order to qualify the college for land-grant funding, even though its faculty was largely composed of men with a traditional liberal arts background. Political economy was taught in the second year of a three-year program by William P. Miles.[70] Primarily an English and mathematics professor, Miles was a native South Carolinian who had graduated from the College of Charleston. No information is available on his choice of texts.

In 1882 the institution was again reorganized as a liberal arts college, and the instruction of history, political science, and political economy went to Professor R. Means Davis. A South Carolina graduate of 1872, Davis was known as a popular teacher but was not an active scholar. The catalogue of 1882–83 notes that political economy was taught to the senior class for one and one-half hours a week, or half the time allotted to Lieber in 1847. The catalogue further states that the first term was devoted to "history of political economy, its different systems, and its fundamental principles." The second term took up the discussion of current economic and social questions with Perry's *Elements of Political Economy* (1866) as a textbook. John Stuart Mill's *Principles of Political Economy* was recommended as a book of reference, along with Blanqui's *History of Political Economy* (1st ed., 1837).[71]

The time allocated to senior political economy was expanded to three hours a week in 1883–84, and Mill's book became the required text in 1884–85. Reference works included Blanqui, Say, Cairnes, Perry, and Walker. The next catalogue reported that Mill's full text had been replaced by the abridgment edited by J. Laurence Laughlin. In 1892–93, class hours were cut back to two a week. Gide's *Principles of Political Economy*, unsupported by supplementary readings, became the textbook in 1893–94. Instruction in mature classical economics thus continued, although the apparent increase in rigor and coverage of the early 1880s dissipated in the 1890s. This was likely a symptom of the severe political buffeting suffered by the institution with the rise of agrarian populism in the state. The Bourbon Redeemers had lost political control and were replaced by representatives of the struggling small cotton farmers of the postbellum South. Led by Governor "Pitchfork Ben" Tillman, they sought to reclaim the land-grant moneys that they felt had been stolen by South Carolina College to teach the sons of the privileged classes. With the help of an endowment from Thomas Clemson, a new land-grant university was established in the state, and the college was stripped of its land-grant funds and its influence. For a brief period, the state's financial support of the college even fell below that for the state teachers' college for women.[72]

As the turn of the century approached, the college, later university, slowly began to recover as the Redeemers gradually regained some of their lost power. Better times for the instruction of political economy began in 1899, when George McCutchen, a graduate of the class of 1898 and subsequently a graduate of the Law School in 1903, was hired as an instructor in economics. The university's first teacher to specialize completely in economics, McCutchen nonetheless taught courses in constitutional and international law until 1906. McCutchen introduced his students to neoclassical and institutionalist thought. This reflected McCutchen's summer studies at major graduate schools of the day: Wisconsin in 1900 and 1908, Chicago in 1901, and Harvard in 1902. Although McCutchen never earned an advanced degree in economics, he was exposed to the diverse viewpoints of such prominent American economists as Richard T. Ely and J. L. Laughlin.

The catalogue of 1905–6 lists McCutchen's text as Bullock's *Introduction to the Study of Economics,* with Gide and Seligman used as reference works. In the following year, work in economics expanded to two three-hour courses as McCutchen's law courses were reassigned. The Introduction to Political Economy class used Fetter's *Principles of Economics,* and the subsequent Theory of Political Economy course relied on Seligman's text, supplemented by references to Gide, Hadley, Marshall, and Thomas Cooper. In addition, McCutchen offered a separate course in banking using Dunbar's *Theory and History of Banking.* Although the research tradition in economics was not to revive at South Carolina for many years to come, the turn of the century did witness the specialization of economics instruction at the university. The final step in this process came in 1910 with McCutchen's formal separation of an Economics Department from partnership with history and political science.[73]

AN ASSESSMENT OF THE COOPER–LIEBER LEGACY AT SOUTH CAROLINA COLLEGE

The case of South Carolina College and the evolution of its curriculum in political economy is extraordinary in the history of academic economics in America. Most of the pioneering institutions in this subject managed to sustain a reasonably strong scholarly emphasis down to the current day. In South Carolina, on the other hand, there was a discontinuity. The early strength of political economy there was too dependent on the unique abilities of Thomas Cooper and Francis Lieber and on a political environment permitting commitment to intellectual excellence. When the personalities and the commitment were gone, the best the college could offer was a nostalgia that encouraged thorough instruction in the classical school of political economy—at least whenever the political situation allowed a very poor state to devote adequate resources to the school. Even this nostalgia may have had its negative aspects. Neoclassical and institutional alternatives to the classical school did not appear until after 1900 in the college's curriculum, substantially later than these perspectives left their mark on the profession and on the research universities of the nation.

The rise and fall of intellectual freedom at South Carolina emphasize dramatically the crucial roles of economic strength and public attitudes toward education. South Carolina College was strongest when the state was one of the more wealthy in the nation. As the state declined economically, its financial commitment to the college could be maintained only by bringing the views of the institution more into line with those of the public. When Thomas Cooper was hired, the state of South Carolina was willing to pay for able scholars and to allow them to create knowledge and to transmit it to their students and the public—all in relative freedom. When Cooper was removed and Lieber hired, the state was still willing to pay for scholars. By the time of Lieber's departure, the state's willingness to support independent thinkers was exhausted. It wished instead to buy only acceptable opinions.

4

Political Economy from the Top Down: Brown University

WILLIAM J. BARBER

POLITICAL ECONOMY had an impact at Brown at an earlier date than at any of the other colleges in New England. One man—the Reverend Francis Wayland—was responsible for this phenomenon.

The institution Wayland took over when elected president in 1826 was a struggling one. Founded in 1764 as Rhode Island College, it needed to establish an identity to distinguish it from its primary rivals, Harvard and Yale. Part of the process of differentiation came easily. Rhode Island College was intended to provide a base for members of the Baptist denomination, but in colonial New England their numbers were small. The viability of the new institution was thus likely to turn on its ability to attract a wider constituency.

From the beginning, creedal orthodoxy was given a more elastic reading in Rhode Island's higher education than in Connecticut or Massachusetts. The college's charter specified that the president of the institution should be a Baptist, but it also provided extraordinary representation for other denominations in its governing structure. Two bodies were created: the trustees (who were charged with the selection of the president and the final determination of institutional policies) and the fellows (who awarded degrees and maintained operational control over instruction). Together they formed "the Corporation." A majority of the fellows, however, were to be Congregationalists or Presbyterians. Moreover, the charter stipulated that no sectarian test should be imposed on appointments to the faculty or on the admission of students. This did not mean that the college was totally indifferent about matters of faith. Believ-

The author gratefully acknowledges the able assistance of the staff of the Brown University Archives in the gathering of materials for this essay.

ers—Jewish as well as Christian—were welcome, but there was no room for atheists.[1]

This type of partnership between Baptists and others widened the base for the college. Even so, its condition was far from flourishing in the late eighteenth and early nineteenth centuries. To attract students, it deliberately kept its tuition rates below those of regional competitors and scheduled a long vacation during winter months to enable students to earn by teaching in the common schools. Enrollments had risen to slightly more than 100 by 1800, but finances remained precarious. This prompted a number of expedients—among them, the organization of lotteries for the benefit of the college and a proposition, advanced in 1803, to permit a donor of $5,000 to designate its permanent name. Nicholas Brown, a graduate of the college and a Providence merchant, responded to this invitation in 1804.

Although a spirit of religious tolerance distinguished Brown from a number of early colleges (and most notably from Yale), there were still limits beyond which this tolerance could not be stretched. In 1826 the Reverend Asa Messer, who had served as president since 1802, was obliged to resign. He had lost the confidence of the Corporation, which suspected that he had lapsed from his original commitment to the Baptist conviction and had become sympathetic to Unitarianism. His successor, the Reverend Francis Wayland, could not be faulted on this score. He had prominently established his credentials as the minister of the First Baptist Church in Boston.

WAYLAND'S VERSION OF POLITICAL ECONOMY

Soon after his arrival as president in 1827, Wayland made clear that he was interested in educational reform and determined to leave his mark on Brown. The institution then had a teaching strength of six: the president, three resident professors (in mathematics and natural philosophy, in moral philosophy and metaphysics, and in Greek and Latin), plus two tutors. The curriculum Wayland inherited was largely in the classical mould characteristic of the New England colleges of the period (though it also advertised some instruction in chemistry, surveying, and navigation). One of the new president's early innovations was a course of lectures (given by himself) in political economy.

Concerned with more than bringing new subject matter to the

curriculum, Wayland cared about pedagogical style and commitment. He banned the use of textbooks at recitations (apart from those in the "learned languages") because he wanted to press both teachers and students to think on their feet. He also insisted that all members of the faculty should be resident at the college and should contribute to the maintenance of social discipline. Among other things, this ruling had the effect of stifling a medical school, which had been affiliated with the college and staffed by Providence physicians who taught part-time with payment by fees. The latter were not willing to satisfy Wayland's stipulations about full-time residence.

With respect to the content of the curriculum, Wayland soon gave political economy a position of some prominence in the course of studies. This subject matter entered into his presidential lectures on moral philosophy during his first term of teaching at Brown, and in the academic year 1828–29 political economy was officially listed in the catalogues as part of the program in the second and third terms of the senior year. In the early going, Wayland relied on Prinsep's translation of Say's *Principles* as a text, but he also worked out his own lectures.[2] These lectures, in turn, became the basis for Wayland's own text, *The Elements of Political Economy*, first published in 1837. Once this work was in print, Wayland changed his teaching style. His instruction then took the form of presiding over recitations on the principles embodied in his textbook.[3] This publication was to have an influence that went well beyond Rhode Island. It was the most widely read text on political economy in pre–Civil War America and went through eighteen editions before 1861.[4]

In Wayland's view, there was no incompatibility between political economy and religious conviction. On the contrary, they were mutually reinforcing. He declared his position on this matter forcefully in an address to the American Sunday School Union in 1830:

the moral system of the Bible is the moral system of the universe. A striking truth of the general principle . . . may be found in the history of political economy. This science has been, to say the least, most successfully cultivated by men who had no belief in the Christian religion. And yet, reasoning from unquestionable facts in the history of man, they have incontrovertibly proved that the precepts of Jesus Christ, in all their simplicity, point out the only rules of conduct in obedience to which either nations or individuals can become either rich or happy. So far as science has gone, then, every new truth in physics or in morals has furnished a new argument for the authenticity of revelation. Thus will it be to the end.[5]

This view was articulated even more specifically in the opening pages of Wayland's textbook, *The Elements of Political Economy.* He there defined political economy as the "science of wealth." A science, he informed his readers, was "a systematic arrangement of the laws which God has established, so far as they have been discovered, of any department of human knowledge," whereas wealth referred to "any object, having the power of gratifying human desire, which is capable of being appropriated."[6] Laying bare the nature of those laws was the task he assigned to himself as an author. He took on this work because he believed that existing treatises were not sufficiently well ordered to "be most serviceable either to the general student, or to the practical merchant." He was aware that his qualifications for such an undertaking might be challenged because he had no practical business experience. His rejoinder was that "principles belong to all men." Moreover, the practical men were likely to be too busy to perform the needed work of enlightenment.[7]

For Wayland, Adam Smith's "invisible hand" should properly be understood as the divine hand. Even so, his organization of the subject matter of political economy still drew heavily on the classical tradition, as transmitted through the works of Say and McCulloch. Many of the central propositions of this tradition he took over without modification. Free markets were beneficent, and a widening division of labor was the carrier of progress. Government's role should be carefully delimited, and its central function should be to protect the institution of private property (a precondition for an orderly and progressive society). Exchange values could largely be explained on the basis of labor content—with direct and indirect labor time taken into account. Moreover, he accepted those later classical positions which held that general gluts were an impossibility and that the Luddite view of technological unemployment was fallacious.

But Wayland's interpretation of the message of political economy was more than a replay of later classical doctrine. At a number of crucial points, he rewrote standard classical argument. He challenged its view that labor in the services sector was "unproductive" and suggested that it was an irrational prejudice to hold such an opinion. In his scheme of things, the work of those "laborers" who engaged in the "industry of discovery or investigation" was essential to the welfare of the community. These "philosophers" were engaged in identifying fundamental "laws" and making them known to the public. Similarly, professional labor generally was distinctively productive. As he put it:

The business of the clergymen is to teach us in what manner we may avail ourselves of the *moral laws* of the Creator. The lawyer teaches us how to avail ourselves of the laws of that *civil society*, of which we are members. The physician teaches us how to obey the *physiological laws* under which we are created, so that we may be relieved from sickness, or preserved in health.[8]

Wayland also revised the Ricardian doctrine of rent. The "natural and indestructible powers of the soil" might account for part of the differential in land rents—but for only a part. In any event, the course of American history did not fit the Ricardian model, which implied that the most fertile lands would be brought into cultivation first and that population growth would require the margin of cultivation to be extended to less fertile acreages on which costs of production would be higher. The facts of America's westward expansion belied that line of argument. Even so, it did not follow that land rents on the eastern seaboard would fall, despite the relative inferiority of its acreages for agricultural purposes. The demand for land—and the rent associated with its ownership—depended on more than the inherent fertility of the soil. Rents were also determined by the attractiveness of land for commercial, industrial, and residential purposes. Advantages of situation, particularly accessibility to means of transport, were important. But Wayland further insisted that "the price of land depends much on the intellectual and moral character of a neighborhood." He observed that

there are towns in New England in which, within a few years, the price of real estate has doubled, for no other assignable reason, than that of the literary and moral advantages which they hold out to residents. . . . Hence we see, that, besides the advantages which intelligence and virtue confer upon the character of a people themselves, there is also an additional advantage, in the rise of property which they produce.[9]

In Wayland's reading of the "laws" of political economy, there were no overtones of inherent divergences in the interests of various classes in the community, nor was there any suggestion that economic growth might be halted by the emergence of a stationary state. His world was one of natural harmonies. There was no reason why economic improvement could not continue without interruption. The essential requirement was a sustained accumulation of capital to increase the demand for labor and, in turn, to banish Malthusian fears about excessive population. Wayland held that the prospect for this happy outcome was bright because the acquisition and application of new knowledge to the production process should make continued investment attractive. Nevertheless, there would be clouds on the horizon if the population succumbed to indolence, intemperance, vice, and wasteful extravagance. The laws of the Creator and of political economy were at one in denouncing such behavior and in calling for remedies to such deficiencies in character.

This doctrinal position had clear implications for economic policy. Free trade was the natural order of things (though a modest tariff for revenue purposes only could be tolerated). Indeed, the principle of comparative advantage should be understood as part of God's plan.[10] Charity for those who were poor from indolence—as opposed to those poor "by visitation of God"—should be avoided because the "strongest inducement to industry" was necessary to "accomplish the designs of our Creator."[11] Governments had a responsibility for the coinage because individuals could not be trusted to perform this function, but they had no right to interfere with the import or export of specie. Nor should governments attempt to influence the terms of private lending and borrowing through enacting usury laws. These positions were all a part of the standard classical package, though, in Wayland's treatment, they were sanctified.

On issues of particular contention in American public debate at the time, Wayland occasionally introduced a qualification or two. With respect to the role of government in the promotion of "internal improvements," he maintained that any projects that were potentially profitable should be undertaken by private associations. The work would thus be carried out at lower cost and without the risk of corruption through political favoritism. But publicly worthwhile projects that the private sector would not absorb should be paid for by the local beneficiaries rather than by a tax on the wider community. Some exceptions were recognized: for example, "works . . . of such magnitude, or . . . so great national importance, that they must be executed and controlled by the public at large." The major case in point was "that class of improvements which reduce the expense, and lessen the risk of *external* commerce." This embraced such activities as harbor improvement, the erection of lighthouses, the preparation and publication of accurate navigational charts. These were the "most economical form of national investment. . . . [A] nation offering these advantages, becomes a better market for all other nations, and they will the more readily resort to her for exchanges."[12]

On the troubled issue of banking in early nineteenth-century America, Wayland was at odds with the Jacksonians in his support for a national bank. He defended note issues by private banks, subject to the condition that they be backed by specie and redeemable on demand. For textbook purposes, he scrupulously avoided discussion of the vexed topic of slavery. In other contexts, however, he took the position that the federal government had no constitutional basis for intervening in this matter and that it was solely within the jurisdiction of the states. Nevertheless, he opposed the potential extension of the area of slavery permitted by the passage of the Kansas–Nebraska Act in 1854. When word of his attitude on this legislation reached the southern states, his textbook was banned from colleges in the South.[13]

THE PRINCIPLES OF POLITICAL ECONOMY AS APPLIED TO THE CRITIQUE OF AMERICAN HIGHER EDUCATION

Wayland took his understanding of political economy seriously. For him, it was not enough to profess it. It was also important to apply its lessons to the problems of practical life. This meant that its insights should also guide the line of "business" he knew at first hand: college education.

In 1842 Wayland presented to the national audience his *Thoughts on the Present Collegiate System in the United States*. Part of its content was inspired by reflections on the condition of American higher education arising from an academic leave in 1840–41, which he had spent in England, Scotland, and France.[14] But the structure of the argument was also informed by the views he had already come to about economic efficiency and the efficacy of markets.

As Wayland saw matters at this time, the American higher education "industry" was in a sorry state. Potentially, higher education should be in great demand. After all, this should be the instrument for moral and cultural uplift and for the transmission of useful knowledge, which—when applied—would contribute much to economic advance. Yet far too few people took advantage of the productive services it could supply. This was all the more remarkable because college education was priced below its cost. From the perspective of political economy, this was "unnatural." When elaborating this point, Wayland presupposed that the "natural price" should be equal to the "cost of production." And he calculated the relevant cost of production as follows: "We should first estimate the amount of capital invested in buildings, libraries, apparatus, and charge upon this sum the ordinary rate of interest. We should add to this, the salaries of professors and other teachers at the rate of remuneration ordinarily earned by persons employed in similar labor." [15] Though he did not use the term, Wayland had an intuitive grasp of the concept of "opportunity cost"—and he was convinced that able faculty members were substantially underpaid by comparison with professional men with comparable abilities, skills, and responsibilities.

If college education was thus priced below its natural value and still could not attract customers in the socially desirable volume, how could this outcome be explained? Wayland was convinced that "this state of things is neither owing to the poverty of our people nor to their indifference to the subject of education." [16] The root of the problem instead was that colleges were not offering the public what it wanted. This mismatch between what colleges supplied and what the public demanded had two separable, though related, aspects: (1) inadequacies in performance within the established curricular framework; and (2) shortcomings in the offerings of the program of studies.

In Wayland's diagnosis, the quality of work performed in colleges had suffered severely because the incentive mechanisms of the market had not been allowed to operate. Teachers were normally paid at fixed salary scales stipulated for their respective ranks. Rewards were thus not linked to performance. Such a system, he argued, was assuredly ill designed to call forth maximum effort. Moreover, the problem was compounded by the fact that faculty salaries in the first instance were not competitive with the earnings of such professionals as lawyers and doctors. This meant that many of the country's ablest minds could not be attracted to an academic career. What then was the remedy? For Wayland, it was self-evident that market principles should be invoked. Fixed stipends should be eliminated; instead, teachers should be remunerated by fees collected from the students they attracted. He was persuaded that the consumer would soon learn to recognize quality and would be prepared to pay for it. Such a system would weed out the incompetent, reward the competent, and attract able new entrants. One of the results would be that the price of education would probably go up, but as things stood, it was too low for the good of education.[17]

But this was only part of his scheme for improving the educational environment. An academic career could also be made more attractive by relieving faculty members of the burdens they were now obliged to carry on "police duty," that is, in supervising student conduct in dormitories. This could be done away with by eliminating requirements obliging students to reside in college-provided housing. Not only would such a reform spare good teachers from petty distractions, it would also free up financial resources that could strengthen a college's ability to perform its central function. In short, capital locked up in buildings for student residences could be reallocated to libraries and laboratories. But such a step, Wayland recognized, would not be feasible unless colleges required more of their students at the point of entrance—in particular, that they be old enough to exercise self-discipline without the need for paternal supervision from college officers. This objective could be met in part by making admission examinations more demanding and by introducing "premiums" (cash prizes) to reward outstanding achievement in these exercises. The premium system should also be used to recognize excellence in academic work in college. In short, market incentives should stimulate qualitative improvement in the performance of students as well as of faculty. Wayland was not comfortable with financial grants to needy students on the ground that those who get something for nothing will fail to value it. His formulas were designed to reward academic productivity at all levels.

If these proposals were not revolutionary enough, Wayland was even more radical in his recommendations for redesign of the curriculum. Many of the ills of higher education, he maintained, could be traced to the fact that there was little to distinguish the product of one institution from that of another. Most of them provided a standardized traditional menu, with little to choose between them. This system could be faulted on two counts. In the first place, the number of prescribed subjects was excessive—too large to permit a student to pursue any one of them in depth. This implied that there should be more scope for concentration within the pattern of studies: "instead of learning *many* things *imperfectly,* we should learn a *smaller* number of things *well.*"[18]

Second, colleges should open up a wider array of choices of subject matter. The public, he believed, was hungry for learning. It was now time for colleges to adapt to its tastes. This meant reaching out to a new clientele and, when doing so, to break the lockstep of the existing pattern. There was nothing sacred about arrangements that expected colleges to cater primarily to candidates for a B.A. degree, acquired after four years of residential study, mainly by students who aspired to enter one of the learned professions. Courses should be offered to persons who did not necessarily seek a degree, residential requirements should be waived, and a variety of certifications of study should be introduced (with no rigid term assigned to the time required to qualify for them).

In 1842 Wayland did not offer a detailed blueprint for a new scheme of academic organization and of degree structures. But the orientation of this thought was already well defined. "Why should not professors in Colleges deliver courses of lectures which would be attractive to the whole community," he asked,

and why should not the means which are at present available to a part be made available to the whole? It would open to the instructor a wide and attractive field of professional exertion. It would enlist in favor of the College all the sympathies of the public, and it would spread before the whole people such means for intellectual improvement as the necessities or tastes of each individual might demand.[19]

In Wayland's judgment, this scheme had two other recommendations: It "would tend so strongly to promote the growth of wealth and civilization and refinement among us"; and it "would so surely annihilate that division of the community into classes, which, already, in spite of our democratic institutions, threatens the direst evils to our republic."[20]

APPLICATION OF THE NEW MODEL TO COLLEGIATE REFORM AT BROWN, 1850–1855

Wayland's *Thoughts on the Present Collegiate System in the United States* received little attention in the 1840s. Even at his own institution, he had not managed to persuade the governing authorities to adopt much of his platform. As early as 1841—before the publication of his book on the subject—Wayland had urged the Brown Corporation to give serious thought to his recommendations for reform.[21] A few modest changes were, in fact, made: Cash prizes for superior performances by students were introduced in 1842–43 and an "English and Scientific Course" of one or two years duration was launched in 1847–48, attracting seven students in the following year. (The catalogue described the objective of this program as follows: "It is believed that such a course will furnish to those who are preparing for Mercantile pursuits, or for the higher employments of Agriculture and Manufactures, the means of securing, at moderate expense, an education specially adapted to their wants.")[22] Meanwhile, Brown's overall position had deteriorated. Enrollments were again on the decline, and the resulting loss of revenues led to dismissals of tutors and salary cuts for the remaining professors. By the close of the decade of the 1840s, Wayland was willing to play for higher stakes.

Faced with this situation, Wayland made a dramatic move. In 1849 he submitted his resignation to the Corporation. Presumably this was a tactic to spur the governing body to action. When asked to withdraw his letter of resignation, he readily did so—subject to the condition that a special "Committee of Advice" be formed to work with him in charting the institution's future. The upshot of this exercise was a "Report to the Corporation of Brown University on Changes in the System of Collegiate Education," which was submitted in March 1850.

The substance of this document was largely Wayland's handiwork. The central themes of his 1842 book were reiterated. The standard curriculum was indicted for spreading studies too thinly. In the words of the report: "We have now in the United States . . . one hundred and twenty colleges pursuing in general this course. All of them teach Greek and Latin, but where are our classical scholars? All teach mathematics, but where are our mathematicians? We might ask the same questions regarding the other sciences taught among us."[23] It was small wonder that colleges had fallen out of favor. The report concluded that "our colleges are not filled because we do not furnish the education desired by the people. . . . Is it not time to inquire whether we cannot furnish an article for which the demand will be, at least, somewhat more remunerative?"[24]

With specific reference to what should be done at Brown, the committee recommended an arrangement to provide greater scope for concentration in selected studies in accordance with student preferences. The objective was a framework in which "every student might study what he chose, all that he chose, and nothing but what he chose." In addition, new courses of instruction should be introduced "as the wants of the various classes of the community require." The fixed term of four years of study should also be scrapped.[25]

To those familiar with Wayland's views on higher education, there were no surprises here. In arguing the rationale for these changes, the language was forceful. The proposed reform was "just." Every man willing to pay for them, has a "right," the report asserted, "to all the means which other men enjoy, for cultivating his mind by discipline, and enriching it with science." But important groups in the community had been shunned by educators. In the whole country, it was noted, there was not a single institution "designed to furnish the agriculturist, the manufacturer, the mechanic, or the merchant with the education that will prepare him for the profession to which his life is to be devoted." Moreover, it was "expedient" to provide knowledge of the "useful arts."

A knowledge universally diffused of the laws of vegetation, might have doubled our annual agricultural products. Probably no country on earth can boast of as intelligent a class of mechanics and manufacturers, as our own. Had a knowledge of principles been generally diffused among them, we should already have outstripped Europe in all those arts which increase the comforts, or multiply the refinements of human life.[26]

The report recognized that a sweeping reform along these lines would require fundamental changes in the conduct of university business. Augmenting the number of subjects to be offered (particularly in the "practical" studies)—when combined with consumer sovereignty—meant that the "corporation cannot pretend any longer to hold themselves responsible for the support of every professor. . . . Like every other man, the instructor will be brought directly in contact with the public, and his remuneration will be made to depend distinctly upon his industry and skill in his profession."[27] A further consequence was foreseeable: decline in the study of Latin and Greek. The authors of the report were not alarmed by that prospect. As they saw matters: "If by placing Latin and Greek upon their own merits, they are unable to retain their present place in the education of civilized and Christianized men, then let them give place to something better."[28]

All of this was consistent with Wayland's vision of incorporating the allocative mechanisms of a market system into the operations of a university. Wayland personally supported one further reform along these lines—a point also drawn from his thinking in 1842. The college should specialize in the education business and get out of the housing business. This would also release time for faculty members to strengthen their professional competence; no longer would they be expected to serve as dormitory disciplinarians. But when Wayland argued that students should go to the private market for housing, the Brown Corporation balked. It refused to sacrifice the rental income from dormitories and directed that faculty members should tighten up their supervision.[29]

The essential features of Wayland's curricular innovations were implemented, beginning in the academic year 1850–51. A multitrack degree structure was then introduced. The bachelor of arts degree was restructured to serve those "who desire to prepare themselves for the different professions, and yet, from unavoidable circumstances, are unable to pursue a complete course of liberal education. In order to render it accessible to such students, the number of studies is limited, and a large liberty of choice is granted."[30] Meanwhile, the master of arts degree, which had formerly been conferred automatically to graduates with three years' seniority, would now become an earned degree. Apart from provision that a few substitutions could be made for studies formerly prescribed, the requirements for this degree replicated those stipulated earlier for the award of the bachelor of arts. A new degree, the bachelor of philosophy, was introduced with lower requirements for admission to candidacy. It could be completed without any exposure to the ancient languages; its course options included "agriculture," "science applied to the arts," and "chemistry applied to the arts"; and the full course of study could be completed in three years.[31]

To serve the clientele the new offerings were expected to attract, a number of additional professorships were authorized, including civil engineering and natural philosophy, chemistry applied to the arts, and agriculture. At the same time, a chair of "History and Political Economy" was created. This was the first occasion on which this designation was formally used at Brown. (Wayland, though he had taught his own brand of political economy, was styled as "Professor of Intellectual and Moral Philosophy" as well as president.) This innovation, however, bore no indirect relation to the curricular reform. In large measure, it reflected instead the discontent of the Professor of Rhetoric, William Gammell. His correspondence at the time displayed symptoms of "teacher burnout" arising from correcting large numbers of student compositions. Gammell was prepared to resign unless his duties were redefined.[32]

Along with these changes, a modified version of Wayland's scheme for faculty compensation was introduced.[33] For the academic year 1851–52, professors could choose a fixed stipend of

$1,200 or a base stipend of $500 plus the fees they could collect from students. All but two of them elected to try the novel option. The following year the terms were amended: a base stipend of $900 plus half of the fees gathered from students. But no amount of fine-tuning seemed capable of stilling faculty dissatisfaction with this technique for compensation. Opposition was led by the newly appointed Professor of History and Political Economy, who protested that this scheme was offensive because it meant that his income was below that of a number of his junior colleagues.[34] By 1856 the Wayland pay plan had been abandoned.

The initial results of the curricular innovation were decidedly mixed. In the first three years of full operation of the system, total enrollments expanded. Aggregate student numbers, which stood at 174 in 1850–51, reached 283 in 1853–54. It was also noteworthy that the geographical draw of the institution widened: In the last year of the old system, 22 percent of the students came from outside New England, but the representation of this group rose to 28 percent of a larger aggregate in 1854–55. No less impressive was the fact that about half of the students from beyond the New England region were from the mercantile and manufacturing centers of the Middle Atlantic states.[35] Satisfaction could also be drawn from the obvious appeal of the popular lectures delivered by the Professor of Chemistry Applied to the Arts in 1853–54. His course on the chemistry of metals, which was directed to craftsmen working with the precious metals, attracted an audience of more than 330.[36]

But there were disappointments as well. The chair authorized for a professor of agriculture was never filled, and the first two appointees to the new chairs of civil engineering and applied chemistry left abruptly after only a brief tenure. (Ironically, they were both invited to terminate their engagements because they were suspected of being lax in enforcing disciplinary regulations. It will be recalled that Wayland had lobbied unsuccessfully to have professors relieved of this type of duty.)[37] Still more serious was the perception of most of the older faculty that the new system had brought a decline in the quality of academic work. Not only were many of the new arrivals inadequately prepared, they stayed for shorter periods of time than would have been tolerated under the ancien régime. And with degree requirements watered down, academic standards seemed to be eroding across the board.

Insights derived from political economy were thus applied to the problem of academic organization and management at Brown in the early 1850s. Results failed to measure up to expectations. Wayland resigned from office at the close of the academic year 1854–55.

COUNTERREVOLUTION AND RETRENCHMENT, 1856–1881

Wayland had been more interested in using his understanding of political economy to shape the institution than in institutionalizing political economy within the curriculum. Few of the specific reforms he had engineered at Brown survived for long. Disaffection with the "new system" soon emerged in a report to the Executive Board prepared by the new president, Barnas Sears, dated July 5, 1856.[38] Sears summarized the state of affairs as follows:

It seems to be the united opinion of the Faculty that the character and reputation of the University are injuriously affected by the low standard of scholarship required for the degrees of A.M. and A.B. It is well known that the best students of preparatory schools, which would naturally direct their pupils to this college, now go elsewhere. . . . This results chiefly from the interpretation which is generally given to our peculiar and lowered standard of degrees as an open act of underbidding other colleges, and as a scramble for an increased number of students. Even the personal relations of our professors are humiliating, so that their intercourse with the officers of other colleges is a source of mortification rather than of pleasure.[39]

In 1857 the structure of the master of arts and bachelor of arts degrees reverted to the status quo ante. Only the bachelor of philosophy remained. By 1861 the Executive Board could report that, "in the order and the course of study, Brown University does not now differ essentially from her sister Colleges of the United States," though "the increased opportunities for practical education are still offered."[40]

One of Wayland's innovations in the reforms of 1850, it will be recalled, was the formal creation of a chair in History and Political Economy. This change, however, was more semantic than substantive. Though it did signify an organizational reaffiliation of political economy—from adjunct status to moral philosophy to adjunct status with history—continuity with the Wayland tradition was maintained.[41] Gammell, a Brown graduate in the class of 1831, had been one of Wayland's pupils, and his teaching in political economy relied on Wayland's book. Gammell's primary intellectual interests, however, lay elsewhere. His major scholarly works included a biography of Roger Williams and a history of American Baptist missions.

In the early 1860s, it was uncertain whether or not this chair would survive. The university was again in dire financial straits, and one of the remedies proposed by a special committee was that courses in political economy and civil engineering be dropped. Teaching in history would continue, but this part of the professor's work would be reallocated to other staff members when the chair fell vacant.[42] In fact, this did not happen. When Gammell retired in 1864, he was succeeded by J. Lewis Diman in the chair of History and Political Economy.

Under Diman, the Wayland approach to political economy was sustained. A graduate of Brown in 1851, he had done postgraduate work in theology, philosophy, and history and had served as a Congregational pastor for eight years before taking up this chair. Political economy was not his first love, but he enjoyed teaching it because "it admits of such clear analysis and precise statement."[43] As he described the substance of his teaching in his report to the Corporation in 1869, his lectures "included a general introduction to the study, with an examination of the laws of Production, Exchange, Distribution, and Consumption. The general design of the course has been to demonstrate that wealth accumulated strictly in accordance with natural laws; that the interests of Society are harmonious; and that all restrictions upon exchange are injurious."[44] This was indeed Wayland warmed over, and Wayland's *Elements* remained as the principal text. Some change occurred in the mid-1870s when Mill's *Political Economy,* Fawcett's *Manual,* Perry's *Political Economy,* and Walker's *Science of Wealth* were introduced.[45] Diman supplemented this material in his lectures with discussions of such topics as the history of socialism in the United States and the economics of the national debt.[46] Though political economy was an elective course, Diman won a substantial and appreciative audience. He expressed regret that "so little time can be allowed to so important a study. The gross ignorance respecting the simplest truths of the science which prevails in the community, and even among our legislators, renders it the more necessary that Political Economy should hold a prominent place in a course of liberal education."[47]

Diman made no published contributions to political economy. Works of his that found their way into print were devoted to historical and theological topics. He was, however, a man of personal force who was not afraid to take unpopular positions: His preachments on free trade were certainly at odds with prevailing sentiment among Rhode Island manufacturers. In the larger academic world, Diman was highly respected. He was offered chairs at Harvard, Princeton, and Johns Hopkins as well as the presidency of the University of Wisconsin.[48] He declined all of these invitations.

POLITICAL ECONOMY IN A NEW KEY UNDER ANDREWS, 1883–1888

With Diman's death in 1881, the chair of History and Political Economy again was empty. This time around there was no debate about whether or not it should be refilled. The range for electives in the undergraduate course of studies had again been widened. Even though expansion in enrollments in political economy had not kept pace with that in the sciences, an effective demand for instruction in the subject matter was well validated.

A regular appointment, however, was deferred for a year when Elisha Benjamin Andrews was called to fill this chair. Andrews was a Brown graduate in the class of 1870, having entered college after service in the Civil War, which had cost him the sight of one eye. Subsequently, he qualified for the Baptist ministry but held a pastorate only briefly before moving into an academic career (first as president of Denison University and then as professor of homiletics at Newton Theological Institution). Though appointed at Brown in 1882, Andrews elected to postpone taking up his duties until the fall term of 1883 in order to study in Germany.

Andrews's German sojourn—with his primary base at the University of Munich—proved to be formative in the development of his views on political economy. He immersed himself thoroughly in the doctrines of the German historical school and assimilated parts of the "professorial socialism" espoused there. These influences left their mark on his teaching and writing. He described the coverage of his political economy course for the academic year 1886–87 as follows: "Lectures, chiefly from the point of view of Adam Smith, but with appreciative attention to the teachings of Cossa, Knies, Kohn, Roscher, Schaeffle, and Wagner. Discussions. Brief special studies by the class of Fawcett, Mill, Sidgwick, and F. A. Walker."[49] The influence of German thinking was even more marked in his textbook *Institutes of Economics,* completed in 1889, which was based on the materials he had prepared for classes at Brown. The historical school, he wrote, "merits thanks" because it had "refuted the old notions of human nature and social institutions as fixed creations" and because it revealed "how meagre must be a system of economic truths valid for all ages and peoples." Similarly, the Socialists should be credited for showing that "laissez-faire is no absolute principle," that the "existence of thorough natural harmony in interests between different social classes is not proved," and that "government can do much for the betterment of economic conditions without attacking the property right or becoming dangerously paternal." [50] Andrews added the qualification that "in all economic activity the presumption is in favor of individual liberty and free competition (laissez-faire)" and that "the rightfulness of public intervention [was] in no case admissible save after proof." [51] Even so, his doubts about the existence of natural harmonies and the beneficence of the invisible hand moved him a considerable distance beyond the tradition of Wayland. [52]

Nevertheless, one element of continuity with Wayland's perspective remained. In Andrews's view of the discipline, there was still a vital connection between economics and practical Christianity, even though the nature of that linkage had been redefined. The miracles wrought by the "invisible hand" were no longer presented as manifestations of revealed truth. Andrews maintained, however, that the "economic elevation of the poor will prove to be ultimately an ethical and educational work" and that "the Christian religion, . . . rightly understood, includes all true morality." [53] In lectures to ministers, he expanded upon this point. "If it was ever possible," he observed, "to set forth a full gospel without canvassing rights and wrongs connected with wealth, poverty, legislation, and social order, it is so no longer. . . . Political economy is not the Gospel, but it may be made nobly ancillary thereto." [54]

In his teaching at Brown in the 1880s, Andrews became something of a cult figure. He maintained that

in fitness for place in an educational curriculum, Economics perhaps surpasses all other studies, through the remarkable combination which it involves of mental discipline with practical utility. Each of its propositions requires careful thought, while certain of its reasonings challenge the highest powers of mind. On the other hand, though it is a science, not an art, its truths touch every human life. [55]

He obviously conveyed this enthusiasm for the discipline to students. And he expressed regret that Brown's organization at that time did not permit greater concentration on economics. Only a minor fraction of his teaching time could be allocated to the discipline; the bulk of his energy was committed to instruction in history. As he put this point in 1886: "It is . . . impossible for any one man to teach so many subjects with the degree of thoroughness and address which a first-rate institution of learning today has a right to demand."[56] Accordingly, he proposed that the Department of History and Political Economy be subdivided to allow greater specialization.

Andrews's suspicions about automatic harmonies in the economic system and his taste for informed governmental intervention allied him with the "Young Turks," led by Richard T. Ely, who in the mid-1880s sought to found an American Economic Association. He was among the charter members of this group. This, in turn, gave him greater visibility on the national scene. In mid-1888 he left Brown to fill a professorship in economics and finance at Cornell.

CURRICULAR DIFFERENTIATION, 1888–1900

With the departure of Andrews (though he was to return a year later as president), Brown again was obliged to face a choice about the future of political economy at the institution. In the judgment of President Robinson, the moment had arrived to divorce political economy from history in the table of organization and to appoint two officers of instruction to the newly vacated space. The primary recommendation for this change was that political economy "has of late years become an absorbing subject of inquiry throughout our country" and—though it remained an elective in the Brown curriculum—it was a study that nearly every student in the college wished to pursue and in greater depth than had "hitherto been practicable." In addition, it was "especially desired as a department of graduate study." But another consideration also suggested that a new division of labor within the faculty was timely. It could be accomplished, "for the present at least, without any increase of cost to the college."[57] In short, two new junior appointees—one in political economy and one in history—could be absorbed with their joint salaries no greater than the stipend formerly paid to Andrews.

To fill the newly authorized instructorship in political economy, Brown looked to its own. Henry B. Gardner, a graduate in the class of 1884 and a native of Providence, was appointed to this position. He had first been exposed to political economy as one of Andrews's pupils, but in the years subsequent to his graduation he had studied with Ely at Johns Hopkins.[58] With Gardner's arrival, political economy acquired a separate departmental status, even though it was to remain a one-man department for more than a decade.

Despite his subordinate status in the pecking order, Gardner brought a distinctly different style to Brown's political economy. Unlike all save one of his predecessors, he was not a clergyman. On the contrary, he was among the first of the new wave of American-trained products of a professional graduate school. His instruction was built around the non-clerical texts: Walker, Ely, Taussig, Jevons, Marshall. Even though it might have been politic for him to assign Andrews's text when its author was on the premises as president, the available syllabi indicate that he did not do so.[59] Nor did he attempt to win converts for bimetallism, a point on which Andrews held strongly affirmative views. The readings of Gardner listed for his courses on money were dominated by the works of orthodox economists who were sound-money and gold-standard men.[60]

Political economy at Brown was thus secularized in the 1890s. By the end of the decade—even though working single-handedly— Gardner offered a diversified menu of upper-level elective courses (including Money and Banking, Public Finance, The Labor Movement with Special Reference to Trade Unions, Industrial Corporations, Tariff History of the United States).[61] In addition, a few graduate students appeared on the scene.

THE DRAMA OF ANDREWS'S PRESIDENCY

With Andrews's return to Brown in 1889 as its president, political economy was again represented at the top. Andrews personally then offered no instruction in the discipline. His pedagogy from the presidential office was assigned to Intellectual and Moral Philosophy. As an administrator, he pushed forward a number of the features of the program Wayland had fought for at midcentury. The constituency of the institution was broadened: A coordinate college for women was created, an ambitious program of extension courses for the citizenry was launched, faculty strength—most notably in the applied sciences—was enhanced, and instruction for graduate students was expanded. Meanwhile, the elective system was extended in the undergraduate program: By 1896 the senior year was fully elective, and there were only four course hours of required study in the junior year. Wayland's objectives of pluralism, outreach, and consumer sovereignty were thus advanced.

While president, Andrews still had energy left over to testify to truth as he saw it on central economic issues of the day. Given the nature of his views on the relationship between economic science and social morality, he felt under an obligation to do so. He was centrally concerned with one issue in particular: international monetary reform. From his perspective, both the United States and the world had suffered grievously from the decision of the American government in 1873 to suspend free coinage of silver and to identify with those countries that had chosen to use gold as the international monetary base. Monometallism meant that the world's monetary stock was inadequate and had thus imposed deflationary pressures on the world economy. Falling prices, in turn, had provoked commercial crises and discouraged the normal growth of industries. But this was not the end of the evils generated by monometallism. The economic environment it produced had spurred new calls for tariff protection and aggravated the problem of industrial combinations as businesses sought to arrest further reductions in prices. The search for a remedy should begin by enlarging the world's money supply though the remonetization of silver at a fixed parity with gold. Andrews did not believe that a single country could pursue this course successfully on its own. What the world needed was coordinated action on the part of all major trading countries. If they could be brought to agreement on common price ratios for gold and silver, a great many of the world's economic ills would disappear. Andrews was among those urging this approach as a presidentially appointed delegate to the international monetary conference held in Brussels in 1892.

Bimetallism took priority in Andrews's thinking about reforms in the existing system. But there was a tinge of radicalism in some of his other positions as well. He regarded the trend toward industrial concentration as irreversible in modern economies when technological improvements meant that cost reductions were associated with bigness. Here also intervention was called for. Andrews preferred to see the public defended against exorbitant monopolistic pricing through public regulation. But, should any monopoly prove to be "defiant or subversive of the general good," he would "unhesitatingly vote" to have it bought out by the "public power."[62] This would not, however, be the ideal solution. A major danger with socialism was that initiative to innovate would atrophy in the bureaucratization that went with it. On this score, however, Andrews noted that there was little to choose between a public and a private monopoly. The latter could also rest on its oars. Ultimately, the solution would have to be found at a point "where political economy abuts upon ethics. . . . We must have more philanthropy, richer, more solid character, willingness in men to do for love what hitherto only money could induce."[63]

Andrews might also have offended some conservative sensibilities for other reasons. He challenged the view that improvement in real wages had necessarily increased the economic welfare of workers. Much of the gain in real wages, he argued, had probably been offset by increased variability and uncertainty in employment. There was thus a legitimate case in favor of trade union organizations to protect the interests of workers. Nor was he totally out of sympathy with Henry George's doctrines on taxation. He agreed that taxation of land rent would improve distributional equity but saw a danger in the "single tax": He feared that it might so enrich the coffers of the state that its power to spend would not be restrained and liberty would be thereby endangered.

It was on the issue of bimetallism, however, that Andrews's fate hung as president of Brown. His public advocacy of international cooperation on a bimetallist program was well known. In 1896 he reached the conclusion that unilateral action by the United States offered the best prospect for moving the rest of the world to action. He made no public statement on this point, though he communicated his modified view in private correspondence. Without his foreknowledge, the contents of that correspondence reached the press and entered the national debate during Bryan's "free silver" campaign for the presidency against McKinley. Andrews unwittingly had become embroiled in a storm of partisan controversy. This prompted questions from some members of the Brown Corporation, who requested him to exercise "forbearance" in expressing opinions "so contrary to the views generally held by the friends of the University," noting that "the University had already lost gifts and legacies which would otherwise have come or have been assured to it."[64] Andrews responded to this challenge by submitting his resignation, noting that he could not accommodate to the position of the Corporation as he understood it "without surrendering that reasonable liberty of utterance . . . in the absence of which the most ample endowment for an educational institution would have but little worth."[65]

When knowledge of these exchanges became public, Brown became a focal point of national attention. Major academic figures throughout the land—college presidents as well as professors—rallied to Andrews's defense. A special memorial, organized by E. R. A. Seligman of Columbia, was circulated among members of the American Economic Association. There were prominent names on the roster of signers, including many who opposed Andrews's position on monetary questions.[66] In addition, twenty-four of the thirty-six established members of the Brown faculty registered their opposition to the posture of the Corporation. Gardner played a leading role in mobilizing the faculty protest.[67]

The Andrews case put Brown on the map in the late 1890s, and it still stands as one of the most celebrated in the annals of late nineteenth-century discussions of academic freedom.[68] The negative publicity associated with it spurred the Corporation to modify its position. In September 1897 the Corporation voted, with five members abstaining, to request Andrews to withdraw his resignation. Though he did so, this episode left a legacy of scar tissue. Andrews quit Brown in mid-1898 to become superintendent of the Chicago public school system. Two years later he became chancellor of the University of Nebraska.[69]

Political economy at Brown in the nineteenth century was not marked by any novel contributions to theory. The content of teaching was essentially derivative, but its sources changed over time. Wayland drew heavily on the works of the later British and French classical economists, though he translated their message to make it compatible with his vision of revealed truth. The pattern he established dominated the Brown style for half a century. During Andrews's tenure of the chair of History and Political Economy, the clerical approach was mutated by influences from Germany. The 1890s witnessed the divorce of political economy from both moral philosophy and history. Though the scale of operations at Brown was considerably smaller than at other institutions with roots in pre-Independence America, the new "science" as understood by the professionals was by then solidly established there.

But there is still something distinctive about the role of political economy in Brown's nineteenth-century history. Two of its leaders—notably Wayland and, to a lesser degree, Andrews—believed that political economy was more than a body of doctrine to be taught to their students and transmitted to wider audiences through books and lectures. It also provided insights into the ways academic institutions should be organized. Their readings of applied political economy have left a lasting imprint on Brown University.

5

A Quest for National Leadership:
Institutionalization of Economics at
Harvard

BYRD L. JONES

POLITICAL ECONOMY deserves a better position in the College," asserted a report to the Overseers of Harvard College in 1871. Noting that the University of Berlin had four economists, the Overseers' report insisted that

there should be an even greater number here, were it proportioned to the crying necessities of our people. Public and private welfare, principles not only of material, but of moral bearing, interests of the State, the family and the individual, the union of classes, the maintenance of peace and honor, are all dependent, humanly speaking, upon the mastery of economic science, and its application to the experiences through which this nation is called to pass.[1]

At Harvard and elsewhere, political economy had been included in the moral philosophy course taught to all seniors. Adam Smith had explained how competition might yield social progress; but by the 1870s inequalities of income and wealth raised troublesome concerns about social stability and traditional values. Public policy issues such as tariffs, national banks, and internal improvement schemes were discussed, as well as Ricardian rents and Malthusian population growth with their implications for income distribution. Marked by optimism and moralistic commentary, American texts presented simplified analyses derived from English and French authors. Most textbooks followed Frédéric Bastiat in emphasizing an underlying harmony of competitive interests rather than David Ricardo's and Thomas Malthus's dismal prospect of growing rents and impoverished masses.[2]

Under President Charles W. Eliot's leadership from 1869 through 1909, Harvard developed from an undergraduate college with professional schools in medicine and law (though scarcely at the graduate level) into a modern university with distinct academic disciplines. As enrollments increased, Harvard recruited a more secular, cosmopolitan, professional, and specialized faculty. Those changes brought few public controversies because Eliot successfully raised endowments and prestige, and Harvard's Unitarian orientation averted many sectarian disputes raised by Darwinism and empirical studies of social problems. The faculty rather easily substituted science and a tolerant national perspective for sectarian religious support of opinions in moral philosophy, history, political science, economics, psychology, and sociology.

In response to those concerns raised by the overseers' report, Harvard had appointed Charles Francis Dunbar in 1871 as the first full-time professor of economics in the United States. Under his guidance, Harvard advanced an empirical, secular, and modern social science curriculum that encouraged specialization of research and study. Dunbar would not so much lead as adapt to the powerful forces of expansion and modernization affecting Harvard. As the department grew, specialized, published the *Quarterly Journal of Economics,* and strengthened its graduate program, it heeded disputes within the discipline more than public debates. Within a broad tradition of American liberalism that accepted both democracy and capitalism, Harvard sought academic excellence and stability at a time when the nation increasingly looked to educated elites for leadership.

MORAL PHILOSOPHY UNDER BOWEN

During the early nineteenth century, most American colleges covered political economy as a part of moral philosophy. Harvard had done so briefly during the 1830s under Francis Bowen (1811–90) and then largely ignored the subject until Bowen rejoined the faculty in 1852. In 1850 Bowen's appointment had been blocked by elected Massachusetts officials, then on the Board of Overseers, who objected to his support for the Compromise of 1850 with its national Fugitive Slave Law. He had rejected Malthusianism as unduly pessimistic and proudly "advocated the American Protective System and argued strongly against Free Trade"; but those views were not controversial unless linked to immediate legislative issues. Eliot recalled him "as a man of unreliable judgment, but clear, incisive, and kind."[3]

In 1868 Bowen, then Alford Professor of Natural Religion, Moral

Philosophy, and Civil Polity, reported to the overseers on his work for the term:

That during the last Academic term, Sept. 1867–February, 1868, the Senior class recited to him in two divisions, one hour to each, six times a week;—namely three times a week in Logic or Metaphysics, and three times a week in Political Economy. For one of these recitations a lecture was occasionally substituted, on which the whole class attended; and in this way a pretty full course of lectures on Political Economy, and one on Logic as often as the subject seemed to require, were delivered by the Professor.[4]

Bowen assigned Adam Smith's *Wealth of Nations,* John Stuart Mill's *Principles of Political Economy,* and the fifth edition of his text, *The Principles of Political Economy.* During the 1850s, he had assigned Francis Wayland's popular text.

Bowen's text revealed the thrust and central metaphors of what Harvard's seniors were expected to learn. He aimed for "an American Political Economy, the principles of the science being adapted to what is special in our physical condition, social institutions, and industrial pursuits." He recognized "a general science of Human Nature, of which the special sciences of Ethics, Psychology, Politics, and Political Economy are so many distinct and co-ordinate departments." Ricardo, Malthus, McCulloch, and John Stuart Mill had generalized laws for economics, "deriving its principles from their knowledge of human nature, and tracing these down to the outward conduct of men and to the social phenomena which these general motives produce or influence." Bowen found those "universal principles," thus deduced, "comparatively few and unimportant."[5]

Hence, Bowen stressed both institutions and immediate political controversies. "Political Economy is eminently a practical science," he insisted, "and a treatise on it may profitably include much valuable information respecting the habits of business, the course of domestic and foreign trade, and the methods which have been suggested by experience for applying Labor and Capital to the best advantage." He presented detailed accounts of banking and currency, public lands, and public finance, "as might be useful, not only to young men in College, but to those who are about to enter the mercantile profession." Academicians addressed an elite who would apply knowledge and perspective to leadership roles.[6]

Discomfited by his materialistic subject, Bowen would address *"the general well-being of society, so far as this is affected by the moral causes regulating the production, distribution, and consumption of wealth.*" He reiterated a widely shared belief "that wealth is that element of civilization which supports all the others, and that without it no progress, no refinement, no liberal art would be possible." Capital or property allowed a division of labor that freed many persons from "the stern necessity of daily brutish toil on the most repulsive tasks." Beneficent outcomes reflected "the laws affecting the creation and production of wealth,—laws which are, in truth, as constant and uniform as those which bind the material universe together, and evince the wisdom and goodness of the Creator quite as clearly as any of his arrangements in the organic kingdom."[7]

Bowen discerned laissez-faire's divine sanction in its intricate design. Although economic interests reflected selfish motivations, their outcomes served public and moral ends:

society is a complex and delicate machine, the real Author and Governor of which is divine. . . . He turneth their selfishness to good; and ends which could not be accomplished by the greatest sagacity, the most enlightened and disinterested public spirit, and the most strenuous exertions of human legislators and governors, are effected directly and incessantly, even through the ignorance, the willfulness, and the avarice of men. Men cannot interfere with His work without marring it.

Yet Bowen scarcely denounced all state actions.

Vice and crime, for instance, are stumbling-blocks in the path of the community; they obstruct the working of the natural laws, the ordinances of Divine Providence, by which society is held together and all well-meaning members of it are made to co-operate, though unconsciously, for each other's good.[8]

Within that framework, competition among individuals had profound social and moral consequences: "the two fundamental maxims of Political Economy, that labor is the source of wealth, and that the wealth produced is in exact proportion to the labor expended, and is therefore measured by it." Under competition, "each receives in exact proportion to the labor which he has bestowed; the labor of all was equally necessary to present the article in its finished state; and he who finally consumes it, therefore, justly pays all by rendering an equivalent amount of labor." Selfishness became cooperation and interdependence among productive factors;

and the fair rivalry which causes the distribution of values among them, in proportion to their respective industry and skill, ought not to create feelings of mutual jealousy and dislike,—ought not to give rise to the cry that one class is taking more than its due share of the common product.[9]

Nevertheless, Bowen praised savers or capitalists for promoting civilization. "The savage does not amass capital, because he is incapable of foresight and self-denial." Paradoxically, he noted, frugality brought personal and national opulence so that early self-denial allowed later indulgence—although always at some future date.

The moral causes which most effectually stimulate labor and frugality, and therefore make capital accumulate most rapidly, are,—
    1. That the laborer shall be sure of receiving the full amount of his wages, or shall be protected in the ownership of the values which he has produced.
    2. That the skill, intelligence, and education of the laboring classes generally shall be raised to the highest point,—so that, the labor of one well-trained mechanic being as effective at least as that of three raw hands or mere laborers. . . .
    3. That the savings when made, or the capital when accumulated, shall be attended with as high a rate of profit, and as large a measure of physical comfort, social consideration, and political influence as possible.[10]

Bowen condemned hereditary classes or arbitrary inequalities of wealth; but in democratic America he found differences "a spur to industry and frugality." Astonishingly, "even the Irish immigrant here soon loses his careless, lazy, and turbulent disposition, and becomes as sober, prudent, industrious, and frugal as his neighbors." Though Bowen penned fewer offensive condemnations of ethnic groups than many economists of his generation, he asserted his "great faith in the acquired excellences of Anglo-Saxon institutions." Nor were his class biases concealed. For laws requiring inheritance taxes or equal incomes, "the political economist has a right to cry, *Laissez faire!*—let alone! and do not attempt to amend the ways of Providence!"[11]

Bowen's summary arguments for a protective tariff suggested a vision of America's future shared by many free traders as well. Without protection, he asserted, industry would not thrive.

The dispersion of the inhabitants over vast tracts of territory, in the isolated pursuits of agriculture, the great majority of them being doomed to work which would not tax the mental resources of a Feejee-Islander, must be fatal, not only to the growth of wealth, but to many of the higher interests of humanity.

He envisioned flourishing cities valued for their culture rather than for their efficiency. He wished

to give full scope to all the varieties of taste, genius, and temperament; to foster inventive talent; to afford adequate encouragement to all the arts. . . ; to concentrate the people, or to bring as large a portion of them as possible within the sphere of the humanizing influences, and larger means of mental culture and social improvement, which can be found only in cities and large towns.[12]

Characteristically, Bowen "explained" American institutions and conditions as outcomes of steady, though often precarious, progress. He invoked individualism and competition as the means toward social and moral goals. Analyses and illustrations were marshaled to support social or political positions that comforted middle-class aspirations of college students (and their instructors). His eloquent defense of protection for infant industries fell short of schools and public health measures for children of Irish immigrants. He praised professional skills, thriftiness especially among the wealthy, and reduced family size as refutations of Malthusianism and Darwinism.[13]

In preparing a new edition of his text, which he titled *American Political Economy; Including Strictures on the Management of the Currency and the Finances since 1861* (1873), Bowen offended both Boston's banking community and Eliot's preference for separating academic presentations and unpopular political judgments. Liberal Republicans regarded the Civil War as a great moral campaign whose debts must be paid in full, and Boston's moneyed interests had shifted toward a freer-trade stance favored by bankers and investors. In the spring of 1868, thirty business leaders had raised funds for lectures that would present "sound" views on currency. Bowen's public advocacy raised a controversy with potential donors, and Eliot requested Bowen to mute his proposed discount for greenbacks or to remove his identification with Harvard from his new text. He recruited Dunbar and limited Bowen's teaching to ethics and evidences of Christianity.[14]

ELIOT, ELECTIVES, AND EXPANSION

For forty years, Charles W. Eliot led Harvard through example, exhortation, and administrative fiat—shaping educational responses that defined the modern American university. He set a challenge in his inaugural address that would dominate Harvard's goals for decades:

The endless controversies whether language, philosophy, mathematics, or science supplies the best mental training, whether general education should be chiefly literary or chiefly scientific, have no practical lesson for us to-day. This University recognizes no real antagonism between literature and science, and consents to no such narrow alternatives as mathematics or classics, science or metaphysics. We would have them all, and at their best.[15]

A chemist formerly affiliated with the Lawrence Scientific School and the Massachusetts Institute of Technology, Eliot advocated and instituted electives as a means to modernize Harvard's curriculum and foster specialization. Nation building meant developing a university open to modern subjects: natural sciences, modern languages, and the scientific study of society.

Eliot would trust students to choose among solid, well-taught, and carefully monitored courses offered by an outstanding faculty. "The important place which history, and mental, moral, and political philosophy should hold in any broad scheme of education is recognized of all," he noted, "but none know so well how crude are the prevailing methods of teaching these subjects as those who teach them best. They cannot be taught from books alone, but must be vivified and illustrated by teachers of active, comprehensive, and judicial mind." To attract that faculty, Eliot raised salaries, protected tenure and sabbaticals, encouraged specialized courses and research, and fostered a university ethos of national leadership: "A university must be indigenous; it must be rich; but, above all, it must be free."[16]

Eliot advocated a natural aristocracy of talent and morality that was both appropriate for an increasingly secular and organized society and yet resembled his family's values of Unitarianism and good works. "This University aspires to serve the nation by training men to intellectual honesty and independence of mind," he concluded in his inaugural address. "The Corporation demands of all its teachers that they be grave, reverent, and high-minded; but it leaves them, like their pupils, free. A university is built, not by a sect, but by a nation." Perhaps Bowen questioned Harvard's openness to high tariffs and discounted greenbacks, but Eliot's notion of academic freedom was nevertheless broad when compared to that of his peers.[17]

When Harvard named Eliot as president in 1869, twenty-three professors in arts and sciences served some 563 undergraduates; the Lawrence Scientific School had nine faculty and forty-three students; in the Medical School, thirteen faculty taught 306 students (only seventy-eight with previous baccalaureate degrees); and the Law School had four professors and 120 students (half without a college degree). Harvard had neither a Graduate School of Arts and Sciences nor Ph.D. degree programs. When Eliot retired in 1909, the Faculty of Arts and Sciences totaled 165, offering instruction to 2,238 undergraduates and 403 graduate students. The professional schools had raised their requirements and expanded their course offerings (though with little growth in total enrollments), and a Graduate School of Business Administration had opened its doors.[18]

As Hugh Hawkins has observed: "In short, by enlarging the faculty during his first years as president, Eliot sought to lighten the teaching burdens of the ablest professors, to introduce new subjects, to challenge the sleepier teachers with competitors in their fields, and to bring sophistication into the counsels of the university." His achievements occurred within a period of increasing wealth, rising collegiate enrollments, and developing professional schools and research centers. Established institutions grew more slowly than new institutions such as land-grant universities or urban professional schools. Rising national demand for higher education enabled Harvard to expand while maintaining selective admissions and asserting its claims to national leadership.[19]

By organizing Harvard as a great university, Eliot promoted what Talcott Parsons and Gerald Platt have labeled "*institutionalized individualism.*" In the late nineteenth century, industrialization, democratic processes, and educational reforms gained from this "mode of organization of the components of human action which, on balance, enhanced the capacity of the average individual and of collectivities to which he belongs to implement the values to which he and they are committed." Individual freedom, such as unrestricted student choices of electives, depended on institutional responsibilities to offer excellence in each discipline. In retrospect, "this institutional order is possible only if there is some consensus on the relevant values and the basic patterns of cultural orientation with which these are associated."[20] Eliot both represented and articulated a consensus that science and reasoning as fostered in universities and large-scale industrial and commercial organizations could enhance material progress and strengthen individual character.

In conceptualizing a university that was both elitist and egalitarian, Eliot also enlarged his sense of what educated citizens should do for the nation and in turn how governments should serve the people. Distrustful of popular appeals to emotion and offended by public corruption, he believed that college graduates should provide leadership and policy advice. Thus, he had opposed the involvement of elected officials with Harvard's governance—as had prevailed before the 1850s—but he would encourage Harvard faculty and graduates in public roles and the use of private experts in Progressive reforms. Like many liberal Republicans who turned mugwump and then toward a version of reform Darwinism, Eliot looked to institutional frameworks within which individual competition might be harnessed for greater efficiency in meeting long-term social goals.

In 1873, as a serious depression deepened, he complained:

The fact is that the enlargement of the functions of the General Government is the great political sin and danger of these times, and it is to be hoped that the people will soon begin to see and understand the threatening evil. Not a week passes without the promulgation of some new scheme for adding to the activities and powers of the central government. Most of our public men, instead of holding by the American doctrine of leaving the people to take care of themselves, seem to be thoroughly inoculated with the European doctrine that it is the duty of the government to help the people to what is good for them—to more railroads, and more canals, better savings-banks, more various industries and better schools.[21]

Like his friend Dunbar and others of his generation, Eliot's views on government depended more on his perceptions about individual responsibilities and his distrust of democratic politics (for voters lacking a Harvard degree) than on a consistent analysis of competitive markets.

The Economics Department developed within a context of electives with increasing numbers of students selecting both introductory and advanced courses. As Frank W. Taussig, Dunbar's successor to academic leadership, would note:

The backbone of the intellectual content of College work ceased to be Latin, Greek, Mathematics, and came to be the historical and political subjects and the modern languages, especially English. Natural science had its place also, and no small one; but not the place which the moderns and iconoclasts had looked for.

With electives and a broadening of curricular options, some disciplines experienced slight or no growth, despite a doubling of

Harvard undergraduate enrollments. By 1881 the introductory economics course had attracted nearly 150 students, and it would remain one of the most popular offerings. By 1900 total enrollments in economics tripled with the introduction of new and advanced courses.[22]

These organizational developments at Harvard largely reflected national patterns of thought. As two recent commentators on late nineteenth-century intellectual trends have summarized:

> Creating a self-conscious group of scientists and scholars and an organizational structure to promote their work was not an easy task in a society imbued with a pragmatic, egalitarian spirit. However, . . . in the decades after the Civil War, men and women directly involved in the pursuit of knowledge found support and encouragement in a constituency of predominantly college-educated, middle-class Americans. This "cultivated" public was motivated by a variety of impulses: the legacy of the Puritans "to advance Learning and perpetuate it to Posterity"; a sense that knowledge would lead to a better understanding of God's grand design; a romantic interest in the natural wonders of the continent and a curiosity about the new sciences, particularly geology and Darwinian biology, which were challenging accepted ways of thought; a regard for learning as a mark of respectability and social place—a bastion against Jacksonian vulgarity and later against the materialism and corruption of the Gilded Age; a widespread belief in the practical benefits of science; and a desire to equal, and perhaps surpass, the intellectual achievements of Europe.[23]

Harvard's economists had imbibed little Darwinism and less romanticism; they saw providence in broad national outline rather than sectarian strictures; but they reacted against the crassness and corruption of the Gilded Age with a lingering tone of Harvard's Puritan and Boston Brahmin traditions. Eliot's emphasis on science and national leadership provided a major impetus for Harvard's advancement; but as disciplines grew, specialization increased. With it came a professionalization of both knowledge and instruction involving formal study, advanced degrees, research and publication, and a reduced loyalty to one's campus. National organizations communicated current research and analyses and validated their truth by encouraging the criticisms of peers.

DUNBAR'S POLITICAL ECONOMY

Charles Francis Dunbar (1830–1900) graduated from Harvard in 1851 and chose a career in journalism. His editorials for the *Boston Daily Advertiser* indicated a commonsense support for lib-

eral reforms based on "sound" economics. In 1869, the new President Eliot offered him a position requiring both Elements of
Government, with eighteen exercises for juniors, and an elective
course in economics for seniors that would include three exercises
a week for the year. To prepare himself, Dunbar studied independently for two years in Europe. After his return, the introduction of electives and the vacancy created by the Bowen contretemps
prompted his assignment to full-time teaching in economics. For
several years, he offered two courses within the Philosophy Department: an introductory course based on Mill and an advanced treatment of Cairnes and Henry Carey. By 1878 enrollments stood at
120; and a year later Dunbar established a separate Department of
Political Economy.[24]

Asked in 1876 to review "Economic Science in America," Dunbar concluded "that the United States have, thus far, done nothing
towards developing the theory of political economy, notwithstanding their vast and immediate interest in its practical applications."
Busily acquiring wealth, Americans had little time for

an abstract inquiry. The thorough student soon finds that it is necessarily
an investigation as to the direction which human volitions will take under
given conditions and that for its successful prosecution he must first direct
his attention to the mind itself, finding in the complex phenomena of society the test but not the grounds for his conclusions.

Despite its ill-considered policies regarding currency, taxes, and
tariffs, the United States had flourished owing to its rich natural
resources and abundance of land expropriated from native Americans and Mexico. But "the regular course of our development
must, at a point not far distant, disclose to us an imperious necessity for investigating the laws of natural wealth."[25]

Dunbar regarded economics as a developed science—useful for
students interested in public policy and critical reasoning. Although he served as the dean of faculty and later of the Graduate
School, he never used his positions or friendship with Eliot to recruit outstanding researchers or to expand economics as rapidly as
student interest might have allowed. Teaching during a period of
lively, often bitter, debates about historical and institutional approaches as well as the marginal revolution, he accommodated to
new ideas without discarding Mill's text. Dunbar welcomed some
historical studies and included sociologists in his department, but
he explicitly restricted economics as a science to logical treatments
of wealth and distribution.[26]

Dunbar's writings on currency convinced economists and the public of the importance of bank deposits to the money supply. He chided those who accepted popular beliefs linking changes in money supplies with fluctuations in business conditions (such as the long depression of the 1870s). He noted that "in the discussions of the national banking system, the same dread of contraction, or of a supposed popular fear of contraction, constantly appears, and shapes the expedients offered by the opponents, and sometimes by the friends, of the present system." By including deposit accounts in the money supply, the reports by the comptroller of the currency showed little if any contraction after 1876 and a substantial expansion during the 1880s.[27]

Though legislation might make money "more or less sound," Dunbar believed that deposits represented "the adjustable part of our system of credit currency, and the part of it which will continue to adjust itself to the scale of the transactions to which current business naturally gives rise." Hence, redeeming greenbacks and bank notes need not cause a shortage of money; and, in response to public demand, bankers might shift the circulating medium between notes and deposits.

It is, in fact, one of the great services rendered by the national banking system that, for a most critical quarter century, it carried note-issue and deposit banking side by side throughout the greater part of the country, under the management of a class of remarkably sound institutions, giving to the community many of the benefits of free banking, with the minimum of its risks.[28]

Dunbar sought a rapprochement with historical or inductive methodologists by both welcoming their criticisms and indicating their limited impact on major developments in the field. As presented by Smith, Ricardo, Mill, and Cairnes, classical economics begins "from a few simple premises, collected by observation of the nature of man and of his environment, draws from these premises a series of logical conclusions, verifies these conclusions by fresh observation and comparison, and thus ascertains certain relations of cause and effect, which are termed laws." Without current facts, economic analyses lacked political relevance. Thus, historicists— often associated with German-trained economists and later with Johns Hopkins University—performed a valuable service by jarring the deductive theorists with reminders of industrialization, urbanization, and bureaucratization.[29]

Dunbar also adopted a middle ground on the political implications of that *Methodenstreit*. Historical economists attacked an unqualified faith in laissez-faire, which Dunbar insisted was "no part of the logical structure of the old economic doctrine." Overly enthusiastic about the state, German-trained historical economists proposed that "society, as a conscious whole, has duties limited only by the possibility of actively advancing the general well-being of its members; its powers are to be adapted to this end, and, if adapted, are the justifiable, the most effective, and the necessary means of social advancement." That argument, Dunbar noted, would justify "a great and not easily definable extension of the activity of government." Yet, in fairness, he added, "Mill, first or last, suggested legislation as the cure for pretty nearly every evil not deemed positively incurable."[30]

Dunbar disapproved of the openly reformist stance of Richard T. Ely and others who had taken the lead in establishing the American Economic Association:

behind this practical tendency in favor of a more effective use of the authority of the State, lies what seems to be regarded as the chief theoretical characteristic of the new movement, "the reunion of ethics with political economy." The power of society is to be directed by a keen sense of duties, scientifically defined and recognized. The obligation to consider other and higher aims than the mere enriching of the community, the duty of treating the laborer as something more than a certain amount of energy to be made effective by the administration of certain doses of capital, the constraint of Christian brotherhood, are to be enforced as a part of the teachings of political economy.

To Dunbar that was "merely the infusion of emotion into economics," whereas "the business of a science is not to propose or pursue ideals, but to ascertain truths,—a work which ought not to be perturbed by aspirations any more than by any other form of prepossession."[31]

Twenty-five years after beginning teaching, Dunbar noted that "no one of the moral sciences has made a more rapid or solid gain than political economy, either in the extent and importance of its scientific investigations, or in its dignity of method and spirit which characterizes its work, or in its educational value." He separated its scientific reasoning from its political applications:

The circle of emotions, hopes, and moral judgments springing from any economic fact, may be boundless; but the relation of that fact to its cause and its consequences is as certainly a question to be settled by appropriate scientific methods, as the perturbation of a satellite or a reaction observed by a chemist.

When treating a controversial issue, an instructor should "carefully disentangle the scientific considerations from all others, and . . . show their limitation as determined by the supposed conditions which underlie the scientific reasoning."[32]

Dunbar's tone was mature, commonsensical, tolerant, and reformist. He would improve but not radically restructure major institutional patterns. He defended his inclusion of demand deposits as money not by referring to providence but by citing Alexander Hamilton and practical business leaders. Allied with liberal Republicans and reformers associated with the *North American Review,* Dunbar would lower tariffs, condemn monopolies (especially if state-chartered), trust bankers to control money and credit supplies, and praise competition for encouraging efficiency and progress. Educated gentlemen could, presumably, adopt a broad view of political economy as a scientific description of how selfish interests competed, under orderly rules, to enhance both private and public welfare.

Dunbar added new faculty and courses in response to growing enrollments; but he never conceptualized a framework of introductory and advanced courses to cover a well-defined field of study. He preferred instructors who involved students in discussions about current issues without straying far from the positions staked out in Mill's text. He appreciated factual investigations and citation of specific data, but he had no sense that mathematical or statistical tools might open new insights. An Irish commentator on American economics, T. E. C. Leslie, had noted "the absence of long chains of deduction, such as English economists have affected, from the assumption that competition equalizes the wages of labourers and the profits of capitalists in different occupations and locations throughout a country." When commonsense reasoning confirmed their policy preferences, few American economists questioned whether competitive markets described actual conditions.[33]

INSTRUCTORS AND INSTRUCTION: LAUGHLIN AND TAUSSIG

Soon after his appointment in 1871, Dunbar became heavily involved in administrative tasks, and he suffered periodic illnesses followed by long sojourns in Europe. Silas Marcus Macvane served as his assistant for five years before being appointed professor of history in 1878, although he continued to write about economic theory. Macvane was replaced by James Laurence Laughlin (A.B., 1873; Ph.D., 1876, under Henry Adams), appointed instructor in 1878 (when Dunbar became dean of the faculty) and assistant professor in 1883. With Eliot's support, Dunbar dominated the choices and approach of Harvard economists for two decades.

By 1882, enrollments had climbed to 151, and they reached 205 a year later when new courses were added. That expansion led to a division of labor based on the personalities and interests of available staff. Dunbar offered "The Economic History of Europe and America since 1763" as a review of money, taxes, and tariffs in order to illustrate principles from Mill's text. J. Laurence Laughlin introduced "Investigations and Discussions of Practical Economic Questions." An energetic and well-trained teacher, he sought to educate the larger public by relating analysis to current political issues. He was also conservative and dogmatic. His important abridgment of Mill's text both omitted discussions of social philosophy and added charts, data, and illustrations from current American conditions. Thus, Harvard had economic history without historicism and an "issues" course that dispensed "answers."[34]

Frank William Taussig (1859–1940), who followed Dunbar as the dominant figure in Harvard's department, had graduated from Harvard College in 1879. He traveled in Europe for a year before returning to Cambridge as Eliot's secretary and as the second doctoral candidate in economics. In 1883 he received a Ph.D. in the Department of Political Science with a thesis entitled "Protection to Young Industries as Applied to the United States." For three years, he offered a course on tariff legislation while earning a law degree. In 1886 he was appointed assistant professor, in 1892 a full professor, and in 1901 the Henry Lee Professor of Political Economy. According to Edward Mason, Taussig "was a competent theorist and something more than that in the field of international trade. As a teacher of economics, he was unexcelled, and generations of young economists can testify to this excellence."[35]

Dunbar's legacy lay in his emphasis on instruction through class discussions and recitations relating public policy issues to broad principles. According to Taussig's official history of departmental developments:

Naturally the questions which were uppermost with the public at that time influenced the direction taken by the work of the new members. Just as

Dunbar gave most attention to money and public finance, so Laughlin gave most attention to the then-emerging silver controversy, while Taussig plunged into the ever-persisting tariff wrangle. . . . The Department from the first gave attention to economic theory; and the slant which was thus given its work under Dunbar's leadership persisted.[36]

In Europe during 1882–83, Dunbar elicited information from Laughlin and Taussig on their teaching. During the fall semester of Political Economy 2, Laughlin reported that he had "run through Cairnes to International Trade, & reached Adam Smith in the historical lectures, to date." During the spring he would cover tariff legislation. He informed Dunbar that his students indicated "a lively contempt for Carey whose 2nd vol. is nearly finished; but we get abundant discussion about principles, & that works for a better understanding of their own beliefs." He noted a growing interest in economics and drew attention to a students' petition to Eliot about retaining Laughlin. He proposed adding Henry George's book in future spring semesters. "For theses, I have selected (1) the National Banking Question; (2) the Revision of the Tariff; (3) the Railway Transportation question; and (4) the Suspension of Silver Coinage."[37]

In response to Dunbar's detailed questioning, Taussig summarized his year. Students "have liked me reasonably well. At least they have shown interest by asking questions after the lectures, and sometimes (but not often) by questions in the lecture room; and they have come to see me in my room occasionally." He regarded their response positively, "considering that the course attracts a number of average and under-average men." Teaching two sections in order to question students individually, he repeated a few set lectures—"on bimetallism (three), on cost of production of precious metals (chiefly historical), on communism & socialism (descriptive), on foreign exchanges and imports and exports (descriptive), on wages, and on profits in the sense of wages of superintendence." Although "I have done most of the talk in classroom myself," the course "has by no means become a pure lecture course."[38]

During his recitations Taussig aimed "to give them something over and above what was in Mill, in the shape of facts or of more or less correct ideas. Thus in connection with Mill's chapter on a Measure of Value, I explained Jevons's and Walker's notions on a tabular standard of value." He asked for written responses to questions once a week, a system instituted by Laughlin, to keep "informed, after a fashion, of what each man was doing. The fact that I had very few surprises at the mid-year shows that it gives a reasonably good idea of the quality of the men's work." During the spring, Taussig planned "lectures on Cooperation, Trade-Unions, Industrial Partnership, on Protection, and on Taxation."

Looking ahead, Taussig thought Mill indispensable, although inadequate:

There is much that needs to be restated in the book on Distribution; and there is useless and cumbersome dialectical stuff in many chapters. I think it gets the men who do understand Mill into an ultra-orthodox frame of mind that is not desirable; and half of them don't, and never can, understand him. But there seems to be no other book.

On that vexatious wages-fund issue, Taussig added, "I am myself inclined to think that cost of labor is not the best way of approaching the problem of wages and profits, and therefore shake my head over much that is in the chapter on the Progress of Society." Nevertheless, Mill, enriched by lectures and discussions on matters of "practical interest," would have to do.

A dozen years after Dunbar's appointment, the introductory course had become one of the most popular electives among undergraduates. Higher enrollments had led to four sections (of more than fifty students) divided between Laughlin and Taussig. The instructors defended lower tariffs, a sound currency with banks providing the bulk of the circulating medium, and a sense that laborers would benefit most if thrift, entrepreneurship, and industrial competition were encouraged. As Taussig noted, "until about 1890 instruction was still in the main that of the good old days: a textbook, and recitations which were directed rather to ascertaining what the student already knew than to teaching anything he had yet to learn." [39]

After Laughlin's departure in 1888, Taussig lectured three times a week during the year, "hundreds of undergraduates being addressed, exhorted, and more or less instructed. It was bad teaching; not bad of its kind, perhaps, but the kind was bad." Taussig attributed the popularity of lecturing to imitations of German scholarship as well as efficiency of instruction. "Economics as a body of connected doctrine is eminently *not* teachable by lectures, except in its most advanced forms and to the most advanced students." By 1911 he would lecture once a week, following the lecture with two quiz sections. President Abbot Lawrence Lowell emphasized undergraduate instruction by supporting discussion sections and then the tutorial system. Introduced under the leadership of Professor Harold H. Burbank (Ph.D., 1915), it left most introductory teaching in the hands of graduate students or beginning instructors.[40]

For many professors, teaching took precedence over research and scholarly writing. Eliot had raised salaries shortly after taking office, but thereafter they increased only 5 percent until 1900, although general price levels had declined through 1896. As an instructor, Taussig carried a heavy teaching load and reported that he had continued writing for two Boston papers and had "given four public lectures in Sever Hall, evenings, on tariff history" in order to supplement his income and enhance his reputation. Many Harvard faculty repeated lectures for Radcliffe students, taught during summer sessions, and sought other speaking or writing engagements. Most faculty relied on inherited wealth as well as what would later be termed psychic income. Eliot had noted that "inducements are apt to be, not increase of salary, but wider companionship, better access to books, better schools for the children, a wholesome life for the family, more social and educational advantages and the general prestige of the inviting institution." [41]

During his tenure, Eliot hired most of the faculty, and his decision between Taussig and Laughlin for a new assistant professorship revealed something of the qualities he considered important. In 1883 Eliot described Laughlin as

a safe man, not having originality enough to abandon strong leaders. He also is very assiduous, goes to all meetings of the finance club, cultivates students, is petitioned for, and written for weekly in the College newspapers, & is in general trustworthy, precise, & arid person whose face & speech are indices of his mind. . . . Taussig is quick, sometimes inaccurate, incisive but not always judicious, having fluency, clearness and a certain elegance in expounding a difficult subject, not very disinterested by nature, but meaning in general to do his duty, interesting but sometimes brusque to students, not patient with fools & critical with wise men, & self-confident but with some reason. He is an abler & more interesting person than Laughlin; but he might embrace hastily crude theories, & attack rashly well-grounded authorities. I hear reports that his opinions about wages & land differ from Mill's & from yours. Do you know any third candidate? [42]

Laughlin's separation took time and some delicacy. He had considerable writing skills, had organized the Political Economy Club (1883), had adapted Mill's text (1884) for American student use, had published a *History of Bimetallism in the United States* (1885), and had connections with local supporters of Harvard (including Edward Atkinson, a businessman who wrote and lectured on economic issues). Eliot believed that "he harbors a notion that I might have recognized more cordially than I have his services concerning the J. E. Thayer gift." Eliot wanted Laughlin to "change his occupation" and hoped Dunbar could encourage that "without souring his mind or making any kind of break." Through Atkinson's support, Laughlin became the executive for an innovative mutual insurance company that sought to reduce risks of fire. Later, he taught at Cornell University and then became department head at the new University of Chicago.[43]

QUARTERLY JOURNAL OF ECONOMICS

In 1885 a significant event helped Dunbar and the Harvard economists establish national influence over their profession, although the department had neither an outstanding theorist nor an active graduate program. John E. Thayer contributed $15,000 to a publication fund "for the encouragement of investigations and studies in political economy." He suggested "the establishment of a journal of Political Economy." The department considered a publication series similar to one at Johns Hopkins University, but Harvard's graduate program was small. "Otherwise the temptation to permit the publication of papers which are passable but not important, in order to maintain the series, is likely to be felt." Hence, the department supported what became the first professional journal of economics in English. The *Quarterly Journal of Economics* (*QJE*) "would not be the representative of any special doctrine or school of economists, but would be devoted to the advancement of economic science and literature by free investigation, discussion and criticism."[44]

With the launching of *QJE* in 1886 and the appointment of first Dunbar and then Taussig as editors, the Harvard department assured itself a central place in national and international communications among professional economists. Hadley from Yale penned his congratulations: "I hardly know which to praise most—its form or its substance." At the same time he gleefully noted that an essay by Wagner left Richard T. Ely with "the ground pulled out from under the school he has labored to build up." Sidney Webb submitted an article attacking Walker's views on distribution, suggested George

Bernard Shaw as a potential contributor, and complained about the difficulties of establishing an "economic journal here, even with unpaid contributors & editor."[45]

After ten years, Dunbar retired as editor of record and commented on the *QJE*'s achievements and goals: "In the larger universities the opportunities for study and research no longer need fear comparison with those of any other country." The *QJE* and the *Political Science Quarterly* published at Columbia University, both founded in 1886, had encouraged scholarship and open criticism of research by other professionals.

The progress in the equipment of teachers, in the matter and methods of instruction, in the solidity of the contributions to learning, has been promoted in high degree by the opportunities for a full and free discussion, addressed not to a miscellaneous public, but to a circle of critics, investigators, and well-informed readers.

According to the editors, "the diffusion of knowledge and the application of principles may be trusted in large degree to take care of themselves, when once the advantage of scientific thought has set in."[46]

Over twenty years, the *QJE* published 340 articles, as well as notes and reviews. Overwhelmingly, they treated current issues (220 essays) in the United States (185 of those). Some seventy articles were by Harvard faculty or graduates, including thirteen by Taussig and twelve by Dunbar. Distinguished European economists contributed fifteen essays. Table 5.1 categorizes those articles into general topics by five-year intervals. (These categories cover clusters of essays and suggest their importance as viewed by Dunbar and Taussig. Historical topics include a broad range because there were only a few in each period. When an article covered more than one topic—for instance, Charles Beardsley on "The Tariffs and the Trusts"—its placement depended on its implications for policy.)

In keeping with Dunbar's interest in money, particularly in recognizing the place of bank notes in the overall money supply, the *QJE* published a number of articles condemning agitations for silver money and for additional credit facilities in rural regions. The authors supported a conservative stance, for instance, urging Congress to "fix a limit to the present amorphous and anomalous state of affairs" for silver. Seventeen articles on money and banking were published during Dunbar's editorship and twenty-four during Taussig's decade, peaking during the 1890s when silver and rural debts were major political issues.[47]

Table 5.1

	Vols. 1–5 (1886–91)	Vols. 6–10 (1891–96)	Vols. 11–15 (1896–1901)	Vols. 16–20 (1901–6)
Current issues				
State of economics	2	3	8	4
Money and banking	6	11	14	10
Tariffs and trade	4	4	5	6
Monopoly, railroads	8	3	1	3
Monopoly, trusts	1	2	5	8
Monopoly, municipal	—	1	8	1
Economic legislation	—	6	1	1
Labor unions/strikes	5	7	9	9
Census/population	2	1	5	4
Charity/cooperatives	3	3	5	2
Taxes	2	7	2	3
Miscellaneous	5	7	3	10
Subtotals	38	55	66	61
Theory				
Distribution of income	13	5	1	7
Capital, interest, and profit	4	13	3	4
Value	1	4	5	6
Mathematical approaches	1	—	1	—
International trade	1	—	—	2
Subtotals	20	22	10	19
History				
Institutions	6	6	6	11
Doctrine	4	8	3	5
Subtotals	10	14	9	16
Totals	68	91	85	96

Tariffs and trade were discussed in nineteen articles over twenty years, eight of them by Taussig. In his first essay covering tariffs from 1830 to 1860, he conceded that "the growth of manufacturing industries has been greatly stimulated by" protective tariffs. "But experience under the more moderate duties of the earlier period indicates that steady growth would have taken place in any event." By 1900 Taussig noted the declining importance of tariffs and protection.

Other questions—the relations of labor and capital, the functions of the State, the very foundations of the social order—will engage the public mind; and the hoary controversy about protection will be not indeed settled, but disposed of and set aside by the working of other great industrial and political forces.[48]

Historical accounts narrated events without much analysis, except for William J. Ashley's works. Several articles explored the implications for economic theory of pricing policies of railroads and municipal services, including a five-part account of the Boston gasworks by John Gray of Northwestern University. During the first half of the 1890s, William B. Shaw annually summarized the laws passed in various states that moderated the effects of unrestrained industrialization on workers and consumers. There were a scattering of essays on settlement house activities, on cooperatives, on the Knights of Labor, on Bellamy's Nationalist clubs, on history of doctrine resurrecting such figures as Sir William Petty and von Thunen. There were reports on legislative and institutional responses to industrialization in Germany and France. Starting in 1898, *QJE* published a series of articles by Thorstein Veblen on the state of economics.

If the *QJE* established a hallmark during this period it was in articles dealing with the wages fund and the challenge of the marginal revolution to explanations of value based on production costs. That revolution would weaken a common association of price with the effort and sacrifice required to produce a good that had apparently justified existing distributions of income and suggested a providential design underlying competitive markets. After Eugen von Böhm-Bawerk and John Bates Clark had presented their marginal analyses, prices would seem more related to available choices (or opportunity costs, in current terms) and to expectations than to the labor (both immediate and embedded in capital) involved in production. The early disputants in this controversy were Silas Macvane and Francis Amasa Walker, who had left his position as professor of political economy at Yale's Sheffield Scientific School in 1881 to become president of the Massachusetts Institute of Technology. Later, a series of essays by Böhm-Bawerk and Clark clarified the marginal revolution.

The *QJE* published twenty-six articles on the distribution of income shares during its first two decades, half of those in its first five years. Also, it included twenty-four articles on capital, interest, and profits which had implications for the distribution of income, thirteen of them appearing from 1891 to 1896. Between 1891 and 1906, articles treating value more generally appeared at a rate of about one a year. Harvard's faculty (notably Macvane, but also

Taussig) resisted the marginal approach, although in 1888 a Philadelphia businessman, Stuart Wood, published an intriguing approach to marginalist reasoning in the *QJE*. Thirteen years earlier, he had received the first Ph.D. in economics at Harvard (and apparently in the United States) for a modest and critical review of Henry Carey. Wood never taught or wrote much, but he was an active supporter of the American Economic Association.[49]

Whereas early publications of the American Economic Association had described municipal socialism and cooperatives, the *QJE* printed articles about America's utility regulations only after 1896, and then it emphasized regulatory problems. Likewise, William Shaw's compilations of legislation that had an impact on businesses never speculated about why consumers and small competitors sought protection against giant firms. Though scientific and industrial progress was scarcely questioned, economists writing in the *QJE* revealed a distrust of politicians and of workers who aspired beyond their level. According to Taussig, a railway strike in 1886 resulted from workers "endeavoring to secure a share in management beyond that for which they were qualified." Modern industry depended on a militarylike organization: "The rank and file are assigned their duties and their places by the captains of industry."[50]

Dunbar and Taussig made most editorial decisions based on clarity of writing and scholarly merit, yet they established a tone of moderate conservatism in both theory and public policy as the Progressive era unfolded. Nevertheless, the *QJE* helped keep Harvard's economists aware of current scholarship. Taussig corresponded with European economists, especially Alfred Marshall, whose text helped reconcile an emphasis on cost of production as a determinant of income shares with newer marginalist approaches. Rejoinders and letters revealed points of disagreement within the profession; and the publication of Veblen's essays indicated an openness to critical viewpoints. The *QJE* usually required a subsidy, and Eliot used the occasion to voice concern about maintaining Harvard's financial support and attracting students. He saw no need for stronger reminders for Dunbar or Taussig. They well knew the costs of building Harvard's national reputation.

WAGES-FUND DOCTRINE AT HARVARD

For two decades Harvard economists discussed how best to reinterpret the wages fund in their class recitations, lectures, and the pages of the *Quarterly Journal of Economics*. Loyal to Mill and to production costs as the source of value, they resisted the marginalist revolution. This debate also indicated the importance attached to the normative correctness of income distribution in the United States. Mill had argued that laborers ordinarily received payment in advance of the sale of their product, and hence aggregate wages depended on previous savings or capital accumulations. In the third issue of the *QJE*, Walker proposed that wages were a "residual share" after rent, interest, and managerial rewards. An appreciation of entrepreneurial efforts, he urged, would deflate Socialist claims and "have a truly reconciling influence upon the always strained and often hostile relations between employer and employed."[51]

In response to important essays by Böhm-Bawerk and Clark, Macvane restated classical views. While praising the Austrian economist's emphasis on the contribution of capital to roundabout means of production, Macvane concluded that Böhm-Bawerk had "done little more than to put the familiar principle of demand and supply in a new and, as I think, less convenient form." Macvane insisted that "the theory which connects value directly with cost has the great recommendation of putting at the front the important fact that exchange is simply a stage in the existing mode of providing for our individual wants." If value depended purely on subjective assessments of exchanges, then economists weakened their praise for capitalists' cost savings through specialization. In retrospect, these tendentious essays apparently aimed to imbue savers and entrepreneurs with moral virtues.[52]

Thomas Nixon Carver's essay in the *QJE* established a middle ground that allowed the "proper" lessons to be drawn about labor.

On the whole, we have every reason for believing that the standard of living acts as an effective check on the increase of numbers and the supply of laborers in general. Therefore, we conclude that the true theory of wages is to be found in a combination of the "marginal productivity," or the "no rent increment," theory of Professor Clark and the "standard of living," or "cost of production," theory of the classical English economists.

Recognizing that population adjusted slowly, Carver hoped a rising standard of living might allow time for education and fresh aspirations to restrain family size and thus to sustain higher wages. Later, as a member of Harvard's faculty, Carver insisted that an economy in balance at the margins would mean equal prosperity for all groups. "Neither the laborer nor anybody else would need the state or any paternalistic organization to safeguard his interest beyond protecting him against violence and fraud." [53]

Taussig's two articles in the *QJE*, later incorporated in his *Wages and Capital* (1896), preserved a wages fund as a recognition of the particular contribution of previous savers to economic progress. He acknowledged Böhm-Bawerk's analysis of capital and interest and his subjective explanations of value. Taussig emphasized institutional patterns of an industrial economy—that capital values, exceeding annual wages by more than three to one, were always being replenished and that money wages might not equal real income. Hence, both capital and wages were "elastic within limits." He rejected "that pessimistic view which finds its expression in the turgid description of the laborer as the slave of the employer, without going to the opposite extreme of concluding that the laborer is no worse off than the investor." [54]

Instead, Taussig elevated the role of business managers, whose foresight and coordination brought labor and capital together:

As to the hired laborer, his position does indeed show that the ownership of wealth in modern societies is very unequally divided, and in so far is not consistent with that ideal organization which, under ideal conditions, would doubtless bring the maximum of human happiness. But it is consistent with a steady improvement in his condition, in his place and power in the community, and in his sources of happiness; and, therefore, we need not despair—men, manners, and morals being what they now are—if it is perhaps the only position he is likely to have for a long time in the future.

Although the wages-fund controversy had become "barren," nevertheless,

as a mode of describing the methods and sequence of production, the concrete structure of society in its economic aspects, the manner in which a prolonged and complicated series of exertions brings at last the flow of real income, the place which capitalists have in the distribution of income,—on these topics something can still be gained from the discussion. [55]

Taussig emphasized large capital aggregations that made possible the specialization of labor and economies of scale. Since corporate managers exercised discretionary power, he would examine their motives and behaviors in order to understand the forces of economic progress. Sympathetically, he noted that businessmen received an uncertain residual share of money incomes because wages and interest were fixed in advance for any accounting period, but he seldom empathized with workers who faced layoffs during hard times. Instead, he counseled laborers to support incentives for capital accumulations, to emulate middle-class values, and to have patience.

Properly reinterpreted, the wages-fund doctrine allowed Taussig, and later Carver, to update Bowen's strictures against the dismal fate of the working class as depicted by Malthus. If prices, including wages, simply reflected psychological states and the relevant set of choices, then economists could not propound their usual praise for foresight, learning, diligence, and character with the same assurance. Marginal conditions did not easily support moralizing about saving and temperance. In their quest for national leadership, Harvard's economists sometimes confused the interests of the university's benefactors and most of its students with America's welfare. Perhaps that commingling accounts for the tedious discussions of the wages fund as a description of the income distributed to laborers.

ADVANCED COURSES, NEW FACULTY, AND PROFESSIONALIZATION

In the early 1890s, the department depicted its growth to one of the largest and most popular disciplines for Harvard undergraduates on a large, neatly lettered chart (see table 5.2).

Although Eliot had raised salaries for professors to $4,000, he lowered average instructional costs by hiring more instructors and assistant professors at $1,000 per year. Between 1880 and 1892 Harvard's faculty "had expanded by slightly more than half and become decidedly more pyramidal in structure." It included thirty-six professors and fifty-six instructors or assistant professors. Professional and business backgrounds continued to dominate. As McCaughey noted, "seven of Eliot's eleven professorial appointees on the 1880 faculty came from conspicuously wealthy backgrounds." The increased professionalization of academic life, meaning extended probationary period and obligations to publish, worked to diversify the faculty.[56]

In 1880 half of Harvard's faculty had advanced degrees or a period of preparation in Europe; and by 1892 two-thirds had advanced training before their tenure appointments.

Still all male, all white, overwhelmingly Anglo-Saxon in ancestry, Protestant in religion, and comfortably middle-class in social origin, the character of the Harvard professoriate had nonetheless changed in several

Table 5.2

	1867–68	1872–73	1877–78	1882–83	1887–88	1892–93
Professors	1	1	1	1	3	3
Other instructors			1	2		2
Introductory and historical courses	1	2	1	1	2	3
Courses in applied economics					4	4
Advanced courses			1	2	3	5
Hours of instruction per week	1	3.5	6	7	22.5	30
Enrollment of students						
General introductory courses	26	92	108	152	208	335
Historical, advanced, applied courses			28	38	219	371
Total enrollment	26	92	136	190	427	706

significant ways: (1) it was less dominated by New Englanders (more than a third now came from outside the region); (2) proportionately fewer, though still a majority, had attended Harvard College; (3) proportionately fewer could be identified as Unitarians or as having close kinship ties with Harvard; (4) only a handful had their total academic experience circumscribed by Harvard.[57]

In McCaughey's terms, Harvard's faculty became more professional and cosmopolitan throughout the nineteenth century. He offered five behavioral criteria for academics: training in a recognized discipline, time in probationary rank "as a teacher-scholar," academic position with "specialized instruction," "commitment to publishing the results of research for the scrutiny, edification, and approbation of fellow specialists," and "belief in the scholarly function and reputation among fellow specialists as primary, the teaching function and particular institutional connection as secondary." Some two decades after Dunbar's appointment, "control of the Harvard faculty had shifted from the locally rooted, non-specialized, institutionally loyal 'academic gentlemen' to the somewhat more socially heterogeneous, highly specialized, intensely competitive professional academics on the faculty."[58]

As enrollments increased, Dunbar had followed Eliot's policy of adding instructors and junior faculty. In 1889 John Graham Brooks offered the problems course, shifting its emphases from "questions of bimetallism, railroads, currency, and tariff" to "labor arbitration, friendly societies in England, German workmen's insurance, trade unions, profit-sharing, and cooperation." The next year, Edward Cummings returned from a three-year travel fellowship to teach sociology within the Economics Department as a supplement to Francis G. Peabody's work in social ethics. According to Robert Church,

> Cummings was one of those fascinating, confused, contradictory conservatives so prominent at the turn of the century. A Social Darwinist, he used rigidly objective standards of social investigation to show that individual initiative and the free operation of natural selection were essential to social progress. Yet he was a social gospeler and headed many, many charity organizations in the Boston area.[59]

For a decade, Cummings discussed laborers' conditions and theories of social reform before becoming assistant pastor in a Boston Unitarian church. He supported union-managed out-of-work benefits based on workers' "incentives of personal economy in detecting imposition, and aided by intimate knowledge of the special conditions of each trade in seeking employment for those who are idle." He welcomed production cooperatives, or profit sharing; wrote positively about university settlement houses such as Toynbee Hall that issued scholarly reports; praised industrial arbitration for averting strikes; and worried that cooperative stores were "unmistakably premature." He reiterated Plato's charge that charity might result in "protecting the weak, perpetuating the unfit, reversing the law of progress, destroying civilization and sympathy itself." His ideal workhouse would inculcate the virtues and ambitions of the strong.[60]

From 1895 to 1900 his brother John Cummings taught statistics, with references to social problems and population patterns. He forthrightly condemned naive notions of race and ethnicity that flourished among economists and sociologists at the end of the nineteenth century. Instead, he argued,

economic development during this period has tended, and tends more and more, not to dissociate, select, and establish ethnic factors, but, on the contrary, to break down all natural differentiations, to break up and obliterate ethnic stratification, and to substitute a classification and hierarchy of social groups dependent upon economic efficiency and function.

Although "the Cummings brothers were able to introduce some methodological techniques," Church concluded, "they were unable to construct an academic subject."[61]

In 1892 the department appointed William J. Ashley, educated at Oxford and author of *An Introduction to English Economic History and Theory*. Ashley's appointment to a professorship was intended to provide a balance by adding an inductive approach, a defense of protective tariffs, and an advocacy of social reforms through public actions. During his nine years on the faculty, he carried on intellectual warfare with Dunbar and, principally, Taussig. As Church discovered from departmental correspondence, "a decade of strain, intellectual and social, inside the department followed Ashley's appointment." In his introductory lecture, Ashley had asserted that historical approaches had

changed the whole mental attitude of economists towards their own teaching. The acceptance of the two great principles,—which are but different forms of the same idea,—that economic conclusions are *relative* to given conditions, and that they possess only *hypothetical* validity, is at last a part of the mental habit of economists.

Those changes had reached "even the pages of the Harvard *Quarterly Journal of Economics*,—the peculiar home of theory."[62]

Ashley hoped that historical studies would reveal new "conclusions as to the character and sequence of the stages in economic development." New laws would be dynamic rather than static and present a broad philosophy of progress or "economic evolution."

The point of view is here no longer that of a bargain between individuals in given social conditions, but of the life and movement of whole industries and classes, of the creation and modification of social mechanism, of the parallel progress and interaction of economic phenomena and economic thought. The studies of the school are no longer individualist and psychological, but collectivist and institutional.

Thus, economic historians had first to comprehend "what has been the institutional framework of society at the several periods, what has been the constitution of the various social classes, and their relation to one another."[63]

From 1897 to 1900 Guy S. Callender offered a course in American economic history. A student of Ashley's who had taught at Bowdoin College and later accepted a position at Yale, Callender looked at institutional and social factors related to economic developments. His Harvard training helped Callender's initial appointment, but he lacked a conviction that social science justified existing social arrangements. With Ashley, Cummings, Callender, and colleagues among the historians, as well as Peabody in philosophy and later social ethics, the Harvard department might have incorporated an interdisciplinary historical and sociological approach with interesting potential for social science developments in the United States. Instead, it collapsed and rebuilt itself in Taussig's image as a narrowly professional and "scientific" discipline.[64]

In 1900 Harvard's Economics Department virtually disappeared. Its reconstruction testified to the institutionalization of economics at Harvard as well as at other universities that had trained economists who satisfied Taussig's criteria. According to his official account,

> In the opening years of the twentieth century the Department suffered a collapse. Dunbar died in 1900. Edward Cummings (A.B. 1883), whose appointment as Assistant Professor of Sociology in 1893 had marked another enlargement of the scope of Economics, resigned in the same year. Ashley resigned in 1901. For two years (1901–03) Taussig was compelled by ill health to withdraw from teaching. Some time passed before the department could be built up again to full strength. The successive appointments of Carver, Gay, Ripley, Bullock, Day filled the gaps. They made possible not only the maintenance and enlargement of the instruction for undergraduates in Harvard College, but the establishment and development of that offered to graduate students.[65]

When Ashley returned to England to head a new School of Commerce at Birmingham, he was replaced by Edwin F. Gay (A.B., Michigan, 1890; Ph.D., Berlin, 1902). When appointed in 1902, Gay was thirty-five and entering his first job—little known and not a Harvard graduate. He had spent most of the previous twelve years in Europe studying economics, history, and philosophy. According to his biographer's description, Gay fitted the Dunbar–Taussig mold:

> This long apprenticeship gave him a breadth and depth of knowledge which contributed much to the reputation he won as one of Harvard's great teachers. Students who knew him only as lecturer gained from his class such new vistas of history and such an insight into the way a master sought, analyzed, and presented his material that in retrospect they counted the course one of their most valued intellectual experiences. Those who went further, following under his guidance the road to a doctor's degree, learned the high standards of rigorous work he demanded,

but they also discovered the infinite pains he would take and the individual attention he was ready to give to their problems.[66]

Other key appointments included several professors who would carry the department on into the 1920s. Thomas Nixon Carver (A.B., Southern California, 1891; Ph.D., Cornell, 1894) was appointed in 1900 and named David A. Wells Professor in 1904. Carver, a lively though opinionated instructor, published several major studies in addition to a later textbook, including *The Distribution of Wealth* (1904), *Sociology and Social Progress* (1905), and *Principles of Rural Economics* (1911). William Z. Ripley (S.B., Massachusetts Institute of Technology, 1890; Ph.D., Columbia, 1893) was appointed in 1902. Previously he had written *The Races of Europe*, and at Harvard his major work dealt with railroads. Charles J. Bullock (A.B., Boston University, 1889; Ph.D., Wisconsin, 1895) moved from Williams College to Harvard in 1901 and was named professor in 1908. He wrote on the history of taxation and advised Massachusetts officials on tax reforms. Edmund E. Day (S.B., Dartmouth, 1905; Ph.D., Harvard, 1909) became an instructor in 1910 and professor in 1920.[67]

These appointments made the department more cosmopolitan. Only Day had his Ph.D. from Harvard. O. M. W. Sprague, who would join the business school faculty did also, but the new department reflected a variety of educational backgrounds. Carver, who came to seem a typical Harvard professor, had tried dry farming in California before working his way through the University of Southern California and then attending Johns Hopkins and Cornell. His summer jaunts through rural America and Europe developing material for his courses on agricultural economics contrasted with Bowen's earlier celebration of urban values.[68] Under Bullock's guidance after 1912, the department would offer a full array of graduate-level courses and hire many doctoral students as tutors or section heads.

At the turn of the century, a regular visiting committee to examine the Economics Department reported that "a very large proportion of the students take Political Economy, and many take the more advanced courses. The courses seem to be satisfactorily conducted and the lecture system is supplemented by conferences and teaching in sections." It noted Dunbar's death and the addition of new courses related to business. By 1914, the Committee to Visit the Department of Economics reported that total student enrollments had reached 1,634, with 542 taking Economics A, the introductory course. Graduate enrollments had increased fairly steadily from sixteen in 1902–3 to forty in 1913–14.[69]

In keeping with the size and importance of the introductory course, one member of the visiting committee who was a faculty member in education, described its instructional pattern: "On Saturdays a lecture is delivered to the students in a body in the New Lecture Hall. On two other days of the week each student attends a meeting of the section to which he is assigned." Five instructors plus Assistant Professor Day met twenty-one sections with about twenty-five students each. For twenty minutes students wrote their responses to a set question arrived at through discussions among the instructors. "After the answer is written the rest of the two meetings is devoted to a quiz, with explanations and discussions based on the required reading, which is usually from twenty to fifty pages of Professor Taussig's *Principles of Economics*." Attendance and attention were consistently good; but "the quality of the thinking done by the students did not seem to equal their attention. . . . Often their ideas seemed hazy, and too often the whole class seemed unable to answer a question adequately explained in the text."[70]

In Taussig's words, "these later years were marked by a further development of advanced instruction and by a growth of departmental strength. It can be said with confidence that in this subject the first place among American universities was then conceded to Harvard." The major weakness that he saw in the 1920s was "the field of social applications or the implications of the subject." Sociology as taught by Cummings, Carver, or Ripley had emphasized not reforms but the paucity of social applications. "But there was no coordination of all this with other disciplines, such as anthropology, psychology, and ethics, and little recognition of the way in which these might contribute to the understanding of economics or of the contribution economics might make to them." Peabody's social ethics substituted for sociology. "Like economics, social ethics began as a constituent part of ethics and philosophy; it began, too, and continued, with a hortatory flavor supposed to be alien to the cold dry atmosphere of science."[71]

Thus, the Economics Department developed despite internal conflicts, crises caused by illnesses and trips to Europe, an unending quest for instructors who would both heed undergraduate concerns in introductory sections and pursue their own research careers. Dunbar, Taussig, and Carver in turn exercised a dominant voice in setting departmental directions. Each combined effective, noncontroversial teaching with considerable writing about broad topics of contemporary interest from a policy viewpoint. They had personality and stature rather than brilliance. They clarified economic theory rather than adding to it; and their views fit, as Joseph Dorfman has noted, in a mainstream of traditional analysis. Laughlin's comment about Dunbar's approach to bank deposits might have described his successors' contributions: "he gave it such a cogent and lucid exposition that it may now be regarded as a part of our general stock of beliefs."[72]

Not until the 1920s, when Bullock and A. A. Young refocused attention on broad issues of theory and public finance, would graduate instruction dominate departmental thinking. Prior to 1897 Harvard listed only three dissertations in economics: Stuart Wood had reviewed Henry C. Carey's massive *Principles of Social Science* (1875); Taussig began his lifelong study of tariffs; and Howard H. Cook wrote on "The Economic Basis of Irish Emigration" before becoming assistant secretary for the American Iron and Steel Institute. In the next three years, five doctors of philosophy finished and advanced in academic careers, including Sprague and Callender. During the first decade of the twentieth century, eighteen Ph.D. degrees were granted. Most graduates accepted academic positions, but none was notable for his contribution to economic analysis.

In reflecting on those changes at Harvard, Taussig expressed a small regret for both the increased disciplinary focus of younger instructors and the tendency for economics to become professional training for business careers. "The economist is interested in *his* universe, that of human society: in the way this society grows and develops and functions; but not in telling the individual how he can advantageously find his place in the complicated organism." Instead, economics students addressed

great public issues such as they would have to deal with in mature life as citizens, legislators, and public officials. And in this experience they dealt with a set of topics that called for close reasoning, often of an abstract kind, as well as for adequate information and the application of informed common sense.[73]

For Dunbar and Taussig, economics remained a policy science not too distant from Bowen's moral philosophy. Reasoning and reasonableness, applied to understanding material and cultural progress in America, would enable Harvard graduates to contribute to nation building.

INSTITUTIONALIZATION—AND AFTER

Between 1860 and 1900, the underpinnings of political economy shifted from moral philosophy to secular analyses and empirical studies; and economics established itself within American universities that offered specialized, advanced training for both old and new professional classes. Early in the nineteenth century, the American college had been "a marginal institution," as Fritz Ringer has noted:

A private venture, it was typically affiliated with a religious denomination or philanthropic association. It generally catered to a local rather than a national clientele. In its academic standards, it resembled a European secondary school rather than a university.

After reading pre–Civil War congressional debates on such issues as tariffs, currency, and land use, Paul Conkin has concluded that "on any specialized issue a layman could usually gain full equality with experts."[74] By 1900, however, economics increasingly required training in colleges and universities to master a core of value theory in addition to richly detailed studies of commercial and industrial organizations.

As noted by Taussig when a young instructor, value theory remained startlingly simple but difficult to master. A straightforward account of how supply and demand worked through competitive markets to determine prices at the lowest cost of production clarified why division of labor (specialization), increased trade (larger markets), and more capital (saving) accounted for rising prosperity. At the same time, establishing how individual markets might balance when aggregated across all producers and consumers, distinguishing real from money or price-level phenomena, or applying broad generalizations to specific policy issues vexed the subtlest economist. Citizens and doctoral candidates might read Adam Smith or Taussig's text at quite different levels of appreciation. Pragmatically, there might be little difference between competition defended as part of a divine plan or as a scientific guide for efficiency and equity; but, ultimately, trained economists would also comprehend market failures due to increasing returns to scale, externalities, and uncertainties.

Nationwide, the transition from moral philosophy to social science was eased by certain continuities among Smith, Malthus, Darwin, and Herbert Spencer. Population pressures on resources resulted in unrelenting competition that transformed selfish individualism into ultimate progress for society or the species. At Harvard, Bowen and Louis Agassiz rejected the logic of evolution while the economists and sociologists accommodated it into their views. As Jurgen Herbst has suggested, German historicism and a higher criticism of the Bible influenced academic theology and paved the way for systematic reasoning and empirical studies in other disciplines. Harvard's Unitarian affiliation and pre–Civil War concentration of German-trained faculty had facilitated an early acceptance of secular arguments for social ethics. Later, William James, Francis Peabody, and Taussig stressed cooperation, or harmonious outcomes of competition, as a counter to a tooth-and-nail struggle implicit in Social Darwinism.[75]

Although economics has seldom offered practical training for business or commerce, it undoubtedly owed much of its popularity among students at Harvard and elsewhere to its subject matter. Industrial growth brought new factories and products, workers and farmers agitated for a larger share of income, monetary policies had to be adjusted for war and variations in gold and silver production. Cities grew and attracted millions of new immigrants from Europe. Science and technology generated miraculous electric lights, phonographs, interurban lines, and chemistry to improve steels and other metals. Economics "explained" that progress and assured individuals that the system ordinarily worked to their advantage without any political interference. There were useful reforms—lowering tariffs, encouraging cooperatives, regulating railroads, promoting public health—but no need for a radical restructuring of society.

In his presidential address to the American Economic Association, Taussig recognized the difficulties of harnessing selfish desires for wealth to improvements in public services. "Enterprise, invention, the development of the fruitful division of labor, the organization of new schemes, the opening of new lands and the utilization of new resources,—these have been the main conditions and accomplishments of great fortunes," he intoned.

We can no longer hold the semi-theological view reflected in Adam Smith's oft-quoted phrase, that the individual is "led by an invisible hand to promote an end which was no part of his intention," but we may at least be thankful that the impulses which move the strong and ambitious are so often turned to the achievements of peace and industry.

If governmental responsibilities expanded in the decades ahead, the nation would need managerial skills of a high order.[76]

America's Constitution and popular fears of tyranny subjected governments to checks and balances and to popular whims that precluded sound planning and firm direction over time. Only political bosses could manipulate the system into concerted actions. Expert advice and such reforms as city managers and commissions might improve public management, but Taussig counted on intelligence and character to supplant political corruption. Character "is affected, no doubt, by teaching and exhortation, but it rests in the main on inherited qualities and on the example and training which go from parent to child." Thus, Taussig honored "uprightness, steadfastness in work, good faith in the affairs of everyday life, respect for law"—traditional New England values, apparently sanctioned by modern economics.[77]

Deliberateness and judiciousness characterized the external activities of Harvard's economics faculty. Taussig had served on the Cambridge School Committee, and he would serve as first chairman of the United States Tariff Commission. Edwin Gay held a number of important posts in World War I, in which he served as a manager bringing information to bear on difficult political, social, and economic problems. Bullock served on various state boards considering tax reforms. Carver directed the Rural Organization Service in cooperation with the Agriculture Department. Most of the faculty belonged to professional organizations, especially the American Economic Association, and had visited distinguished economists and traveled in Europe. They were respected as gentlemen and scholars, not as iconoclasts or brilliant theorists.

Self-conscious of its role as a leading national university, Harvard purveyed a moderately conservative mainstream viewpoint of social sciences—welcomed by its graduates and students but poor preparation for unexpected crises. Economic, social, political, and intellectual developments in the twentieth century would prove unkind to its economics faculty. Their tolerant and moderate tone suggested muddled beliefs—without restraining them from offering denigrating comments about Irish immigrants, politicians, labor unions, and reformers. During the 1920s, the department's Economic Service pioneered in statistical techniques for forecasting business cycles. Yet no major department would so firmly oppose New Deal recovery measures or undergo such a revolutionary transformation following the publication of John Maynard Keynes's *General Theory* (1936).

From two quite distinct perspectives, the lessons of Harvard economics that had appealed to undergraduates later appeared less compelling to Franklin D. Roosevelt as president and to W. E. B. DuBois, the great black scholar and civil rights activist. In 1936 Roosevelt wrote to honor Taussig, his former teacher: "Thirty-six long years ago I began a more or less intensive study of economics and economists. That course has continued with growing intensity during the last four years." But Harvard could take little comfort from the president's jocular conclusion: "that I know nothing of economics and that nobody else does either." He attributed Taussig's successes to "the delightful twinkle in his eye and his keenness of judgment of men and events." [78]

W. E. B. DuBois had studied economics in depth, submitting his essay on the wages fund for consideration for the Tappan Prize. Tariffs and Populist reforms, he recalled,

were discussed with some clearness and factual understanding at Harvard. The tendency was toward English free trade and against the American tariff policy. We reverenced Ricardo and wasted long hours on the "Wages-fund." The trusts and monopolies were viewed frankly as dangerous enemies of democracies, but at the same time as inevitable methods of industry. We were strong for the gold standard and fearful of silver. On the other hand, the attitude of Harvard toward labor was on the whole contemptuous and condemnatory. Strikes like that of the anarchists in Chicago, the railway strikes of 1886; the terrible Homestead strike of 1892 and Coxey's Army of 1894 were pictured as ignorant lawlessness, lurching against conditions largely inevitable.

Karl Marx was ignored as commercial and industrial donors "made Harvard rich but reactionary." [79]

Although Harvard's economists contributed little to theory, Eliot, Dunbar, and Taussig had reason to be proud of their accomplishments. They had adapted what Oleson and Voss called "the distinctive features of specialization: the acceptance of objective criteria for judging individual ability, a division of labor among experts, and a coordination of efforts achieved through rational methods of control and communication." [80] They had also emphasized active interactions with students and a sense of national leadership by Harvard. Institutionalized as a social science within the university, economics depicted current elites as deserving their position. Harvard economists sought to prepare future leaders imbued with personal values and supportive of public policies that would harness individual responsibility and scientific knowledge to modern organizations capable, it seemed, of producing goods and services in abundance.

The Fortunes of Political Economy in an Environment of Academic Conservatism: Yale University

WILLIAM J. BARBER

DURING THE FIRST century and a quarter of its existence, neither the curriculum nor the organization of Yale College changed substantially. When its foundations were laid in 1701—as the "Collegiate School" in the colony of Connecticut—the institution's purposes were set out clearly: to educate and train a clergy in the Congregationalist tradition of the Christian faith and to nourish intellectual endeavors in the citizenry at large. Though distinctly committed to a sectarian creed, the institution in its early history was also a public institution. The leaders of the Connecticut Colony ran its governmental structure as a theocracy. They were militant in their view about the primacy of what they took to be the "true faith"—as opposed to a debauched version promulgated in the Massachusetts Bay Colony from which they had fled. Congregationalism was to be the established church in their newly settled territories, and there was to be no tolerance for heresy. With church and state united in a common endeavor, it followed naturally that public assistance should be provided to finance the new institution. Private donors, to be sure, were also sought: One of them—Elihu Yale, who had accumulated a fortune as an officer of the East India Company—was responsible for giving the Collegiate School a new name in 1718. Even so, more than half of the gifts to Yale College in the eighteenth century were official contributions from the colony and state of Connecticut.[1]

Though Yale from its earliest days had a clear sense of identity and of the priority of its commitment to serve the Connecticut community, it also recognized an obligation to reach a wider con-

The author is indebted to the Yale University Library for permission to quote from documents held in its archival collections.

stituency. The Congregationalists who inspired and shaped the institution had a missionary zeal about them, including a mission for Yale to spread the true doctrine (particularly to frontier settlements). This implied that it was proper to welcome students from beyond the reaches of Connecticut and to assist in founding satellite educational institutions from which religious truth could be disseminated. Both of these objectives were pursued with vigor. By the end of the American War of Independence, Yale's enrollments outdistanced those of its nearest rival, Harvard, by more than a third. Its student body was also considerably less parochial than that of any other American educational institution. By the early decades of the nineteenth century, about a quarter of its undergraduates were drawn from outside New England with approximately 10 percent from the southern states.[2]

THE EDUCATIONAL PATTERN IN THE EIGHTEENTH AND EARLY NINETEENTH CENTURIES

Yale conferred the bachelor of arts degree on 2,333 of its graduates in its first 100 years. The average size of the graduating classes increased to more than fifty in the first decades of the nineteenth century. Even though the college's total enrollment was the highest in the nation, the scale of operations was still—by latter-day standards—small. In 1817, for example, a population of about 275 undergraduates was served by a faculty of ten.[3]

Despite numerous evidences of dynamism in its early history, the educational product Yale offered remained essentially static. The course of instruction was built around prescribed instruction with emphasis on the study of Latin, Greek, and the Holy Scriptures. The typical program of study also provided some space for elementary mathematics, with a bit of attention to the Newtonian view of the universe, but for little else. Nor did instructional methods provide much scope for the imagination. The accepted pedagogical technique called for "tutors" to perform as drillmasters presiding over daily recitations on all the prescribed subjects. This was held to be the appropriate way to treat young men in an institution committed to equipping them with the disciplines—both intellectual and moral—needed for life. And the young were young indeed: The average age of entry on the four-year course was sixteen, and freshmen were eligible to matriculate after they had "passed the age of fourteen." Accordingly, the institution felt honor-bound to replicate an environment of parental supervision in which there was little free time for mischief. In all of its essential features, the Yale College of this period—along with most other American colleges of the time—was more like a tightly run secondary boarding school for boys than an institution of higher learning.

The organizational structure that kept all this in place was dominated by a president who was charged with general superintendence of the academic program and student behavior, with management of the college's business affairs, and with authority to appoint and dismiss members of the academic and managerial staff. The president, in turn, was selected by the fellows of the "Corporation"—a body controlled by Congregational clergymen resident in Connecticut. In its decision on the selection of a president, the Corporation valued intellectual and executive abilities, but another qualification took precedence: the candidate's soundness on Congregational doctrine as codified in the "Saybrook Confession of Faith." From 1722 to 1823 all members of the faculty were also expected to satisfy this test of orthodoxy as a condition of employment. But still more was called for in the president: He was expected to be an ordained clergyman as well.

The bulk of the instruction in the college was carried out by tutors, characteristically, recent graduates who took on this assignment for a short term while continuing their professional studies (more often than not for a ministerial career). Tutors were responsible for working closely with a subdivision of each of the four "classes" of students in residence, hearing their daily recitations in all the required subjects. Greater scope for academic specialization was afforded to those appointed to "professorships." These were permanent appointments available to senior scholars whose primary duties were to prepare lectures for the more advanced students. By 1800 only three such "chairs" had been created: Sacred Theology (1755); Mathematics and Natural Philosophy (1770); and Ecclesiastical History (1777). It was also standard practice for the president—who usually held the title of "professor" simultaneously—to lecture to students in the final year of their studies.

These arrangements were scarcely hospitable to the introduction of "modern" subjects into the teaching enterprise. A president, were he so inclined, might transcend the constraints of the prescribed curriculum in his work with upper-level undergraduates. Ezra Stiles (president, 1778–95) appears to have exercised such discretion from 1789 onward in introducing seniors to Montesquieu's *Spirit of the Laws* and subsequently to Paley's *Principles of Moral and Political Philosophy*. But such concessions to "modernism" could not be regarded as curricular reforms: These were strictly matters of presidential taste and could easily be reversed. Stiles's successor, Timothy Dwight (president, 1795–1817), made no attempt to disguise his antipathy to European intellectual currents, attacking particularly the works of Voltaire, Rousseau, and "other godless men."[4]

At times, the inherent conservatism of the Yale educational plan provoked calls for reform. Some of them the college could ill afford to ignore. The leveling spirit and the growth of anticlericalism in the years after the close of the revolutionary war prompted petitions to the Connecticut General Assembly calling for change in the institution's mode of governance. In particular, the clerical monopoly of the Corporation should be broken with the appointment of "civilians." And there was an implied threat that the General Assembly should sponsor a competing college in the event that Yale failed to change its ways. The result was a charter revision in 1792 that struck a compromise: The Corporation was restructured to include eight ex officio members: "the Governor, Lieutenant-Governor, and six senior assistants in the Council of this State." This amendment was primarily cosmetic: Majority voting power remained in the hands of the Congregational clergy, who also retained the right to designate their own successors. Meanwhile, the state resumed its financial assistance to the college. Yale thus emerged from this episode with its autonomy intact and with its resources replenished.

Although Yale had resisted external pressures for reform in the late eighteenth century, a number of adjustments internal to the institution in the opening decades of the nineteenth century foreshadowed some redirections that would later gather momentum. These occurred piecemeal, not as a part of preconceived grand design. Yet their cumulative impact was to produce a significant modification in the character of the institution by the mid-nineteenth century. Part of what was at work was signaled in the shifting makeup of the professional interests of Yale College's undergraduate clientele. In the first four decades of the eighteenth century, approximately half of its graduates entered the ministry. For the decade 1805–15, by contrast, less than 18 percent chose a ministerial career, whereas nearly one-third of the total elected to become lawyers.[5] To be sure, it could still be argued—and it was—that the traditional curriculum laid the ideal foundation for subsequent professional training. Nevertheless, a case could be made in favor of an institutional posture that would involve Yale more directly in the post-B.A. professional education of its graduates. The college had long offered opportunities for such study to candidates for the ministry. The bulk of the training of prospective lawyers and doctors, on the other hand, had largely been left to the practicing professionals who took on trainee-apprentices for a fee. There was much to be said for regularizing this professional training by affiliating it with an established educational institution. Yale, situated in the largest city in Connecticut and the only college in the state, was a natural candidate to assume this larger educational role.

As early as 1777, Ezra Stiles had envisioned the teaching of law and medicine in a "Plan of a University," but the unsettlement of war and its aftermath had brought this scheme to naught. The idea resurfaced in 1801 when a professorship of law was created. The incumbent gave little time to academic duties and allocated the bulk of his energies to private law practice and to political affairs. Meanwhile, an able New Haven lawyer with a well-equipped law library and a talent for teaching began attracting pupils, many of them graduates of Yale College. It was not until 1826, however, that these separate strands were integrated. The senior member of the private law school was appointed to the professorship of law (which had been vacant since 1810), and a formal connection between these two enterprises was established. The working relationship was modeled on the pattern established earlier (in 1813) for the creation of a "Medical Institution." Professionals would be affiliated with Yale in a "department" separate from Yale College. Instructors in the professional departments were accorded academic titles, and the award of degrees would be exercised jointly with Yale. For budgetary purposes, however, the law and medical departments had no claim on the resources of Yale College, and the remuneration of their officers would be drawn primarily from their own fees. "Greater Yale" could thus blunt the charges of those critics who alleged that it was indifferent to practical concerns. Meanwhile, Yale College could continue to tread its traditional path.

But even within Yale College there were some departures from traditionalism in the early years of the nineteenth century. Perhaps the most striking was the decision of President Timothy Dwight—a man noted for arch-conservatism and popularly referred to as the "pope of Connecticut"—to create a professorship of chemistry and natural history. No less remarkable was his selection of an appointee for this post. Benjamin Silliman, who was designated for this chair in 1802, had no obvious technical qualifications for the assignment. He knew virtually no chemistry. A graduate of Yale in

1796, he carried with him both the strengths and weaknesses of its educational system. Silliman, however, possessed three qualities that were highly valued in faculty members at the time. He was sound on matters of religious doctrine; he was a son of Yale and understood its mores; and he was obviously a highly intelligent man. Silliman was allowed the better part of two years—most of which he spent in Philadelphia studying chemistry and medicine— to prepare himself for his new tasks and was subsequently supported on a trip to Europe to purchase scientific equipment and demonstration materials. In the eyes of Timothy Dwight, this venture into new subject matters could readily be reconciled with the institution's central commitment: Science was expected to display the marvels of God in His creation of an orderly universe. Assimilating lectures on scientific inquiry into the undergraduate program was not thought to be a compromise in the traiditional curriculum but was considered an extension of it. In fact, this innovation was later to have much more sweeping implications for the structure of Yale.

NEW PRESSURES FOR CHANGE IN THE 1820S

Yale had long enjoyed the position of a "chartered monopoly" in the higher education market in Connecticut, and its officers were anxious to protect it.[6] Among other things, this status offered the prospect that Yale would have access to subventions from the General Assembly. The future of this arrangement, however, was crucially dependent on a larger political environment over which Yale and its officers could exercise no direct control. Toward the close of the second decade of the nineteenth century, it was clear that public attitudes in Connecticut were changing. The decision of the General Assembly in 1818 to disestablish Congregationalism as the state religion suggestcd that the days of Yale's monopoly were numbered. Soon thereafter Episcopalians registered their desire to found a college in Hartford (which was to begin as Washington— later Trinity—College in 1825), and Methodists were shortly to follow by founding Wesleyan University (1831) in Middletown. Though Yale was unsuccessful in warding off these challenges, it reformed some of its practices in its attempt to do so. In 1823 the requirement that faculty members should subscribe to the Saybrook Confession of Faith—a stipulation that had been in place for more than a century—was dropped.

The attitudes of politicians also prompted Yale to rethink other aspects of its internal business in the 1820s. State officials formed a minority of the Yale Corporation, but their goodwill was seen as having an important bearing on the fate of requests for public moneys. It was thus a matter of consternation when a state senator (and Yale graduate) proposed in 1827 that the curriculum should be overhauled by dropping the "dead languages" and that they should be replaced with modern and more practical subjects.

Yale's response to this challenge took the form of a lengthy "Report on a Course of Liberal Education," prepared by the president and faculty, issued in September 1828. In the main, this was a spirited defense of the classical curriculum. At the same time, the report argued that the college had not been as inflexible as some of its critics had alleged it to be. Recently, the report observed, "whole sciences have, for the first time, been introduced: chemistry, mineralogy, geology, political economy, etc."[7] With respect to the natural sciences, this was an obvious reference to the work Silliman had initiated. Studies in political economy, however, were far less systematic. It appears, however, that seniors were given some exposure to this subject matter at this time.[8]

Though attention was thus directed to some evidences of change, the central message of the 1828 report was an articulation of the case for clinging to the tried and true principles of the traditional pattern in undergraduate education. The purpose of the college was to train the mind and to build character. This could best be done by giving students the disciplines of a classical training. This did not mean that all educational institutions in the United States should necessarily proceed along the same path. America was a new, large, and diverse country in which there was scope for a healthy pluralism. But, as far as the posture of Yale College was concerned, there should be no compromise.

None of this was taken to preclude the possibility that a more diverse pattern of studies could be made available to "resident graduates . . . if suitable arrangements were made."[9] The experience of European universities, the report noted, might offer some guidance on ways to accommodate a wider array of subjects within the existing institutional framework. The German mode of university organization had "of late gained the notice and respect of men of information in this country."[10] This suggested that a "School of Philosophy"—intended for graduate students—might be entertained as a supplement to the professional schools. But such an innovation could be considered only on the understanding that the integrity of Yale College's program should remain intact. There the status quo should be protected. In sum, the authors forcefully rejected the proposition "that our colleges must be new-modeled; that they are not adapted to the spirit and the wants of the age; that they will soon be deserted unless they are better accommodated to the business character of the nation."[11]

Yale College thus resisted the pressures of the 1820s to "modernize" its curriculum. In 1830, however, it did initiate one modest reform in its procedures: Tutors were then allowed to specialize by subjects, rather than to cover the texts in all of the required fields. In addition, the report of 1828 opened up the possibility that new things might be done at the graduate level. The sticking point here was money. Yale might consider a move in this direction if someone else paid for it, but the resources of Yale College were not to be made available for these purposes.

THE SCIENCES AND INTERNAL PRESSURES FOR CHANGE IN THE MIDDLE DECADES OF THE NINETEENTH CENTURY

More by accident than by design, a momentum for institutional reorganization was set in motion in the late 1840s that would ultimately produce an environment in which the teaching of political economy would have an established place on the Yale scene. The cutting edge in these developments was supplied by a small group of enthusiasts for the natural sciences. President Dwight's gamble on Silliman to bring chemistry and natural history to Yale had paid off in ways that had not altogether been anticipated. Though Silliman's teaching had been primarily confined to lecturing and demonstrations, he had won an appreciative audience. His laboratory facilities were meager—far too modest to be integrated with his instruction to undergraduates—but they did permit him to work privately with a few apprentices. One of them, John Pitkin Norton, was later to pursue studies in Europe in chemistry as applied to agriculture. When he returned to the United States as the leading American authority on this subject, Silliman took the initiative in persuading the Yale Corporation to take advantage of Norton's skills. Here was an opportunity to link scientific knowledge with the world's work. The Corporation responded by creating a professorship in agricultural chemistry—subject to two important provisos: that the professor would offer "instruction to graduates and others not members of the undergraduate classes" and that "the support of this professor is in no case to be chargeable to the existing funds or revenues of the College."[12] In other words, Yale was prepared to accept this venture as a free good so long as it was kept at arm's length from the college.

The enabling legislation for this innovation created a title for a resident professor, but otherwise it amounted to little more than a license to free-lance in New Haven. How then could the relationship between Yale and the applied scientists on the periphery be given more positive content? An interim solution was worked out in 1847. Yale was at that time organized administratively into four "departments": the "academical" (i.e., the B.A. program, which was always regarded as the core) and the three professional departments (theology, law, and medicine), each of which was expected to be self-sufficient financially. The amendment of 1847 created an additional department in which instruction could be made available to students who were neither undergraduates nor enrollees in the professional schools. This new vehicle—styled as the Department of Philosophy and the Arts—was intended "to embrace philosophy, literature, history, the moral sciences other than law and theology, the natural sciences excepting medicine, and their application to the arts."[13]

Yale thus moved a step in the direction of the German model of university organization as foreshadowed in the report of 1828. Though this authorization provided considerable scope for the pursuit of advanced studies over a wide range of fields, enrollments in the Department of Philosophy and the Arts were in fact dominated by students interested in applied chemistry and in civil engineering (which was added to the offering soon after). But a stable equilibrium had still not been achieved. The pioneering instructors in the applied sciences could not be indifferent to the concerns of students: Teachers were dependent on student fees for a livelihood. For their part, students were interested both in substantive learning and in some form of public recognition for their effort. These considerations prompted the creation of two degrees to be awarded on the recommendation of the faculty in the Department of Philosophy and the Arts: the B.Phil. (a first degree awarded to students specializing in the applied sciences) and the Ph.D for advanced study. The latter was formally authorized in 1860, supported by the argument of the scientists that this move would "enable us to retain in this country many young men, and especially students of science who now resort to German universities for advantages of study no greater than we are able to afford."[14] The doctorate was first awarded in the United States in 1861 at Yale when three students (one in physics, one in philosophy and psychology, and one in classical languages and literatures) qualified for this degree.[15]

It was, however, the B.Phil. degree in the science program that was to be the source of the greatest academic ferment in the Yale of the mid-nineteenth century. Yale's reputation for work at the forefront of American science spread quickly, attracting increasing interest among students and potential donors. One major contributor to this cause gave the science program a new name as the "Sheffield Scientific School." But the very success of this venture generated a new problem in academic politics. The accommodations of the 1850s had produced an institution that awarded two first degrees: the B.A. from the college, with qualification in the "dead languages" as a condition of entrance and a prescribed curriculum for the subsequent four years; and the B.Phil.—which could be earned in a shorter period—for scientists, for whom the requirements in the ancient languages were relaxed. From the beginning these separate tracks had been regarded as noncompeting spheres. Indeed, one of the recommendations of this formula to the "traditionalists" was that it might permit Yale to respond to pressures to adapt to the modern world in a manner that would allow Yale College to carry on its business as usual.[16] But this scheme had another consequence: Students and faculty in the Scientific School were systematically segregated from those in the "Academical Department" and treated as second-class institutional citizens. Similarly, remunerations of instructors in the Scientific School were considerably lower than those of Yale College faculty, even after some endowments had been found to relieve the former's exclusive dependence on income from fees.

In this atmosphere, the Scientific School tended to attract to its staff two types of persons: (1) scientists with a sense of mission about their cause (and usually with some independent income); and (2) educational reformers—not necessarily scientists—who were frustrated with the hidebound conservatism of Yale College and who sought a setting in which they might have a freer hand to experiment. The prime exemplar of the latter category was Daniel Coit Gilman, a Yale graduate in the class of 1852. After a postgraduate tour in Europe during which he was caught up in debates about the "new education," he returned to New Haven uncertain about the course he should pursue. For the next several years, he was employed variously as a fund raiser for the Scientific School and as a Yale College librarian, and he obtained a license to preach in the Congregational church.[17] Educational reform—in which some reconciliation could be struck between the sciences and the humanities—was his abiding passion. His central faith was set out as follows:

Never, probably in the history of the country, was it more desirable that the study of History, Law, Political Economy, Philosophy, Literature and all the humanities should be kept up, and that young men should learn to value the lessons of the past, and to take counsel from the thoughts of wise men of every age and country. Heretofore, the complaint has been, that the classics have been the only means of liberal education. Henceforward, science will offer its aids to intellectual culture in organized schools. Both classes of institutions will flourish side by side, and each will be strong in the other's strength. The Creator and his laws, man and his development, or, in other words, science and history, alike offer abundant discipline for the mind and appropriate preparation for the active life of work.[18]

Gilman was one of the main contributors to the design of the "Select Course" launched in the Scientific School in the 1860s. In the first two years in this program, a student was expected to study the rudiments of the various sciences and mathematics in addition to English literature, history, and a modern language. The third year included political economy, moral philosophy, theology, logic, and commercial law. This was indeed education for the generalist. Its formulation was at once an indictment of the narrowness of the Yale College curriculum and an opportunity for the student who wished to develop an acquaintance with the sciences without committing himself prematurely to specialization in any one of them. But this program could also be understood as an attempt to enhance the status of the Scientific School on the local scene and as a model from which Yale College might borrow if it had a mind to do so.

For the better part of a decade, Gilman was responsible for much of the teaching in political economy at the Sheffield Scientific School, even though his appointment was "Professor of Physical and Political Geography."[19] Gilman's larger purpose—to generate some momentum for change in the Yale College curriculum—was, however, frustrated. Though championed for the presidency of Yale by younger alumni in the early 1870s, his candidacy was a nonstarter in the eyes of a Corporation controlled by conservative clergymen. In 1872 he accepted appointment as president of the University of California and subsequently carried his vision of educational innovation to Johns Hopkins as its first president.

Though Gilman left Yale a disappointed man, he had still left a legacy. His own teaching in "political economy"—which appears to have been oriented more to political and economic history than to economic analysis—reached only a small number of students in the Select Course program in the Scientific School. Even so, the exposure he provided to this line of inquiry was more than the typical student in Yale College was likely to get. President Woolsey (whose scholarly training had been primarily in Greek language and literature) taught with Francis Lieber's works on political science in his course with seniors during this period and produced a text of his own, *Introduction to the Study of International Law, Designed as an Aid in Teaching Historical Studies* (1860).[20] An impression of what he conveyed on political economy can be gleaned from the recollections of William Graham Sumner, a graduate in the class of 1863. Sumner reported reading and reciting from Wayland's *Political Economy* but said that this had left a lesser mark on his thinking than his reading of Harriet Martineau's *Illustrations of Political Economy*—which he had come upon by chance—at the age of thirteen or fourteen.[21]

Gilman could at least depart from New Haven with the satisfaction of knowing that he had established a secure beachhead for political economy at the Scientific School. His replacement—Francis Amasa Walker—was a man of remarkable credentials. He had risen to the rank of brigadier general during the Civil War and subsequently had directed the statistical work of the 1870 federal census. Not only did he have a quantitative bent, he had also collaborated with his father, Amasa Walker (a teacher of political economy at Amherst College), in the preparation of a textbook entitled *The Science of Wealth,* published in 1866. Walker was invited in 1872 to join the faculty of the Sheffield Scientific School with the title of "Professor of Political Economy."[22] This was the first time such a designation was accorded at Yale. To be sure, this appointment was made outside the mainstream of the Yale establishment. Given prevailing attitudes among Yale's senior administrators, it is doubtful that Walker, despite his eminence, would have been welcomed to a post in the Academical Department. He was after all a graduate of Amherst, not of Yale.

SCENERY SHIFING IN THE 1870S AND 1880S

Noah Porter, Professor of Moral Philosophy and Metaphysics, ascended to the presidency of Yale in 1871. A Yale graduate and a Congregational clergyman, he was decidedly a man of the old school. In his inaugural address, he reaffirmed the priority to be attached to defending the classical curriculum of Yale College. Though Harvard might institute President Eliot's "elective" reforms, there was no place for such heresies at Yale's core. Modern subjects could be tolerated when segregated in the Scientific School and, to some extent, in postgraduate programs of study. But these concessions at the periphery simply reinforced his conviction that the purity of Yale College should be preserved.

At the same time, Porter was well aware that his vision was not shared by an increasingly vocal number of alumni and younger members of the faculty. A "Young Yale" movement had formed in the late 1860s with two primary items on its agenda. The first was reform in Yale's structure of governance, which would bring alumni into the Corporation and crack the hegemony of the self-perpetuating clerical membership. Part of this objective was reached—with the aid of active lobbying by Gilman—in 1871 when the Connecticut Assembly was persuaded to amend Yale's charter to permit six alumni to take over the six seats allocated to senior state senators. This did not immediately shift the balance of power and, in any event, this change was not effective until the unreformed board had called Porter to the presidency. Nevertheless, the charter amendment signaled that the curricular stand-patters could no longer expect to be unchallenged.

A voice in institutional governance was the instrumental but not the final objective of the Young Yalers. Their substantive goal was to move the college curriculum into closer contact with the contemporary world. A brochure produced by the Executive Committee of the Society of Yale Alumni put the matter as follows in 1870: "it would be easy to name important departments of learning which are not yet represented in the scheme of professorships." Its enumeration included the history and philology of the English language and "the wide field of political science (in which instruction has been given by President Woolsey), including the philosophy of government, the law of nations, and political economy."[23]

These were realities with which Porter had to reckon, however distasteful he might find them to be. He was not far into his administration before the issue was no longer whether an appointment to cover political economy and related subjects should be made but how it should be made. Some teaching in this subject matter had been institutionalized under Woolsey as part of the president's work with seniors. Porter had no disposition to sustain this precedent himself: His own preoccupation in teaching was in moral philosophy, metaphysics, and the "evidences of Christianity." Offloading part of the presidential duty (as defined by his predecessor) on someone else was thus not an unattractive proposition. On July 3, 1872, Porter wrote to William Graham Sumner, then an Episcopal minister in Morristown, New Jersey:

> I think I ought to apprize you that your name has been prominently mentioned as a suitable person to fill the chair of political economy and political science. . . . One other person has been urged who is not a graduate of the college. Those who urge him urge very strongly and those who object to him are very decided in their objections. All the members of the faculty would like to have you here in some capacity. The proposition has been made to have you here as a third professor in Greek and Ancient History and to raise whatever endowment might be necessary.[24]

In a number of respects, this was a remarkable invitation. Sumner had already identified himself as an agitator for reform as one of the prime movers among the Young Yale alumni. Nor did he have visible credentials as a scholar in the social studies. Following his graduation from Yale in 1863, he spent three years in Europe, but his studies there—first at Geneva, then at Göttingen, and for a brief spell at Oxford—were primarily in the ancient languages, church history, and biblical criticism. One might also have questioned the substantive utility of his three-year stint as a tutor at Yale (1866–69), when he taught mathematics and Greek, to the new work for which he was being considered. These considerations, however, were overridden by others: Sumner had the Yale blue in his blood and, as an ordained clergyman (though not a Congregationalist), he seemed to be sound on questions of faith.[25]

If some might have questioned the adequacy of his preparation for the proposed professorship, Sumner entertained no self-doubts. As he later observed:

> When I came to write sermons, I found to what degree my interest lay in topics of social science and political economy. . . . It was not possible to preach about them, but I got so near to it that I was detected sometimes, as, for instance, when a New Jersey banker came to me, as I came down from the pulpit, and said, "There was a great deal of political economy in that sermon."[26]

Sumner began his duties at Yale College in the fall term, 1872. His title was styled as "Professor of Political and Social Science." "Political Economy," though suggested by Porter in his initial correspondence, had been dropped.

In the evolution of Yale College, Sumner's appointment was a signal event. But it was one thing to create a regularized platform for this subject matter and quite another to provide the man professing it with a substantial audience. The structure into which Sumner's teaching was initially supposed to fit relegated political economy to a part-time study available only to seniors. It is not surprising that Sumner soon began to push for greater scope. In company with colleagues from the sciences, he managed to press through a modest modification in the curriculum in 1876 which provided a bit more flexibility. President Porter continued to drag his feet, but his critics could now advance a new argument for departing from the lockstep of required studies. The post–Civil War generation of undergraduates were older than their fathers had been during their college years. The typical age of entering freshmen had now risen to eighteen. Thus, the prescriptions that might have been desirable in an earlier period were no longer self-evidently appropriate for classes of students with more maturity and presumably better preparation at the point of entry.

The infighting of this episode created a number of "optionals" in the program of studies. (The term "electives" was deliberately avoided; this language had been contaminated by the radical innovations emanating from Harvard.) In fact, the optionals offered little scope for student choice. The work of the first two years was unchanged, with all of a student's curricular time committed to required courses in the ancient languages and mathematics. In the junior year, further work in the classics and mathematics was dropped as a requirement and a number of sciences were prescribed instead. The student was then expected to supplement the required third-year menu by selecting from a number of options. Latin, Greek, mathematics, and French accounted for three-quarters of the subjects on the optional list (which did not include political economy). In the senior year, political economy was required in the first term and political science in the second, and the range of options was widened. There were, however, more choices available in the ancient languages than in any other field. Moreover, optional courses were scheduled to meet in the afternoons, with the mornings reserved for work in the required courses. Even so, the new regime, which not only prescribed political economy in the first term of the senior year but made additional study available in the second term for those who chose to continue, suggested that there was considerable pent-up student demand for this material. In the first year of this experiment (1876–77), the supplementary political economy option outdrew the other optional studies by a considerable margin.[27]

This was a breakthrough of a sort. But it was far from sufficient to satisfy the aspirations of a new generation of reformers. In the academic year 1883–84, the battle lines were formed once more in a campaign for a thoroughgoing scheme of electives. Sumner again was in the thick of the fight, serving on a faculty committee to draft reforms. But he also went public with his message. He laid down a widely read indictment of the traditional regime in an essay entitled "Our Colleges before the Country," published in the *Princeton Review* in March 1884. He then charged that "college officers are, for many reasons, unfit for college management. . . . Certainly the notion that any body of men can now regulate the studies of youth by what was good for themselves twenty, forty, or sixty years ago is one which is calculated to ruin any institution which they control." The old way of doing things was a form of "mandarinism" which produced people disqualified for useful work. In the same vein, he asserted that "a college which is a refuge for mere academicians, threshing over the straw of a dead learning, is no better than a monastery." He lamented the waste of his energies in attempting to teach political economy to classically trained students but added that those who were the best in political economy were usually the worst in the classics. The proper route was to give students complete liberty in their choice of fields but to place requirements within fields.[28]

The outcome of this phase of the debate was a compromise in which one-half of the junior year and 80 percent of the senior year were liberated from requirements. This was far short of what Sumner wanted but far more than Porter wished to recommend to the Corporation. Porter's resistance was broken when Sumner and his faculty committee colleagues sequestered him in his office for several hours and wore him down. This reform—like the one before it—was immediately followed by a rising demand for instruction in political economy.

THE STYLE AND CONTENT OF SUMNER'S TEACHING

Sumner was a thorn in the flesh of President Porter for reasons that went well beyond his ardent advocacy of curricular reform. Sumner also wanted to break the conventional mould in the way subjects were taught. The hallowed procedure in the classical curriculum was daily recitations from the assigned texts, a technique that rewarded skills in rote memorization but not critical thinking. Sumner set out to challenge his students. As he stated his views in the preface to a collection of problems in political economy published in 1883:

I have long used problems and fallacies as auxiliaries to my other classroom work. The object of such exercises is to break up the routine of textbook recitations, to encourage wider study of scientific treatises, and to develop some power of independent thinking, and of applying the principles which have been learned. In the present state of political economy it seems especially desirable to study subjects, and not text-books.[29]

The phrasing of some of Sumner's "problems" for students, however, might incline a latter-day observer to wonder just how much independence in thought he was prepared to inspire in his classroom.[30] Nevertheless, Sumner's pedagogical style and his procedures for evaluating students provoked Porter's displeasure.[31]

A more serious tension between the two men was sparked by Sumner's use of Spencer's *Study of Sociology* in his classes. When this information came to Porter's attention, he bluntly informed Sumner of its unsuitability for undergraduates because of the "unfairness with which [Spencer] attacks every Theistic Philosophy of Society and History." Porter felt assured "that the use of the book will bring intellectual and moral harm to the students, however earnestly and vigorously you may strive to counteract its influence—and that the use of it will inevitably and reasonably work serious harm to the reputation of the college. . . . I am presumed to authorize the use of every text book. I must formally object to the use of this."[32] Sumner turned this issue into a cause célèbre as an infringement of academic freedom and threatened to resign if this administrative censorship were not lifted. Though he gained enough publicity to establish his point—presidential intervention in textbook selection did not occur thereafter—Sumner neither resigned nor assigned the book.[33]

Sumner did not need to assign Spencer's work directly to students in order to convey its message. By 1880 it was built into what Sumner had to say. Society was ordered by immutable natural laws, one of the most fundamental of which was the law of natural selection. To deny the survival of the fittest, Sumner insisted, was to guarantee the survival of the unfit. The outcome of the struggle should prevail. There was no place for sentiment about the result: The drunk in the gutter should not be picked up because he was exactly where he belonged. Nor was there any place for governmental intervention to cushion the harshness of the competitive contest. Sumner saw himself as a spokesman for the "forgotten man"—whom he identified as the thrifty, prudential, hardworking citizen—who always ended up being victimized by schemes promoted by misguided social reformers. This was full-blooded laissez-faire with particularly pronounced antipathy to anything that smacked of socialism, protectionism, or bimetallism.

Although a Spencerian flavor was certainly embodied in the material Sumner provided to undergraduates, he also relied on a number of standard texts in his courses (which carried a catalogue listing as "Political and Social Science"). In his first year of teaching, Perry's *Political Economy* was prescribed in the first term of the senior year and Lieber's *Civil Liberty* in the second term, thus following the pattern Woolsey had established. In the academic year 1873–74, Mill's *Principles* replaced Perry. From 1874–75 through the mid-1880s, Fawcett appears to have been the standard text, though it was supplemented by Laughlin's edition of Mill from 1884 onward.[34]

In his instruction to graduate students, Sumner pursued the same themes. Notes on his lectures taken by J. C. Schwab during the academic year 1886–87 are revealing about the manner in which the central argument was developed. Sumner was fond of displaying statistics, and he took the full sweep of world history as his province. He surveyed the state of knowledge on the history of population and technology, on land tenure systems, on international patterns of production and trade, on the practices of governments in property law and commercial legislation. But underlying all this illustrative material were a number of integrating threads: that the laws of population, diminishing returns, and money are timeless and universal; that "harmony and equilibrium in the industrial system" are established by natural laws beyond the control of men; that the evolution of economies beyond the subsistence level necessarily is associated with inequality in the income distribution.[35]

Sumner was predictably polemical and forceful in everything he did. Latter-day interpreters have been inclined to write him off as the arch-apologist of late nineteenth-century robber-baronial capitalism in America. For his part, Sumner never thought of himself as a conservative. His style instead was "to set the cat among the pigeons" by attacking what he took to be sentimentalism and sham. This technique probably won him more enemies than friends, but it was one he was prepared to deploy consistently both on campus and off. At the height of his powers as a contributor to economic debate in the 1880s, he was prominent nationally on the lecture platform and in the press as an uncompromising advocate of free trade and sound money. Certainly his denunciation of protectionism—which he depicted as a form of moral corruption that eroded the integrity of the body politic—outraged many of the established economic interests of his time. In his view, a well-ordered society was one in which there should be both a separation of state from church and a separation of state from markets. He saw little prospect, however, that popular democracy would generate an order that would match his image of economic rationality.

The message Sumner conveyed was dogmatic, but it still served as a mind-opener to many of the students with whom he dealt. Many—including a number who would later become members of Yale's faculty—attributed their choice of career to the stimulus of his teaching.[36] They may have parted company with him on particular points of doctrine and their implications for economic policy, but they still stood in awe of Sumner the man.

But Sumner's outspokenness had other consequences. It alienated many professional colleagues in other colleges and universities at a time when political economists were attempting to establish a professional identity on a national scale. Some promoters of an American Economic Association indeed defined their central purpose as counteracting Sumner's influence. Certainly Richard T. Ely, one of the charter sponsors of the organization, was unambiguous on this point in the 1880s.[37] The polarizing effect of Sumnerism, in turn, isolated Yale's political economists from these national trends for the better part of a decade. Sumner and his colleagues preferred to associate with members of the Political Economy Club, an organization composed largely of New England academicians and businessmen, most of whom were like-minded on controversial issues of the day.[38]

Despite Sumner's prominence in the 1880s when his intellectual activity was most heavily concentrated on problems of political economy, he left little mark on the subsequent development of economic theory. He wrote no textbook that might shape the course of thought outside New Haven (though his book of "Problems" attracted some attention and went through five editions between 1884 and 1893).[39] Much of his published commentary on economic issues was in essay form and sermonlike in style. The books he produced in these years, on the other hand, were structured as treatises on topics in American history in which he surveyed practices in monetary management and in finance. In fact, however, they were "message-oriented" documents designed to show the follies of misguided intervention and of monetary experimentation.

Sumner's eagerness to convey the "correct" conclusions on current issues also precluded analytic novelty. His vision of the virtues of the competitive order was presented quite differently from the way later champions of laissez-faire have typically argued their case. Sumner did not address questions about the structural conditions required for the achievement of optimal allocative efficiency. Formal argument at this level was of no interest to him. Questions about monopoly or about labor organization could be handled much more simply. "Trusts" were bad only if bigness enjoyed protective shelter from governments. The case of "natural monopolies" was recognized, but regulation was a doubtful remedy because public authorities simply did not know enough to do their job intelligently. Nor was he concerned that the development of trade unions might prove to be a threat to the competitive order. Organizations of whatever type were simply a manifestation of the underlying social forces, and whether they survived or not was a matter to be resolved not by legislation but by their ability to adapt successfully to societal needs.

DEVELOPMENTS AT YALE'S PERIPHERY IN THE 1870S

Sumner rocked the boat at Yale College in the 1870s and early 1880s. Meanwhile, political economy had a hearing at Yale—and sometimes an impressive one—outside its central establishment. The first permanent inroads for the discipline had been made at the Scientific School. In 1871 this entity, aided by additional endowment, gained greater autonomy with a charter amendment that removed the school from the direct control of the administration of Yale College. The affiliation with Yale remained, but an independent governing board was to guide the destiny of the institution, rechristened as the Sheffield Scientific School. Its enrollments continued to grow: Indeed, this unit was responsible for the bulk of the enlargement in Yale's undergraduate numbers in the 1870s.[40]

Within the framework of the Scientific School, the subject matter of political economy entered the required senior-year program of students in the Select Course, then officially described as "preparatory to other higher pursuits [i.e., not specialized scientific ones], to business, etc."[41] Walker expanded that base—which he had inherited from Gilman—not long after his arrival as professor of political economy. In the academic year 1874–75, instruction in political economy was pushed into the third term of the junior year (based on the Walkers' *Science of Wealth*), and lectures in the subject continued to be required for Select Course students throughout the senior year. This format remained until Walker's departure in 1881, though Rogers's *Manual* became a textbook for juniors in 1877–78.

Students in the Select Course at the Scientific School got more instruction in political economy than did their contemporaries in the Academical Department of Yale College, but their numbers were not large. Graduating classes at the Scientific School in the late 1870s and early 1880s were in the forties and fifties, and typically only about one-third of the new B.Phil.'s took the Select Course.[42] If Walker had aspired to win a wider undergraduate audience at Yale for the new social science, he must surely have been disappointed. Two primary factors excluded him from participation in the central power structure of Yale: his assignment to the Scientific School and his lack of a Yale pedigree. He allocated much of his time in New Haven to his own scholarly pursuits and to part-time consulting engagements on the statistical programs of the federal government. As his biographer has put it, the "chief value" of his Yale sojourn was that it afforded him an opportunity to systematize his thoughts in writing.[43]

Why did not Walker and Sumner collaborate in advancing the curricular status of political economy at Yale? As critics of the traditional curriculum, they were agreed. Each, in his own way, brought current data to his pedagogy. Moreover, their teaching activities intersected in one of Yale's peripheral enterprises, the fledgling graduate program. Beginning in 1873–74 and continuing for the duration of his time at Yale, Walker was regularly announced as offering instruction to graduates in public finance and the "statistics of industry." Meanwhile, Sumner's offerings were more varied, with such titles as "History of Politics and Finance in the United States," "Political Economy," "Constitutional Law," "History and Science of Self-Government," "Sociology." With each man afforded an opportunity to teach in areas of personal interest, the risk of jurisdictional disputes between them must have been minimal.

Even so, this was not an altogether promising site for fruitful partnership. Graduate instruction at that time was loosely structured and served only a very limited clientele. In 1874–75 a total of twenty-nine students was recorded, with twelve enrollments in "political science" courses. Though the total number of students taking graduate instruction rose to sixty in 1875–76, there were only fifteen enrollments in "political economy" courses.[44] In the later 1870s, the demand for Yale's graduate offerings contracted, largely in response to the entry of Johns Hopkins into this market as the first specialized graduate program in the United States.[45] Indeed, only five Ph.D.'s were granted by the "Economics, Sociology, and Government" component of Yale's graduate department between 1872 and 1890 and none at all during the decade of the 1880s.[46]

Even though Walker and Sumner might potentially have been allies as academic politicians, there was too much distance between their views on economic policy issues to convert that potential into reality. Friction between the two men was on public display in the later 1870s over the issue of bimetallism, on which Walker had expressed himself sympathetically. Sumner lost no time in denouncing such heresy in an essay published in 1878. Subsequently, personal relationships between the two, which had never been close, deteriorated and, though formally correct, were distinctly cool.[47]

Though Walker's years at Yale were productive for his scholarly development, they must also have been frustrating ones. He never felt completely at home there and was certainly receptive to alternative employments. When Gilman tried to recruit him to join newly founded Johns Hopkins, however, he felt obliged to decline on the grounds that he had recently returned from a period of leave and thought it would be ungentlemanly to depart so soon thereafter. (He did, however, accept a part-time appointment as a nonresident lecturer at Johns Hopkins in the newly formed Department of National Economics.)[48] Had another possible opportunity come to fruition, it is highly probable that he would have left not long after. The presidency of Amherst College, his alma mater, intrigued him. He was strongly endorsed for this post, though his most ardent supporters recognized that he lacked one of the qualifications still regarded there as indispensable: He did not have the title "Reverend." When the call came to head an institution in which this condition was not essential, he accepted with alacrity. In 1881 Walker departed to shape the destinies of the Masschusetts Institute of Technology as its president. Like Gilman before him, Walker set out to do elsewhere what he had not been allowed to do at Yale.

CHANGES IN THE LINEUP, 1881–1891

The mid-1880s brought changes in the institutional climate at Yale that were to have a significant bearing on its receptivity to political economy. The most striking was the partial victory of the reformers in opening space for optionals in the regular undergraduate program. But a new set of attitudes about the role of graduate studies was also taking shape at this time. This was evident in the charter amendment pushed through in 1887 by a new president, Timothy Dwight (grandson of the man who held this office in the early decades of the century), to change the name of the institution from Yale College to Yale University. Dwight was in the conservative mould of the Congregational clergy, but he nevertheless made it part of his agenda to strengthen graduate studies, which had fared badly in the preceding decade.

The way in which these larger institutional adjustments affected the teaching of political economy, however, was a matter primarily under Sumner's control. He remained the dominating force in the social studies wing of the faculty and handled personally the bulk of the instruction in the enlarged undergraduate program and in the graduate department. Even though the effective demand for teaching in political economy had increased, the entry of faculty newcomers remained far from easy. Nevertheless, three new figures appeared on the scene—Henry W. Farnam, Arthur T. Hadley, and John C. Schwab—and each of them was to hold the title of "Professor of Political Economy" at some point in his Yale career. Though their talents and interests were diverse, they shared a number of attributes. From the local point of view, they were all "establishment figures"—that is, each held a B.A. degree from Yale. All of them were from the Sumner stable in the sense that the early training of each had been shaped by his teaching. In addition, all of them had undergone a period of postgraduate studies in political economy in Germany.

Special circumstances surrounded the terms on which each of them participated in the affairs of the Yale faculty. The first of the new arrivals, Henry W. Farnam, had taken his B.A. in 1874 and had stayed on to complete an M.A. in political economy in 1876.[49] He had then set off for Germany to pursue advanced studies in political economy and earned a doctorate at the University of Strasbourg (1878), presenting a dissertation on the doctrines of Colbert and Turgot.[50] By the standards of the day, Farnam returned from Germany with impressive paper credentials to instruct in political economy: Few Americans could rival his achievement of a doctorate in political economy. The academic appointment made available to him upon his return to New Haven, however, was a tutorship in Latin in the Academical Department, a post he took up in 1878. Such an appointment had been mooted in mid-1876, with an indication that a vacancy was not likely to be available until 1878. Farnam had then been reluctant to commit himself and had advised the secretary of the Corporation that he preferred to direct his career to political economy. Yale, however, was not then interested in exploring that possibility. Franklin B. Dexter, writing for the Corporation, observed that he "could appreciate your wish to make all your work bear on the topics which you expect to make your future study. But it is contrary to our system to commit any part of senior year to temporary officers [i.e., tutors], and there is no opportunity for these studies in the lower years."[51]

Farnam's status changed dramatically in mid-1880. He was then notified that the Corporation had elected him to a "professorship in political economy" in the Department of Philosophy and the Arts.[52] This was a title but little more. As the official letter of notification put it: "The appointment thus made not having any regular duties of instruction connected with it, the Corporation are not able to offer any salary, except such as may accrue from the fees paid by graduate students who may seek your instruction."[53] Farnam's circumstances were such that he could afford to be a "gentleman scholar." The new professor's father had accumulated a considerable fortune as a railway entrepreneur and subsequently had become one of the college's most generous donors. There was also some evidence already that the son was prepared to carry on the philanthropic spirit.[54]

Farnam's assignment was made more specific in mid-1881 when he was appointed a member of the governing board of the Sheffield Scientific School and Professor of Political Economy and History in that branch of the institution. This move nominally filled the space vacated by Walker and was a salaried position. (It appears that Farnam did not, in fact, draw the stipend to which he was entitled but left it to accumulate as a "credit," which he might subsequently direct the Corporation to allocate.) Though Farnam took over the political economy teaching for students in the Select Course, the scale of this activity was cut back. In the last four years of Walker's tenure, political economy was prescribed throughout the senior year and for one term of the junior year. For the first five years after Walker's departure, on the other hand, the political economy requirement was reduced to one term of study in the senior year.[55] Though Farnam was not a forceful presence as a teacher, he was still actively engaged in promoting political economy in other ways. In early 1881, for example, he made known his willingness to underwrite a "working library" for students of the political and social sciences designed to include "chiefly works on statistics, government reports, laws and in general the raw material for original investigation."[56]

The rise of a second newcomer to professorial rank was far less meteoric and marked by a number of frustrations along the way. Arthur T. Hadley aspired to an academic career from a young age, but upon his graduation from Yale in 1876 he was still unsure about a field of specialization. He set off for Europe to explore and, while in Berlin, developed a taste for political economy. Though he was far from sympathetic to some of the doctrines to which he was exposed there, the experience broadened his perspective. On his impressions of Wagner's seminar, he wrote: "Wagner, I am sorry to say, is a socialist. It is astonishing how nearly impossible it is for a German scholar to keep his head straight when he gets hold of such a subject as political economy. But there are more sides to some of these questions than Billy Sumner would have us believe."[57] He also reported that he had developed an interest in Marx and, "while very far from agreeing with him," had concluded that his work had a "higher scientific aim than almost any work on political economy in the last half century."[58]

Hadley returned to New Haven in late summer 1879 without an advanced degree but with uncertainties about his preferred career path resolved. Political economy was the field he was determined to cultivate. But the only academic employment offered to him was a tutorship in Greek at Yale. He stayed on as a tutor for four years, following the year of Greek with one in Latin and two in German. None of this teaching was to his taste, but he had accepted these assignments with the expectation that something might be found for him in political economy. When he was denied a position of the type he wanted—in spring 1883—he resigned from Yale to try his hand at free-lance writing on economic subjects. He described his situation as follows in a letter to a friend:

My plan is now to write all I can . . . until I can make such an impression on the public as to command some first-rate place as professor of pol. economy, pol. science or history. Of course I had much rather that such a place would be in New Haven than anywhere else; but if it were a choice between the right kind of work somewhere else and the wrong kind of work here, I should choose the former."[59]

This was a bold move for a young man without any significant private income. Yale responded to it by offering him a title as "instructor in political science" in the graduate department, but it was not prepared to provide a stipend. In short, Hadley had a courtesy title and was allocated space in which he could teach. But, as the income he might be able to earn from fees paid by those attending his lectures was unlikely to meet his needs, he was obliged to continue with his plans for free-lance writing This he did energetically, working particularly on problems of the railway industry. For a brief period (1885–87), he also served as the commissioner of labor statistics for the state of Connecticut.

Yale had only opened the door a crack to Hadley's interests, but it had still enabled him to keep a toe inside the halls of academe. Hadley enjoyed his teaching, and his lectures, if not notably remunerative, were well received. Though he might have preferred to have more time available for academic work than his circumstances then allowed, his outside involvements were productive in his development as a professional economist. His immersion in "real-world" problems was a learning experience different from the one college libraries could provide. Moreover, his work in applied economics inspired a novel contribution to economic theory—namely, the finding that firms with heavy fixed costs may find it advantageous to continue operations even though revenues fall short of costs. This type of analysis was quite different from what Sumner provided.

By 1886—after his pioneering study, *Railroad Transportation: Its History and Its Laws,* had been published—Hadley had something distinctive to offer to academic audiences. At this point, Henry W. Farnam intervened: He requested the Corporation to use "the $8000.00 standing in my credit in the Treasury" to provide a salary for Hadley over the next five years.[60] The Corporation complied and awarded Hadley the title of "Professor of Political Science." This partial salary enabled Hadley to spend more time on academic pursuits. Beginning in the academic year 1886–87, he joined with Sumner in some of the undergraduate teaching while continuing his work in the graduate program.

A third newcomer, John C. Schwab, joined the faculty in 1890. He entered through the familiar pipeline: B.A., Yale, 1886; M.A., Yale, 1888; and a doctorate from the University of Göttingen, 1889. He too was a protégé of Sumner. But Schwab was the first of the younger generation to begin teaching in the field of his choice, rather than as a tutor in one of the subjects hallowed in the traditional curriculum. On his arrival, he was accorded the title of "lecturer in political economy," though without salary. In the following year, however, he was appointed to regular faculty status as an "instructor in political economy."

The restructuring of the undergraduate curriculum and of the graduate program set in motion in the mid-1880s obviously widened the market for teaching in political economy. Expansion in the size of the market, in turn, provided greater scope for specialization. By the academic year 1890–91, a division of labor had been worked out. In the undergraduate B.A. program, an introductory course was offered for juniors, meeting for two hours per week in both terms. This course was a prerequisite for "advanced political economy" in the senior year (two hours per week in both terms). Sumner was in charge of this instruction. In addition, qualified seniors could elect a course in finance (one hour per week for two terms) under Sumner. Two advanced elective courses were offered by Hadley: "Industrial History of the United States since 1850" (described as calling for "original work in collecting and arranging statistics"); and "Modern Economic Theories" (described as "an account of some of the attacks upon the current doctrines of Political Economy, especially on the part of the Socialists"). These met for two hours per week for one term only. For the first time, in the academic year 1890–91, seniors—with the permission of Sumner, the instructor—could enroll in a research seminar labeled the "School of Political Economy." This was designed for students who wished to make this subject their "chief study during the year," and they were "expected to investigate an assigned topic thoroughly and prepare a series of papers upon it."[61]

In the graduate school, Sumner typically offered a selection from a standard menu, which included "Finance and the Science and Art of Politics in the History of the United States"; "Industrial Organization of Modern Society"; "Sociology"; and "Anthropology." For 1890–91, it was announced that, in collaboration with Schwab, a version of the School of Political Economy research seminar would be available to graduate students. Hadley's graduate courses typically concentrated on such topics as "Railway Administration," "Corporations," and "Industrial Legislation," with "Methods of Studying Political Events" added in 1890–91. The standard topics listed for Farnam (who was first announced as offering graduate instruction in 1886–87) were "Principles of Public Finance" and "History of Labor Organizations." Meanwhile, Farnam continued to be charged with organizing the instruction in the Sheffield Scientific School.

The response of undergraduates in the B.A. program to these innovations was impressive. Enrollments boomed, and political economy was well on the way to becoming one of the most popular studies in the college. There was no similar trend, however, in the graduate program. Farnam particularly found this disturbing. As he lamented to Sumner in the autumn of 1888: "The outlook in general is discouraging. . . . We must make the graduate courses a success in some way."[62] Strengthening the graduate program was to become one of his major preoccupations, and he began to do something about it in the later 1880s by circularizing major undergraduate colleges in search of strong candidates.

Even though the faculty roster in political economy had been enlarged by 1890, there could still be no confusion about who was in command. Sumner was the only spokesman for political economy at Yale with first-class permanent status in the university. His personal stamp was evident in the description of the rationale underlying the structure of undergraduate offerings:

The instruction in the elements of Political Economy is intended to give familiarity with the method and doctrines of the so-called "orthodox" economists, as the proper introduction to what the student should have to the science, and used as the basis for whatever may be offered later. Textbooks are used with set lessons, constant examinations, both written and oral, discussions, and illustrations.[63]

His control over the graduate program was even more explicit. The catalogue description of the graduate program, beginning in 1887–88, read: "Candidates for a degree are required to pursue, and to be examined on, a course of reading in the leading textbooks of Political Economy which will be prescribed by Professor Sumner for each student upon consultation."[64]

REALIGNMENTS IN THE 1890S

In 1891 Sumner's grip on the direction of political economy at Yale weakened. His health had broken, and he went to Zurich to recover. Even if he had remained on the spot, it is likely that some structural realignments would still have occurred. His own intellectual interests had shifted increasingly toward sociology, and it was with that field that he later made his primary professional identification. For Sumner, this was a natural transition. He had long held that political economy was really a subbranch of the science of sociology. His absenteeism, which extended over the better part of two years, meant that some restructuring was unavoidable.

Hadley took over most of the political economy teaching vacated by Sumner and at the same time was rewarded with promotion to regular faculty status as Professor of Political Economy. The goal he had set for himself eight years earlier had finally been reached. Schwab's duties were enlarged to take over courses in "Finance" (described as covering "money, banking, taxation, and public debts"). Farnam's, on the other hand, were not. He advised Sumner in September 1892 that he was willing to help in any way possible but feared that he was "hardly prepared to take up any of your graduate classes."[65]

Another name entered the table of organization in the academic year 1891—92 when Irving Fisher offered an undergraduate course entitled "Mathematical Theory of Prices," open to students "who besides studying political economy have taken or are pursuing a course in calculus." Fisher had the standard qualification for a faculty appointment: He was a Yale graduate in the class of 1888 and had stayed on to complete a Ph.D. in 1891. This was the first instance in which a product of Yale's own doctoral program was to teach political economy. Strictly speaking, his doctorate was awarded by the faculty of mathematics, and his appointment in 1891 was as a "tutor in mathematics." But, as indicated by the title of his dissertation, "Mathematical Investigations in the Theory of Value and Prices," he was well equipped to bring a new approach to the teaching of political economy. Nor was it simply the formal mathematical treatment that made his pedagogy different. For purposes of classroom demonstration of the properties of general equilibrium, he constructed a "hydro-static mechanism" to illustrate market interdependencies by means of water flows. The costs of constructing this device were paid by Henry W. Farnam.[66] In 1895, Fisher's title was changed from "Instructor in Mathematics" to "Assistant Professor of Political and Social Science."

Hadley had now become the dominant presence in Yale economics. In his view, a new science of economics was in the process of taking shape, and it was quite different "in its methods of analysis and powers of explanation" from the tradition inherited from John Stuart Mill. Two separate strands of argument had coalesced to contribute to this change: 1. "the principle of natural selection," which could be invoked "to explain the development and present shape of industrial ideas and institutions"; and 2. the marginal utility doctrine, "to account for the actions of individual men in pursuing their own interests under the ideas and institutions thus developed."[67] Hadley appropriated the latter approach in his teaching and writing when developing the concept of demand diagrammatically.[68] This technique, he maintained, made a positive contribution to expositional clarity, though he rejected the claims made for this procedure by some of the more enthusiastic among the new generation of "marginalists." With reference to Jevons and the Austrians, he observed that "much of the work of this school . . . seems to belong rather to the domain of psychology than of economics, and to have a very remote application to the practical problems of business and legislation."[69] It was precisely to those problems that the reconstituted "science" needed to speak.

As Hadley saw matters, a host of new practical problems had arisen on which insight was needed. Most of them were rooted in the emergence of large concentrations of capital, particularly in the industrial and transportation sectors of the modern economy. This phenomenon had important implications for economic theory. As he put it, "the size of units of capital is so large that free competition often becomes an impossibility, and theories of economics which are based upon the existence of such competition prove blind guides in dealing with modern price movements." There was no mystery about what had brought about this situation: The principle of natural selection was at work in weeding out inefficient smaller units.[70] This component of the argument had overtones of Sumner's influence. But Hadley was prepared to move well beyond Sumner in his view of the way the problem should be analyzed.[71]

With respect to the proper approach to the matter, Hadley insisted that the facts of modern life should be investigated quantitatively, with particular attention to the properties of costs. This built on his earlier investigations of the railway industry, from which he had concluded that the conception of a "normal price" that matched the cost of production was erroneous in industries with heavy commitments of capital. Unit costs would vary considerably with the volume of output and, when there was unused capacity, they were likely to fall as outputs increased. At any particular moment, it would be impossible to determine what unit costs would be in future time periods. But uncertainty about the true cost of production was compounded by the likelihood that industries of this type would generate a high degree of price volatility. In periods of slack demand, producers might well sell below costs rather than shut down. This loss-minimizing strategy—though rational in the short term for enterprises in which fixed costs were sizable—could not long be sustained. It was inevitable that the industry would evolve in the direction of monopoly.

The inherent tendency toward combination and concentration thus implied that some qualifications to old-fashioned doctrines of laissez-faire were in order. In Hadley's opinion, that phrase had taken an "exaggerated hold on the public imagination, and has been regarded as a fundamental axiom of economic science, when it is in fact only a practical maxim of political wisdom, subject to all the limitations which experience may afford."[72] Increased concentration obviously posed a threat to the public interest by exposing consumers to price gouging and by blunting the stimuli to efficiency and innovation that a genuinely competitive market should provide. How then should the public welfare be defended? Legislation to mandate competition, he maintained, was likely to be futile when economies went with bigness.[73] Governmental regulation was likely to be practicable in only a very limited number of cases: The types of information on costs necessary to form judgments on "fair prices" were rarely available, and misjudgments would generate unfortunate allocative distortions. Nor was governmental ownership of large enterprises a satisfactory option; this would simply breed the inefficiencies that necessarily flowed from politicization. Hadley placed his best hope on the development of "far-sighted management in the affairs of monopolies." If natural selection worked as it should, the most talented of men would rise to the leadership of these enterprises.[74] They, in turn, would need to realize that they occupied a position of public "trust" and that it was in their self-interest to order the affairs of business in a way that served the welfare of the public. Should they fail in the exercise of that trust, there would be penalties. On this point, Hadley observed: "If they will not accept the full measure of responsibility which goes with their industrial power, they must expect to be deprived of responsibility and power together, by a popular movement in the direction of socialism."[75] Hadley had no taste for that prospect. At the same time, he had moved well beyond the position of those who held that the natural interplay of market forces automatically generated the outcomes that were socially optimal.

Hadley's teaching to undergraduates attracted large audiences, and his introductory course in political economy became the most popular course in the college. In 1899 some 253 students elected it.[76] Altogether, the offerings listed under "political science"—the departmental category under which economics teaching was still grouped—accounted for 13.1 percent of the education of students graduating in the class of 1899 by contrast with 3.5 percent of the educational experience of the class of 1886. This was by far the highest rate of growth of any of the departmental categories.[77] Meanwhile, the absolute size of both the student body and numbers of faculty teaching undergraduates approximately doubled in the 1890s. By 1899–1900, 1,224 undergraduates were enrolled in Yale College, and they were taught by a teaching staff of 106.[78]

No less striking was the revitalization of the graduate program. By contrast with the decades of the 1880s (when no Ph.D.'s were produced in the Political Economy, Sociology, and Government branch of the graduate program), the decade of the 1890s witnessed the award of fourteen.[79] By the end of the century, the total number of graduate students approached 300. Growth in graduate enrollments in the 1890s was aided by the development of a limited program of fellowships and scholarship awards, as well as by the decision—taken in 1892—to open graduate instruction to women. In tandem with these developments came a mushrooming in the number of "professorships in political economy": Hadley (1891), Fisher (1898), and Schwab (1898).

By the mid-1890s, curricular offerings had also become more variegated. Hadley handled most of the lecturing in the large introductory courses, frequently assisted by Fisher, who ran recitation sections; and Hadley's text was assigned as the standard source. Fisher also taught statistics and a course in advanced economic theory (using Marshall's *Principles of Economics*). In 1897–98 he added a course on "Vital Statistics and Life Insurance" for graduates. Hadley and Schwab often collaborated in courses on topics in economic policy, with Hadley treating issues in industrial organization and Schwab focusing on money and banking, public finance, and international trade. In addition, Schwab's offerings included courses in American economic history, and Hadley, on occasion, offered the "History of Political and Economic Theories." Farnam's listings for graduates treated public finance, labor organization, and the "economics of poor relief." Meanwhile, Sumner's work— listed as "Social Science"—was primarily sociological and anthropological in its content.

REDEFINITIONS IN THE EXTERNAL RELATIONS
OF YALE ECONOMISTS

While realignments were taking place on the inside in the 1890s, some changes in the external relations of Yale's cadre of political economists were also occurring. The latter might not have happened so easily if Sumner had been on the campus without interruption. In the preceding decade, Yale had largely isolated itself from the movement to organize the community of professional economists on a national basis. This posture was linked with the friction between Sumner and Ely, the leading exponent of committing the American Economic Association to the position that the state had a positive role to play in economic life. The resulting situation was one with which neither the younger members of the Yale faculty nor some of the more moderate charter members of the American Economic Association felt comfortable. Edwin R. A. Seligman of Columbia (one of the organizers of the AEA), for example, argued as early as 1887 that the language of its draft charter should be amended in order to bring men like Hadley and Farnam into the membership.[80] In 1892—when Sumner was out of the country—Farnam expressed his willingness to cooperate. As he wrote to Seligman: "In the beginning I kept out, partly on account of some phrases in the platform, and partly because I felt (perhaps erroneously) that Sumner had been slighted in the matter. These reasons have long since disappeared."[81] Both Farnam and Schwab attended the 1892 AEA meetings in Chautauqua, New York, and informed Sumner after the fact. Farnam wrote as follows in September 1892: "This is the first time that Yale has been represented at one of these meetings by one of its professors and I think that it created a good impression to have one of them there." Farnam added that he had been made a vice-president of the organization. "In view of these changes," he inquired, "do you not think that you would like to join? I know that there is a strong desire to have you and that you would find yourself quite in sympathy with the present spirit of the society."[82] Sumner declined this invitation—and all subsequent ones—to become a member of the American Economic Association. Three of his colleagues, however, were later to become presidents of the AEA: Hadley (1898), Farnam (1911), and Fisher (1918).

The visibility of Yale political economy on the national scene was further enhanced in the 1890s by the acquisition of a journal to be edited by members of its faculty. Farnam was the moving spirit behind this enterprise. Not only did he inspire the creation of the *Yale*

Review as a "quarterly journal of history and political science," he acted as its financial backstop and covered its persisting deficits. Farnam's central objective was to promote the image of Yale political economy, though in the original design of the enterprise prominence was also given to general historical scholarship. This decision on coverage was prompted in part by Farnam's desire that Yale should compete in the learned journal market with rival institutions, particularly Harvard (which had launched the *Quarterly Journal of Economics* in 1886), Columbia (the sponsor of the *Political Science Quarterly,* which had begun publication in 1886), and the University of Chicago (which was about to found the *Journal of Political Economy*). At the same time, some product differentiation was thought to be desirable. Thus, the *Yale Review*'s receptivity to historical materials would set it apart from the Harvard and Columbia products. This was an important consideration in light of the fact that all three of these journals were to have the same publisher in New York. For market reasons, complementarity should be emphasized rather than competition.

This venture into the learned journal market began with the publication of the first number in May 1892. When recruiting Yale colleagues to contribute their energies to this undertaking, Farnam argued that a successful journal would put Yale's social sciences on the map and should also make a positive contribution to the promotion of the graduate programs. Apparently, Hadley and Schwab found these arguments persuasive and agreed to join the original Board of Editors along with two professors of history. Sumner—in Europe when the preparatory planning was moving forward—was not invited to become one of the editors and was first informed about the whole enterprise after most of the commitments had already been made.[83]

In 1896 the character of the enterprise changed. When the American Historical Association then founded its own journal, the senior historians on the editorial board of the *Yale Review* withdrew. Irving Fisher joined the ranks, and the journal's purpose was restyled as "a quarterly journal for the scientific discussion of economic, political and social questions." Fisher, however, was less active in this capacity than the other political economists involved in this undertaking.[84] His specialized interests did not mesh with the substantive content of the journal. The *Yale Review* offered no space for articles in mathematical economics, though it covered a wide variety of topics in applied economics—money and banking, taxation, transportation, public utilities, labor economics—and contained a liberal sprinkling of surveys of economic institutions and policies in other countries.

The *Yale Review* in these years provided a ready outlet for the scholarly production of both members of the faculty and their graduate students. It also involved them as reviewers of the new literature from around the world. But Farnam was determined to make it more than an institutional house organ. Largely through his efforts, articles were commissioned from leading economists at other institutions: among them, John Bates Clark (Columbia), E. Benjamin Andrews (Brown), Francis Amasa Walker (Massachusetts Institute of Technology), Edwin R. A. Seligman (Columbia), Frank Fetter (Indiana), Jacob Hollander (Johns Hopkins). Not all of their contributions meshed with the local line on controversial points of doctrine and policy. But this very hospitality to diversity helped to break down some of the insularity that had formerly characterized Yale's approach to political economy.[85]

THE FIN-DE-SIÈCLE SITUATION

By 1899 a permanent position for political economy at Yale had been solidly established. The agenda of the curricular reformers, however, had not been completed. The amount of time an undergraduate could allocate to this line of study was still constrained by mandatory commitments to the traditional subjects. Timothy Dwight's decision to step down from the presidency suggested that the moment might have arrived for another wave of reforms.

The background of Dwight's successor, Arthur T. Hadley, might have been read as auguring well for this prospect. Certainly his credentials as an enthusiast for political economy were abundantly visible, not just as one who professed the subject from the lecture platform but also as one who had served as president of the American Economic Association and had authored a widely read textbook. In addition, he had championed the cause of the discipline as the first dean of the graduate school (1892–95). But there was something even more promising about Hadley's election to the presidency of Yale: He was the first to hold this position who was not ordained as a Congregational clergyman. Ironically, some of Hadley's colleagues who were close to him in professional interests were less than enthusiastic or ambivalent about his elevation to this office. Sumner was openly opposed. Fisher thought well of Hadley personally but also maintained that "If an equally good man of equally favorable age can be found who has been connected with some other university than Yale, I should think it better. Yale is too self centered. It needs fresh blood."[86] When writing to Hadley, Fisher assured him that he was his choice among Yale faculty members mentioned for this post but added:

If no one from the faculty is to be chosen I wish the choice could be someone connected with another university. Our ruts of Yale tradition are very deep and hard. Yale begets Yale and we suffer from "in and in breeding." . . . If the Corporation is so mediaeval that it cannot break away from ecclesiasticism, or give us a young man, or a man who will study questions of curriculum, who will know the professors and their work, who will build up departments rather than dormitories, who will accommodate salaries to the men we want and not men to the salary we fix, who will go in for quality rather than quantity, who will coordinate the scientific and academical departments and economize instead of duplicating their courses, then I say Yale is doomed. We cannot wait another quarter of a century when we are that much behind Harvard already.[87]

In fact, Hadley was disposed to approach the issue of further curricular reform as a matter to be sorted out by evolution, not through revolution. As far as the status of economics was concerned, there were changes at the margin, including a number of shifts in personnel. Hadley's presidential duties afforded him little time for teaching (though he continued his lecturing in the introductory course during his first year as president). Replacement for Fisher—who began a three-year medical leave of absence to recover from tuberculosis—was also called for. John Bates Clark of Columbia took over much of Fisher's repertoire in 1898–99, and in the two subsequent years some of Fisher's graduate students filled in. In 1899 Henry Crosby Emery, whose specialty was international trade and commercial policy, was appointed as a professor of political economy. This marked a "first" for Yale. As a graduate of Bowdoin College, with an M.A. from Harvard and a Ph.D. from Columbia, Emery was the first "nonnative" to achieve this rank.

Under Hadley, the framework of the late nineteenth-century organizational pattern altered little. No separate Department of Economics was formed—indeed, that did not happen until 1937. Economics was classified under Social and Political Science (a category that included sociology). From the longer-term perspective, the inroads that political economy had made into the traditional curriculum were nevertheless impressive. It had taken a long time to secure them. More so than most other major American universities, Yale had resisted significant "modernization" in its core curriculum for undergraduates. There was no welcome mat for political economy at the front door. This kind of subject matter could be tolerated at the side doors—in the Scientific School and in the graduate program—so long as there was no claim on the financial resources of Yale College. It was only through the efforts of Sumner—who was appointed with the expectation that he would instruct in the clerical pattern of moral philosophy but who turned out to do something else—that greater curricular space for political economy was initially created within Yale College. Even so, there was only a grudging hospitality to the discipline for a considerable period. The central administration was disinterested in finding money to support others in this type of activity. Only in the 1890s did this attitude undergo significant change.

Yale's posture of academic conservatism, combined with the preference it accorded to its own sons, had two larger consequences. Indirectly and unintentionally, it contributed to significant innovation elsewhere in American higher education in the nineteenth century. Yale's failure to appreciate and to assimilate the talents of Gilman and Walker was its loss, though Johns Hopkins and the Masachussetts Institute of Technology were assuredly the gainers. But the quality of institutional hubris that frustrated the energies of these potential innovators had another side: It bred an intense loyalty among many of the college's alumni. They wanted to be part of the place but also to have an opportunity to pursue and promote intellectual interests that had not been well represented in the traditional curriculum. Sumner drove an opening wedge. Farnam, a man whose pen made no memorable contributions to the literature of political economy, proved to be an effective catalyst in advancing the cause of the discipline on the local scene. His role as an "in-house angel" certainly made it easier for his younger colleagues (and most particularly Hadley) to get on with their work, and it enhanced the attractiveness of Yale to graduate students as well. The agents of change were these loyalists who had standing to work within the system and who did so with a dedication that sometimes overrode their private financial self-interest.

7

From Recitation Room to Research Seminar: Political Economy at Columbia University

FRANEK ROZWADOWSKI

IN 1870 COLUMBIA was a small, stagnant, clerical college. Years before, in 1830 and especially 1857, there had been attempts to introduce new subjects and graduate courses, but these had failed, allowing the disapproving trustees and faculty to slump back into self-satisfied apathy. A tradition of superior instruction in political economy, established by John McVickar and bequeathed to Francis Lieber, had proven fragile: Lieber's successor was painfully inadequate. But ten years later, in 1880, the School of Political Science was founded and began to flourish. The School led the transformation of Columbia into a largely graduate institution. Its resounding success was the best answer (though also a threat) to the opponents of advanced education, and it became the model for Columbia's other graduate schools. Finally, it brought together the ingredients—graduate students, seminars, library—that made it possible to create a modern Economics Department where research and advanced teaching could nourish each other.

The history that follows falls into two parts, reflecting the two phases in Columbia's history. In the first, collegiate phase, the "Department" of Political Economy is one of the several departments (others were Moral Philosophy, History, Belles Lettres) carried by a single member of the faculty. In the second, university phase, the department takes on an institutional and administrative structure and grows in size so that there are several men in the department rather than several departments to a man.

I am grateful to B. Cisco for comments on an earlier draft.

COLUMBIA COLLEGE: THE YEARS OF DISCOURAGEMENT

Governance, Finances, Curriculum

King's College was founded in 1754 by royal charter, but neither the name nor the source of its authority was destined to last. In 1784 the school of Alexander Hamilton and John Jay was given the more suitable name Columbia, and its government fell to the Regents of the University of the State of New York, created by an act of the state legislature. Three years later another act transmitted control to a self-perpetuating corporation, the Trustees of Columbia College.

From the beginning, talk of the new college raised a storm of controversy over its prospective ties with the Church of England. An early illustration shows the spire of Trinity Church rising behind the college while a cluster of other spires stands nearby.[1] The "low" churches, Dutch Reformed, Presbyterian, Lutheran, Huguenot, were strongly represented in New York and regarded the foundation of the college as a power play by their "high" church brethren. One resentful publicist dubbed it "Trinity Church College." On the defensive, Trinity Church, which planned to cede land to the college, added two conditions: The president must be in communion with the Church of England, and college prayer must use the liturgy of that church. These stipulations were written into the charter of the college, bringing to a close the first of a series of skirmishes that was to divide the college against itself and sour relations with the state and the city of New York. After the Revolution, Trinity's stipulations were struck from the charter, and religious tests were forbidden. This put Columbia in an odd position because the test was still a condition for the gift of land. Matters came to a head in 1811 when the Reverend John M. Mason, not an Episcopalian, was the strongest candidate for the presidency. The trustees avoided the issue by creating a new position, provost, with more power than the president. Mason was made provost, and the presidency went to the Episcopalian Dr. W. Harriss. So a generous bending of the rules prevailed over narrow sectarianism, leaving an unsatisfied minority who complained that the charter had been violated.[2]

These incidents show the trustees using tact to appease two opposing constituencies. The college remained nominally Episcopalian, but enforcement could be lax. For example, the liturgy of the Episcopal church, which was used until the presidency of Harriss (1811–29), subsequently fell into disuse so, at the inauguration of

President Charles King, the Reverend John McVickar felt the need to urge: "Let not the dust again gather upon it."[3] Yet the trustees continued to be overwhelmingly Episcopalian, and they were quite capable of fueling New Yorkers' fear that Columbia was an exclusively Episcopalian enclave; this was unfortunate because the college charter came from the suspicious state Senate, which was petitioned repeatedly, unsuccessfully, for funds.

The nature of the Board of Trustees emerges clearly in light of the Gibbs affair of 1854. At issue was who should succeed James Renwick in the chair of chemistry. Wolcott Gibbs, the obvious choice, was a Unitarian, so the powerful and obstructive trustee Gouverneur Ogden led the six clergymen on the board in a bitter fight to give the post to Richard McCulloh instead. Gibbs was supported from within the board by his friend Samuel Ruggles and by Ruggles's son-in-law, the diarist George Strong, but Hamilton Fish, whose assistance was sought, would not take a stand, and Ogden's faction was successful. Their religious prejudice and plain obstructiveness provoked an angry response in the New York press and led to an investigation by a committee of the New York State Senate. Though the committee found Gibbs had been discriminated against, it declined to censure the Board of Trustees, drawing a distinction between the motives of individual trustees and the "corporate act of the body."[4] This was a wise evasion: The trustees were chastened by the anger they had provoked (feelings ran so high that celebrations of Columbia's centennial were canceled), so there was no need for the legislature to be drawn into the mire.

George Strong was exceedingly annoyed by his fellow trustees, and not only on this occasion. In 1855 he complained that the board was "the corporate embodiment of respectability & inertia." And here is how he described a meeting in 1860: "Barely a quorum. Some work done and some small monies appropriated for sundry expenses, mostly on Mr. S. B. R.'s [Ruggles's] motion, and with a few feeble reluctant gruntings by the treasurer and others, but on the whole with lazy indifferent good nature. What an inert, blase, non-feasant set they are!"[5] The shining exception, if Strong is to be belived, was Ruggles. Born with the century and graduated from Yale in 1814, Ruggles was a Columbia trustee from 1836 until he died in 1881. A lawyer by trade, his interests ranged across the practical issues of his time. He argued effectively for enlarging the Erie Canal and expanding the railroads; he represented the United States at the Fifth International Statistical Conference in

1863 and at the International Monetary Conference of 1867; his work on the coinage shows some ability as an empirical economist. At Columbia, Ruggles was the trustee with clearest vision. In 1854, in a pamphlet published in defense of Gibbs, he issued a prophetic and influential call for a "great national University."[6] Through the years Ruggles lent his support to plans for advanced education, notably in the Law School, of which he was a trustee, but it was not until 1880 that the seed that he planted in the Gibbs Manifesto sent forth a shoot.

In every aspect of campus life there was painfully slow growth during the first six decades of the nineteenth century and a dramatic flowering during the last two. At first there was only the college and a loosely affiliated Medical School. In 1857 the Law School was founded, followed by the School of Mines (later Applied Science) in 1864, the School of Political Science in 1880, and Barnard College in 1889. Until 1850 the number of bachelors' degrees awarded fluctuated erratically around an average of twenty-two but showed no trend; sixty-nine bachelors' degrees were awarded in 1860, and 274 in 1900. In 1881 the college had its first resident graduate students; in 1900 the university awarded 104 A.M. degrees and twenty-one Ph.D.'s. The faculty grew steadily at first, from four in 1800 to eight in 1825. A spurt in 1830, when the faculty increased to twelve, was followed by a long period of no growth at all: in 1862 there were only thirteen professors. Thereafter, growth was more rapid. There were twenty professors in 1869, 100 in 1880, and 339 in 1898.[7]

Salaries followed a similar pattern. In 1818 John McVickar was hired at $2,500 per annum plus a residence worth $500 per year. From 1843 to 1857 professors were paid a base salary of $1,200 plus ten dollars for every fee-paying student (plus accommodation); with enrollment fluctuating around 100–120 students this represented a small cut in expected value with an increase in uncertainty. In 1857 fixed salaries were reinstated at the level of $3,000 per annum (plus $1,000 if lodging was not provided). This remained the base salary (though there were cuts during the Civil War and temporary increases after the mid-1860s) until 1875 when the level of professors' salaries was fixed at $7,500.[8]

Although the takeoff after 1870 was impressive, this was a late start, particularly in view of the rapid growth of New York City. The reason, President Barnard explained to a critical press in 1882, was financial; since its foundation the college had never commanded adequate resources. At first revenues grew slowly, and there were persistent and growing deficits. In 1805 the income of the college was a little more than $14,000; forty-five years later, in 1850, it was only $20,000, of which $4,000 was committed to servicing a debt of $68,000. The debt would reach $166,000 in 1857. Only then did Columbia's fortunes reverse themselves; revenues began to increase so that by 1872 the debt was extinguished (largely by the sale of greatly appreciated real estate). And to those who have, more will be given: Fund raising during the last decades of the century was spectacularly successful.[9]

The financial difficulties of the early years were in large part the result of religious differences between town and gown. The citizens of New York, out of sympathy with the Episcopalian bent of the college, drew their purse strings tight. Frequent pleas by the trustees to the state Senate were rewarded with grudging response, and private donors were not more liberal. The same cause may also be responsible for disappointing enrollment, both in the regular college course and in the experimental extension courses offered in 1830. In turn, this meant that tuition charges were not a constant or reliable source of revenue until the 1860s.[10] Columbia was caught in a vicious circle: Financial straits led to a bare-bones operation which was not attractive to students. For years the most visible sign of penury was the new wing to the original building, which lay unfinished, a half-built ruin. In addition, the library was inadequate; scientific equipment was incomplete through breakage and disrepair; the faculty was overburdened. These were, President Butler put it later, the "long years of discouragement."

During the first seventy years of the century, the rhythm of instruction at the college changed little. At nine each morning there was compulsory chapel; the rest of the morning was divided into three lessons, each an hour long. Teaching methods varied across subjects and changed gradually over time. In the classical subjects recitation was the norm: One by one, the students would read from prepared texts and be quizzed on them. This took time and made classes larger than twenty cumbersome, so, as enrollments increased in the 1850s, the college was compelled to split the underclass courses into sections. Some professors preferred to lecture, but the "lecture" was really dictation: Students would inscribe the professor's notes word for word. As the century wore on, there was some change. By 1855 (and probably much earlier) McVickar was teaching political economy in a format that mixed dictation of the main points with a freer exposition and elaboration. His successor, Francis Lieber, lectured in a fashion that was more responsive to the class; he claimed that he never delivered the same lecture twice, which is more revealing about the norm than about himself. Yet these changes were more a matter of personal taste than of institutional commitment; as late as 1876 Charles Nairne reverted to recitation in his version of the political economy course.

At the turn of the century Columbia statutes required professors to teach fifteen hours a week. The actual teaching load was close to this at first, but by 1855 the average was ten hours a week. In the 1860s Lieber taught for four hours, but this was unusual; more typical was the ten hours taught by Nairne. So, although the faculty had tripled in number since 1810, the teaching load had fallen by only a third; the difference is explained by the fact that the underclass courses had been divided into sections. These seem fairly heavy teaching loads by modern U.S. standards, but there was more repetition and less preparation than would be necessary today.

In 1810, after reviewing the state of education in the college, the trustees laid out a curriculum that was to have influence well into the century. They prescribed in detail what was to be covered in Classics (Greek and Roman literature and history), in English Rhetoric (grammar, declamation, composition) and in Mathematics (Euclid, trigonometry, algebra). Tellingly, the content of other courses is laid out in much less detail or not at all. These second-class citizens of the college were Geography, History, Science, Ethics, and, in the senior year, the Law of Nature and Nations, which course bore the germ of political economy.

The curriculum of 1810 brought nothing new; on the contrary, it was an attempt to reaffirm traditional standards and enforce them more vigorously. It was the embodiment of a theory of education that emphasized moral and intellectual discipline, and scorned what the Trustees' Committee on the College Course would later call the "mere acquisiton of learning." [11] That barb is pointed at the German universities, whose curriculum had greater scope and relevance, more room for modern, useful subjects. In 1830 the German challenge was brought home by discussions preparatory to the creation of New York University along "modern" lines. Columbia's powerful Professor John McVickar was unsupportive of the project. He was equally unenthusiastic about Columbia's defensive response in 1830, to create extension courses of its own, the so-called Scientific and Literary Course. In the event, New York University was placed on a conventional foundation, and Columbia stood firm. When the extension courses failed, McVickar felt vindicated, declaring with a note of triumph that "these loose schemes of education are more showy than sound, and can never become the substitute for the regular study and discipline of youth." [12]

As the years went by, cracks developed in this too smooth classical edifice. In 1855 the trustees set up a Committee on the College Course, which questioned the college president, Charles King, and each of the professors about every aspect of their teaching: how they ran their classes, whether textbooks were used, how students were examined, how class discipline was maintained. The professors indicated that they were under pressure. McVickar found that he was unable to fit all his material in the allotted time, yet he was unwilling to drop any topic, a hint that his newfangled subject was by now firmly wedged into the curriculum. And he felt stretched too thin by the large variety of courses he taught. In his report President King requested an increase in the size of the faculty in order to be able to split large classes into sections and divide the responsibilities of some professors. He also hinted that it might be desirable to provide an "option" to students. At the same time, enrollments were up, straining the physical facilities. In spite of these signs of strain, the committee celebrated the traditional style of education in its report, but it did admit that its conservatism "does not meet with universal sympathy or acquiescence." [13]

Meanwhile, Ruggles's call for a university, contained in his Gibbs Manifesto of the preceding year, had circulated widely in New York. He asserted

that a great national University is needed—not a college, in our narrow sense of the term,—a mere gymnasium, or grammar school, where some half dozen professors repeat year after year, the same rudiments,—but a broad, comprehensive seat of learning, science and art, where every student may pursue any path he may select, to its extremest attainable limit, and above all, where original research and discovery by the ablest men the world can furnish, shall add daily to the great sum of knowledge. [14]

In the same year a Trustees' Committee proposed a university course, but the proposal was noncommittal and there was no progress until after Columbia had moved to Madison Avenue from its original site behind Trinity Church.

At last, in July 1857, the trustees adopted a new set of statutes. These preserved the old, compulsory curriculum for the first three "collegiate" years but made the senior year an elective "university year." Seniors would select one of three options, each taught by a different department. The Department of Letters taught the traditional, classical, senior year; the Department of Science taught mechanics, physics, and astronomy; the Department of Jurisprudence taught political economy and modern history as well as law. On completing the senior year, students were awarded a bachelor's degree as before. But the departments were told to offer an A.M. degree as well, on the completion of two further years. Several chairs were divided, and new faculty was engaged to fill them. In particular, McVickar's crowded chair was split into three: The older man kept up his course in Evidences of Religion, Francis Lieber was brought in to teach History and Political Science, and Charles Nairne was hired as Professor of Moral and Intellectual Philosophy and (English) Literature. The additional teaching strength permitted most courses below the senior year to be taught in sections.

The plan of 1857 failed. It is not clear why. In his history of Columbia, Munroe Smith asserts, with the benefit of hindsight, that this was "not because of intrinsic defects, but because it was put into operation at least two decades before the American public was ready for it." The apathy of the trustees, the uneasy relationship between Columbia and the city, and recurring financial difficulties provide some gloss to that "explanation." Anyway, the graduate courses never materialized, and in 1861 the trustees ended the threefold division of the senior class. But the experiment had important side effects. The Law School survived; the faculty was stronger for the addition of distinguished men; professors' responsibilities became more focused. These improvements, added to an attractive new location and lower tuition, contributed to a steady increase in enrollments during the following decade. More important, the long deliberation that preceded the changes had left a mark on the trustees. Whereas in 1855 they had put down the idea of "progressive knowledge" with a haughty irony, by 1857 the chairman of the Committee on the College Course, William Betts, predicted enthusiastically that the new senior year would "emancipate the student gradually from the trammels of catechetical teaching." [15] The battle over curriculum was by no means over, and the conservative faction of the trustees remained powerful, but the idea of electives and the idea of the university would not be uprooted. In the 1870s election would be extended to much of the senior and junior years, and President Barnard would become a persuasive and insistent promoter of graduate education. Even the use of the senior year as a university year would reemerge after 1880, when, presumably, the American public was "ready for it."

The Department of Political Economy

John McVickar (1787–1868) was the first Professor of Political Economy at Columbia and the last Professor of Moral Philosophy.[16] It is tempting to interpret this twin distinction as the mark of a transitional figure with one foot planted in the past, the other directed at the future. This would be too simple. McVickar's every instinct was for tradition and orthodoxy. Whether the subject was politics, morals, education, or literature, his views were consistently respectable. But he had the interest, the wit, and the perseverance to ground himself thoroughly in the method and doctrines of classical political economy and to recast them in a mold that helped them spread in the United States. It is likely, indeed, that his impeccably conservative credentials were a necessary ingredient to his success.

In 1817 McVickar was made Professor of Moral Philosophy, Rhetoric, and Belles Lettres at Columbia, with a salary of $2,500 plus accommodation worth $500 a year.[17] Although the influence of his father-in-law, Samuel Bard, played a role in getting him the chair, this was not an appointment that would raise eyebrows. On the contrary, by the standards of the time, McVickar was admirably qualified for the position. He was well connected by marriage and by birth; he was a Columbia alumnus who had graduated, in 1804, at the top of a class of thirty-one; he had studied under Bowden, whose death left the chair vacant; he was, finally, an ordained minister of the Episcopal church.

Who could have known then what a long shadow this short, earnest young man would cast on the college? Within eight years, deaths and departures made him the faculty member of longest standing; for forty years he was to be a pillar of Columbia. During these years of stagnation he was one of the "strong men who fought the fight which saved the university for the 20th century."[18] The rhythm of academic life would be much the same at McVickar's retirement in 1864 as it had been at his arrival, but there is no reason to believe that this stability disturbed him. McVickar's fight, and his contribution, was to preserve, not to change. For him education was "our Anglo-Saxon inheritance—solid, classical religious training," and not mere learning as in the German universities.[19] If expansion meant more of this, he would support it, but newfangled "learning," as was proposed for New York University, was suspect.

His teaching load was large and diverse. In 1846 McVickar taught seniors immediately after chapel and devoted the second and third hours to juniors and sophomores, respectively. He taught religion and philosophy, rhetoric and English composition, history and political economy. His lectures were part dictation of maxims for the young, part discussion. Students' notebooks were devoted largely to fair copy from authorities, yet they wrote weekly essays too. They were encouraged to think for themselves, but within fairly narrow bounds. And so it was for forty years with only minor variations in course scheduling and course content.

It is possible to reconstruct the lectures in some detail. In his first years McVickar would read them; later he delivered them from notes, "guiding the analysis of the subjects but not controlling the words," as he put it. Toward the end of his career he explained that

long experience has satisfied me that the only efficient manner of instruction in aesthetic, moral and intellectual science is by free, conversational lectures, aided by a general textbook, but mainly dependent on wider reading—a manner of teaching which encourages a student to independent inquiry, awakening the talent and informing opinion, not by dogmatic teaching but by voluntary study.

Every day students would be examined on the material of the previous lecture; it is fair to assume that this was the first order of business. The lecture proper would begin with a list of main points, which the students took down verbatim; then McVickar would enlarge on each point in turn "with reference to authorities" but slowly enough for note taking. Students were given the opportunity to ask questions.[20]

After the class, students would write out their notes neatly, lecture notes on the right-hand page and quotations from authorities (Gibbon and Lauderdale as well as Smith and Ricardo) on the left. The latter were chosen by the students "by reference to general reading." The notebooks were handed in once a week for evaluation by the professor; they were also handed in at examination time. The notebook prepared in 1849 by E. Babcock, which survives, is meticulously written in a careful hand that must have won the praise of the professor. It is divided into twenty "subjects," each corresponding to a lecture, each containing two or three double pages of notes. They read like a catechism, to be memorized. Typically, a thesis is stated, then objections are raised and answered, then the next thesis is stated, and so on. A striking feature of this notebook is that it contains a diagram (illustrating the distinction between market price and natural price) and instructions for drawing others.[21]

An odd puzzle relates to the scorn McVickar heaped on text-books in his interview with the Trustees' Committee on the College Course in 1857. He wished, he said, "to study subjects rather than books." Textbooks tended to load the students' memories with opinions rather than train their minds. This was not an unusual statement to make at that time: Columbia's statutes enjoined the teaching of "*subjects* rather than whole books," and at Yale Sumner would stress the same distinction.[22] Yet we know that McVickar did not object to all textbooks. He consistently used Whatley for rhetoric, and his own *Outlines of Political Economy* had been pre-pared as a textbook after his search for a suitable one, in 1822, had failed. Perhaps he had changed his mind about textbooks since then. Or perhaps he had come to reject what he had written thirty years previously.[23] At any rate, by 1856 his practice was "to give the class a list of the best [textbooks], any one of which would be satisfactory."[24]

McVickar's schedule, with thirteen "contact hours" per week plus essays and notebooks to inspect, was a full one, especially in view of the number of subjects he taught. On the other hand, he taught much the same material from year to year, so perhaps the danger of boredom was greater for this vigorous man than the dan-ger of overload. Nevertheless, in 1856 he found the efficiency of his department "lessened by crowding too many subjects in one chair."[25] At seventy, he was having unaccustomed difficulty maintaining discipline. He did not wish to drop any subject from the curricu-lum; instead, he asked that his subject be divided and a tutor be engaged. Accordingly, his chair was split in three and for the next seven years, until his retirement, McVickar continued to teach, on a part-time basis, the Evidences of Religion.

In his writings and in the lecture rooms McVickar taught a ver-sion of classical political economy that was congenial to one of his class and station. His peers, those who shared his connections with commerce, insurance, and banking, praised his work and some-times commissioned it. The great landowner James Wadsworth had first interested him in publishing a textbook; the *Outlines of Politi-cal Economy* was accordingly dedicated to him. The financier and banking reformer Isaac Bronson induced him to write the *Hints on Banking*.

To sketch his teaching in broad strokes is to affirm his member-ship in the classical school: The production of wealth is facilitated, first, by a government that is strong (insuring security of property and person) and liberal (not interfering with commerce); second, by the division of labor, including internationally; and, third, by the accumulation of capital. Tariffs are anathema. Mercantilism is refuted. Wealth (income) is distributed among three classes who receive, respectively, rent, profits, and wages. Market prices, which depend on supply and demand, gravitate toward natural prices, which reflect costs of production. An increase in wages is at the expense of profit. There is a declining rate of profit. Government is to be circumscribed, especially insofar as it interferes with commerce.

For the most part this doctrine was satisfactory: McVickar's method was to start with the classical doctrine and modify it where necessary, by adding emphasis or corrections or commentary helpful to an American audience. The most striking example of this modus operandi is McVickar's *Outlines of Political Economy*, really an annotated American edition of McCulloch's article "Political Economy" in the 1824 Edinburgh Supplement to the *Encyclopaedia Britannica*. McVickar added dozens of footnotes, often several pages long, and a couple of short essays. But this is not an isolated example: *Interest Made Equity*, published in 1826, included an article by McCulloch from the *Britannica*, and McVickar's last extended statement, the *Essay upon the Principles of Political Economy*, published a dozen years later, is still recognizably derivative of McCulloch. This indicates a lack of originality, but McVickar was an intelligent and critical disciple, not a slavish one. He had read and admired Smith and Say as well as Ricardo and Mill and was quite capable of refuting McCulloch's positions; furthermore, he in fact prefers Smith over Ricardo so often that one comes to doubt Dorfman's judgment in calling him "Ricardian."[26]

McVickar was a vigorous promoter of political economy, and the terms of his advocacy are a key to his distinctive vision. First, simply, he believed that this new science was the road to truth, that theory would root out unreliable conclusions derived from the application of untrained common sense, that science takes no sides: "The language of political economy is the language of reason and enlarged experience, blinded by no prejudices, drawn aside by no private motives, coloured by no sectional feelings."[27] Such a science could and should be used to guide national economic policy, for example, on issues of monetary institutions, poor laws, and free trade.

But McVickar was not content to defend political economy as an impartial, useful science. It is also, he maintained, "the moral instructor of nations." "It is to states what religion is to individuals, the 'preacher of righteousness'—what religion reproves as wrong, Political Economy rejects as inexpedient."[28] These are ringing words, even if they do ring false in modern ears. Of course, the religion and the morality McVickar has in mind have little to do with the beatitudes or with the tongue-lashings of the Old Testament prophets; they have more to do with the Protestant work ethic and a sense that poverty, like wealth, is earned. In his *Introductory Lecture,* addressed to the upright citizens of New York, he enumerates the ways in which political economy is moral. First, "Though it be but the science of wealth yet does it shew *that* wealth to be the result of the moral and intellectual as well as the physical powers of man." The wealthy could rest easy: Their fortunes were the result of their own higher powers and not only the base physical labor of others. Second, political economy teaches the pursuit of wealth, an activity that is "decidedly favorable to the formation of moral character." This would remove the indigent from the streets of temptation and put them on the road to respectability. Finally, it teaches nations "the all important lessons of peace and mutual benefits." The reference here is to the gains from trade and the costs of waging war. In short, political economy was moral because it taught moral lessons.[29]

It taught the right political lessons too. McVickar feared democracy, feared the extension of the suffrage, feared that when the poor obtained political power they would redistribute property. Ignorant, they would split the foundation of prosperity and bring down the rich and civilization too. In the *Introductory Lecture* he proposed that the remedy was to teach the legislator and the electorate the lessons of political economy, "that science which demonstrates the comforts of the poor to be linked inseparably with the prosperity of the rich, which gives the best pledge of security to wealth, by making every man, however poor, feel himself interested in the laws for its preservation." The role of the university in this is spelled out explicitly: It serves the rich, "for [its] own safety, [it] well knows, is bound up in the ancient land marks—in building up a dike, against the rising flood, that is swelling up from beneath."[30] This is the contemptuous language of a dignified gentleman among his moneyed peers. Though it smacks of a fund-raising speech, it is vintage McVickar.

So the "liberal system" taught by political economists drew into a consistent whole not only matters relating to prosperity but also a political and a moral vision. McVickar was taken by this harmony; he saw it not as unlikely coincidence but as corroboration of the truth of the liberal system: "That science and religion eventually teach the same lesson, is a necessary consequence of the unity of truth, but it is seldom that this union is so early and satisfactorily displayed as in the researches of Political Economy." Modern science shows:

the beauteous and harmonious union of public virtue and public wealth, of peace and benevolence uniting nations by the bonds of mutual interest, and national prosperity the result of all those internal and external regulations, which a good man would desire for their own sake, and a religious man choose on the score of duty and conscience.

He was confident that the liberal doctrines, though unpopular, were "destined eventually to triumph, and to form the prosperity and pride of the nation that first models itself on them."[31]

These views color many of the threads that McVickar wove into his version of the classical doctrine. The *Outlines* is a good place to look for what is distinctive to its editor since the text of McCulloch stands as foil for McVickar's footnotes and commentary. It is instructive to look at some of these in some detail.

For one thing, McVickar rejected Smith's distinction between productive and unproductive labor. The point of refuting this "invidious distinction" was to establish that the labor of the financier or banker, not to mention the university professor or cleric, was productive; to quash the "vulgar prejudice against the rich, as if they were supported by the poor." This explains McVickar's passion. But he argues the case with insight as well, and this is also in character. He sees this as part of a broader question, whether political economy "relates to exchangeable value in general, or solely to that value which resides in material products." He rejects the materialist alternative by pointing out that it leads to anomalies and would have us call Watt, Whitney, and Fulton unproductive.[32] And he insists, consistently, that neither the capital stock nor national product ("wealth") is made up of material items alone. Again, it is characteristic that none of this was original: McCulloch had made a strong case against Smith's dichotomy; Say had written with clarity on human capital. McVickar restates and elaborates; he lays out the conceptual structure of theory and examines how its parts lock together; he has a sharp eye for sloppy definitions and inconsistency. These are not sufficient qualities for original thought, but they are marks of a fine teacher.

McVickar professed himself "attached to the liberal system, or that which identifies individual profits with national benefit." The

sharpness of this identification of private with social gain is striking, but the case made for it is weak, being simply that the national
wealth is the sum of individual wealths. On the other hand, he
points out exceptions, which Dorfman believes are the "first of
their kind in the Anglo-Saxon literature." These are, first, the provision for war; second, the extraction of profit from the miseries of
others (for example, slavery and gambling, which, though profitable to the individual, are harmful to society); and, third, speculation, in which wealth merely changes hands.[33]

On value and price, the footnotes to the *Outlines* present a
mélange of classical views. McVickar accepts the classical synthesis
in which natural price, regulated by the cost of production, is the
center around which market price fluctuates, moved by supply and
demand. But he departs from McCulloch with the assertion that
"as a practical principle" the concept of market price is more
useful, being entirely general and relating to the actual price; the
oscillations of price around the natural price may be large and en-
dure long, rendering the latter "inapplicable in many important
cases." In addition, McVickar occasionally twits McCulloch for
failing to use supply and demand where appropriate or for mis-
using the technique.[34]

He also rejects McCulloch on the labor theory of value. Insisting
that labor and capital are distinct and obey different laws, he balks
at reducing capital to dead labor; the idea that labor is the only
determinant of exchange value he regards as false, or, at best, a
misuse of language.[35] But he is inconsistent and confused on this
point: Notes taken from his lectures assert that "Capital is only
Reserved Labor."[36] And in the *Essay,* where only traces of the labor
theory of value remain, there appears the odd statement that "the
doctrine of many political economists, which refers the production
of exchangeable utility entirely to labor, if not an error, is yet an
unnecessary refinement." There is evidence he was groping for a
demand side, but his use of the compound term "exchangeable utility" is evidence of confusion and perhaps also its cause.[37]

With regard to the theory of distribution, McVickar betrays
some ambivalence. He celebrates the theory of rent as "the great
glory of the school of Ricardo" but warns against neglecting other
factors (unspecified) that could modify or change the result. The
problem is that Ricardo used the theory to show, contrary to
McVickar's doctrine of a harmony of interests, that profits and
wages stand in an inverse relation. McVickar praised the analysis
that lies behind the inverse relation but insisted that the wage in

question is not the same as the real wage that determines the well-being of the worker; the former is part of a firm's output; the latter is a bundle of consumer goods. "This consideration tends somewhat to diminish the value of the novel principle laid down by Ricardo, viz., that of the inverse ratio of wages and profits, and to explain further the anomalous fact of high wages and high profits existing together, as they unquestionably do in this country."[38] Since modern theorists uphold Ricardo on this score, it is no surprise that McVickar's assault was ineffectual; what is telling is that he made it.

In addition to theoretical elaborations, the thorough editor inserted discussions that referred to America. For the most part, these were merely familiar instances of general principles: canals as examples of investment, American examples of the behavior of wages, rents, and profits. But the Americanization of political economy was effected mainly by two essays, one on "Economical Science in America," the other on "Great Britain and Her American Colonies." The former, which may be the first history of American economic thought, contains praise for the mainly practical contributions of Benjamin Franklin (who argued for free trade and devised a successful scheme for paper currency in Pennsylvania) and the Columbia alumnus Alexander Hamilton. In the second essay America is presented as the cradle of liberalism, at least in practice:

The American colonies were established, generally, in the spirit of freedom,—it was the purchase which repaid the colonists for exile,—and so far as they were left free to pursue their own measures, they were in accordance with the liberal principles of the science of Political Economy,—arrived at, not indeed by speculation, but by the clear-sightedness of men who pursue their own interests, unshackled by the arbitrary restraints of government.

Britain attempted to check their liberty, and the result was the American War of Independence. After the war free trade returned and brought prosperity, thus settling, "we may consider conclusively, the greatest of all questions in the science of political economy."[39]

On the role of government, McVickar argued for minimal intervention, consistent with his belief that "peaceful labour and unrestricted interchange constitute the *only* source of the wealth of nations." Government should provide defense and enforce law. It may encourage commerce in a general way (by building canals or ports or insuring that the financial system works smoothly) but must not favor particular industries by tariff or subsidy since this would create monopolies. It is not obvious that the government must support the poor since this would encourage indolence. McVickar analyzed the financing of government spending with some care. He studied tax incidence and the effects on the economy of taxes and government borrowing. Taxes retard society and are at best a necessary evil. They should be low and cheap to collect; they should fall on luxuries and favor good morals. Government borrowing is a disguised tax; it may stimulate the economy in the short term but will cripple it in the long run.[40]

But his major contribution to public policy lay in the field of banking. The *Hints on Banking* was an eloquent and influential plea for an end to the system of chartered banking. Instead, he insisted, there should be free entry combined with regulations designed to insure the safety of banks. Eleven years later these provisions were reflected in the Free Banking Act of New York, which McVickar supported energetically, though with reservations. In 1841 he joined the controversy relating to a National Bank. The charter of the second National Bank had expired in 1836, four stormy years after President Jackson's veto had delivered the killing blow. Now, in the midst of financial disorders, McVickar published an article in the *New York Review* which argued that a National Bank is the only security against overexpansion of the money stock and fluctuations in credit. The National Bank he envisions is modern in several respects. It is the only issuer of currency; it maintains convertibility; it is, finally, independent of the executive and protected from the whims of the legislature.[41]

When McVickar's chair was divided into three, Francis Lieber was hired to teach History and Political Science. Lieber (1800–72) was a Prussian whose nationalism and liberalism had led him to exile in England in 1826 and to America a year later. A vain and energetic but often thwarted self-promoter, he made himself known in intellectual circles as the father and editor of the *Encyclopaedia Americana,* which appeared in 1833. In 1835, when it was clear he would not obtain the chair he coveted at a major urban college, he went to South Carolina College where he inherited Thomas Cooper's chair in History and Political Economy.[42] During the twenty years he was to spend there he wrote his major treatises, in political theory. In 1855, when he was passed over for the presidency of the college, he resigned in a huff. The appointment to Columbia came two years later with the backing of Samuel

Ruggles, whom Lieber had cultivated assiduously and who was later to support him in adversity.

Unlike McVickar, Lieber was enthusiastic about modern learning. In his inaugural address he held up the German university as a model to be imitated and, commenting on the functions of a college, gave the transmission of information pride of place over character building. Of course, this was the direction in which Columbia had just pointed itself: It was typical of Lieber to sing in harmony. But, unfortunately for him, the movement in this direction was halting (no graduate courses materialized) and subject to reversal (the elective senior year was abolished in 1861), so by 1862 Columbia looked much as it had before McVickar's chair had been divided. In this context Lieber's large salary (he was paid the going Columbia rate for a full professor: $4,000, including $1,000 for housing) and small teaching load (four hours a week) appeared extravagant to the traditionalists among the trustees, especially since his teaching had mixed reviews. His annoying stream of petitions for special treatment (a change in his academic title, exemption from freshman teaching, a reduced teaching load, salary gripes) won him no friends, whereas the disorder of his classroom and his laziness made him vulnerable to his enemies. Among the latter was the newly installed President Barnard who, in 1865, abolished Lieber's chair and transferred his subjects to Charles Nairne, the Professor of Moral and Intellectual Philosophy and Literature. Lieber's influential friends, the trustees Samuel Ruggles and Hamilton Fish and ex-president Charles King, were unable to stay the ax but did manage to get him a position in the Law School.[43]

Although his own contribution was to political theory, Lieber was a keen promoter of political economy. He expanded the course from McVickar's twenty lectures in the spring of the senior year to one hour a week throughout the year and pressed for two hours a week.[44] His case for political economy, made at his inaugural lecture, has political overtones that resonate with McVickar's but lack the older man's moralizing. Political economy, he declares, has taught nations that exchange benefits all; the refutation of mercantilist doctrine has had a salutary effect on diplomacy. Then again, political economy checks industrial violence by teaching workers "that a factory cannot be kept working unless the master can work to a profit." Like McVickar, he defends political economy against the charge that it is materialistic; again like his predecessor, he disputes the claim that only "practical" men can understand it. To the charge that economists disagree about everything, he responds with force that "there is greater unity of opinion, and a more essential agreement among the prominent scholars of this science, than among those of any other, excepting, as a matter of course, mathematics."[45] Such defensiveness is interesting in view of the fact that McVickar had been teaching political economy at Columbia for fifty years and had made much the same case twenty-eight years previously. Perhaps Lieber had detected the ambivalence among the trustees.

There are mixed reports about Lieber's performance in the classroom. He himself objected to the old style of "lecturing" and advocated instead a vigorous and engaged presentation, extemporaneous, up-to-date, and responsive to the needs of the class. This was hard work; he estimated that each lecture took three hours to prepare. Lieber innovated further by introducing weekly in-class examinations instead of the more time-consuming, less searching recitations.[46] Sixty years later, in 1921, President Nicholas Murray Butler wrote that "history was never better taught to college students than by Francis Lieber." But Lieber's contemporaries were harsh. John Burgess, whom Ruggles later brought to Columbia to fill Lieber's shoes, declared that his lectures on law were a "distinct failure." President Barnard wrote (to Hamilton Fish) that in the college course "the instruction is substantially thrown away." George Strong had heard that Lieber's lecture room was "in chronic, scandalous disorder, insubordination and row," though he also pointed out that the discipline of Lieber's lectures "cannot be worse than that of Renwick's in my days and of McVickar's afterwards." Freidel's explanation, which is confirmed by Barnard and also by one of Lieber's students, is that the lectures were of high quality but were appropriate for graduates, not undergraduates. Still, it is remarkable that after thirty years of teaching undergraduates Lieber was unable or unwilling to get through to them.[47]

What he served up to his classes was standard fare, based on the sixty-year-old *Political Economy* of J. B. Say. As for his own economic thought, his lecture notes, published as "Notes on Fallacies of American Protectionists," give us a feel for its texture.[48] He begins by laying out first principles. Exchange is one of the distinguishing practical characteristics of man, comparable to speech; protection is wrong because it interferes with the natural course of exchange; trade brings material benefits, which are the result and the sign of interdependence. Lieber then proceeds to refute, one by one, twenty-two fallacies that are to be found at large. In the refutation there is clarity and sound economic reasoning; Lieber is particularly effective against those who argue that domestic capital (or labor) is threatened by cheap foreign capital (or labor). He also presents the usual reply to mercantilism, Smith's "new statesman-ship," which follows from the proof that trade brings mutual advantages. But there is no form to Lieber's arguments, which bear down relentlessly in a uniform single file. It is not hard to see why his public lectures were ill attended.

With Lieber's departure in 1865, and until Richmond Mayo-Smith took over in 1877, the courses in history and political economy were added to the responsibilities of Charles Murray Nairne (1808–82). In 1865–66, the Columbia catalogues relate that Nairne was Professor of Moral *and* Intellectual Philosophy *and* English Literature in the Department of Philosophy, History, Political Economy, *and* Belles Lettres.[49] One need say no more about the nature of his burden. During 1865–66, President Barnard, who, as the architect of Lieber's overthrow, was interested in Nairne's success, reported approvingly that the senior class "recited two hundred and twenty five pages of Wayland's *Political Economy.*[50] But in truth Nairne was not interested in political economy and shrank the course back into the second half of the spring semester of the senior year. To his credit, he did cast about for a suitable textbook though he did not find one that satisfied him. He used Millicent Fawcett's vulgar *Political Economy for Beginners* for some time and for one year used the superior *Manual for Political Economy for Schools and Colleges* written by J. E. T. Rogers of Oxford.[51] In his autobiography John Burgess is dismissive of this odd man: "As a teacher he was a joke. He did not know one of his students from another, marked them all alike, and remonstrated only mildly when they played ball in his recitation room. . . . He had a tutor named Quackenbos who did most of his teaching for him. Naturally he had no disciples."[52]

THE GENESIS OF THE UNIVERSITY

Burgess and the School of Political Science

In 1876, when John Burgess (1844–1931) came to the campus as Professor of History, Political Science, and International Law, he found Columbia a "small old fashioned college" where the classics and mathematics were taught and not much else.[53] The expansion and curricular changes of 1857 had been reversed almost entirely.

There was no graduate instruction; there were few electives; the library was inadequate. McVickar and Lieber had not been replaced, so the less able Nairne was saddled with almost as heavy a burden as McVickar had borne thirty years before. Powerful forces were arrayed against change: The Board of Trustees had a strong clerical party, and the faculty and alumni tended to conservatism and apathy. Yet two men, the trustee Samuel Ruggles and the president, Frederick A. Barnard (1809–89), were determined to see a university rise out of the college; Burgess would help them shape it.

For the elderly Ruggles this was another battle in a long campaign. In 1854 he had called for an expanded curriculum. In 1857 he had urged Lieber's appointment. Now, two decades later, he told Burgess, "You are the man we have been looking for ever since Lieber's death. You must come to Columbia." There was opposition among the trustees, but Ruggles and Barnard were able to send Burgess an invitation, which he found "cordial and flattering" and which he accepted after some agonizing. His salary was at the level Columbia had fixed the previous year for full professors, $7,500.[54]

Burgess was a southern gentleman whose college education, begun at Cumberland University in Tennessee, was interrupted by the Civil War. He joined the northern forces, more because he objected to secession than because he objected to slavery. In 1864 he went to Amherst College where his philosophy professor, Julius H. Seelye, impressed him with his intellect and learning and also with his Socratic teaching methods. After graduating, Burgess was apprenticed to a Springfield, Massachusetts, jurist for a year, then taught briefly at Knox College in Illinois before making the European tour, which in his case took him to Göttingen, Leipzig, and Berlin.[55] In 1873, while still in Berlin, he was invited for a first time to teach at Columbia's Law School, but he chose instead to accept the offer by Seelye to be the first occupant of a new chair of history at Amherst.

The twenty-nine-year-old Burgess believed that his calling was to establish a school of political science and that he could do this at Amherst by devoting all his efforts to the history course for seniors. The course was a resounding success, and seven seniors asked Burgess to take them on for a further year. He agreed, and thus was born an informal graduate school, a seminar that met twice a week to discuss students' research. But a suspicious faculty placed obstacles in Burgess's way, first by loading him down with teaching Greek and Roman history to freshmen and then, when this had failed to stop him, by informing him that it would be "detrimental to the proper interests of the college" (in Burgess's words) for him to continue the graduate instruction.[56] When Columbia made a second offer, Burgess accepted; though he was a devoted alumnus and though he loved the countryside, his calling was the more compelling passion.

Burgess and Ruggles were long-standing supporters of university education, but Barnard's support signaled a change of mind. The elderly president did not abandon his long-held belief that the traditional training and mental discipline were essential; what changed was where he felt the college fit in. Initially he had believed—with everyone else—that such training was precisely the function of the college. New subjects, even if elective, would interfere with discharging this sacred trust and could not be taught in enough depth anyway; they should be discouraged. This was the cast of mind Barnard brought to Columbia in 1864; indeed, it had led to Lieber's dismissal. But by 1876 Barnard's views had changed. In a retrospective essay, contained in his 1886 annual report, he writes that the change was neither in deference to popular demand nor a passive response to the crowding in of new subjects, as appeared to be the case at other colleges.[57] Rather, it was the result of his personal research into the character of the student body and his finding that the college student of the 1870s matriculated two years older than had his antecedents. Juniors were now at an age, about twenty, when the "period of mental growth" had ended and students had begun to develop particular faculties, such as language or science or philosophy. Only with an elective system could a mature student choose a subject suited to his interest and ability and pursue it in depth. "Training" was no longer appropriate: In fact, "when this point is reached, to compel an individual to occupy himself with efforts for which he is constitutionally unfit, is a serious educational error." Once he had decided that higher learning was desirable, Barnard became an enthusiastic advocate. Year after year his annual reports call for a full-fledged university and rehearse the advantages of electives. Such protestation points to its opposite: There was opposition among the trustees and opposition among the faculty. But Barnard was largely successful. Eight of the fifteen senior hours were made elective in 1872, the rest in 1884; in 1880 thirteen junior hours were elective but in 1884 this number was reduced, over Barnard's protest, to five.[58]

In 1880 Burgess and Barnard moved, separately at first, then in concert. Burgess had suffered a setback in 1876, when plans for an expanded program in law were tabled, and he feared that the Law School would continue to stress professional training to the exclusion of "Ethics, History and Public Law."[59] The spark that fired his imagination, in 1878, was a letter from a student, Clifford Bateman, who wrote from Europe about the Ecole Libre des Sciences Politiques, which had been founded to train civil servants. In 1880 Burgess wrote to Barnard that the training of civil servants was a "bounden duty" and great opportunity for the university, and he presented a plan for a department whose curriculum drew heavily on that of the Ecole Libre des Sciences Politiques.[60] Barnard, who was then preparing his own proposals (to the Trustees' Committee on the Course) for graduate instruction, was enthusiastic. He forwarded Burgess's letter to the committee and added to his own document a proposal for what he called a "School of Preparation for the Civil Service." The committee was satisfied that the training that Burgess had in mind was worthwhile. Accordingly, it proposed that the trustees found "a school designed to prepare young men for the duties of public life, to be entitled a School of Political Science."[61] However, the committee was not persuaded that the time had yet come when superior qualifications would help young civil servants, so it played down that aspect of the proposal.[62]

There ensued a long and painful debate in the deeply divided Board of Trustees. Fearing that graduate education would slip his grasp yet again, Burgess lobbied actively. To Hamilton Fish, then chairman of the trustees, he wrote that the question was whether Columbia would advance to the first rank of colleges or drop into the third. Two points were essential, "the establishment of graduate courses in every direction" and a wholly elective senior year. Fish feared a "dwarfing, if not eventual annihilation of the undergraduate course," and he was not alone in this.[63] But, Fish was willing to graft the graduate school onto a healthy college, while others, notably Gouverneur Ogden, resisted the very idea of a graduate school. The issue was so highly charged that Fish stepped down from the chair rather than steer the debate. So the lineup was as it had been over the Gibbs affair twenty-five years earlier: Ogden obstructive and reactionary, Ruggles open-minded and visionary, Fish shrinking from the engagement. This time Ruggles won, by a narrow margin and in the nick of time: A year later he was dead.

Burgess, whom Ruggles had dispatched to Paris to study the Ecole Libre, leaped into action. Joined by his young colleague Richmond Mayo-Smith and assisted by Munroe Smith and Clifford Bateman, students he had "marked as colleagues," he drew up a plan for the School of Political Science. If Burgess's reminiscences can be trusted, they planned with great foresight. Teaching was to be "by lecture, reference reading, examinations every few days on the lectures and the references, and research work in the seminar conducted by each professor." The proposed teaching methods, especially the seminar, were based on German and French models, though students at Columbia were to be kept under closer supervision. All in all, Burgess's vision of graduate instruction, penned somewhat later, has a modern, if wistful, ring: Lectures transmit the professor's own views and the results of his research; students fill out their education by reading in a great library. The aim is independent judgment and comprehensive knowledge both for instructor and for instructed. In addition, the school would edit and publish a journal of political science, an Academy of Political Science would be formed as a sort of alumni association, and a series of monographs would be published.[64]

What emerged from the resolutions of the trustees and the vigorous efforts of Burgess's group was a rough-hewn, lopsided creature. The new School of Political Science provided a three-year course in history, law, political economy, and philosophy, which students might enter after their junior year. At the same time the Faculty of the Arts (really the undergraduate college) was to give graduate instruction across the board. At first, owing to rivalry with the Faculty of Arts, the School of Political Science was not empowered to award the degrees of A.B. or A.M.. Instead, it awarded the less prestigious degree of Ph.B. after one year and the Ph.D. to graduate students. Later, this anomaly was removed by stages. First, in 1885, the School of Political Science received authority to award the A.M. at the end of the second year.[65] Then, in 1895, the Ph.B. was scrapped; thereafter, undergraduates could credit courses taken in the School of Political Science to their A.B. degree, which was awarded exclusively by Columbia College.

To earn the Ph.D., students were required to write and defend a dissertation, pass an oral examination on the three-year course, and show competence in Latin and either French or German. In 1883 the first three dissertations were accepted; one by F. B. Herzog, on *The Railroad Transportation Question,* was Columbia's first dissertation with an economic subject. During the first decade three or four dissertations were defended per year in the School of Political Science; by 1886 these had attracted the favorable comment of the president for their originality and systematic investigation.[66]

The School of Political Science flourished, but graduate instruction under the Faculty of the Arts wilted through neglect. There was considerable opposition to the School, and there were attempts, in 1883–84, to have it reabsorbed into the college. Burgess replied aggressively with a pamphlet arguing that graduate faculties should be recognized in the university statutes and represented on a university senate. Statutory recognition would protect the graduate faculties from attacks from the still dominant college, and the creation of other graduate faculties, notably in philosophy, would end the isolation of the School of Political Science. Burgess's plan (which would allow the Faculty of the Arts to concentrate on gymnasial education of the traditional stripe) was nevertheless opposed strenuously by that faculty, which anticipated its own eclipse. But Burgess and his colleagues fought tenaciously too and had the support of Presidents Barnard and Low. In addition, the exemplary success of the School of Political Science was itself a strong case for university reorganization. The combination was decisive, and the plan that the trustees approved in May 1890 contained the main provisions Burgess had fought for. So, fourteen years after his arrival at Columbia College, the university was born; in 1896, when Columbia formally began to call itself a university, this was merely recognition of its new estate.

Burgess also agitated repeatedly and effectively for improvement in the library. In the 1870s there were some 25,000 volumes, catalogued by author; the librarian, one "Reverend Betts," resisted making new acquisitions and returned half of his funds unspent to the trustees! The building was open for only an hour and a half a day, from 11:00 A.M. Characteristically, Burgess struck out on his own. First, in 1880, he obtained a room and a librarian, Isaac Rice, for books in history and political science. When Rice resigned in 1883, the collection had 3,000 volumes but was still inadequate to the needs of the School of Political Science. In the same year, Burgess was instrumental in the appointment of his Amherst student Melvil Dewey, who had already worked out a scheme for cataloguing books by subject and would bring the Dewey decimal system to Columbia. During Dewey's first year at Columbia, lending increased fivefold; during his five-year tenure, the collection, which had doubled in the previous seven years, doubled again, reaching 100,000 volumes.[67] Books in history and political science from the several libraries were added to the political science library to form a collection numbering 12,000 volumes in 1884; this increased to 18,000 by 1890.

But Burgess's major contribution to Columbia was a stableful of young and brilliant disciples from his days at Amherst. Their names have already been mentioned, but it is useful to remember how many they were. Melvil Dewey was father to the Columbia libraries; more important were Richmond Mayo-Smith (the first instructor hired by Columbia for his expertise in political economy), Munroe Smith (the first managing editor of the *Political Science Quarterly*), and Clifford Bateman (the first of the founders of the School of Political Science to die, only a year and a half after he began teaching.) Together they formed a core of men with common experience and vision: They created the School of Political Science and exerted considerable influence in university affairs.

The Department of Political Economy and Social Science

Ruggles had brought Burgess to Columbia with the express purpose of replacing the classical political economy taught by Nairne with the newer inductive methods used by the German historical school. So Columbia was to be injected with a dose of German political economy to complement its new German educational philosophy. In the event, Burgess taught jurisprudence, and the new economics was brought in by Mayo-Smith (1854–1901), who was to be the founder of Columbia's Department of Political Economy and Social Science. Born in 1854, Mayo-Smith had studied under Burgess at Amherst College where he received his bachelor's degree in 1875. That summer he went to Europe for a two-year stint, studying political economy at Heidelberg and Berlin. In 1877 Burgess invited him to be one of his assistants; two years later he was promoted to adjunct professor, and in 1887 he was made professor of political economy and social science.[68] Although he was an able economist and lectured on a wide range of subjects, his reputation is due mainly to his work on statistical methods. He was, indeed, the leading American statistician of his generation and was elected to the National Academy of Science, a rare honor for a social scientist. Mayo-Smith's courses on statistics at Columbia were the first in America, and his paired volumes *Statistics and Sociology* and *Statistics and Economics* were widely used as textbooks.[69] In 1901, at the peak of his career, he died suddenly.

When he came to Columbia, Mayo-Smith tripled the amount of time devoted to political economy. In 1878, for the first time, a junior course was taught; this met two hours a week for a semester and worked from Rogers's *Manual of Political Economy*. The course was "to prepare such as should elect the subject, during

Senior Year, for higher work; and to give the entire class an outline of the science and as full discussion of practical questions as was possible in the time." To seniors he taught an elective course which met for two hours a week all year; the textbook for this course was J. S. Mill's *Principles of Political Economy*. This classical diet was spiced with references to other authors and to "documentary and statistical works." Later he delivered lectures on institutions: one on land tenure in Europe, two on the monetary systems of Europe and America, eight on the financial history of the United States.[70] Mayo-Smith's undergraduate courses were popular—he regularly addressed the controversies of the day—and he continued to teach them after most of his energies were directed toward the graduate program at the School of Political Science.[71] But it was in the latter theater that the truly dramatic innovations of the 1880s and 1890s were staged.

The graduate program changed utterly the relationship between the emerging university at Columbia and the emerging profession of economics. Prior to 1880 the college was merely a channel through which doctine generated in Edinburgh, Paris, or London was transmitted (often with several decades' lag) to American students in the recitation room and, through the published tracts of professors, to the educated public. McVickar and Lieber, it is true, rephrased European works in an America idiom and occasionally added penetrating critical insights, but this was not original research and the flow of new ideas was overwhelmingly inward. Now the department became an intellectual workshop and marketplace of ideas engaged on equal terms in the give-and-take of scholarly discourse. An astonishing amount of original research was generated and published; on the other hand, new ideas from outside were examined, criticized, and absorbed rapidly.

It was Mayo-Smith who first taught the graduate course in political economy. By 1883 he was teaching a series of courses that effectively set the agenda until the end of the century. The first-year graduate course, also the senior elective, met for two hours a week. The fall semester was devoted to a History of Politico-Economic Institutions and the spring to Taxation and Finance. His teaching method was historical; students would learn the history of institutions and study their present form before proceeding to analysis. Mayo-Smith continued to teach a variant of this course, later entitled Historical and Practical Political Economy, until the end of his life. In the late 1890s he added a small reading class devoted to Marshall's *Principles of Economics*. The second-year course, Statistical Science: Methods and Results, bore his personal stamp. Here he taught not only methodology but also (to paraphrase) that body of knowledge which is gained mainly by observation. To third-year students he gave a year-long course entitled Communistic and Socialistic Theories, where they were confronted with the teachings of George and Owen as well as Marx and Engels.[72] Such open-mindedness was the fruit of self-confidence, not sympathy: Mayo-Smith felt that the best bulwark against the influence of these ideas was a wide knowledge of them. In addition, he instituted a "seminarium" on political economy in which students' work, written under supervision, was presented to the class and instructor for discussion and criticism. During the next few years the seminar was to divide and grow into an increasingly important role in the department.

As the pioneer class moved into its second and third year and new classes entered, the burden on Mayo-Smith increased. In 1880–81 there were eleven students; in 1883–84 there were forty-two; by 1890 the number had risen to 197.[73] Without relief, his exhausting course load would have prevented any further expansion. But three new members swelled the roster of the Department of Political Economy and Social Science to four in 1895. The increased size was immensely important. It contributed to the department's emerging as an administrative unit with a degree of autonomy. It permitted a greater variety in course offerings and seminars and freed up the time needed for research and publishing projects. Finally, the three individuals hired were exceptionally productive: E. R. A. Seligman and J. B. Clark in the field of economics and F. H. Giddings in sociology.

The first to arrive was Seligman (1861–1939), whom Burgess and Mayo-Smith had groomed most carefully. Born in 1861, he graduated in 1879 from Columbia, where Burgess "marked him immediately for a colleague."[74] His European tour (1879–82) took him to Berlin for one semester, to Heidelberg for three, and to Paris for a year. He returned to Columbia and enrolled in the Law School and the School of Political Science. There he earned the Ph.D. in 1885, after defending a dissertation on the "Mediaeval Guilds of England," written under Mayo-Smith. In 1885 he was awarded one of the three-year prize lectureships that the School of Political Science provided, with a stipend of $500. In 1888 he was appointed adjunct professor and in 1891 was promoted to full professor of Political Economy and Finance. He became the pivotal figure in the department, which he was later to head, and in 1904 he was named the McVickar Professor of Political Economy. He retired in 1930.[75]

Born into privilege, well connected in financial and business circles in New York, Seligman was liberal with his time and his money. He served the city of New York, the federal government, and the League of Nations as an advisor on issues of taxation and finance. Dorfman suggests that this set the stage for more frequent consultation of academics by government officials.[76] He served his profession by helping Ely found the American Economic Association, by his participation in the Academy of Political Science, and by overseeing the publication of the *Encyclopaedia of the Social Sciences* as editor-in-chief. Finally, he served his students at Columbia not only by discharging his assigned duties but also by making available his superb library, which was sold to the university at his death.

Seligman is remembered mainly for his contributions to public finance (especially taxation) published in the 1890s.[77] Although he opposed Henry George's single tax, Seligman used the Georgian criterion "ability to pay" to argue, cautiously, for a progressive inheritance tax. He was in favor of income taxation but believed that a progressive income tax was not practicable; in this belief he was overtaken by events. Seligman also painted on broader canvases. In 1901–2 he published in the *Political Science Quarterly* a series of articles entitled "The Economic Interpretation of History," which described the method of "historical materialism" and encouraged its use, stressing that this method had no necessary connection with Marx's economics. The essays were in such demand that they were later collected in a small volume.[78]

Seligman began his prize lectureship with a course entitled the History of Political Economy that was to become a staple of the offerings at the school. His other standard course was public finance, which he taught in a number of variations (e.g., the Financial History of the U.S., the Science of Finance, the Industrial and Tariff History of the U.S.). Finally, he taught sporadically a course in the then pressing Railroad Problems, Economic, Social, and Legal.[79]

He and Mayo-Smith joined forces to build up the seminars. By 1890 there were two: a Preliminary Seminar in Political Economy run by both men and an Advanced Seminar in Finance run by Seligman alone. Five years later Mayo-Smith was running a second advanced seminar in political economy and introduced a statistical laboratory. The seminars performed two functions: They were a forum for the new ideas of students and professors and a structured setting in which to confront new ideas from abroad. The first function was performed mainly by the presentation and discussion of essays written by A.M. and Ph.D. candidates. For example, in 1894–95 Seligman's finance seminar met biweekly to discuss seventeen student papers grouped under four headings (The Railway Question, Taxation, Theory of Distribution, Miscellaneous). The three main topics spell out Seligman's research agenda: By influencing the essay topics, he focused the seminar on his concerns and turned it into a workshop for his own research as well as that of his students. This is confirmed by a list of the papers presented in 1899–1900. One group of seven is devoted to Marx on materialism or to economic interpretations of specific historical episodes; two years later Seligman published his own "Economic Interpretation of History" in the *Political Science Quarterly*. Another six papers are case studies of corporate taxation in various states; these are spin-offs from Seligman's article on that subject in 1889. This sort of team effort was a new phenomenon at Columbia; it multiplied the power and comprehensiveness of research and is an early model of joint research by large teams. To the second function, reviewing recent literature, Seligman devoted half an hour of each biweekly meeting; the task was farmed out to members of the seminar. Mayo-Smith's seminar in political economy also read recent works; in 1894 the topic was the theory of value, and the books covered were Smart's *Introduction to the Theory of Value on the Lines of Menger, Wieser, and Böhm-Bawerk* and von Wieser's *Natural Value*.[80]

The same two functions were performed by the *Political Science Quarterly*, which was first published in 1886, a fecund year that gave birth to the *New Princeton Review* and Harvard's *Quarterly Journal of Economics* as well. The *Quarterly* found its form almost imediately: Each volume ran to 700 pages with twenty-five to thirty articles and about 100 reviews. It was run in-house: Professor Munroe Smith was the managing editor, and five of the six other editors were on the Faculty of Political Science. Each year it contained a number of articles by members of the faculty, who also contributed the overwhelming majority of the reviews in early years and a large fraction (more than a third) later on. It is likely that the need to write these reviews set the agenda for discussion of recent publications in seminar. The contributions were of a high quality, and after a few years of struggle the journal became self-supporting. Two further publishing ventures point to the ambition and scope of the emerging school. One was a series of systematic treatises prepared by the faculty on the subjects they taught, but the series appears not to have made a great impact.[81] The second was a series containing the better doctoral dissertations, published as Studies in History, Economics, and Public Law under Seligman's editorial supervision. The series was a success and was to be long-lived; in 1954 it was renamed Columbia Studies in the Social Sciences.[82]

In 1892 Franklin H. Giddings (1855–1931) was appointed lecturer in sociology; two years later he became Columbia's first Professor of Sociology. The son of a minister, he had trained as an engineer at Union College and obtained his bachelor's degree from Oberlin in 1877. Prior to joining Columbia he had taught politics at Bryn Mawr. Though best known as the founder of a theoretical, quantified sociology, Giddings had contributed articles to economic journals and had collaborated with his friend J. B. Clark on a book entitled *The Modern Distributive Process* (1888).[83] At Columbia he and Mayo-Smith made up a subgroup within the department that was the germ of the future Department of Sociology.

The name of John Bates Clark (1847–1938) completes the roster of nineteenth-century economists at Columbia. Clark arrived in 1895, one of three professors hired as a result of Burgess's adamant refusal to allow women, in particular Barnard College seniors, in the courses students were required to take at the School of Political Science. Under a scheme worked out by President Low, Clark was paid by Barnard College but did most of his teaching at the School of Political Science; in return, the school provided separate instruction for Barnard seniors.[84] A graduate of Amherst College (class of 1872), Clark had been one of the first American political economists to make the European tour. He had been in Europe for three years, 1872–75, mainly at Zurich and at Heidelberg where he had fallen under the influence of Karl Knies. When Columbia engaged him he was already an accomplished scholar, a cofounder of the American Economic Association. He had published many articles, several in the *Political Science Quarterly,* and three monographs; he had taught at Carleton College in Minnesota, where Veblen had been his prize student, and later at Smith (1881–93) and Amherst (1893–95); he was lecturing concurrently at Johns Hopkins. Now forty-eight, he was the oldest member of a young department. Nonetheless, his most influential work lay before him.

Unlike Burgess or Seligman or Mayo-Smith, Clark joined a fully articulated department. Indeed, the fact that it was a fully articulated department was crucial to his decision to accept Columbia's invitation and to reject one made at the same time by Johns Hopkins.[85] Fourteen years after its foundation, the department's curriculum, as also its methods of instruction and research, was firmly in place, and the task of raising a departmental structure was complete: Clark's contribution would be the intellectual output for which he is remembered today.

Though he was schooled in German historicism, Clark's strength was deductive reasoning, and he had the independence of mind to pursue it. His first major treatise, *The Philosophy of Wealth,* shows not only the grandeur of his vision (Clark the Christian Socialist hopes that cooperation will replace competition on the marketplace) but also the penetration of his analysis (it is here that he develops the notion of marginal utility, which he calls "social effective utility"). In 1899 he published *The Distribution of Wealth,* where he presented systematically his thoughts on marginal productivity, a "natural law" which he asserts, incorrectly, "would give every agent of production the wealth which that agent creates." In this work, Clark analyzed the distribution of wealth under static equilibrium conditions; later, in *The Essentials of Economic Theory* (1907), he made a first stab at a dynamic theory, a "provisional statement of the more general laws of progress."[86]

While probing at dynamics Clark was also concerned with impediments to his "natural law." In 1901 he published *The Control of Trusts* (coauthored with his son, J. M. Clark) and in 1904 *The Problem of Monopoly.* He opposed monopolies in testimony to the Senate Interstate Commerce Committee and also in articles addressed to professional and nonprofessional readerships. His influence on policy was thus exerted in a distinctly modern way. Instead of appealing to an influential elite, as the publicists McVickar and Lieber had done, Clark (as also Seligman) addressed himself first to the economics profession and second, using his academic credentials, to the lawmaker. The age of the expert advisor had come.

Like Mayo-Smith and Seligman, Clark developed a repertoire of courses that matched his research interests closely. Four courses, each meeting two hours a week, became his standard offerings. Economics 9 and 10 made up a year-long sequence in, respectively, the Static Laws of Distribution and the Dynamic Laws of Distribution. Here were presented the marginal productivity theory and Clark's groping toward a dynamic theory. The lectures delivered for this course were worked up into the volume *Essentials of Economic Theory* with the help of J. M. Clark. His other courses were

Socialistic Theories (Econ 11) and Social Reforms (Econ 12). Under Clark's guidance the seminar on economic theory took up a wide range of subjects, though usually a cluster of related papers provided some focus. In 1895–96 the Socialists Proudhon, Fourier, and Lassalle were studied and also communistic experiments in the United States; in 1898–99 the emphasis was on theories of price, value, and rent; the next year there were papers on trusts and monopolies as well as organized labor.

Columbia's response to the increasing size, specialization, and complexity of the operation of departments in the School of Political Science was to give them an increasing amount of autonomy, particularly in regard to curriculum and staffing. This trend, more pronounced after 1890, accompanied a fractioning into more focused departments. The School initially fell into three groupings: Jurisprudence, Political Economy and Social Science, and History; by the end of the century these corresponded to three autonomous departments.[87] Sociology split away from economics gradually during the first decades of the twentieth century.

By 1900 the School of Political Science was firmly established, with an enrollment that fluctuated between 200 and 270.[88] Of this number, about one-half were full-time members of the School; the rest merely took courses there. There were eleven professors and three other instructors. Within the School the Department of Economics and Social Science had four professors, all of whom were able economists (though Mayo-Smith put half of his time in statistics and Giddings taught sociology only). In 1899–1900 the department offered eight courses in economics plus two seminars that met weekly and alternated between Political Economy and Finance (Seligman) and Economic Theory (Clark).[89] The offerings varied slightly from year to year, so the range of options over three years was greater than this would suggest. The class size ranged from sixty-five (including perhaps twenty college seniors) in Mayo-Smith's first year course to twenty-two in Clark's advanced course on the dynamic laws of distribution; the average was thirty-five.[90]

It is clear that by 1880 the climate was right for graduate studies, particularly in the social sciences. Similar developments had taken place at other American universities; Johns Hopkins had been founded with graduate education and research as express goals. But Columbia's School of Political Science grew with exceptional vigor mainly because of the vision and careful planning of Burgess and his Amherst cabal. It is not difficult to identify the ingredients of this success. First, they designed the program so as to encourage cross-pollination among graduate teaching, research, and publication. Drawing on a study of methods, particularly the seminar, that had stood the test of time at the great European universities, they planned so well that the School sprouted fully shaped. There was growth after 1880, but this did not bring changes in form; rather, it filled out the existing structures. Second, Burgess (who was, after all, a student of constitutional law) had the vision to establish a delicate balance between the School and Columbia. The School of Political Science had to resist reabsorption into the college, which could not be relied upon to initiate or implement graduate education; the demise of the plan of 1858 had made that clear. On the other hand, the second-class status of a loosely affiliated school (such as the Sheffield Scientific School at Yale or Lawrence Scientific School at Harvard) was to be avoided. Burgess's plan for university organization struck the right balance by making the Faculty of Political Science one of several equal faculties of the university. This freed him and his colleagues to throw their energies into research and graduate instruction. The first fruits were gathered early; by the end of the century the harvest was rich.

Political Economy in the Flagship of Postgraduate Studies: The Johns Hopkins University

WILLIAM J. BARBER

WHEN THE Johns Hopkins University opened its doors in 1876, it did so with the sense that it was bringing something genuinely fresh to the nation. It began life without the sponsorship of either church or state, and those charged to chart its destiny took pride in their independence from political and ecclesiastical influences. They also were alert to the fact that they had a unique opportunity to innovate. Their mission, as they came to perceive it, was ambitious: to elevate the intellectual life of America. The Johns Hopkins University was born amid the celebration of the centennial of the nation's birth, and it was a time at which numerous commentators on America's first century deplored the absence of significant contributions by Americans to the world's stock of fundamental knowledge. Though Americans had established their credentials as a nation of "doers," they commanded little respect as a nation of thinkers.

The trustees of a corporation established by a wealthy Baltimore businessman, Johns Hopkins—who at his death left shares of Baltimore and Ohio Railroad stock then valued at $3.5 million with instructions that a university bearing his name should be built—had an unprecedented capacity to contribute to the cultural elevation of the New World. Never before had an educational benefaction of such magnitude been recorded. The twelve citizens of Baltimore administering this trust included seven businessmen, four lawyers, and one doctor. Seven of their number were Quakers (as the donor had been).[1] All of them were committed to the promotion of good works in the service of the wider community. None, however, claimed any professional expertise in educational matters. The man whom they selected to be the university's first president, Daniel Coit Gilman, certainly could do so.

Gilman's career had been dedicated to the promotion of a "new education," one with an orientation toward the discovery and dissemination of knowledge as opposed to the traditionalism of the classical curriculum. He had been one of the architects of reforms along these lines as a member of the staff of Yale's Scientific School in the 1860s and early 1870s. But this achievement, significant as it was for the development of his own thinking, was marginal within the larger institutional context of Yale, where traditionalists remained the dominant force in the academic power structure. Disappointed that his hopes to have a greater impact were frustrated, he accepted the presidency of the University of California in 1872. This setting offered him greater scope for innovation, but it also exposed him to the political hazards to which a state institution can be vulnerable.[2] When Johns Hopkins's trustees invited Gilman to consult with them on the design of a new institution in Baltimore in late 1874, he accepted with alacrity. His recommendation was that it should be "the means of promoting scholarship of the first order . . . by only offering instruction to advanced students which other universities offer in their post-graduate courses." If appointed to head such an institution, Gilman indicated that he would

select as professors men now standing in the front rank of their own fields; . . . [he] would give them only students who were far enough advanced to keep them constantly stimulated to the highest point; and he would exact from them yearly proof of the diligent and faithful cultivation of their specialities by compelling them to print somewhere the results of their researches.

All of this would be aimed to advance the "intellectual progress and fame of the United States."[3]

From the beginning, Johns Hopkins was structured primarily as a research center for senior scholars and for younger men of promise who aspired to scholarly careers. The institution was confident that it had the resources to attract the best of talents. It could afford to pay above the market for distinguished investigators with established reputations for whom the title "professor" was reserved. It also planned an ambitious program of nonresident professorships to bring scholars of prominence to Baltimore as visiting lecturers. Other titles—"assistant," "associate," and later "associate professor"—were assigned to staff members with temporary appointments. Still more innovative was the inauguration of a program of "fellowships" to attract the best of the nation's postgraduates to study at Johns Hopkins. For the first year of operations, provision was made for twenty "fellows"—to be selected from a national competition—who would be relieved from the payment of tuition and fees and awarded the then princely stipend of $500. Nothing like this had been seen before in the land, and it attracted attention.[4] In the first round of the competition, 152 applications for fellowships were filed by candidates from forty-six different colleges, and 107 in this entry were deemed to be well qualified.[5] But not all graduate students had to be "hired" to be attracted to the opportunities for study at Johns Hopkins. In the first academic year (1876–77), fifty-four graduate students were in residence, of whom only a minority enjoyed the status and stipend associated with designation as a fellow.[6]

Th early signs were thus favorable that Johns Hopkins could make an impressive impact. This setting, in principle, would appear to be hospitable to the nurturing of new learning in political economy. Constraints that had inhibited the advance of the discipline elsewhere on the American academic landscape were absent at Johns Hopkins. Battles over finding space for such material in a course of studies shaped by educational traditionalists were unnecessary there. Johns Hopkins could write on blank slate. Its leaders did not need to be persuaded that the field of public affairs called out for detached scholarly inquiries and interpretations. Certainly Gilman was personally committed to the importance of the social studies. That was clear from his work in championing a place for such study at Yale's Scientific School and at the University of California, as well as from his affiliation with the American Social Science Association (an organization to which he would be elected president in 1879). His convictions were also set out in his inaugural address as president of Johns Hopkins when he observed:

There is a call for men who have been trained by other agencies than the caucus for the discussion of public affairs; men who know what the experience of the world has been in the development of institutions, and are prepared by intellectual and moral disciplilne to advance the public interests, irrespective of party, and indifferent to the attainment of official stations.[7]

From the earliest days, political economy was incorporated into the Johns Hopkins program of study. Even so, the university did not make a permanent appointment to a full professorship in political economy until 1904. Nevertheless, in the 1880s and 1890s, Johns Hopkins occupied center stage in national controversies about the nature of economic "science." The intra-institutional turbulence associated with those debates explains part of the delay in achieving first-class status for political economy within its academic hierarchy. But that turbulence, in turn, contributed to the crystallization of a professional identity for the national community of economists in the United States.

POLITICAL ECONOMY IN THE EARLY YEARS (1876–1881)

The scheme put in place at the opening of Johns Hopkins's first academic year called for an organization of studies into six "departments," one of which was designated as "Moral and Historical Sciences, including Ethics, Political Economy, History, International and Public Law." This was consistent with Gilman's conception of the proper way to approach the social studies. These interrelated subjects should be grouped, with the expectation that students should be exposed to each, though they would also be called upon to specialize in one of them. There was, however, some elasticity in nomenclature, and a number of years were to pass before terminology stabilized. One point, however, was clear from the outset: The man Gilman wanted to head this branch of studies was General Francis Amasa Walker, a man of unquestioned eminence whom Gilman had come to know and respect in days when their paths crossed at Yale's Scientific School. Walker was approached in February 1876 to be a nonresident lecturer during the inaugural academic year in what was then described as a "Department of National Economics."[8] To this invitation Gilman added: "Privately, please tell me whether any other proposition looks attractive and feasible. It if does, I desire to urge its consideration upon the Committee."[9] During the following month, Gilman and Walker corresponded about a plan for a "department of public affairs," which Walker regarded as "feasible and admirable," though he cautioned against giving "prominence to the special feature of proximity to Washington."[10] Gilman believed that it would "take a year to develop the scheme."[11] Before the close of 1876, Gilman was ready to propose firm longer-term arrangements. He then formally invited Walker to take a chair and to assume the direction of a "department of political and economical science." Though Walker found this prospect intriguing and described the invitation as the "most flattering" he had ever received, he declined out of a sense of obligation to colleagues at Yale's Scientific School who had covered for him during his absence in the preceding months when he was working with the Centennial Exhibition in Philadelphia.[12]

This disappointment was but one of many Gilman faced in his initial attempts to recruit faculty for the Johns Hopkins University. To put the institution on the map, he wanted stars for professorial appointments and was not prepared to settle for less. Like Walker, many of his preferred candidates were not movable for permanent positions. When this was the case, Gilman gladly welcomed them on "second-best" terms as nonresident professors to give courses of lectures. Walker performed this role in the spring of 1877 when he delivered twenty lectures on "money," and he returned as a visiting lecturer in the spring of 1878.[13] Such arrangements were not optimal, but they at least meant that various fields could be represented at a high level. Meanwhile, the absence of a full-time and resident professor in political economy did not mean that the field could not profitably be pursued by graduate students. After all, candidates for the Ph.D. were expected to do much of their learning independently and in informal discussions with their peers. Recognized professionals could always be brought in from the outside when needed as advisors and examiners.

One member of the charter class of fellows, Henry Carter Adams, indeed chose to specialize in political economy and successfully completed the requirements for the Ph.D. in 1878 with the presentation of a thesis on the "History of Taxation in the United States, 1789–1816." A native of Iowa and a son of the manse, he had been inspired to take up this line of study by the conviction that it promised to uplift society. The success of his early studies suggested that the new style of postgraduate education in the United States was off to a flourishing start.[14] Indeed, in his first year as a graduate student, Adams had planned (with the concurrence of Gilman and Walker) to teach a class in introductory political economy. This project was aborted when he was called to Iowa because of the illness and subsequent death of a sister.[15] Henry Carter Adams's interest in teaching political economy at Johns Hopkins did not wane. While in Germany in 1878–79 for a postdoctoral year, he proposed a "complete system of lectures upon Economy . . . to meet the wants of the University." These included courses on economic principles, public finance, American technics ("composed of technics of agriculture, manufactures, and transports"), and the financial history of the United States. He personally was eager to begin implementing this scheme at Johns Hopkins in the acacdemic year 1879–80.[16] Gilman, however, was not prepared to make this kind of commitment to a younger man. Instead, Adams was invited to deliver a series of lectures at Johns Hopkins on "National Debts" during the spring term, 1879–80, to supplement his part-time employment at Cornell during that academic year. He again taught courses in political economy and in finance—to a total of nineteen students—in the fall term of the academic year 1880–81 before departing to teach at the University of Michigan.[17]

Henry Carter Adams was thus the first person with a doctorate in political economy to offer resident courses in the discipline at Johns Hopkins. He was not, however, the first member of the university to teach a class in the subject matter there. Herbert Baxter Adams (no kin) taught an introductory class in the spring term, 1879. He had arrived at Johns Hopkins as one of the original fellows with a Ph.D. from Heidelberg already in hand. Though his primary academic specialty was in history, he had studied political economy under Knies while in Germany. Brimming with ambition and self-confidence, Herbert Baxter Adams was eager for academic preferment at Johns Hopkins and ready to make himself useful in any way that might advance his position. His contribution to the academic program was acknowledged with the award of the title "assistant"—a step above the status of fellow, though one far short of his aspirations.

Though political economy lacked a regular full-time representative at Johns Hopkins in its early years, this was not for want of attempts to find one. Gilman persisted in the search for a senior scholar to direct the branch of studies that had come to be described as "Historical and Political Science." When Francis Amasa Walker could not be persuaded to take a permanent assignment, Gilman made overtures to J. L. Diman, Professor of History and Political Economy at Brown, and to Thomas L. Cooley of the University of Michigan Law School. For a time, there was some hope that Hermann von Holst, a professor of history at the University of Freiburg with an interest in the study of the American past, could be wooed to a chair in Baltimore. Though each of these scholars graced the Johns Hopkins lecture series as a visitor, none could be induced to accept a full-time position.[18] In the face of these disappointments, Gilman chose to temporize. Spokesmen for political economy were on and off the scene, but they were visitors or junior scholars struggling for a place.

ADDITIONS TO THE ROSTER IN THE 1880S

Strategy for the development of the Historical and Political Science wing (which included political economy) changed in the 1880s. An attempt was then made to build from the ground up by giving younger men a chance to realize their potential. The first step—taken in May 1881—was to advance Herbert Baxter Adams to the rank of "associate" for a two-year term. This assignment carried with it the expectation that Adams would be responsible for the general direction of the work of this department. The second step was the appointment of Richard T. Ely, initially to give twenty lectures on the history of political economy during the fall term, 1881. Gilman had also hoped to have lectures on political economy from a senior scholar in the program for the academic year 1881–82. With this in mind, he had turned to Simon Newcomb, a mathematician and astronomer with the U.S. Navy. Political economy was not Newcomb's primary specialty, though he had published books and articles and delivered lectures at Harvard on the subject. As president of the Political Economy Club—an organization of East Coast academicians, businessmen, and journalists—he was also in touch with current debates on economic issues.[19]

As events unfolded for the academic year 1881–82, Newcomb, in fact, did not deliver the lectures expected from him, begging off on grounds of ill health and pressure of other work.[20] On the other hand, Ely—who had been contracted originally for a short stay during the fall term—began a residence at Johns Hopkins that was to last for the next eleven years.

Ely had discovered economics as a graduate student in Germany where he had gone after graduation from Columbia in 1876 with the intention of studying philosophy. Though he had received some exposure to economics as an undergraduate, it had then left little mark on him.[21] But the German approach to the discipline was different. At the University of Heidelberg, he came under the influence of Karl Knies—whom Ely regarded as his "master"—and completed a Ph.D. in 1879. The experience in Germany was useful to Ely in other ways as well. He there met Andrew D. White, president of Cornell, who was then on leave as American minister in Berlin, and at White's invitation Ely prepared a survey of the city's administration.

Armed with enthusiastic letters of recommendation from White, Ely sought academic employment on his return to the United States. This support, in turn, could not have failed to impress

Gilman. (Gilman and White had been friends and contemporaries at Yale and had spent a *Wanderjahr* in Europe together in the 1850s; White had also been a leading champion of Gilman's candidacy for the presidency of Johns Hopkins.)[22] Even so, Gilman proceeded cautiously, offering Ely only a short-term appointment in the fall term, despite Ely's statement that he "would not like to makke any engagement for less than a year."[23] Ely's lectures were sufficiently well received to justify an extension of his contract for the full academic year. In his report on teaching activities in 1881–82, he observed that he had conducted two courses: (1) History of Political Economy, for both graduates and undergraduates, with "27 regular hearers"; and (2) a lecture course for seven graduates on Roscher's *Grundlagen der Nationalökonomie*.[24] On the strength of this performance, his contract was renewed for a year, during which he proposed advanced courses in Finance (dealing "at length with such practical topics as banking, paper-money, monometallism, bimetallism and taxation") and in the Theory and Practice of Administration with Special Reference to Civil Service Problems and Municipal Reform; a series of six public lectures on the History of French and German Socialism; and two undergraduate courses (The Principles of Political Economy and Historical Systems of Political Economy).[25]

The content of Ely's offerings was clearly moulded by his conversion to the methods and the conclusions of the German historical school. He had returned from Heidelberg fired with a sense of mission to spread the "correct" approach to economic problems in the United States. In this reading of matters, the influence of British classical economics needed to be purged. It was out of touch with the living reality, too ahistorical, and too wedded to the view that economic life was organized around immutable and universal natural laws. Moreover, its predisposition in favor of laissez-faire was pernicious. Not only was competition often wasteful and destructive, its very morality was questionable. The "old" economics, Ely alleged, was organized around the analysis of the baser acquisitive instincts of the human species. The sights of economists should instead be set on serving more humane purposes in the interest of the common good. This indeed, he maintained, was the only course compatible with Christianity. The message of Ely's version of a social gospel was resoundingly clear: The right-minded citizen should work for the uplift of society's downtrodden, should encourage the formation of voluntary associations (such as labor unions and cooperatives) to protect the weak, and should promote active intervention by the state to correct injustice in the distribution of income and of economic power. The economist, in this reading of matters, had an obligation both to reveal the truth about the existing social order and to point the direction in which it should be reformed. Not only did Ely preach this message in the classroom and from the lecture platform, he also spread it prolifically in columns for the popular press and in articles for national periodicals.

Ely won an appreciative and devoted audience among students at Johns Hopkins and was rewarded with promotion to the rank of associate in mid-1883. Nevertheless, he was dissatisfied with the salary—set at $1,250—that went with this advancement. He stated his case for a raise to Gilman as follows in September 1883:

My work is attracting more attention than you are probably aware of and opportunities are continually being presented which would enable me to call attention to the work of my department and bring the Johns Hopkins University favorably before the public, were not my salary so small as to make it impossible for me to avail myself of them. . . . If you reflect upon what is expected of a modern political economist, you will understand that his work is more expensive to him than any other university work. He must travel, be a man of the world and associate with bankers, manufacturers, merchants, lawyers and public men. I often learn more in half an hour's conversation with a lawyer or manufacturer than in reading half a day. But it costs more than I can afford to mingle with men. I am asked to join clubs which would enable me to make acquaintances of value to one in my position but poverty compels me to decline them as all other invitations. I cannot take the positions in the world which others almost force on me and I appear surly and unsocial. I am continually humiliated and mortified. . . . When people compare my work with that of Prof. Sumner they do not stop to consider that he receives three times the salary I do and has consequently better advantages.[26]

This appeal succeeded in extracting an additional $500 from the Johns Hopkins administration for the academic year 1883–84, though Gilman was still uncertain about whether Ely would have a future at the university. A memorandum of September 28, 1883, on a "President's Office" letterhead in Gilman's hand describes the situation as follows:

In fixing Mr. Ely's salary, consideration was given to two points: (1) the proper organization of the group of studies in Historical and Political Science, & (2) the probable adaptation of Mr. Ely to the future requirements of the University. On neither of these points was a conclusion reached.

Though Ely was granted an increment in pay, an understanding was noted that he would be advised before the middle of the following April "if the engagement is not renewed."[27]

Gilman's thinking about the "proper organization" of studies in Historical and Political Science took clearer shape during the academic year 1883–84, and it was influenced in part by initiatives of Herbert Baxter Adams. Adams, who had been associated with the university since its opening day, was certainly aware that the status an individual faculty member could enjoy there was often linked with success in promoting the image of the institution in the scholarly community at large. This was self-evidently the case in other branches of the university, where the resident professoriat had launched scholarly journals—first in mathematics, subsequently in chemistry, biology, and philology. These enterprises won the applause of Gilman and the trustees. They aided in establishing the identity of the new institution and served the larger cause of elevating standards of American scholarship as well. In this spirit, Adams brought forward a proposition that the university should also support the publication of scholarly monographs in the social studies. In 1882 a series entitled Johns Hopkins University Studies in Historical and Political Science was born, with Adams as its editor.[28] Not long thereafter, in 1883, Adams was advanced to the newly created rank of associate professor. Subsequently, he was charged to direct the work of the Department of Historical and Political Science.

As constituted for the academic year 1884–85, the graduate program of the deparment centered on a "seminary" required of all students, meeting weekly throughout the year, under the general supervision of Adams. Three lines of inquiry were pursued, "represented by the three instructors": American Institutions of Government (Adams); History of Political Economy in the United States, "with reference not only to the progress of the science but to the history of taxation and of economic administration in certain representative cities and states" (Ely); and Representative State Constitutions (Jameson, an assistant in history).[29] Though the substantive content of the seminary varied somewhat from year to year, there was continuity in its style. Students were assigned topics for research, and their findings were subjected to general discussion and criticism. The best of the seminary projects ultimately found their way into print in the Johns Hopkins Studies in Historical and Political Science. Though the seminary experience formed the core of the graduate program and was regarded as a research laboratory, students were also expected to select among history, political science, and political economy as a major field of specialization. Those electing political economy as a major did advanced courses with Ely.

On the whole, Ely and Adams worked well together. Indeed, they had a lot in common. Both were products of the University of Heidelberg. Both were energetic and ambitious, not only for themselves but also for the propagation of their approaches to their respective disciplines. Both were natural academic entrepreneurs: Adams was to be the moving force behind the formation of the American Historical Association, and Ely was to play a similar role in the organization of the American Economic Association. In addition, they collaborated, from 1884 through the early 1890s, in bringing their messages to popular audiences at the Chautauqua summer school. Ely nevertheless pressed for autonomy for his work at Johns Hopkins. Gilman was unmoved by such pleas.[30] But a bit more scope for political economy was conceded in 1889. All graduate students in the Historical and Political Science Department were still required to participate in the common seminary, but those declaring political economy as a major could also attend the "Economic Conference," a separate seminar conducted weekly by Ely. These additional sessions attracted enrollments of eight students in 1889 and ten in 1890. For the academic year 1890–91, he introduced a variation in the format of the Conference: Every fourth meeting was to be "a journal evening, devoted to a discussion of recent economic periodical literature."[31]

A decade after Ely's arrival at Johns Hopkins, political economy still occupied subordinate status in its table of organization. Even so, a full-time resident spokesman for the discipline had been built into the structure. From this there was to be no turning back.

THE OUTBREAK OF INTRAMURAL CIVIL WAR IN THE MID-1880s

Though political economy found a lasting place in the curricular pattern in the 1880s, the precise form that it would take remained a matter of considerable dispute. The issue turned on two distinct views of the nature of the discipline. The central antagonists were Richard T. Ely and Simon Newcomb. Neither was a newcomer to the Johns Hopkins scene when the friction began in 1884. Ely was already on the spot as the resident political economist. Newcomb—though appointed to the chair in mathematics, effective from September 1884—had already established his credentials as a Johns Hopkins man through his ties as a consultant with Gilman on appointments in the sciences and as a sometime visiting lecturer on astronomy and, potentially, on political economy.

In their approaches to political economy, Ely and Newcomb were at opposite poles. Ely's vision called for the scholar to be engaged in setting the world to rights, and he viewed theoretical abstractions with suspicion. Newcomb, on the other hand, aspired to make economics a positive science, free of contamination from normative judgments. When the issue betwen the two was joined in earnest in 1884, Newcomb had published more on economic topics (even though these matters were secondary to his primary field of intellectual endeavor) than had Ely. In addition, Newcomb had prepared a textbook, *Principles of Political Economy,* which was to appear in 1885. Their divergent perspectives set the stage for a major debate on the future direction of economic studies in the United States.

The spark igniting this *Methodenstreit* was an essay by Ely, entitled *The Past and Present of Political Economy,* which appeared in the 1884 issue of the Johns Hopkins Studies in Historical and Political Science. Ely had there set out a characteristic indictment—from the German historical point of view—of the deficiencies of the "old" style of political economy with its pretensions to imitate the natural sciences. Newcomb was aroused by this charge and wrote to Gilman that he hoped for an

opportunity to say a few words about your department of political economy before the impulse which has been given me by Dr. Ely's pamphlet entirely dies out. It looks a little incongruous to see so sweeping and wholesale attack upon the introduction of any rational or scientific method in economics come from a university whose other specialties have tended in the opposite direction.[32]

Newcomb took particular exception to one passage in Ely's paper "where he most clearly emphasizes his dissent from what seem to me to be sound views," especially because Newcomb thought he "could claim the paternity of the sentence selected for criticism."[33] The passage in question in Ely's monograph read as follows:

To put it positively, the political economy of the past was a pure science, which was considered apart from policy, which is as a changeable, fluctuating factor, introduced a disturbing element into what was otherwise immutable. "Until economical questions," writes an adherent of this method in *The Nation,* "are considered and answered from a purely scientific standpoint without respect to any considerations of policy, it is vain to hope for any advance in our means of judging them." That is to say, political economy is a science in an older and narrower sense which limits science to the discovery of truth without regard to its practical applications.[34]

On this point, the swords were drawn. Newcomb prepared a rebuttal, a copy of which he sent to Gilman for comment, with a covering note in which he observed that he had "never been able to see any essential difference between the objections raised against political economy from the new school point of view and the general objections of the public against the value of theoretical science."[35] In the published version of this statement—which appeared in the November 1884 issue of the *Princeton Review*—Newcomb cited "a brochure by Dr. Ely, recently issued by the Johns Hopkins University," as an example of fundamental intellectual confusion. The objections raised against English political economy, he maintained, were founded on "misapprehension." All science was necessarily linked with hypotheses, and the "great mistake made by the objectors is that of supposing that the economist considers all his hypotheses as susceptible of universal application without any restriction or modification." This was patently not the case. In all scientific endeavors, the enunciation of "natural laws" was always qualified by specifications of "other conditions being equal." Those who criticized deductive procedures had failed to understand that they were "an essential process in every rational explanation of human affairs." The "disciples of a new school," on the other hand, professed to "start from the great facts of history and statistics" while rejecting "certain hypothetical principles of human nature." This approach to economic study, Newcomb argued, was as misguided as "commencing physics by taking the student around to see all the machinery in a city at work." Altogether, he concluded, those who rejected the "commonly perceived propositions" of political economy were "guilty of a proceeding so irrational that only the number and strength of [their] following entitle [them] to serious refutation."[36]

Newcomb was not willing to let the matter rest there. In May 1884 he had asked for a "good opportunity" to deliver a lecture at Johns Hopkins on "political economy as a science."[37] Such an opportunity arose in February 1885 when Newcomb addressed the university's Scientific Association. His lecture was entitled "On the Possibility of Applying Mathematics to Political Economy," and his demeanor on this occasion has been described as one of "irritating assertiveness."[38] Two days later, Charles Levermore, one of Ely's students, opened a discussion of "Newcomb on Mathematical Economy" before the Historical and Political Science Association to an audience predisposed toward Ely's position.[39] There was no ground on which the positions of the central antagonists in this controversy could be readily reconciled, and the tone of the exchanges between the rival camps was deteriorating.

Despite his buoyant self-confidence, these must have been uneasy days for Ely. He lacked security of tenure at Johns Hopkins, whereas Newcomb held a permanent professorship. But, in his attempts to bolster his position at the university, Ely could draw on resources that Newcomb could not match. In the first place, Ely had influence over a group of able and articulate graduate students who were prepared to argue his cause on the local scene and in the public periodicals. In addition, Ely had access to a network of German-trained younger economists who might, in principle, provide external buttressing to his position. Gilman's propensity to look with favor on members of his faculty who could promote the name of Johns Hopkins before the national scholarly community was well known. In his autobiography, Ely later wrote that the organization of professional associations was the "sort of thing . . . in the air at the Johns Hopkins and was encouraged by the authorities."[40] But there was also an element of personal opportunism in his decision to go forward in 1885 with a plan to form an American Economic Association. When communicating with Gilman about this activity, Ely reported that a revised platform of the proposed AEA had been

submitted to a large number of the younger economists of the country and favorable replies have been received in every case with no exceptions. . . . The proposals seem to be very favorable for an influential movement which will help in the diffusion of a sound, Christian political economy. At the same time, I trust it may benefit the Johns Hopkins University.[41]

Ely succeeded in bringing the American Economic Association into being in September 1885, with Francis Amasa Walker installed as president and with himself as secretary. In candid moments, he acknowledged that his major objective was to mobilize younger economists who shared his perspectives to do battle against "the Sumner, Newcomb crowd."[42] But he was also at pains to broaden the membership to include economists of more moderate views.[43] Indeed, it was something of a coup to bring Walker into the fold and to persuade him to accept the presidency. His presence provided a bridge between the older and the younger generations.[44] And it certainly did Ely no harm in his relations with Gilman.

No doubt some type of national organization of economists would have emerged in late nineteenth-century America. But both the timing and the early shape of the American Economic Association owed something to the ethos of Johns Hopkins in the mid-1880s and to the tensions within its faculty over the correct approach to economic inquiry.

THE ELY—NEWCOMB CONFLICT: PHASE 2

Ely began the academic year 1885–86 at Johns Hopkins with a stronger hand to play. But rivalry with his local adversary did not diminish; on the contrary, it intensified. The Ely camp took the offensive with a hostile review of Newcomb's *Principles of Political Economy,* which had appeared in 1885. The author was Albert Shaw (an Ely pupil and disciple), but he was largely guided by Ely. Newcomb's approach to political economy was characterized as that of "an astronomer who *has* seen the stars, and nothing else, all his life." His eminence as an astronomical mathematician was acknowledged, but this very achievement was treated as disqualifying him as a commentator on political economy. "[I]n matters of social organization," Shaw wrote, "his astronomical bias is vitiating. . . . It is hardly necessary to say that the book exhibits, throughout, the mental habit of the mathematician. . . . Unfortunately, it does not meet a want."[45]

But Newcomb was still a potential threat to Ely's position at Johns Hopkins. Newcomb had a voice in the conduct of the university's affairs, and it was one that Gilman listened to. In May 1886 Newcomb was asked to serve as an examiner of Ph.D. candidates in political economy and was blunt in his comments to Gilman on the quality of the instruction to which Ely's graduate students had been exposed:

The examination in economics seemed to me to show that the teaching was not directed in the line required by the exigencies of the times. The candidates showed an almost deplorable want of training in the power of logical analysis of the economic theories which move men and determine the course of our industry at the present time. The impression that I got . . . was that they were amply able to grapple with the subject, had it only been presented to them, but that it was quite new to their minds. In such processes as tracing out the effects of Chinese cheap labor, and irredeemable paper money, they seemed to be quite untrained. The main teaching seemed to have been directed towards the administrative and economic policies of the leading countries of the world, especially Germany.[46]

On receipt of this report, Gilman invited Newcomb to submit recommendations on the course of instruction at the university. Newcomb spoke plainly about his sense of where the pedagogical priorities should lie: The main concentration should be on developing the student's capacity to analyze economic phenomena. And he reiterated his impression—"drawn from the examination and all other sources"—that "very little attention is paid to the analytic process" in current teaching at Johns Hopkins.[47]

The controversy between the two men resurfaced in a public forum in June and July 1886. Both had been invited by the editor of *Science* (the journal of the American Association for the Advancement of Science) to contribute to a series on the differences between economists, old-style and new. Ely's submission restated familiar positions: that concern with what ought to be was inherent in the work of the political economist; that the task of economists was to understand the "laws of progress" and to show how they could be directed to promote the economic and social growth of mankind; and that the ethical ideal was "simply the Christian doctrine of talents committed to men, all to be improved."[48] Newcomb's rejoinder also sounded some predictable notes: It was a "contradiction in terms" to regard discussions of what ought to be as "science"; the principle of "non-interference" in economic affairs also favored progress but sought its achievement by giving individuals the widest possible latitude of choice; public intervention was suspect because governments were incapable of acting on "sound business principles." But Newcomb also aimed a personal barb at Ely, characterizing him as an "expounder" of the "socialistic school."[49]

Ely could ill afford to let this charge go unchallenged. In a rebuttal he attempted to play down the suggestion that he was a Socialist, dismissing it as "doubtless inadvertent" on the part of his "learned colleague." But he, in turn, implied that Newcomb lacked the credentials to speak on political economy because he "fail[ed] to distinguish between mathematical sciences and those which are more descriptive in their nature, and have to do with growing, changing bodies." This shortcoming precluded Newcomb from understanding the moral obligation imposed on the expert in economics to work to improve society. "Who," Ely asked, "can so well treat of social remedies as he who has studied society? Why stop when we have reached that point which renders our science useful?" [50]

In Newcomb's response to this submission, there was more than a hint that a basis for accommodation could be found among the various schools struggling to establish proper procedures for economic inquiry. The debate over the priority of "deductive processes from general principles" versus "the study of the facts as developed by history and statistics" was not a matter of "either-or." Sound results could not be obtained "except by a judicious combination of both processes." In their teaching, Newcomb maintained, "all economists should agree . . . to emphasize both the understanding of principles and the investigation of facts." [51]

If there were signals that a truce might be in the offing in mid-1886, they were short-lived. Internecine warfare broke out again in the autumn and at an escalated level of hostility. This time the focal point of controversy was no longer one of method but rather one of substantive interpretation of an economic issue then at the forefront of public attention. Ely and Newcomb both produced books dealing with the "labor question" in 1886, and the moment of their publication was one of high tension between capitalists and organized labor. That year strikes doubled the record set earlier, and the movement for the eight-hour day had triggered violence in the Haymarket bombing in May.[52] It was small wonder that the role of organized labor and its claims was the "hot" issue on the national agenda.

As might have been expected, Ely and Newcomb took diametrically opposed positions on this question. In Ely's reading, the labor movement was an instrument of social redemption, and he described it as "the strongest force outside the Christian Church making for the practical recognition of human brotherhood." [53] The fostering of voluntary associations of workers—and the development of a sense of solidarity among them—promised to be a force for universal peace and a device to unite black and white in the American South. Cooperative activities—in both production and distribution—could be built on these foundations. In this vision, "competition and its wastes" could be eliminated with savings sufficient "to bring comfort to all people in the United States." [54] Newcomb, on the other hand, saw labor organizations as more likely to be a curse than a blessing. He allowed that they might have legitimate functions if they confined their activities to improving productive efficiency—for example, through pooling information on work techniques, through education, through dissemination of facts on employment opportunities and their terms. But work stoppages, wage rigidities, and limitations on the hours of employment should not be countenanced. By interrupting production and reducing efficiency, they ran counter to the welfare of society and of its individual members.[55]

At this stage in the ongoing dispute, tempers were strained. The Elyites—with Albert Shaw as their spokesman—depicted Newcomb as an incompetent amateur. "Professor Newcomb's 'Plain Man's Talk on the Labor Question,'" Shaw wrote "might better have been called 'An Astronomer's Talk on the *So-called* Labor Question.'"[56] Newcomb's review of Ely was even more biting. He characterized Ely's book as displaying "a lack of logical acumen" and "an intensity of bias . . . to which it would be hard to find a parallel elsewhere than in the ravings of an Anarchist or the dreams of a Socialist." The review concluded with the following comment: "Dr. Ely seems to us to be seriously out of place in a university chair."[57]

This kind of indictment in a national periodical could obviously have damaging implications for Ely's career prospects at Johns Hopkins and, potentially, for the reputation of the university as well. Certainly Ely was conscious of his vulnerability. A number of students rallied to his aid by writing and inspiring favorable notices of Ely's work. But he survived this crisis and came out ahead.[58] In June 1887 he was elevated to the rank of associate professor with a three-year contract at a salary of $2,500 per annum. Meanwhile, Newcomb retired from the fray and concentrated his energies thereafter on mathematics and astronomy. Even so, there must have been some residual doubts in the minds of Gilman and his trustees about whether Ely was the right man for a permanent place at Johns Hopkins.[59]

CHANGES IN STRUCTURE, PERSONNEL, AND STYLE IN THE 1890S

The fortunes of Johns Hopkins University underwent a sea change in the 1890s. When the institution opened, its endowment seemed more than ample to underwrite its ambitions. That confidence weakened in the late 1880s when dividends on Baltimore and Ohio Railroad stock (in which all of the university's financial assets had been placed) shrank and subsequently were suspended. Various emergency appeals for funds kept the institution's existing programs going, but there were no resources to spare for new ones. The atmosphere of affluence in the 1870s had been replaced by one of austerity in the 1890s.

The reputation for quality in graduate studies established in the early years meant that the institution was still a magnet for able students. Even so, its relative position in American higher education had declined. At the beginning, Johns Hopkins had enjoyed a near monopoly position in the Ph.D. market. But its success in this enterprise had attracted imitators. Harvard, Yale, and Columbia, for example, had expanded their graduate programs, and two new entrants in the 1890s—the University of Chicago and Stanford—began life with resources far greater than Johns Hopkins had commanded even in its palmy days. In the 1890s these changes in the national academic environment exposed Johns Hopkins to much livelier competition for faculty and for graduate students than it had ever faced before.

These developments on the outside, in turn, left an imprint on the shape of the Department of History and Political Science at Johns Hopkins. In 1891 its two ranking members—Herbert Baxter Adams and Ely (both then associate professors)—were being courted to join the newly formed University of Chicago. Both men, however, preferred the atmosphere of Johns Hopkins. But the Chicago negotiations did provide an opportunity to bargain for promotion. Adams was elevated to a professorship in 1891; Ely was not, and he felt slighted.

In December 1891 Ely formally requested three changes in his "situation" at Johns Hopkins. One was that he be made a full professor on the grounds that his "subordinate position does not correspond to the position which I occupy among the economists of this and other countries." Second, he asked that political economy be divorced from history and made a "distinct department by itself." He also asked for additional assistance, setting out the case as follows:

the field of economics has become so large that no one man can possibly cover it satisfactorily in a great university like the Johns Hopkins, having both graduate and undergraduate departments. Any attempt to do so must result in work of a quality which does injustice to the one who undertakes it, and cannot be regarded as worthy of the University. . . . As at present understood, political economy includes the treatment of pure theory, banking, money, taxes, public debts, the history of economic thought, a critical discussion of socialism, and numerous other topics. . . . There is no other institution of anything like the rank of the Johns Hopkins University which asks one professor to do all the work in economics.[60]

Even though Ely informed Gilman that he had an offer in hand to go elsewhere, Gilman did not exert himself to satisfy Ely's demands. In correspondence during January 1892 Gilman advised Ely that he and the Executive Committee of the Board of Trustees had concurred that "the time has not yet come to constitute a department of political economy distinct from the department of historical and political science"; that the matter of a full professorship involved questions of general university policy on which no action could immediately be taken; and that Ely should make his decision about a position elsewhere "on its merits."[61] In February 1892 Ely submitted his resignation, effective at the close of the academic year, and announced that he had accepted a post at the University of Wisconsin.

Gilman did not record his innermost thoughts about this parting of the ways. He could certainly have retained Ely's services had he had a mind to do so. Why did he not? One can only speculate. A number of factors must have influenced him, however. Gilman's sense of the university's budget constraints no doubt dampened his enthusiasm for requests for additional staffing. Perhaps as well he had lingering doubts about whether Ely was the man to head an independent department that might be moulded to a "party line" at a time when the contours of the discipline were changing.[62] But there was also a conflict in the perceptions of the two men about the place political economy should occupy within the university's framework. Gilman believed that there were valid educational reasons for continuing to meld history, political science, and political economy. On the other hand, the maturing sense of professionalism among economists—to which Ely had been a catalyst—was pushing the discipline rapidly in the direction of specialization.

The task of filling the gap left by Ely's departure proved to be a time-consuming one. As he had done before, Gilman kept the instructional program going by making junior appointments and by calling on visiting lecturers. For the academic year 1892–93, John Bates Clark (then at Smith) was recruited to deliver twenty-five lectures on "The Economic Theory of Distribution" during the fall term and Henry Carter Adams (then dividing his time between the University of Michigan and the Interstate Commerce Commission) to deliver twenty lectures on "Finance" in the spring term. Resident instruction in political economy was placed in the hands of Sidney

Sherwood, a Johns Hopkins Ph.D. in the class of 1891, who had spent the academic year 1891–92 on the faculty of the University of Pennsylvania and was called back as an "associate." Though Sherwood had been one of Ely's students, he was far more sympathetic than his mentor to the use of mathematics in economics, and his style brought Johns Hopkins's political economy closer to the mainstream of the discipline. During his first year as chairman of the Economic Conference for graduate students, Sherwood invited Simon Newcomb to deliver a paper.[63] It is unlikely that Newcomb's remarks on "The Relation of the Economist to the Public" would have been hospitably received had Ely remained in the chair.

This general pattern was repeated in the two subsequent academic years, though Gilman recognized that such a mix of juniors and visitors was less than ideal. He wanted to confer a professorship of political economy on a luminary and was not to be hurried into a hasty decision. In early 1895 he believed he had found the man for the job in John Bates Clark. Clark (then at Amherst College and newly elected as president of the American Economic Association) was certainly no stranger to Johns Hopkins. He had alrady served three tours as a visiting lecturer. In correspondence with Gilman, Clark made clear that "the character of the work to be done at the Johns Hopkins University" was "attractive" to him.[64] But, in the interval between Clark's indication of his willingness to accept such a proposition and formal action by the trustees of Johns Hopkins to confirm the offer, events took an unexpected course. Columbia University made a bid for Clark's services, and he accepted. When explaining this decision to Gilman, Clark wrote: "As invitations to different positions have come to me, the test question that I have invariably asked has been 'Will the proposed change increase or diminish my opportunity to influence the development of economic theory?'" As he then assessed matters, Columbia offered "special advantages" in that "it would associate me with other coordinate teachers, and relieve me from all incidental care in so far as a large part of the department of economics is concerned. It would limit my own lecturing to the subject of pure theory."[65]

Gilman was bitterly disappointed. He had been prepared to accord departmental autonomy to political economy if its direction would be placed in the hands of a man of Clark's stature. When this recruiting effort fell short, he settled for a more modest arrangement. Sherwood was advanced to the rank of associate professor in 1895 (a position he held until his death in 1901), and younger men were nurtured within the Johns Hopkins fold to carry on instruction in political economy—notably, Jacob Hollander (Ph.D., Johns Hopkins, 1893) and George E. Barnett (Ph.D., Johns Hopkins, 1901). Formal creation of a separate Department of Political Economy occurred in 1901, a year when Herbert Baxter Adams and Sidney Sherwood died and Gilman retired from the presidency. Hollander was named as director of this department, and in 1904 he became the first to hold the title of Professor of Political Economy at Johns Hopkins.

THE ACHIEVEMENTS OF A QUARTER CENTURY

Though the program in political economy had not evolved in the way Gilman wanted, he could certainly take satisfaction from the overall results of his handiwork. Johns Hopkins had provided the yeast for raising the standards of American scholarship. During the twenty-five years of his administration, Johns Hopkins had produced a grand total of 579 Ph.D.'s (double the number of its nearest rival in graduate education, Harvard).[66] And there was no lack of distinguished names among them.[67]

Certainly the Johns Hopkins of the late nineteenth century left an impressive mark on the development of American economics and in the diffusion of its study throughout the American academic landscape. The overwhelming bulk of its graduate students chose to pursue academic careers. A number of them were to discover that the expression of controversial views at other colleges and universities was less acceptable than it had been at Johns Hopkins, and their names dominated the roster of "academic freedom" cases in the 1890s.[68] But no less than eleven of its graduate students during Gilman's leadership of the institution were to reach the professional eminence associated with the presidency of the American Economic Association.[69] In addition, three who taught at Johns Hopkins during these years—Francis Amasa Walker, John Bates Clark, and Richard T. Ely—served the economics profession from this office. Even without a full professor of political economy, the Johns Hopkins of the nineteenth century had an impact on American economics far greater than that of any other institution in the land.

An Uneasy Relationship: The Business Community and Academic Economists at the University of Pennsylvania

STEVEN A. SASS

Few business communities were more serious about their economics than that of nineteenth-century Philadelphia. The city became a great manufacturing center over the course of the century—indeed, it became the nation's largest industrial complex—and its businessmen were vigorous champions of high protective tariffs. So eager for protectionism was the Philadelphia business elite that it nurtured its own guru of high-tariff economics, Henry C. Carey (1793–1879). Philadelphia manufacturers helped integrate Carey's program into the new Republican party's platform in 1860 and, during the war for the Union, saw it successfully enacted. But the University of Pennsylvania, the city's titular center of higher learning, provided no support for high-tariff economics through the first two-thirds of the nineteenth century.

The institution that was to become the University of Pennsylvania could trace its roots to Benjamin Franklin's dream for a civic-sponsored and nonsectarian college at which the youth of the Pennsylvania Colony could be trained in practical subjects while being spared the adornments of the ancient languages. Part of his vision was realized, and part was not. The "College of Philadelphia"—chartered to award degrees in 1755—was initially funded by laymen of the city who steered clear of identifying it with any particular church. In its early decades, however, day-to-day administration was controlled by clergymen who shaped its curriculum along classical lines familiar elsewhere in colonial

I wish to thank Thomas M. Jacklin, who taught me much of what I know about American ideology. See his forthcoming study of American ideology in this period, *The Civic Awakening*. Much of this essay derives from my *Pragmatic Imagination: A History of the Wharton School, 1881–1981* (Philadelphia: University of Pennsylvania Press, 1982).

America. When reconstituted after the American War of Independence, the institution acquired a new name: the University of Pennsylvania. This elevation in status could then be justified by the presence of a medical school. But the undergraduate college remained a small and local operation throughout the period before the Civil War. Within the overall university, the professional schools (initially in medicine and later in law) predominated. These schools scarcely dealt with tariffs or political economy. The undergraduate college did so, though it seldom catered to more than 150 or so young men aged fourteen through eighteen.[1]

In the classical curriculum pursued in the undergraduate college before the Civil War, economics had no independent standing. The subject appeared only in courses on moral philosophy that ranged widely over the broad field of civics and social ethics. When the school's longtime moral philosopher, Henry Vethake (1792–1866), lectured on economics—as he did from 1837 to the 1860s—he rather conventionally followed the lead of David Ricardo. And Vethake's instruction included Ricardo's famous defense of free international trade. In the eyes of the city's growing community of manufacturers, the university thus did worse than shirk its civic duty to advance the protectionist standard. Instead, it promoted what Philadelphia's industrial fathers saw as that pernicious British evil, free trade.[2]

THE ACCOMMODATION TO PROTECTIONIST DOCTRINE IN THE 1870S AND EARLY 1880S

Philadelphia's manufacturers saw their influence expand over the course of the nineteenth century, and when they were able they remedied this civic embarrassment at the University of Pennsylvania. They sat on the institution's Board of Trustees in increasing numbers and paid a growing portion of the university's bills. The industrial community supported the adoption of an elective system in 1866–67: This was the critical break with the unified classical undergraduate curriculum that would allow the development of economics in a more vocational and present-minded program. Students would henceforth elect one of several curricula offered by the university, in either science, classics, modern foreign languages, or general contemporary education. In line with this shift toward practicality, the manufacturing community also improved, to its way of thinking, the quality of economics instruction at Pennsylvania. The school began teaching Francis Bowen's mild protectionism in 1860–61. Then, in 1864–65, during the highpoint of the nationalist campaign to save the Union, the university embraced Carey and full-blooded Philadelphia protectionism. Finally, in the 1869–70 academic year, Careyite social science became a required course in the general, or "English," elective curriculum.[3]

The industrial community's influence on the city's higher education reached a climax in 1881. In that year Joseph Wharton, a local metals manufacturer, donated $100,000 to the university to establish a school for educating businessmen and public leaders. The Wharton School of Finance and Economy, the first of its kind in the United States, established a new undergraduate curriculum, which students could elect after two years of general liberal education. Students passing through the program were to be trained for executive positions in business and government—for the world of practical affairs. Wharton was most insistent on rectifying wayward economics instruction. He believed free trade to be a "fungus . . . which healthy political organisms can hardly afford to tolerate" and insisted that "no apologetic or merely defensive style of instruction must be tolerated upon this point, but the right and duty of national self-protection must be firmly asserted and demonstrated." Should Pennsylvania slacken in its teaching of protectionism, Wharton reserved the right to reclaim his gift. And for nearly 100 years thereafter, the university housed all economics instruction at Joseph Wharton's school.[4]

The protectionist businessmen's chief ally on the university's faculty was Robert Ellis Thompson (1844–1924). A Pennsylvania graduate and ordained Presbyterian minister, Thompson had first joined the Pennsylvania faculty as an instructor of Latin and mathematics. But he became a Carey enthusiast and in 1868–69 took on the university's new course in "social science." Thompson thus became the first in the nation to carry the title of Professor of Social Science in 1874 and thereafter developed an expanding economics curriculum under that Careyite rubric. His presence on the faculty indeed helped convince Wharton, an active trustee at nearby Swarthmore College, to launch his program at the University of Pennsylvania. Wharton and Thompson knew each other quite well by 1881. Both regularly attended Carey's Sunday afternoon salon, the focal point of the Philadelphia school of economics. Wharton had also financed the publication of Thompson's 1875 protectionist *Social Science and National Economy*. Not surprisingly, this text became the basis of economics instruction at the university's young Wharton School.[5]

Thompson's economics, like the Careyite original, developed in opposition to Ricardo's free-trade orthodoxy. Thompson's and the Philadelphia school's economics nevertheless had a classical base. Thompson, like Carey, constructed his alternate system on a basic premise of Adam Smith's economics—that the division of labor was the source of national wealth—and he used it to refute Ricardo's pessimistic forecast of an inevitably overpopulated planet. Thompson reasoned that the division of labor, and thus productivity, rose with the growth of population. Increasing numbers pushed "men into closer and more helpful association, and [led] them to adopt wiser and better methods."[6] More consumers also meant expanded markets for specific goods and services, allowing efficient production by divided labor and specialized investment. Thompson confidently predicted that these forces making for increasing returns to population would outweigh Ricardo's emphasis on diminishing returns (a conclusion based on the inferior fertility of marginal lands), and he invoked historical evidence to support his claims. Following Carey, Thompson reviewed the development of agriculture, the activity with the greatest exposure to the Ricardian law of diminishing returns, to show that rising population widened the division of labor and increased productivity.[7]

Despite this glorification of specialization and exchange, the Philadelphia economists nevertheless opposed free international trade. Thompson presented his students with two arguments frequently heard in the city. First, he claimed that the English defenders of free trade ignored the basic *social* reality of economic affairs. Whereas the classical economists had derived the division of labor from each individual's "propensity to truck, barter, and exchange," the Philadelphia school emphasized the force of *association*. They reasoned that it was social cohesion rather than self-interest that allowed individuals to specialize; that fellow feeling, more than the market, determined the extent of the division of labor. Nations, the basic social unity in modern times, had a duty to preserve this cohesion by protecting producers from external disruptions.[8]

The second Philadelphia argument was more classical. It emphasized a fact well known to English free-trade economists—that is, the limited scope for the division of labor found in agriculture as against the high division found in industrial pursuits. By Smith's postulate, industry would thus offer more productive potential.

Should a nation turn from industry to agriculture because of international specialization, it would sacrifice future economic strength for the sake of current consumption. That nation, they continued, would eventually experience a contraction in its division of labor and hence a reduction in economic productivity. On the other hand, its trading partner, by expanding its industry and thereby its division of labor, would further enhance its competitive power in manufacturing. To the Philadelphians the process seemed cumulative, with the first nation ending as a raw materials exporter and the second capturing all the gains of economic development. The Philadelphia economists presented case after case where free trade had led to a concentration of manufacturing in the more advanced nation and the virtual abandonment of industry by its trading partner. For nations with a comparative advantage in agriculture, such as the United States, the Philadelphia school predicted economic decay as the outcome of a free-trade policy.[9]

THE EVOLUTION OF THE UNIVERSITY IN THE LATER 1880s AND 1890s

With the founding of the Wharton School, the views of the Philadelphia business community gained in influence over economics teaching at the University of Pennsylvania. This institutional innovation helped promote economics instruction from an addendum in the moral philosophy course to a major portion of the new two-year undergraduate major. More critically, business influence had installed Careyite doctrine, as interpreted by Thompson, as the school's prevailing orthodoxy. Students had only a passing acquaintance with English economists: Wharton used elementary finance texts by Henry Fawcett and W. S. Jevons, but mature English work was absent from its program. The triumph of business influence proved, however, to be short-lived. Already in the early 1880s, it was threatened by a revolution in American academic life—by the rise of the German-style research university, by the Ph.D., and by disciplinary specialization. A new form of learning was quickly taking hold, and either the university adjusted to the new standards or it would be left behind. The Reverend R. E. Thompson, although a brilliant lecturer and energetic civic figure, did not fit the new academic mould. He resisted specialization in academia. He refused to keep up with the latest academic literature and instead maintained a thriving side practice as a journalist and editor. Regarding Thompson as an obstacle to progress, the university leadership sought fresh blood for its economics program. In time, the students themselves began clamoring for more analytical and conventional instruction.[10]

The first attempt to address the problem led to the appointment, in 1883, of Edmund J. James (1855–1922) as head of the Wharton School. Born and raised in Illinois, James traveled to Germany where he earned a Ph.D. in economics at Halle under Johannes Conrad. He was hired to teach public finance and administration, an instructional area ranging from taxation systems to constitutional structures. But more importantly, James was expected to bring German neocameralistic economics—the science of state economic policy making—to Pennsylvania. Moreover, James's brand of midwestern Republicanism meshed well with the local scene. Both branches of the GOP favored positive governmental programs such as education and internal improvements. Both demanded protection from what they saw as unfair competition: The midwesterners feared slave labor and plantation agriculture, whereas Philadelphia feared British industrialism. German economics suggested a design for the development of a business-oriented program at Wharton. James divided business research and instruction as the Germans divided economics, on the basis of practical problems rather than on the basis of categories suggested by economic theory. His first organizational scheme examined specific industries: railroading, insurance and manufacturing. But he soon recast the program along functional lines: accounting, finance, marketing, and management. Economics played a role in the general education of James's business specialists, but it did not become a major object of study, as Joseph Wharton had believed that it should be in his conception of business education.[11]

James also sought to create an American equivalent of the Verein für Socialwissenschaft, a leading German organization devoted to promoting scientific research on policy issues and bringing its results to the attention of government officials. James first attempted to establish a "Society for the Study of the National Economy" and circulated a draft constitution among younger American economists that stressed the importance of governmental intervention to "promote all the conditions for a sound industrial system." This initiative, taken in 1884, failed to win widespread support (though Richard T. Ely subsequently built on its foundations when launching the American Economic Association in 1885). James had much greater success with two other organizations: the American Academy of Political and Social Science (founded in 1889) and the National Municipal League (founded in 1893). Here he fashioned a working symbiosis between the economist and society, with academicians researching and civic leaders promoting good government policy. These institutions were essentially exercises in the liberal Republican, or mugwump, tradition of the 1880s; they campaigned to replace corrupt machine politics with university-trained civil servants and independent professional opinion. James's own exposé of Philadelphia's municipal gas system established a model of such cooperation. Of course, he could not control the institutional development of American professional economics. But with the American Academy and the National Municipal League, he created impressive platforms for practical-minded policy analysis.[12]

James's specialty, government finance and administration, was central to the German economics profession. But in America the field was peripheral to the mainstream academic concern: the principles underlying the functioning of market systems. As a student of political institutions and government administration, James would today be called a political scientist rather than an economist. Instruction in economics per se thus remained in Thompson's increasingly old-fashioned hands. Mounting discontent among students and faculty eventually led, in 1888, to a change. Thompson was reassigned to the Pennsylvania history faculty, and Simon Patten (1852–1922) was brought in as the university's new professor of economics. Patten and James were well acquainted from their student days at Halle. Patten, however, had been decidedly less successful than James upon his return to America. He remained unemployed on his father's Illinois farm until James called him to Philadelphia. He never cut a figure, as did James—indeed, many confused him with the school janitor. But his intellect and his insightful readings of the economic literature soon won Pennsylvania a broad reputation. Most important for his position in Philadelphia, Patten was a protectionist. Perhaps at James's instigation, he wrote *The Economic Basis of Protection* soon after his arrival. This allowed James to reassure university officials, anxious over Joseph Wharton's sensibilities, that "Dr. Patten . . . can be trusted to look after [protectionist economics]. He is regarded by nearly all economists . . . as the leading scientific representative of this policy." And when Joseph Wharton sent an inspector through the school in 1892, he found Patten sound and the student body well versed in the protectionist gospel.[13]

Though he parted company with the position of classical authors on the matter of free trade, Patten had a high regard for their analytical style and believed that "one cannot too much emphasize Ricardian clearness." His classes traced developments in the classical tradition, through the development of marginalism, and incorporated readings in economic history and the history of economic analysis. Before 1894–95 students entered the Wharton School as juniors, and Patten typically introduced them to economics through Adam Smith's *Wealth of Nations,* Francis A. Walker's *Political Economy,* and one of his own theoretical volumes (either *Protection* or *Dynamic Economics*). The senior class read J. S. Mill (later Marshall) and J. K. Ingram's *History of Political Economy* (later C. Gide and C. Rist). Unlike Thompson, Patten thus presented his innovations, such as his defense of protectionism, within a pedagogical framework recognizing the main lines of theoretical development.[14]

PATTEN'S CONTRIBUTION TO ECONOMIC DOCTRINE

Patten's own thinking, though analytically sophisticated, was formulated within the tradition of unorthodox anti-Ricardianism. Like the German academic school in which he was trained and the amateur school of his adopted city, Patten countered the classical "law" of diminishing returns with a "law" of increasing returns. He traced the springs of a rising per capita output to the steadily widening division of labor, to ongoing technological adaptation, and to the emergence of larger and more powerful organizations. To these conventional anti-Ricardian arguments, Patten added his own extended analysis of consumption. Consumption was then at the forefront of scientific speculation with Ernst Engel, William Stanley Jevons, Leon Walras, and Carl Menger all building their theories around the analysis of demand. In fact, Jevons, Walras, and Menger were constructing a general microeconomic theory in which subjective utility was treated as the ultimate determinant of economic value. They extended Ricardo's key conception of diminishing returns by applying it to consumer behavior. With the aid of the concept of diminishing marginal utility from consumption, they presented a system of gracefully equilibrating neoclassical symmetries.

Patten gave a novel anti-Ricardian twist to the debate over marginal utility by arguing that human societies often experienced increasing returns to all forms of economic activity—that is, to consumption as well as to production. Patten maintained that in a progressive society the power of increasing variety and combination in consumption steadily overcame the tendency toward satiety. In a dynamic economy, Patten held, the multiplicity of new delights grew faster than did the tendency of people to tire of any particular good. In addition, such societies were forever combining old products into savory new items of consumption. Patten pointed out that eating beef with salt, for example, yielded far more pleasure than consuming either by itself. When combining his view of steadily increasing utility with the Philadelphia/German anti-Ricardian premise of steadily rising productivity, he fashioned a tremendously optimistic economic vision.[15]

Keeping faith with his new civic sponsors, Patten deployed his analysis of the ever-expanding progressive economy to the defense of high tariffs. Patten argued that Ricardo's case for free trade, based on the theory of comparative advantage, applied only to technologically static economies. In the course of economic development, Patten held, advances occurred at different times in different sectors. It was thus prudent for a country to diversify its productive base. Productivity in ferrous metals, for example, might rise sharply in one decade and stagnate in the next. In another sector—say the chemical trades—the timing could be reversed. If, under a regime of free trade, a nation specialized in ferrous metals and reduced (or perhaps even dismantled) its chemical capacity, it would be likely to miss out on a future technological revolution in chemicals. As one of Patten's graduate students in the early 1890s summarized this aspect of his mentor's teaching: "Often industries that give the greatest temporary return are not those that give the greatest permanent return."[16] It was Patten's position that sustained economic dynamism was the fruit of social development and was not tied to any particular productive sector. "Civilization causes intelligence," Patten wrote, "and intelligence gives productive power." To the extent that free trade located entire industries in isolated environments, remote from the general advance of scientific knowledge, it thus lowered the long-run rate of economic progress.[17]

Patten solidified his position by presenting a specifically American case for protection. In so doing, he ingeniously combined two classic Ricardian theorems. According to Ricardo's law of comparative advantage, the land-rich United States should concentrate on agricultural production. Moreover, according to Ricardo's theory of rent, a rise in agricultural production would increase the proportion of national income flowing to landlords. Like Ricardo, Patten viewed landlords as a parasitical and unenterprising lot, the natural enemies of labor and enterprise. Both economists felt that a rise in the share of income going to rent would slow the pace of economic development. Thus, in a free-trade regime, the ever more agricultural America would languish whereas its industrial trading partner (say, Britain) would smartly advance.[18] Patten's extended defense of protectionism naturally pleased Joseph Wharton, who held an effective veto over economics instruction at Pennsylvania. Patten's credentials as a theorist meanwhile satisfied the students and the university's academic evaluators.

Patten's tenure at Pennsylvania coincided with a critical juncture in the history of social science. Neoclassical economists were then fast closing in on the central riddle of their discipline: the analysis of market price. This progress was achieved, however, by restricting the focus of the science to short-term relationships of a narrowly economic sort. Only within such a limited framework could economists assume simple and predictable human responses and stable productive patterns. Moral philosophers (such as Adam Smith) and earlier economists (such as John Stuart Mill) had concerned themselves with long-term economic progress. They had discussed the economic influence of religious, social, and psychological forces. Patten, like many of his talented contemporaries, resisted the dramatic movement of theoretical economics toward preoccupation with short-term market equilibriums. Nevertheless, many economists proceeded with the marginalist revolution, pushing it on to its formal conclusions. Others, including Patten, Max Weber, Vilfredo Pareto, and Joseph Schumpeter, insisted on taking a larger view. Patten claimed that there could be "no full discussion of economic problems without bringing political and moral principles into relation with the economic." He defined the "laws" of economics not as stable, objective market relationships but as "what qualities must be impressed upon men in their struggle for that higher civilization which the conditions of life permit."[19]

Patten's major work, *The Development of English Thought*, was published in 1899 after a decade's study of history, psychology, and sociology, as well as economics. Although the book did not exert a great influence on American economics, it had a profound effect at Pennsylvania—on its economics instruction, on the programmatic direction of the Wharton School, and on relations with the Philadelphia elite. Patten began with two simple dichotomies: between will and passivity and between rational and nonrational action. Using these distinctions, he identified four human types. "Clingers" were timid and unthinking folk who readily exchanged everything for survival and a bit of security; "sensualists" were a vigorous and domineering class whose insatiable "strong appetites" thwarted their capacity for rational thinking; "mugwumps" had a highly developed capacity for analytical thought but lacked the will to act against the established structure; finally, "stalwarts" combined rational thought processes with the drive to carry out their programs. "Mugwumps" and "stalwarts" were names for factions within the Republican party and, by making the latter his heroes, Patten signaled a break with James and his mugwump affiliation with the Philadelphia elite. Asserting his own identity, Patten put his faith in a more militant, grass-roots, and midwestern Republicanism.[20]

Patten believed that the degree of success experienced by each psychological type depended, in large measure, on material historical conditions. In the crude stages of human history, the constant struggle for survival denied much play to rational thinking. The swift, instinctual action of the sensualists best mastered the intense, localized conflicts. But with the appearance of wider markets and significant surpluses in fifteenth-century Europe, universalizing rationality became more useful. The Puritans, Patten's first successful stalwarts, developed a capacity for manipulating symbols that permitted them to rise "above custom and tradition." And this mode of thought led to democratic ideals as well:

Democracy would not have its present force if the common qualities of men had not been idealized. Only when the differences and defects of men are overlooked can the concept of free citizens, born with certain natural rights, become vivid enough to control society. The citizen is taught to pride himself on these common qualities. . . . It is upon these instincts that modern societies are built: without them no co-operation would be possible.

The whole anti-Ricardian tradition held that cooperation was the fundamental wellspring of progress. The stalwarts thus emerged as its carrier, but they had to dominate the sensualists if they were to perform their historical mission.[21]

Patten reasoned that a new age of abundance, which he divined in his economic theorizing, required the triumph of the rational classes. Economic scarcity had favored sensualists and clingers. Their "strong appetites"—stuffing their mouths with anything available—kept them alive. Under the domination of sensualists, clingers were also adept at producing large quantities of simple staples, goods requiring little thought but providing basic sustenance. Survival, however, was no longer the overriding economic objective. Greater fulfillment now lay with the rational mugwumps and stalwarts, whose patterns of economic demand and supply had to "be impressed upon men in their struggle for that higher civilization which the conditions of life permit." In consumption, mugwumps and stalwarts thoughtfully avoided excess while searching for variety and new delights. In supply, they were the skilled artisans and professionals who produced such valued and esoteric goods and services.[22]

Victory for the rational classes, Patten feared, was by no means assured. Popular attitudes were slow to adapt to changes in economic circumstances, and much of the population remained mired in habits developed during the era of scarcity. Moreover, he saw the rise of big business as a critical threat. Patten viewed industrial concentrations as vehicles through which rejuvenated sensualists could exploit masses of unskilled and uneducated clingers. This capitalist/proletarian system produced staples more effectively than did artisans and professionals and demanded goods of their own production, rather than the finer output of the rational classes. A specter of a new industrial slavery, in which small independent producers were outcompeted, haunted this transplanted midwesterner. The place of the modern economist, Patten argued, was to lead the nation's stalwarts—its forceful, rational element—in their struggle for abundance. The economist's proper task was to educate and energize middle-class opinion. In his 1908 presidential address before the American Economic Association, Patten demanded that economists take their place "on the firing line of civilization," asserting that "by education and tradition" they were to be "revolutionists." Indeed, their "vehicle should be the newspaper and magazine, not the scientific journal."[23]

THE IMPACT OF PATTEN AT PENNSYLVANIA

American economists followed Patten's presidential advice with the inattention typically lavished on such ceremonial admonitions. But back at Pennsylvania, Patten had real impact. He taught upper-level undergraduates and was especially influential with those studying economics rather than business. Patten was at his best in small graduate seminars, and over the course of the 1890s and 1900s the university built up a strong Ph.D. program. Students came to Philadelphia to study with Patten and to join in his campaign for reform. They also came because the university found money for their support. Charles H. Harrison, who sold his family business to the American Sugar Refining trust and retired to the university provostship in 1895, endowed a host of graduate fellowships. A rapidly growing Wharton undergraduate student body—rising from 59 in 1892, to 150 in 1901, and to 625, in 1912—also generated demand for graduate student instructors. As Pennsylvania then hired many of these students to the faculty, the influence of their mentor became even stronger. Finally, Edmund James, leader of the Wharton program and Patten's good friend and sponsor, had been sacked in 1895 by the incoming provost Harrison. Thus, more by default and serendipity than by design, Patten and his ideas moved to the center of the Wharton program.[24]

Many of Patten's graduate students became leaders in the Progressive movement on the city, state, and national level. A number of the most vigorous also won appointments to the Pennsylvania faculty. Scott Nearing, who joined the economics faculty, was director of the state Child Labor Committee. Clyde King, professor of political science, and William Draper Lewis, future dean of the university Law School, figured prominently in the Progressives' 1914 battle with the Philadelphia Electric Company. Edward T. Devine (a product of Patten's graduate program, though not a member of the faculty) and Roswell McCrea, who would become dean of the Wharton School, served in the vanguard of the nation's young social work profession.[25]

Patten also believed that Pennsylvania undergraduates should be brought into the stalwart crusade. To this end, he encouraged instructors to mobilize the energies of their students as well as to nurture their intellects. Patten took a special interest in Wharton's required freshman survey of contemporary economic problems. This course had been part of the school's curriculum since 1894–95 when Wharton first extended its curriculum over all four years. Patten put Scott Nearing in control of the course and directed him to develop the moral and political dimensions of current economic events. He would have the students experience—not merely analyze—the human dimensions of economic society. Nearing enthusiastically took on the task. Through the text he wrote for the course, through assigned book reviews on the latest Progressive literature, and through his charismatic lecturing style, Nearing introduced incoming students to the full gamut of Progressive issues and sensibilities. Drawing freely on local examples of capitalistic excess, Nearing discussed how specific families made fortunes through such questionable practices as the use of child labor or the

sale of tainted products. With other courses in economics and social science reinforcing this political perspective, the Wharton
School became a hotbed of Philadelphia progressivism.[26]

Meanwhile, the local elite was losing much of its earlier enthusiasm for a liaison with academic economists. The rise of big business, culminating in the great merger wave at the turn of the
century, provided business with a much desired insulation from the
uncertainties of the competitive marketplace. In the new regime,
profit became more predictable and less dependent on the shelter of
tariff protection. Businessmen thus concerned themselves less with
market dynamics—the province of professional economics—and
more with internal corporate management. Protectionism, the
great cause of nineteenth-century Philadelphia, became a minor
issue, and Frederick Taylor, evangelist for scientific management,
replaced Henry Carey as the city's business guru. The pursuit of
honest and efficient government, which had led business to support
James's policy research program, also gave way to a policy of accommodation with the urban machine. And those businessmen
who maintained an interest in academic economics typically found
the profession too theoretical, too hostile, or too obsessed with
regulatory detail.[27]

In the years between 1900 and 1915, a serious rift thus developed between Pennsylvania's economics program and its post-1870
sponsor, the local business establishment. Driven by Patten's ideology, which pictured unbridled big business as the people's main
adversary, the university's economists grew increasingly hostile to
the Philadelphia establishment. Indeed, they supplied inspiration
for the national political movement to tame giant enterprise. The
establishment, for its part, no longer felt an acute need for academic allies to defend protection. The consensual chain between
Pennsylvania's academics and the local elite had reached an end.
Indeed, their relations became more strained than they had been in
the days of Henry Vethake and moral philosophy. Always linked
with Republican ideologies, Philadelphia's economists and businessmen drew apart just as the Republican party itself divided into Bull
Moose and regular factions.

PARTING OF THE WAYS

The rupture came in the summer of 1915. After most members of
the faculty had left campus, and in violation of standard university
practice, the trustees dismissed Scott Nearing. Although the trust-

ees never disclosed their specific reasons, they clearly had several things on their minds. Nearing's agitation over child labor had irritated members of the state legislature, who now threatened to withhold state funds for the university as long as the young economist remained on the faculty. Trustee Joseph Rosengarten, an old friend of the now departed Joseph Wharton, had a simpler complaint. He objected to the fact that

men holding teaching positions in the Wharton School introduce there doctrines wholly at variance with those of its founder and go before the public as members of the Wharton School faculty and representatives of the University, to talk wildly and in a manner entirely inconsistent with Mr. Wharton's well-known views and in defiance of the conservative opinions of men of affairs.

Edward Stotesbury, a university trustee and the most prominent businessman in the city, certainly took offense when Nearing humiliated his stepson, a student in the freshman economics survey class. Nearing had taken a newspaper report of a party at Stotesbury's mansion and had contrasted the food and dress of the guests with that of Philadelphia's working class. He then had detailed the business dealings of those invited, accusing them of monopoly, political corruption, and moral insensitivity. So, despite vigorous faculty and student protest, Nearing's dismissal stood.[28]

Following Nearing's departure, the trustees encouraged a general exodus of Progressive economists. By 1917 their victory was complete: They then rid themselves of Simon Patten. The trustees refused their great economist permission to remain on the faculty after he had reached the age of sixty-five. This was a privilege they normally extended to distinguished scholars. But the trustees viewed Patten as their chief troublemaker and were determined to clean house. A disheartened Patten spent the remaining five years of his life in loneliness and isolation, watching World War I consume the promise of American progressivism. With the departure of Patten and his followers, the university had chosen to do without an intellectually vigorous economics faculty rather than to put up with one so contentious.[29]

Pennsylvania economists, since the abandonment of moral philosophy, had always engaged in policy advocacy. In the early years this strategy had led to growth and creative development. Robert Ellis Thompson had brought Careyite economics to the academic arena. Edmund James had fashioned significant organizational linkages between scholars and practical men for the analysis of public policies. Simon Patten—the central figure in the institutionalization of economics at Pennsylvania—had made impressive analytical contributions while apologizing for protectionism and promoting progressivism. Pennsylvania's economists thus did not take the "objective" road that Mary Furner has discerned in other parts of the United States: They had not abandoned partisan political involvements to augment their authority as impartial scientific experts. But, unlike the story developed by Furner, the failure of "advocacy" at Pennsylvania owed little to internal professional debates; the external environment was clearly most critical. "Advocacy" was a very risky long-run strategy for serious pre–World War I academics. The social context of the profession—the American social and business establishment—could stand only so much insult. And when business finally sued for divorce, Pennsylvania's Progressive economists were the ones who had to relocate.[30]

10

Political Economy in an Atmosphere of Academic Entrepreneurship: The University of Chicago

WILLIAM J. BARBER

R OME WAS NOT built in a day. The University of Chicago almost was. When it opened its doors on October 1, 1892, it did so with a larger complement of students and faculty than any American institution of higher learning possessed before the Civil War. By 1909 the scale of its operations exceeded that of all save two American universities (Columbia and Harvard).[1] This achievement was primarily the result of the collaboration of two men—William Rainey Harper and John D. Rockefeller. Harper supplied the bulk of the ideas required for this rapid institution building, and Rockefeller supplied the bulk of the money.

Rockefeller—flush from his triumphs with the Standard Oil trust—was indeed lavish in his support. By 1910 he had committed more than $36 million to this enterprise and was later to describe this investment as the best he ever made. Money was obviously an essential ingredient to the university's instant creation: It could not otherwise have been "born full-fledged," as Harper had insisted it should be. But access to extraordinary financial resources was not sufficient to account for the arresting speed of the institution's early development. The additional element was Harper's entrepreneurial zeal in devising an innovative mix of educational products and in promoting them aggressively.[2]

Harper (1856–1906) was no stranger to Chicago when he was invited to assume the presidency of the new institution. From 1879 to 1886 he had lived in the city's Morgan Park suburb while serving as Professor of Hebrew and the Cognate Languages at the Baptist Union Theological Seminary located there. He then migrated to

The author gratefully acknowledges the assistance of the staff of the University of Chicago Archives in the gathering of materials for this essay.

Yale (where he had earned a Ph.D. before celebrating his nineteenth birthday). From an academic base in New Haven, Harper acquired an international reputation as a scholar in Old Testament criticism. But he also won prominence as an educational innovator, both through his regular academic activities and through his summer work in the Chautauqua lecture and correspondence courses. He also served as the administrative head of Chautauqua's "College of Liberal Arts."

Rockefeller's links with higher education in Chicago came later. Understandably, the fortune he had amassed attracted attention. Himself a devout Baptist, he was besieged in the later 1880s by petitioners for worthwhile causes—and not least from his co-religionists. Rockefeller was sympathetically disposed toward appeals for financial aid to uplift Baptist higher education, but the form his philanthropy would take was initially far from clear. Forceful arguments were presented to him to underwrite the creation of a major Baptist university in New York or in Washington. Champions of Chicago's cause argued, on the other hand, that educational uplift in the "West" should take precedence. The absence of a major Baptist-sponsored institution in the region, they maintained, entailed the risk that the young of the denomination would be diverted to state universities for their education. Chicago's importance as the economic hub of mid-America further strengthened its cause. But another argument had persuasive power. Baptists had earlier attempted to found a university in Chicago, but that institution had been forced into bankruptcy in 1886. It was thus a matter of honor to expunge this initial failure and to salvage the remnants of the Baptist divinity school. In 1890, when the leadership of the denomination endorsed the Chicago plan, Rockefeller was ready to make financial commitments. The charter then drafted for the new institution provided that the president of the University of Chicago should be a Baptist and that two-thirds of its Board of Trustees should subscribe to the Baptist faith. No religious test, however, was to be applied to members of the teaching staff or to the admission of students to the university.

THE ORIGINAL DESIGN

One of the implied conditions associated with Rockefeller's initial bequest was that Harper should lead the new institution. Harper, in turn, found this proposition attractive on the understanding that he would be allowed to act and think big. He had no taste for building an institution incrementally—for example, by starting with a small undergraduate college and expanding cautiously as the way opened. Instead, the structure of the entire enterprise should be in place from the beginning.

Harper's vision was indeed on a grand scale. The first *Official Bulletin*—published more than a year before formal operations were begun—set out the overall plan. The university was to be organized into three "divisions": (1) the "University Proper," that is, undergraduate and graduate faculties, including professional schools such as the Divinity School; (2) the "Extension Division," that is, off-campus instruction through lectures and correspondence courses; (3) the "Publications Division," that is, sponsorship by the university of scholarly publications through a university press and through professional journals to provide outlets for the research produced in each of the departments.[3] Wags might characterize all of this as "Harper's Bazaar," but Harper was in dead earnest about it.

In the larger scheme of things, the university was to be the vehicle for general cultural uplift and for creative innovation. Instruction, Harper maintained, was an obvious purpose of the institution, but it should be subordinate to investigation. A university's overriding purpose was to expand the frontiers of knowledge. Once that task had been performed, it had an obligation to disseminate its findings widely. Dissemination, in turn, should take forms that would be appropriate to multiple audiences. Novices were welcome in the undergraduate programs, which were divided into two "colleges": a Junior College in which the work of the first two years would be undertaken, with the expectation that a range of disciplines would be explored; and a Senior College in which undergraduates would begin specialization in a major discipline. Postgraduates were to be welcomed to graduate programs, once they had demonstrated their capacity to conduct independent research. But the wider public was also invited to taste the fruits of higher education through the extension program. To top it all, the publications of the university's researchers would enrich the scholarly community throughout the world. Some of the functions that Harper envisaged had, of course, been anticipated by other institutions. Johns Hopkins had led the way in the development of postgraduate research, and by the early 1890s Harvard, Yale, and Columbia had moved in the direction of meshing undergraduate and postgraduate studies. In its comprehensiveness, however, there was nothing to match Harper's project.

Harper was no less innovative in his approach to organizational details. Day-to-day operations at Chicago were to be conducted in a novel way. The academic year was to be divided into four quarters of twelve weeks each (as opposed to the conventional autumn and spring semester pattern). The facilities of the university would thus be in use throughout the year, without the usual break for summer vacation. This calendar, in Harper's judgment, had a number of recommendations. It permitted students to accelerate their progress toward completion of a degree. It made it possible for faculty members—whose contracts prescribed a normal load of teaching in three of the four quarters of the year—to accumulate credits that could be converted into vacations from teaching for a year or two at full salary. It also afforded the university an opportunity to engage outstanding teachers, whether from the United States or abroad, as visitors during the summer quarter while on vacation from their home institutions. In addition, it promoted efficiency through full utilization of the university's physical plant.

Harper's sense of orderly structure also brought to Chicago a more fully articulated table of organization than then characterized most American institutions. In consultation with the president, decisions on personnel and programs were to be made by "departments," each representing a field of knowledge. (In the original design, provision was made for twenty-six such departments, and teaching was conducted in twenty-three of them from the opening day.) A "head professor," in turn, would direct the work of each department. Subordinate ranks were carefully specified. Though professors and associate professors were considered as occupying permanent positions, term appointments were to be made at lesser ranks. (In order of precedence, they were assistant professor, instructor, tutor, docent, reader, lecturer, and fellow.) The age of hierarchy and bureaucracy in higher education had arrived, with Chicago in the vanguard.[4]

Filling all of these slots in short order—between the formal chartering of the university in September 1890 and its scheduled opening on October 1, 1892—was an impressive achievement. Harper encountered some of same difficulties that Daniel Coit Gilman had faced a decade and a half earlier when he set out to build Johns Hopkins from scratch. Many established scholars in major universities were reluctant to move to an untested institution. In one sense, the challenge facing Harper was more formidable than the one Gilman had confronted: Harper planned to fill a much larger number of positions. In a more important sense, Harper's task was easier: For the stars he most wanted, he could produce terms that were compellingly attractive. The scale ultimately set for head professors was a salary of $7,000 per year (at a time when the senior professors at Harvard or Yale were seldom paid more than $4,000). Some nationally significant scholars could be lured at these rates. In fact, nine of his appointees for the first year resigned from presidencies of colleges and universities to take positions at Chicago.[5] The recruiting effort that attracted the most contemporary comment, however, was Harper's "raid" on Clark University. A distinguished group of scientists had been assembled there, and Harper bought nearly half of them—fifteen in all.[6] Harper's takeover bids earned him some enemies in the national academic community, but the publicity accorded to them left no one in any doubt that the University of Chicago was a force to be reckoned with, even before its first students had matriculated.

THE PLACE OF POLITICAL ECONOMY IN THE STARTING LINEUP

By contrast with many of the older institutions of higher learning, curricular advocates for political economy did not have to wage a battle for recognition at Chicago. It was present at the creation. Nor was a struggle necessary there in order for the discipline to gain autonomous departmental status. When Chicago was founded, political economy was linked with history and political science at Johns Hopkins, with political science at Columbia, and with "social science" (and more particularly with Sumner's brand of sociology) at Yale. Chicago began with separate departments of political economy, political science, history, sociology, and philosophy. Even though the dividing lines between these fields were blurred—a matter that would subsequently generate some jurisdictional frictions between departments—Harper's Chicago started off with a disciplinary division of labor that was lacking in older institutions.

At Chicago there was thus never a question about the legitimacy of political economy as a separate field of inquiry. The relevant questions instead were "What kind of political economy?" and "By whom should it be taught?" The answers, however, were not altogether easy to come by. To head his new department, Harper obviously wanted a man of stature with a record of accomplishment that would heighten the institution's prestige. Some of the polemical extremism of the mid-1880s between the "new" and the "old" schools had moderated by the time Harper began to select his faculty. Nevertheless, there was still a potentially awkward problem of choice: All of the potential candidates for head professor—that is, those eligible in the sense that they would add luster to the university—would necessarily have been identified with one camp or the other in the battles of the preceding decade. Harper hoped to form a Department of Political Economy with a mix of perspectives. At the same time, his conception of administrative order presupposed that the head professor would exercise considerable authority over departmental appointments. The extent to which substantive balance could be achieved was thus heavily dependent on the head professor's tolerance for diversity.

In his search for a head professor to lead the Department of Political Economy, Harper turned first to Richard T. Ely, then an associate professor at Johns Hopkins. From Harper's perspective in 1891, Ely's candidacy for this position had much to commend it. Ely had acquired national prominence through his writings and through his activities in forming the American Economic Association. Moreover, Ely's deep commitment to Christian social activism meshed well with Harper's conception of the brand of political economy appropriate in an institution with Baptist sponsorship. In addition, the two men were well acquainted through their joint work in the Chautauqua summer school. Ely, for his part, was receptive to serious discussions about prospects at Chicago. He was then less than satisfied with his situation at Johns Hopkins, where he was pressing for promotion to a full professorship, for more money, and for an autonomous Department of Political Economy under his jurisdiction.[7] Meanwhile, Harper was also negotiating with Herbert Baxter Adams (Ely's superior as head of the Department of History and Political Science at Johns Hopkins) as a potential head professor for Chicago's Department of History.

For more than a year, Harper and Ely communicated about possibilities at Chicago. As early as November 1890, Ely submitted a plan for staffing a new department there. Not surprisingly, his recommendations for junior colleagues—Albert Shaw and Amos G. Warner—were both former students of his at Johns Hopkins.[8] In March 1891 Ely offered a modified and more detailed organizational plan, in which he "would manage the department and take certain aspects of general sociology, social ethics and finance."[9]

But Ely wanted to bargain for more than control of departmental management. He wanted a salary fixed to his specifications. As Harper's discussions with Ely came early in his "headhunting" expeditions, the stipend first mentioned was $4,000. (It was only later—in December 1891—that Harper managed to push the scale for head professors to $7,000.) Ely held out for a minimum of $5,000, stating the case as follows:

It seems to me . . . that you must raise your prices somewhat in order to get the men who will make the university the success which we desire. . . . In political economy we have the saying that high priced labor is the cheapest labor. I think this is eminently the case with regard to universities. The best man for a place is worth, not twenty per cent more than the second best, but a hundred per cent more.[10]

Ely added: "I cannot put myself in the attitude of a candidate. I can only name conditions which I would consider seriously, saying that the sooner you make me an offer the more likely I will be to accept it."[11] Harper did not meet Ely's terms, noting that he regarded $4,000 as "a first class offer," and counseled Ely not to refuse any proposition that Gilman of Johns Hopkins might propose in order to keep him there.[12] Meanwhile, Ely was trying to exploit his Chicago discussions to his advantage at Johns Hopkins. In mid-March 1891 he represented to Gilman that he had declined an offer of the head professorship of social and economic science at the University of Chicago at a salary of $4,000 (to be increased to $5,000 in three years) and with the assurance that he would have three assistants.[13]

Ely overplayed his hand in the spring of 1891. He secured a raise of $500 at Johns Hopkins—to an annual stipend of $3,000—but he remained an associate professor and his appeals for additional staff went unheeded. Nor did he get what he sought from Harper. In his memoirs, written more than four decades after the fact, Ely suggested that he had doubts about working with Harper at that time. In this retrospective account, he reported that Harper was "anxious" to recruit him to head the department but that, on the basis of their association at Chautauqua, he feared Harper would be "too stern a master" who "cracked the whip over his associates."[14] Technically, Ely never received an official offer from the University of Chicago (though he was later to protest to the contrary). No formal appointment was ever approved by the university's Board of Trustees. Nevertheless, he was presented with terms which—had he agreed to them—would have formed the basis for an official invitation. Ely chose to play for higher stakes, and he lost. If Harper had chosen to meet them—which he did not—Chicago economics might well have been launched under Ely's direction. Ely's circumstances at Johns Hopkins were deteriorating to the point that a change was in the offing. Harper's terms in March 1891 were considerably better than those Ely settled for a year later when he moved to the University of Wisconsin.

More by happenstance than by design, Harper identified another candidate for the head professorship in J. Laurence Laughlin. Their paths crossed in the autumn of 1891 when Harper was on a recruiting trip to Cornell, the primary purpose of which was to persuade a professor of Latin there to migrate to Chicago. The two men met socially on this occasion, and Harper came away impressed. In early December 1891 Harper had an opportunity to observe Laughlin in action while defending monometallism in a debate sponsored by the Baptist Social Union of New York. Before the evening was over, Harper proposed that he take on the position at Chicago. Laughlin held out for more money and won: The salary scale for head professors was then established at the $7,000 figure. On December 29, 1891, Chicago's Board of Trustees officially confirmed Laughlin's appointment.[15]

Laughlin (1850–1933) and Ely were studies in contrasts. Laughlin was a major spokesman for "old-school" economics and had little but contempt for Ely's passion for interventionist solutions to social and economic problems. He distanced himself from what he took to be the dangerous doctrines associated with the organizers of the American Economic Association and identified instead with the conservative orientation of the Political Economy Club (of which he had been one of the founding members).[16] Whereas Ely had maintained that economics at Chicago should aspire "to make its influence felt on political life and to elevate practical politics,"[17] Laughlin believed that a new department should devote at least part of its energies to exploring the practical problems of concern to businessmen.

Laughlin obviously had qualities that Harper valued in a department head. He was a figure of prominence through his writings— which included the preparation of a textbook edition of John Stuart Mill's *Principles of Political Economy* as well as articles in the journals of the day—and through his speeches to popular audiences in defense of sound money. He had respectable academic credentials: A.B. (1873) and Ph.D. (1876) from Harvard. He had a solid reputation as a teacher as an instructor and assistant professor at Harvard (1878–88) and as a professor at Cornell (1890–92). In addition, he had administrative experience in his background, acquired as the president of an insurance company in Philadelphia during a two-year furlough from academic life.[18]

THE INITIAL ATTEMPT TO BALANCE THE TICKET

Harper was well aware of the crossfire between the rival camps in American economics in the early 1890s, and he wanted Chicago to have a foot in each. After appointing Laughlin, he approached Edward W. Bemis, an Ely disciple then teaching at Vanderbilt University, who had also lectured in the Chautauqua summer school. Bemis would certainly add variety to Chicago economics. Its work otherwise would be exclusively in the hands of Laughlin and three of his transplants from Cornell (Adolph C. Miller as an assoicate professor, William Caldwell as a tutor, and Thorstein Veblen as a fellow). Laughlin, however, balked at the proposition that Bemis be included in the regular roster of the department.

Laughlin's attitude on this point came as no surprise to Harper. Anticipating it, he proposed to bring Bemis in through a side door. Bemis's appointment would officially be designated as an associate professor in the Extension Division of the university where he could operate outside Laughlin's jurisdiction. This was agreeable to Bemis, who informed Harper that it would be "most embarrassing and hazardous for myself or indeed any man of the new economic movement" to be placed in a position subordinate to Laughlin. But, at least in Harper, Bemis believed he had a champion—and one who "did not intend to have any one school of economics dominate in the U'v's'ty, but would have all sides represented on an equal footing." Ultimately, Bemis hoped that he would be able to enjoy equivalent status with Laughlin, not just independence from him. He presented his conception of the optimal arrangement in the form of a question to Harper.

Would it not be possible to recur to your idea of representation of both schools and to make my call and work independent of Prof. L—— and representative of the historic school, creating, as it were, a possibility of a double department in the future when you might wish to call another head professor to be equal with Laughlin?[19]

By keeping Bemis's primary responsibilities on a track separate from the Department of Political Economy, it appeared that possibilities for friction could be minimized. But they could not be eliminated altogether. Bemis expected to enjoy his work in the Extension Division, but he did not wish to allocate all of his professional time to that enterprise. As he described his aspirations to Harper: "I hope to do my fundamental work and build my reputation chiefly upon work inside University walls and upon economic writing."[20] As a condition of accepting employment at Chicago, Bemis insisted that part of his assignment should be within the University Proper. Accordingly, the terms Harper negotiated called for him to work full-time in the Extension Division for two quarters of the academic year and to teach in the University Proper during the third quarter. This formula was not likely to be entirely trouble-free: Laughlin still had doubts about Bemis's competence (or, for that matter, about the competence of any Ely-trained economist). For his part, however, Bemis did his best to establish a modus vivendi.[21] But, in the event that mutually acceptable working relationships could not be established between the two men, it seemed possible to satisfy Bemis's demand for space within the University Proper through an affiliation with the Department of Sociology. Its head professor, Albion Small, had overlapped with Bemis during their graduate studies at Johns Hopkins. Small stood ready to offer hospitality to Bemis, writing that "I know and value your work, and shall be glad to have some of it in the department of sociology." But there was also a cautionary note in Small's reaction to this proposition: "it would please me if you would make your courses largely descriptive, and only incidentally and secondarily controversial."[22] During the first year of the university's operations, Bemis was, in fact, listed on the masthead of both the Department of Political Economy and the Department of Sociology. His teaching assignment in economics, however, was peripheral. The mainstream teaching of the department was carried on by Laughlin and his three colleagues imported from Cornell. Between them they offered a varied menu of courses, the integrating aim of which (in the words of the department's official statement of purpose) was "to teach methods of work, to foster a judicial spirit, and to cultivate an attitude of scholarly independence."[23]

Chicago's Department of Political Economy also got off to a fast start in establishing its presence before the wider professional community. The first issue of its *Journal of Political Economy* was published before the university had been in operation for a full three months. This undertaking was part of Harper's vision of the mission of the University of Chicago: Each department there was expected to produce a scholarly journal. The Department of Political Economy was the first to rise to this challenge.[24] When introducing the first issue, Laughlin set out its credo: The academic community had a responsibility to enlighten the public on the proper way to approach the complex economic problems the nation confronted. In his judgment, there was a "desire to learn to think correctly in these subjects" and the need for learning was great. "Never in our history," he asserted, "have venerable fallacies and misinterpretations been more widely current. . . . We seem to be passing through what may be called an exceptional development of the heart without a corresponding development of the head."[25] Academic economists had an obligation to redress this situation through "new means of communication between the investigator and the public." This was especially important "in view of the practical opportunities for investigation in the central states of the Union." The *Journal of Political Economy* was thus to be "devoted largely to a study of practical problems."[26]

FURTHER TURMOIL OVER BEMIS

Relations between Laughlin and Bemis had never been easy, and they deteriorated during the first year of their association at Chicago. In August 1893 Laughlin advised Harper that Bemis's presence—even though only part-time—"seriously impair[ed] the *morale* of his department" and recommended that Bemis's assignment within the University Proper be transferred to the Sociology Department. If that could be accomplished, he would then pose no objection to Bemis's role in the Extension Division, "even though I do not believe he is competent to treat a difficult economic problem."[27] Meanwhile, Harper was beginning to have doubts about Bemis's longer-term usefulness to the university. Bemis's lectures in the Extension Divison had not lived up to expectations: Indeed, Harper regarded them as essentially a failure. Accordingly, the president advised Bemis in January 1894 that he would do well to seek his future elsewhere.[28] Bemis was being urged, though not compelled, to leave. But, if he stayed on, his work within the University Proper would be assigned to Sociology.[29]

Laughlin was no doubt relieved to have Bemis become Small's problem rather than his. At the same time, he did not wish it to be said that his department could not live with diversity. Others were better qualified than Bemis—as Laughlin saw matters—to represent divergent perspectives. He nominated two candidates for Harper's consideration. John Graham Brooks—whom he characterized as being in "great demand" in Boston for his lecturing and advising on such topics as the "liquor traffic, workingmen's insurance, labor organizations, the unemployed, etc."—deserved a try.[30] In addition, he supported David Kinley of the University of Illinios, whose work he regarded as "of a radically different kind from

Bemis', and yet he is one of Ely's men."[31] Brooks, in fact, joined the Extension Division staff of the university with privileges to teach part-time within the regular Department of Political Economy. The Kinley nomination, however, proved to be a nonstarter.

Bemis was on notice as early as January 1894 that his status at the university was problematic. It became even more so in the following July. The city of Chicago was then the storm center of bitter controversy occasioned by the Pullman strike. What had begun as a work stoppage by employees of the Pullman Company over wage cuts had escalated into a sympathetic boycott ordered by Eugene Debs, the leader of the American Railway Union, who instructed his members not to handle Pullman cars or equipment. The resulting disruption of rail traffic into and out of Chicago set in motion a chain of events that culminated in the arrest of Debs and the dispatch of federal troops to Chicago, where a state of insurrection was alleged to exist. Passions over the claims of capital and labor had seldom run higher when Bemis participated in a panel on "Some Lessons of the Strike" convened at Chicago's First Presbyterian Church. Bemis then took the following position:

If the railroads would expect their men to be law abiding they must set the example. Let their open violations of the Interstate Commerce Law and the relation to corrupt legislatures and assessors testify as to their part in this regard. . . . [B]oycotts on the part of railroads are no more to be justified than a boycott of the railroads by strikers. Let there be some equality in the treatment of these things.[32]

By late twentieth-century standards of public discourse, such comments would be dismissed as innocuous. But in Chicago in mid-summer 1894, the atmosphere was different. Prominent figures in its business community were angered, and none more so than Marvin Hughitt, president of the Chicago and Northwestern Railroad. As a member of Bemis's audience, Hughitt denounced such utterances by a man holding a position at the University of Chicago.

Harper liked publicity, but not publicity of this kind. He admonished Bemis to "exercise very great care in public utterances about questions that are agitating the minds of the people" during the remainder of his connection with the university, adding that Bemis's speech had "caused him a great deal of annoyance."[33] To Laughlin, Bemis's behavior was proof positive of his incompetence. He advised Harper that it was time to let the public know "that he goes because we do not regard him as up to the standards of the University in ability and scientific methods." Bemis, Laughlin observed, was "wholly one-sided on this railway question." Laughlin further intimated that Bemis had damaged the prospects of one of his pet schemes: the creation of a center for the study of railway economics within the Department of Political Economy. As he put the matter: "in antagonizing Pres. Hughitt he is making very difficult the establishment of a great railway interest in the University."[34]

During the academic year 1894–95, the atmosphere in Chicago's departments dealing with the social sciences remained unpleasant. Bemis was still on the premises. In March 1895, however, Harper and Small officially asked for his resignation. He might continue in the Extension Department, but, if he did so, his remuneration would henceforth be based on student fees rather than on a contractual salary.[35] Bemis, who made no claims to effectiveness in his extension lecturing, understood that he needed another job. Finding one was another matter. His attractiveness elsewhere would not be enhanced if his difficulties at Chicago were construed as turning on his competence (as Harper, Laughlin, and Small maintained). On the other hand, his attractiveness to other employers might be increased if his problems there were perceived as stemming instead from his expressions of views that angered the rich and the powerful. Bemis thus had a stake in presenting himself as a casualty of political victimization.

Bemis needed allies, and he turned naturally to his old Johns Hopkins mentor, Richard T. Ely. Ely lent sympathetic support, but for reasons that were as much anti-Chicago as they were pro-Bemis. To be sure, Ely's position on social issues of the day meshed with those espoused by Bemis. At the same time, Ely had personal as well as intellectual reasons for casting senior members of the University of Chicago in the role of villains. None of the regular members of its Department of Political Economy had supported him—though prominent economists of differing persuasions at other institutions had done so—during his difficulties with the regents of the University of Wisconsin during the summer of 1894.[36] Perhaps even more distressing to Ely was Harper's decision, communicated in January 1895, to dismiss him from the Chautauqua faculty.

Between them, Ely and Bemis contrived to present the impression to the public that the University of Chicago was the captive of big business interests and that they, in turn, were responsible for Bemis's undoing. Bemis and Ely had no evidence to document the claim that outsiders intervened in the university's personnel decisions. But there was enough in the context of the situation—for example, the university's link to massive private wealth, the displeasure of university officers with Bemis's prolabor sympathies—to stir the imaginations of the suspicious. Ely added fuel to the fire by passing the word that he had declined the head professorship in political economy "because the institution was supported in part by a monopolist."[37]

This campaign took a particularly ugly turn in August 1895—just as Bemis's connection with the university was being severed—when he and Ely arranged to plant an anonymous letter in the *New York World* asserting that Harper had "denied" that Ely had ever been offered a professorship at the University of Chicago.[38] Ely followed this up with a letter to Harper stating that he found it "incredible that you could have made any such statement. You repeatedly offered me the head professorship of Political Economy in the University of Chicago."[39] Ely requested Harper to correct the statement attributed to him, threatening that, if Harper failed to do so, "it might compel me to state some things which I would prefer to keep to myself. . . . I have never made public the reasons why I declined your offers."[40] Harper did not rise to this bait. He must, however, have regretted his choice of phrase in correspondence with Ely more than four years earlier when he referred to a $4,000 salary as a "first class offer" when Ely was insisting on a minimum of $5,000. But Ely must also have known that there was a limit beyond which he could not press his threat to embarrass Harper publicly. If challenged to produce evidence of an official letter of appointment at the University of Chicago, Ely would not have been able to deliver the goods.

Meanwhile, Bemis was becoming increasingly desperate. In October 1895 he released a statement to the press suggesting that only the pressure of monopolists could account for his dismissal. This did provoke a response. The university's official statement in rebuttal argued that

the prominence which this case has attained through the press is not the result of misunderstanding, but . . . it is the carrying out of a deliberate design to misrepresent the facts. We believe that Mr. Bemis has received advice which has made him the tool of private animosity toward the University. . . . Both Mr. Bemis and his mentor have refused to act in accordance with the positive testimony of those who knew the facts, and have persisted in misconstruction of indirect evidence to suit their purpose of detraction.[41]

Ely's name was not mentioned, but there can be no doubt about the identity of the "mentor" referred to in these remarks.

Indicative of the form of publicity in circulation at the time was a letter received by Albion Small, Head Professor of Sociology and editor of the *American Journal of Sociology,* from an unidentified correspondent in Boston:

I can look for no lasting good from a work that is conducted by an educational institution founded by the arch-robber of America and which already, by its treatment of Professor Bemis, exhibits a determination to throttle free investigation of sociological or economic subjects whenever there is any danger of running counter to plutocratic interests.[42]

Small felt obliged to respond at length to this indictment in the journal's first issue.

The first attempt to blend divergent approaches to economics into a common enterprise at Chicago thus ended disastrously. But the effort to bring balance to the ticket was not totally abandoned. Brooks was reengaged as a visitor. More significant was the appointment of Edmund Janes James (of the University of Pennsylvania) to a professorship in the Extension Division. James, along with Ely, had been in the forefront of the "new" economics movement of the German-trained economists in the 1880s. His arrival at Chicago, which Laughlin opposed, kept a "new-school" perspective on the scene. James's departmental affiliation within the University Proper was with Political Science as a Professor of Public Administration. Harper steered clear of Laughlin when arranging James's assignment.

Following his departure in August 1895, Bemis was treated as a nonperson in Harper's annals of the achievements of the university.[43] In the volume produced to celebrate the publications of Chicago's faculty during the university's first decade, Bemis (whose work had been published in the *Journal of Political Economy*) was omitted. This cannot be explained as a clerical oversight. Publications of other departed faculty members were included, as were those of faculty members—such as James—whose primary responsibilities were in the Extension Division. Bemis was quite deliberately excluded.[44]

THE WORK OF THE DEPARTMENT, 1895–1902

The Bemis affair put Chicago economics in the headlines. Less conspicuous was the ongoing work of the Department of Political

Economy, which became increasingly systematized in the mid-1890s. Beginning in the academic year 1895–96, its courses were grouped into four categories:

1. Introductory (in which Laughlin's edition of Mill served as a basic text)
2. Theoretical (e.g., courses in Scope and Method, Unsettled Problems in Economic Theory, History of Political Economy, Socialism)
3. Practical (e.g., courses in Social Economics, Money, Statistics, Railway Transportation, Tariff History, Financial History, American Agriculture, Banking, Finance)
4. Seminars (usually conducted for graduate students under Laughlin's guidance) [45]

Students responded positively to these arrangements. Enrollments steadily increased. Analysis of the distribution of elective courses selected by students receiving a bachelor's degree prior to June 1901 revealed that 66 percent of the men had chosen courses in political economy (with only the Department of History recording a higher percentage).[46] Meanwhile, there was a lively interest in the department's graduate program, which produced eleven Ph.D.'s during the first decade.[47] Five in this early crop of Chicago doctorates in political economy were to hold teaching posts in the department of the student of this period who was later to leave the most significant mark on the development of American economics—Mitchell).

In a typical year in the later 1890s, the department carried six regular staff members, and their ranks were supplemented on occasion by visitors for a quarter or two.[48] Of the regular members, however, only three—Laughlin, Miller, and Veblen—were on the payroll continuously throughout the first ten years. In the judgment of the student of this period who was later to leave the most significant mark on the development of American econonics—Wesley C. Mitchell—there was a valuable complementarity in their work.[49] Laughlin won respect for his dedication to the welfare of his students, many of whom referred to him affectionately as "Uncle Larry." Though he came through as rigid and dogmatic, these qualities nonetheless made for effective pedagogy: Students were inspired to think hard about issues on which they disagreed with him. Miller was polished, clear, and precise in his presentations to the point that the most complex material appeared to be deceptively straightforward. Veblen's unorthodox style, with its skeptical and satirical qualities, provided a counterpoint. Mitchell regarded Veblen as a fundamental influence on his own intellectual development. Veblen challenged his students to rethink the way in which economic phenomena should be analyzed and understood. Those who grasped his message—and not all of them did—could not thereafter look at economic theory in quite the same way. He was an antidote to intellectual complacency.[50]

In keeping with Harper's conception of the linkage between instruction and investigation, members of the Department of Political Economy during its first decade meshed teaching with scholarship. Laughlin's scholarly interest was primarily in monetary economics, which he approached from the perspective of "sound" money— that is, a gold-based monetary standard. His central contribution to the debates of the 1890s was a critique of the quantity theory of money. The form in which he espoused that position was, in turn, shaped by his hostility to claims advanced by the advocates of free silver. In his view, the argument that expansion in the money supply through the free coinage of silver would raise the price level (and, among other things, ameliorate the grievances of farmers) was unsound. He took it to be an obligation of "scientific" economists to expose the fallacies of this doctrine and to educate the untutored in the citizenry who had been beguiled by it. Neither theory nor empirical observation, Laughlin insisted, could establish a direct connection between enlargement in the money supply—which he defined narrowly as the monetary metals, thus excluding bank deposits—and the behavior of the general price level. Price levels instead were determined by longer-term conditions governing costs of production. When technological change generated efficiencies in the production process, the normal competitive environment would naturally tend to generate price reductions. These changes were quite independent of the money supply.

Laughlin's line of attack on the quantity theory was sharply criticized by many of his non-Chicago professional colleagues. (It was, in fact, a critique of the crude quantity theory rather than of the more sophisticated statement of the equation of exchange.) But this approach suited Laughlin's immediate polemical objective: an assault on the free-silverites. In 1895 and 1896 Laughlin came into public prominence in debates with William H. ("Coin") Harvey, the author of the widely circulated popular tract supporting the Populist position on free silver. The tone of Laughlin's comments on "unsound" money proposals was more intensely partisan than Bemis's remarks had been at the time of the Pullman strike. Laughlin genuinely believed, however, that there was a crucial distinction between his own role in the discussion of controversial issues and the one Bemis had played. Laughlin regarded his intervention as an effort to enlighten the public on truths based on "scientific" findings. Academicians should be engaged, but with the head, not with the heart.[51]

Miller's work had no comparable public drama associated with it. His primary teaching assignments were in the fields of public finance and taxation, with some attention as well to questions of money, industrial organization, and international trade. He produced no major book while at Chicago, though a number of articles emerged from his pen. These were competent professional performances but not ones that left memorable marks on the flow of professional discussion. All were published in the *Journal of Political Economy*.

Veblen's teaching responsibilities were more varied. They evolved gradually and in a manner that reflected his own intellectual interests. During the academic year 1892–93 (while still a "fellow"), he developed a course on "Socialism." He enlarged his repertoire in the following year. He was then advanced to the rank of reader and added a course on "American Agriculture," a by-product of two articles he had prepared for the *Journal of Political Economy*.[52] By the middle 1890s, Veblen's teaching had been extended to include the History of Political Economy. But his most original contribution to the curriculum was the creation of a course entitled "Economic Factors in Civilization," the scope of which was described as follows:

The course is intended to present a genetic account of the modern economic system by a study of its beginnings and the phases of development through which the present situation has been reached. To this end, it undertakes a survey of the growth of culture as affected by economic motives and conditions. With this in view, such phenomena as the Teutonic invasion of Europe, the Feudal system, the rise of commerce, the organization of trade and industry, the history of the condition of laborers, processes of production, and changes in consumption, will be treated.[53]

This course served as a laboratory in which themes that found their way into *The Theory of the Leisure Class* were worked out.

But the scope of the professional work of the department's members extended well beyond their individual activities in teaching and scholarship. The work initiated there through the *Journal of Political Economy*—with Veblen serving as its managing editor—enriched the national and international discourse among professional economists. Much of the material in the first issues was produced "in-house"—that is, by faculty members and by graduate students. But contributions from leading figures in the discipline in the United States and abroad also appeared.[54] Nor was it necessary to subscribe to a particular party line in order to have articles appear within its pages. Bemis was published in the early issues. Moreover, despite Laughlin's strongly held views on sound money, material critical of his position appeared.

These were notable achievements, and they owed much to Laughlin's doggedness and enterprise as an organizer. He took his position as head professor seriously. As he understood it, his duty required a determined defense of the prerogatives and of the autonomy of his department. At times, this brought him into conflict with the university's central administration. In the intrauniversity infighting, he lost at least as many battles as he won. But Harper was frequently reminded that Laughlin was perhaps the least pliable of his head professors.[55]

Among the battles that Laughlin did win, one gave him great satisfaction: the creation of a College of Commerce and Administration, which began operations in 1898. Laughlin had long believed that the university was excessively preoccupied with training future teachers to the exclusion of studies preparing students for practical careers in business. In his view, the latter were as worthy as any others for systematic treatment within the halls of academe. Laughlin stated the case as follows:

> For the great professions of Railway Management, Banking, Insurance, Trade and Industry, Diplomacy, Politics and Journalism, a student would be at a loss to know where to find schools adapted to his purposes. . . . The men and women wishing to enter professions above indicated, should, no longer step directly from the high school to the desk and counter, but they should find a course of liberal training open to them, which at the same time will train them to deal fitly with problems of their future careers and give them a wider outlook and profounder insight into the active life upon which they are entering.[56]

The new venture was initially organized as a collaboration among the departments of Political Economy, Political Science, History, and Sociology. Early results were disappointing: In the academic year 1901–2, only 7 of 311 baccalaureate graduates completed their work in the College of Commerce and Administration.[57] Even so, the seeds of what would ultimately become a professional school of business had been sown.

REASSESSMENTS AND REALIGNMENTS, 1902—1905

When the university celebrated its tenth anniversary in 1902, the prevailing mood was one of self-congratulation. A series of Decennial Publications was commissioned acclaiming the accomplishments of a decade and celebrating the scholarly performances of faculty and students. Harper, however, was then less than euphoric about the state of the Department of Political Economy. Two of its members, Adolph Miller and Wesley C. Mitchell, had decided to leave in favor of the University of California and for reasons that Harper found to be disconcerting.[58] His discussions with both men, he advised Laughlin, led to the following conclusion:

There is a strong feeling that the Department of Political Economy in our University is isolated from the work of Political Economy throughout the country; that the members of our staff do not come in contact with other men interested in the same subject, and with the work at large; that perhaps by going to some other institution a better relationship with the outside economic world can be secured.[59]

Laughlin was stunned by this indictment of his management of departmental affairs and replied at length. With respect to the charge that his department was isolated "from the work of Political Economy throughout the country," he wrote:

That refers either (a) to me, or (b) to other members of the corps. (a) If to me, I beg to say that I am intimately informed as to the work going on elsewhere; and my personal relations with such men as H. C. Adams, J. W. Jenks, R. T. Ely, J. B. Clark, A. T. Hadley, H. W. Farnam, etc. are very friendly and cordial. (b) If to other instructors, they all know perfectly well they are free to form any personal relations they please with other men elsewhere. This point is rather absurd. If they are "isolated," they are so only in the sense that any scholar, in any department, is isolated—because of engrossing occupation in study, or lack of means to travel,—or to inertia (in one possible case). And each man, in his specialty, keeps himself (with one well-known exception) well informed as to the work done elsewhere, not merely in this country, but in Europe.[60]

Laughlin took strong exception as well to the allegation that "members of our staff do not come in contact with other men interested in the same subject." In his opinion, "We see more outside economists in Chicago than they do at Cornell or Harvard." Men like Henry Carter Adams and John A. Hobson had been invited. Not all members of the staff necessarily bothered to meet visitors when they were on hand: Department members were at liberty to come and go to special lectures. If they failed to make contact with colleagues from other institutions, it was their own fault. Laughlin dismissed the charge that Chicago economists were out of touch "with the work at large" as "incomprehensible." As he put it:

The "work at large" is done either (a) by teaching, or by (b) publication. (a) I think we know the methods of teaching as well as any others of our guild,—or even better. (b) As to publications, very few institutions in the world have better means than ours (with the *Journal,* etc.) of keeping in touch with the progress of thinking in our subjects.[61]

What then could account for an impression that members of his department might secure "a better relationship with the outside economic world" by moving? Laughlin suggested that two factors could explain such a misperception. The first was his refusal "to pool our publications with the Econ. Association," a position that had "excited a feeling that we propose to separate ourselves from the others." A number of the leaders of the American Economic Association had come to "regard Chicago as their most efficient rivals," and "they are ready to make difficulties for us." Much of this friction, Laughlin suggested, could be eliminated if Chicago were to abandon its separate publications, but he had "too much spirit to yield to this kind of pressure." A second source of misunderstanding, in Laughlin's view, could be traced to "the Bemis affair, and attacks upon the University as an organ of great capitalists." This had led to "persistent attempts . . . to misrepresent the economic attitude of our department. . . . We have been represented as intolerant, rigid in our views, narrow, old-fashioned, and unwilling to take new departures." This, of course, was "false, all through." No one had "ever been able to refer to a written, or spoken, statement of mine which justified any such characterization of the department." Indeed, in his own work on money, he had departed so far from the "conservative classical school" that he believed he might "possibly be called an iconoclast. In teaching the general principles, my classes know that I have introduced the most recent points of view—changing and leaving very little of Mill."[62]

Few men are endowed with acute faculties for critical self-analysis: Laughlin was not one of them. In this *apologia pro vita sua,* however, there was an implicit acknowledgment that Chicago economics just might be somewhat segregated from the national mainstream. But, in Laughlin's judgment, this resulted from the jealousy of other institutions and from animosities lingering from the ideological warfare of the 1880s. He further implied that

Harper's initiative in involving the university with Bemis was responsible for mistaken impressions about the character and quality of the work of the department. Laughlin's sincerity and depth of conviction on these matters were beyond dispute.

If Harper had intended to nudge Laughlin to shift the orientation of Political Economy in the direction of significantly greater diversity, he did not succeed. Herbert Davenport and John Cummings—both products of the Chicago Ph.D. program—were engaged in 1903 to cover part of the space vacated by Miller and Mitchell. There was, however, a change in the approach offered within the department to the study of industrial organization. Veblen replaced Miller in this assignment and restyled it as follows:

Organization of Business Enterprises—Trusts. A discussion of the growth of the conditions which have made large business coalitions possible, the motives which had led to their formation, the conditions requisite to their successful operation, the character and extent of the advantages to be derived from them, the drawbacks and dangers which may be involved in their further growth, the chances of governmental guidance or limitation of their formation and of the exercise of their power, the feasible policy and methods that may be pursued in dealing with the trusts.[63]

The ideas that were to flower in Veblen's *Theory of Business Enterprise* (published in 1904) were being developed in this context.

To Laughlin's taste, a quite different alignment in the work of the department—initiated in the academic year 1904–5—was more palatable. Course offerings were then restructured into eight "groups": (1) Introductory and Commercial; (2) Advanced Business Courses (including insurance, accounting, and commercial law); (3) General Economic Fields; (4) Labor and Capital; (5) Money and Banking; (6) Railways; (7) Statistics; and (8) Seminars.[64] The practical subjects, especially those with application to the business world, were thus elevated in status and assigned increased representation. Laughlin wrote with particular pride about the development of studies in the economics of railways. "From the foundation of the university," he asserted, "it had been planned to make the instruction in railway subjects correspond in some degree to the magnitude of railway interests in the greatest railway center of the greatest railway country in the world."[65] That dream now seemed to be approaching realization. Hugo R. Meyer—whom Laughlin described as a man who had made transportation economics "his life-work"—had been engaged to offer new courses on railway rates and on European railway experience. In addition, the curator of Chicago's Museum of Commerce (E. R. Dewsnup) had been appointed as a professorial lecturer on railways, offering evening courses to many who were employed by railways. As a result of this activity, "a new interest and vitality" in this field had been "excited," and the "influence of the University at home and abroad [had] been signally enlarged." Laughlin noted that this effort had been "aided by an Advisory Board, consisting of high officials appointed by the railways themselves" and anticipated that it might lead to the creation of a "Railway College intended for all those looking forward to a railway career."[66]

In the aftermath of the reevaluation prompted by the departure of Miller and Mitchell, the contacts of Chicago economists with academic colleagues throughout the nation expanded somewhat. Laughlin joined the American Economic Association in 1904, and the university invited the historical and economic associations to a joint meeting in the city.[67] Meanwhile, the department's contacts with the Chicago business community expanded considerably. Veblen's presence meant that the department still had an anti-establishmentarian voice. Veblen's days at Chicago, however, were drawing to a close. That he survived there as long as he did was an outcome that owed much to Laughlin's interventions on his behalf. The two men could hardly have been more different in their styles, in their temperaments, and in their view of what economics was really about. Yet Laughlin respected Veblen's intelligence. It was Laughlin, after all, who had rescued Veblen from academic oblivion by finding fellowship money to support him at Cornell in 1891, and it was he who had brought him to Chicago in 1892. Laughlin would have preferred to see Veblen direct his talents into more conventional channels and was disappointed when Veblen did not do so. Even so, Veblen was useful. His knowledge of languages was a departmental asset.[68] And his erudition was valuable in the editorial work of the *Journal of Political Economy*. Moreover, unlike Bemis, Veblen did not involve himself in political agitation.

Veblen's nemesis at Chicago was Harper. In the president's eyes, Veblen was anything but an ornament to the university. He appeared to be uncouth and, at times, irresponsible.[69] In addition, his teaching—though it made an indelible impression on some of his students—was far from satisfactory in other ways. Very few undergraduates elected his courses. Veblen seemed to live in a private intellectual world and to be unable to adapt to the routine demands of pedagogy.[70] In 1899 Harper informed Veblen that there would be no objection if he resigned, observing that he "did not advertize the University." (Veblen's response was that he had no intention of doing so.)[71] He did manage to stay on and—with the aid of Laughlin's advocacy—he was advanced to the rank of assistant professor in 1900 at a salary of $2,000.[72] He never enjoyed any security of tenure during his years at Chicago; meanwhile, men much younger and less published than he received preferment. Veblen was forced out in 1906. His personal conduct, not his professional conduct, was the straw that broke the camel's back. His wife's absence and his alliance with another woman were more than Harper could tolerate.

Veblen's sojourn at Chicago, where he held a job for longer than he did anywhere else during his career, left no lasting imprint on Chicago's economics. No attempt was made to replicate his brand of iconoclasm. Indeed, had a serious effort been made to do so, it would have been fruitless: What Veblen offered was unique. But the Chicago experience left an indelible mark on Veblen's later writing. *The Higher Learning in America,* subtitled *A Memorandum on the Conduct of Universities by Business Men* (published in 1918), was an undisguised critique of Harper's university.[73] In Veblen's reading, business culture was the dominant force in the shaping of the university. His central thesis, however, was quite different from the one advanced by some of the university's external critics at the time of the Bemis affair: that the institution's association with a "monopolist" compromised freedom of academic expression.

Veblen's main argument was that academic institutions moulded within the environment of a business culture necessarily operated in ways that stifled creativity. This followed, he maintained, because universities had imitated the organization and behavior of the modern corporation. They were led by "captains of erudition" who competed in the marketplace to sell "merchantable instruction." In their struggle to succeed, they were guided by a principle of "sane business practice" that called for "economy of cost as well as a large output of goods." This implied that "it is 'bad business' to offer a better grade of goods than the market demands, particularly to customers who do not know the difference, or to turn out goods at a higher cost than other competing concerns." This approach to academic management meant that instructors should be engaged "at competitive wages and to turn out the largest merchantable output that can be obtained." Moreover, in the interests of efficiency, their instructional product should be packaged in a standardized format. In such an environment, those who conformed—and in ways that enhanced the university's public image—were rewarded, whereas those with the imagination to see beyond routine were likely to be penalized. The end result was a mediocrity that deadened creative thought.[74] This was a far cry from Wayland's judgment in the 1850s that American higher education was stagnating because it was too unbusinesslike in its methods. To the contrary, Veblen insisted that what mattered most in higher learning was being sacrificed because universities had become too businesslike in their operations.[75]

NINETEEN SIX AND THE CLOSE OF AN EPOCH

Harper died and Veblen departed in 1906. Laughlin remained until his retirement a decade later. There were no repetitions of the turbulence that surrounded the Department of Political Economy in its first decade and a half.

The Harper era was decisive in the shaping of Chicago economics. At a number of points in the early going, the direction of its work might have taken a different course. Starting up at a time when American economics was intellectually and ideologically polarized, a new institution could not insulate itself from the internal conflicts in which the discipline was engaged. Harper's attempts to achieve a representative mix of perspectives turned out to be counterproductive. There was no common ground on which Laughlin and the Elyites could meet. One camp was disposed to dismiss its rivals as "unscientific" and "incompetent"; the other camp was inclined to treat its adversaries as morally corrupt and deficient in social conscience. Such attitudes precluded harmonious coexistence. At the same time, Laughlin's department, though it had a well-defined point of view, was not rigidly orthodox. After all, it nourished Veblen for fourteen years.

Learned disputations still rage about whether or not a distinctive "Chicago school" of economics actually exists.[76] Regardless of the way one might choose to characterize Chicago economics in the late twentieth century, one point is indisputable: The observable outcome has been influenced by institutional decisions made in the late nineteenth century.

Political Economy in the Far West: The University of California and Stanford University

MARY E. COOKINGHAM

CALIFORNIA WAS a haven for migrants after World Wars I and II, a place with spectacular scenery, fertile farmland, abundant natural resources, a wonderful climate, and a booming economy. Nineteenth-century reports were equally enthusiastic, and thousands of easterners, southerners, and midwesterners were drawn west by the state's opportunities. In the last half of the nineteenth century, two major institutions of higher education were founded in the state, both of which have produced outstanding economics departments. The early histories of the two schools—one public and one private—are intertwined yet separable, as are the histories of their economics departments. Both rose in eminence in the twentieth century, despite troubled beginnings in the nineteenth century.

California entered the Union as a free state as part of the Compromise of 1850. With this legislation, three centuries of Spanish, Mexican, and American territorial rule ended. The new state had little political infrastructure, a huge land area, and a very sparsely settled population. The economy depended on cattle ranching, mining, and fur trading. According to the census of 1850, only 8 percent of the population was female, and consequently the birth rate was very low. Despite the fact that there were then few children in the state, the committee drafting California's constitution in 1847 chose to follow Iowa's example by stipulating that a public university be established but set no specific date for its creation. Over the next twenty years, the state's political, economic, and demographic structure changed dramatically. Amid this flux, the University of California came into being.

California's entry into the Union had been accelerated by the gold rush. In the winter of 1848–49, gold was discovered in the foothills of the Sierra Nevada. As word of this strike spread, thousands headed to California. Initially, the migration consisted mostly of single men, but it soon included families as hundreds of wagon trains carrying "Argonauts" moved across the country. In one year, 1850, fully 50,000 people moved into the state. By 1852 California's population was recorded at 250,000, up from only 15,000 four years earlier.

The state's political, judicial, and educational institutions struggled to cope with this population explosion. With the initial announcement of the discovery of gold, towns and ranches were deserted as residents rushed to the banks of the American River. As the mania lessened, miners moved to the towns, and cities like San Francisco faced severe problems maintaining public order.[1] Real estate prices skyrocketed. Meanwhile, municipalities were hard-pressed to provide even minimal public services. In such an environment, little energy and few resources could be devoted to education.

Under Spanish rule, California's educational, social, and political system had depended on Jesuit and Franciscan missions. Throughout the New Mexican territory and all along the California coast, missionaries had erected settlements where reading and writing were taught in conjunction with the principles of Christianity. This system dissolved in 1821 when Mexico obtained its independence from Spain. A series of provisional Mexican governors did little to replace the control of the missions. Although the common-school philosophy of New England was imported by mid-nineteenth century, it was grafted only slowly on to the remnants of the mission system. Educational standards in the West thus lagged behind those of the East.[2]

Although the state had achieved a reasonable measure of political stability by 1860, the Civil War proved to be disruptive: Californians enlisted in both the Confederate and the Union armies. With the end of the conflict and the completion of the transcontinental railroad in 1869, many thousands more migrated to California. The claims of these new residents further strained the limited budgetary resources of the young state, and the educational system was forced to concentrate on widening its coverage rather than deepening it. As a result, California had few students with the equivalent of a high school education by 1870.[3]

THE FOUNDING OF THE UNIVERSITY OF CALIFORNIA

Despite deficiencies in primary and secondary educational facilities when Congress passed the Morrill Act in 1862, California's legislators perceived the opportunities this legislation presented and arranged to take advantage of the federal aid it provided before the congressional deadline of 1866. The Morrill Act gave a state 30,000 acres of public land for each senator or congressman, with the proviso that proceeds from land sales be invested to form an endowment for at least one college of agricultural and mechanical arts. In this manner, the University of California was initially funded and founded in 1868.

California's land-grant college was nonsectarian and coeducational. Women were admitted as full degree candidates in 1870 without any of the controversy that surrounded coeducation at other schools. Northern California was selected as the location for the new institution, primarily because the vast majority of the state's population was then concentrated there. In addition, its original location in Oakland afforded access to several buildings formerly the property of the College of California, an institution sponsored by Presbyterians and Congregationalists that was dissolved as the state university was being formed. These facilities provided a temporary home for the University of California until a new campus could be built on a large unsettled tract (to be known as Berkeley) some five miles to the north.[4]

The university opened in 1869 with forty students and nine faculty members but without a president or a clear sense of direction.[5] Its governing body, the Board of Regents, was dominated by elected public officials and political appointees, and its members were divided about the emphasis to be given to the teaching of practical subjects (in the spirit of the Morrill Act) and to the perpetuation of a "College of Letters" (which the state had inherited from the College of California and had agreed to sustain). Some residual bitterness from the Civil War further strained their deliberations. Former Confederate sympathizers within their ranks sought to minimize the influence of New England educational ideas and preferred to see the new school shaped more along the lines of a military academy. These considerations prevailed in the initial choice of a president. In 1869 General George B. McClellan—whom Lincoln had dismissed from command of the Union armies and who later ran against Lincoln in the presidential campaign of 1864—was offered this post. When McClellan declined, a pro–New England faction of the Board of Regents mobilized enough strength to invite Daniel Coit Gilman, a man whose credentials as an advocate of educational innovation were already well established at Yale's Sheffield Scientific School.[6] Gilman did not take up this first invitation. In 1872, after he had been passed over as a candidate for the presidency of Yale, he accepted a renewed call from California. In the interim, the new university was administered directly by the regents, who hired its faculty for the first year of operations, and by the former president of the College of California (who was brought out of retirement to act as a caretaker from 1870 to 1872).

Gilman then saw an opportunity to build an institution in which "modern" subjects (particularly in the sciences) could be given equal standing with the liberal arts disciplines. His conception of a "university idea" further called for the creation of professional schools offering technical training in such fields as law, medicine, dentistry, and pharmacy. Ultimately, these schools would coexist with the six "colleges" mandated in the university's charter: colleges of agriculture, mechanics, mining, civil engineering, chemistry, and letters. The obstacles to implementing this program proved, however, to be formidable. Ample funding was an obvious necessity, and this was not readily available. The institution could receive no income from tuition fees; state legislation had prohibited such charges. Moreover, the endowment funds acquired from sale of the 150,000 acres of federal land could not be used to cover current operating expenditures. The university was thus largely dependent on annual appropriations voted by the legislature.

Gilman soon discovered that he could not count on sympathetic support from the state's legislators. This was dramatically demonstrated in 1872 when the balance of political power in the state shifted toward a coalition of farmers and mechanics who made the administration of the university a prime political target. The charges brought by this group were fueled, in part, by Henry George, editor of the *San Francisco Daily Evening Post*, who asserted that "the original idea was that the University should be a college of industry" and that the regents had "perverted the University from its original design into a college of classics and polite learning." George called upon the legislature to destroy all of the institution except the colleges of agriculture and mechanics.[7] One of the consequences of this agitation was the enactment of a "Political Code"— with effect from January 1873—that placed the Board of Regents under the jurisdiction of the legislature. From Gilman's perspective, this legislation meant that the fate of the university was at the mercy of the state's volatile political moods. Its enemies, he feared, would "turn it into a sort of low manual-labor school."[8] Moreover, the possibility that the institution "might be swept away in an hour" frustrated his efforts to attract private donors who might give it a measure of financial independence.[9]

By 1875 Gilman saw little prospect that he could accomplish what he had set out to do, given the political climate of California. When the call came to him to head a new private university to be established in Baltimore with a healthy endowment from the estate of Johns Hopkins, he accepted with alacrity.[10] During his California years, he had at least managed to produce a blueprint of what a great state university might look like, although decades would pass before his vision approached reality. As far as the discipline of political economy was concerned, Gilman had another claim to recognition there: He was the first to present this subject matter to University of California students. During his first year as president, he taught political economy and physical geography to members of the senior class, and in his second year he offered instruction in political economy and history.[11]

For the better part of a quarter-century following Gilman's departure, the university lacked strong academic leadership. Meanwhile, a number of difficulties that had plagued Gilman's administration persisted. The university remained vulnerable to political interference, and many who served as regents were ill qualified for their responsibilities. Uncertainties about financial support further damaged faculty morale. Salaries were periodically cut, as in the budgetary crisis of 1881–82. Job security was also a major concern: Faculty members of all ranks could be—and were—fired at the will of the Board of Regents. A series of weak presidents (who were themselves former faculty members) were unable to ease the professors' anxieties by restraining intervention by the regents.

In the early 1890s, however, the creation and initial success of a new university only fifty miles to the south encouraged major changes in the administration, staff, and curriculum of the University of California. In the judgment of a California alumnus writing two years after Stanford's opening,

The State University has been gaining in wealth and influence these many years, but the greatest gain that has come to it is due to the establishment of its coadjutor in the field of higher education, the Leland Stanford Junior University. The good will already manifested between the faculties of the two institutions, and the healthy, honest rivalry between the students, have raised the standards everywhere. The friends of the older institution feel that their hands have been strengthened by the vigorous university of Palo Alto, and it has been said, with much truth, that if Senator Stanford had chosen to endow the State University with his millions, he would have helped it less than he has done by establishing a sister university . . . to aid, support, and encourage the entire educational system in California.[12]

THE LAUNCHING OF STANFORD UNIVERSITY
AND ITS SIDE EFFECTS

Like the Johns Hopkins University, Stanford was created by a railroad tycoon, Leland Stanford, and began with no church or state affiliation. Stanford was an executive of the Central Pacific (the western section of the transcontinental railroad) as well as president of the Southern Pacific. He had left a law practice in Wisconsin to seek a new life in California and was soon a successful merchant. He helped organize the Republican party in California and was elected governor in 1862 and U.S. senator in 1885. Through his network of railways he amassed a huge fortune, and upon the death of his only child from typhoid fever in 1884 decided to found a university in the boy's memory.[13]

When governor, Stanford had expressed interest in higher education, and in 1884 he agreed to serve on the Board of Regents for the University of California.[14] He was, in fact, officially nominated for a position as a regent, but an election intervened before his appointment could be confirmed by the legislature. The incoming Democratic administration chose to withdraw all unconfirmed nominations and elected not to resubmit Stanford's name, which the public associated with wealth and monopoly power. Later that same year Stanford began planning a new university to be named for his deceased son, Leland Stanford, Jr. If Stanford had been confirmed as a regent, it is likely that much of his fortune would have gone to the University of California. Prior to the withdrawal of his nomination as regent, Stanford had told its president that he planned to "do something" for the university.[15] Stanford, however, adapted his plans to the changed political circumstances and decided that designing a new school might better relieve the family's grief over the premature death of an only child.[16]

Initially, Stanford had talked of the importance of practical training for the men and women of California, and his original plans called for the creation of a technical school. Later, he expanded his goals:

I design that the amplest provision shall be made for all the branches of what is known as a liberal education, and every facility given for the prosecution of all professional studies. . . . It is my hope that the university may afford to both sexes an opportunity for technical education which will enable every student to earn a living and something more than a living. . . . It is our intention to provide primarily for the masses. The rich can take care of themselves, but will always be welcome here. . . . The institution is to be an example of economy, but not of stinginess or meanness, and will put the highest education within the reach of all.[17]

The cornerstone for this new university was laid in 1887, and classes began in the fall of 1891.[18]

Before the institution opened, Leland and Jane Stanford traveled extensively throughout the East, gathered ideas for the school, and tried to recruit a founding president. Their first choice was General Francis Amasa Walker, then president of the Massachusetts Institute of Technology and author of *Political Economy* (1883). Walker declined the offer, and the Stanfords proceeded to Harvard, Yale, Cornell, Columbia, and Johns Hopkins. Both Gilman of Hopkins and White of Cornell strongly recommended David Starr Jordan for the position. Jordan was promoted as a bright, young scientist with remarkable organizational ability and good common sense.[19] Jordan had been in Cornell's first graduation class and was currently president of Indiana University. In Jordan, the Stanfords found a young man who was prepared to emphasize "reality and practicality."[20] Under his direction, Stanford University was initially structured around groupings of studies designed to prepare students for vocational specialties. Hence, a department of philosophy was not represented in its original table of organization. Meanwhile, Jordan assigned importance to technical assistance for the local community and himself offered extension lectures to fruit growers on the control of crop-damaging insects.[21]

Most contemporary observers assumed that Jordan's energy combined with Stanford's money insured the school's success. The press estimated that the school's endowment would be in excess of $20 million, yielding an income that would compare favorably with that of Harvard or Yale. However, skeptics stressed Jordan's relative inexperience and the problems a new university might encounter when situated in such close proximity to an established one. (On at least one count, the new institution would not be at a competitive disadvantage with the older one: By direction of the Stanfords, their university would have no tuition charges.) Frequent allusions were made to the prospect that Stanford's professors would lecture to empty benches in marble halls built in the middle of wheat fields.[22] Despite such grim forecasts, Stanford opened with 559 students and thirty-five faculty members.

The administration of the University of California was quickly made aware of Stanford's presence in the competition for students, faculty, and prestige. By the time Berkeley was thirty years old, its complement of students and faculty members was only slightly more than double that of Stanford in its first year. A series of "conscientious but inexperienced and unqualified" presidents[23] had not convinced the state legislature and recalcitrant Boards of Regents of the need for major changes—in particular, for more money and for more aggressive leadership. When the presidential office fell vacant in 1899, the regents began to deal with these problems by recruiting a vigorous young scholar from Cornell to head the University of California. Benjamin Ide Wheeler had been recommended to the regents by President Charles Eliot of Harvard and Adolph C. Miller, a California alumnus then teaching at the University of Chicago. Although Wheeler's academic specialty was classical philology, a field in which he had earned a Ph.D. at the University of Heidelberg, he arrived in California with aspirations to expand the number of departments and to strengthen existing ones. He insisted on having a freer hand to build than his predecessors had enjoyed: One of the conditions he set for accepting the presidency was that he be guaranteed sole authority over appointing and removing faculty members and in determining their salaries. In the early years of his twenty-year tenure, he concentrated on recruiting senior faculty members from east of the Rocky Mountains and on building up the library. Accelerating the development of the social science departments was also high among his priorities.

POLITICAL ECONOMY IN THE LATE NINETEENTH CENTURY AT THE UNIVERSITY OF CALIFORNIA

Although Benjamin Wheeler built up political economy at the University of California, Bernard Moses (1846–1931) was the first regular faculty member to teach the subject there. When invited to join the faculty at Berkeley, he was asked to teach history and either philosophy or political economy. He chose the latter—"a narrow escape from becoming a philosopher," [24] as he later put it—and was accorded the title of Professor of History and Political Science in 1876. Soon after his arrival, however, some thought apparently was given to the creation of a separate chair in political economy. At least Henry George understood that his name had been mentioned for such an appointment, and he actively pursued this possibility. In early 1877, he delivered a guest lecture at the university on "The Study of Political Economy." Some of the ideas that were to emerge two years later in *Progress and Poverty*—the sterility of orthodox political economy, its neglect of the interests of the workingman, its failure to address the recurring problem of depression—were then set out in embryonic form. The university authorities did not explore further George's candidacy for an academic position.[25]

Over the last quarter of the nineteenth century, Moses was the major figure in this field at Berkeley as well as in all the social sciences at Berkeley. An 1870 graduate of the University of Michigan, Moses subsequently studied at Berlin, Leipzig, and Heidelberg and spent almost a year in Sweden and Italy. He returned to Heidelberg in 1873 to complete the necessary examinations for a doctorate and is believed to have been the first American economist to obtain a Ph.D. in Germany.[26] Between 1876 and 1890, Moses taught two courses in political economy every year, offering one each semester. One was described as "a critical study of the history of economic thought," the other as "a general view of the principles and laws of political economy in its present position."[27] Very little information on the exact nature of these courses exists, although the university course register for the academic year 1881–82 identified the textbooks as Perry's *Elements of Political Economy,* Fawcett's *Manual of Political Economy,* and Cossa's *Guide to the Study of Political Economy.* These courses continued to be listed in the History and Political Science Department until 1901. One presumes that Moses integrated historical methods into his economic analysis, as he had been trained to do at Heidelberg. Even so, he saw historical analysis as necessary but not sufficient in understanding problems of political economy. In his words:

History . . . furnishes us material absolutely essential to the formation of an economic science, absolutely essential also to the formation of that grander science of which economics is a part; but it would be a wrong use of terms to call either economics or sociology a science, or a philosophy, of history. . . . history must be summoned to our aid, but history can give only a partial explanation.[28]

Throughout the bulk of his career at California, Moses was *the* social scientist for the university. During his first seven years there, he taught all history courses (with the exception of ancient history) in addition to all courses in political economy. When a Department of History and Political Science was organized in 1883, he was appointed as its chairman. He was then listed as a professor of political science and, as such, taught all of the courses offered in that field. Moses wanted to give greater visibility to the social sciences at Berkeley and founded a journal—entitled the *Berkeley Quarterly: A Journal of Social Science*—in 1880. This enterprise, however, survived for only two years, its demise being attributed to an insufficient number of submissions. Moses's own scholarly interests ranged widely: His contributions to the national economic journal literature treated such diverse topics as the nature of sociology, the economic history of sixteenth-century Spain, legal tender notes in California, and the economic situation in Japan in the 1890s.

On the Berkeley campus, Moses was a major figure—one who was a candidate for the university's presidency in 1892 and 1899. In the judgment of a local observer in 1892, "the University [was] regarded strongest in the department of history and economics and social science, under Professor Moses."[29] He had significantly less impact on the wider world of learning. It could hardly have been otherwise. He was working in an environment geographically remote from the mainstream of national scholarly debates and one in which he was obliged to spread himself over a multiplicity of subjects. Unlike others of his generation who absorbed German teaching in political economy, he did not participate in the affairs of the American Economic Association in its formative years (although later, in 1903, he did participate in the founding of the American Political Science Association). Given the difficulties under which he worked, it is noteworthy that he achieved as much wider recognition as he did.[30] Opinions differ on the impact of his teachings. Joseph Dorfman has characterized Moses as a conservative because of his opposition to Germany's compulsory workmen's accident insurance and his support of the free enterprise system.[31] Certainly, however, one could not describe many of the students he trained as conservatives. Indeed, Jessica Peixotto, for example, was an enthusiastic supporter of government intervention in the economy, especially in the form of social welfare insurance and government spending programs during the Great Depression. She claimed Moses as her mentor and credited him with strongly influencing her thinking in his class on the Economic Condition of Laborers in England.[32] Today Moses is infrequently cited in studies of nineteenth-century economists. He is now primarily remembered as a political scientist, presumably because his teaching and research immediately prior to his retirement fit most clearly into that discipline. For most of his career, however, Moses was the central figure in political economy at Berkeley.

In the 1890s, new courses in political economy were added, several new instructors were hired, and graduate courses began to be offered. This trend began when Moses took a year's leave in 1890 and was accelerated by the opening of Stanford. Adolph C. Miller (California, class of 1887) was brought back as a visitor in 1890. Miller had received an A.M. at Harvard after his graduation from Berkeley and then proceeded to Europe where he studied at Munich and Paris. Although he taught at Berkeley for only one year before moving to positions at Cornell and Chicago with J. Laurence Laughlin, he gave Moses's major political economy course, a four-hour class taken primarily by upperclassmen, as well as courses in economic theory, finance, and economic history.[33]

Additional instructors in political economy were recruited as course offerings expanded in response to student interest in the major changes then occurring in American industry. Carl C. Plehn was hired as an assistant professor in the Department of History and Political Science in 1892. Plehn, Moses, and a changing group of lecturers and assistants taught all the political economy courses until 1902. Courses then included classes on economic theory, economic history, finance and taxation, banking and currency, statistics, theories of social progress, and the condition of laborers in England. Plehn's presence also freed Moses to teach the course entitled Economic Theory, described as a "critical study of writers and systems; discussion of unsettled problems in political economy; socialism."

Carl Copping Plehn (1867–1945) had moved to Berkeley after teaching at Middlebury College in Vermont. He had earned an A.B. from Brown and a Ph.D. from Göttingen. His German education clearly affected his approach to economics. As he later described the atmosphere of the times:

From about 1880, or perhaps a little earlier, young Americans flocked to Germany to study under the masters of the new historical school of Economics. They returned to spread the new gospel at home. The scorn with which we of the new school (for I was one of the pilgrims) looked down upon those "closet philosophers" of the old school who imagined that they could construct "out of their own head" by deductive methods a working theory of "living human economic society" was not, I fear, always successfully concealed by a thin veneer of politeness. A great war, wordy in the extreme, was waged over the scope and method of Economics. Looking back, those pompous arguments, in which such deadly terms as deductive, inductive, empirical, and metaphysical and all the other "ives" and "cals" were hurled about seem somewhat amusing. Then they were serious enough.[34]

In 1898, when a College of Commerce was opened at California to provide practical training for businessmen, Plehn became its first dean. He saw its goals in this light:

Commercial organization on a large scale is the order of the day, and the successful administration of the vast aggregation of capital, the buying and selling of goods in the world markets under the conditions of world-wide competition requires the broadest mental training and the widest knowledge that can possibly be obtained.[35]

Plehn continued to teach political economy courses while holding his position as dean of the College of Commerce. His Introduction to Political Economy included among its readings Marshall's *Principles of Economics*, volume 1, Mill's *Principles of Political Economy*, Smith's *Inquiry into the Nature and Causes of the Wealth of Nations*, and Ingram's *History of Political Economy*, as well as works by J. B. Clark, Cossa, Lalor, Schönberg, Roscher, Cohn, Böhm-Bawerk, and Cairnes.[36] He also taught classes in Public Finance, Banking and Currency, and the Industrial and Commercial History of the United States. His major scholarly interest was in problems of taxation. His book, *Introduction to Public Finance*, was published in five different editions between 1896 and 1926, and a number of states (including California) utilized his ideas in the formation of their tax systems. Plehn was elected president of the American Economic Association in 1923.

EXPANSION AND DIFFERENTIATION DURING WHEELER'S ADMINISTRATION OF THE UNIVERSITY OF CALIFORNIA

As part of Wheeler's development program for the university, Political Economy became an independent academic department in 1902. The following year it was renamed "Economics." The organizational linkages with history and political science of the Moses era were thus severed. To head the separate department, Wheeler turned to Adolph C. Miller (1866–1953), then a professor of economics at the University of Chicago, whom he had known when they were both at Cornell. Miller, in turn, persuaded two of his younger colleagues at Chicago to join him: Wesley C. Mitchell (in 1903) and Henry Rand Hatfield (in 1904). The Chicagoans migrated to the West with the expectation that they would have wider scope for scholarly pursuits there than would be the case in a department dominated by J. Laurence Laughlin.[37]

For his part, Mitchell made good use of this opportunity. While at Berkeley, he taught classes on money, banking, foreign exchange, labor, economic crises and depressions, but he also launched some of his most innovative research.[38] His study of *Gold, Prices, and Wages under the Greenback Standard* appeared in 1908. The most significant fruit of this period in his career, however, was his investigation of business cycles. His pioneering work on this subject appeared in book form in 1913. It was at once a survey of major theories of the cycle, a detailed statistical investigation of the experience of the United States, England, France, and Germany, and a statement of Mitchell's own analysis of the manner in which the institutions and habits of a capitalist economy contributed to cyclical fluctuations.[39] This work was a major step forward in the development of techniques for national income and product accounting.[40] Moreover, its suggestion that business cycles could be moderated, if their nature were properly understood, set the agenda for a fresh set of discussions about the conduct of economic policy. The publication of *Business Cycles* established Mitchell as a major figure in the American economics profession.

In his efforts to strengthen the university, Wheeler often looked eastward for recruits to his faculty. But he also looked with favor on homegrown talent. In 1904 he added Jessica Peixotto, a Moses student, to the departmental staff as a lecturer. Two years later she was promoted to an assistant professorship. Her research and teaching interests were initially focused on economic systems other than capitalism and on ways that capitalism could be adapted to make it more responsive to the needs of the poor, sick, and elderly. In her first years at California, she exchanged ideas with Mitchell and began to document the standard of living of workers and to study the factors affecting its change. Much of her early work extended ideas that she had discussed with Moses. She developed a course entitled Contemporary Socialism, which was described as "a study of the program and methods of the contemporary socialist parties; a critical investigation of the theories on which the programs are based" that broadened to cover "current schemes for the partial and total reconstruction of industrial society."[41]

In the first decade of the twentieth century, the Economics Department at Berkeley took on a distinctly institutionalist flair. Solomon Blum (1883–1926), Carleton Parker (1878–1918), Stuart Daggett (1881–1954), and Ira Cross were all hired during the Wheeler administration. Blum, a Johns Hopkins Ph.D., came to Berkeley in 1909 and staffed the department's labor classes. Unsatisfied with marginal and classical wage theories, he tried to merge an institutional framework with the more orthodox teaching he had received at Johns Hopkins under Hollander and Barnett. Like Parker (who joined the department in 1913), Blum died in his early forties, leaving most of his research incomplete. Both men, however, utilized Veblenian concepts and added to the heterodox perspectives of Moses, Peixotto, and Mitchell in Berkeley's Economics Department.

Parker, a native-born Californian who had graduated from the university in 1904, had been encouraged by Adolph C. Miller to abandon such western pursuits as mining, ranching, and rafting for a more stable profession—teaching.[42] He attended Harvard, then went to Germany and obtained a Ph.D. at Heidelberg in 1912. The following year he was hired at Berkeley as an assistant professor of industrial economics to teach labor. Although on leave part-time to be the executive secretary to the California Immigration and Housing Commission, Parker had a major impact on Ira Cross, who arrived in Berkeley in 1914.[43] Parker was intensely involved as a mediator in numerous labor disputes: The relationship between psychology and economics intrigued him, and he wanted to explain both the militant tactics of the Industrial Workers of the World (IWW) and the discontent of migratory workers.[44] In the summer of 1916, he traveled throughout the country talking about his ideas with (among others) Veblen, Mitchell, and Commons. To Berkeley's misfortune, Parker was recruited by the University of Washington in 1917 to head its Economics Department and was soon made dean of its College of Commerce. He died a year later.[45]

Stuart Daggett, the Economics Department's first Harvard Ph.D., was appointed in 1909 as an assistant professor of railway economics. He taught courses on transportation and wrote his *Principles of Inland Transportation* and *Chapters on the History of the Southern Pacific*. Like most California faculty members, he also served as an academic expert on a number of government committees, including the California Commission for Railroad and Water Facilities. Daggett was the last surviving member of the Berkeley Economics Department created by Wheeler.

By World War I, the department offered forty economics classes, had fifteen full-time faculty members, and was secure in its place in the university. Graduate degrees were now granted. Even so, there were losses as well as gains. Wesley Mitchell departed in 1913 to accept an appointment at Columbia, and Adolph C. Miller left in 1914 to become a charter member of the Federal Reserve Board.[46] Nevertheless, the momentum established in the first decade of the century meant that Berkeley was well on its way toward becoming both nationally and internationally recognized. In the 1920s, three of its faculty members were elected as officers of the American Economic Association.

POLITICAL ECONOMY IN STANFORD'S FIRST DECADES

Despite the optimistic predictions that accompanied its opening, Stanford University soon encountered financial problems. Leland Stanford died in 1893 before the university's endowment fund was complete. It had been Stanford's practice to forgo regular dividends from his railroad investments; he preferred to "borrow" money periodically from retained earnings. With his death, his personal and corporate financial holdings were immediately frozen pending probate. A federal suit filed against the estate for repayment of government railroad loans further complicated an already messy financial situation. As a result, the university faced severe short-run financial difficulties after being open for only two years. It had no income from endowments and no revenues from tuition charges. The court, however, granted an allowance to Stanford's widow, the university's sole trustee. By calling professors her personal servants, she was able to pay the faculty a portion of their contractual salaries. No funds were available, however, for the expansion of facilities or for the replacement of faculty members who left. Fiscal austerity continued until 1898 when a sum of approximately $14 million was allocated to Stanford University, much of it arising from the sale of Central Pacific stock.

Even so, the university's financial problems persisted until after Mrs. Stanford's death in 1905. After the federal suit against her husband's estate had been settled, she sought to complete the building program they had jointly planned. As a result, a large proportion of funds available to the university were spent on construction rather than on the recruitment and retention of the high-quality faculty President Jordan wanted. Salaries were frozen for the academic years 1903–4 and 1904–5, and hiring was postponed whenever possible. Jordan referred to this period in the university's history as the "Stone Age." In Laurence Veysey's judgment, "around 1904, morale at Stanford had reached the lowest point—apart, perhaps, from the darkest days at Clark—ever to be observed at a major American university."[47] Ironically, the earthquake of 1906 leveled many of the buildings that Mrs. Stanford erected at the expense of support to faculty and to program development before her death.

When he was appointed as president, Jordan had hoped to have a significant economics program in place at the university's opening. On the national academic scene, the question of whether or not political economy deserved representation in the university curriculum had largely been answered by the early 1890s. The remaining issue was the brand (or brands) of economics that should be introduced. Jordan wanted to convince a major figure in political economy to head the new department but discovered that

men who have already made their fame and their fortune in Eastern Colleges . . . are not willing to leave their present positions at any salary which would not be simple extravagance. They are unwilling to take any of the risks of pioneer work unless heavily paid for it. But rising young men who will grow for twenty years to come, and some of whom are sure to be famous, are greatly attracted by the prospects of the University, and among them I can take almost any one I choose.[48]

In economics, offers were made to Frank Taussig (Harvard), Jeremiah Jenks (Cornell), and Henry Carter Adams (Michigan) for the first year, but all three declined.[49] Even so, ten courses were listed as options for students in the very first year, although only three were actually taught.[50] Orrin Leslie Elliott—a Cornell Ph.D. whose primary assignment was as registrar and secretary to the president—handled this work as an acting instructor in economics.[51]

For Stanford's second academic year, Amos G. Warner (1861–1900)—a John Hopkins Ph.D. and protégé of Richard T. Ely who had served as superintendent of charities in Baltimore—was engaged to head the department. In 1892–93, all political economy classes were listed in the course catalogue under Economics and Social Science. The department then had four members, two professors (Warner and Ross), and two assistant professors (F. C. Clark and Elliott). Courses were available in three subfields: Political Economy, Statistics and Finance; Sociology; and Political Science. Warner and Ross taught classes in all three areas. Walker's *Political Economy* was the textbook generally used for the first semester of the introductory course, followed by a second class where students wrote papers, attended occasional lectures, and concentrated on readings such as Mill and Marshall.[52] Warner taught Elements of Economics in the fall of 1893, which was focused on the works of

Ely and Andrews. But more than books were involved in the Stanford style of instruction. Warner made a distinctive contribution with his "friendly woodyard" of tramps and migrants. He used free meals as an opportunity for his students to observe the problems of the poor and unemployed at first hand.[53] For his class on Charities and Corrections, he had his students tour jails, almshouses, asylums, police courts, and city halls. All of this was compatible with Jordan's belief that the university should be involved in the community. Owing to recurring illness, however, Warner was unable to hold regular classes after 1894 and died six years later, a young man "only at the beginning of a career of distinguished usefulness."[54]

With Warner incapacitated, effective leadership of the department passed to Edward Alsworth Ross (1866–1951), another graduate of Ely's program at Johns Hopkins who had been elected to the secretaryship of the American Economic Association in 1892. Jordan had recruited Ross for the faculty at Indiana shortly before his departure to take up the presidency at Stanford. In 1893, Jordan again called upon Ross (by then at Cornell) and appointed him to a professorship of economic theory and finance at Stanford. Jordan clearly had high regard for Ross, whom he once described to Mr. Stanford as follows:

I think of all the younger men in the country in this line of work, Dr. Ross is the most promising. He has originality, energy, and force of character, and in his investigations of financial and administrative questions, he shows himself entirely free from either political prejudices or the prejudices of books.[55]

Ross initially taught a public finance class that focused on Bastable, Ely, and Adams as well as on the work of Wagner, Cohn, and Leroy-Beaulieu. In addition, he lectured on statistical and dynamic sociology as well as on current economic problems. The latter course was listed as

A study of the signs and causes of existing discontent; of the nature, benefits, and evils of the industrial revolution; and of the complaints of the farmer, the workingman, and the consumer. The various reforms demanded on their behalf, including land nationalization, state socialism, and collectivism.[56]

In 1896–97 he offered a course entitled Transportation, described as "A study of the laws of movement and of the economic, social and political consequences of improvements in transportation. Special studies will be made on roads, waterways and street railways"; the second semester was "a study of railroad problems."[57]

Ross held strong views on industrialists, trusts, railroads, and easy money. He advocated social and economic reform both in his classes and in public. He gained national prominence, however, primarily through his extracurricular activities. In 1896 Ross publicly supported the candidacy of William Jennings Bryan for president of the United States. As a "free silver" advocate, Ross favored inflation of the currency as a means of helping farmers and debtors. Mrs. Stanford was unhappy that a member of "her" faculty took a public stance in an election and asked President Jordan to remove him.[58] Jordan argued on Ross's behalf but warned him of the cofounder's unhappiness. In 1897 Ross was "demoted"—as he described his status—to a professorship in sociology as a partial reprimand and relieved of teaching courses in finance.[59]

For Ross, this redefinition of his duties was quite acceptable: His central academic interest had now shifted to sociology.[60] His reassignment, combined with Warner's persisting ill health, meant that there were gaps in the economics program. Dana Durand, who was appointed as an assistant professor of finance and administration in 1897, was expected to fill part of them, but he soon took a leave of absence to engage in statistical work in Washington. In 1898 Jordan turned to Frank R. Fetter, a Halle Ph.D. then teaching at the University of Indiana. Fetter accepted an appointment as professor of economics on the condition that he soon be permitted research leave.[61]

In 1900 Ross again angered Mrs. Stanford over a speech he made in San Francisco. This time he argued that Asian workers lowered the American standard of living and recommended tightened restrictions on immigration. This position was popular in California and important in national politics as well. Chinese coolies, however, had helped construct the Central Pacific Railway, and Mrs. Stanford was extremely sensitive to criticisms of their employment. She was also unhappy with Ross's public advocacy of municipal ownership of public utilities: Southern Pacific owned a number of urban transit systems in California. "God forbid," she told Jordan, "that Stanford University should ever favor socialism of any kind."[62] Mrs. Stanford immediately informed Jordan that she wanted Ross's resignation. Jordan resisted taking this step and attempted to work out a compromise: Ross would be reappointed for the academic year 1900–1 on the understanding that he would actively look elsewhere for a position and that he would submit a letter of resignation, which the president could accept at his discretion. Ross complied with these terms in June 1900. Mrs. Stanford, however, remained adamant in her insistence that Ross be dismissed. In November 1900 Jordan was obliged to accept the letter of resignation Ross had drafted in the preceding June.[63] Ross then released a statement to the press asserting that he had been denied academic freedom.[64] Ross subsequently was hired by the University of Nebraska (where he joined E. Benjamin Andrews, who had also encountered academic freedom difficulties when at Brown) and later migrated, in 1906, to the University of Wisconsin where Richard T. Ely had arranged a position for him.

The "Ross incident" rekindled anti-Stanford sentiment in the press. Of the four founders of the Central Pacific, Stanford had been the most ostentatious with his money. His house on Nob Hill, his private railroad car, and eventually his university were the most visible symbols of his wealth. Ambrose Bierce, a muckraking journalist, took delight in writing of him as "£eland $tanford." It was Stanford's connection with the Southern Pacific, however, that especially aroused public ire: The SP was the state's largest landowner and employer. The railroad was alleged to have manipulated the state legislature in the 1870s and 1880s with bribes and extortion practices.[65] Robert Cleland, the historian of California, summarized the public's view: "Long after the men who complacently accepted the title of the 'Big Four' had been gathered to their fathers, the Southern Pacific machine still remained an arrogant and hateful reality to the people of California—the personification of all that was dictatorial and corrupt in state politics."[66]

Ross's forced resignation by Stanford's widow had major repercussions on the university and especially on the Economics Department. Ross was a popular and important instructor. When Warner had been ill and on leave, Ross had covered many of his classes. In addition, seven members of the Stanford faculty—two of whom were economists (Frank Fetter and Morton Aldrich, an assistant professor who had been appointed in 1899)—resigned in protest over the dismissal or its aftermath. Members of the American Economic Association organized a committee to conduct an unofficial investigation of the case, and its report supported Ross and censured Stanford. Edwin Seligman, John Bates Clark, Richard T. Ely, Henry Carter Adams, and Frank Taussig—all major figures in the profession—signed the resulting document.[67]

As early as May 1900, Jordan anticipated that difficulties might lie ahead in the staffing of the Economics Department, and he looked to Frank Fetter to take the lead. He asked Fetter to find an assistant professor—"a man with a future if possible"—to replace Ross or Burt Estes Howard in the event either of them resigned or did not return.[68] After Ross had been dismissed in November, Jordan invited Fetter's opinion of several economists who might fill the vacant space, including Adolph C. Miller (then at Chicago) and Thomas Nixon Carver (then at Oberlin College).[69] The following month Jordan asked Fetter, who was then on leave on the East Coast, to return to Palo Alto to head the troubled department, assuring him that Ross's dismissal was the result of no one incident and that academic freedom was not violated in any way.[70] Fetter declined to come back to California in the middle of the academic year because of commitments in the East, but he promised to recruit actively during the American Economic Association meetings in Detroit later that month. Fetter, however, was clearly discouraged: "I can not think of the unexpected wreck of our hopes of the department without the grief that comes from the loss of years of earnest effort. It is all to do over again. But when the time comes I hope to summon courage and go on with good heart."[71]

In his recruitment efforts, Fetter obviously encountered a great deal of skepticism about Stanford's treatment of Ross. By the end of January 1901, Fetter had decided that he was unwilling to chair the department without a firm, formal statement of administration policy. He then wrote:

The kind of men we want, men of promise, usually have assured positions and the prospects of advancement elsewhere, and they will be only reasonable in asking for a positive declaration of the attitude the University takes toward the work in economics. . . . I should feel chagrined if unable to meet such requests with an authoritative and emphatic statement.[72]

Jordan, however, refused to issue the type of statement Fetter wanted, observing instead that "The customary 'unwritten contract' will hold: liberty of thought, speech and action, on the one hand; reasonable discretion, common sense and loyalty on the other."[73] Consequently, Fetter resigned, although with much regret. The *San Francisco Chronicle* commented on Fetter's departure as follows: "He was considered one of the strongest men on the faculty and was noted for his liberal opinions. [His] withdrawal . . . leaves the already weakened economics department in a bad way. It will be necessary to secure at least two strong men to bring the department up to its former standard."[74] He accepted an appointment at Cornell and later held a professorship at Princeton where he remained until his retirement.

The Ross incident cast a shadow over Stanford for a number of years.[75] Although no formal boycott of the Stanford Economics Department was ever instituted, many influential economists urged their students to take positions elsewhere.[76] In 1906 Ira Cross, who then arrived from Wisconsin as a graduate student to study labor in San Francisco, was warned by his friends that he would probably not last six months in light of Stanford's intolerance for freedom of speech as evidenced by the Ross case.[77] Meanwhile, staffing of the economics program was largely a patchwork affair. The university register for 1901–2 lists John J. Halsey (on a leave of absence from Lake Forest College) as an acting professor, Simon James McLean and Mary Roberts Smith as associate professors, Burt Estes Howard as an acting associate professor, and two instructors as the department faculty. Harry A. Millis and Albert Conser Whitaker were added the next year as an assistant and an instructor, but both Halsey and Howard were gone. In 1904–5, a year of salary freezes and budget cuts, only three names were listed under Economics and Social Science: McLean, Millis, Whitaker. Economics at Stanford had no chairman, no full professor, and a very uncertain future.

In 1906, Jordan attempted to rebuild by engaging Allyn A. Young (1876–1929) as a full professor to head the department. A Wisconsin Ph.D. and collaborator with Richard T. Ely, Young was indeed "a man of promise." Young, in turn, recommended that an offer be extended to Thorstein Veblen, informing Jordan that he did not think that Veblen "has an equal among American economists in breadth of scholarship and subtlety of analysis."[78] Veblen was also available: He had been dismissed from his post at the University of Chicago and had no other employment prospects in sight.[79] Even so, it was not clear that Veblen could be persuaded to move west. Veblen's correspondence with Jordan at this time indicates that he was concerned about the way his association with Stanford would be regarded in the profession. Jordan initially offered him a position for one year at $2,500. Veblen responded by asking for a guarantee that no one in the department be paid more or hold a higher rank.[80] Ultimately, he accepted the title of associate professor and acknowledged that Young deserved higher salary and status in light of his administrative responsibilities.[81] Veblen accepted Stanford's offer in mid-May 1906 and began teaching there in January 1907. Young took up his duties in the fall of 1906.

With Veblen's arrival, Stanford added a "name"—although a rather heterodox one—to its economics faculty. His reputation was already well established through the publication of *The Theory of the Leisure Class* and *Theory of Business Enterprise,* as well as through his work as managing editor of the *Journal of Political Economy.* That Veblen could be a difficult personality and that his private life was unconventional were well known to those who arranged his appointment at Stanford. He was still attractive to an institution that needed to refurbish its image for tolerance. (He was hired, however, with the understanding that he would bring his wife.) For Jordan, Veblen's presence had another recommendation: It might provide some counterweight to pressure from his trustees for heavier concentration on vocational training.[82] Jordan had arranged an appointment for Veblen that permitted him to teach as little as he wanted in order to devote time to writing.[83] His principal course offerings at Stanford were Economic Factors in Civilization and The History of Economic Thought, both of which he had developed while at the University of Chicago. Reports by Robert Duffus and Ira Cross suggest that he did not enjoy teaching undergraduates, was a poor lecturer, and actively tried to keep his classes small.[84] Cross described Veblen as follows:

He was a curious fellow. He always made a very great impression on women. He wore rather heavy tweed clothes; he had a scraggly beard and a moustache. He appeared half awake when lecturing to his small classes as well as when engaged in ordinary conversations. There was something hypnotic about him. I took one of his courses, but I got very little out of it because he usually mumbled to himself and used long words. He was a brilliant man in his field, very original.[85]

In 1909 Jordan was again pressured into obtaining the resignation of a well-known member of the Economics Department whom he had personally recruited. As had been the case at Chicago, Veblen was asked to leave Stanford because of the way he conducted his private life, not because of his performance as a teacher or scholar. In both instances, the president of the university was drawn into the discussion of the Veblens' marital problems.[86] In October 1909 Jordan wrote as follows about this matter to President Judson (Harper's successor at the University of Chicago):

I have been able, with the help of Mrs. Veblen, to find out the truth in detail as to Professor Veblen's relations. . . . It is fair to say, that on my final talk with him, he carried himself in manly fashion, with no attempt at denial or evasion. He has tendered his resignation to take effect at my discretion. This will probably mean with July of next year, for the University cannot condone these matters, much as its officials may feel compassion for the individual.[87]

Veblen's departure initiated another round of instability for Stanford's Economics Department.[88] Young resigned in 1911 to take up a professorship at Washington University in Saint Louis.[89] Apparently, Young was quite unhappy at Stanford. He felt he was underpaid and that Jordan was unwilling to give him jurisdiction over personnel decisions. Young twice recommended that Veblen be promoted; Jordan refused.[90] Harry Millis, who had held an assistant professorship since 1903, departed in 1912 to join the faculty at the University of Chicago. Cross stayed on after completing his doctorate in 1909 to teach classes in labor, immigration, charities, and corrections until 1914. He impressed Jordan with his book, *The Essentials of Socialism,* and felt that he could have remained at Stanford if he had wished.[91] However, through Solomon Blum and Jessica Peixotto, he was recruited to the University of California where he taught until his retirement.[92] Of all those who taught economics at Stanford in the years before the outbreak of World War I, only two—Albert C. Whitaker and Murray Shipley Wildman—built a career at Stanford.

It is small wonder that economics at Stanford in its early decades developed the image of a "swinging door" department. Jordan's repeated efforts to build a respected Economics Department had failed, and he himself retired from the presidency in 1913. He had been able to attract some remarkable talents but had been unable to keep them. Three members of the economics faculty during Jordan's administration later served as presidents of the American Economic Association (Fetter, Young, and Millis), and one (Veblen) was nominated for this post but declined to serve. None of them achieved eminence, however, for work done while at Stanford.

TWO DEPARTMENTS, TWO DIFFERENT GROWTH PATTERNS

During the first decade of the twentieth century, Stanford's Economics Department floundered, whereas California's experienced a period of growth that would continue until the 1930s. In essence, the two departments reversed the positions they had held in the early 1890s. California's development was stimulated by the foundation of a Political Economy Department at the new institution, whereas Stanford's was sidetracked by a series of unfortunate and sometimes unavoidable conflicts.

Stanford's Economics Department failed to retain most of the bright, committed, and ultimately productive economists it recruited. President Jordan could not overcome Mrs. Stanford's interest in, and control of, personnel matters. Moreover, Stanford had no tenure policy and offered faculty only annual contracts. Salaries were frequently frozen, and faculty members were hard-pressed to provide for their families, let alone to travel and cover research expenses. Jordan could offer faculty members little hope that the situation would soon change to permit him to implement his plans to build a nationally respected institution. Moreover, the dismissals of Ross and Veblen badly damaged Stanford's image. No major figure in economics stayed in residence long enough to train a significant body of graduate students or to attract other well-known economists to Palo Alto. No "school" developed, as at Wisconsin or Chicago. Instead, Stanford was a stopover point for a series of economists who moved frequently between universities.

By contrast, Berkeley largely grew from within. Besides retaining some of its own graduate students, California's department recruited a number of its own undergraduates who had gone elsewhere for postgraduate training. The department projected an image of a congenial place where members undertook research on a variety of topics without being dominated by a "head professor" as at Chicago. In Benjamin Ide Wheeler, Berkeley had a strong president who convinced the California state legislature to increase funding for the university and who fought to retain valued faculty members, although not always successfully. Moreover, no major scandal or adverse publicity tainted the department in these years. Although some members (such as Miller and Mitchell) eventually left, those remaining maintained contact with them and made use of these associations when recruiting faculty. By World War I, the department was neither second-rate nor provincial and, in the following two decades, its economists played important roles in the American Economic Association and in the formulation and implementation of government policy.

12

Mind and Hand: Economics and Engineering at the Massachusetts Institute of Technology

RICHARD P. ADELSTEIN

ON THE GREAT SEAL of the Massachusetts Institute of Technology stand a scholar and an artisan, each facing outward, on either side of the lamp of learning. The lamp in turn rests on a foundation of Science and Art, beneath which is inscribed the institute's motto, *Mens et Manus*. For its determined founder, William Barton Rogers, the "practical usefulness" of the Institute's "happy union of science and art"[1] to the industrial and social life of the nation was the centerpiece of an educational philosophy that has guided the school to the present day. This emphasis on the practical in higher education placed Rogers squarely with those reformers who sought to supplant the traditional study of Scripture, ancient languages, and classical mathematics with a "modern" curriculum, more responsive to the commercial and cultural demands of a rapidly industrializing, secular society.

But he vigorously denied that an education centered on engineering or applied science was best achieved in departments or affiliated schools which, like the Lawrence Scientific School at Harvard or the Sheffield Scientific School at Yale, had been created specifically for this purpose at established colleges. Instead, Rogers's Institute itself was to be an experiment, combining rigorous professional training in engineering with the breadth of outlook offered by sustained exposure to the liberal arts within a single, independent technical university. Its graduates, he believed, would be uniquely qualified to grasp and apply continuing advances in scientific knowledge and to provide both the sophisticated technical

I am indebted to Loretta Mannix for helpful comments on and criticisms of an earlier draft of this essay.

skills and the entrepreneurial leadership the emerging industrial age would require.

In this joining of mind and hand, Rogers captured precisely the spirit of the new age. For the promise of technology was control, not merely over stone and metal but over the economic and social affairs of human beings as well, through the purposeful application of scientific theory to practical problems in both engineering and administration. As the nineteenth century gave way to the twentieth, spectacular advances in the technologies of production, transportation, and communication transformed the nation's economic landscape and began to induce equally significant changes in political thought and the structure and functions of government. These parallel and interrelated revolutions in technology, organization, and ideology brought America to an age of concentration in which scientific rationality and conscious control over nature and man were to become pivotal cultural values. In all of this, MIT reflected the mood and aspirations of the time and, through the scholarly and professional leadership of its political economists, contributed in important and lasting ways to the development of the discipline throughout this critical period.

William Barton Rogers was born in Philadelphia on December 7, 1804, the second of four remarkable sons of Patrick Kerr and Hannah Blythe Rogers. Each of the Rogers brothers was to achieve distinction in his own right as a scientist and educator, and they collaborated with one another on a host of projects throughout their lives. In 1819 the family moved to Williamsburg, Virginia, where Patrick, trained as a physician, had been elected professor of natural philosophy and chemistry at the College of William and Mary. William entered the college that autumn, quickly completed the prescribed studies, and, by the age of twenty, had translated an important French work on the differential calculus. After pursuing independent studies in physics and mathematics and assisting his father in the laboratory in Williamsburg, he joined his brother Henry in experimenting briefly with the organization of a technical high school at the Maryland Institute in Baltimore.[2]

When Patrick Rogers died in 1828, young William was chosen to succeed him at William and Mary, taking on teaching responsibilities in mathematics for a short time as well. Stimulated by his brother Henry, who was to become professor of geology at Pennsylvania in 1835, William turned his energies to research in geology.

Appointed in 1835 by the state legislature to conduct a geological survey of Virginia, he won national recognition for his work and was soon named professor of natural philosophy at the University of Virginia. Here his reputation continued to grow, and in 1840 he helped found the Society of Geologists and Naturalists, which seven years later became the American Association for the Advancement of Science.

In 1844 Rogers took his turn as chairman of the faculty at Virginia, the school's chief administrative officer. It was an unhappy time for the university. The campus was racked by violent disturbances, in one of which Rogers's predecessor as chairman was killed in his doorway by riotous students. The legislature seriously considered withdrawing the state's support from the university, but Rogers stayed its hand with an eloquent recital of the significance of scientific and literary education for the cultural development of the nation.[3] Despite this success and the eventual restoration of peace on the campus, Rogers began to consider finding a more tranquil place to live and work.

Geological research and professional contacts drew him to Boston, as did his deepening relationship with Emma Savage, whom he married in 1849. Henry was now settled there as well, having resigned his post at Pennsylvania to lecture and consult in the Boston area. During their frequent visits, they discussed the ideas William had expressed in his message to the Virginia legislature and the extension of higher education into technological fields, which were not then well represented in American colleges. In 1844, Henry was invited to deliver a series of talks at the Lowell Institute, established twelve years earlier by the Lowell family to offer free lectures on scientific subjects to the public. By 1846 Henry had interested John Amory Lowell, the Institute's trustee and the dominant member of the Harvard Corporation, in the possibility of creating at the Lowell Institute a scientific and technical school such as he and William had discussed. Lowell asked Henry to submit a plan in writing, and Henry appealed to William in Charlottesville for help. The result was two letters from William, dated March 13, 1846, and called "A Plan for a Polytechnic School in Boston."

New England, with Boston at its heart, seemed the ideal place for such a venture. For decades it had been a leader in industrial development and a source of capital and enterprise for the nation's expanding economy. During the War of 1812, Francis Cabot Lowell built the first complete factory in America at Waltham around a newly invented power loom, providing a model and spur to the growth of the region's great industrial cities over the next forty years.[4] By 1850 Boston capital was instrumental in financing railroads and mining operations in the Middle West, and New England's industry had become the most active and diversified in the United States.

The idea of an advanced technical school that could meet the increasing demand for men trained in science and skilled in its application had been in the air for many years.[5] Those early American engineers who had not been self-taught were primarily graduates of West Point, which had offered formal training in military engineering since 1802. Slowly, however, schools offering instruction in civil engineering as well began to emerge, and in 1835 the first American degree in civil engineering was conferred at the Rensselaer Institute in Troy, New York. By the 1840s, even these schools could not keep up with the demand for trained engineers, and the instruction they undertook was too narrow and vocational to provide the practical but liberal education that the Rogers brothers believed their "polytechnic school" could offer.

Apart from its stress on the cultural and practical value of a higher education built upon the scientific disciplines, the Rogers plan is noteworthy both for its commitment to the laboratory method of instruction, a "daring innovation" at the time,[6] and for its provisions for serious offerings in applied science to artisans and foremen who supervised work on the shop floor. But the plan foundered when it was held that the Lowell bequest could not be used to support such an enterprise, and in the following year new schools of applied science were opened at both Harvard and Yale. Disappointed but still convinced that a scientific and technical college must be free to develop independently of a great university if its educational potential were to be fully realized, the brothers held fast to their dream. In 1853 William left his chair at Virginia to move to Boston and, after Henry's departure in 1855 to become Regius Professor at Glasgow, continued to pursue their vision alone.

When opportunity smiled, Rogers was ready. In a message to the Massachusetts legislature in 1859, Governor Banks urged that newly filled land in the Back Bay be devoted in some way to the development of public education in the commonwealth, and the idea of establishing a new educational institution on a portion of this land quickly gained favor in influential circles. Rogers, able to draw upon both the political skills sharpened in his own dealings with the Virginia legislature and the active support of important industrial and commercial leaders who wanted a technical school in Boston, went straight to work. After two false starts, he and four associates produced the "Objects and Plan for an Institute of Technology," and on April 10, 1861, an Act to Incorporate the Massachusetts Institute of Technology, "having for its objects the advancement of the Mechanic Arts, Manufactures, Commerce, Agriculture and the applied sciences generally, together with the promotion of the practical education of the industrial classes," was signed by Banks's successor, Governor John Andrew.[7]

Now the Civil War intervened, and the problem of financing the Institute remained. In 1862 Congress passed the Morrill Act, granting federal funds to "provide Colleges for the benefit of Agriculture and the Mechanic Arts." Governor Andrew proposed that this money be used to support a grand plan to unite Harvard, the fledgling MIT and a new agricultural college at Amherst. Rogers spoke forcefully against this plan and its implied submission of the Institute to a dominant Harvard, and the governor gracefully withdrew. In the end, seven-tenths of the federal grant was used to create the agricultural college, with the remainder given to MIT. This, coupled with generous gifts from private sources, was sufficient to proceed.

The strain took its toll on Rogers. In 1864 he traveled to Europe to recuperate in his brother's company and to observe developments in scientific education there. He was impressed most by the Polytechnic Institute at Karlsruhe and returned refreshed to Boston late in 1864 to prepare to admit students that winter. Elementary courses in mathematics, physics, chemistry, drawing, and French were assembled and announced, and on February 20, 1865, Rogers exulted in his diary: "Organized the school! Fifteen students entered. May not this prove a memorable day!"[8]

When the first regular session began in October of that year, with seventy students enrolled, the faculty roster numbered ten, all with the rank of full professor. Besides Rogers, who taught physics and geology, the staff included not only such men as John D. Runkle in mathematics and Charles W. Eliot in analytical chemistry and metallurgy, but also Ferdinand Bôcher in modern languages and William P. Atkinson in English language and literature.[9] The early presence of these humanists and the equality of rank they enjoyed make clear that from the outset Rogers's intent was to offer more than just focused professional training in engineering. He meant as well, as the first catalogue put it, "To furnish such a general education, founded upon the Mathematical, Physical, and

Natural Sciences, English and other Modern Languages, and Mental and Political Science, as shall form a fitting preparation for any of the departments of active life."[10]

Rogers's insistence on educating engineers rather than simply training them led him to reject the sequential model of independent exposure to the liberal arts followed by concentrated technical work, as in medicine or law. He believed instead in the integration of scientific, literary, and social studies in a single four-year program. This view came less from a desire to conserve his students' time and resources, though this was an important consideration given the modest circumstances of the typical aspiring engineer, than from Rogers's conviction that engineers must be conscious of the cultural values implicit not only in the humanities but in the forms and assumptions of technological practice itself. The ability to understand and criticize one mode of thought or discourse in light of another, the mark of an education in breadth, could be achieved only by the concurrent, interactive study of contrasting disciplines.[11]

Still, Rogers knew that young men and women[12] would come to MIT to study science and engineering, not liberal arts. He designed for them a common program of required subjects.[13] In the first two years, comprehensive studies in basic science and technique were leavened with substantial work in English composition and literature, French, and German. At the beginning of the third year, students were expected to select one of five (after 1873, eight) courses offered in the scientific and technological disciplines. Here too their sustained exposure to liberal studies was insured by further requirements in biological science and four broad areas of humanistic endeavor: modern languages; history, political economy, and the "science of government";[14] logic, rhetoric, and the history of the English language; and mental and moral philosophy.

But Rogers also understood that there would be some students for whom the prospect of concentration in a specific technical discipline would no longer seem as attractive as it once did, and he sought to insure that there would be a course for them, too, a path to the bachelor's degree that did not entail their transfer to another school. From 1865 to 1904, there was such a course, formally identified over the years as Science and Literature, the Elective Course, or General Studies, but known popularly from 1873 on as Course IX. Concentration in Course IX did not mean a radical switch from a technical discipline to a wholly different specialization in a single area of the humanities or social sciences. Instead, it would be a continuation of the same diversified program of liberal studies that had accompanied the student's professional education from the start, albeit in somewhat greater depth than was demanded of engineering majors. Nor would the technical disciplines be abandoned; in place of an intensive sequence in one of the engineering fields, Course IX upperclassmen were required to select, as their interests dictated, subjects in physics, chemistry, geology, zoology, and the various branches of engineering. For them, the change would thus be from a greater to a lesser degree of technical specialization. Though its focus would be widened and its cultural setting enriched and enlarged, the central emphasis on science would remain uncompromised.[15] Never a large program in terms of student majors,[16] Course IX was nonetheless treated throughout this period with the respect Rogers himself had exemplified, as a full partner in the educational aspirations of a technological university.

The task of making these ambitious plans a reality in the classroom fell largely to William Parsons Atkinson. Born in Boston in 1820, Atkinson graduated from Harvard in 1838 and spent the years until his appointment at MIT in preparatory education as a private tutor and, briefly, as principal of the Brookline High School. Remembered by his students as a "quiet and genial personality [who] made 'history hour' a relief from the more abstract and trying engineering studies,"[17] he struggled manfully to assemble the lectures and exercises promised by Rogers's expansive vision. In addition to his subjects in English composition and literature, he developed teaching materials in history, philosophy, political economy, and business law, and in 1871 his title was changed to professor of English and history to reflect the range of his responsibilities more fully. By 1873 Atkinson had constructed an imposing program of upperclass studies, which included year-long subjects in British and American Constitutional History and the History of Commerce and Industry, and one-semester offerings in History and Literature, Political Economy, Business Law, and Political and Industrial Geography.[18]

A bit of the flavor of these subjects, as well as Atkinson's difficulties in teaching across so wide a spectrum by himself, is given by his report on the activities of the "English Department" in 1872:

With the fourth year's class my attention has been mainly devoted to Political Economy and the Commercial and Economical aspects of History. Adopting the smallest and least controversial manual that I could find [otherwise unidentified], I have made it the text for a series of readings and oral lessons, designed mainly to interest the class in the investigation of the various politico-economical subjects, which have so close a connexion with their professions and future occupations in life. No subjects belonging to the English department are more important, or have proved more interesting to the students as these; but in the more technical parts of Political Economy, the subjects of Currency, Banking, &c., I have to lament my own lack of practical knowledge; and I would respectfully suggest that a brief course of non-controversial lectures on these topics, explanatory of the ordinary course of business, and given by a practical business man, would be very useful.[19]

Atkinson's pleas for more staff so that he might increase the effectiveness of his own teaching by narrowing its scope were answered in part by the appointment in 1871 of George H. Howison as professor of logic and the philosophy of science. In 1873 Course IX was joined as an alternative to concentration in a specific technical discipline by a new course in philosophy, and Howison was eager to begin the work of curriculum development in this area. But the Institute's trustees prevailed upon him to assist Atkinson in political economy as well, so in the spring of 1873 he taught the fourth-year class from Amasa Walker's *Science of Wealth*, "taking pains," he wrote,

to present the points in which other leading writers differ from him, and to develop with special clearness both sides of the great dispute between Protection and Free Trade. The class have shown great interest in the subject, and at the final examination . . . not a single member was conditioned, while the great majority passed at a very high grade.[20]

In 1874, over the strong protest of Atkinson,[21] the work in political economy, which had previously been required of all students, was made optional for all but concentrators in Course IX. Atkinson continued to plead for more staff and resources in the humanities and social studies, but by now the "spectre of poverty stalked the Institute."[22] Increasingly severe financial difficulties forced the Institute not only to deny this request but to reduce the staff in several other areas and, in 1878, to withdraw the Course in Philosophy entirely.

Finances had been a serious problem for the Institute from the very beginning. Much of Rogers's time and energy during the early years was consumed in the search for funding, and in October 1868 he suffered a slight stroke while attending a faculty meeting. John D. Runkle was appointed acting president in December of that year while he recovered, but age and weariness forced Rogers to submit his formal resignation on May 3, 1870. Yet, even before Runkle's succession to the presidency became official in October, the Institute's independence was threatened by its own financial weakness and the considerable ambitions of the new and energetic president of Harvard.

Harvard had for many years been receptive to the ideals of technical education. As early as 1847, it had committed itself to instruction in the applied sciences by establishing the Lawrence Scientific School, but it could never resolve to its own satisfaction the question of what the status of technical studies within the university should be. Successive administrations showed a continuing bias toward pure science rather than its applications, and the prevailing opinion within the university was that professional training should be appended to rather than combined with the traditional liberal arts curriculum. That the Lawrence School never prospered in such circumstances is not surprising, and proposals to merge the new MIT with Harvard were heard with regularity.[23]

Rogers, as we have seen, fought tenaciously for the Institute's independence and held to the view that the proper place for engineering training was in a four-year undergraduate program, where it could effectively be combined with liberal studies to produce a sound and useful education. In 1869, however, the Harvard Corporation reached into the Institute's faculty to select Charles W. Eliot as the university's new president. Their choice was not unanimous; many members feared that the traditional Harvard curriculum was not safe in the hands of this young reformer, with his scientific background, his avowed sympathy with the new technical education, and his harsh criticism of the unresponsiveness of American colleges to the economic and technological imperatives of the time.[24] For his part, Eliot intended to build a university in the largest sense at Harvard, and for forty years he pursued the goal of making MIT a part of it.

There was much to commend such a merger. The Institute's coffers were all but empty, though the apparent success of its educational experiment had already begun to win it a reputation for excellence. Harvard, on the other hand, had money, but the Lawrence School had never been able to achieve the standards the university and the Lawrence family had set for it. In his courtship of the Institute, Eliot stressed not only the financial rewards of a merger with the university but, perhaps misreading the temper of his intended, the great honor MIT would enjoy in becoming a part of Harvard as well.[25]

Despite some sentiment in favor of the association within his own faculty, Runkle, with the strong support of the recuperating Rogers, successfully resisted Eliot's advances. But the collapse of the merger plan late in 1870 left the Institute's financial difficulties unresolved. Enrollments, which had been 224 in 1870, peaked at 348 in 1872 and, in the lean years following the depression of 1873, dropped year by year to a low of 188 in 1878.[26] Runkle struggled to keep the Institute alive, and though suggestions that the staff be reduced and faculty salaries lowered were never taken up, the few new appointments that were possible could be made only at the lowest ranks. By 1878 Runkle's energies were exhausted, and he resigned the presidency for a two-year leave of absence in Europe. Rogers himself was called from retirement to succeed him and, at the age of seventy-four, managed to raise over $60,000 in new funds and reverse the alarming decline of enrollments. By the time Runkle returned in 1880 to resume his professorship in mathematics, the financial emergency had been weathered and the Institute's prospects brightened once again.[27]

Now Rogers could look forward to a hard-earned second retirement. The MIT Corporation had elected his successor in 1881, and an inaugural ceremony was planned as a part of the graduation exercises in Huntington Hall on May 30, 1882. After an emotional tribute to the greatness of his vision and leadership, the old man, visibly moved, rose to reply. "His voice," said one who was there,

was at first weak and faltering, but, as was his wont, he gathered inspiration from his theme, and for the moment his voice rang out in its full volume and in those well-remembered, most thrilling tones. Then, of a sudden, there was silence in the midst of speech; that stately figure suddenly drooped, the fire died out of the eye ever so quick to kindle at noble thoughts, and, before one of his attentive listeners had time to suspect the cause, he fell to the platform instantly dead.[28]

Thus was the torch passed to this stunned witness, Francis Amasa Walker. At forty-one, he had already been a soldier, a public servant, a scholar, and a teacher, winning in each of these endeavors distinction enough in the eyes of his contemporaries to fill a lifetime. Now, with the enthusiastic concurrence of Rogers himself, Walker assumed leadership of the institute as its third president. In the seventeen years of his tenure, MIT would grow from a fragile school of slender resources and great ambitions to an institution of national reputation, a leader by example in the revolutionary modernization of American higher education. By 1897 the construction and purchase of several buildings in the Back Bay would more than double the worth of the Institute's physical capital, the number of students and teachers would quadruple, and the endowment would rise almost fifteen times in value.[29] Instruction was introduced and departments created in technical fields that were just then being born, and in nurturing a genuine Department of Political Economy at MIT Walker contributed greatly to building the scientific and empirical foundations he believed so essential to the development of his own discipline. But, as if to illustrate the truth of Rogers's perception that the values and assumptions of technology itself would gradually permeate the wider culture, Walker's own economic thought during this period came increasingly to encompass a kind of technological art, an informed and purposeful interference in the processes of economic life by a state committed to furthering "the public interest."

The second son of Amasa Walker, Francis was born on June 2, 1840, just as his father was abandoning a successful career in manufacturing to devote the remainder of his life to public service and scholarship. The family soon settled near Amherst, Massachusetts, where Amasa embarked on the teaching and writing that would establish him as a leading American economist of his day. Young Francis entered Amherst College at fifteen. Despite a serious eye malady that kept him back a full year, he excelled both in his studies and at boxing, an activity well suited to the quickness of his hands and temper. Upon his graduation with honors in 1860, he joined the law firm of Devens and Hoar in Worcester and drilled with a local rifle company during the critical winter of 1861. When war erupted that spring, his older brother enlisted immediately, but Amasa forbade Francis to join him until he reached the age of majority. Volunteering that August as a sergeant major, Francis began four years of military service distinguished by bravery and pluck. Quickly promoted to staff officer, he saw action in Virginia, sustaining heavy wounds at Chancellorsville and falling into enemy hands near Petersburg in the summer of 1864. A daring attempt at escape was unsuccessful, and Walker languished in the Libby Prison at Richmond until he was exchanged and sent home late that year. In March, not yet twenty-five, he was breveted brigadier general for gallantry and meritorious service.[30]

With his recovery complete and the war over, Walker took a teaching position at Williston Seminary in Easthampton and assisted his father by lecturing from time to time at Amherst. Like John Stuart Mill, he also contributed to his father's scholarly work, helping Amasa prepare his treatise *The Science of Wealth,* published in 1866. Though decidedly in the classical English tradition against which Francis was later to react, the elder Walker's ideas made a strong and lasting impression on his son's thinking. Both insisted on a scientific approach to political economy based on the confrontation of theory with empirical evidence and labored to free the subject from what they saw as the limiting and distorting effects of treating it as a branch of theology or moral philosophy. Both maintained a lifelong interest in monetary problems, and Francis significantly extended and developed Amasa's insightful distinction of entrepreneurship from capital as a factor of production. Early in 1868, however, Francis left the academy, briefly writing editorials for Samuel Bowles's *Springfield Republican.* Declining an offer to return to Amherst as a part-time lecturer, he immersed himself instead in Washington politics to gain experience for a career in journalism.[31]

In 1869 Walker was deputized by David A. Wells, then special commissioner of the revenue, to reorganize the Treasury's Bureau of Statistics, and his work there led to an appointment in 1870 as superintendent of the Ninth Census. Walker saw the job of collecting statistical data as a serious scientific endeavor; as early as 1868, he had written that the latest election returns from Melbourne or the ordinary police blotters of American cities held more "interest to the student of political science than all the speculations of all the philosophers."[32] With the support in Congress of his friend James A. Garfield, Walker sought unsuccessfully to professionalize the operations of the census by basing the selection of enumerators on ability rather than patronage. Still, he was able to gather data with unprecedented thoroughness, winning the admiration of statisticians around the world with his imaginative presentation of the results in the exhaustive *Statistical Atlas* of 1874 and his candid assessment of the survey's errors and shortcomings.[33] The huge mass of facts and figures that now filled his head, moreover, fueled his growing impatience with the dry, lifeless abstractions of English orthodoxy. When the empirical methods of German historicism promised to put this mountain of information to productive scientific use, Walker would be prepared to recognize the advantages of the new approach and treat the young economists who argued for it with sympathy and respect.

As the work of the census continued through 1871, Walker's thoughts turned increasingly to his own future. After negotiations for an editorial post with the *New York Times* came to naught, he accepted President Grant's appointment to the scandal-ridden commissionership of Indian Affairs so that he might finish his census work despite the expiration of its funding. By Christmas of 1872, discouraged by the corruption and inefficiency he had seen in Washington, Walker was preparing to return to Massachusetts and a position with his brother-in-law's manufacturing concern when a new opportunity appeared unexpectedly. The census had engaged him in a cordial and fruitful collaboration with Daniel Coit Gilman of the Sheffield Scientific School at Yale, and when Gilman left Yale in 1872 to become president of the University of California, Walker was asked to join the Sheffield faculty as its first professor of political economy and history.[34]

Walker's seven years at Yale were busy and productive. Though somewhat shy as a public speaker, teaching appealed to him, and the deep and genuine concern he showed for the welfare of his students made the erect, soldierly professor with the full moustache and glossy silk hat a well-loved figure on the campus.[35] His fascination with data and their analysis never waned; he inaugurated one of America's first courses in statistics at the Yale Graduate School and maintained his ties to the census by serving from New Haven as its unsalaried superintendent until 1874. The impact on Walker's thinking of this continuous exposure to "the flesh and blood of actual, vital Political Economy," to "man and societies as they are,"[36] was profound. More sensitive than they to the vast complexities of the American economy, he showed correspondingly less of the dogmatic assurance of many of his academic contemporaries.[37] Nor did Walker abandon his interest in politics and practical affairs. He served on both the local and the state boards of education, went to Paris in 1878 as the American delegate to the International Monetary Conference to argue for universal bimetallism, and, at Garfield's urging, directed the census once more in 1880.[38]

But the most lasting and significant product of Walker's Yale years was his scholarship, embodied primarily in *The Wages Question* (1876) and a book that was to become a leading college economics text in the United States for twenty years, *Political Economy* (1883). In these works, Walker developed a theory of entrepreneurial profits closely analogous to the Ricardian theory of rent and challenged the reigning wage-fund doctrine by asserting a relationship between wages and the productivity of labor. He developed this latter insight into a general (and controversial) theory of distribution that linked the returns to capital, labor, and entrepreneurship to the contribution each makes to the value of current production.[39] Walker's analysis lacks the precision of John Bates Clark's later articulation of the marginal productivity theorems, prompting one not unsympathetic historian to observe that Walker's theory "amount[s] simply to the statement that each factor in turn gets what is left over when the others have been paid."[40] Yet the very interrelatedness of allocational outcomes in this sense anticipates the style of contemporary general equilibrium theory and, accordingly, Walker continually drew attention to conditions of perfect competition as the guarantor of a "harmonious and beneficent"[41] economic order. Where real conditions diverge from the ideal of perfect competition, he maintained, government, clumsy though it might be, could properly legislate as required to establish or restore competitive conditions.[42]

Yet, despite the corrective role for government implied by the centrality of competitive conditions, Walker remained faithful throughout this period to the doctrine of laissez-faire. Influenced perhaps by the incompetence and venality he had seen in Grant's Washington, his views at this moment, expressed in two letters written in 1879, are worth quoting at length:

> The social and industrial relations of every community, even the most primitive, are a web finer and more intricate than gossamer; and when the clumsy foot of the law, as of a ruminating or meditative ox, is brought down upon it, rending and crushing what all the art of all the legislators in the world cannot restore, I say "brutal." . . .
>
> That is why I am a free-trader—not because I doubt that capital and labor make mistakes, when left to themselves . . . nor because I doubt that it would be possible for a central authority, directed by superior intelligence, so to order them as to produce appreciably larger results; but because I know of what sort of stuff legislators and committees are composed—what sort of bargaining and dickering goes on . . . what sort of compromises are made . . . what sort of influences prevail. . . .
>
> For these reasons, I would rather trust the sense of individual interest, imperfect as it is often found to be, than submit industry to the discussions of any Legislature that ever was assembled.[43]

Productive though it was, Walker's time at Yale must have been frustrating as well. His relations with the "cantankerous" William Graham Sumner, never close, deteriorated over time as the differences in their views became sharper, and Walker's lack of a Yale pedigree and association with the slightly déclassé Sheffield School consigned him to the periphery of campus life.[44] He regretfully declined Gilman's offer of a professorship at Johns Hopkins in 1876 to redeem the obligation he felt to those colleagues at Yale who had taken on his classes while he had been on leave. But he did deliver a series of lectures on monetary questions at Johns Hopkins in 1877 which brought him into closer contact with the German historicism newly transplanted in Baltimore by Herbert Baxter Adams and alerted him to the quality of the students at Gilman's new university. When Rogers sought him out in June 1880 to offer the presidency of MIT, Walker's responsibilities to the census and the possibility of a cabinet post in the new Garfield administration caused him to hesitate, but he accepted at last in the spring of 1881. Delayed and saddened by the subsequent murder of his old friend the president, he set out in November of that year for yet another career, this time in Boston.[45]

A "doer" all his life, Walker was stimulated by the challenge of building a young institution as vibrantly committed to the "New Education" as he was.[46] He stood foursquare with Rogers in his belief in the soundness and utility of a liberal education rooted in science and technology and saw in it a way not only to provide the nation with young people trained to meet the demands of modern life but to extend the moral and developmental advantages of higher education to a broader class of students as well. Classical studies, he argued in his *President's Report for 1883,* would only rarely provide the spark needed to engage the labors of the young in scholarly work, but rigorous, practical training in science would generate enthusiasm for study in all the disciplines and spare students the boredom and idleness that pervaded traditional colleges. "I believe it to be equally true," he went on, "that the faculties of clear perception, of careful discrimination, and of just generalization are developed by the study of natural history, of chemistry, of physics, as they can be through no other educational means."[47]

A proper history of the Institute's impressive growth in size and stature in the years before 1900 and the role played in it by Walker's leadership has yet to be written. The new president worked hard to improve the school's precarious financial health, cajoling substantial support from both private benefactors and the state and steadfastly preserving the Institute's independence in the face of continuing overtures from Eliot's Harvard. He moved immediately to broaden the curriculum and, despite his own lack of experience at the frontiers of technology, made a series of brilliant appointments in the scientific and technical disciplines, including Silas Holman in physics, George F. Swain in civil engineering, and William T. Sedgwick, a graduate of the Sheffield School at Yale, in biology, which established the school's eminence in these fields for decades to come. Yet, when the Institute moved to its present site in Cambridge in 1916, the building chosen to bear Walker's name housed neither classrooms nor research laboratories. Instead, the Walker Memorial has to this day been a comfortable place for students to eat and a home to dozens of extracurricular organizations and activities.

From the beginning of his presidency Walker strove to promote the physical and emotional well-being of his charges. When he arrived in 1881, the Institute maintained no housing for its students, and the single dining facility was a small lunchroom hidden in a corner of the shed used for military drill. Students came with seriousness of purpose and well-defined career objectives, largely from families of limited means and no traditional college loyalties, and their full class schedules and the time spent in travel left them very little opportunity for diversion or organized recreation. Under Walker's guidance, a true campus life began to emerge. Constantly accessible to students and their parents, a good part of his working day was spent in conversation with lonely or discouraged young people. He cheerfully supported a host of budding student organizations in mustering a wholesome spirit of community and slowly cultivated a strong loyalty to the Institute in its growing body of alumni. Here, even more than at Yale, Walker inspired the respect and love of hundreds of students to whom he was both teacher and mentor.[48]

For Walker himself, the chance to create at MIT a Department of Political Economy where none had existed before must have been irresistible, and he plunged instantly into this particular labor of love. As if in answer to Atkinson's prayers, the catalogue for 1881–82 announced: "The instruction in Political Economy and International Law is given by the President,"[49] enabling a grateful Atkinson to return to teaching in English and history, the fields he knew best. By 1883 Walker had stiffened the requirement in liberal studies for concentrators in all disciplines; in addition to substantial work in English literature and modern languages, all science and engineering majors now took a sequence that included three subjects in history and one, taught by Walker from his own text, in political economy. In 1882 the Course in Science and Literature was reorganized and renamed the Course in General Studies, though it continued to be known informally as Course IX. Built as before on a demanding base of science and mathematics, Course IX now encompassed extended work in history, political economy, public law, geography, and statistics. In its emphasis on the inter-relatedness and empirical foundations of all these studies, more-over, it began to reflect the influence of the German historicism to which Walker himself was increasingly drawn. Until 1886 Walker and Atkinson between them taught nine subjects in General Studies each year, and in these years every regular student at the Institute was exposed to the president's energy and commitment to his field in the introductory lectures in political economy. And for Walker, whose admiration for the "captains of industry" and the activity of entrepreneurship was strong and deeply rooted, the presidency of MIT offered a unique opportunity to reach and influence the development of dozens of young entrepreneurs-to-be.[50]

But Walker's purpose from the outset had been to build a teaching department around the Course in General Studies whose excellence and commitment to scholarship would equal that of the Institute's scientists and engineers. As the everyday burdens of administration left him less and less time for the classroom, Walker's thoughts turned to the question of new appointments in history and political economy. Given his own growing dissatisfaction with English classicism and his long-standing, cordial relationship with Gilman and his colleagues at Johns Hopkins, the search would prove to be an easy one.

In September 1885 the American Economic Association (AEA) was born in Saratoga Springs, New York, and Walker, who himself had felt "the need of such moral support from fellow workers in political economy as might come from formal association and concerted action,"[51] agreed to serve as its first president. The initiator of this venture was Richard T. Ely, a vigorous and provocative young scholar who had returned from graduate work at Heidelberg in 1880 and joined the faculty at Johns Hopkins the following year. Along with his older colleague Herbert Baxter Adams, the founder in 1884 of the American Historical Association, Ely had drunk deeply of German historicism. Greatly impressed by the empiricism of the historical school and the active role for the state in economic affairs that its doctrines implied, Ely hoped to create an association of progressive economists who, like him, repudiated laissez-faire as a scientific doctrine and sought ways not only to explain the economic order but to improve its ability to produce wealth and distribute it justly as well.[52] "They were concerned," as Joseph Dorfman has aptly put it, "not only with analysis, but—in an in-cipient way of course—with social engineering."[53]

In this, Ely's views were at one with those of the German economists who had formed the Verein für Sozialpolitik in 1872. Rejecting the rigid formalism of English theory and its emphasis on natural rights and immutable laws of nature, the Verein economists were strongly influenced by the success of the inductive, experimental method in the natural sciences and committed to a political philosophy that reified the organic state and asserted its plenary authority over the individual.[54] They attached great importance to the gathering of statistical data by government agencies and its application to what they called the "Science of Finance," the study of the "wants of the state and the means by which they are supplied."[55] When John Kells Ingram of Trinity College, Dublin, offered a sympathetic summary of their views to the British Association for the Advancement of Science in 1878, he might just as easily have been quoting from the statement of principles adopted by the AEA at its founding seven years later. The Verein, he said,

seeks to understand present economic phenomena through the study of their historical development, and to ascertain them as accurately as possible through statistical investigations. It uses the knowledge of the nature of man's intellect and will for the rational explanation of economic facts, but does not construct those facts themselves out of one-sided assumptions respecting the nature of men.

It . . . recognizes the right of the state to positive intervention in the economic relations of the community, for the support of the weak and the strengthening of public spirit. As the Political Economy of the last century applied itself chiefly to the liberation of the economic forces from antiquated and useless restrictions, so the new school specially meets the acknowledged need of new social arrangements, the need of social reform in opposition to social revolution on the one hand and to rigid *laissez-faire* on the other.[56]

But in the 1880s such young men as those gathered around Ely at Saratoga Springs could not successfully challenge the abstract, deductive orthodoxy alone. Their attempts to bring empirical substance to economic theory through historical and statistical research and to create an active role for the state in economic policy needed a champion from the older generation of established economists. They found him in Walker. Though he opposed the association's original (and short-lived) statement of activist principles on the tactical ground that it would divide economists rather than unite them and never subscribed to policies of state intervention quite so radical as Ely's, Walker nonetheless saw great merit in the approach of the historical school[57] and threw the weight of his considerable prestige behind the efforts of its young American adherents.[58] He had always been deeply concerned to establish his discipline as a positive science rather than a prescriptive art or a form of moral discourse. The economist's business, he told his students, was simply "to trace economic effects to their causes, leaving it to the philosopher . . . the moralist or the statesman, to teach how men and nations should act in view of the economic principles so established."[59] Though his respect for classical doctrine remained strong, Walker came increasingly to fault its sterile deductivism and often stubborn normative predisposition to laissez-faire. Classical writers, he argued in 1879, had been led to "avoid some of the most fruitful sources of economic discovery, to employ less and less the historic and inductive methods, and to resort more and more to the *a priori* and deductive, and especially to effect a simplicity in classification of which the subject matter is not susceptible."[60]

At Sumner's Yale, such an appeal to experience and empirical procedure could be made, if at all, only apologetically.[61] But at MIT, the banner of inductivism flew proudly over disciplines whose magnificent achievements were there for all to see, and Walker's confidence in the value of methods of physical science and engineering to the study of economic problems grew accordingly. In his *President's Report for 1883*, as we have seen, he had commended the study of physics to all educated men and women as a model of clear thinking and discriminating perception. By 1890, in a letter to Alfred Marshall, his claims regarding the place of physics in the education of the economist had become substantially bolder:

> But the physicist . . . has a truly enormous advantage in studying the phenomena of industrial society, in watching the propagation of economic shocks, in tracing the lines of fracture from commercial or financial disasters, in appreciating and estimating the degree and direction of industrial forces making for good and of industrial disturbances making for harm.
>
> I have been much impressed by this thought as I read your work. It seems to me that only a man who had profoundly studied the mechanics of heat, light and sound could exhibit so much insight into the nature of economic forces and so much at once of capacity and of restraint in judging and even estimating their effects upon human society.[62]

If the analogy of economics to classical physics was a powerful influence on Walker's economic epistemology during these years, it is hardly surprising that his views on economic policy too came increasingly to reflect the ambition of technology so brilliantly realized at MIT, the subjugation of nature by man's purposeful application of physical science. Walker's attachment to laissez-faire had never been one of principle; indeed, as we have noted, he had no doubt that a central authority guided by a "superior intelligence" *could* intervene to achieve the purpose of increasing production by drawing upon the principles of a well-developed, disinterested social science. His objection was rather that real lawmakers were too venal or, at best, simply too clumsy or ignorant to fashion legislation sufficiently responsive to the complexities of economic life to improve upon the results of free dealings between labor and capital. But now the undeniable successes of technology in the physical world offered the promise of something better, a neutral and effective economic engineering derived from the new social science inspired by Newton and Maxwell. Accordingly, Walker became more receptive to carefully crafted legislation designed to achieve specific, limited public purposes.

To be sure, Walker retained to the end of his life a firm belief in free competition as the cornerstone of a healthy and just economic order and a corresponding skepticism regarding the efficacy of state intervention.[63] But he came more and more to recognize that the realities of industrial life were often a far cry from the ideal of perfect competition, and in these cases he believed that only supervision or regulation of business by the state offered the hope of correcting the imperfections. He could, for example, distinguish the effects on competition of older, looser forms of business organization from those of the large corporations and trusts of his own day. Partnerships and small firms, he wrote in 1887,

are always subject to dissolution, by reason of antagonisms developed, suspicions aroused, separate interests appearing; and the expectation of such dissolution attaches to them from their formation. The cohesion excited, as between the particles of the economic mass which the theory of competition assumes to be absolutely free from affiliation and attractions, is certain to be shifting and transitory. The corporation, on the other hand, implies the imposition of a common rule upon a mass of capital which would otherwise be in many hands, subject to the impulses of individual owners. But it is because the hand into which these masses of capital are gathered is a *dead hand* that the deepest injury is wrought to competition. . . . [H]ow deeply the industrial corporation violates the principle of competition, and how absurd it is to claim for it the protection of *laissez-faire*.[64]

Thus, Walker favored both a vigorous antitrust policy and the formation of trade unions in particular industries to address the threat to competition represented by the imbalance of economic power in the industrial combines.[65] Toward this latter end, he supported much social legislation as well: acts regulating wages, hours, and working conditions, the provision of free primary education for all, and the regulation of banking to safeguard the savings of working men and women.[66]

The faith of the AEA's young founders in the efficacy and moral value of purposeful state intervention informed by impartial social theory and administrative science was itself an influential component of a larger shift in the terms and assumptions of American political discourse during this period. As the nineteenth century drew to a close, the Progressive ideal of conscious managerial control over social outcomes in the interest of the public at large and the refinement of bureaucratic techniques for securing it exerted a growing influence on the nation's political thought and practice.[67] Led by such intellectuals as Ely, Lester Ward, and Herbert Croly, American Progressives began to conceive of society itself as a concrete, living entity. Its purposes and interests were understood to be entirely its own, distinct from and superior to those of its human constituents. The active agent of this reified society in the world of affairs was the state, and it, they held, must be given pervasive powers to direct individual behavior and manipulate social outcomes in the interest of "society."[68] Politics, as Woodrow Wilson suggested, could now be separated from administration; whereas the former concerned itself with the often vexing problems of identifying and articulating the common good, the latter could draw upon the neutral theories of management science to devise ways to bring it about.

Though Walker never traveled as far down the ideological path toward public management of economic processes as did Ely and his disciples, the strong and timely encouragement he offered those who did makes him an important transitional figure in the history of American economics. Moved both by the teachings of the German historicists and by the confident assurance of technological mastery over nature that pervaded the institute he represented to the world, Walker firmly rejected the complacent quietism of laissez-faire. Instead, he came increasingly to see law and administrative regulation as tools of the state, "social technologies" made possible by the growth of scientific knowledge and designed to enable the outcomes of complex social processes to be manipulated in the public interest. In this affirmation of the engineer's aspiration in the realm of human affairs, he helped lead his discipline into the twentieth century and lay the foundations for the political economy of hierarchical organization and allocation by plan in both the public and private sectors that has come to characterize our own time.

But just as the reification of society in both its German and its American variants carried the seeds of a virulent, often racist nationalism, which would burst forth in the Great War, Walker's cautious attraction to the imperatives of the public interest had its darker side as well. The new ideology did indeed allow the separation of politics from administration, but now, as it sought to identify and articulate the common good, Progressive politics necessarily became collectivist, and sometimes xenophobic. On questions of race and immigration in particular, Walker's ideas exerted a considerable influence on Progressive opinion. From his quarter-century of immersion in demographic statistics, Walker had by 1896 distilled what he called the "displacement principle," the notion that immigration does not add to the total population because it induces a compensating decline in the birth rate of the native population.[69] He drew the necessary conclusions for policy with stark candor:

The entrance into our political, social, and industrial life of such vast masses of peasantry, degraded below our utmost conceptions, is a matter which no intelligent patriot can look upon without the greatest apprehension and alarm. These people have no history behind them which is of a nature to give encouragement. They have none of the inherited instincts and tendencies which made it comparatively easy to deal with the immigration of the olden time. They are beaten men from beaten races; representing the worst failures in the struggle for existence. . . .

The present situation is most menacing to our peace and political safety. In all the social and industrial disorders of this country since 1877, the foreign elements have proved themselves the ready tool of demogogues in defying the law, in destroying property, and in working violence. . . . The problems which so sternly confront us today are serious enough, without being complicated and aggravated by the addition of some millions of Hungarians, Bohemians, Poles, south Italians, and Russian Jews.[70]

In the last twelve years of his life, Walker's partial conversion to the politics of state intervention in the interests of "society" was given strong impetus by the intellectual presence and energetic teaching of the staunch Germanist Davis Rich Dewey. The elder brother of the generally like-minded philosopher John Dewey, Davis was born in Burlington, Vermont, on April 7, 1858. After his graduation with honors from the University of Vermont in 1879, he spent four years as a teacher of Latin and Greek and principal of various academies in Vermont and Hyde Park, near Chicago. In 1883 Dewey began graduate work in history, politics, and economics at Johns Hopkins, traveling two years later with his mentor Ely to Saratoga Springs to sign the original statement of principles of the AEA. Dewey's deep attachments both to the association and to German historicism lasted until the end of his life in 1942. His *Financial History of the United States,* first published in 1903 and dedicated to his beloved teachers at Johns Hopkins,[71] is a model of the integrative methods Dewey first learned at Hopkins and remained in print for over thirty years in twelve editions. Equally loyal to the association, he became its president in 1909 and served continuously as editor of the *American Economic Review* from its founding in 1911 to his retirement in 1940.

When Walker determined to make a new appointment in General Studies for the academic year 1886–87, his thoughts turned naturally to the committed young man he had met at Saratoga Springs. For Dewey too, the prospect of working at the very citadel of inductive science with so eminent and sympathetic a figure as Walker must have been an exciting one, and he eagerly accepted the invitation to join the Institute's faculty as instructor in history and political science in 1886. The years that followed saw Walker's gradual withdrawal from teaching and, under Dewey's increasingly confident leadership, a remarkable development in the scope and depth of the Institute's offerings in economics and the related historical and political studies that both Walker and Dewey saw as essential to them.

Indifferent to abstract theorizing divorced from empirical reality, Dewey insisted that the application of economic knowledge to the practical problems of government and business administration was the central calling of the academic economist.[72] From the beginning of his long service at the institute, he brought this point of view into the classroom. By 1888 Dewey, now assistant professor of economics and statistics,[73] was teaching ten (!) different subjects each year, ranging from introductions to political economy, statistics, commercial geography, and industrial history to practical studies in governmental administration, commercial practice, railroad management, and national taxation and budgets to advanced work in such areas as socialism and the history of economic theory.[74] Nor were the related disciplines ignored. As William Atkinson, who had taught every one of the Institute's regular students since 1865, prepared to retire, his position in history was filled (and Dewey partially relieved) first by Charles H. Levermore, another of Ely's students at Johns Hopkins, who served from 1888 until he was called to head what is now Adelphi University in 1893, and then by Charles F. A. Currier.

The program assembled in General Studies by these men is distinguished by both the breadth of its offerings and the clear influence of Dewey's commitment to the interdisciplinary, empirical approach of German historicism. By the early 1890s, all students were required to take (in addition to subjects in English and modern languages) modern political history in the first year, American history in the second, and political economy and industrial history in the third. Students in Course IX not only pursued greater depth in all these studies but availed themselves as well of elective sequences in a wide range of fields, including political theory and public law, sociology, and anthropology. Course IX majors seeking a concentration in economics and other interested students were offered a rich menu of advanced subjects falling into five general areas. Finance and Taxation included a class in financial history taught by Dewey that made extensive use of primary sources and government documents, a subject in the history and theory of taxation using Bastable's *Public Finance,* and a class in banking that, reflecting Walker's strong interest in the subject, included detailed treatment of the question of bimetallism. Two subjects in the area of Commercial and Industrial History were offered, as well as introductory and advanced work in statistics. A single subject in Socialism (later retitled Theories and Methods of Social Reform) considered "the economic systems proposed, particularly during the present century, to change the existing distribution of wealth [in addition to] systems of cooperation, profit-sharing, and governmental control of industries," and the concentration concluded with an integrative subject in the History of Economic Theory.[75]

Yet the institute was far from a passive receptor and propagator of the Gospel according to Johns Hopkins. We have already noted the dramatic impact of Walker's close exposure to classical physics and its practitioners on his methodological thinking. But the culture of science and technology that permeated the Institute made an equally deep impression on Dewey and pushed him on to intellectual territory still uncharted by the Germanists themselves. By 1891 they had both to come to see the natural and social sciences as parts of a single whole, a unified science of nature and man that implicitly extended the promise of control through technology from the world of objects to the world of men and women. The catalogue for 1891–92 expressed it this way:

The curriculum [in Course IX] has been arranged in the belief that the origin, growth and laws of political and industrial society can best be approached through the methods used in natural science. The general requirement of the Institute in chemistry and physics is substantially preserved in this course. From the study of biology, including botany and zoology as a basis, the student is prepared to proceed to the study of man in society, and to consider the history and significance of social institutions, such as the family, the state, and the church. Physical science, biology, anthropology, social science, and history, political and industrial history, and international law thus present, throughout the course, a definite progressive relationship. . . .

The instruction in Social Science and History has been arranged so as to connect the instruction in Biology with that in History. These two departments present an unbroken sequence of related studies extending through three successive years of the Course IX curriculum. This series rests upon the fundamental knowledge of living forms and of prehistoric man that is presented in general Biology, Zoology, and Anthropology. In the classes in Social Science and History the student passes to the consideration of rudimentary social organisms, or primitive political and religious conceptions, and of ethnological questions [and thence to modern politics and international law].[76]

Walker's pride in the accomplishments of the faculty and students in General Studies shines through his *President's Reports* for these years. He and Dewey sought to attract the best minds possible for the program and often found them; between 1892 and 1895, a lively and popular course of lectures in business law was given on Saturday mornings by the Boston attorney Louis D. Brandeis. But no appointment could have made them prouder than that of William Z. Ripley, first as instructor in political science in 1893 and then as assistant professor of sociology and economics in 1895. For Ripley, like many of the most illustrious faculty members in the technical disciplines, then and now, was one of the institute's own. He had graduated in 1890 with a degree in civil engineering but had stayed on for another year to study economics and history with Dewey and Levermore. In 1891 he became a fellow in the School of Political Science at Columbia, receiving his Ph.D. in 1893 and returning to the Institute to teach and begin the research in transportation economics that would later bring him renown.[77] In so hospitable an institutional climate as this, General Studies grew and prospered, and by Walker's death in 1897, Dewey, Ripley, and the geographer William Niles taught a full fourteen subjects each year in economics and statistics, Ripley and Currier offered four in political science and sociology, and Currier alone taught seven in history.[78]

But the strong commitment to political economy and its related disciplines that marked Walker's presidency would soon be withdrawn, if only briefly. A three-year interregnum under James Mason Crafts of the Chemistry Department followed Walker's death in 1897, and both it and the short, unhappy administration of Henry Smith Pritchett that succeeded it were dominated by the vexed and recurring question of merger with Harvard. Crafts had managed to repel Eliot in 1898,[79] yet when the issue arose once more in 1904, Harvard at last found in Pritchett a leader of the Institute who responded to the proposal with enthusiasm.

But the faculty would not follow Pritchett's lead in this great controversy. Aloof and self-assured, he had alienated many by his cavalier treatment of personnel matters, and now the faculty felt that the president had been less than frank with them regarding his own position on the merger and the various considerations that had been raised in support of it. A decision on a technical point by the Supreme Judicial Court of Massachusetts quashed the merger plan once again in September 1905, but the residue of bitterness and hostility was not easily dispelled.[80] Writing about the president to his colleague Robert H. Richards in October of that year, the normally calm and balanced Dewey found himself "so influenced by resentment and discouragement that I do not feel great confidence in my own judgment."[81]

The roots of Dewey's feelings ran far deeper than the merger plan alone. At Pritchett's insistence, the Course in General Studies was abolished in 1904 and replaced with a program in General Science, which sharply reduced the breadth of social and humanistic studies in Course IX and refocused its curriculum on elective subjects in natural science and engineering. The Course in General Science was explicitly directed to prospective "businessmen" and high school teachers of science[82] and reflected Pritchett's own deep skepticism about the value of what he called "culture studies" at a technological institution:

The very earnestness which pervades a technical school, the spirit which prompts the student to bend himself to the task before him, tends to place a light value on any studies which do not lead to visible results. It is difficult to convince him that such subjects have for him a value comparable with the more direct utilitarian subjects; and to study them in this atmosphere and with this spirit is to achieve a very much smaller result than would be possible in a different atmosphere with a different spirit.

As a matter of fact, we men in the college of technology need to recognize that it is not the study of Literature, nor of Economics, nor of History, nor of any other subject, that *per se* brings culture and a broad sympathy with men. Chemistry, Physics, and Mechanics may be taught in such a way as to develop great humanistic interests as effectively as any of the so-called culture studies. . . . If we desire to increase in our colleges of technology a spirit of true culture and to bring about a larger common interest, the effective way to do this is to bring into our colleges teachers [of science and engineering] who are themselves exponents of this culture and of this wide human interest.[83]

The impact of this change on Dewey's department was immediate and devastating. Though the introductory subject in political economy was still required of all third-year students, its scope was reduced to include only the most practical and descriptive elements of the subject, and Dewey complained in 1903 that "in no way can it be regarded as comprehensive."[84] Perhaps reading the handwriting on the wall, Ripley resigned in 1902 to accept a chair at Harvard and was replaced the following year by Carroll W. Doten. By 1906 the roster of offerings in economics beyond the introductory subject had been reduced to six and reoriented toward the practical, with Dewey teaching Banking and Finance, Organization of Industry, and Economics of Corporations and Doten offering Railroad Economics, Labor Problems, and Economic History.[85]

Dewey held the decimated program together with hard work and the establishment of popular tutorials and personal conferences attached to the introductory subject,[86] and the skies over Course IX soon brightened once again. Pritchett was gone by 1908, replaced the following year by the physicist and lawyer Richard Cockburn Maclaurin. Born in Scotland and raised in New Zealand, Maclaurin's legal training at Cambridge and the breadth of his educational vision made him far more sympathetic to the ideals of General Studies than Pritchett had been, and though his attention in the years before 1916 was primarily devoted to the Institute's planned relocation in Cambridge, he gave Dewey and Doten the encouragement they needed to carry on.

At the request of the Department of Electrical Engineering, Dewey had for many years offered its majors a required subject in the Economics of Corporations, which considered "the nature of corporations and their legal development, accounting, valuation of bonds, holding companies, lighting companies, street railway franchises, and the taxation of corporations."[87] Now, with the explicit support of Maclaurin,[88] he expanded this core into an entire Course in Engineering Administration, established in 1914 and known to the present day as Course XV. Specifically designed for those "who expect to enter positions concerned with the management or administration of manufacturing, construction and transportation enterprises which demand a knowledge of scientific and engineering principles,"[89] the new Course encompassed separate options for civil, chemical, and mechanical or electrical engineers. Though its emphasis was most decidedly in the building of practical business skills,[90] it nonetheless provided a necessary haven for economic studies at the Institute in a period of great stress and uncertainty for them. The school that had produced Alfred P. Sloan and Gerard Swope[91] thus turned itself to the explicit training of managers and administrators, an undertaking it has proudly sustained ever since. In this way, Dewey managed to save economics at the Institute by casting it in its most obviously "useful" and worldly form, as business administration. At MIT, this was not only sufficient, it was precisely the point.

13

Political Economy and the Service of the State: The University of Wisconsin

JOHN P. HENDERSON

THE UNIVERSITY is not a party separate from the State. It is part of the State—as much a part of the State as the Capitol itself." As president of the University of Wisconsin, Charles Kendall Adams spoke those words in 1896.[1] The link between the state government and the state university took a distinctive form in Wisconsin in the late nineteenth and early twentieth centuries, and it was one in which academic economists played a significant role. What came to be known as the "Wisconsin Idea" had two important ingredients: that academic experts should work in alliance with public officials to promote reforms and that the academy had a responsibility to enlighten the citizenry at large through ambitious programs of publications and extension courses. In the heyday of the Progressive era, the Wisconsin conception of education as a catalyst to the solution of society's problems brought the state's university into national, even international, prominence.

Schemes for state-sponsored institutions of higher education did not originate in Wisconsin. The southern states had blazed the trails. With his plans for the University of Virginia, Thomas Jefferson had best articulated the ideal model for such institutions. The Jeffersonian conception of secular higher education supported by the public purse came into fullest flower, however, on the "free soil" of the states created from the Northwest Territories. Jefferson had drafted the Northwest Ordinance of 1787—the only lasting monument of the national government organized under the Articles of Confederation—which stipulated that civil and religious rights would be guaranteed and slavery prohibited in the territories of the Northwest. Five states were later organized from this area—Ohio,

The author would like to thank Daniel W. Bromley, W. Lee Hansen, Robert J. Lampman, and Julie Nelson of the University of Wisconsin for their kind cooperation in gathering material for this paper.

Indiana, Illinois, Michigan, and Wisconsin—and each created a notable state university.

THE BEGINNINGS AT THE UNIVERSITY OF WISCONSIN

The University of Wisconsin was established in 1848, the same year that the state was admitted to the Union. These two institutional structures—one educational, one political—had begun to take shape, however, when Wisconsin was still a territory administered from Detroit. Indeed, the original constitution for the state explicitly mandated "the establishment of a state university, at or near the seat of state government."[2] The founders set ambitious objectives for the state university. It was to perform a vital public function in training leaders for the responsibilities of government. In that spirit, the governing body of the university, the Board of Regents, made provision for a professorship of civil polity whose holder was expected to impart "such knowledge and discipline as may be calculated to prepare liberally educated young men to become good and useful citizens." It was further expected that the state university should provide training fitted to the practical and professional requirements of the community, with attention to "the application of the Sciences to the useful arts, including every industrial occupation which ministers to the well-being of society."[3]

In the University of Wisconsin's opening decades, these goals were easier to state than to reach. In the first instance, the pool of students prepared to undertake college-level work was limited. When the first classes met in 1849, all students were enrolled in a preparatory program because none had a high school diploma. Nearly a decade was to pass before student numbers in regular college courses exceeded those in preparatory and special classes. Moreover, public and legislative support for the new institution was often less than enthusiastic. In the mid-1850s, the legislature seriously considered proposals to reallocate moneys earmarked for the University of Wisconsin to the several privately sponsored colleges already established in the state. Some of these were then markedly stronger than the struggling university.[4] The university was vulnerable to criticism for its early failure to include a program of "practical" studies in its curriculum. Despite rhetoric to the contrary, its course of college-level studies looked very much like the conventional "classical" curriculum. Within that framework, the administrative head of the institution—originally assigned the title of chancellor, later redesignated as the president—provided instruction "in Theoretic and Practical Morality, in the Science of Government, in International and Constitutional Law, and in the laws regulating the Production, Distribution, Exchange, and Consumption of material wealth."[5]

Political economy thus was represented in the curriculum through the president's lectures to seniors, as was standard practice in most colleges at that time.[6] This type of instruction in "modern" subject matter was not sufficient, however, to satisfy those critics who wanted a much more pronounced "utilitarian" emphasis in the university's work. In the late 1850s, committees of the legislature indicted the management of the university for failure to differentiate it from "ordinary" colleges and insisted that the university's work

be adapted to popular needs, that its courses of instruction shall be arranged to meet as fully as possible, the wants of the greatest number of our citizens. The *farmers, mechanics, miners, merchants, and teachers* of Wisconsin, represented in this legislature, have a right to ask that this bequest of government shall aid in securing to themselves and their posterity, such educational advantages as shall fit them for their pursuits in life.[7]

The Civil War initially aggravated, but ultimately eased, the university's problems. As the state's young men entered military service, enrollments plummeted: only sixty-three students were in residence during the winter term, 1862–63. In order to justify remaining open, the university authorities enlarged their constituency by creating a "normal" (or teacher training) department to which women were admitted. By the fall term of 1863, total enrollment had risen to 229, with 162 students in the normal department (of whom nearly three-quarters were women). Expediency had thus provided an opening wedge for coeducation, although full status for women (i.e., one that would permit them to study in all departments of the university) was delayed until 1874.[8] The war years also contributed in other ways to the emergence of a new sense of direction for the university. With the passage of the Morrill Act in 1862 and the state's decision to accept the federal land grants it provided, the university undertook to organize a program of agricultural education in 1867, even though most faculty thought the project to be too practical. Shortly thereafter, further opportunities for more practical and professional studies were added through the creation of a Department of Engineering and a School of Law.

EDUCATION IN THE PUBLIC INTEREST: REDEFINITIONS
UNDER PRESIDENT BASCOM, 1874–1887

With the election of John Bascom (1827–1911) to the presidency
in 1874, the university acquired a forceful leader and the first to
leave a personal stamp on the institution.[9] Educated at Williams
College and the Andover Theological Seminary, Bascom resigned
a professorship in rhetoric and oratory at Williams to take up
his new duties at Wisconsin. His intellectual interests, however,
were not accurately conveyed by his title at Williams. Curti and
Carstensen have described Bascom as "almost the last American
who attempted to feel at home in every field of knowledge."[10] During the course of his career, his writings embraced political economy, sociology, theology, psychology, mathematics, and literary
aesthetics. His first book, published in 1859, was a text on political
economy.

Bascom's early work in economics was orthodox, so orthodox
that his text was used at Yale in the early 1860s. Indeed, Bascom
was more rigidly utilitarian than John Stuart Mill. The laws of political economy, he then maintained, demonstrated the existence of
a natural harmony of interests among groups in the community,
and any tampering by governments with the market forces should
be viewed suspiciously. He held it to be important that these principles be clearly understood by the people in order to enable them
to promote wise legislation. There were, of course, imperfections in
the existing economic order, but they should be addressed primarily through improvements in education, particularly for the laboring classes.[11]

By the time he arrived at Madison, Bascom had begun to reject
his earlier support for individualism and laissez-faire. He taught a
course for seniors, which—although listed as Mental and Moral
Philosophy—was as wide-ranging as the mind of the president. He
continued to stress the role of the individual, but he shifted the
emphasis from the promotion of self-interest to concern for the welfare of the larger community. The measure of the "good-will of the
state," he wrote in 1880, was

the interest it takes in the progress of all its citizens. If the state in some
way feels with, and peculiarly represents, the well-to-do classes, then it is
no longer the state, but a fragment of it. If the pride of power rises and
hisses contemptuously among the wealthy, then will the hydra-heads of
communism rise and hiss defiantly among the poor.[12]

One of the central purposes of the university was thus to produce public officials of "intelligence, integrity, and independence" who could promote the general good.[13]

No doubt a number of factors contributed to Bascom's conversion to liberalism (as Joseph Dorfman has characterized his intellectual career).[14] High among them, however, was his growing sympathy for the ideals of the Prohibition movement. If the individual did not have the strength to refrain from the evils of alcohol, then the state had a responsibility to interfere. In company with many advocates of prohibition, Bascom was also a strong supporter of women's rights, including the suffrage. Much of the poverty of the time, he maintained, was caused by men who consumed their wages on alcohol and neglected the needs of their families. From him the people of Wisconsin also heard that workers had the right to join trade unions and to strike for higher wages and improved working conditions. In the pages of leading periodicals, he supported the Knights of Labor. When Richard T. Ely's *Labor Movement in America* appeared in 1886, Bascom wrote that he was "quite in harmony" with the book's aims and spirit and that the volume had his "hearty endorsement."[15] As Bascom later summarized his position, competition required a "parity of conditions between purchasers and sellers," a requirement that could no longer be satisfied in labor markets if workers' organizations were lacking or in product markets in which monopoly power was unrestrained. Accordingly, he argued that it was the

permanent duty of the state to perpetually re-establish the conditions of favorable production. When any class is permanently worsted in the competition of trade, that class becomes . . . an object of solicitude. It at once accrues, as an urgent duty, on the part of the state, to check in all practical ways such a tendency, and to restore, if possible, to their feet those who have fallen.[16]

In Bascom's thinking, all of this was integrated into a vision of Christian socialism. In his final address at Madison, he asserted:

The University of Wisconsin will be permanently great in the degree in which it understands the conditions of the prosperity and peace of the people, and helps to provide them; in the degree in which it enters into the revelation of truth, the law of righteousness, and the love of man, all gathered up and held firm in the constitution of the human soul and the counsel of God concerning it.[17]

Bascom's teachings on social responsibility and on the role of education in uplifting the quality of public life were not conveyed just in his classes for seniors and in his writings and public addresses. Perhaps some of his most effective pedagogy occurred in his conversations with students in Sunday afternoon "open houses." Two of the men who later consolidated the alliance of state and university were strongly influenced by Bascom. A future governor, Robert M. La Follette, a member of the class of 1879 who became the dominant force in Wisconsin progressivism, regarded him as a major contributor to his own thinking. Charles R. Van Hise, also a member of the class of 1879 who was to guide the university as its president from 1903 to 1918, described Bascom as "among the prophets who from time to time have appeared to rejuvenate man and to arouse in him the invincible determination so to live as to advance the human race toward the goal never attained and never attainable of illimitable power, complete understanding, and spiritual perfection."[18]

Despite his popularity with students, Bascom's tenure at Madison was marked by friction with the Board of Regents. He made no attempt to conceal his low regard for the qualifications of most of the political appointees on the board. They, in turn, regarded Bascom as a "crank" and a meddler. A number of regents took particular offense at Bascom's extracurricular activities in support of the Prohibition party and his denunciations of the city of Madison for alleged failures to enforce laws banning the sale of alcoholic beverages to minors. These views were out of touch with prevailing opinion in the state of Wisconsin, particularly among the large segment of the population that identified with the German beer-drinking tradition. Bascom was forced out of office in 1887 and returned to Williams College where he taught until his retirement.

FRESH DIRECTIONS IN THE LATER 1880s AND EARLY 1890s

When Bascom left the presidency, the University of Wisconsin had an enrollment of some 500 students. The thirteen years of his administration had witnessed only a modest growth. Nor was his tenure marked by any significant changes in curriculum: The program of the academic departments departed little from the pattern he inherited. His personal efforts to promote a sense of social conscience among students left an imprint, to be sure, on several generations of undergraduates. In other ways, however, he was not an innovator. He had little sympathy for an expanded role for the sciences or for the more "practical" studies at the university. Instruction in the Department of Agriculture was essentially dormant as the state's practicing farmers showed little interest in "classroom farming." During the Bascom years, Wisconsin was overshadowed by the state universities in neighboring states.[19]

This pattern began to change soon after Thomas C. Chamberlin (1843–1928) assumed the presidency in 1887. A native Wisconsinite, he had received a classical education at Beloit College and subsequently had pursued graduate studies in geology at the University of Michigan. At the time of his appointment at the age of forty-four, he headed the glacial division of the United States Geological Survey. Chamberlin maintained continuity with the earlier conception that the function of the state university was to serve the needs of the state's citizenry. But he took that mandate to mean that the university should assign greater weight to the promotion of original investigation and that its results should be widely disseminated to the populace. Accordingly, research was accorded an enhanced status, and junior members of the faculty were put on notice that their retention and advancement required the completion of a Ph.D. and continued scholarly activity. Chamberlin stimulated the development of graduate programs and managed to win appropriations from the regents to provide fellowships for graduate students. In addition, he revitalized the College of Agriculture and brought its research work to the attention of practicing farmers and dairymen through short courses and "institutes." By the academic year 1891–92, such outreach to the public was enlarged to include extension lectures on general "cultural" subjects at sites scattered around the state.[20] The meaning of the state university's function in the service of the state had indeed been broadened.

Political economy did not initially fare well under Chamberlin's regime. What Bascom had offered was not replaced. Strictly speaking, a part-time professor of civil polity and political economy was on the premises: John B. Parkinson, a former regent who also served as vice-president of the university, had held this title since 1876. The available evidence suggests, however, that Parkinson's instruction made little impact. In the judgment of the university's official historians, Parkinson "lacked profound scholarship and had little contact with many of the new developments in his field."[21] By the early 1890s, there were stirrings to strengthen coverage of economic subjects. The executive committee of the Board of Regents recommended in 1891 that a professorship of finance and statistics be created along the lines of the Wharton School at the University of Pennsylvania. The regents intended that the university should better serve the needs of students planning careers in business.[22]

Before this scheme could be implemented, events took an unexpected turn. Leadership in the development of research programs in the social sciences was then in the hands of Frederick Jackson Turner (1861–1932), Professor of American History. His enunciation of the "frontier thesis" was still ahead of him, but Turner had already established a local reputation as an original thinker and as one of the men of stature on the faculty. Following his graduation from the University of Wisconsin in 1884, Turner had stayed on as an instructor in history. At Chamberlin's behest, he had embarked in 1888 on studies for a Ph.D. at Johns Hopkins, where he was a member of the seminar conducted by Herbert Baxter Adams and Richard T. Ely. Although Ely had attempted to persuade Turner to remain in Baltimore as one of his assistants, Turner elected to return to Wisconsin as an assistant professor of history with an assurance from Chamberlin that his candidacy for promotion to a full professorship would be given an early review. (Turner was, in fact, promoted to a full professorship of history in 1891 at the age of thirty).[23]

By the autumn of 1891, Ely was unhappy with his situation at Johns Hopkins and informed Turner of his interest in making a move.[24] Turner leaped at this prospect, informing Ely that he knew from their association in Baltimore "how great a privilege it would be to have you on our faculty."[25] Turner relayed the word of Ely's availability to Chamberlin, who was also favorably disposed toward this possibility. Not only was Chamberlin interested in improving on the work Parkinson had handled; he was also eager to bring nationally recognized scholars to Wisconsin, lest it lose out to the University of Chicago in the competition for graduate students.[26] Ely was clearly a "catch." In order to get him, Chamberlin persuaded the regents to redefine the specifications for the newly authorized chair in finance and statistics and to create a "School of Economics, Political Science, and History" with Ely appointed as its director.[27] The latter step was necessary to justify the unprecedented salary of $3,500 that Ely had demanded. In addition, the regents established a new assistant professorship in political economy, made provision for graduate fellowships, and allocated a sum of $5,000 for the purchase of books.

The formation of the School of Economics, Political Science, and History was announced with considerable fanfare. It would put Wisconsin on the cutting edge of research in the social sciences. For his part, Ely saw this venture as an opportunity to do "university work of the highest character in economics, political and historical science," in the context of "a civil academy to do somewhat for the civil service that which West Point and Annapolis do for the military and naval services respectively."[28] The training of future civil servants had been one of the motivating forces behind the creation of the Faculty of Political Science at Columbia in 1880 and the School of Political Science at the University of Michigan in 1881. Wisconsin was now preparing to challenge them.

THE EMERGENCE OF WISCONSIN POLITICAL ECONOMY UNDER ELY

The University of Wisconsin catalogue for 1892–93 set out the goals of the new school as follows:

The purpose of the School of Economics, Political Science, and History is to afford means for advanced study and research in the economic, political, social, and historical sciences. These subjects are treated largely from the investigative and scientific point of view. It is an especial aim to promote a more liberal study of the branches that are basal to the practice of law, journalism, the ministry, and other professions directly concerned with human relations. It is adapted to those who wish to supplement their legal, theological, or other professioinal studies with courses in general social science. Such courses, being strictly non-partisan and non-sectarian, will furnish a liberal and comprehensive equipment for those who wish to enter upon public life, the law, the ministry, business pursuits, or to become teachers of history and the political and economic sciences in schools and colleges. It is an especial endeavor to foster those studies which tend to raise the standard of good citizenship.
    The school embraces both undergraduate and graduate courses, but its leading endeavors center in the latter. The degree of Doctor of Philosophy is conferred upon those who successfully meet its requirements. The undergraduate courses are more extended than those usually offered in the college curriculum.[29]

Ely got the program off to a fast start by bringing three of his Johns Hopkins students to Madison with him. William A. Scott, who had just received his Ph.D., came as an assistant professor with a salary of $1,500. Charles J. Bullock had won a fellowship at Boston University in 1891, which allowed him to do graduate work at any university, but had chosen to go to Johns Hopkins to study with Ely; when Ely went to Wisconsin, Bullock followed. David

Table 13.1

University	Number of credit hours for academic year 1892–93
Pennsylvania	1,020
Chicago	996
Columbia	764
Michigan	756
Harvard	735
Yale	645
Wisconsin	612
Cornell	408
MIT	375
Oberlin	337

Source: "Courses of Study in Political Economy in the United States in 1876 and in 1892–93," *Journal of Political Economy*, October 1892, pp. 143–51.

Kinley moved from Johns Hopkins as well, accepting a $750 fellowship, which Ely had recommended him for at Wisconsin.

Ely also moved fast in providing a large number of courses at Wisconsin. Some indication of the scale of his effort can be seen in Table 13.1, which displays a ranking of institutions on the basis of the total credit hours of course offerings in political economy for the academic year 1892–93.

Some sixty-five institutions responded to the survey that produced these findings. (It should be noted, however, that the coverage did not include a number of institutions in which teaching in political economy was well established—among them, Johns Hopkins, the University of Virginia, and Amherst College.) Whatever the limitations of these data, it is still noteworthy that Ely was able to propel Wisconsin into such national prominence in his first year.

Wisconsin offered three year-round courses: the Economics Seminary; Public Finance; and the introductory course, Outlines of Economics. Ely was responsible for the seminary, which met in his home every Tuesday evening; Scott taught Public Finance; and Kinley, the introductory course. One-semester courses were offered in the Distribution of Wealth, History of Political Economy, Money, Statistics, and Recent Economic Theories. Scott taught Distribution, Money, and Statistics. Ely took care of the historical courses. In addition, special (or "Synoptical") lectures were given by Albert Shaw (on cities), Amos G. Warner (on pauperism), F. H. Wines (on criminology), and Simon N. Patten (on economic theory). Shaw and Warner were former students at Johns Hopkins, the other two old friends. In view of Ely's interest in organized labor, it may seem strange that no course was offered on the subject. On the other hand, with only three economists on the faculty, it was impossible to cover everything. Of the sixty-five institutions reported on in the *Journal of Political Economy* survey, only two, Michigan and Vassar, then listed offerings in labor economics.

The style of work that Ely brought to Wisconsin was by no means restricted to classrooms in Madison. He organized field trips for his students to investigate such problems as the administration of charities and solicited donations from the public to help defray the costs of these expeditions. In addition, he took an active part in lecturing in the extension program. His extension lectures on "socialism," in which he advocated public ownership of the natural monopolies, attracted sizable audiences throughout the state in his early years there. Ely threw himself into these tasks with enthusiasm. At this point in his career, he had largely disengaged himself from his earlier involvements in the activities of the American Economic Association, an organization he then believed to have been taken over by his opponents. The work in Wisconsin thus consumed the bulk of his abundant energies.

Even so, Ely was not totally satisfied with his situation at Wisconsin. He was dismayed that he was expected to teach undergraduates; he much preferred working with graduate students, as he had done at Johns Hopkins. He was disappointed when the state's citizens failed to contribute generously to the funding of special projects at his school (a prospect for which he had entertained high hopes before his arrival at Madison). He had been outraged to discover that Parkinson—who still held the title of Professor of Civil Polity and Political Economy—had successfully lobbied with the regents to have his son appointed as an assistant. With some justice, Ely regarded this as an affront to his jurisdiction over staffing in the social sciences. But Ely was even more disturbed by Chamberlin's decision, in mid-1892, to resign the presidency in favor of an appointment as the head professor of geology at the newly opened University of Chicago. Ely understandably feared that Chamberlin's successor would not feel bound to honor Chamberlin's commitments of administrative support for the new school.[30] In fact, this concern proved to be groundless. Charles Kendall Adams (1835–1902)—formerly president of Cornell and a recognized historian from his professorial days at the University of Michigan—

championed vigorously the development of the School of Economics, Political Science, and History.

In mid-1895, however, Ely had very good reason to feel that his position at the University of Wisconsin was in jeopardy. The Democratic party had won control of the state government in 1892, and its upset political victory had also brought into office a new state superintendent of public instruction, Oliver E. Wells. By virtue of this position, Wells also served as an ex officio member of the university's Board of Regents. Wells turned on Ely in a letter to the *Nation* of July 12, 1894, under the title "The College Anarchist," alleging that Ely was a purveyor of "pernicious doctrines" that "furnish a seeming moral justification of attacks on life and property."[31] Moreover, Ely was alleged to have provided advice and hospitality to a "walking delegate" (or "agitator") of a union and to have broken a contract with a nonunion printing firm. In a climate conditioned by the passions aroused over violence in the Pullman strike, these charges were bound to attract attention—and they did.

Ely denied all of these allegations and protested that his economic philosophy, properly understood, was essentially conservative. In addition, he qualified his earlier support for organized labor. By 1895 he maintained that strikes against the public services were intolerable. Indeed, organized labor had acted beyond the bounds of legitimacy in the railway boycotts. In a statement prepared in his own defense, Ely went so far as to say that Wells's charges against him, if true, should properly disqualify him from teaching.[32] Ely's students and colleagues at the University of Wisconsin rallied to his support, as did a number of prominent economists at other institutions. Not least, Ely had strong backing with the regents from President Charles Kendall Adams. After conducting public hearings into the facts of the case in 1895, the regents rejected Wells's charges. Not only did they spare Ely, they put on record a memorable statement of the importance of academic freedom: "Whatever may be the limitations which trammel inquiry elsewhere we believe the great State University of Wisconsin should ever encourage that continual and fearless sifting and winnowing by which alone the truth can be found."[33]

The Wells incident notwithstanding, the university prospered during the decade of the 1890s. The administration of Charles Kendall Adams was regarded as an "era of good feeling" in which enrollments nearly trebled, crossing the 3,000 mark in the early

years of the twentieth century. It was also a period in which graduate programs flourished, with the School of Economics, Political
Science, and History leading the way. More than half of the doctorates awarded by the university up to 1900 were earned by its
graduates. In its first decade, the school produced twenty-one
Ph.D.'s (of whom sixteen earned this degree in the economics component of the program).[34] Even when the school was less than five
years old, Adams proudly asserted to the regents that "we are entitled to feel that in no institution in the country, unless it be in the
School of Political Science in Columbia College, is there more thorough and comprehensive work done than that we are now giving in
this important department of the University."[35] Meanwhile, the demand for undergraduate teaching in economics expanded. Fifteen
courses were listed in 1895–96, eight of them taught by Scott,
including a new offering on the economics of agriculture, which
was required for students enrolled in the short course in the College of Agriculture. Ely handled five courses, one of which was the
seminary for graduate students. With Kinley's departure for the
University of Illinois following the completion of his Ph.D., two
graduate students, Edward D. Jones and Helen Page Bates, were
added to the faculty.

RESTRUCTURING IN THE FIRST DECADE
OF THE TWENTIETH CENTURY

The year 1900 brought two changes in the structure of Ely's
"school." The first was occasioned by Adams's determination to
create a post for Turner that would be sufficiently attractive to dis-
suade him from moving to the University of Chicago where he had
been offered a much higher salary. This matter was resolved by
creating a separate "School of History" with Turner as its director.[36] Ely's jurisdiction was diminished still further at this time by
the creation of a College of Commerce with Scott appointed as its
head. This innovation reflected the desire of the regents—expressed
as early as 1891—to provide training for future business leaders at
the university, an objective Ely's school had not met. Courses in
accounting and business administration were at the core of the new
college. Scott described the purpose as follows:

> It was the result of an endeavor to make a four-year undergraduate
> course, parallel with the other four-year courses leading to degrees, which
> would do for the prospective business man what the four-year long course

in agriculture, the engineering courses, the law course, and the course in pharmacy were doing or attempting to do for men who were planning to enter as a vocation, after leaving college, agriculture, engineering, law, or pharmacy. It is to the development and improvement of such a course that the greater portion of our energy and resources devoted to business training has been given.[37]

Another consideration also entered the deliberations over the provision of business-oriented education. The United States in the post–Spanish-American War period, it was argued, was acquiring responsibilities overseas that called for well-trained administrators and business leaders equipped to work in international markets.[38]

Ely was dismayed over these truncations in his empire. In 1903 his school in its reduced form (i.e., as the School of Economics and Political Science) even lost its semiautonomous status within the university when it was assigned the status of a "department" within the College of Letters and Science. (This redesignation, however, was part of a general administrative reorganization within the university and did not represent a slackening in the institution's commitment to work in economics.)[39] In these years, Ely was ready to look elsewhere. He tried unsuccessfully to obtain invitations from Johns Hopkins and Harvard and even gave some thought to shifting from an academic to a public career.[40] Meanwhile, Ely had reentered the work of the American Economic Association, serving as its president in 1900–1.[41]

Ely's skill as an academic entrepreneur came into prominence at Wisconsin once again in 1904 when he mobilized funding from private sources to create an American Bureau of Industrial Research.[42] The purpose of this enterprise was to produce a general history of labor in America, a project Ely regarded as a sequel to his *Labor Movement in America*, published in 1886. To direct the research work of the new bureau, he called on another former student from Johns Hopkins days: John R. Commons (1862–1945), a man who originally had been inspired to embark on graduate studies at Johns Hopkins by his enthusiasm for Ely's 1886 book. As a graduate student, Commons had assisted Ely in the preparation of his *Introduction to Political Economy* (the text produced to accompany Ely's lectures at the Chautauqua summer school). The two men had also collaborated in an abortive attempt to establish an American Institute of Christian Sociology in early 1893.[43]

Commons arrived in Madison with an appointment as a professor of political economy at a salary of $3,000 (two-thirds of which was paid from funds supplied by private contributors).[44] Before reaching Wisconsin, Commons had been unable to maintain an academic post. In the academic year 1890–91, he had succeeded Woodrow Wilson at Wesleyan University as a tutor in political economy but had been dismissed for ineffectiveness in teaching after only one year. In 1895 his propensity to identify with populist causes had eroded his position at the University of Indiana: Although not technically dismissed there, he was instructed by its president to accept "at once" an invitation to fill a newly created chair in sociology at Syracuse University.[45] Four years later, his chair was abolished. This time troubles arose initially over Commons's advocacy of baseball on Sunday, a position regarded as sacrilege by some of the college's financial supporters, who threatened to close their purses so long as he remained a member of the Syracuse faculty.[46] Five years of exile from academia followed. Commons, however, used them productively in developing his skills as an investigator and in deepening his understanding of practical problems. During this period, he served as secretary of the United States Industrial Commission (which involved him particularly in studies of the impact of unrestricted immigration on American workers) and as a member of the staff of the National Civic Federation (an organization designed to bring business and labor leaders together in the interests of promoting industrial peace).[47]

The Commons who reached Wisconsin in 1904 had not abandoned his earlier zeal for economic and social reform, but his views were now tempered by a heightened sense of realism. Public intervention would be effective only when it was informed by command of the relevant facts. This required detailed and painstaking empirical investigations that went well beyond the gathering of numbers. The significance of the technical economic data had to be interpreted within the context of the larger cultural and legal environment. There could be no shortcuts in this exercise. Conclusions arrived at deductively through the techniques of "old-school" economic theorizing were inadequate. Nor was it any more satisfactory to interpret modern industrial society (at least in America) with the aid of Marxian categories of "class consciousness." As Commons came to understand the American labor movement, workers combined in pursuit of their individual self-interest but were not motivated by an abstract conception of collective "class" interest. His approach to economics was to become the hallmark of Wisconsin "institutionalism" in the early decades of the twentieth century.

Although never an impressive lecturer, Commons brought the pulsebeat of the "real world" into his classrooms by sharing the fruits of his investigations with his students. In his first year at Wisconsin, he offered a course on "Race Elements in American Industry," drawing on his earlier work with the United States Industrial Commission. In subsequent years—as the findings of the American Bureau of Industrial Research were beginning to emerge—he taught courses on labor and industrial history.[48] In 1907 he introduced a course on the regulation of public utilities, an innovation reflecting his growing involvement with public commisions established by the state government in Wisconsin.[49] Some of Commons's students felt his tutelage to be deficient in that it lacked a systematic theoretical core. Commons himself acknowledged difficulties in systematizing his thinking, but this was not central to his concern. The ultimate point was to solve practical problems, not to generate grand theories for which claims for universal applicability could be asserted. His method was one of "reasonableness," which he defined as "idealism limited by practicality."[50]

Commons won an enthusiastic and loyal following among students, and his style was to become the leitmotiv of Wisconsin economics until his retirement in 1932. But his recruitment was by no means the only significant development in the work of the department in the first decade of this century. By 1911 the department had grown to be the largest in the country, with six full professors and eleven assistants.[51] Thomas S. Adams became its first external appointee of the Ely era when he joined the faculty in 1901 with a newly minted Ph.D. from Johns Hopkins, and his work in public finance and taxation strengthened the department's offerings in these fields. In 1902 Henry C. Taylor, whom Ely had encouraged to take up the study of land economics as a graduate student at the university, began to develop a program in agricultural economics.[52] These enlargements in the scope of Wisconsin economics met with Ely's hearty endorsement, as did the appointment of Edward A. Ross to a post as a professor of sociology. For a number of years after Ross's dismissal from Stanford, Ely had hoped to promote a place at Wisconsin for his former pupil. It was 1906, however, before he succeeded.[53]

At the same time, the scholarly productivity of the department was sustained at an impressive level. Particularly noteworthy was the manner in which senior professors engaged their students and colleagues as collaborators. The 1908 revision of Ely's textbook, *Outlines of Economics,* was coauthored, for example, by Allyn A.

Young (Ph.D., Wisconsin, 1902), Max Lorenz (Ph.D., Wisconsin, 1906), and Thomas S. Adams.[54] The most productive scholar was Commons, and between 1904 and the end of the decade he published seven articles in Harvard's *Quarterly Journal of Economics.* Two graduate students—John Bertram Andrews and Helen Laura Sumner (both of whom earned Wisconsin Ph.D.'s in 1908—served with Commons as coeditors of portions of *The Documentary History of American Industrial Society.* Altogether, ten volumes in this series appeared, beginning in 1910. But these achievements were not free of frictions. At one point, Ely and Commons were scarcely on speaking terms: Commons's pace of work was too slow for Ely's taste. In addition, misunderstandings arose over the distribution of royalties from *The Documentary History* and over the direction of the work of the Bureau of Industrial Research. Commons charged that Ely sought to preempt credit for the bureau's achievements and that Ely's role had been "a narrow and petty financial one rather than a broad and scientific one."[55] Ely, on the other hand, maintained that Commons had the business sense of a "new born babe."[56] Only through the intervention of the university's president as a mediator (in 1909) was a *modus vivendi* worked out between the two men.

THE UNIVERSITY AND THE SERVICE OF THE STATE IN THE ERA OF HIGH PROGRESSIVISM

Charles R. Van Hise (1857–1918) was installed as the university's president in 1903, and his accession to office added momentum to trends that had been visible in the preceding two decades. Van Hise was a Wisconsinite through and through. During his undergraduate years at the university, he had been impressed by Bascom's teaching on the social responsibilities of the educated and had stayed on at the university to complete a doctorate in geology and to become a professor in the faculty of geology. In the latter capacity, he had been an active participant in the extension lecture programs and in research to advance the conservation of the state's natural resources. As president, Van Hise built on the foundations he inherited, but he also expanded them dramatically. Under his leadership, the extension program touched all corners of the state, and its substantive coverage was comprehensive. All subjects taught within the university's walls were being made available to the citizenry through special lectures and correspondence courses. Increasingly, the practical results of the research work conducted at

the university were transmitted through special institutes and research bulletins. The earlier dream of making the university serve
the needs of the state's farmers, mechanics, and so on, first articulated in the 1850s, seemed to have become the reality. In 1909 the
journalist Lincoln Steffens wrote enthusiastically about the Wisconsin experiment, describing it as one in which the university was
prepared "to teach anybody—anything—anywhere." Indeed, the
whole state seemed to be going to college.[57]

Meanwhile, control of the state government had been won in the
elections of 1900 by one of Van Hise's classmates and a fellow
Bascom disciple, Robert M. La Follette. As governor, La Follette
saw opportunities to link the university with the state in still other
ways. The policy agenda of his Progressive program called for government to curb abuses of monopoly power. Bigness per se was not
the enemy: Large concentrations of capital could bring gains in
efficiency that should not be sacrificed, a principle endorsed by Van
Hise. The task of the future, as the Progressive reformers saw it,
was to control price making in the larger public interest. There was
thus a compelling case for regulation of the natural monopolies,
particularly of the railways and the public utilities. But the form it
took should be sensitive to the need for private enterprises to earn a
reasonable rate of return. This was a call not for public ownership
but for public control through informed intervention.[58]

Intelligent regulation, in turn, required that the authority to exercise it be placed in the hands of trained experts who would be
immune from the potential corrupting influences of partisan politics. La Follette looked to the university for counsel on his legislative agenda. He invited Commons to draft a civil service bill,
passed in 1905, which established performance in competitive examinations as the basis for employment in public positions. He
called upon him as well to give shape to legislation to create a
regulatory commission for railroads (in 1905) and one for public
utilities (in 1907).[59] Commons subsequently was the central figure
in designing workmen's compensation legislation (enacted in 1911),
which was widely regarded as the most advanced in the nation.[60] In
these years, the labors of bill drafting were coordinated by Charles
McCarthy, a Wisconsin Ph.D. of 1901, who served university and
state simultaneously as head of the Legislative Reference Library
and as a lecturer in political science (without compensation).

The output of McCarthy's "bill factory" created still more opportunities for academicians to serve the state. By 1908 some
forty-one members of the university's staff held membership on at

least one state commission. (Van Hise personally was a member of no less than five.)[61] Expertise provided by the university was sweeping in its range: For example, professors of geology were to be found on the Conservation Commission; professors of engineering on the Railroad Commission; professors of agricultural bacteriology on the State Livestock Sanitation Board; professors of agronomy on the State Seed Inspection Service.[62] Among the economists, Thomas S. Adams held an appointment on the Tax Commission, Commons on the Industrial Commission, and Balthasar H. Meyer (who earned his Ph.D. at the university in 1897 with a thesis on the "History of Railway Legislation in Wisconsin" and later joined the faculty of the College of Commerce) on the Railroad Commission. It is small wonder that some observers referred to the university as the "fourth department of state," supplementing the executive, legislative, and judicial branches.[63]

The enthusiasts for the alliance of university and state were convinced that it brought benefits to both parties. In the first instance, expertise supplied by the academy promoted good government. As Charles McCarthy saw matters:

If the legislature may not secure expert service save that paid for by private interests, it will never reach the scientific basis of these great questions now before us which must be solved by the aid of the expert's technical knowledge. The university should not be blamed for having men upon whom the legislature may call for advice. They are paid from public funds; why should the public not avail itself of their services?[64]

But involvement in the day-to-day work of government, it was claimed, also enhanced the quality of instruction at the university. Direct participation in public affairs by members of its faculty brought dimensions of reality into classrooms in ways that gave a special quality to the University of Wisconsin. McCarthy entertained no doubts on this score:

Certainly the teacher of political science or political economy who is worthy of consultation upon governmental matters can give the students a better idea of those great subjects than some mossback whose theoretical learning was acquired by carefully keeping away from the only laboratory which could be of any service to him. . . . Indeed it is a healthy sign—a sign that a department of economic or of political science is not sleeping when its men are constantly attacked by those who, session after session, have crowded the legislative halls in opposition to every constructive piece of legislation.[65]

Why should the state of Wisconsin have been in the vanguard of Progressive reforms in the first decade of this century? Some participant-observers were inclined to explain this phenomenon as a by-product of the convergence of two influences imported from Germany. Much of the state's population was of German extraction, the heirs to the tradition brought by refugees of 1848. As Charles McCarthy saw them in 1912, they were "noted for their steadfast love of liberty and the systematic way in which they proceed with government."[66] In the structuring of the University of Wisconsin, this spirit had been fused with New England educational ideals, such as those Bascom had represented with his calls for social morality in statesmanship. But another German ingredient entered the mix with Ely's arrival in Wisconsin. McCarthy maintained that it was a "singular coincidence" that "the pupil of Knies and Wagner, coming from Germany with his German political ideals, succeeded Bascom as a teacher of political economy in the German university of the German state of Wisconsin."[67] It was thus not surprising that doctrines supporting active intervention of the state to promote economic welfare "found better soil" in Wisconsin than they did elsewhere in America. Indeed, it was "only natural that the legislation of Wisconsin should receive an impetus from men who believe that laws can be so constructed as to lead to progress and at the same time preserve to the fullest all human betterment; that the advice of scholars may be sought."[68] In 1914 Ely echoed this assessment. "The German universities," he then wrote,

have for two centuries or more held a position in German life like that which American universities, especially the University of Wisconsin, have begun to occupy in the life of the American nation. They have been largely engaged in preparing men for civic life, for positions as civil servants.[69]

Commons, on the other hand, challenged such appraisals. Writing in 1934, he argued that "the Germans in Wisconsin, although exceeding in numbers any other of its many nationalities, have been the least active, politically, of all. The civil service law was sprung on the state by one man, La Follette."[70]

THE RUPTURING OF THE PROGRESSIVE ALLIANCE
OF UNIVERSITY AND STATE

The Wisconsin Idea had passed its high-water mark by the time of the outbreak of the First World War. The conservative wing of the

Republican party had recaptured control of the state government in the elections of 1914, and its leaders were markedly unsympathetic toward the direction in which Van Hise had led the university. Grievances, which had been accumulating for some time, received an attentive hearing. The university was accused of financial extravagance, of encouraging its faculty to neglect teaching duties in favor of research and extracurricular activities (such as work with governmental commissions), and of harboring "radicals" who were out of touch with prevailing opinion in the state. Many of these charges had been simmering for decades, and the conservative Republicans, "the stalwarts," were waiting. Perhaps still more threatening to prospects for appropriations requested from the legislature was the charge that the university was attempting to dominate the state. As one of its critics—a regent—put the issue in 1912, Wisconsin would have "a university state instead of a state university" unless the people were aroused to ward off a power grab.[71] Certainly, Van Hise was increasingly sensitized to the fact that close involvement of academicians with politicans could be a two-edged sword. After 1914 he appeared to back away from his earlier positions, particularly with respect to encouraging faculty members to hold official appointments. He even expressed his "repugnance" toward "use of the phrase 'The Wisconsin Idea.'"[72]

With America's entry into World War I, little remained from the coalition of the university with La Follette progressivism. The German dimension of Wisconsin life—which had been lauded as a source of strength only a few years earlier—was by now a source of tension. La Follette responded to this element in his constituency by voting against the declaration of war with Germany in April 1917. On this issue, the bulk of his former academic allies turned against him. In 1918 an overwhelming majority of the university's faculty signed a petition denouncing him. Ely and Commons—each with a son in military service—were among the signators and leaders of the opposition to La Follette.

Even so, the University of Wisconsin had established a solid tradition in political economy by the close of the first decade of the twentieth century, and it was one that spoke with a distinctive voice. In addition, it remained influential on the national scene. Six of those associated with its work as faculty members or as graduate students up to 1910 achieved the prominence of the presidency of the American Economic Association: Richard T. Ely (1900–1); David Kinley (1913, then at the University of Illinois); John R. Commons (1917); Allyn A. Young (1925, then at Harvard); Thomas S.

Adams (1927, then at Yale); and Harry A. Millis (1934, then at the University of Chicago). These years also left a legacy in the public servants that the University of Wisconsin supplied to the federal government, most notably George C. Taylor at the Bureau of Agricultural Economics, Balthasar H. Meyer at the Interstate Commerce Commission, Helen Laura Sumner at the United States Department of Labor, and Harry A. Millis at the National Labor Relations Board. They pioneered an extension of the Wisconsin Idea to the corridors of the federal bureaucracy.

14

The Educational Revolution and the Professionalization of American Economics

A. W. COATS

The institutions of higher education in any nation are always a faithful mirror in which are sharply reflected the national history and character. In this mobile nation the action and reaction between University and society at large are more sensitive and rapid than in stiffer communities. Charles Eliot, Inaugural Address, Harvard, 1869

IT IS NO COINCIDENCE that the modern social science professions as we know them today first appeared in the United States during the post–Civil War decades. It was an era of dramatic economic, social, and cultural transformation of the kind commonly depicted in such portmanteau terms as industrialization, urbanization, modernization, and bureaucratization, and these processes generated demands for many new kinds of specialized knowledge, skills, and training, which the old-time college curriculum was incapable of supplying—although the seeds of future growth had already been sown in the prewar era. With the increasing social division of labor there were innumerable new opportunities for careers in manufacturing, commerce, agriculture, and the public service, for as William J. Goode has observed, "an industrializing society is a professionalizing society."[1] By comparison with other countries, undoubtedly the most striking feature of American experience of the period is the sheer pace of change, which meant that the nation quickly caught up with and passed its European rivals. But it also had the effect of compressing (and thereby exacerbating) social tensions and exposing conflicts of ideas, ideals, and interests that were either concealed or muted in more slowly evolving communities built on entrenched traditions and inhibited by powerful institutional constraints. In the United States new values and standards had to be devised and articulated, and new institutions created virtually *ab initio* to cope with immediate and pressing needs. This is not to say that the processes of change were either purely or uniquely American. Some lessons were learned from European experience, and certain features of European society were consciously imitated, usually with appropriate modifications to suit domestic conditions, since many American viewed the European heritage with skepticism and accordingly embraced it selectively.[2] As a result, many of the solutions to perceived problems bore a distinctly hybrid character reflecting both the mixture of sources and the confusion of objectives.

This was especially true in the educational field, where the English concept of the general culture of the educated gentleman and the German idea of the pursuit of knowledge as an end in itself were combined with the American belief that the university should directly serve the needs of its society. Even in the case of Johns Hopkins, where intellectual values were strongly emphasized, President Gilman announced in his inaugural address that the institution's purpose was "to develop character—to make men. It misses its aim if it produces learned pedants or simple artisans, or cunning sophists, or pretentious practitioners."[3] Perhaps his declaration was calculated to propitiate the burghers of Baltimore, but like other leaders of the educational revolution Gilman was a man of antispeculative bent whose primary contributions were in administration and publicity. It is noteworthy that the only wholehearted plea for pure scholarship in the entire American education canon emanated from that distinguished but disappointed maverick, Thorstein Veblen.[4] After a relatively brief flirtation with the ideals of pure scholarship and research, there was a reaction toward the end of the century in favor of more practical considerations, as epitomized in the work of John Dewey and his disciples. In his immensely influential *School and Society,* published in 1899, Dewey complained that contemporary education was "dominated almost entirely by the medieval conception of learning," that it appealed "simply to the intellectual aspect of our natures . . . not to our impulses and tendencies to make, to do, to create, to produce, whether in the form of utility or art," and consequently tended to perpetuate "the division into 'cultured' people and 'workers,' the separation of theory and practice."[5] Admittedly, this attack was directed mainly at the lower levels of the educational ladder, but the American practice of describing institutions of higher learning as "schools" suggests that more exalted institutions were not far from Dewey's mind.

It was the state university, especially in the West, that most clearly embodied the American quest for self-improvement and fulfillment through education. It mirrored the temper of the people, "for its main standards were quantitative, its main concerns materialistic, its educational bias utilitarian, and its outlook optimistic."[6] No doubt utilitarian considerations predominated in the public mind, as reflected in the Morrill Act of 1862, which awarded grants of federal land to institutions committed to "teach such branches of learning as are related to agriculture and the mechanic arts," albeit "without excluding science and classical studies." The so-called land-grant or agricultural and mechanical colleges were especially responsive to the pressing claims of practicality that threatened to convert higher educational bodies into mere service stations catering to every change in consumers' tastes. But of course no single institutional species was typical. As earlier chapters have demonstrated, society's demands were met in a variety of ways. At Harvard a prestigious traditional college was converted into a great new university, whereas at Yale fierce resistance from a conservative faculty successfully protected the old curriculum but could not prevent the growth of genuine university work above and around it. In the expanding state universities, especially beyond the Alleghenies, the established B.A. rapidly disintegrated with the proliferation of new departments specializing mainly in practical or vocational subjects, and at Johns Hopkins and later in Chicago there was a radical break with the past as graduate teaching and research were given priority over undergraduate instruction. In each case the outcome was determined by a combination of circumstances, including local beliefs and traditions, powerful personalities, the sources of financial aid, and the activities of pressure groups.

No Royal Commission seeking to bring Britain into the mainstream of modern science and scholarship, no French or German minister of education charged with the direction of higher education and research, not even a group of American scientists or scholars with sufficient authority and wealth would have set out to create such a decentralized pluralistic structure. Yet implicit in this structure were the sources of strength and vitality that would distinguish the American organization of learning: the opportunity to borrow selectively from European institutions of higher education and research; the flexibility to change organizational forms, invent new structures, and incorporate emerging fields; the refusal to erect barriers between pure and applied research, between the discovery and application of knowledge; the openness to recruit and reward excellence without regard for the traditional social hierarchies that constrained European intellectual life; the need to rely on a multiplicity of patrons and constituencies and thereby to cultivate broad public support; and the inevitable impulse among regions, institutions, and individuals to compete for recognition.[7]

Perhaps the most surprising development in this so-called Gilded Age, much derided by later intellectuals because of its unrestrained quest for pecuniary gain, its vulgarity, and its materialism, was the manner in which a handful of conspicuous *nouveax riches*—Commodore Vanderbilt, Ezra Cornell, Johns Hopkins, Jonas Clark, Leland Stanford, John D. Rockefeller—provided munificent endowments for new centers of learning that were destined to rival or outstrip their counterparts elsewhere in the Western world. Less surprising than this competitive philanthropic emulation was their success, as in their business enterprises, in finding able academic entrepreneurs to head their new creations: energetic, farsighted men like Andrew D. White of Cornell, Gilman of Johns Hopkins, and Harper of Chicago. These "captains of erudition," as Veblen so aptly dubbed them, had their peers both in the older colleges and in some state universities—men such as Eliot of Harvard, James B. Angell of Michigan, and Nicholas Murray Butler of Columbia. As their academic undertakings expanded apace, the resemblances to the new giant business corporations became increasingly obvious, and both reflected the general trend toward more "nationally oriented, impersonal, hierarchical organizations" in American society.[8] The growing scale and, within limits, structural uniformity in the "order of learning" toward the end of the century and beyond partially counteracted the bewildering variety of aims, institutions, and functions that was so disconcerting to some contemporary commentators.

The impact of the educational revolution on the curriculum can be broadly characterized as a broadening of the base and a narrowing at the top of the educational pyramid, a process whereby the range of offerings spread outward to embrace new subjects—as permitted by the elective system—and upward into more advanced, specialized study and research. These two trends, though distinct, were interdependent, for the rising student demand for new subjects generated a derived demand for a new generation of qualified teachers, which in turn stimulated the growth of training facilities at the graduate level. This explains why, once the sequence began, the Americans were able to catch up with the German universities so rapidly. The system's capacity for expansion and adaptation was remarkable. According to one estimate, the number of university and college students in the United States increased four times as fast as the total population between 1870 and 1910.[9] Despite numerous earlier unsuccessful efforts, serious graduate work did not begin effectively until Johns Hopkins opened in 1876, but by "1900 about 1500 institutions were committed to graduate study—though less than a third of them to doctoral work—and were developing faculties and programs to that end." Even more striking, by the time the Association of American Universities (AAU) was inaugurated in 1900, almost 90 percent of the earned doctorates were produced by only fourteen institutions, and 55 percent of the total came from California, Chicago, Columbia, Harvard, and Johns Hopkins.[10]

To American readers it will come as no surprise to find that the drive for academic consolidation, standardization, and conformity (even in such matters as academic robes) proceeded entirely without central direction or guidance. The AAU, like the American Economic Association (AEA) and innumerable other national learned societies and scholarly bodies, was a spontaneous internal growth from within the academic community representing the effort to establish acceptable standards at a time of bewilderingly rapid change. Yet matters might have been different had any of the various schemes for a national university come to fruition.[11]

Proposals for such an institution in one form or another date back to the Constitutional Convention, and they received enthusiastic support from George Washington (who left money in his will for the purpose), James Madison, Thomas Jefferson, and many others. Oddly enough, among other motives, Washington wanted to discourage American students from studying abroad, whereas some of the opponents of the idea feared that a national institution would be dominated by un-Christian foreign scholars. It is of interest that the project's proponents regarded social and political subjects as appropriate parts of the institution's curriculum, but of course there were objections on financial and constitutional grounds. At one stage, though, Jefferson was prepared to support a constitutional amendment to clear the way. In the early 1870s the manifest inferiority of American universities led the National Teachers' Association (later the National Educational Association) to recommend the foundation of a great new university backed by federal funds, but the plan encountered formidable opposition from Charles Eliot, then newly enthroned as president of Harvard, who depicted it as yet another symptom of the "deep seated disease" of government interference.[12] By the mid-1870s this phase of the debate was over and the opportunity had gone, for the subsequent boom in higher education conclusively demonstrated America's capacity to compete both domestically and internationally. Nevertheless, the idea remained alive, and efforts to establish an elite national center for scholarship and research have recurred periodically during the present century.

The impact of the educational revolution on the social sciences, a group of subjects that barely even existed at the close of the Civil War, was especially dramatic, and the economists were in the vanguard. Various statistical indicators of the subsequent expansion can be cited. Until the 1870s there were no opportunities for advanced training in political economy anywhere in the United States, and only three Ph.D.'s were awarded during that decade—at Harvard (1875), Yale (1877), and Johns Hopkins (1878). In 1880 there were only three men in the leading schools who "devoted most of their time to political economy,"[13] and during the next ten years eleven more Ph.D.'s were awarded by five different institutions. By 1890 the pace had quickened considerably: There were then twenty chairs in the subject, fifty-one by 1900, and in the intervening period a further ninety-five Ph.D.'s had been awarded. There is no reliable index of the increase of teaching in the subject, partly because it was often still combined with other social sciences, but incomplete figures published in the first issue of Chicago's *Journal of Political Economy* suggest that the number of teaching hours had increased about sixfold between 1876 and the early 1890s.[14] Changes in quality were no doubt more important than changes in quantity. The practice of teaching by recitation and rote learning began to give way before prepared lectures and critical discussion; and as graduate training spread, the seminar method of learning, based more or less on the German model, was widely adopted.

Advanced study in political economy moved from self-guided reading outside academic institutions to self-study with professional guidance inside institutions. The new advanced elective courses justified granting specialized teachers more time to work with fewer and more interested students in a single subject area. . . . The ambitious group of young economists exploited the new environment with unbridled gusto and ingenuity. For every economic problem they could develop a college course. Political economy began to unfold in every direction. It literally exploded. There are few parallels in the history of higher education.[15]

Rather than attacking the traditional curriculum directly, thereby arousing the opposition of the established disciplines, the economists often used more subtle strategies, such as introducing the second course (if there was already an undergraduate offering) or even the first one (if there was not) at the graduate level, and opening up graduate courses to advanced undergraduates. Consequently, "with persistence as well as ingenuity the economists worked their way down through the curriculum. By 1900 they were able to offer political economy even to freshmen."[16] In the early years of the AEA, there were even several discussions of the opportunities for and desirability of political economy teaching in high schools.[17]

At the advanced level, the Americans modified the German seminar system in a variety of ways: for example, either having all members study the same topic prior to discussions with the professor as seminar leader, or having individual students study separate topics with advice from the professor and seminar presentations when they were ready. This made the seminar

a revolutionary step towards professionalism. Scientific investigation became the authority. Both teacher and student contributed to the subject matter. The number of topics to be covered could be expanded greatly. Professional skill in research, analysis, presentation, became more important than the accumulation of facts. More abundant library resources permitted specialization which in turn led to more productive scholarship and the basis of all professions—a larger and growing literature.[18]

The cooperative, mutually exploratory atmosphere of the American seminar was usually much more egalitarian than its German counterpart, where attitudes toward the professoriate were, and were expected to be, much more deferential. The German system of a single lofty and prestigious professor surrounded by a host of dependent and sometimes sycophantic *dozents* did not suit American attitudes and social conditions. As John Higham has noted, unlike the continental European situation, in the United States it was assumed that "every academic person should not only have his own distinct speciality" but should be able "to aspire to his own sphere of influence. Every Ph.D. who chose to teach should be able some day to become a professor," whereas in Germany, "so jealously were professional prerogatives guarded that provision for new fields of study usually came slowly and reluctantly. Specialization was confined within strict limits."[19]

The more egalitarian American atmosphere had organizational

as well as strictly intellectual consequences as the university department emerged as a "society of equals." Again quoting Higham:

in a department, several relatively autonomous teachers shared responsibility for a field of knowledge. Every one of them could have unchallenged control of his own little subdivision of the field. By the 1890's departments were developing a busy, independent life which they conducted for the most part on a collegial basis. The department could easily expand to accommodate new specialists; it facilitated the coexistence of a considerable number of full professors, and its self governing procedures acknowledged the juridical equality of all specialists. As the departments rose in importance after 1900, they acquired power that had earlier belonged to the university presidents. The age of strong presidents passed, and that too promoted specialization.[20]

This departmental structure was admirably suited to the competitive climate of the age. For the individual there were opportunities for internal promotion, and for those at the top, as indeed for some of the promising stars lower down, there was scope for geographical mobility since any department, provided it could command the requisite resources, could in principle find a place for an additional specialist and would seek to replace one who left for greener pastures. (The possibility of dismissal will be referred to later, in connection with academic freedom issues.) The importance attached to specialization, increments to the sum of knowledge, and publication also had a marked effect on the quality of Ph.D. output. Contrary to later impressions, the Ph.D. in German universities was

not the highest on an ascending scale of academic degrees, as it proudly became in America. It was the basic and almost the only degree the philosophical faculty (i.e., arts and sciences) awarded. There was no B.A., no graduate school, and no clear differentiation between the few students who hoped for a career in science and scholarship and the many students who were simply preparing themselves for secondary school teaching or some other profession. . . . In addition to writing a brief dissertation, candidates underwent examination in three broad subjects, such as history, geography, and mathematics. Neither the dissertation nor the examinations were very concentrated or demanding.[21]

Somewhat the same was probably true of the early American Ph.D.'s in economics, but by the end of the century conditions were very different, at least at the leading graduate schools. The absence of any central monitoring agency led to an enormous proliferation of different types and qualities of degree. The danger of competitive debasement was obvious, and strenuous efforts were required to maintain reasonable standards. Here the pressures of specialization and interinstitutional rivalry helped to relieve the situation. According to Parrish,

Dissertations became longer, more sophisticated and more specialized, i.e., they were no longer the mark of a cultured gentleman but the demonstration of professional skill. By 1900 the Ph.D. in political economy (as in many other subjects) had won out over all other degrees and the "no degree" school as the symbol of top level professional training.[22]

Several of the larger graduate institutions in economics began to issue monograph series consisting largely of completed Ph.D. dissertations. Others encouraged their students either to publish in these outlets or to offer their products to the AEA's Publication Series, which was periodically starved of suitable material. And for those who produced shorter works there was a growing number of periodicals such as the *Quarterly Journal of Economics, Political Science Quarterly, Journal of Political Economy, Annals of the American Academy, Yale Review,* and so on, all of which published articles on economic questions by up-and-coming as well as established economists. As with the proliferation of degrees, the rapid multiplication of publications was disquieting to those whose institutions lacked their own economic outlets or who were concerned at the mediocre quality and limited supply of material available to the AEA. In the end, after a decade or more of anxious discussion,[23] the association decided to abandon its monograph series and launch its own journal, the *American Economic Review,* in 1911, an addition the profession managed to absorb as the supply of potential authors was also increasing.

Needless to say, the younger generation of economists played a notable part in these educational developments. Among the AEA's founders and early members, several became university presidents (e.g., Francis A. Walker at MIT; William Watts Folwell at Minnesota; Edmund Janes James at Northwestern and Illinois; and Arthur T. Hadley at Yale), and doubtless many others turned down opportunities to follow their lead. Even more important to the discipline were the founders and/or influential leaders of major departments or schools, such as Charles Dunbar and Frank Taussig at Harvard, Henry Carter Adams at Michigan, and Richard T. Ely at Wisconsin. In addition to their teaching, direction of research, editorial work, and publishing, many of them provided expertise for a variety of federal, state, and local bodies and to private businesses far too numerous to cite here.[24] Their collaborative work on the successive national censuses serves as a conspicuous example of the marriage of scholarly expertise and public service.

Prior to the 1870s, the primary cultural and institutional influences on political economy were still British rather than continental European. The implications of this state of affairs, both for the subject's content and for its status in the college curriculum, cannot be fully appreciated without reference to the European scene. And when we consider the later part of the century the impact of European precedents on American ideas and practices becomes increasingly obvious.

As previous chapters in this volume reveal, political economy was widely taught in the early American colleges as an integral part of the traditional liberal arts curriculum—more widely, in fact, than in Britain, its country of origin. This proved to be a mixed blessing. As befitted a subject tracing its intellectual lineage back to Adam Smith, political economy was usually added onto or incorporated into the final year's standard course in moral philosophy conducted by the college president, the institution's most visible personality, on whom it was greatly dependent for its academic standing and even its financial viability. This gave the subject a secure and recognized place in the instructional program; but it was also inhibiting, for the teaching was elementary, often only barely competent, and intellectual innovation was generally discouraged.[25] As the college's mental atmosphere was seeped in theology, it is hardly surprising that popular introductory textbooks sometimes stressed the compatibility between the laws of political economy and the laws of God. The pedagogical creed emphasized the disciplined inculcation of accepted truth rather than the quest for knowledge, and it is suggested that the preoccupation with character formation rather than intellect represented a workable early compromise between the classicists and the devout in the struggle between learning and piety.[26] The proper balance between character and intellect was hotly debated during the educational transformation, and it may be an index of Yale's conservatism that as late as 1910 its economist president, Arthur T. Hadley, still saw the possibility of conflict between the two.[27]

Not surprisingly, as in England, the few notable American contributions to economic thought came mainly from outside academia, and economic writers were widely regarded, not entirely without justification, primarily as spokesmen for free trade or protection. Possibly the subject would have had a more lively and independent existence had it been viewed, as in England, as a science rather than merely as an adjunct to the humanities. The natural sciences were not unknown even in the traditional colleges, though they occupied (like political economy) a subordinate position. By midcentury, they were being taught in a growing number of educational institutions and, as at Harvard, Yale, and Dartmouth, occasionally in newly established units separate from but affiliated with older foundations.[28] Had the traditional curriculum been completely resistant to change, political economy would surely have flourished eventually in these newer environments, for there was an irresistible growth of public interest in economic affairs. As it transpired, the established college program was prized open by a series of reformers who prepared the ground for Charles Eliot's introduction of the elective system,[29] and political economy, breaking away from the claustrophobic embrace of moral philosophy, became one of the principal beneficiaries of the new dispensation.

On the European mainland the situation was quite different. There the early teaching of economics occurred mainly in the context of law and public administration (e.g., Cameral Science and Staatswissenschaft); the climate of thought was more secular and scientific than theological; and the clientele consisted primarily of prospective lawyers, public officials, and civil servants, rather than clergymen and broadly educated citizens, as in the United States. There is, of course, some danger of exaggerating the intellectual and institutional differences between the two continents, for European conditions were by no means uniform. In some countries the prevailing *étatisme mentalité* encountered a strong and growing nineteenth-century challenge from advocates of liberal economic ideas and policies who owed their allegiance to Adam Smith and the physiocrats. These doctrines, especially in their more speculative manifestations, flourished in France, Italy, and elswhere in the Mediterranean, for they appealed to the Latin *mentalité*, although everywhere they encountered resistance from established beliefs and vested interests. Yet it was from more northerly territories, especially Germany, where economic liberalism was a distinctly minority creed, that continental influences came to exert a major impact on American intellectual life and higher education even well before large numbers of native sons returned home from their studies abroad in the 1870s and 1880s.

The influence of the young Americans' *Wanderjahren* is difficult to summarize briefly and accurately if only because so much depended on the individual's background, personal character, interests, and goals.[30] Above all, they went abroad for educational reasons, to savor the opportunity for foreign travel and get the advanced scholarly and professional training that was lacking in the United States before the 1880s. Moreover, they had the expectation of returning home with enhanced career prospects. Of course, there was no uniform reaction to the experience of study abroad, although in most cases in the earlier period it was strongly favorable, even enthusiastic. They could hardly fail to be impressed by the superior faculties of the German universities with their renowned seminars conducted by famous professors, well-equipped laboratories, and numerous research institutes dedicated to specialized scholarship of a kind rarely encountered across the Atlantic. The gap in standards between the two regimes was obviously substantial, yet it constituted no serious obstacle: Entry conditions in Germany were easy, and the requirements for the Ph.D. degree far from exacting. Thus, the Americans had ready access to a wide range of subject matter, skills, and conceptual tools in an environment of serious commitment to scholarship as a profession. For many of them the sense of freedom was almost overwhelming. There was a startling contrast between the intellectual and social constraints imposed by the typical American college and the genuine independence enjoyed by the German students, many of whom were reacting against the strict discipline of the *Gymnasium* years. The feeling of liberation was further reinforced by the fact that the Americans were far from home, in control of their own affairs often for the first time, at an age when they were maturing rapidly—intellectually, socially, physiologically, and sexually. Generally speaking, the climate of economic, social, and political opinion in Germany was congenial to them in the 1870s. Germany had expressed strong support for the northern cause during the Civil War, and the young Americans were stimulated by the confident and expansive mood of the newly unified, rapidly industrializing nation. They were probably unaware of the political conditions affecting senior university appointments, so impressed were they by the prestige, high status, emoluments, and respect accorded to the professoriat,[31] all of which undoubtedly enhanced the attractions of an academic career.

By the turn of the century, however, conditions had changed. The leading American academic institutions had largely, if not entirely, caught up with their German counterparts, and American students were much less favorably impressed by what they saw abroad. Indeed, in some cases they reacted strongly against the increasingly arrogant and strident nationalism expressed by some German professors, as well as by politicians and the press.[32] After 1900 the great student exodus was largely a thing of the past.

German economic ideas, methods, and policies were being vigorously discussed in the United States from the early 1870s,[33] but the most striking evidence of their influence came a decade later in the form of two distinct but interrelated proposals to establish a scholarly and scientific organization on the lines of the Verein für Sozialpolitik (Union for Social Policy), which had been founded in Germany in 1872. Both schemes derived their inspiration from Johannes Conrad of Halle, a founder member of the Verein, who urged his American students to launch a similar body in the United States. After much deliberation, Edward Janes James and Simon Nelson Patten of the University of Pennsylvania produced a plan for a Society for the Study of National Economy (the German equivalent, *Nationalökonom,* had a more distinctly statist sound) in June 1885, but on their failure to win the necessary support Richard T. Ely of Johns Hopkins, who had been present at the Halle discussions, took the initiative and circulated his proposal for an American Economic Association (AEA), which was duly adopted at Saratoga Springs, New York, in September of that year.[34] The occasion proved to be a watershed marking the effective beginning of the economics profession, not only in the United States but throughout the world, for the AEA's example was soon copied in Britain and elsewhere, and the organization has since become the largest and most influential learned body in its field. The historical conjucture of the background, setting, and detailed implementation of Ely's scheme is fascinating, affording rich insights into the contemporary intellectual and educational scene, the interaction of personal and institutional interests and rivalries, and questions of professional strategy.

Clearly the time was ripe for a union of American economists. During the 1870s and 1880s some 200 new learned societies were formed in the United States, a veritable explosion of knowledge organization that signaled the nation's metamorphosis from a cultural backwater into potential world leadership in science and scholarship. The selection of Saratoga Springs as the birthplace of the AEA was calculated, as it was the annual meeting place of the American Social Science Association (ASSA), and the assembled company would include a number of those who had already undertaken to support the new body. It was also a symbolic choice, for the AEA proved to be but one of a series of new social science associations that would eventually bring the quietus to the older body.[35]

The ASSA had been formed in 1865 under the sponsorship of the Massachusetts State Board of Charities by a group of New England gentlemen educators and men of affairs who wished to study and find solutions to various social problems, especially those resulting from rapid urbanization and immigration. They also sought to establish a "community of the competent" who would not only accumulate useful knowledge but also raise the standards of scientific investigation, and they were subsequently reinforced by a number of prominent rising educators, including some of the previously mentioned captains of erudition who were in the process of reforming American colleges and universities. By the 1880s the ASSA had expanded, not without difficulty, to the point where the activities of its several "departments" embraced most of our present-day social science disciplines, and it began to produce a number of specialist offspring which reflected the increasing division of labor among the educated cadres. Strictly speaking, the first of these was the American Historical Association (AHA), founded at Saratoga a year before the birth of the AEA, but the latter was the more significant of the two from the ASSA's standpoint.

There had been no specifically historical section within the existing body, and the "teachers and friends of history" had declined to form one despite the ASSA president's warning that "the tendency of scholarship in this country was towards excessive specialization."[36] In the economists' case, however, there were already two departments of the ASSA within their general field: Social Economy and Finance, both of which had economist secretaries (E. J. James and H. C. Adams) who were active proponents of the new body. The decision to break away was a clear indication of the ASSA's inability to retain control over its rapidly expanding bailiwick. It also signified that leadership in the establishment of authoritative sources of knowledge was passing from the gentlemen amateurs who had founded the older body to a new generation of university professionals.

The vigorous discussion of ends and means at the AEA's foundation and during its early years, which revealed the complex mixture of motives and interests involved, will be considered shortly. At this point it is appropriate to observe that from the mid-1880s the ASSA went into a slow but inexorable decline, eventually giving up the ghost in 1909 after the formation of the American Sociological Society in 1905 and the American Political Science Association in 1909, both of which were direct offshoots from the AEA. It is also significant that both the historians' and the economists' associations were direct products of the vigorous entrepreneurial activities of Johns Hopkins, the new graduate and partially German-inspired university that was currently heading the academic procession. President Gilman actively encouraged his young faculty members to establish national learned societies for the promotion of knowledge in general and the university in particular, so it was no coincidence that the historian Herbert Baxter Adams became the founder and first secretary of the AHA, while his colleague Ely occupied a similar position in the AEA.[37] Curiously enough, a few years earlier, the ASSA's secretary had proposed a merger between his association and Johns Hopkins, then only two years old, and although for a time Gilman seemed interested, on becoming president of the ASSA (in 1879–80) he did not take up the offer but simply recommended that a department of historical studies should be added to the existing structure. It is intriguing to conjecture what might have happened had Gilman implemented the scheme, for he was poised "on the very edge of the transition from amateur to professional social science." By the mid-1880s the ASSA's fate was sealed. As John Higham has observed, the emergence of the modern social sciences involved a drive for cultural consolidation comparable to the trust movement in American business.[38] It was the product of an egotistic quest for status and power, threatening the old established elites, the last generation of amateurs, as the aspiring professionals used their cognitive skills to capture the expanding markets for their services. In intellectual terms it involved a crisis of authority among both the older and the new generations; and, as we shall see, it posed serious problems concerning the interrelationships between advocacy of social reform and assertion of authoritative claims to neutrality and scientific objectivity.[39]

Although there were striking similarities among the origins, structure, and objectives of the AHA and the AEA, there were also significant differences in their social composition. Unlike its younger sister, the AHA was dominated by an older cadre of patrician leisured amateurs until the early years of the century, and although there were already fifteen full-time professors of history, five full-time assistant professors, and about thirty graduate students in the mid-1880s, it was not until 1907 that a "purely and exclusively" professional historian was elected president.[40] By contrast, partly owing to its initial domination by the young men newly returned from Germany, the AEA was always led by an academic economist, and only one nonacademic ever served in any of the executive offices. In other words, the new generation of professionals seized and retained control.

When Ely circulated prospective supporters of his new organization in the summer of 1885, he enclosed a provisional statement of "objects" and a draft "Platform" for the AEA because, as he explained at the inaugural gathering, "it is not easy to arouse interest in an organization that professes nothing." If this was indeed his intention he certainly succeeded, for the platform was the focus of a lively debate at Saratoga, where it was referred to a committee for redrafting; and even after it was "toned down," rechristened as a Statement of Principles and approved for publication with the proviso that it was "not to be regarded as binding on individual members," it remained the subject of controversy until it was eventually dropped in 1888.[41]

As there was a direct line of descent from the Verein für Sozialpolitik through the James--Patten prospectus for a Society for the Study of National Economy and Ely's platform to the published Statement of Principles, the various formulations are worth examining briefly for, taken in conjunction with the Saratoga proceedings, they provide revealing insights into the range of opinions, aims, and aspirations among the central figures in the late nineteenth-century professionalization process. As Ely had been the prime mover, his views were obviously prominent, but they were neither consistent nor calculated to generate a consensus, and during the inaugural discussions it became clear that they were not representative. For example, in clause 4 of his platform he had complained that economists had been "too ready to assert themselves as advocates," yet at Saratoga he argued that advocacy was both unavoidable and necessary in order that "intelligent men and women should distinguish between us and certain economists in whom there is little faith." The platform was broad enough, he maintained, to include "all those who can cooperate advantageously with us. It advocates simply certain methods of study and the accomplishment of reforms by certain means which alone seem to us to promise valuable results." How far this was compatible with the professed desire for "perfect-freedom in all economic discussions," he did not explain.[42]

Ely did not specify which reforms were essential or the means of achieving them, doubtless realizing that to do so might prove highly contentious. But he was much more explicit about methods of study. They should "part company," he declared, with those who did not "believe in historical and statistical enquiries and examinations into actual conditions [because] we have little faith that the methods advocated by certain economists will ever lead to valuable results." Whether method was in fact a key issue has been questioned by some modern commentators, probably because Ely declared in his autobiography, published more than fifty years later, that it was not fundamental but merely "the way of breaking down barriers in the path of progress and preparing the ground for something new and constructive."[43] Yet surely this was an important function. There was a general consensus that the AEA's first "Objects" should be "the encouragement of research" and "the publication of economic monographs," and some measure of agreement on scientific procedures was essential if acceptable professional standards were to be established. Questions of method figured prominently in the well-publicized debate between representatives of the so-called old and new schools in the series of articles that appeared in *Science* magazine the following year,[44] and, as Mary Furner has noted, the choice of the first two protagonists—Ely and his Johns Hopkins colleague, the astronomer-economist Simon Newcomb— virtually guaranteed that the issues would appear in an unnecessarily polarized form.[45] There was in fact no sharp dichotomy between the two schools on methodological issues, merely an important difference of emphasis and degree. Yet there was substantial justification for Ely's contention that, by contrast with "the final statement that characterized the political economy of a past generation," the young professionals claimed "superiority" only on the humble grounds that "we know better what we do not know."[46]

The outcome of the discussion of Ely's platform was that his derogatory references to "final statements" and to the laissez-faire doctrine as "unsafe in politics and unsound in morals," were deleted, in an effort to win moderate support, and replaced in the Statement of Principles by a vague expression of appreciation for "the work of earlier economists." However, the reference to the need for historical and statistical studies, a trace of German influence, remained with only a minor change of wording.

A major bone of contention at Saratoga as, indeed, throughout the AEA's subsequent history was whether, and if so how far, the organization should, as a body, become directly involved in economic and social policy issues. It is here that the difference between the American project and its German antecedent is most marked, and it was on this issue that the need for compromise was most vital during the AEA's early years, a compromise that eventually pointed the way to the future of the economics profession in the United States.[47] To assert that "Behind all the protests against Ely's platform lay a single fear: that people would get the idea that the so-called new economists were all socialists"[48] is an oversimplification; but it highlights one essential part of the truth. The Verein's critics had dubbed its leaders *Kathedersozialisten* (Socialists of the Chair), and the James–Patten program appeared to substantiate that charge, for their proposals were far longer, more detailed, and more far-reaching than anything contemplated at Saratoga.

After questioning "the widespread view that our economic problems will solve themselves" and the bias of "our laws and institutions" in favor of "individual instead of collective action," they asserted that "the state is a positive factor in material production and has legitimate claims to a share of the product. The public interest can be served by the state's appropriating and applying this share to promote public ends."[49] Taken in conjunction with the rest of the document, these general statements constitute a preamble to a comprehensive scheme of national planning embracing a redistribution of constitutional powers among municipal, state, and federal governments and potentially radical departures in the fields of education, sanitary conditions, wages and hours, restrictions on large units of production, control of transportation, and the conservation and improved utilization of natural resources to achieve a more "symmetrical development." All this was buttressed by the general argument that the quality of public administration is inversely related to efforts to diminish public expenditure and narrow the scope of government action. "True economy in government affairs does not necessarily consist in a reduction of public revenues, but in such a distribution and administration of public expenditures as will in the most efficient manner promote public ends."

It is easy to imagine the reactions of most educated middle-class Americans to such an ambitious program at a time when the tide of opinion was just beginning to turn from the exuberant early post–Civil War laissez-faire ethos toward the fin de siècle conception of a general welfare state.[50] To conservatives it must have been anathema, whereas moderates—assuming they accepted the idea that a learned society should actively promote policy changes—generally favored piecemeal solutions to contemporary economic and social evils rather than a comprehensive scheme of state intervention. This is not to say that the James–Patten initiative sank without a trace. Both Ely's platform and the Statement of Principles acknowledged that the state had a positive role to play as an "indispensable condition of human progress" and, together with the church and science, as an aid in finding a "solution" to "the conflict of capital and labor." Both documents contained a declaration of belief in "a progressive development of economic conditions, which must be met by a corresponding development of legislative policy." This too bears a German imprint, notwithstanding Ely's insistence that the association had arisen "spontaneously in answer to felt needs" and that "Nothing was more marked than its American character."[51]

There was, however, at least one distinctively American feature in Ely's platform and the Statement of Principles that was lacking in the James–Patten constitution and in the Verein's program: the reference to the role of the church. This directly reflected Ely's personal influence as an active Christian Socialist and believer in the interdependence of economics and ethics; but it was a deterrent to those who preferred a more secular and strictly scientific approach to economics dissociated from the clerical Ricardianism that had dominated earlier American college teaching of political economy. For those who questioned whether the AEA needed any platform, there was a dual force in Newcomb's caustic comment that Ely viewed the AEA as "a sort of church, requiring for admission a renunciation of ancient errors and an adhesion to the supposed new creed."[52]

Of course, Ely was by no means the only dedicated Christian among the young "new-school" economist founder-members: H. C. Adams, Clark, James, and Patten had broadly similar religious backgrounds and were equally sincere believers. But the question was: Should the AEA be as closely identified with contemporary religious social reform activism as Ely desired? Among the fifty who joined the AEA at Saratoga, there were about twenty-three current or ex-ministers, several of whom—including Washington Gladden and Lyman Abbott—were well-known leaders of the so-called Social Gospel movement, and Ely energetically campaigned to increase their numbers.[53] Many members of that movement sought a via media between laissez-faire and socialism; but some were radicals who could legitimately be regarded as Socialists, and critics of the AEA were hardly disposed to discriminate carefully among them, for the lines were blurred.[54] Moreover, although advocacy of Socialist measures was one shortcoming in a would-be social scientist, sentimentalism was another, and even some of Ely's closest allies were dismayed by his habit of occasionally expressing his views in exaggerated and emotional language.[55]

Underlying the inaugural discussion of questions of method, the role of the state, the desirability and character of reform, and the relationship between economics and ethics was the more fundamental and delicate issue of the need to define the "community of the competent"—or, as Ely put it, to "include nearly all those who can cooperate advantageously with us." Apart from Ely's opening remarks, the only reference to this matter in the official record was E. B. Andrews's expressed hope that the platform could be framed so as "to exclude no earnest economist," but no doubt this problem was in the minds of most of those present. As Ely recalled in his autobiography, there was "an inclusive as well as an exclusive aim." The statement of principles was "a compromise on behalf of catholicity" in an effort "to win the great body of economists. . . . it aimed to gather together like-minded men, congenial men who it was supposed could profitably work together. Not every economist was at first asked to join, although no economist who expressed a desire to join was refused enrollment," and no one was asked to sign the statement of principles.[56] Even so, it proved to be seriously divisive. Before the problems it caused are described, one further feature of the AEA's initial plan deserves consideration.

Like James and Patten, and before them the Verein, Ely conceived of "cooperation" among the AEA members in quite specific terms. The formation of a series of standing committees charged with the task of investigating and producing a report on a specific topic to be presented and discussed at one of the council meetings was directly modeled on the Verein's procedures, whereby teams of scholars produced numerous substantial monographs, which revealed a "relentless will to dig" for historical and statistical data.[57] If the Germanic conception of economics had reigned unchallenged in the United States, something of the same kind would presumably have occurred under AEA auspices, and indeed historical and descriptive monographs dominated the association's publications until after the turn of the century. However, these were produced by individuals, not by groups; the Bureau of Information, another of the organization's initial objects, proved to be little more than a communication center, mainly owing to lack of funds; and there were no substantial standing committee reports.

During the AEA's first three years (i.e., prior to the abandonment of the Statement of Principles), the Executive Committee's[58] primary concern was to enlist the support of those "like-minded, congenial" economists (as Ely termed them) who had either refused invitations to join or were holding back until it became clear how the organization would develop. Contrary to the impression created by the *Science* debate, there was, in fact, a spectrum of opinion rather than a sharp division between the old and new schools, and a good many economists were unwilling to align themselves with either party. Of course there were some whose membership was neither desired nor solicited, including, for example, Newcomb, who had been in dispute with Ely since 1884, and William Graham Sumner, the Yale professor of political and social science and leading American spokesman for laissez-faire. Knowledge of the opposition to Sumner proved especially embarrassing to his former students and young colleagues, Arthur T. Hadley and Henry W. Farnam, who, despite certain reservations, were favorably disposed to the AEA. Somewhat similar misgivings applied in the case of Charles Dunbar and Frank W. Taussig of Harvard. Some of the AEA's founder members maintained contact with the outsiders through the small private Political Economy Club founded by J. L. Laughlin in 1883, with Newcomb as president.[59] Curiously enough, in the following year Ely and F. A. Walker, who were to become the AEA's secretary and president, respectively, from 1885 to 1892, had considered the possibility of "asserting ourselves aggressively" within the club rather than launching a brand-new organization.[60] Such a strategy was hardly feasible, however, for despite Laughlin's hope of making it a genuinely scholarly dining-discussion circle rather than a free-trade clique, the leading members were far more interested in current policy and political affairs than in academic questions.

By contrast with the Political Economy Club, the AEA marked the emergence of a more mature, complex, and scientific approach to economic thought and policy. Notwithstanding some initial unnecessary boldness and defiance in the attitude toward the ruling orthodoxy, most of the organization's prime movers were flexible and open-minded. Though they differed among themselves on basic issues of method, theory, and policy, they nevertheless shared a common commitment to the advance of scientific investigation and the exchange of ideas and information, and they became less aggressively partisan as they became more confident that the organization could not be captured by the older generation.[61] As the membership expanded, the AEA ceased to be regarded as the organ of a particular school or approach, as had been the case with most of the earlier organizations concerned with economic affairs, and its annual gatherings—which were not confined to fully paid-up members—provided an open forum in which any inclinations toward dogmatism or intellectual intolerance were constrained by the accepted conventions of scientific procedure and the etiquette of formal debate. Consequently, attendance at these meetings proved reassuring to doubters.

The gradual and occasionally delicate process of transforming the AEA into a truly representative scholarly and scientific body need not be recorded in detail here for it is already well documented.[62] Given the limited numbers involved at the outset, personalities necessarily played a significant part, especially those of Ely and Walker, the AEA's first two principal officers. Ely's boundless energy, enthusiasm, and willingness to take the initiative were undoubted assets in the organization's formative stages, and it is no exaggeration to say that during the 1880s and early 1890s the general public's response to the AEA was largely determined by the various reactions to his ideas and writings. As indicated earlier, however, within the emerging scientific community his aggressive self-importance, coupled with his views and his mode of expression, soon became recognized by the moderates as a liability. An example of the younger conservative reaction is that of Laughlin, who responded to the news of his election to the AEA's Council by refusing to join "a class of disciples" or support a body with "any constitution save love of truth." His unwillingness to be "another rag tied on to Ely's kite to steady his erratic movements" may have been influenced not only by his distaste for Ely's ideas but also by the realization that the AEA would undermine support for the Political Economy Club.[63] Whatever the reasons, he did not join the AEA until 1904, being the last prominent academic economist to do so.

By contrast with Ely, Walker was unquestionably the ideal choice as president. A respected member of the older generation, well known at home and abroad for his economic writings and his distinguished record of public service, Walker was also sympathetic to the new professionals. In 1884 he had written to Ely:

Perhaps no one has had more occasion than myself to feel the need of such moral support from fellow workers in political economy as might come from formal association and concerted action. When I first started out in 1874, I suffered an amount of supercilious patronage and toplofty criticism which was almost more than I could bear. Downright abuse would have been a luxury.

Subsequently, in one of his AEA presidential addresses, Walker recalled the days when laissez-faire "was not made the test of economic orthodoxy, merely. It was used to decide whether a man were an economist at all," and the fact that he had experienced difficulties with Sumner at Yale may also have helped to endear him to the younger generation. In the difficult period of negotiation over the AEA's Statement of Principles, its general strategy, and the temporary crisis caused by Ely's decision to organize the 1892 annual meeting at Chautauqua, Walker consistently adopted a statesmanlike attitude and was clearly a strong force for unity.[64]

The AEA's internal history is a major source of insights into the forces shaping the development of the economics profession in the United States. The initial uncertainties and disagreements over the organization's purposes, strategy, and management proved to be transitory. The role of personalities necessarily diminished as the scale of its activities and membership expanded; and in the 1890s the main internal problems stemmed from institutional rivalries and regional differences of interest and outlook.

The fact that the original proposal for an organization of economists had come from the University of Pennsylvania, an institution closely associated with the nationalist tradition in American political economy and with protectionism, a policy unpopular with the majority of economists, may help to account for the failure of the James–Patten project. By contrast, Ely's initiative derived from Johns Hopkins, then unquestionably the leading institution in the modernization of American higher learning. That Harvard and Yale initially appeared as possible centers of resistance to the AEA has already been noted, and after the spectacular launching of the University of Chicago that institution appeared as a threat to the union of the economists. Quite apart from Laughlin's refusal to become a member, his independent decision to launch the *Journal of Political Economy* aroused Taussig's and Dunbar's "disgust at this intrusion into the field. It is a clear case of not having the interest of science at heart; though it may be a question whether this interest is pure and undefiled in the breast of any of us. We all have a concern for our institutions.[65]

Needless to say, Taussig's outburst reflected his interest in Harvard's *Quarterly Journal of Economics,* but it came at a time of growing concern about the multiplication of university publications in economics, which was making it difficult to obtain a sufficient supply of suitable material for the AEA's series. This problem continued through much of the following decade, and the failure to reach agreement on cooperation among the leading institutions eventually led to the decision to inaugurate the AEA's own journal, the *American Economic Review*.[66]

Another, more deep-rooted, and potentially more serious source of disunity within the community of economists at this time was the emergence of a distinctive regional pattern of opinion reflecting contemporary political, social, and intellectual tensions, a state of affairs that directly affected the AEA through the expansion of economic training in the Middle and Far West. It is obviously impossible to consider in detail the problems involved in analyzing regional variations in social and cultural conditions and in tracing their effects on the work in a particular social science discipline.[67] The evidence is limited and difficult to interpret, although the chapters in this volume on Berkeley and Stanford (Chapter 11), Wisconsin (Chapter 13), and Chicago (Chapter 10) convey a useful preliminary impression. The issues involved were persuasive, because the selection of faculty was often directly influenced by local prejudices in both private and state institutions,[68] and the number of summary dismissals and academic freedom cases (which will be touched on later) made painfully clear the penalties of defiance of local sensibilities. Of course, these incidents reveal that at least some economists openly resisted local pressures; and others were protected by the courage and goodwill of their university authorities or were discreet enough not to cause trouble. Nevertheless, especially in the turbulent political and social climate of the first half of the 1890s, when there were clearly marked regional differences of interest and outlook over such issues as free silver, the tariff, and the trusts, it is hardly surprising that these differences were reflected in the attitudes of many academic economists. When Walker and Ely ended their terms as president and secretary of the AEA in 1892, to be replaced by Dunbar and E. A. Ross (a Johns Hopkins graduate under Ely) of Cornell, many of Ely's sympathizers interpreted the change as a move toward conservatism and suspected that Ely had been driven out by an eastern cabal, an impression reinforced by his decision to move to Wisconsin.[69]

As usual, the facts were more complex than this conspiracy thesis suggests, and Ely did little to clarify the situation. There was indeed a sense in which the adoption of a more scholarly and scientific stance entailed the AEA's withdrawal from active participation in contemporary economic and social reform movements, which had been one of the founders' initial objects. Yet this was also a move toward a more academic, detached, and neutral approach to economic affairs, one that reflected the prevailing mood of the economics profession. Interpreted broadly, the growing interest in marginal utility and marginal productivity analysis in the 1890s was not merely a reaction against the divisive methodological and doctrinal controversies of the preceding decade but also a manifestation of the economists' yearning for scientific status and prestige. This they sought to achieve by dissociating themselves from the past and establishing economics (rather than political economy, old-style) as an independent scholarly discipline free from theological, ethical, historical, and sociological encumbrances, and, above all, free from the taint of missionary zeal and political partisanship. In this they were continuing the process that had begun with the breakaway from the American Social Science Association, and it was part of a general trend toward professionalism in the social sciences, as in American society generally.[70]

Needless to say, not all the AEA's members welcomed this trend, especially those most closely associated with Ely or sympathetic toward his approach. At a time when radicalism was rife in the Middle West, there was a growing belief that the national body had become more conservative and that it was unduly dominated by eastern academics. Accordingly, various efforts were made to form an alternative or rival organization to cater to the special needs of those in colleges and universities where contemporary issues and vocational needs were given priority over academic specialization and research. In part, the division of opinion and interests was ideological, but it was also professional, in the narrower sense of that term, and geographical. The sheer size of the country made it difficult and expensive for those in the distant interior to attend annual meetings, which were invariably held in the eastern cities, and therefore to become fully participating members in the professional community. Several of Ely's former students pressed him to take the lead in forming a new association, which might have become a breakaway movement, but he refused, partly because of his desire to avoid the taint of socialism or radicalism, especially after his "trial" at Wisconsin in 1894.[71]

In 1895 the AEA's officials were alarmed at the news that a Political Science Association of the central states had been formed and that it either might be dominated by an "Ely–Commons faction" or might be captured by the predatory academics of the University of Chicago,[72] an institution widely regarded as a ruthless rival to the established leaders of American academic life. As it transpired, both fears were exaggerated, for the association's leaders began by passing a resolution expressing their determination "to arrange its future meetings so as to avoid conflict with the two national organizations in which we are all interested." As its secretary, G. W. Knight of Ohio State University, explained, its purpose was to discuss "the many questions of pedagogy and methodology in connection with these fields [i.e., sociology, history, economics, and political science], and *peculiar to the institutions of this section of the country,* or at least away from the seaboard." [73]

A key figure in this situation was H. C. Adams, a respected founder-member of the AEA, head of the Economics Department at the University of Michigan, which was widely regarded as the leading state university, and a moderate skeptic toward current theological tendencies in economics. After considerable debate within the AEA, an acceptable compromise was reached whereby the two associations would meet jointly in Indianapolis, not only because it was close to the Political Science Association's birthplace but also because the University of Indiana and John R. Commons, in particular, were under severe attack in the state legislature. It was thought desirable to show "the people of Indianapolis and of the state the determination of the economists of America, no matter what their opinions, to insist upon the freedom of instruction and investigation." At this meeting H. C. Adams was elected president of the AEA, a move that was fully justified by his standing in the profession, and doubtless also influenced by a conscious desire to conciliate the westerners.[74]

During the latter half of the 1890s, the threat of a regional split within the AEA passed away almost as rapidly as it had arisen, and it is not entirely fanciful—if too facile—to draw a parallel between the rise and fall of midwestern discontent among the economists and the contemporaneous swings in the Populists' political fortunes, which reached a climax in William Jennings Bryan's dramatic but unsuccessful bid for the presidency in 1896. As noted by Joseph Dorfman, the doyen of American historians of economics, this was the first presidential campaign in American history "to center on economic theory" [75]—that is, the question of the respective merits of gold and silver as the basis of the nation's money supply. The dilemma this situation posed for some conscientious economists is perfectly exemplified in the case of H. C. Adams who, as we have seen, was a key link between the western dissenters and the eastern establishment. As he told his mother, at first he had decided to "throw my vote away" on the minority gold Democrat, John M. Palmer; but in the end he backed Bryan:

All my reasonings and arguments, said vote for McKinley, but at the booth I gagged, and could not swallow the [Republican] party that, as I believe, has not a disinterested sentiment, in it. The election has postponed the struggle, for a struggle is bound to come, and I am glad that it will not come on an erroneous analysis like that of free silver.[76]

Soon after the election, support for the Populists faded rapidly, especially with respect to the demand for free silver, as economic growth, expanding urban demand, and the rise of prices undermined the farmers' case for inflationary policy measures. The struggle for reform referred to by Adams did not cease; it was taken up by the Progressives who, as William Allen White, the Kansas journalist, so aptly remarked, "caught the Populists in swimming and stole all their clothing, except the frayed underdrawers of free silver."[77] The Progressive movement was more national than sectional or regional, more urban than rural (as it reflected the underlying population movement), and it received more substantial support from the academic and intellectual communities than had the Populists. Needless to say, disagreement and controversy persisted among the economists; but there is substantial justification for W. J. Ashley's view that, after the AEA's leadership had passed from Ely and Walker to Dunbar and Ross, there was a new "spirit of tolerance and mutual charity among political economists which has not always been found within their circle."[78] Ashley was in a good position to judge, for he had recently moved from Toronto to a chair of economic history at Harvard, the first of its kind in the country, and he was English by background and strongly sympathetic toward the historical school. No doubt his impression of the professional situation was affected by the fact that some of the midwestern dissenters, including Ely, had temporarily absented themselves from the AEA's annual meetings. But there was also at that time a more conciliatory mood among economists in Britain who found that Marshall's *Principles*, first published in 1890, provided an admirable basis for consensus on fundamentals, and even in Germany the echoes of the *Methodenstreit* had at least partly died away. By the end of the decade there

were some who felt that the economists were becoming too complacent. Even Laughlin had conceded, in 1892, that the new
school's attacks had been "stimulating to the development of the
science, because they have caused further examination of fundamental postulates, and drawn attention by severe logical processes
to the proper statement of principles," while by insisting on the
value of the historical method and the verification of reasoning by
facts they had encouraged the careful and extensive collection of
data.[79] On the whole, the *Science* debate had demonstrated that the
gap between the two sides was not as great as the more extreme
protagonists had claimed and that there was a genuine basis for an
agreement to differ. However, H. H. Powers, a member of the AEA's
Publications Committee, may have exaggerated when he informed
Ely that

The Association seems now to have outlived the day of dissension. Perhaps
its chief danger now is from indifference. With Laughlin out and Hadley
graduated into a higher sphere I think no angular spirit of any influence
remains. But with the disappearance of discord there has seemed to me to
go something of the energy of earlier days. . . . I cannot but hope that your
devotion and earnestness will revive something more of these qualities
in the Association and do much towards making our traditions more
exacting.[80]

This somewhat myopically internalist assessment of the situation
undoubtedly reflects concern at the lack of enthusiasm and support
for the AEA's publications program mentioned earlier and the fact
that the organization's membership was growing sluggishly by com-
parision with that of the American Statistical Association and the
AHA.[81] Of much greater significance to the economists as a body,
however, was the external threat posed by a number of disturbing
academic freedom cases involving well-known economists. As
these affairs have been admirably described and analyzed by previous scholars, it is unnecessary to consider them in detail.[82] Instead,
attention will be focused on the insights they provide into the economists' recognition of the need for collective solidarity, especially in
response to the cases of E. B. Andrews at Brown University in 1897
and E. A. Ross at Stanford in 1900. These experiences evoked a
coordinated reaction in defense of the victims and a growth of professional self-consciousness which clearly reveals the extent of the
institutionalization of political economy in the United States at the
end of our period.

The rise of the new school of political economy in the 1880s was part of a wider educated public's reaction against certain disturbing trends in political, economic, and social life, such as the apparently unconstrained power of great wealth, the growing conflict between capital and labor, and the manifest evils of expanding urban industrial centers. The repudiation of laissez-faire and Sumner's conservative Social Darwinist doctrine, according to which any interference with the "natural" course of events was both futile and harmful since it would insure "the survival of the unfittest,"[83] put the economists and other social reformers into the same camp as Sumner's most effective critic, the sociologist Lester Ward, who insisted on the human capacity for intelligent control of social evolution. "The negative school of political economists," he argued, in terms that most of the AEA's early members would have endorsed, "insist upon nothing so strongly as that the natural processes of society must be left undisturbed." By contrast, according to a reform Social Darwinist like Ward, whereas "the environment transforms the animal . . . man transforms the environment. . . . The paradox, therefore, is that free competition can only be secured through regulation." Moreover, deftly turning the tables on Sumner and his allies, he added that the social reformers were themselves a "natural" phenomenon since they represented a response to society's inertia and its failure to react to the need for change.[84] Irrespective of whether they were prepared to be regarded as reformers, many of the economists found themselves thrust willy-nilly into the forefront of public debate as the result of the intense interest in such contentious questions as the tariff, the currency, the relations between labor and capital, and the trusts. Few of them were inclined to retreat into their ivory towers, which were, in any case, usually too close to the marketplace to afford effective protection; nor were the university authorities generally in favor of pure scholarship for its own sake. More often than not, institutions of higher learning were viewed as public service stations, with an obligation to promote the interests of their local community or the nation.

The public preoccupation with economic affairs brought tribulations as well as opportunities for public service. As one economist put it, "nobody cared what we taught so long as we dealt in abstractions and investigated only hypothetical cases. . . . But when we talk about railways, sugar trusts, labor unions, strikes, and municipal monopolies, the conversation grows personal."[85] The reference to the personal element in this passage is apt, for complex changes were taking place both within the academic community and in society at large. An examination of the late nineteenth-century academic freedom cases reveals how, in each instance, the outcome was determined by a complex and shifting combination of intra- and extraprofessional circumstances, including the individual's institutional location, his ideological position, professional standing, and personality traits; and the university authorities' behavior. If, as the historian Carl Becker reputedly said, "a professor is a man who thinks otherwise," it is easy to understand how the shift of pedagogic activity from the inculcation of established truths in callow youth to the communication of the latest research skills and findings to eager career-oriented graduates could affect the social scientists' conception of their relationship to the public. The young new-school economists' assertiveness did not merely result from their desire to overthrow the ruling economic orthodoxy: It also reflected their claims to expertise and their novel conception of the professor's role in American society, a conception profoundly influenced by the German experience. As Walter Metzger has noted, there were significant differences between the German and American versions of academic freedom, which were generally accepted by academics of widely differing political persuasions. Generally speaking, the German professor expected to be in unfettered control in the lecture hall and seminar and was often both aggressive and partisan in his presentations, but he was prepared to exercise self-restraint in his public utterances. By contrast, his American counterpart acknowledged the duty to be neutral in the classroom treatment of controversial matters and silent on topics outside his competence but claimed the right to extramural freedom of speech enjoyed by all American citizens.[86]

Prior to the Andrews case in 1897, it is doubtful whether more than a handful of American economists really appreciated the need for a concerted effort to insure their collective security, although a number of leading figures had been groping their way toward that conclusion for some time. The decline of controversy within their ranks and the repudiation of Ely's emotional style of Christian social reformism were obviously helpful; so too was the adoption of a more self-consciously "scientific" approach, for as Charles Eliot had observed some thirty years earlier, unlike the "established sciences," professors in "philosophical subjects" could not speak with authority but should confine themselves to mere exposition because of the prevalence of "disputed matters, open questions, and bottomless speculations."[87] Needless to say, most of the younger professional social scientists were not prepared to restrict themselves so narrowly; but until the university authorities and the relevant outside public were prepared to grant them the status and autonomy they demanded, the threat of interference with academic teaching and research would inevitably persist. And of course this reinforced the need for some kind of code of acceptable professional conduct.

The gradual emergence of a tacit but nonetheless increasingly recognized code of behavior is a central theme in Furner's generally excellent account of the *fin-de-siècle* professionalization of American social science. And as the economists were in the vanguard of the process it is also a central theme in the institutionalization of their discipline. Given the heterogeneity and rapidly changing character of higher education, there is inevitably a temptation to oversimplify the story by imposing "more order than ever existed," for there was a significant gap between the leadership and the rank and file in "the order of learning." As Furner concedes, at the time of the Andrews case the majority of scholars probably still

thought of their own positions as political sinecures where advocacy that conformed to local expectations was properly expected. . . . Professionalization had not progressed so far in 1897 that a principled defense of the economists' right of advocacy had become an aspect of professional identity.

Nevertheless, the situation was changing significantly. Although the AEA as a body refrained from taking an official position with respect to any particular violation of academic freedom, it came within a hair's breadth of doing so after the Ross case, and the published report by the unofficial committee of economists that had been established with support from those in attendance at the Detroit annual meeting was a decisive step en route to the formation of the American Association of University Professors in 1915.[88]

The repeated attacks on well-known economists not only served to strengthen the sense of professional identity and esprit de corps; they also

contributed to the gradual narrowing of the range of dissent that seemed safe for professional social scientists. Too much involvement, too much taking of sides where the public remained divided, undermined the scholarly authority of all social scientists and threatened their freedom to continue working. . . . For better or worse, these troubles taught many academics to conserve their image and preserve their instititions, to prepare to defend themselves but avoid the necessity, to exert influence quietly as experts rather than noisily as partisans. . . . Out of all the cases emerged a rudimentary discipline which identified the degree and type of advocacy that was entitled to collective security. Within limits where agreement could be reached on goals and tactics, the economists had exchanged the capricious discipline provided by powerful external opponents for the more steady influence of national professional control.[89]

The sense of unity among the economists was significantly enhanced in 1899 when Ely returned to the fold after having absented himself from the annual meetings for several years, and there was a further step in the same direction when Laughlin at last joined in 1904. Yet there were still significant differences of opinion within the community of economists with respect to appropriate professional conduct and their responsibility toward the public. This was revealed in a memorable exchange between Hadley, then president of Yale, and John R. Commons, then without an academic post, after Hadley's second presidential address to the AEA, in which he argued that the economist could most effectively enhance his influence by preserving a

dispassionate and critical attitude . . . as a man who stands above the clouds of prejudice and therefore sees farther than those about him; that it is his mission to be the representative and the champion of the permanent interests of the whole community, in face of conflicting claims from representatives of temporary or partial ones.[90]

In response, Commons, who had been invited to lead the formal discussion, flatly disagreed. Acknowledging that the economist should strive to be impartial and scientific in his analysis of contemporary problems, he denied that influence could be obtained or the professor's responsibility could be fulfilled by holding aloof from contending economic and social forces and seeking to promote the general good. "If we must wait for public opinion, led by economists and social moralists, to control the bosses in industry and politics," he warned, "then we are only waiting for a harsh despotism to become a paternal despotism." Class differences were endemic in society, and to deny their existence would simply be to accept the status quo, thereby playing into the hands of the ruling class. Representative government was in danger of breaking down, not because it represented class interests but precisely because it failed to do so. The patriotic course for the economist was not to remain hors de combat but to participate actively in the policy-making process seeking to bring about those changes that his scientific analysis led him to consider necessary and desirable. Appealing to his fellow economists, Commons declared:

We would be on safer ground if, when our conclusions lead us to champion the cause of a class . . . we should come out squarely and admit that this is so; not because the class interest is foremost in our minds, but because the class is the temporary means of bringing about the permanent interest of the whole.[91]

Needless to say, Commons was in a minority on this occasion. His professional colleagues had no desire to be regarded as spokesmen for a class interest, however scientific the economic analysis underlying that posture. Nevertheless, his views are significant in several ways. They demonstate that the professional consensus was still far from complete, which is hardly surprising. They testify to the continuing existence of a dissenting and reformist component in the discipline, which was in fact about to gather renewed momentum with the aid of Thorstein Veblen's powerful, if muted, critique of contemporary society and his disturbing exposure of the preconceptions of economic orthodoxy.[92] And, in addition, they reveal Commons's penetrating conception of the representation of interests in American society, which was to be a prominent theme in the progressive literature during the next two or three decades.

Although Commons could legitimately be regarded as untypical—an outsider, or at least a failure in terms of his career achievement at the time of his confrontation with Hadley—he was by no means alone in reacting against Hadley's type of complacent eastern elitism.[93] A similar outlook was expressed by Adams, who had certainly been successful professionally (after certain initial difficulties) and had become somewhat more conservative with age. In 1889 Adams had been attacked in the *Detroit Tribune* for having propagated free-trade doctrine under the auspices of a university financed by a state most of whose voters favored protection. The threat to the university's appropriations by the state legislature led the *Springfield Republican* (of Massachusetts) to mock that "this science of political economy . . . is subject to change at the polls on election day by the will of the people, and college professors must take notice." Meanwhile, Adams's friend Seligman declared: "Things are coming to a pretty pass in this country when the arbiter of scientific opinion is to be the *hoi polloi*." Nevertheless, Adams's faith in democracy was unshaken. Ten years later he informed a correspondent, in commenting on the respective merits of state and private institutions: "I believe that the people even have a right to make fools of themselves rather than that they should be controlled by a privileged class of any sort. . . . Education supported by the gifts of the wealthy must inevitably respect and support the interests of the wealthy classes."[94] After the sorry affairs at Brown and Stanford it was clear, if it had not been earlier, that public institutions were not the only offenders. And it is clear that by the turn of the century the adverse publicity resulting from academic freedom cases was beginning to serve as a check on the university authorities, as well as on the academics themselves.[95]

At the beginning of this chapter, it was noted that the professionalization of economics in the United States occurred at a time of extraordinarily rapid economic and social changes, which generated a vastly increased demand for new kinds of knowledge, skills, and training. Generally speaking, as we have seen, the economists were able to take advantage of this expansion. Yet the difficulties they encountered, and the uncertainties and disagreements they expressed with respect to their individual and collective social roles and objectives were not due simply to the transitional pressures of the times: They also reflected deep-rooted cultural tensions, which various historians have regarded as distinctively American. For example, according to Daniel Boorstin, as far back as colonial times American society had "proved uncongenial to any special class of 'knowers,'" and the leading intellectual historian of his day, Merle Curti, devoted a series of lectures to what he termed *The American Paradox: The Conflict of Thought and Action*.[96] The essence of this paradox, he argued, lay in the coexistence of two conflicting attitudes toward education and intellectual activity: on the one hand, a passion for education; on the other, a deep-rooted suspicion of intellectualism as a basis of social stratification. It was the passion for education that inspired the early settlers to build schools, endow colleges, and create state universities; and a similar motivation influenced the programs of labor unions, the enthusiastic audiences at public lectures, lyceums, and Chautauquas, the innumerable subscriptions to correspondence courses, and the large sales of encyclopedias and popular works of knowledge. Yet at the same time there was a persistent current of what Jacques Barzun has termed "primal" antiintellectualism,[97] which was a legacy of the European background, wherein the intellectual was invariably associated with the leisured aristocracy and with the claim of one individual or group to superiority over another. The stereotype of this "Jacksonian" prejudice was to be found on the frontier, the place where success supposedly went to those who could tame the wilderness or the virgin forest by means of brute strength and skills acquired in the rugged school of experience, in which book-learning played little or no part. Despite the intensity of the passion for education, it seems clear that for most Americans knowledge or learning was viewed pragmatically, as a means to material gain and to social and occupational advancement rather than a source of intellectual or cultural fulfillment. Specialization and the concomitant claims of experts to superior knowledge and influence posed peculiarly acute problems in a society ostensibly dedicated to democratic and egalitarian values. As John Higham has perceptively noted:

of the leading countries in the Western world, the United States in 1830 was perhaps the least specialized and surely the most committed to the omnicompetence of the ordinary citizen. By 1920, however, America had embraced the specialist and sanctified the expert with an enthusiasm unmatched elsewhere. For European critics and imitators alike, the American assembly line with its minute subdivision of labor and the American university with its cafeteria style of education were becoming emblems of the future.

The conflict between a deep-rooted distrust of privileged intellectual elites—for example, as assembled in a hierarchical body such as an academy of the European type—and the irresistible advance of specialized knowledge "was resolved by widening immensely the opportunity to specialize and restricting the opportunity to dominate," a process facilitated by the sheer size of the country, which inhibited any tendency toward centralization in the nation's capital, such as frequently occurred in Europe. A "democracy of specialists" was created through learned societies with broad, usually open, membership and representative officers; yet whether this egalitarianism could be sustained in practice is debatable.[98] By the turn of the century, as Furner has emphasized, in the case of economics there was already substantial evidence of the progress of cultural consolidation:

the profession was national, hierarchially organized and dominated by senior, mostly eastern economists in major universities. Standardized professionalization procedures gave the leading professors a large measure of control over the mobility and advancement of junior scholars. A maturing network of communications through organizations and journals that were accepted both within the profession and outside it as authentic forums for professional economists gave even more authority to the top academics in important schools who selected editors and officers. Managed by a powerful professional elite, the academic freedom cases had isolated unacceptable practices and underscored areas of consensus on doctrine, method, mission, and protocol which economists had reached in the 1890s.

Readers familiar with the subsequent history of American economics may well protest that this portrayal is overschematic, that it homogenizes a still diverse and fluid situation. Dissent has, after all, been an enduring feature of American economics; the early years of this century saw the beginnings of institutionalism, which has usually been regarded as a distinctively American phenomenon; and this was the period of a flourishing "revolt against formalism" in the social sciences. Nevertheless, even though Furner's comment may exaggerate the extent, it accurately conveys a sense of the direction of the institutionalization of American economics during the course of the nineteenth century.[99]

Notes

CHAPTER 1 POLITICAL ECONOMY AND THE ACADEMIC SETTING

1. The first generation of American colleges (i.e., those founded in the colonial period) included nine institutions: Harvard (1636), William and Mary (1693), Yale (1701), Princeton (1746), Columbia (1754), Pennsylvania (1755), Brown (1765), Rutgers (1766), and Dartmouth (1769). They are identified by their permanent names. The dates given are the years in which a charter granted or clearly implied the authority to award degrees.

2. For a detailed account of patterns of governance in the early American colleges, see Jurgen Herbst, *From Crisis to Crisis: American College Government, 1636–1819* (Cambridge, Mass.: Harvard University Press, 1982).

3. Michael J. L. O'Connor, *The Origins of Academic Economics in the United States* (New York: Columbia University Press, 1944), pp. 20–21.

4. Thomas Cooper, *Lectures on the Elements of Political Economy*, 2nd ed. (1829), p. 263.

5. Ibid., pp. 106, 107.

6. O'Connor, *Origins of Academic Economics*, p. 32.

7. Colin B. Burke, *American Collegiate Populations: A Test of the Traditional View* (New York: New York University Press, 1982), p. 54.

8. *The American Almanac and Repository of Useful Knowledge for the Year 1855* (Boston: Phillips, Sampson, 1855), pp. 196–99.

9. Burke, *American Collegiate Populations*, pp. 213–16.

10. It should be noted that some of the initial land-grant appropriations—especially on the eastern seaboard—were allocated to established private institutions with the understanding that they would diversify their offerings appropriately. In New England, for example, Connecticut first allocated land-grant moneys to Yale, Rhode Island to Brown, and New Hampshire to Dartmouth.

11. Charles F. Dunbar, "Economic Science in America, 1776–1876," *North American Review*, January 1876, pp. 124–54.

12. Thomas Edward Cliffe Leslie, "Political Economy in the United States," *Fortnightly Review* 28 (October 1880); reprinted in *Essays in Political Economy*, 2nd ed. (Dublin and London, 1888), pp. 126–54.

13. For an excellent survey of the developments in the later nineteenth century, see Laurence R. Veysey, *The Emergence of the American University* (Chicago: University of Chicago Press, 1965).

CHAPTER 2   WILLIAM AND MARY AND UNIVERSITY OF VIRGINIA

1. For general background, see Michael J. L. O'Connor, *The Origins of Academic Economics in the United States* (New York: Columbia University Press, 1944), esp. pp. 6–63; Joseph Dorfman, *The Economic Mind in American Civilization, 1606–1865* 2 vols. (New York: Viking Press, 1946), esp. pp. 527–66, 881–934; Elbert V. Wills, "Political Economy in the Early American College Curriculum," *South Atlantic Quarterly* 24 (April 1925): 131–53; Edwin R. A. Seligman, "The Early Teaching of Economics in the United States," in Jacob H. Hollander, ed., *Economic Essays Contributed in Honor of John Bates Clark* (New York: Macmillan, 1927).

2. Although long projected, a definitive history of the college is still awaited. See, however, John E. Morpurgo, *Their Majesties' Royall Colledge: William and Mary in the Seventeenth and Eighteenth Centuries* (Williamsburg: College of William and Mary, 1976); Wilford Kale, *Hark upon the Gale: An Illustrated History of the College of William and Mary* (Norfolk, Va.: Donning, 1985); Parke Rouse, Jr., *A House for a President: 250 Years on the Campus of William and Mary* (Richmond: Dietz Press, 1983); John M. Jennings, *The Library of the College of William and Mary in Virginia, 1693–1793* (Charlottesville: University of Virginia Press, 1968). Older works still retaining interest are Herbert B. Adams, *The College of William and Mary: A Contribution to the History of Higher Education with Suggestions for Its National Promotion*, U.S. Bureau of Education Circular of Information, no. 1 (Washington, D.C.: Government Printing Office, 1887); *The History of the College of William and Mary (Including the General Catalogue) from Its Foundation, 1660, to 1874* (Richmond: Randolph and English, 1874). Much miscellaneous information about the college's history is to be found in the *William and Mary College Quarterly Historical Magazine* (now *William and Mary Quarterly*), ser. 1, 1892–1919; ser. 2, 1921–43; ser. 3, 1944–present.

3. Kale, *Hark upon the Gale*, p. 17.

4. Records of matriculation list seventy-nine students before 1752 and an average of sixteen for the years 1752–76, with a peak of thirty-five in 1771 (see the 1874 *History*). These records are inexact.

5. For impressive lists of famous pre-1861 William and Mary products, see Lyon G. Tyler, *The Making of the Union: The Contribution of the College of William and Mary in Virginia* (Richmond: Whitter and Shepperson, 1899). See also the complete listing of matriculants in the 1874 *History*.

6. Hugh Jones, *The Present State of Virginia, etc.* (London: Clarke, 1724). See Dorfman, *Economic Mind*, pp. 122, 135.

7. Andrew A. Lipscomb and Albert E. Bergh eds., *The Writings of Thomas Jefferson,* 20 vols. (Washington, D.C.: Thomas Jefferson Memorial Association, 1903), 1:74. Other significant changes were the abandonment of compulsory Latin and Greek and the introduction of an elective system of study.

For details of the 1779 reforms, see Morpurgo, *Royall Colledge,* pp. 184–87; Robert P. Thompson, "The Reform of the College of William and Mary, 1763–80," *American Philosophical Society Proceedings* 115 (1971): 187–213; Roy J. Honeywell, *The Educational Work of Thomas Jefferson* (Cambridge, Mass.: Harvard University Press, 1931), pp. 54–56.

8. At some time, Emmerich de Vattell's *Law of Nations* (1st American ed., New York: Berry and Rogers, 1787) was introduced as a law text; it was already established at William and Mary in 1803. It covered aspects of commerce, money, foreign exchange, and foreign trade. See O'Connor, *Origins of Academic Economics,* p. 21.

9. See the entries on Madison in the *Dictionary of American Biography* and other biographic reference works such as the *National Cyclopedia of Biography* (New York: White, 1893), 3:234, 7:216.

10. Lyon G. Tyler, president of the college from 1888 to 1919, argued in a series of publications that political economy teaching might have begun as early as 1784. (This date is included in "priorities" listed on a plaque attached to the college's Wren Building; see Kale, *Hark upon the Gale,* p. 109.) Tyler's arguments were subjected to trenchant criticism by Seligman, "Early Teaching," pp. 204–32, where Tyler's writings are listed. See also O'Connor, *Origins of Academic Economics,* pp. 20–21; Thomas D. Willett and Tipton R. Snavely, "William and Mary: The Cradle of Academic Economics in America?" *Southern Economic Journal* 34 (April 1968): 572.

11. "The Statutes of the University of William and Mary, 1792," *William and Mary College Quarterly Historical Magazine,* ser. 1, 20 (July 1911): 52–59. As Morpurgo, *Royall Colledge,* p. 220, suggests, these statutes involved a degree of wishful thinking. Students for the B.A. had to be acquainted with "Logic, the Belles Letters [*sic*], Rhetoric, Natural Law, Laws of Nations and the general principles of Politics." In 1795 St. George Tucker observed similarly that "In moral philosophy the students are examined on the ablest writers in logic, the belles lettres, ethics, natural law, the law of nations, and politics." See Lyon G. Tyler, "Education in Colonial Virginia. IV. The Higher Education," *William and Mary College Quarterly Historical Magazine,* ser. 1, 6 (January 1898): 171–187, at p. 183.

12. Samuel Miller, *A Brief Retrospect of the Eighteenth Century* (New York: Swords, 1803), 2:503–4.

13. See "Letters from William and Mary College, 1798–1801," *Virginia Magazine of History and Biography* 29 (April 1921): 129–79, at pp. 159–60. The letters are from Joseph Shelton Watson to his brother Robert and are dated January 17 and April 1, 1801, respectively. See also "Letters to David Watson," *Virginia Magazine of History and Biography* 29 (July 1921): 257–86; Seligman, "Early Teaching," pp. 300–301.

14. Tyler, "Education in Colonial Virginia," p. 181; "Letters from William and Mary College," p. 159n.; Seligman, "Early Teaching," p. 297.

15. Madison's scientific interests are amply documented in his letters to Thomas Jefferson, printed in *William and Mary College Quarterly Histori-*

cal Magazine, ser. 2, 5 (April, July 1925): 77–95, 145–58. William Barton Rogers, founder of MIT and himself educated at William and Mary in the early 1820s (he succeeded his father as professor of natural philosophy in the college in 1828), recalled that Madison had delivered there "the first regular courses of lectures on physical science and political economy ever given in the United States." *The Life and Letters of William Barton Rogers, edited by his Wife* (Boston: Houghton Mifflin, 1896), 1 : 401. Student notes on Madison's natural philosophy lectures are preserved in the William and Mary Archives.

16. Madison, "Manifestations of the Beneficence of Divine Providence towards America" (Richmond: Thomas Nicholson, 1795).

17. Meade, *The Evergreen* (1846), quoted in Tyler, "Education in Colonial Virginia," p. 182. Meade's report was based on hearsay as he had not studied under Madison.

18. See Lyon G. Tyler, "Glimpses of Old College Life, Part Two," *William and Mary Quarterly Historical Magazine*, ser. 1, 8 (April 1900): 213–27, at p. 213. Unfortunately, the notes by Andrew Reid, Jr., have not been traced.

19. See O'Connor, *Origins of Academic Economics*, p. 20; Seligman, "Early Teaching," p. 301; Wills, "Political Economy," pp. 133–35; Willett and Snavely, "William and Mary." Seligman (pp. 293–94) records earlier coverage of practical economic material at Columbia.

20. Matriculations averaged sixteen for 1777–1812, with a peak of fifty in 1798 (from lists in 1874 *History*). Kale, *Hark upon the Gale*, p. 69, reports forty-four students in attendance in 1812, matriculations in 1811 having been thirty-eight.

21. See Morpurgo, *Royall Colledge*, pp. 209–22.

22. By the early 1820s almost half of Princeton's matriculants were from Virginia. See Phillip A. Bruce, *History of the University of Virginia, 1819–1919*, 5 vols. (New York: Macmillan, 1920); 1 : 84.

23. See Dumas Malone, *Jefferson and His Time*, 6 vols. (Boston: Little, Brown, 1948–77), 6 : 233–40; Honeywell, *Educational Work;* James B. Conant, *Thomas Jefferson and the Development of Public Education* (Berkeley: University of California Press, 1962); Bruce, *History*, 1 : 45–55.

24. Honeywell, *Educational Work*, p. 209; for the full text of the 1779 bills, see pp. 199–210.

25. Jefferson to Priestley, January 18, 1800, in Lipscomb and Bergh, *Writings*, 10 : 133–43, at p. 140. See also Honeywell, *Educational Work*, pp. 215–16.

26. "I had proposed that William and Mary, under an improved form, should be the University, and that was at that time pretty highly Episcopal, the dissenters after a while began to apprehend some secret design of preference for that sect"; Jefferson to Priestley, January 27, 1800, in Lipscomb and Bergh, *Writings*, 10 : 146–49, at p. 147. See also Jefferson's remarks in his autobiography on the subject; 1 : 71. Washington College subsequently became Washington and Lee University.

27. Ibid., 10 : 141. Priestley's response made no mention of commerce or

political economy. It is reproduced in Gilbert Chinard, *The Correspondence of Jefferson and Du Pont de Nemours with an Introduction on Jefferson and the Physiocrats* (Baltimore: Johns Hopkins University Press, 1931), pp. 15–18.

28. Lipscomb and Bergh, *Writings*, 10:142.

29. See Malone, *Jefferson and His Time*, 2:3–20; Chinard, *Correspondence;* Dumas Malone, ed., *Correspondence between Thomas Jefferson and Pierre Samuel Du Pont de Nemours* (Boston: Houghton Mifflin, 1930); Gilbert Chinard, *Jefferson et les idéologues d'après sa correspondence inédité avec Destutt de Tracy, Cabanis, J-B Say, et Auguste Comte* (Baltimore: Johns Hopkins University Press, 1925); see p. 275 for reference to Dugald Stewart.

30. The faculty comprised eight or so distinguished scholars and scientists, some known personally to Jefferson. There was even a hint that the mathematician Lagrange might join them. See Bruce, *History,* 1:61–63; Neil M. Shawen, "Thomas Jefferson and a 'National' University: The Hidden Agenda for Virginia," *Virginia Magazine of History and Biography,* 99 (July 1984): 309–35. In 1789 Jefferson had been drawn, rather unwillingly, into a grandiose scheme for a French-American Academy of Arts and Sciences, centered in Richmond. The promoter was a grandson of Quesnay, the famous physiocrat. See Bruce, *History,* 1:55–60; Shawen, "Thomas Jefferson."

31. This characteristically Gallic scheme does not seem to have appealed to Jefferson, who showed little interest in proposals for a national university. See Malone, *Correspondence,* pp. 8–26, for the relevant letters. A translation of the second French edition (1812) of Du Pont's essay is in Bessie G. Du Pont, ed., *National Education in the United States of America* (Newark: University of Delaware Press, 1923). Also see Shawen, "Thomas Jefferson," and Bruce, *History,* 1:63–65.

32. Jefferson to Du Pont, April 12, 1800, in Malone, *Correspondence,* pp. 8–9.

33. Jefferson to Pictet, February 5, 1803, in Lipscombe and Bergh, *Writings* 10:355–57, at p. 355.

34. Malone, *Jefferson and His Time,* 6:234. A long letter from the *Richmond Enquirer,* February 1, 1805, describing a scheme for a university in the central part of the state, is reproduced in the *William and Mary College Quarterly Historical Magazine,* ser. 2, 4 (October 1924): 266–67. There is also a significant unpublished letter of January 5, 1805, from Jefferson to Littleton W. Tazewell in the University of Virginia's Jefferson Papers, Alderman Library.

35. Jefferson to Joseph C. Cabell, June 27, 1810, in Nathaniel Francis Cabell, ed., *Early History of the University of Virginia as Contained in the Letters of Thomas Jefferson and Joseph C. Cabell* (Richmond: Randolph, 1856), pp. 1–2.

36. Jefferson to Cooper, January 16, 1814, in Lipscombe and Bergh, *Writings,* 14:59–60. For details of other inquiries Jefferson made around this time, see Honeywell, *Educational Work,* p. 171.

37. Jefferson to Carr, September 7, 1814, in Honeywell, *Educational Work,* pp. 222–27; quotations are from p. 222. Honeywell argues (pp. 163–65) that the proposals of the Carr letter were influenced by the views of Destutt de Tracy.

38. Ibid., p. 224.

39. Dumas Malone, *The Public Life of Thomas Cooper, 1783–1839* (New Haven: Yale University Press, 1926), p. 227.

40. For comments by Jefferson on these writers, see Lipscombe and Bergh, *Writings,* 8:31; 10:447–48; 11:1–7, 222–26, 274–76; 13:404–33; 14:82, 223–24, 459–61; 19:196, 249.

41. See, e.g., Joseph Dorfman, "The Economic Philosophy of Thomas Jefferson," *Political Science Quarterly* 55 (March 1940): 98–121; William D. Grampp, "A re-examination of Jeffersonian Economics," *Southern Economic Journal* 12 (January 1946): 263–82; Malone, *Jefferson and His Time,* 6:137–50. For examples of Jefferson stressing the practical importance of political economy, see Honeywell, *Educational Work,* p. 250; Lipscombe and Bergh, *Writings,* 14:224, 256; 19:263–64.

42. Jefferson to Duane, January 22, 1813, in Chinard, *Jefferson et les idéologues,* pp. 105–6. Duane declined to undertake publication. For a detailed account, with relevant correspondence, see pp. 97–188.

43. Ibid., pp. 31–96. Jefferson's recommendation of this book to William and Mary is mentioned in the fourth section of this chapter.

44. Lipscombe and Bergh, *Writings,* 19:367. The complete minutes of the Visitors of Central College and the University of Virginia until the time of Jefferson's death are reproduced in this volume, pp. 361–499.

45. For details of the long campaign that led to the opening of the University of Virginia in 1825, see Bruce, *History,* vols. 1 and 2; Malone, *Jefferson and His Time,* 6:251–82, 365–425; and, most graphically, Cabell, *Early History.* The struggle was complicated by regional and sectarian antagonisms, as well as by a mistrust of Jefferson in some quarters.

46. See Malone, *Public Life,* pp. 227–47. For details of extensive unpublished Cooper correspondence held at the University of Virginia, see the annotated list in *The Jefferson Papers of the University of Virginia* (Charlottesville: University of Virginia Press, 1973). Cooper also had some negotiations with William and Mary in 1817–18 about a professorship of chemistry.

47. Cabell, *Early History,* p. 36. See Lipscombe and Bergh, *Writings,* 11:1–3; 14:223–24, 258–67; 19:248–50. At this time Say was in some disfavor with Napoleon and had recently sold his textile business. His prior experience had been of public life and business; only later did he become an academic. See the entry on Say in David L. Sills, ed., *The International Encyclopedia of the Social Sciences* (New York: Macmillan, 1968).

48. The complete text of the report is to be found in Honeywell, *Educational Work,* or Cabell, *Early History.* The quotations are from Honeywell, pp. 252–53. The report defined "Ideology" as "the doctrine of thought" (p. 253).

49. Cabell, *Early History,* p. 448.

50. See Lipscombe and Bergh, *Writings,* 19 : 433–44, meetings of April 7, October 4, 1824. The quotations that follow come from pp. 434–35; the restriction to U.S. citizens is on p. 436.

51. Subsequently, degrees of M.A. and then B.A. were added, requiring graduation in specified groups of schools. Otherwise, the structure remained largely unchanged until well after the Civil War. The number and coverage of the schools were designed to be flexible, and some changes occurred over time.

52. Letter of February 3, 1825, in Cabell, *Early History,* p. 339; see also pp. 303–4, 353, and Honeywell, *Educational Work,* pp. 121–23. Jefferson to Destutt de Tracy, December 26, 1820, in Chinard, *Jefferson et les idéologues,* p. 203. Destutt de Tracy's *Commentary* would not have been appropriate for the list of books on U.S. government.

53. *Catalogue of the Library of the University of Virginia Arranged Alphabetically* (Charlottesville: Gilmer Davies, 1828).

54. Chinard, *Jefferson et les idéologues,* p. 216n.

55. Lipscombe and Bergh, *Writings,* 19 : 461.

56. For information on Tucker, see Robert Colin McLean, *George Tucker: Moral Philosopher and Man of Letters* (Chapel Hill: University of North Carolina Press, 1961); Tipton R. Snavely, *George Tucker as Political Economist* (Charlottesville: University of Virginia Press, 1964); "The Autobiography of George Tucker, 1775–1861," *Bermuda Historical Quarterly* 18 (autumn and winter 1961): 82–159. Tucker's early essays were collected in his *Essays on Various Subjects of Taste, Morals, and National Policy* (Georgetown: Milligan, 1822), published under the pseudonym "A Citizen of Virginia."

57. See Bruce, *History,* vol. 2, for an account of the university's turbulent first twenty years.

58. Tucker, "Autobiography," p. 139.

59. George Tucker, *The Laws of Wages, Profits, and Rent, Investigated* (Philadelphia: Carey and Hart, 1837), p. iii. Tucker's later *Political Economy for the People* (Philadelphia: Sherman, 1858) was "a compendium of the lectures on Political Economy delivered by the author in the University of Virginia, with such alterations as his further experience and reflection have suggested" (p. iii). Tucker was aged eighty-four when this book appeared.

60. George Tucker, *The Theory of Money and Banks Investigated* (Boston: Little, Brown, 1839). The book does not appear to have been drawn from Tucker's lectures. Tucker was a frequent contributor to contemporary debates on banking questions.

61. For further consideration of Tucker's teaching of political economy, see Snavely, *George Tucker,* pp. 23–33, and Tipton R. Snavely, *The Department of Economics at the University of Virginia, 1825–1956* (Charlottesville: University of Virginia Press, 1967), pp. 12–27; see p. 14 (or pp. 25–26 of the earlier book) for a sample of Tucker's examination questions on the subject.

62. Notes on Political Economy 1840–41, by Robert Lewis Dabney (1820–

98), Dabney Family Papers (38/219), Alderman Library, University of Virginia. These notes, which cover sixty-four closely written pages, are referred to extensively in Snavely, *George Tucker*. Interestingly, Dabney was far from being an unqualified admirer of Tucker's teaching in general; see McLean, *George Tucker*, p. 34.

63. Among Tucker's books, these lectures are closest to his later *Political Economy for the People*.

64. See Bruce, *History*, 2:128–34.

65. On these matters, see Snavely, *George Tucker;* also John R. Turner, *The Ricardian Rent Theory in Early American Economics* (New York: New York University Press, 1921), pp. 83–109. The treatment of Tucker in Dorfman, *Economic Mind*, pp. 539–51, 881–89, is somewhat carping. Mention ought also to be made of Tucker's important and pioneering statistical work in his *Progress of the United States etc.* (New York: Hunt's Merchants Magazine, 1843).

66. Minutes of the Faculty, Manuscripts Division, Alderman Library, University of Virginia. For comparison, over the academic years 1831–32 to 1844–45 registrations in all moral philosophy courses were 57, 42, 70, 50, 67, 48, 80, 64, 78, 45, 46, 22, 24, and 55, respectively, whereas overall numbers of students attending the university were 140, 158, 205, 211, 250, 269, 230, 247, 243, 171, 170, 128, 158, and 194, respectively (see *Catalog*, 1866–67, p. 19). About two-thirds of the students were typically from Virginia, and many left after one year.

67. Kale, *Hark upon the Gale*, p. 69. It is unlikely that political economy was taught during this interval when Bracken served as professor of moral philosophy.

68. For details, see the entry on Smith in the *Dictionary of American Biography*.

69. This statement is reproduced in *William and Mary College Quarterly Historical Magazine*, ser. 1, 25 (April 1917): 238–41.

70. *The Officers, Statutes, and Charter of the College of William and Mary* (Philadelphia, 1817).

71. Notes taken by Gerald B. Stuart on the Moral and Political Philosophy Lectures of John Augustine Smith (1981.49); Notes on the Wealth of Nations, etc., 1821 (1981.52), College Archives, Swem Library, William and Mary. The Stuart notes cover twenty-two or more lectures and work through to book 4, chap. 6, of Smith.

72. John Augustine Smith, *Syllabus of the Lectures . . .* (Philadelphia: Hobson, 1817), having appended "A Discourse by the same Author on the Manner in which Peculiarities in the Anatomical Structure affect the Moral Character."

73. Ibid., preface. For the indirect communication with Jefferson, see Cabell, *Early History*, pp. 47, 53, 69. The last page referenced suggests that Smith was contemplating in 1816 switching from Adam Smith to Say or Destutt de Tracy as political economy text, but no change was made.

74. Ibid., pp. 19–20, 74–77.

75. Titles were flexible. Law was altered from Oeconomy in the Faculty Minutes (College Archives). At various points Dew listed his professorship as "Political Economy, Metaphysics, etc.," "History, Metaphysics and Political Law" (see the title pages of his 1829 and 1834 publications, cited below, in nn. 78 and 83).

76. *Laws and Regulations of the College of William and Mary* (Richmond, 1830).

77. The first-year courses were the Junior Moral, the Junior Mathematical, the Chemical, and the Junior Political (covering "Civil history, ancient and modern, the Law of Nature and Nations, and Government"). The second-year courses were the Senior Moral, the Senior Mathematical, the Senior Political, and the Natural Philosophical.

78. The 1829 *Lectures* was published by Shepherd, Richmond. The *Review* was published by White, Richmond, in 1832, and in amplified form in Thomas R. Dew, *An Essay on Slavery* (Richmond: Randolph, 1849). The *Digest* was first published in 1853 by Appleton, New York.

79. Dew, *Lectures*, preface. *Lectures* was dedicated to John Augustine Smith under whose tutelage Dew must first have studied Adam Smith.

80. See esp. Lecture 2, in *Lectures*, pp. 20–37.

81. See ibid., pp. 104–5.

82. *Catalogue for 1840–1*, p. 9.

83. Dew, *Essays on the Interest of Money . . .* (Shellbanks, Va.: Farmer's Register, 1834), pp. 2, 3.

84. "Substance of a course of Lectures on Political Economy Delivered by T. R. Dew, President of William and Mary College, to the Senior Political Class 1841–2 Ses." [Whitaker Harris], 204 pages (pp. 186–204 covering lectures on government), College Archives, Swem Library, 1981.36; see also 1981.37, 1984.8, for other, less satisfactory, sets of notes.

85. Dew's views on the latter topics had been set out in his *Great Question of the Day: Letter of President Thomas R. Dew of William and Mary College Virginia to a Representative in Congress from That State on the Subject of the Financial Policy of the Administration and the Laws of Credit and Trade. Originally published in the Madisonian* (Washington, D.C.: Thomas Allen, 1840). See also Dew's usury essay and articles he published in the *Farmer's Register* for June 1835 and June 1836. A summary is provided by Dorfman, *Economic Mind*, pp. 899–903.

86. The details in this paragraph are drawn from the *Catalogue for 1840–1*. Dew's educational philosophy is further revealed in his inaugural lecture as president: *An Address Delivered before the Students of William and Mary, at the Opening of the College, on Monday October 10th, 1836* (Richmond: White, 1836). For further details on Dew's work at William and Mary, see Stephen Mansfield, "Thomas Roderick Dew at William and Mary: 'A Main Prop of that Venerable Institution,'" *Virginia Magazine of History and Biography* 75 (October 1967): 429–42.

87. On Dew as a social and economic thinker, see Dorfman, *Economic Mind,* pp. 895–909; Lowell Harrison, "Thomas Roderick Dew: Philosopher of the Old South," *Virginia Magazine of History and Biography* 57 (October 1949): 390–404; Stephen C. Mansfield, "Thomas R. Dew: Defender of the Southern Faith" (Ph.D. diss., University of Virginia, 1968).

88. See the matriculation records in the 1874 *History* and the more accurate post-1826 lists in "Register of Students of William and Mary College, 1827–81: Parts 1–6," *William and Mary Quarterly Historical Magazine,* ser. 2, 3–5 (October 1923–April 1925). In this later period, at least, a student matriculated every year he attended.

89. See Beverley D. Tucker, *Nathaniel Beverley Tucker: Prophet of the Confederacy, 1784–1851* (Tokyo: Nan'un Do, 1979), p. 427.

90. On this episode, see ibid., pp. 425–36; Rouse, *House for a President,* pp. 113–18.

91. See *Catalogue for 1855.*

92. On Tyler, see John E. Hobeika, *The Sage of the Lion's Den* (New York: Exposition Press, 1948).

93. See *Catalogue for 1890–1.*

94. These developments are detailed in Snavely, *Department of Economics,* pp. 39–134, where the economic courses and views of each of the actors are described. See also Dorfman, *Economic Mind,* pp. 889–90, 920–28 and entries in the *Dictionary of American Biography.*

95. The *Catalogs* show enrollments for the thirteen academic years 1857–58 to 1869–70 as, respectively, 633, 625, 606, 604, 66, 46, 50, 55, 255, 490, 475, 452, 464. Enrollments then hovered around 360 through the 1870s. The rapid postwar recovery reflected the large number of youthful ex-soldiers, the dislocation of other southern colleges, and perhaps a turning away from traditional northern choices. Non-Virginians, who had comprised about 45 percent of the student body in the immediate prewar years, made up about 60 percent in the years 1867–68 to 1869–70. But there was no marked change in their geographical distribution.

96. For details, see Bruce, *History,* vols. 3 and 4; Paul B. Barringer, ed., *The University of Virginia* (New York: Lewis, 1904), 1 : 165–218.

97. By 1892–93 the teaching of economics was established in other Virginia institutions: Randolph-Macon College and Washington and Lee University at least. (See the appendix to J. Laurence Laughlin, "The Study of Political Economy in the United States," *Journal of Political Economy* 1 (December 1892): 143–51.) For brief histories of these other institutions, see Herbert B. Adams, *Thomas Jefferson and the University of Virginia,* U.S. Bureau of Education Circular of Information, no. 1, pt. 2 (Washington, D.C.: Government Printing Office, 1888), pp. 227–305.

98. Dew, *An Address,* pp. 17, 21.

CHAPTER 3   SOUTH CAROLINA COLLEGE

1. Cooper to Jefferson, February 16, 1804, Thomas Cooper Papers, South Caroliniana Library, University of South Carolina. Dumas Malone, *The Public Life of Thomas Cooper, 1783–1839* (New Haven: Yale University Press, 1926), pp. 164–70.

2. Cooper to Jefferson, September 22, 1814, Cooper Papers.

3. Edwin L. Green, *A History of the University of South Carolina* (Columbia, S.C.: State Company, 1916), pp. 11–15. Minutes of the Board of Trustees of the South Carolina College, November 30, 1815. Also cited in Daniel Walker Hollis, *University of South Carolina*, 2 vols. (Columbia: University of South Carolina Press, 1951), 1:48.

4. Peter A. Coclanis and Lacy Ford, "The South Carolina Economy Reconstructed and Reconsidered: Structure, Output, and Performance, 1670–1985," manuscript, 1985; William W. Freehling, *Prelude to Civil War: The Nullification Controversy in South Carolina, 1816–1836* (New York: Harper and Row, 1965), pp. 1–24, 89–91.

5. Clement Eaton, *The Freedom-of-Thought Struggle in the Old South* (New York: Harper and Row, 1964), pp. 3–31; W. F. Cash, *The Mind of the South* (New York: Knopf, 1946), pp. 3–28, 53–58.

6. Hollis, *University of South Carolina*, 1:3–21; Eaton, *Freedom-of-Thought Struggle*, p. 216.

7. Malone, *Public Life*, pp. 227–47.

8. Frank Freidel, *Francis Lieber: Nineteenth-Century Liberal* (Baton Rouge: Louisiana State University Press, 1947), pp. 116–17; also see Hollis, *University of South Carolina*, 1:99.

9. Maximilian La Borde, *History of the South Carolina College* (Charleston, S.C.: Walker, Evans, and Cogswell, 1874), pp. 96–104; Green, *History of the University*, pp. 31–33. Cooper to Jefferson, June 18, 1823, Cooper Papers.

10. Hollis, *University of South Carolina*, 1:51–76.

11. La Borde, *History of the College*, pp. 364–69.

12. Cooper to Jefferson, June 18, 1823, Cooper Papers. Hollis, *University of South Carolina*, 1:98–101. Malone, *Public Life*, pp. 259–76.

13. Gladys Bryson, "The Emergence of the Social Sciences from Moral Philosophy," *International Journal of Ethics* 42 (1932): 304–23; and "The Comparable Interests of the Old Moral Philosophy and the Modern Social Sciences," *Social Forces* 11 (1932): 19–27.

14. La Borde, *History of the College*, pp. 55–58, 95–96, 364–65, 436; William Paley, *The Principles of Moral and Political Philosophy*, 15th ed., 2 vols. (London, 1804); Michael J. L. O'Connor, *The Origins of Academic Economics in the United States* (New York: Columbia University Press, 1944), pp. 80–81; Joseph Dorfman, *The Economic Mind in American Civilization*, 5 vols. (New York: Viking Press, 1946, 1949, 1959), 2:512.

15. A tantalizing, yet unfortunately inconclusive, piece of evidence regarding

instruction in moral philosophy at South Carolina College is found in the current university's library copy of the 1804 Paley text. Hand-written margin notes and underlining seem to indicate that this particular copy was used by students and/or professors of the college in the nineteenth century. Specifically, there are apparent signatures from both 1817 and 1857 in the text, as well as the following comment on the heading page of the aforementioned political economy chapter: "Finance and Economy Omitted." On the other hand, notes and underlining, in what appears to be different handwriting, are scattered throughout this same chapter. Pending a more scientific analysis of this copy of Paley, the actual instruction of political economy before Cooper remains quite uncertain, although the signature of 1817 does argue that perhaps the book was used by one of Henry's predecessors before 1818. The University of South Carolina Library also yielded another possible indication that its early students were left with an interest in political economy issues. One of its copies of Adam Smith's *Wealth of Nations* (1814 edition) is signed "Edward Gordon Palmer—1822." Mr. Palmer is listed as a graduate of the class of 1819 (La Borde, *History of the College*, p. 441) and so would have been a senior student of Professor Henry in his moral philosophy course. However, he would have left before Thomas Cooper arrived and began his explicit instruction in political economy.

16. Hollis, *University of South Carolina*, 1:78–82.

17. Minutes of the Board of Trustees, April 28, 1823; also cited in Hollis, *University of South Carolina*, 1:81, and Malone, *Public Life*, p. 303.

18. Cooper to Jefferson, June 18, 1823, Cooper Papers. Minutes of the Board of Trustees, November 27, 1823; December 3, 1823. Cooper was not able to get the metaphysics course abolished, although he managed to get a committee appointed to study the possibility. See La Borde, *History of the College*, p. 167.

19. Thomas Cooper, *Lectures on the Elements of Political Economy*, 1st ed. (Columbia, S.C., 1826), p. iii.

20. Ibid., p. v.

21. *Charleston Southern Patriot*, November 18, 1826; *Southern Review* 1 (February 1828): 192–218; *American Quarterly Review* 1 (June 1827): 309–31; *North American Review* 25 (October 1827): 408–25; *Encyclopaedia Americana* (1828), pp. 223–24.

22. *American Quarterly Review*, 1827, p. 309; *North American Review*, 1827, pp. 413–15; O'Connor, *Academic Economics*, p. 56; J. R. McCulloch, *The Literature of Political Economy* (London, 1845), p. 19.

23. Thomas Cooper, *Public Political Essays* (Northumberland, Penn., 1799), pp. 39–43; Malone, *Public Life*, p. 303; *On the Proposed Alteration of the Tariff* (Charleston, S.C., 1823). *A Manual of Political Economy* (Washington, D.C.: 1834); O'Connor, *Origins of Academic Economics*, pp. 218–20.

24. Our analysis of Cooper's economic thought is indebted to William C. Whitten, "The Economic Ideas of Thomas Cooper," in *South Carolina Economists: Essays on the Evolution of Antebellum Economic Thought,*

ed. B. F. Kiker and R. J. Carlsson (Columbia, S.C.: Bureau of Business and Economic Research, College of Business Administration, University of South Carolina, 1969), pp. 44–82.

25. Malone, *Public Life*, p. 98; Cooper, *Lectures*, pp. iii–v.

26. Cooper, *Lectures*, p. 19. Review of Cooper in *Southern Review*, 1828, p. 196.

27. Cooper, *Lectures*, pp. 14–20.

28. Malone, *Public Life*, pp. 290–94; O'Connor, *Origins of Academic Economics*, pp. 33–34; Dorfman, *Economic Mind*, 2:536, 576–77, 895–99.

29. Cooper to Jefferson, December 4, 1808, Cooper Papers.

30. Thomas Cooper, *Letters on the Slave Trade* (Manchester, 1787); Eaton, *Freedom-of-Thought Struggle*, pp. 18–31; Freehling, *Prelude to War*, pp. 49–86.

31. Malone, *Public Life*, pp. 376–85. After he left South Carolina College, Cooper wrote several letters to Biddle urging him to run for the presidency of the United States.

32. See, e.g., the evaluation of La Borde, *History of the College*, pp. 164–70. La Borde was a graduate of the class of 1821 under Cooper and later joined the faculty in 1842 after a successful career as a physician and state politician.

33. Cooper, *Lectures*, p. v; O'Connor, *Origins of Academic Economics*, p. 49. Hollis, *University of South Carolina*, 1:80–81, 84–93.

34. Cooper, *Lectures*, pp. v–vi. O'Connor, *Origins of Academic Economics*, pp. 123–24.

35. The most apt comparison was between Cooper's text and Wayland's, which translated the classical school in terms acceptable to the clerical colleges. The Wayland text was just as rigorous as Cooper's, but having been stripped of almost all references to the great economists of the day and their works, it was surely less likely to have stimulated its readers into a deeper exploration of the field.

36. *Charleston Southern Patriot*, November 18, 1826; La Borde, *History of the College*, pp. 170–72; J. Marion Sims, *The Story of My Life* (New York, 1884), p. 82. Sims, a graduate of the class of 1832, is also cited in Hollis, *University of South Carolina*, 1:79–80.

37. Malone, *Public Life*, p. 303; and W. E. Dodd, "Contributions of the South to Economic Thought and Writing to 1865," in *The South in the Building of the Nation*, 12 vols. (Richmond, Va., 1909), 5:567. Both cite the general opinion in South Carolina at the time that Cooper was the first American instructor of political economy. Besides the previously noted statement in Cooper's commencement address of 1824, he wrote a letter to the *Columbia Telescope*, January 1, 1830, that was reprinted in the Washington *Banner of the Constitution*, January 13, 1830, in which he declared: "Who, prior to myself, ever recommended or delivered lectures on political economy in the United States?" The *Banner of the Constitution*, February 24, 1830, published a letter from an alumnus of Columbia College in New York (possibly

McVickar, a graduate of the class of 1804), claiming McVickar's 1817 priority in political economy instruction.

38. Freehling, *Prelude to War*, pp. 25–48; Alfred G. Smith, *Economic Readjustment of an Old Cotton State: South Carolina, 1820–1860* (Columbia: University of South Carolina Press, 1958); Eaton, *Freedom-of-Thought Struggle*, pp. 144–61.

39. Freehling, *Prelude to War*, pp. 49–86.

40. Eaton, *Freedom-of-Thought Struggle*, pp. 300–34; Cash, *Mind of the South*, pp. 59–99; Hollis, *University of South Carolina*, 1:171–75.

41. Malone, *Public Life*, pp. 307–36; Hollis, *University of South Carolina*, 1:102–6.

42. Malone, *Public Life*, pp. 281–306.

43. Ibid., pp. 309–10.

44. Freehling, *Prelude to War*, pp. 128–297, 324–27.

45. Malone, *Public Life*, pp. 337–67; Hollis, *University of South Carolina*, 1:106–16; Sims, *Story of My Life*, p. 83.

46. Green, *History of the University*, p. 437.

47. Freidel, *Francis Lieber*, pp. 1–81.

48. Hollis, *University of South Carolina*, 1:115–22; La Borde, *History of the College*, p. 367. After Cooper's departure, his political friends arranged for him the task of editing a work on the legal statutes of the state, on which he worked until two months before his death in 1839 at the age of seventy-nine; see Malone, *Public Life* pp. 368–91.

49. Freidel, *Francis Lieber*, p. 118. Lieber had sought or been approached about positions at New York University, Girard College, Harvard University, and Transylvania College. In the last three instances, he had made heavy use of his acquaintances with, respectively, Nicholas Biddle, Associate Justice of the Supreme Court Joseph Story, and Henry Clay.

50. Ibid., pp. 117–22.

51. Ibid., pp. 124–26; Hollis, *University of South Carolina*, 1:122–25; Lieber to *Columbia Telescope*, July 16, 1835. While in South Carolina, Lieber attended services at the Episcopal church and purchased a slave housekeeper.

52. Semiannual reports of the Professor of History and Political Economy to the president of South Carolina College, dated May 10, 1837; November 24, 1840; May 1, 1843; November 22, 1847; April 29, 1848; in Francis Lieber Papers, 1833–1879, Manuscripts Division, South Caroliniana Library. The nature of any relationship between Cooper and Lieber is uncertain. The only apparent connections uncovered to date are Lieber's citation of Cooper's text in the *Encyclopaedia Americana*, Lieber's use of the Cooper text before switching to Say, and a letter from Cooper to H. C. Carey, November 4, 1835, cited in Freidel, *Francis Lieber*, p. 127, in which Cooper evidently wrote of meeting Lieber and forming a friendship with him. Freidel attributes the lack of public interaction to Lieber's caution in being connected to the disgraced Cooper. However, Lieber's continued use of Cooper's text would probably have been common knowledge. For example,

a letter to the *Charleston Mercury,* November 25, 1845, comments favorably on Lieber's use of Say's textbook.

53. Lieber's 1840 report states that during the fall term he had covered Say's book 3 but, for want of time, had to leave the subject of distribution of wealth untouched. O'Connor, *Origins of Academic Economics,* p. 123, cites a course outline of book 1 inserted in Lieber's personal copy of Say (see n. 58, below).

54. A useful summary of Lieber's views on political economy is contained in A. C. Flora, "The Economic Ideas of Francis Lieber," in *South Carolina Economists,* ed. Kiker and Carlsson, pp. 83–104. Francis Lieber, *Manual of Political Ethics* (Boston, 1839); *Essays on Property and Labour* (New York, 1841); *On Civil Liberty and Self-government* (Philadelphia, 1853); "Notes on Fallacies of American Protectionists," in *Miscellaneous Writings of Francis Lieber,* 2 vols. (Philadelphia, 1880), 2:390–459.

55. Lieber, *Essays on Property and Labour,* pp. 79–80.

56. Freidel, *Francis Lieber,* pp. 235–42, 400–2; Lieber, "Plantations for Slave Labor: The Death of the Yeomanry," Manuscripts Division, South Caroliniana Library.

57. Semiannual report, May 1, 1843.

58. O'Connor, *Origins of Academic Economics,* p. 123. The outline as cited by O'Connor is as follows: "1. Machinery; 2. Division of Labor; 3. Formation of capital; 4. Transformation of capital; 5. Lectures on capital and interest; 6. Unproductive capital; 7. Say—Chapter XIV; 8. Product for product; 9. Regulations prescribing the nature of production; 10. Exports and imports; 11. Protectionism in America; 12. Balance of trade; 13. Money."

59. Freidel, *Francis Lieber,* pp. 137–39; Hollis, *University of South Carolina,* 1:188–89. Giles J. Patterson, *Journal of a Southern Student, 1846–48* (Nashville, Tenn., 1944), made many entries in regard to Lieber and his course. In addition, see La Borde, *History of the College,* pp. 405–7; and Green, *History of the University,* p. 61.

60. Eaton, *Freedom-of-Thought Struggle,* pp. 216–66.

61. Hollis, *University of South Carolina,* 1:114, 160–76; La Borde, *History of the College,* p. 331; Cash, *Mind of the South,* p. 80. Avery Craven, *The Coming of the Civil War* (New York: Scribner, 1942), p. 14. An honor member of the class of 1831 and a favorite student of Cooper, Thornwell converted to Presbyterianism shortly after graduation and testified against Cooper—although with some reservations—at the trustees' hearing of 1832. It is nonetheless a mistake to caricature as totally intolerant a man who was in fact quite complex. It is generally acknowledged that it was Thornwell who most effectively championed the desirability of a state-supported nonsectarian South Carolina College among the institution's religious opponents.

62. Hollis, *University of South Carolina,* 1:142, 177–93; Freidel, *Francis Lieber,* pp. 130–34, 141–42, 198–200, 207–10, 281–82.

63. Freidel, *Francis Lieber,* pp. 213–22, 230–35, 249–58, 280–91.

64. The reaction of the northern press is typified by the *New York Daily Trib-une*, May 12, 1856.

65. During the war, Lieber became an influential moderate Republican. He was called upon to codify standard rules of war to govern Union armies in the field and, after the war, to prepare the government's legal case for the trial of Jefferson Davis. His final years before his death in 1872 were occupied with work and writings dealing with various questions of international law.

66. Hollis, *University of South Carolina,* 1:194–211; Green, *History of the University,* pp. 63–67.

67. This conclusion is based on evidence found in a copy of Say (1847 edition) located in the current university's library.

68. Hollis, *University of South Carolina,* 2:19–60. Catalogues of the University of South Carolina, 1866–1910.

69. Hollis, *University of South Carolina,* 2:61–79; Green, *History of the University,* pp. 409–15.

70. Hollis, *University of South Carolina,* 2:80–97.

71. Ibid., pp. 98–127; Green, *History of the University,* p. 126. On the character of the Perry text, see O'Connor, *Origins of Academic Economics,* pp. 274–75.

72. J. Laurence Laughlin, "The Study of Political Economy in the United States," *Journal of Political Economy* 1 (1892): 149; Hollis, *University of South Carolina,* 2:128–96. Winthrop College for Women was also a creation of the agrarian movement, along with Clemson University. Its purpose was to provide a "decent" alternative to employment in the new cotton mills for the daughters of the impoverished farmers.

73. Hollis, 2:197–221. C. McFerron Gittinger, *Broadening Horizons: A History of the College of Business Administration, the University of South Carolina* (Columbia, S.C., College of Business Administration, University of South Carolina, 1974), pp. 18–23. On Bullock's economics, see Joseph A. Schumpeter, *History of Economic Analysis* (New York: Oxford University Press, 1954), pp. 944, 1165.

CHAPTER 4   BROWN UNIVERSITY

1. Walter C. Bronson, *The History of Brown University, 1764–1914* (Providence: published by the University, 1914), pp. 98–99.

2. *Catalogue of the Officers and Students of Brown University for the Academic Year, 1828–29.*

3. Wayland, "Report on Instruction to the Corporation," 1843.

4. Michael J. L. O'Connor, *The Origins of Academic Economics in the United States* (New York: Columbia University Press, 1944), p. 324. In addition, some 13,000 copies of an abridged version were in circulation by 1854. About 50,000 copies of the unabridged edition were in circulation by the late 1860s. James O. Murray, *Francis Wayland* (Cambridge: Houghton, Mifflin, Riverside Press, 1891), p. 208.

5. Wayland, "Encouragements to Religious Effort: A Discourse delivered in Philadelphia at the request of the American Sunday School Union, May 25, 1830," as reprinted in Wayland, *Occasional Discourses* (Boston: Loring, 1833), p. 146.

6. Wayland, *The Elements of Political Economy*, 2nd ed. (New York: Robinson and Franklin, and Boston: Crocker and Brewster, 1838), pp. 15, 16.

7. Ibid., pp. iii, iv.

8. Ibid., p. 50.

9. Ibid., pp. 358, 359.

10. As Wayland wrote: "God intended that men should live together in friendship and harmony. By thus multiplying indefinitely their wants, and creating only in particular localities, the objects by which those wants can be supplied, he intended to make them all necessary to each other" (ibid., p. 92).

11. Ibid., pp. 123, 124–25.

12. Ibid., pp. 190, 191.

13. Murray, *Francis Wayland*, p. 140. Wayland's text, however, was again used in some southern institutions after the Civil War, notably at South Carolina College and at Auburn.

14. During his visit in London, Wayland attended a meeting of the Political Economy Club, at which Senior, Torrens, and Tooke were present. Francis Wayland and H. L. Wayland, *A Memoir of the Life and Labors of Francis Wayland, D.D., LL.D.* (New York: Sheldon, 1868), 2:32.

15. Wayland, *Thoughts on the Present Collegiate System in the United States* (Boston: Gould, Kendall and Lincoln, 1842), p. 134.

16. Ibid., p. 17.

17. Wayland was prepared to speculate about what might have happened if this scheme of compensation had been put in place in American higher education from the beginning: "A professional career would have been opened to every collegiate instructor as wide and as far reaching as to men in every other department of intellectual exertion. Talent of the highest rank would have been attracted to our colleges. Emulation of the loftiest character would have been awakened. Instead of a great number of small and ill supported Colleges, we should have had a small number of real and efficient Universities. I believe that this change alone would have increased the learning and intellectual vigor of the nation a hundred fold" (ibid., p. 75).

18. Ibid., p. 108.

19. Ibid., p. 144.

20. Ibid., p. 156.

21. Wayland, "Report on Instruction to the Corporation," 1841.

22. *Catalogues of the Officers and Students of Brown University*, passim.

23. "Report to the Corporation of Brown University on Changes in the System of Collegiate Education," March 28, 1850, pp. 17–18.

24. Ibid., p. 34.

25. Ibid., pp. 51, 52.

26. Ibid., pp. 56–58.

27. Ibid., p. 62.

28. Ibid., p. 74.

29. Bronson, *History of Brown*, p. 295.

30. *Catalogue, 1850–51.*

31. Ibid.

32. Gammell to Wayland, March 4, 1850, Wayland Papers, Brown University Archives.

33. For a fuller treatment of Wayland's reforms, see Theodore K. Crane, "Francis Wayland: Political Economist as Educator," Brown University Papers, Brown University Press, Providence, 1962.

34. Bronson, *History of Brown*, pp. 293–94.

35. Ibid., pp. 284, 289.

36. Ibid., p. 277.

37. Ibid., pp. 296–97. Both of the professors in question immediately migrated to Yale where they joined the Scientific School then taking shape there, and they took a number of their better students along with them.

38. Sears, a graduate of Brown in the class of 1825, had been a Baptist clergyman and had held various academic positions, including the presidency of the Newton Theological Institution.

39. President Barnas Sears to the Executive Board of the Brown Corporation, July 5, 1856, as quoted in Bronson, *History of Brown*, p. 321.

40. "A Sketch of the History and Present Organization of Brown University," by the Executive Board of the Brown Corporation, 1861, as quoted in Bronson, *History of Brown*, p. 325.

41. The *Catalogue* for the second term of the academic year 1850–51 offered the following description: "The course in Political Economy is associated as closely as possible with the course in History. It is designed to explain the nature of national wealth, and the laws which regulate its production and accumulation, and the prosperity of nations, with examples from the history of legislative enactments and economical arrangements which have prevailed in different ages and countries. In all which reference will be constantly made to the industrial progress and interests of our own people." Under the new arrangements for electives, this course was open to students pursuing any of the degrees and to those who were not candidates for a degree at all.

42. Bronson, *History of Brown*, p. 322.

43. Caroline Hazard, comp., *The Rev. J. Lewis Diman* (Cambridge, Mass.: Houghton, Mifflin and Company, The Riverside Press, 1887), p. 200.

44. Jeremiah Lewis Diman, "Report on Instruction," 1869.

45. *Catalogue, 1876–77.*

46. An impression of the substance of his teaching can be gleaned from the notes taken on his lectures by a graduate in the class of 1881 (and future chief justice of the Supreme Court of the United States). See Charles Evans Hughes, "Lectures in Political Economy, by J. L. Diman, Brown University, February–June, 1880," Brown University Archives.

47. Diman, "Report on Instruction," 1872.

48. In 1872 Diman was also championed by some members of the Yale faculty for the position that was ultimately awarded to Sumner.

49. *Catalogue, 1886–87.*

50. Elisha Benjamin Andrews, *Institutes of Economics* (Boston: Silver, Burdett, 1891), p. 25. Andrews dedicated this work to J. A. R. von Helferich, Professor of Economics and Finance in the University of Munich.

51. Ibid., p. 26.

52. Andrews's copious citations indicate that he was well read in the current literature of economics—American, British, and French as well as German. Wayland's work is scarcely mentioned.

53. Andrews, *Institutes of Economics,* p. 226.

54. Andrews, *Wealth and Moral Law,* Carew Lectures for 1894 (Hartford: Hartford Seminary Press, 1894), pp. 9, 10.

55. Andrews, *Institutes of Economics,* p. 28.

56. Statement by Andrews in the "Annual Report of the President to the Corporation of Brown University," 1886, p. 38.

57. "Annual Report of the President to the Corporation," 1888, p. 5.

58. Gardner completed his Ph.D. at Johns Hopkins in 1890 and achieved the rank of professor at Brown in 1898. He was to serve as president of the American Economic Association in 1919.

59. Only in the academic year 1889–90, when Willard Clark Fisher substituted for Gardner, was Andrews's *Institutes of Economics* cited as the text. Statement by Willard C. Fisher, "Annual Report to the President of the Corporation," 1890, p. 57.

60. Course notes in the Henry B. Gardner Papers, Brown University Archives.

61. *Catalogues,* passim.

62. Andrews, *Wealth and Moral Law,* p. 27.

63. Ibid., p. 49.

64. Statement of a Committee of the Brown Corporation to Andrews, July 16, 1897, as quoted in Bronson, *History of Brown,* p. 463.

65. Statement of Andrews, July 17, 1897, as quoted in Bronson, *History of Brown,* p. 463.

66. Economists rallying to Andrews's defense included John B. Clark (Columbia), Irving Fisher (Yale), Richard T. Ely (Wisconsin), Frank Fetter (Indiana), F. W. Taussig (Harvard), J. Laurence Laughlin (Chicago), Henry C. Adams (Michigan), W. F. Willcox (Cornell), Woodrow Wilson (Princeton). William Graham Sumner (Yale) and Charles Dunbar (Harvard) registered their support for Andrews, though they associated themselves with the memorial submitted by college presidents rather than with the statement circulated by Seligman through the network of the American Economic Association. See *The Andrews Controversy: A Compilation of the Several Letters, Memorials, and Protests Relative to the Recent Action of the Brown Corporation* (Providence, 1897).

67. The petition presented by the faculty called upon the members of the Corporation to "follow the nobler traditions of Brown University," reminding

them that "Francis Wayland, in a protectionist community, for so many years taught the doctrines of free trade" both inside and outside the walls of the university. "Remonstrance of Twenty-Four Members of the Faculty," July 31, 1897, as reprinted in ibid., p. 21.

68. Richard Hofstadter and Walter P. Metzger, *The Development of Academic Freedom in the United States* (New York: Columbia University Press, 1955), esp. p. 458.

69. Ironically, while in Nebraska (a hotbed of "free silver" sentiment), Andrews retracted his earlier pronouncements on this issue and supported the gold standard, arguing that he had formerly underestimated the amount of gold that new production could make available to the world's monetary system. See Dorfman, *Economic Mind,* 3:180.

CHAPTER 5   HARVARD UNIVERSITY

1. Overseers Reports, Academic Series, 2:18, Harvard University Archives (HUA).

2. For the flavor of instruction in economics, there is no substitute for perusing a text. Also see Michael J. L. O'Connor, *The Origins of Academic Economics in the United States* (New York: Columbia University Press, 1944).

3. Bowen to G. B. Dixwell, January 31, 1882, Bowen Papers, HUA. Eliot's assessment paraphrased in Hugh Hawkins, *Between Harvard and America: The Educational Leadership of Charles W. Eliot* (New York: Oxford University Press, 1972), p. 10.

4. Francis Bowen, Reports to Overseers, May 5, 1868, HUA.

5. Francis Bowen, *American Political Economy* (New York: Scribner, 1870), pp. iv, v. Male references prevailed among Harvard's economists, reflecting then common conventions and a biased definition of human beings. Such gender limitations jar modern sensibilities, and I have minimized their appearance in quoted matter while leaving some as a reminder of social prejudices among social scientists—including those who lectured at Radcliffe.

6. Ibid., p. v. On the social and economic background of Harvard students, see Seymour E. Harris, *Economics of Harvard* (New York: McGraw-Hill, 1970), pp. 7–20. In 1870–75, "21.2 percent of the Harvard students came from professional backgrounds and 43.4 percent from proprietor, managerial and official class" (p. 12).

7. Bowen, *American Political Economy,* pp. 13–14, 15; italics in original.

8. Ibid., pp. 18, 19.

9. Ibid., pp. 36, 41.

10. Ibid., pp. 66–67.

11. Ibid., pp. 67, 106, 107.

12. Ibid., p. 495.

13. See Francis Bowen, "Malthusianism, Darwinism, and Pessimism," *North American Review* 129 (November 1879): 447–72.

14. This story is well told in Hawkins, *Between Harvard and America.*

15. Eliot's address in *The Development of Harvard University: Since the Inauguration of President Eliot, 1869–1929,* ed. Samuel Eliot Morison (Cambridge: Harvard University Press, 1930), p. lix.

16. Ibid., pp. lxii, lxxiv.

17. Ibid., p. lxxiv.

18. Data compiled from Appendix in Samuel Eliot Morison, *Three Centuries of Harvard, 1636–1936* (Cambridge: Harvard University Press, 1936), p. 460.

19. Hawkins, *Between Harvard and America,* p. 63. Also see Colin B. Burke, *American Collegiate Populations: A Test of the Traditional View* (New York: New York University Press, 1982), esp. pp. 212–62.

20. Talcott Parsons and Gerald M. Platt, *The American University* (Cambridge: Harvard University Press, 1973), pp. 1, 1–2; italics in original.

21. Quoted in Hawkins, *Between Harvard and America,* p. 149.

22. Frank W. Taussig, "Economics," in Morison, *Development of Harvard University,* p. 196; also see charts on preceding pages.

23. Alexandra Oleson and John Voss, eds., *The Organization of Knowledge in Modern America, 1860–1920* (Baltimore: Johns Hopkins University Press, 1979), p. ix.

24. Eliot to Dunbar, April 25, 1894, Dunbar Papers, HUA.

25. Charles F. Dunbar, "Economic Science in America, 1776–1876," *North American Review* 122 (January 1876): 140, 146, 154.

26. Information from Robert L. Church, "The Economists Study Society: Sociology at Harvard, 1891–1902," in *Social Sciences at Harvard, 1860–1920: From Inculcation to the Open Mind,* ed. Paul Buck (Cambridge, Mass.: Harvard University Press, 1965), pp. 24–27.

27. Charles F. Dunbar, "Deposits as Currency," *Quarterly Journal of Economics* 1 (July 1887): 402.

28. Ibid., pp. 410, 413.

29. Charles F. Dunbar, "The Reaction in Political Economy," *Quarterly Journal of Economics* 1 (October 1886): 2.

30. Ibid., pp. 19, 21, 22.

31. Ibid., pp. 23, 24, 26.

32. Charles F. Dunbar, "The Academic Study of Political Economy," *Quarterly Journal of Economics* 5 (July 1891): 397, 401, 415.

33. Thomas Edward Cliffe Leslie, "Political Economy in the United States," *Fortnightly Review* 28 (October 1, 1880): 139.

34. Robert L. Church, "Economists Study Society," pp. 27–32.

35. Edward S. Mason, "The Harvard Department of Economics from the Beginning to World War II," *Quarterly Journal of Economics* 97 (August 1982): 394. Only after 1894 were Ph.D.'s identified as in "political economy," although the department had adopted the modern term of "economics" during 1892–93.

36. Frank W. Taussig, "Economics," p. 190.

37. J. Laurence Laughlin to Charles F. Dunbar, November 23, 1883 and Laughlin to Dunbar, March 18, 1883, Dunbar Papers, HUA.

38. Frank W. Taussig to Charles F. Dunbar, March 17, 1883, Dunbar Papers, HUA. (Italics in original.) Also following two paragraphs.

39. Frank W. Taussig, "Economics," pp. 196, 196–97.

40. Ibid., p. 197; italics in original.

41. Taussig to Charles F. Dunbar, March 17, 1883, Dunbar Papers, HUA. On salaries generally, see Harris, *Economics of Harvard*, pp. 140–71; Eliot quoted on p. 141.

42. Eliot to Dunbar, April 18, 1883, Dunbar Papers, HUA. Also see Eliot to Dunbar, January 11, 1883.

43. See Alfred Bornemann, *J. Laurence Laughlin: Chapters in the Career of an Economist* (Washington, D.C.: American Council on Public Affairs, 1940), pp. 2–3. Also see Harold F. Williamson, *Edward Atkinson: The Biography of an American Liberal, 1827–1905* (Boston: Old Corner Bookstore, 1934).

44. Department of Political Economy to President and Fellows of Harvard College (draft), December 12, 1885, Dunbar Papers, HUA. Taussig preferred plain "Economics," but Laughlin would later adopt Thayer's suggested title for a journal when at the University of Chicago.

45. Arthur T. Hadley to Dunbar, October 25, 1886, and Sidney Webb to Dunbar, October 20, 1887, Dunbar Papers, HUA.

46. *Quarterly Journal of Economics;* Index of vols. 1–10, pp. iii, iv.

47. S. Dana Horton, "Silver before Congress," *Quarterly Journal of Economics* 1 (October 1886): 75.

48. Frank W. Taussig, "The Tariff, 1830–1860," *Quarterly Journal of Economics* 2 (April 1888): 364; and Frank W. Taussig, "The Iron Industry in the United States," *Quarterly Journal of Economics* 14 (August 1900): 508.

49. See George J. Stigler, "Stuart Wood and the Marginal Productivity Theory," in his *Essays in the History of Economics* (Chicago: University of Chicago Press, 1965), pp. 287–301. On the marginal revolution generally, see Craufurd D. Goodwin, "Marginalism Moves to the New World"; Joseph J. Spengler, "The Marginal Revolution and Concern with Economic Growth"; Donald Winch, "Marginalism and the Boundaries of Economic Science"; and G. L. S. Shackle, "Marginalism: The Harvest," in *The Marginal Revolution in Economics: Interpretation and Evaluation,* eds. R. D. Collison Black, A. W. Coats, and Craufurd D. Goodwin (Durham, N.C.: Duke University Press, 1973).

50. Frank W. Taussig, "The South-Western Strike of 1886," *Quarterly Journal of Economics* 1 (January 1887): 219.

51. Francis A. Walker, "The Source of Business Profits," *Quarterly Journal of Economics* 1 (April 1887): 288. Also see Robert Cooter and Peter Rappaport, "Were the Ordinalists Wrong about Welfare Economics?" *Journal of Economic Literature* 22 (June 1984): 507–30.

52. Silas M. Macvane, "Boehm-Bawerk on Value and Wages," *Quarterly Journal of Economics* 5 (October 1890): 25–27.

53. Thomas N. Carver, "The Theory of Wages Adjusted to Recent Theories of Value," *Quarterly Journal of Economics* 8 (July 1894): 396, and "Some

Probable Results of a Balanced Industrial System," *American Economic Review* 10 Supplement, *Papers and Proceedings* (March 1920): 74.

54. Frank W. Taussig, *Wages and Capital: An Examination of the Wages Fund Doctrine* (New York: Appleton, 1896), pp. 80–81, 102.

55. Ibid., pp. 80–81, 325.

56. Robert A. McCaughey, "The Transformation of American Academic Life: Harvard University, 1821–1892," *Perspectives in American History* 8 (1974): 293, 310.

57. Ibid., p. 310.

58. Ibid., pp. 243, 246.

59. Church, "Economists Study Society," pp. 33–34, 37.

60. Edward Cummings, "The English Trade-Unions," *Quarterly Journal of Economics* 3 (July 1889): 435; idem, "Co-operative Production in France and England," *Quarterly Journal of Economics* 4 (July 1890): 357–86; idem, "University Settlements," *Quarterly Journal of Economics* 6 (April 1892): 257–79; idem, "Industrial Arbitration in the United States," *Quarterly Journal of Economics* 11 (April 1897): 279; and idem, "Charity and Progress," *Quarterly Journal of Economics* 12 (October 1897): 27.

61. John Cummings, "Ethnic Factors and the Movement of Population," *Quarterly Journal of Economics* 14 (February 1900): 210. For more pernicious comments, see especially Edward A. Ross, "Recent Tendencies in Sociology," *Quarterly Journal of Economics* 17 (November 1902): 82–109. Also see Church, "Economists Study Society," p. 61.

62. Church, "Economists Study Society," p. 62, and William J. Ashley, "On the Study of Economic History," *Quarterly Journal of Economics* 7 (January 1893): 117–18, 120; italics in original. See Church, "Economists Study Society," pp. 67–72, for more on Ashley's appointment.

63. Ashley, "Study of History," pp. 121, 122, 131.

64. See Church, "Economists Study Society."

65. Taussig, "Economics," pp. 191–92.

66. Herbert Heaton, *A Scholar in Action: Edwin F. Gay* (Cambridge, Mass.: Harvard University Press, 1952), p. 2.

67. Taussig, "Economics," p. 191.

68. See Thomas N. Carver, *Recollections of an Unplanned Life* (Los Angeles: Ward Ritchie Press, 1949).

69. Arthur T. Lyman, Report, June 5, 1901 and "Report of the Committee to Visit the Department of Economics," April 13, 1914, HUA.

70. "Report of Committee to Visit the Department of Economics," April 13, 1914; appended report by John Wells Morss, pp. 228–29, HUA.

71. Taussig, "Economics," pp. 192, 193. For a more restrained assessment, especially the delayed introduction of mathematical approaches, and later developments, see Mason, "Harvard Department of Economics," pp. 408–30.

72. Laughlin's review cited in Joseph Dorfman, *The Economic Mind in American Civilization*, vol. 3: *1865–1918* (New York: Viking Press, 1949), p. 66.

73. Taussig, "Economics," pp. 200, 201; italics in original.

74. Fritz K. Ringer, *Education and Society in Modern Europe* (Bloomington: Indiana University Press, 1979), pp. 247, 247–48, and Paul Conkin, *Prophets of Prosperity: America's First Political Economists* (Bloomington: Indiana University Press, 1980), p. 313.

75. Jurgen Herbst, *The German Historical School in American Scholarship* (Ithaca, NY: Cornell University Press, 1965), pp. 92–97, and Sidney Kaplan, "Taussig, James and Peabody: A Harvard School in 1900?" *American Quarterly* 7 (Winter 1955): 315–31.

76. Frank W. Taussig, "The Love of Wealth and the Public Service," *Publications of the American Economic Association*, 3rd ser. 7 (February 1906): 9.

77. Ibid., p. 22.

78. Roosevelt to Joseph Schumpeter, December 18, 1936, PPF, F. D. Roosevelt Library, Hyde Park, N.Y.

79. W. E. B. DuBois, *Dusk of Dawn* (1940), quoted in *The Harvard Book: Selections from Three Centuries*, ed. William Bentinck-Smith (Cambridge, Mass.: Harvard University Press, 1982), p. 256. DuBois's essay on the wages fund is in the Archives, University of Massachusetts at Amherst.

80. Oleson and Voss, *Organization of Knowledge*, p. xix.

CHAPTER 6   YALE UNIVERSITY

1. Brooks Mather Kelley, *Yale: A History* (New Haven: Yale University Press, 1974), p. 11.

2. Ibid., pp. 102, 138.

3. George Wilson Pierson, *Yale College: An Educational History, 1871–1921* (New Haven: Yale University Press, 1952), p. 700; Kelley, *Yale*, pp. 142–43.

4. Kelley, *Yale*, pp. 109, 122.

5. Ibid., p. 123.

6. At the same time, Yale was decidedly on the side of competition in the academic marketplace beyond Connecticut's borders. Generating rivals to Harvard—where the doctrine taught was regarded as impure—accounts for part of Yale's assistance and encouragement in the founding of Williams (1793) and Amherst (1821). Strictly speaking, Amherst did not receive a charter until 1824, though teaching began there three years earlier.

7. "Report on a Course of Liberal Education," as published in the *American Journal of Science and Arts*, January 1829, p. 299.

8. Political economy was first mentioned in the catalogue for the academic year 1825–26 when it appeared as a subject for study in the third term of the senior year. Recitations on Say's *Political Economy* were specified in the official announcements from 1827 through 1836. In 1837 Wayland's *Elements of Political Economy* became the prescribed text. *Catalogues of the Officers and Students in Yale College with a Statement of the Courses of Instruction in the Various Departments*, passim.

9. "Report on a Course of Liberal Education," p. 310.

10. Ibid., p. 315.

11. Ibid., p. 300.

12. "Resolution Passed by the Yale Corporation," August 19, 1846, as quoted by Russell H. Chittenden, *History of the Sheffield Scientific School of Yale University, 1846–1922* (New Haven: Yale University Press, 1928), 1:37.

13. "Report to the Corporation, August 19, 1847," as quoted in Chittenden, *History of Scientific School*, p. 41.

14. As quoted in Pierson, *Yale College*, p. 704.

15. Kelley, *Yale*, p. 185.

16. It is noteworthy that Yale College seriously questioned whether or not it was desirable to create a professorship in history as late as 1850–51. The upshot of the discussion was that the college would be willing to accept an endowment for this purpose if it were offered, though no effort was made to raise the required funds. An endowment for this purpose was not forthcoming until 1865. Kelley, *Yale*, pp. 176–77.

17. For details of Gilman's life and career, see Fabian Franklin, *The Life of Daniel Coit Gilman* (New York: Dodd, Mead, 1910).

18. As quoted in Chittenden, *History of Scientific School*, pp. 144–45.

19. Funding for this chair had been found through the award of land-grant funds provided through the Morrill Act in 1863. Gilman had lobbied vigorously in favor of the allocation of these moneys to the Scientific School.

20. Kelley, *Yale*, p. 175.

21. "Sketch of William Graham Sumner," *Popular Science Monthly*, June 1889; as reprinted in *Sumner Today*, ed. Maurice R. Davie (Westport, Conn.: Greenwood Press, 1971), pp. xii–xiii.

22. In urging Walker to accept this invitation, Gilman wrote as follows on September 24, 1872: "The associates you would have, the opportunities to teach, write and talk which are open to you, the nearness to Boston and New York, and above all the chance to help on modern studies in a conservative and substantial way—all this will attract you." Gilman to Walker, September 24, 1872, as quoted in James Phinney Munroe, *A Life of Francis Amasa Walker* (New York: Holt, 1923), p. 149.

23. "Yale College in 1870," by the Executive Committee of the Society of Yale Alumni, p. 6.

24. Porter to Sumner, July 3, 1872, William Graham Sumner Papers, Yale University Archives, Yale University Library.

25. The alternate candidate for this appointment was J. Lewis Diman, Professor of History and Political Economy at Brown. Diman was clearly the more experienced of the candidates and was ordained as a Congregational clergyman as well. He was, however, a graduate of Brown, not of Yale.

26. "Sketch of Sumner," in Davie, *Sumner Today*.

27. Pierson, *Yale College*, p. 707.

28. William Graham Sumner, "Our Colleges before the Country," *Princeton Review*, March 1884. There is a striking parallelism between the imagery used here and that later employed by Thorstein Veblen in his attacks on "the higher learning in America."

29. Sumner, *Problems in Political Economy* (New York: Holt, 1883), p. v. The problems were set out as a series of questions—366 of them—followed by references to works in which the issues were discussed. The texts referred to with greatest frequency were Adam Smith (Thorald Rogers's edition), John Stuart Mill, Jevons, Marshall (*The Economics of Industry*), Cairnes, Francis Amasa Walker, (*Political Economy*), and Cossa (*Guide to the Study of Political Economy*). Not surprisingly, students were also directed to a number of Sumner's works.

30. For example, Problem no. 9: "It has been said that the free play of economic forces would produce, not the best conceivable, but the worst conceivable state of society. Show the absurdity of this statement." Sumner, *Problems in Political Economy*, p. 4.

31. On January 20, 1876, Porter reproved Sumner as follows: "I was startled to see it announced in the newspapers that you have given notice to the class that . . . you should not mark them at their daily recitations but only at the term examinations. I think if you will give a second thought to the matter, you cannot fail to see that this must be considered by every member of the faculty as a breach of that common understanding which is the condition of any success in the administration of the college. No one would think of interfering with your own individual method of marking or reporting marks. But to announce without consulting anyone that you should depart from a method of procedure on which the whole system of discipline and honors is founded can only tend to the demoralization of the students and the faculty." Porter to Sumner, January 20, 1876, Sumner Papers.

32. Porter to Sumner, December 6, 1879, Sumner Papers.

33. Spencer's *Study of Sociology* is, however, referred to as a useful source in Sumner's published set of *Problems in Political Economy*.

34. *Catalogues of the Officers and Students in Yale College.*

35. J. C. Schwab, "Notes on a Course of Lectures in Political Economy, 1886–87," Sumner Papers.

36. Irving Fisher, for example, was among them. See his memorial comment, "William Graham Sumner: The Inspirer," *Yale Review*, May 1910, pp. 5–7.

37. Ely wanted "simply an association of the younger progressive elements, and the platform must be broad, yet it must not include men of the Sumner type." Ely to E. R. A. Seligman, June 9, 1885, as quoted in Dorfman, *The Economic Mind in American Civilization* (New York: Viking Press, 1949), 3:206.

38. J. Laurence Laughlin of Harvard was the principal organizer of this group. Writing to Sumner in the autumn of 1883, he observed: "You will remember the suggestion of a plan for the organization of the political economists in this country for mutual cheer (and quarrelling). . . . Even the dentists have annual seasons of good fellowship and mutual encouragement." Laughlin to Sumner, November 12, 1883, Sumner Papers. Laughlin's choice of imagery may have an interesting resonance to those who recall the language John Maynard Keynes used in his 1930 essay entitled "Economic Possibilities for

Our Grandchildren." Keynes then wrote: "If economists could manage to get themselves thought of as humble, competent people, on a level with dentists, that would be splendid."

39. Michael J. L. O'Connor, *The Origins of Academic Economics in the United States* (New York: Columbia University Press, 1944), p. 321.

40. Pierson, *Yale College*, p. 722.

41. *Catalogues of the Officers and Students in Yale College.*

42. *Statistics of the Class of 'Eighty-One, Sheffield Scientific School, Yale College,* published in New Haven, 1881.

43. Munroe, *Life of Walker*, p. 155. During these years, Walker published three books—*The Wages Question* (1877), *Money* (1878), *Money in Its Relations to Trade and Industry* (1879)—and did the bulk of the work on two others, his textbook, *Political Economy,* and *Land and Its Rent,* both of which appeared in 1883.

44. Executive Committee of the Society of the Alumni, "Yale College in 1875," "Yale College in 1876."

45. Not all of Johns Hopkins's early customers were totally satisfied. Thorstein Veblen left Johns Hopkins to attend Yale where he was entered in the "Philosophy and Psychology" component of the graduate department. He was awarded a Ph.D. in 1884 with a thesis on "The Ethical Grounds of a Doctrine of Retribution." Veblen was later to call on Sumner for letters of recommendation to support his candidacy for academic employment.

46. *Doctors of Philosophy of Yale University with the Titles of Their Dissertations, 1861–1927* (New Haven: Yale University, 1927).

47. Walker was later to describe Sumner as a "cantankerous man"; as quoted in Dorfman, *Economic Mind,* 3 : xxviii. When acknowledging receipt of a complimentary copy of Sumner's *Problems in Political Economy,* Walker observed: "I think I could 'make it lively' for you at two or three points, if I were in your class room; but, life being what it is, I can only envy those younger men who enjoy that privilege." Walker to Sumner, January 13, 1884, Sumner Papers.

48. Munroe, *Life of Walker,* pp. 182–83. For additional details, see Chapter 8, herein.

49. Farnam was among the first to be awarded an earned M.A. at Yale. Before reforms that took effect in 1875, this degree had automatically been conferred on B.A.'s after three years of "good conduct" and the payment of a fee.

50. Farnam's studies in Europe were actively encouraged by his father, who urged him to remain abroad until he had become the master of this new discipline. The father anticipated that his son would have no difficulty in finding a suitable appointment in political economy at Yale when he was ready to take on such an assignment.

51. Dexter to Farnam, July 7, 1876, and September 25, 1876, Farnam Family Papers, Yale University Archives, Yale University Library.

52. Farnam acknowledged this official communication with a touch of humil-

ity. On September 8, 1880, he wrote as follows to Franklin B. Dexter, secretary of the Yale Corporation: "Your note of July 1 informing me of my appointment to the Chair of Political Economy in the Department of Philosophy and the Arts reached me in Europe during the vacation. This will, I hope, excuse my delay in replying. Will you kindly express to the Corporation my warm appreciation of the distinction they have conferred upon me and say that I will put myself at the service of the College after January first next. Let me thank you, in closing, for your expressions of personal good will and congratulations. Such words are doubly welcome when the work to be done is so vague and success so difficult and necessarily slow, where moreover so much depends on the advice of those who have had experience." Farnam to Dexter, September 8, 1880, Farnam Family Papers.

53. Dexter to Farnam, July 1, 1880, Farnam Family Papers.

54. Henry W. Farnam, as a tutor in Latin, was on record as returning salary checks to the president with instructions that the money be allocated to poor students needing assistance. Farnam to President Noah Porter, April 1, 1879, Farnam Family Papers.

55. *Catalogues,* passim.

56. Farnam to Porter, April 13, 1881, Farnam Family Papers.

57. Hadley to Charles Willcox, February 16, 1879, as quoted in Morris Hadley, *Arthur Twining Hadley* (New Haven: Yale University Press, 1948), p. 32.

58. Hadley to E. D. Worcester, July 29, 1879, as quoted in ibid., p. 32.

59. Hadley to Worcester, July 10, 1883, as quoted in ibid., p. 47.

60. Farnam to Sumner, April 27, 1886, Sumner Papers. Dexter acknowledged this transaction as follows: "I beg to assure you that I express the feeling of the Corporation in emphasizing their high appreciation of the purpose of this gift, and their confident expectation that Mr. Hadley's eminent attainments will be of great service in building up a very important portion of the Department in which he is to instruct." Dexter to Farnam, May 21, 1886, Farnam Family Papers.

61. *Catalogues,* passim.

62. Farnam to Sumner, October 17, 1888, Farnam Family Papers.

63. *Catalogue, 1887–88,* p. 50.

64. Ibid., p. 99.

65. Farnam to Sumner, September 5, 1982, Sumner Papers.

66. Irving Fisher, *Mathematical Investigations in the Theory of Value and Prices* (New Haven: Yale University Press, 1925), p. iii.

67. A. T. Hadley, *Economics: An Account of the Relations between Private Property and Public Welfare* (New York: Putnam, 1897), p. iii.

68. In his presentation of a demand schedule, however, prices were measured on the horizontal axis and quantities on the vertical one.

69. Hadley, *Economics,* p. 80.

70. Ibid., p. iii.

71. In the preface to the general work in which his mature thinking on economics is most fully expressed, Hadley acknowledged aid from two col-

leagues: Irving Fisher and J. C. Schwab. Sumner was not mentioned in this connection, nor was Farnam.

72. Hadley, *Economics*, p. 12.

73. It is arresting to note that Hadley's single mention of the "Sherman Act of 1890" refers to legislation of that date requiring purchase of silver by the Treasury, not to the antitrust statute enacted in 1890.

74. Hadley, *Economics*, p. 175.

75. Ibid., p. 120.

76. Hadley, *Arthur Twining Hadley*, p. 73.

77. George W. Pierson, *A Yale Book of Numbers: Historical Statistics of the College and University, 1701–1976* (New Haven: Yale University Press, 1983), p. 267. This trend was noted in the early 1890s when the *Yale Review* surveyed the effects of the first ten years of experience with "electives." The percentage of juniors studying "political science" had risen from zero in 1884 to ninety-six in 1893. The percentage of the seniors devoting two-fifths or more of their time to political science had risen from zero in 1884 to thirty-one by 1893. As political science was among the few fields "into which students are not driven at one time or another in their four year's course," it was conclusive that it stood on its "own merits." "Comment," *Yale Review*, November 1894, pp. 237–40.

78. Pierson, *Yale Book of Numbers*, p. 261.

79. *Doctors of Philosophy of Yale University*. The hand of Hadley was obvious in two dissertations dealing with the problems of railroads.

80. Dorfman, *Economic Mind*, 3:208.

81. Farnam to Seligman, June 5, 1892, Farnam Family Papers.

82. Farnam to Sumner, September 5, 1892, Sumner Papers.

83. Writing to Sumner on April 9, 1892, Farnam observed: "I trust that the plan will meet with your approval, and that we can count on you as a contributor." Farnam Family Papers.

84. In 1892 Fisher had suggested that the *Yale Review* might usefully publish an English translation of a number of Pareto's articles on mathematical economics. Nothing was to come of this suggestion. Fisher to Farnam, December 12, 1892, Farnam Family Papers.

85. The *Yale Review*'s character as a journal for economic discussion ended in 1911. The quarterly was then restructured to publish material on a wider array of subjects, with priority given to articles reflecting scholarly work at Yale. The timing of this change was influenced by the fact that the American Economic Association—of which Farnam was then president—had decided to launch a specialized journal of its own as the *American Economic Review*. Even so, Farnam still undertook to subsidize the *Yale Review* during the first five years of its new incarnation.

86. Fisher to Sumner, undated (but apparently written during the winter of 1898–99), Sumner Papers.

87. Fisher to Hadley, December 6, 1898, President Arthur T. Hadley Papers, Yale University Archives, Yale University Library.

CHAPTER 7   COLUMBIA UNIVERSITY

1. Columbia University, *A History of Columbia University, 1754–1904* (New York: Columbia University Press, 1904), facing p. 32.
2. Ibid., p. 98.
3. See Columbia College, *Addresses at the Inauguration of Mr. Charles King as President of Columbia College* (New York, 1849), p. 6.
4. Daniel G. B. Thompson, *Ruggles of New York: A Life of Samuel B. Ruggles* (New York: Columbia University Press, 1946), pp. 80–81, 89.
5. Strong Diary, May 9, 1855, quoted in ibid., p. 90; see also p. 163.
6. S. B. Ruggles, *The Duty of Columbia College to the Community and its Right to Exclude Unitarians from Its Professorships of Physical Science, by One of Its Trustees* (New York, 1854); cited in Thompson, *Ruggles of New York,* p. 86 (this paragraph draws heavily on the latter work).
7. Strictly, the figures for bachelors' degrees are noncomparable. They all exclude the Medical School, but the figure for 1860 includes twenty-eight from the Law School, and the 1900 figure includes eighty-eight law degrees as well as thirty-nine from Barnard College and forty-nine from the School of Applied Science. As for faculty, the 1862 figure includes members of the Law School and the "Academical" Department but not the Medical School. Figures are from Columbia University, *Catalogue of Officers and Graduates of Columbia University from the Foundation of King's College in 1754* (New York: Columbia University Press, 1916); M. H. Thomas, *Columbia University Officers and Alumni, 1754–1857* (New York: Columbia University Press, 1936). Figures for 1869, 1880, and 1898 include the Schools of Law and Mines; see Columbia University, *Catalogue,* and Columbia University, *History,* p. 264.
8. Columbia University, *Resolutions Passed by the Trustees of Columbia College, 1820–1868* (New York: Van Nostrand, 1868), p. 127; Columbia University, *Resolutions Passed by the Trustees of Columbia College, 1874–79* (New York, 1879).
9. Columbia University, *Annual Report of the President of Columbia College* (New York: Columbia University Press, 1882).
10. It would be interesting to know whether the sharp changes in tuition fees were calculated to increase revenues. In 1811 the fee was reduced from $100 to $50. Subsequent changes were to $80 in 1815; $90 in 1820; $50 in 1857; $100 in 1862; $150 in 1880. See Columbia University, *Annual Report of the President, 1882.*
11. Columbia University, *History,* p. 126. The work of that committee is discussed below.
12. J. McVickar, *Introductory Lecture to a Course of Political Economy; Recently Delivered at Columbia College, New York* (London: John Miller, 1830). p. iv.
13. Columbia College, *Statements of Prof. McVickar,* appended to *Report of a Committee of the Trustees of Columbia College* (New York, 1858). p. 7; Columbia University, *History,* p. 127.

14. Ruggles, *Duty of Columbia College;* cited in Thompson, *Ruggles of New York,* p. 86.

15. See Columbia University, *History,* pp. 135, 204, 217.

16. So much is sure. He was not the first to teach political economy in the United States; priority in that goes to Cooper at South Carolina College. It is known that McVickar intended to teach political economy in the spring of 1818. The subject appears in the Columbia statutes of 1821 and is part of McVickar's title in the 1826 catalogue. See J. Dorfman and R. G. Tugwell, *Early American Policy: Six Columbia Contributors* (New York: Columbia University Press, 1960), pp. 109–11.

17. Ibid., p. 108.

18. Nicholas Murray Butler, quoted in J. B. Langstaff, *The Enterprising Life: John McVickar* (New York: St. Martin's Press, 1961), p. 398.

19. Langstaff, *McVickar,* p. 398; Columbia College, *Addresses,* p. 12.

20. Columbia College, *Statements of McVickar,* pp. 2, 4, 5.

21. Ibid., p. 5. E. Babcock, "Notes," Rare Books and Manuscripts Collection, Columbia University Library. Dorfman points out that George Tucker used diagrams at Virginia at least as early as 1840.

22. Columbia College, *Statements of McVickar,* p. 4. See Chapter 6, herein. Columbia University, *History,* p. 107.

23. This would explain the sometimes glaring differences between what McVickar wrote in 1826 and what his students inscribed in their notebooks in the 1840s.

24. Columbia College, *Statements of McVickar,* p. 4.

25. Ibid., p. 1.

26. J. McVickar, *Outlines of Political Economy: A republication of the article upon that subject contained in the Edinburgh Supplement to the Encyclopaedia Britannica* (New York: Wilder and Campbell, 1825). J. McVickar, *Essay upon the Principles of Political Economy: Designed as a Manual for Practical Men* (New York: Theodore Foster, 1837); published under the pseudonym "An American." J. Dorfman, *The Economic Mind in American Civilization,* 3 vols. (New York: Viking Press, 1946), 2:516, 713.

27. McVickar, *Outlines of Political Economy,* p. 186.

28. Ibid., pp. 186–88.

29. McVickar, *Introductory Lecture,* pp. 5–8.

30. Ibid., pp. 24, 25.

31. McVickar, *Outlines of Political Economy,* pp. 69, 186.

32. Ibid., pp. 161, 162, 164.

33. Ibid., p. 90. J. Dorfman, "On the Naturalization of Ricardian Economics in the United States," in Dorfman, ed., *Outlines of Political Economy* (New York: Augustus Kelley, 1966), p. 9. McVickar, *Outlines of Political Economy,* p. 91.

34. Ibid., pp. 112, 114, 125.

35. Ibid., pp. 105, 114, 130, 131, 142.

36. Cited in Dorfman and Tugwell, *Early American Policy,* p. 127.

37. McVickar, *Essay upon the Principles of Political Economy,* p. 13.

38. McVickar, *Outlines of Political Economy*, pp. 129, 144, 149.

39. Ibid., pp. 44–48, 72–75, 73.

40. McVickar, *Introductory Lecture*, p. iii; *Essay upon the Principles of Political Economy*, pp. 54–55; *Outlines of Political Economy*, pp. 172–74. He was later to modify this opinion, arguing that government bonds provide a necessary stability to financial markets. See the treatment in Dorfman and Tugwell, *Early American Policy*, p. 145.

41. The article was reprinted as a pamphlet; see J. McVickar, *A National Bank: Its Necessity and Most Advisable Form* (New York, 1841).

42. See Chapter 3, herein.

43. George Strong wrote in his diary: "Lieber's laziness is a sore impediment to his friends' efforts on his behalf. He is unwilling to undertake work enough to justify us in asking the Trustees to help him in the School on a full salary." A. Nevins and M. H. Thomas, eds., *The Diary of George Templeton Strong: Post War Years, 1865–75*, 4 vols. (New York: Macmillan, 1952), 4:23. Lieber's friends fought to protect his salary, but his continued laziness made his position precarious (4:208, 235).

44. Dorfman and Tugwell, *Early American Policy*, p. 294.

45. J. Dorfman and R. G. Tugwell, "Francis Lieber: German Scholar in America," *Columbia University Quarterly* 30 (1938):350, 351.

46. Columbia College, *Communication of Prof. Francis Lieber*, appended to *Report of a Committee of the Trustees of Columbia College* (New York, 1858), pp. 4–6. Columbia College, *Catalogue of the Officers and Students of Columbia College for the Year 1864–65*.

47. Columbia College, *Annual Report of the President, 1921*, p. 28. F. Freidel, *Francis Lieber: Nineteenth-Century Liberal* (Baton Rouge: Louisiana State University Press, 1947), pp. 365–68. Nevins and Thomas, *Diary of Strong*, 4:6. Strong also blames Barnard, who should have intervened to check the disorder.

48. F. Lieber, "Notes on Fallacies of American Protectionists," in *Contributions to Political Science*, 2 vols. (Philadelphia: Lippincott, 1881), 2:389–459. This piece was based on lecture notes "in connection with a course of Political Economy," probably Lieber's course of public lectures, not his college course.

49. Columbia University, *Catalogue*, for 1865–66, 1866–67, 1868–69. Nairne also taught in the Law School where, during 1860–78, he was Professor of Ethics and Jurisprudence. See Columbia University, *General Catalogue of the Officers and Graduates of Columbia University, 1754–1916*.

50. Columbia College, *Annual Report of the President, 1886*, p. 6.

51. Columbia College, *Catalogue* (various years), and Columbia University, *History of the Faculty of Political Science* (New York: Columbia University Press, 1955), p. 168. According to the *Catalogues*, he used Wayland until 1871–72; Fawcett from 1872–73 to 1876–77.

52. J. Burgess, *Reminiscences of an American Scholar* (New York: Columbia University Press, 1934), p. 170. Richard Ely had the misfortune to be his

student but was by no means a disciple. For Ely's reaction to Nairne, see Chapter 8, herein.

53. Ibid., p. 160.

54. Ibid., pp. 151, 152. Columbia University, *Resolutions Passed by the Trustees of Columbia College, 1874–79* (New York, 1879).

55. His *Reminiscences* open with an anecdotal and sentimental defense of the antebellum slaveowning aristocracy. Burgess, *Reminiscences*, pp. 3–5, 52–54. Columbia University, *History of the Faculty of Political Science*, pp. 5–6.

56. Burgess, *Reminiscences*, pp. 139–47.

57. Columbia College, *Annual Report of the President, 1865*, pp. 13–14. Barnard was not above pointing out that some potential students had been sent elsewhere because of the limits placed on junior-year electives at Columbia (*1886*, p. 23).

58. Ibid., *1886*, pp. 29, 34.

59. Quoted in Columbia University, *History of the Faculty of Political Science*, p. 9.

60. Another influence was the University of Strasbourg. See ibid., p. 12.

61. Ibid., *History of the Faculty of Political Science*, p. 15. As Burgess tells the tale, it was Ruggles who submitted his plan to the trustees. See Burgess, *Reminiscences*, pp. 191–92.

62. The committee wrote: "It is not to be assumed that, as political affairs are now managed, the possession of superior qualifications will necessarily afford the aspirant to place any very substantial preliminary advantage." Cited in Columbia University, *History of the Faculty of Political Science*, p. 15.

63. Ibid., pp. 16, 17.

64. Burgess, *Reminiscences*, pp. 197–202, 198, 349–68. Columbia University, *History of the Faculty of Political Science*, p. 24.

65. Columbia University, *History of the Faculty of Political Science*, p. 36.

66. Columbia College, *Handbook*, 1883, p. 163. Columbia University, *History of the Faculty of Political Science*, p. 307. Columbia College, *Annual Report of the President, 1886*, p. 63.

67. Burgess, *Reminiscences*, pp. 174–76, 211–12, 217. Columbia University, *History of the Faculty of Political Science*, pp. 39–40.

68. Columbia University, *History of the Faculty of Political Science*, pp. 7, 170, 313. According to Seligman, the promotion was in 1883. See E. R. A. Seligman, "Richmond Mayo-Smith," *Columbia University Quarterly* 4 (1901):42.

69. Like Lieber before him, he was interested in improving the methods used at the census. See Columbia University, *History of the Faculty of Political Science*, p. 173; Seligman, "Richmond Mayo-Smith," p. 42.

70. T. Rogers, *Manual of Political Economy* (Oxford: Clarendon Press, 1868). Columbia College, *Annual Report of the President, 1878*, pp. 5–6, 7; *1880*, p. 87.

71. In the 1880s about a quarter of the senior class elected political economy.

72. Columbia University, *Annual Report of the President, 1880*, pp. 172, 183; *1900*, p. 178. Columbia University, *History of the Faculty of Political Science*, pp. 24, 172; Columbia College, *Handbook*, 1883, pp. 158–9; Columbia College, *Catalogue*, 1886.

73. Columbia University, *History of the Faculty of Political Science*, pp. 27–29; and Columbia College, *Annual Report of the President, 1890*.

74. Burgess, *Reminiscences*, p. 186.

75. Columbia University, *History of the Faculty of Political Science*, pp. 32–33, 174–76.

76. Ibid., p. 175.

77. E. R. A. Seligman, *The Shifting and Incidence of Taxation* (1892); *Progressive Taxation* (1895); *Essays in Taxation* (1895).

78. E. R. A. Seligman, "The Economic Interpretation of History I," *Political Science Quarterly* 16 (1901): 612–40; idem, *The Economic Interpretation of History* (New York: Columbia University Press, 1902), p. 24.

79. The political economy course appears to have been taught for a semester each to second- and third-year students; see Columbia College, *Annual Report of the President, 1886*, p. 137. See also *Annual Report of the President, 1890*, p. 87; *1893*, p. 115; *1895*, p. 121.

80. Columbia College, *Annual Report of the President, 1895*, p. 123; *1900*, p. 182; *1895*, p. 124. See Smart, *Introduction to the Theory of Value on the Lines of Menger, Wieser, and Böhm-Bawerk* (London and New York: Macmillan, 1891), and von Wieser, *Natural Value* (1889).

81. Mayo-Smith's two-volume *Science of Statistics* (1895, 1899) and Seligman's *Shifting and Incidence of Taxation* (1892) are the sort of study that would be in the series. But I have no other evidence that it got off the ground.

82. Columbia University, *History of the Faculty of Political Science*, p. 140.

83. Ibid., pp. 61, 176–77, 285–88.

84. To sweeten the pill, Low personally paid Clark's salary for the first three years.

85. For details of this episode, see Chapter 8, herein.

86. J. B. Clark, *The Distribution of Wealth* (New York: Macmillan, 1899), p.v.; idem, *Essentials of Economic Theory* (New York: Augustus Kelley, 1968), p.v.

87. The Department of Political Economy and Social Sciences was renamed Economics and Social Science in 1892 at the instance of Seligman. See Columbia University, *History of the Faculty of Political Science*, p. 60.

88. Columbia University, *Annual Report of the President, 1896*, p. 38; *1899*, p. 51.

89. Columbia University, *Annual Report of the President, 1900*, p. 178.

90. This calculation excludes the seminar (twenty-one students) and the Readings in Marshall (eight students).

CHAPTER 8   JOHNS HOPKINS UNIVERSITY

1. Hugh Hawkins, *Pioneer: A History of the Johns Hopkins University, 1874–1889* (Ithaca, N.Y.: Cornell University Press, 1960), pp. 4–5.
2. At one point in 1874, Gilman's tenure of his position at the University of California was in jeopardy. The specific issue prompting an investigation by the state legislature into his administration concerned arrangements for the construction of buildings at the university. Agitation on this point, however, had been sparked by malcontents on the university faculty who opposed Gilman's programs for educational reform. They, in turn, aroused Henry George, then editor of a daily newspaper in San Francisco, to mount a publicity campaign to harass Gilman. See Fabian Franklin, *The Life of Daniel Coit Gilman* (New York: Dodd, Mead, 1910), pp. 142–54.
3. The substance of Gilman's remarks to the trustees was conveyed to his friend, E. L. Godkin, editor of the *Nation*, who summarized them in the edition of January 28, 1875 (as reprinted in Franklin, *Life of Gilman*, pp. 188–89).
4. Though postgraduate studies were the main focus, some undergraduate students were also admitted (despite the fact that undergraduates had been excluded in Gilman's initial vision). This modification was a concession to strengthening the institution's public relations on the local scene. A majority of the "matriculates"—i.e., undergraduates—were residents of Baltimore and surrounding areas in the state of Maryland. Until well into the 1890s, graduate students consistently outnumbered undergraduates. See data in the Johns Hopkins *Circulars*, passim, and the Daniel Coit Gilman Collection, Letterbook 4, Special Collections, Milton S. Eisenhower Library, Johns Hopkins University.
5. Hawkins, *Pioneer*, p. 81.
6. Francesco Cordasco, *Daniel Coit Gilman and the Protean Ph.D.: The Shaping of American Graduate Education* (Leiden: Brill, 1960), p. 86.
7. Gilman, "Hopkins Inaugural," as quoted in Hawkins, *Pioneer*, p. 68.
8. Walker to Gilman, February 14, 1876, Gilman Collection.
9. Gilman to Walker, February 7, 1876, Gilman Collection, Letterbook 1.
10. Walker to Gilman, March 1876, Gilman Collection.
11. Gilman to Walker, March 30, 1876, Gilman Collection, Letterbook 1.
12. Walker to Gilman, December 11, 1876, Gilman Collection.
13. The topic of Walker's lectures underwent some modification in the course of his negotiations with Gilman. Originally, he had planned to draw on his work with the United States Census by lecturing on the theme of statistics and "their graphic illustration." This was subsequently amended when Walker wrote: "The universal agitation of the Currency Question, arising out of the silver problem, seems to make this a singularly favorable occasion for taking up that question historically and scientifically. I think I could do for this question what I have done for the Wage Question, sweep away much that obstructs the proper discussion of it, and at least put the issues involved

in a distinct form, even if I could not contribute greatly to their solution." Walker to Gilman, December 11, 1876, Gilman Collection. These lectures were subsequently published in book form under the title *Money.*

14. A young man who was also to leave his mark on American economics— John Bates Clark—was an unsuccessful candidate for a Johns Hopkins fellowship in 1876. His shortcoming for competitive purposes was that he lacked written work to submit. Cf. Joseph Dorfman, *The Economic Mind in American Civilization* (New York: Viking Press, 1949), 3 : 189. This rejection did not deter Clark from making known his availability for a faculty appointment, observing: "I understand that there is not, as yet, an associate professor of Political Economy at your university. . . . I have, in the intervals of my work in the State University at this place [the University of Minnesota], commenced a little treatise on the subject and a certain part of it is sufficiently complete for examination." Clark to Gilman, November 4, 1876, Gilman Collection.

15. Adams to Gilman, March 2, 1877, Gilman Collection.

16. Adams to Gilman, dated January 7, 1878 (though the dateline from Berlin indicates that the year 1879 was intended), Gilman Collection.

17. Adams to Gilman, February 27, 1880, and December 18, 1880, Gilman Collection.

18. Hawkins, *Pioneer,* pp. 170–73.

19. When Gilman was negotiating with Newcomb about the projected lectures in June 1881, Newcomb observed that he "appreciate[d] the honor" of the invitation and that the "only difficulty" he had "is giving an exact designation to my lectures. One lecture would be principally devoted to the general subject of the study of political economy and another to the practical details of taxation. The intermediate one would probably include general principles covering both subjects." Newcomb to Gilman, June 18, 1881, Gilman Collection.

20. Newcomb to Gilman, May 10, 1882, Gilman Collection.

21. In later life, he was often to speak disparagingly about this aspect of his college education, describing as "ridiculous" a course at Columbia which met once a week for recitations on Mrs. Fawcett's *Political Economy for Beginners.* See, e.g., Richard T. Ely, *Ground under Our Feet: An Autobiography* (New York: Macmillan, 1938), p. 35.

22. In light of the friction that was later to arise between Ely and William Graham Sumner of Yale, it is ironic that one of the letters of introduction White wrote for Ely was addressed to Sumner. Ely sent a copy of that letter to Gilman in support of his availability for an appointment at Johns Hopkins, noting that he had "not yet been able to see Prof. Sumner." Ely to Gilman, March 18, 1881, Gilman Collection.

23. Ely to Gilman, August 20, 1881, Gilman Collection.

24. Ely to Gilman, May 23, 1882, Gilman Collection.

25. Ely to Gilman, May 26, 1882, Gilman Collection.

26. Ely to Gilman, September 27, 1883, Gilman Collection.

27. President's Office Memorandum, September 28, 1883, Gilman Collection.

28. John C. French, *A History of the University Founded by Johns Hopkins* (Baltimore: Johns Hopkins University Press, 1946), pp. 50–55.

29. *Johns Hopkins University Circulars,* June 1884, pp. 114–15.

30. When advising Ely of his promotion to an associate professorship for a three-year term in mid-1887, Gilman observed that the trustees were "not prepared to separate the course in Political Economy from those in History, and they desire that for the present Dr. Adams should remain the head of the course in History and Political Science." Gilman to Ely, June 10, 1887, Gilman Collection.

31. *Johns Hopkins Circulars,* November 1889, p. 13; June 1890, p. 98; November 1890, p. 10.

32. Newcomb to Gilman, May 14, 1884, Gilman Collection.

33. Newcomb to Gilman, June 1, 1884, Gilman Collection.

34. Richard T. Ely, "The Past and Present of Political Economy," *Johns Hopkins Studies in Historical and Political Science* 2 (1884): 15.

35. Newcomb to Gilman, June 1, 1884, Gilman Collection.

36. Simon Newcomb, "The Two Schools of Political Economy," *Princeton Review,* November 1884, pp. 291–301.

37. Newcomb to Gilman, May 3, 1884, Gilman Collection.

38. Hawkins, *Pioneer,* p. 81.

39. *Johns Hopkins Circulars,* March 1885, p. 66.

40. Ely, *Ground under Our Feet,* p. 135.

41. Ely to Gilman, July 11, 1885, Gilman Collection.

42. Ely to Albert Shaw, May 7, 1885, as quoted in Hawkins, *Pioneer,* p. 181.

43. For an excellent discussion of the formation of the American Economic Association, see Mary O. Furner, *Advocacy and Objectivity: A Crisis in the Professionalization of American Social Science, 1865–1905* (Lexington: University Press of Kentucky, 1975), esp. pp. 59–80.

44. Once the AEA was in being, Ely informed Gilman that it gave him pleasure to report that the organization had received "prominent attention" and invited Gilman to join. Gilman, however, did not do so. Ely to Gilman, September 19, 1885, Gilman Collection.

45. Albert Shaw, "Recent Economic Works," *Dial,* December 1885, pp. 210, 211. The Elyites, however, failed to appreciate one of the distinct merits of Newcomb's book: his reformulation of the quantity theory of money which, in all essential respects, anticipated work that was to bring Irving Fisher fame some two decades later.

46. Newcomb to Gilman, May 24, 1886, Gilman Collection.

47. Newcomb to Gilman. May 28, 1886, Gilman Collection.

48. Richard T. Ely, "Ethics and Economics," *Science,* June 11, 1886, pp. 529–33.

49. Simon Newcomb, "Aspects of the Economic Discussion," *Science,* June 18, 1886, pp. 538–42.

50. Richard T. Ely, "The Economic Discussion in *Science,*" July 2, 1886, pp. 3–6.

51. Simon Newcomb, "Can Economists Agree upon the Basis of Their Teachings?" *Science*, July 9, 1886, pp. 25–26.

52. Furner, *Advocacy and Objectivity*, p. 135.

53. Richard T. Ely, *The Labor Movement in America* (Boston: Crowell, 1886), p. 138.

54. Ibid., pp. 207, 296.

55. Simon Newcomb, *A Plain Man's Talk on the Labor Question* (New York: Harper, 1886), passim.

56. Albert Shaw, "Seven Books for Citizens," *Dial*, November 1886, p. 150.

57. [Newcomb], "Dr. Ely on the Labor Movement," *Nation*, October 7, 1886, pp. 293–94. Though this review was published anonymously, Newcomb's authorship was accepted by Ely.

58. Conceivably, Ely might also have found himself in trouble at Johns Hopkins for other reasons as well. His staunch advocacy of public ownership of railroads was hardly calculated to endear him to all members of an institution whose financial fate was linked with the fortunes of the Baltimore and Ohio Railroad. To the credit of the Johns Hopkins University, there is no evidence that Ely's outspokenness on this issue figured in the evaluation of his future at the university.

59. Gilman's papers contain undated correspondence (which appears to have been written during the academic year 1890–91) in which Ely took pains to point out that the review in the *Nation* in 1886 had positive as well as negative effects. Ely's submissions included letters expressing outrage at the unfair and vindictive tone of the review. In addition, Ely reported that Frank W. Taussig of Harvard—who had originally declined to join the American Economic Association—had reversed his position because of the malicious treatment to which Ely had been subjected and that John R. Commons (then teaching at Wesleyan University and one of the stellar products of the graduate program) had been attracted to Johns Hopkins after reading the review.

60. Ely to Gilman, December 12, 1891, Gilman Collection.

61. Gilman to Ely, January 4, 1892, Gilman Collection, Letterbook 5.

62. Indeed, some of Ely's original allies in the formation of the AEA were uneasy about the use he was making of his position as secretary and its impact on the public image of the profession. His commitment to the anti-laissez-faire language of the platform had come to be regarded as divisive. Questions were also raised about the preference Ely accorded to works by his students in the AEA Publication Series. In addition, in the eyes of many of the professionals, Ely was more a popularizer than a scholar. At the meeting of the American Economic Association of August 1892, Ely was eased out of the secretaryship and replaced by one of his students, Edward A. Ross, then at Cornell. For a valuable discussion of this episode, see Furner, *Advocacy and Objectivity*, esp. pp. 107–24.

63. Minutes of the Economic Seminary (Series 1), Records of the Department of Political Economy, no. 04.140, Ferdinand Hamburger, Jr., Archives, Johns Hopkins University.

64. Clark to Gilman, January 3, 1895, Gilman Collection.
65. Clark to Gilman, February 18, 1895, Gilman Collection.
66. Cordasco, *Daniel Coit Gilman*, p. 111.
67. Included among the notables were John Dewey and Josiah Royce (philosophy); Frederick Jackson Turner (history); Albion Small (sociology); and Woodrow Wilson (the only president of the United States to have earned a doctorate).
68. Economists with a Johns Hopkins background who encountered such difficulties included Edward W. Bemis (at Chicago), Edward A. Ross (at Stanford), Henry Carter Adams (at Michigan), and Richard T. Ely (at Wisconsin).
69. Johns Hopkins graduate students of this period who became presidents of the AEA (with their institutional affiliations at the time of their tenure of office) were the following: Henry Carter Adams (University of Michigan); Davis R. Dewey (Massachusetts Institute of Technology); David Kinley (University of Illinois); Thomas Nixon Carver (Harvard); John R. Commons (University of Wisconsin); Henry B. Gardner (Brown); Jacob H. Hollander (Johns Hopkins); Henry R. Seager (Columbia); Thomas Sewall Adams (Yale); Fred M. Taylor (University of Michigan); and George E. Barnett (Johns Hopkins).

CHAPTER 9   UNIVERSITY OF PENNSYLVANIA

1. Edward P. Cheyney, *History of the University of Pennsylvania* (Philadelphia: University of Philadelphia Press, 1940), passim.
2. For Henry Vethake's moral philosophy, see his *Principles of Political Economy*, 2nd ed. (New York: Augustus Kelley, 1971). Also see Paul K. Conkin, *Prophets of Prosperity: America's First Political Economists* (Bloomington: Indiana University Press, 1980), pp. 123–34; Donald H. Meyer, *The Instructed Conscience* (Philadelphia: University of Pennsylvania Press, 1972), pp. 99–105; Gladys Bryson, "The Emergence of Social Science from Moral Philosophy," *International Journal of Ethics* 42 (1932): 514–18; Carl W. Kaiser, Jr., *History of the Academic Protection–Free Trade Controversy in America before 1860* (Philadelphia: University of Pennsylvania Press, 1934), pp. 90–97; A. D. H. Kaplan, *Henry Charles Carey* (Baltimore: Johns Hopkins University Press, 1931).
3. Cheyney, *History of the University*, pp. 276–77; Charles J. Stille, *Reminiscences of a Provost, 1866–1880* (Philadelphia, 1880).
4. Joseph Wharton, "Is College Education Advantageous to a Business Man?", address before the Wharton School Association, February 20, 1890 (Philadelphia: Wharton School, 1890), p. 15; Joseph Wharton, "National Self-Protection," reprinted from *Atlantic Monthly*, September 1875 (Philadelphia: American Iron and Steel Association, 1875), p. 8; Wharton to the Trustees, Minutes of the University Trustees, March 1, 1881.
5. Richard Montgomery, "Robert Ellis Thompson: A Memoir," *Barnwell Bul-*

letin for Central High School of Philadelphia 12 (October 1934):15–29; James H. S. Bossard, "Robert Ellis Thompson: Pioneer Professor in Social Science," *American Journal of Sociology* 35 (1929):239–42; Joseph Wharton, "International Industrial Competition," *Penn Monthly Magazine* 1 (1870):476–93; Robert E. Thompson, *Social Science and National Economy* (Philadelphia: Porter and Coates, 1875), p. iii.

6. Thompson, *Social Science,* p. 50.

7. Ibid., pp. 50, 69, 70–129; Kaplan, *Henry C. Carey,* pp. 49–50. For the economics of Henry C. Carey, see Henry C. Carey, *Principles of Social Science,* 3 vols. (Philadelphia: Lippincott, 1858), and *The Past, the Present, the Future* (New York: Augustus Kelley, 1967); also see Conkin, *Prophets of Prosperity,* pp. vii–ix, 123–34, 261–305.

8. Adam Smith, *The Wealth of Nations* (New York: Modern Library, 1937), pp. 13, 16; Thompson, *Social Science,* pp. 12, 13, 19, 32ff., 232, 400–3; Kaplan, *Henry C. Carey,* p. 61.

9. Thompson, *Social Science,* pp. 40, 46–48, 234–35, 249.

10. Richard A. Swanson, "Edmund J. James, 1855–1925: A 'Conservative Progressive' in American Higher Education" (Ph.D. diss., University of Illinois, 1966), pp. 77–78; Donald Fleming, *William H. Welch and the Rise of Modern Medicine* (Boston: Little, Bown, 1954), p. 32; Frederick Rudolph, *The American College and University: A History* (New York: Knopf, 1962), pp. 264–86, 329–54; Cheyney, *History of the University,* p. 290; Minutes of the University Trustees, April 7, 1891; Minutes of the Wharton Faculty, November 12, 1887, November 19, 1887; Minutes of the University Trustees, January 5, 1886, February 2, 1886, December 6, 1887, February 7, 1888; Albert S. Bolles, *Practical Banking* (New York: Homans, 1884), p. v; E. Otis Kendall [Dean of the College Faculty], *First Annual Report of the Wharton School of Finance and Economy,* May 1, 1884, Wharton School File, Archives of the University of Pennsylvania (hereafter cited as Archives), pp. 2–4.

11. Swanson, "James," pp. 22–45; Daniel M. Fox, *The Discovery of Abundance: Simon N. Patten and the Transformation of Social Theory* (Ithaca, N.Y.: Cornell University Press, 1967), pp. 21–25; Edmund J. James, "Political Economy in German Universities," *Nation* 35 (1882):261–62; Brian Chapman, *The Profession of Government* (London: Allen and Unwin, 1959), pp. 23–24, 100; *University of Pennsylvania Catalog* (hereafter cited as *Catalog*), 1883–84, p. 31, and 1887–88, p. 62; Kendall, *First Annual Report,* p. 2; Edmund J. James, "The Science of Finance," *Cyclopedia of Political and Social Science,* 2:196–206, and "The Relationship of the Modern Municipality to the Gas Supply," *Publications of the American Economic Association* 1 (1886):p. 61; see William Roscher, "Roscher's Programme of 1843," trans. William J. Ashley, in William J. Ashley, *Surveys Historic and Economic* (London: Longman's, Green, 1900), pp. 33–34. Roscher was the founder of the German historical school of economics. See also Thomas L. Haskell, *The Emergence of Professional Social Science: The*

American Social Science Association and the Nineteenth Century Crisis of Authority (Urbana: University of Illinois Press, 1977), pp. 24–47, 234–56.

12. Edmund J. James and Simon N. Patten, "Society for the Study of National Economy," reprinted in Richard T. Ely, *Ground under Our Feet: An Autobiography* (New York: Macmillan, 1938), p. 297. Fox, *Discovery of Abundance*, pp. 37–39; Swanson, "James," pp. 95–99; Mary O. Furner, *Advocacy and Objectivity: A Crisis in the Professionalization of American Social Science, 1865–1905* (Lexington: University Press of Kentucky, 1975); Edmund J. James, *Instruction in Political and Social Science* (Philadelphia: Philadelphia Social Science Association, n.d. [1895?]).

13. James to Pepper, undated, Robert Ellis Thompson File, Archives; Edward Shils, "The Order of Learning in the United States from 1865 to 1920: The Ascendancy of the Universities," *Minerva* 16 (1978):186–87; Swanson, "James," pp. 90–94; Montgomery, "Thompson," p. 36; Thompson to Wharton, April 16, 1892, Thompson File; Elder to Wharton, May 23, 1892, Wharton School File; John R. Everett, *Religion in Economics* (New York: King's Crown Press, 1946), pp. 99–134; Rexford G. Tugwell, "Notes on the Life of Simon Nelson Patten," *Journal of Political Economy* 31 (1923):158–70; Fox, *Discovery of Abundance*, pp. 13–31, 36; Simon N. Patten, *The Premises of Political Economy* (Philadelphia: Lippincott, 1885).

14. Simon N. Patten, "The Educational Value of Political Economy," *Publications of the American Economic Association* 5 (1890):473, 474, 484, 486–87, 491, 494–95; *Catalog*, 1892–93, pp. 154–56; 1893–94, pp. 109–11; 1894–95, pp. 66–69; Rexford G. Tugwell, "To the Lesser Heights of Morningside," memoir, pp. 144, 144n. Tugwell's manuscript has been edited and published as *To the Lesser Heights of Morningside* (Philadelphia: University of Pennsylvania Press, 1982).

15. E. K. Hunt, "Simon Patten's Contribution to Economics," *Journal of Economic Issues* 4 (1970):40–48; James Boswell, *The Economics of Simon Nelson Patten* (Philadelphia: University of Pennsylvania Press, 1934), pp. 46–101; Fox, *Discovery of Abundance*, pp. 44ff.

16. Henry R. Seager—later a professor of economics at Columbia—recorded this summation (as quoted in Joseph Dorfman, *The Economic Mind in American Civilization* [New York: Viking Press, 1949], 3:183).

17. Simon N. Patten, *Economic Basis of Protection* (Philadelphia: J. B. Lippincott, 1890), pp. 127; see also 5–53, 66, 90–91, 123–33, 162–69.

18. Ibid.

19. Simon N. Patten, "The Formulation of Normal Laws," *Annals of the American Academy of Political and Social Science* (1896):426–34; Patten, "Educational Value," pp. 481, 496–97; Simon N. Patten, *The Development of English Thought: A Study in the Economic Interpretation of History* (New York: Macmillan, 1899), p. 407. See Talcott Parsons, *The Structure of Social Action* (New York: McGraw-Hill, 1937), and Joseph Schumpeter, *The Theory of Economic Development* (Cambridge, Mass.: Harvard University Press, 1934 [1911]).

20. Patten, "Normal Laws," pp. 434–49, and *English Thought*, pp. 1–31; Fox, *Discovery of Abundance*, pp. 71–72.

21. *English Thought*, pp. 118, 122, 123–24, 134–42; Patten, "Normal Laws," p. 435.

22. Patten, *English Thought*, pp. 142–263; Boswell, *Economics of Patten*, pp. 46–48; Everett, *Religion in Economics*, pp. 111–12.

23. Simon N. Patten, "The Making of Economic Literature," in *Essays in Economic Theory by Simon Nelson Patten*, ed. Rexford G. Tugwell (New York: Knopf, 1924 [1909]), pp. 244, 247; Everett, *Religion in Economics*, pp. 108–9; Fox, *Discovery of Abundance*, pp. 51, 63–65, 71–72, 83–85, 94–103; Boswell, *Economics of Patten*, pp. 125–27.

24. Minutes of the Wharton Faculty, October 9, 1895; Roswell C. McCrea, "The Wharton School," *Alumni Register* 17 (1915): 294–95, 298; Emory R. Johnson, *The Wharton School: Its First Fifty Years, 1881–1931* (Philadelphia: University of Pennsylvania Press, 1931), p. 20; Cheyney, *History of the University*, pp. 299, 337–39.

25. See Sass, *Pragmatic Imagination*, pp. 105–16. Also see Tugwell, *To the Lesser Heights*, pp. 3–70.

26. Patten, "Economic Literature," p. 245; Simon N. Patten, "University Training for Business Men," *Educational Review* 29 (1905): 232; Patten, "Economic Literature," p. 244; Scott Nearing, *Educational Frontiers: A Book about Simon Nelson Patten and Other Teachers* (New York: Seltzer, 1925), pp. 16–17; Leo S. Rowe, "University and Collegiate Research in Municipal Government," *Proceedings of the Chicago Conference for Good City Government* (Philadelphia: National Municipal League, 1904), pp. 242–43, 247; Edwin O. Lewis, "College Men in Philadelphia Politics, from a City Party Point of View," *Red and Blue* 19 (January 1907): 2–7; Lloyd M. Abernathy, "The Insurgency in Philadelphia, 1905," *Pennsylvania Magazine of History and Biography* 87 (1963): 3–20; Scott Nearing, *The Making of a Radical* (New York: Harper and Row, 1972), pp. 56–58; Lightner Witmer, *The Nearing Case* (New York: Huebsch, 1915), pp. 113–17; Morris L. Cooke, *Our Cities Awake* (New York: Doubleday, Page, 1919), pp. 150–57, 174; Tugwell, "To the Lesser Heights," pp. 67–68; Clyde King, "Municipal Markets," *Annals of the American Academy of Political and Social Science* 50 (1913): 102–17; Donald W. Disbrow, "Reform in Philadelphia under Mayor Blankenburg," *Pennsylvania History* 27 (1960): 386; Jeffrey S. Feld, "The Whartonians: An Examination of the Relationship between Philadelphia Municipal Reform and Professors of the Wharton School, 1906–1916" (senior thesis, Department of History, University of Pennsylvania, 1980), pp. 87–88, table 5-2.

27. For the organizing success of American business and its new concern for "scientific management," see Alfred D. Chandler, Jr., *The Visible Hand* (Cambridge, Mass.: Harvard University Press, 1977).

28. Witmer, *Nearing Case*, p. 84 (for Rosengarten quotation); ibid., passim; Nearing, *Educational Frontiers*, pp. 45–48, 78–79; Minutes of the Whar-

ton Faculty, October 22, 1915; Tugwell, *To the Lesser Heights,* pp. 66–70; also see Sass, *Pragmatic Imagination,* pp. 121–24.

29. Resolutions of the University of Pennsylvania Board of Trustees, October 14, 1915, in Edward Robins (secretary of the university) to Roswell McCrea, October 12, 1915, Minutes of the Wharton Faculty, October 22, 1915; Witmer, *Nearing Case,* pp. 3, 31, 75, 84; Nearing, *Making of a Radical,* pp. 83ff., 87; Witmer, *Nearing Case,* pp. 1–14, 32–36; Nearing, *Educational Frontiers,* p. 13; Feld, "Whartonians," p. 96; Tugwell, "To the Lesser Heights," p. 243; Fox, *Discovery of Abundance,* p. 126.

30. See Furner, *Advocacy and Objectivity.*

CHAPTER 10   UNIVERSITY OF CHICAGO

1. Enrollment figures at this time were as follows: Columbia, 6,232; Harvard, 5,558; Chicago, 5,487. Three other institutions then had student populations in excess of 5,000: Michigan, 5,259; Pennsylvania, 5,033; and Cornell, 5,028. Laurence R. Veysey, *The Emergence of the American University* (Chicago: University of Chicago Press, 1965), p. 339.

2. Historical background on the early years of the University of Chicago is drawn from Richard J. Storr, *Harper's University: The Beginnings* (Chicago: University of Chicago Press, 1966), and from Thomas Wakefield Goodspeed, *A History of the University of Chicago Founded by John D. Rockefeller: The First Quarter Century* (Chicago: University of Chicago Press, 1916).

3. *The University of Chicago: Official Bulletin,* no. 1 (January 1891), pp. 7–8.

4. Ibid., p. 11.

5. Particularly notable in this group were Albion Small, head professor of sociology (formerly president of Colby College), and Thomas Chamberlin, head professor of geology (formerly president of the University of Wisconsin).

6. G. Stanley Hall, president of Clark University, reacted bitterly to this transaction, commenting that Harper's action "was like that of an eagle who robbed the fish-hawk of his prey." Hall also threatened "to make a formal appeal to the public and to Mr. Rockefeller himself to see if this trust magnate (who was . . . at the height of his unpopularity and censure, and who was said to have driven many smaller competing firms out of existence by slow strangling methods of competition) would justify such an assassination of an institution as had . . . been attempted here"; as quoted in Joseph Dorfman, *Thorstein Veblen and His America* (2nd printing, New York: Viking Press, 1935), p. 91.

7. For details of Ely's circumstances at this time, see Chapter 8, herein.

8. Ely to Harper, November 15, 1890, Presidents' Papers, University of Chicago Archives. Shaw, the editor of the *Review of Reviews,* had rejected many invitations from universities, but Ely believed that he could be drawn to Chicago "if we could offer sufficient inducements." Warner was then teching at the University of Nebraska and was regarded as a prospect for the

United States Senate. With respect to Warner, Ely observed: "He is still a young man, and would soon gain a foothold in Illinois such as he now has in Nebraska. It would be a fine thing for the University of Chicago to have a professor in the United States Senate."

9. Ely to Harper, March 6, 1891, Presidents' Papers.

10. Ibid.

11. Ibid.

12. Harper to Ely, March 20, 1891, Ely Papers; as quoted in Clair Edward Morris, Jr., "J. Laurence Laughlin: An Economist and His Profession" (Ph.D. diss., University of Wisconsin, 1972), p. 35.

13. Ely to Gilman, March 13, 1891, Gilman Collection, Special Collections, Milton S. Eisenhower Library, Johns Hopkins University.

14. Ely, Ground under Our Feet (New York: Macmillan, 1938), p. 175.

15. Morris, "J. Laurence Laughlin," pp. 28–30.

16. Laughlin, in fact, stayed outside the American Economic Association until 1904. By that time its membership and orientation had changed considerably.

17. Ely to Harper, March 6, 1891, Presidents' Papers.

18. Cf. Chapter 5, herein, for a discussion of Laughlin's experience at Harvard. Additional biographical details are contained in Alfred Bornemann, J. Laurence Laughlin: Chapters in the Career of an Economist (Washington, D.C.: American Council on Public Affairs, 1940).

19. Bemis to Harper, February 21, 1892, William Rainey Harper Papers, University of Chicago Archives.

20. Bemis to Harper, February 19, 1892, Harper Papers.

21. Bemis explained his position to Laughlin as follows: "As to my economics position, i.e., my opinions and their expression, which I would necessarily have to retain wherever I taught save as my views change, I suppose I believe in a somewhat more active governmental policy than do you. . . . Into my U'v's'ty Extension work I try to throw the same enthusiasm as did Toynbee, whom I don't claim to rival but whose economic views I much admire, though I fully agree with recent writers like Marshall in seeing less difference than was supposed a few years ago between the so-called orthodoxy and the historical school"; Bemis to Laughlin, February 27, 1892 (copy), Harper Papers.

22. Small to Bemis, March 31, 1892, Harper Papers.

23. University Register, 1892–93, p. 40.

24. Arrangements for the production of the Journal of Political Economy were set in motion in March 1892 when the trustees appropriated $1,000 from a fund for incidental expenses "for the support of a journal in the department of Political Economy during the first University school year"; Minutes of the Board of Trustees, March 17, 1892, University of Chicago Archives.

25. J. Laurence Laughlin, "The Study of Political Economy in the United States," Journal of Political Economy, December 1892, p. 2.

26. Ibid., p. 19.

27. Laughlin to Harper, August 31, 1893, Presidents' Papers.

28. Storr, *Harper's University*, p. 84.

29. The Minutes of the Board of Trustees, April 3, 1984, contain the following entry: "That in case Asso. Prof. Bemis remains connected with the University during the year beginning July 1, 1894 he shall be transferred from the Department of Political Economy to the Department of Social Science [i.e., Sociology]."

30. Laughlin to Harper, February 21, 1894, Presidents' Papers.

31. Laughlin to Harper, August 6, 1894, Presidents' Papers.

32. Remarks by Bemis, reported in the *Chicago Times*, July 16, 1894; as quoted in Morris, "J. Laurence Laughlin," p. 64.

33. Bemis quoted Harper to this effect in a letter to Ely, August 13, 1894; as quoted in Morris, "J. Laurence Laughlin," p. 68.

34. Laughlin to Harper, August 6, 1894, Presidents' Papers.

35. Morris, "J. Laurence Laughlin," p. 76.

36. For details of this episode, see Chapter 13, herein.

37. Word of such a statement by Ely had come to the attention of Laughlin, who asked Harper whether it was true that Ely "was offered the position I now hold"; Laughlin to Harper, August 6, 1894, Presidents' Papers.

38. The correspondence documenting this scheme is reported in Morris, "J. Laurence Laughlin," pp. 81–83.

39. Ely to Harper, August 17, 1895, Presidents' Papers.

40. Ely to Harper, September 7, 1895, Presidents' Papers.

41. As quoted in Morris, "J. Laurence Laughlin," p. 96.

42. *American Journal of Sociology* 1 (1895–96):210.

43. Thereafter, Bemis held only one academic post—as a professor of economics at the Kansas State Agricultural College from 1896 to 1899. His views recommended him for an appointment there when the Democrats and Populists won control of the state government in 1896, but he was dismissed when the Republicans returned to power in 1899. Subsequently, he joined with John R. Commons in a short-lived attempt to establish a Bureau of Economic Research in New York designed to investigate topical issues from a "non-partisan but progressive viewpoint." From 1901 to 1909 he served a reform mayor in Cleveland as superintendent of the city's Water Department. He later found employment as a member of an advisory board to the Interstate Commerce Commission. Joseph Dorfman, *The Economic Mind in American Civilization* (New York: Viking Press, 1949), 3:288–89, and Richard Hofstadter and Walter P. Metzger, *The Development of Academic Freedom in the United States* (New York: Columbia University Press, 1955), p. 435.

44. See *The Decennial Publications of the University of Chicago: Publications of the Members of the University* (Chicago: University of Chicago Press, 1904).

45. Announcements for 1895–96 in the University Register, 1894–95.

46. *The President's Report, 1892–1902*, pp. 144–45.

47. Ibid., p. 28.

48. Maffeo Pantaleoni of the University of Naples was scheduled to teach during the summer quarter, 1896, though he did not, in fact, arrive. Visitors who did carry out their engagements included Bernard Moses (University of California), Henry C. Adams (University of Michigan), and Stephen Bauer (an economist from Austria who taught "Colonial Economics" during the summer quarter, 1899).

49. Mitchell had entered Chicago as a freshman in the opening class, earned a B.A. in 1896 and a Ph.D. in 1899. His doctoral dissertation, inspired by Laughlin, was the basis of his first book, *A History of the Greenbacks*, published in 1903.

50. Mitchell's impressions of his Chicago teachers are described in Lucy Sprague Mitchell, *Two Lives: The Story of Wesley Clair Mitchell and Myself* (New York: Simon and Schuster, 1953), esp. pp. 85–86.

51. Though Laughlin entered the debate with Harvey with enthusiasm, he did not initiate it. In *Coin's Financial School*, Harvey had written about an imaginary exchange with a "Professor Laughlin" in which "Professor Laughlin" had come out second-best. Laughlin could thus legitimately hold that it was incumbent upon him to set the record straight.

52. These essays—entitled "The Price of Wheat since 1867" and "The Food Supply and Price of Wheat"—represented the first and only work by Veblen involving the manipulation of quantitative data.

53. University Register, 1902–3.

54. Included among the early contributors were American economists of the prominence of Arthur T. Hadley, E. R. A. Seligman, Simon Newcomb, E. Benjamin Andrews, and David Kinley. Major foreign economists whose work was published were Vilfredo Pareto, Gustav Cohn, and F. Wieser.

55. Laughlin, for example, had led the charge against Harper's plan (which came to naught) to bring E. Benjamin Andrews, the president of Brown, to the University of Chicago as a copresident. Laughlin reproved Harper for bypassing the university senate in the discussion of this organizational issue and for acting "consciously or unconsciously, on the Napoleonic Plan." (Laughlin, January 8, 1894, Presidents' Papers.) Laughlin, however, could not block Harper's decision to appoint Edmund Janes James to the Extension Division at the time of Bemis's departure. Nor, despite his vigorous objection, could he later prevent James from organizing a course of lectures "on modern social and economic problems" involving lecturers from other universities. Laughlin took vigorous exception to this enterprise—which involved Edward A. Ross (an Elyite who had recently been dismissed from Stanford University). In a letter of protest to Harper, he wrote: "We are laying up difficulties for ourselves in the future. . . . [A]s in the case of Bemis, I object to certain persons being chosen by the Extension D'p't to go over the country, and make an exposition of economics which is certain to prejudice the scientific quality of our work here." (Laughlin to Harper, December 3, 1901, Presidents' Papers.) Harper brushed Laughlin off, indicating that the inclusion of the word "economic" in the description of the lectures was probably a mistake; their content was really more in the do-

main of sociology. (Harper to Laughlin, December 5, 1901, Presidents' Papers.)

56. Laughlin, Draft Statement of Aims of a College of Commerce and Politics, 1898–99, Presidents' Papers.

57. Storr, *Harper's University*, p. 305.

58. Miller, of course, had been on the original team. Mitchell (following a post-Ph.D. year with the Census Bureau in Washington) had returned to the university to serve as an instructor in political economy.

59. Harper to Laughlin, August 15, 1902, Presidents' Papers.

60. Laughlin to Harper, August 23, 1902, Presidents' Papers.

61. Ibid.

62. Ibid.

63. Course Announcements for 1903–4, contained in the University Register, 1902–3.

64. Course Announcements for 1904–5, University Register, 1903–4.

65. Laughlin, Report on the Department of Political Economy, in *The President's Report, July, 1904–July, 1905*, p. 115.

66. Ibid.

67. These gestures of reconciliation, as Coats has noted, "dispelled the fear that Laughlin might use his considerable influence . . . to spread distrust and hostility towards the Association" and "enabled the economists to present a united front in their efforts to enhance the public prestige and influence of their professional discipline." A. W. Coats, "The First Two Decades of the American Economic Association," *American Economic Review* 50 (September 1960): 572.

68. Veblen's translation of *The Science of Finance* from Gustav Cohn's German text was the pioneering volume in the department's publication series entitled Economic Studies of the University of Chicago.

69. Veblen did not endear himself to Harper during his first year at Chicago when he abandoned in midstream an assignment to prepare a correspondence course in political economy. When withdrawing from this project, Veblen told Harper that the terms of payment were inadequate. Veblen to Harper, July 27, 1893, Presidents' Papers.

70. Veblen's biographer has described the techniques he used to minimize enrollments in his courses: e.g., his casualness about examining and grading, his haphazard organization that frustrated students who were accustomed to taking well-organized notes. Dorfman, *Veblen*, esp. pp. 119–20, 247–49. Dorfman's suggestion that Veblen routinely assigned the grade of C to all his students needs to be qualified. In the academic year 1904–5, for example, the records of the university registrar reveal the following about Veblen's courses: "Autumn Quarter: History of Political Economy: 5 students (3 'B's,' 2 'C's'); Organization of Business—Trusts: 6 students (1 'A,' 3 'B's,' 2 'C's'). Spring Quarter: Economic Factors in Civilization: 3 students: (1 'B,' 2 'C's,'); Socialism: 13 students (3 'A's,' 6 'B's,' 3 'C's,' 1 'incomplete')."

71. Dorfman, *Veblen*, p. 174.

72. Minutes of the Board of Trustees, February 20, 1900.
73. In the preface, Veblen referred to Chicago's first president as the "Great Pioneer" and as the "Strong Man." Veblen, *The Higher Learning in America* (rp., New York: Augustus Kelley, 1965), p. vi.
74. Ibid., pp. 116–18 et passim.
75. It is noteworthy that the issues Veblen raised in *The Higher Learning in America* continue to generate lively discussion among commentators on American education. See, e.g., Hofstadter and Metzger, *Development of Academic Freedom;* Veysey, *Emergence of the University;* and Frederick Rudolph, *The American College and University: A History* (New York: Knopf, 1962).
76. See, e.g., H. Laurence Miller, Jr., "On the 'Chicago School of Economics,'" George J. Stigler, "Comment," and Martin Bronfenbrenner, "Observations on the 'Chicago School(s),'" *Journal of Political Economy,* February 1962; A. W. Coats, "The Origins of the 'Chicago School(s),'" *Journal of Political Economy,* October 1963; and Warren J. Samuels, ed., *The Chicago School of Political Economy* (East Lansing: Michigan State University Press, 1976).

CHAPTER 11   UNIVERSITY OF CALIFORNIA AND STANFORD

1. Robert Glass Cleland, *From Wilderness to Empire* (New York: Knopf, 1970), chap. 3.
2. It was not until 1866 that an elementary education was available to most white California children. School was not compulsory until 1874. Walton Bean, *California: An Interpretive History* (New York: McGraw-Hill, 1968), pp. 158–59.
3. Ibid.
4. The College of California, founded in 1860, was disbanded in 1868, and its buildings were deeded to the new state university. Some of its faculty members were hired by the regents to teach at the University of California.
5. Material for this account of the early years of the University of California is drawn primarily from Fabian Franklin, *The Life of Daniel Coit Gilman* (New York: Dodd, Mead, 1910), esp. pp. 110–81.
6. For background on Gilman's early career, see Chapter 6, herein.
7. As quoted in Franklin, *Life of Gilman,* p. 146.
8. Ibid., p. 155.
9. Ibid., p. 178. See also Verne A. Stadtman, *The University of California, 1861–1968* (New York: McGraw Hill, 1970), pp. 70–80.
10. For an account of Gilman's work in building this institution, see Chapter 8, herein.
11. Franklin, *Life of Gilman,* pp. 129, 136. Gilman was certainly no stranger to these materials. He had offered similar lines of instruction while at Yale's Sheffield Scientific School. In one of his despairing moments about the drift

of affairs at Berkeley, he had entertained the thought of resigning in order to found a monthly magazine "to be devoted to the discussion of modern social problems." As he informed Andrew D. White, his long-standing friend who was then president of Cornell: "Such work as Walker is doing for the U.S. Census could be expanded and multiplied indefinitely. History and political economy might be treated on a scientific basis." Gilman to White, April 5, 1874, as quoted in *Life of Gilman,* p. 156.

12. As quoted in Orrin L. Elliott, *Stanford University: The First Twenty-Five Years* (Stanford, Calif.: Stanford University Press, 1937), p. 80. The alumnus was Charles Howard Shinn.

13. Leland, Jr., was the Stanfords' only child after eighteen years of marriage.

14. Stadtman, *University of California,* p. 95.

15. Ibid.

16. G. T. Clark, *Leland Stanford* (Stanford, Calif.: Stanford University Press, 1931); Elliott, *Stanford University.*

17. As quoted in Elliott, *Stanford University,* p. 19.

18. For a description of Stanford's movement back and forth between wanting to help the common man and wanting to buy the prestige of aristocratic eastern institutions, see Kevin Starr, *Americans and the Californian Dream, 1850–1915* (New York: Oxford University Press, 1973), chap. 10.

19. For Andrew White's description of Jordan to Stanford, see Elliott, *Stanford University,* p. 40.

20. David Starr Jordan, *The Voice of the Scholar,* as quoted in Laurence R. Veysey, *The Emergence of the American University* (Chicago: University of Chicago Press, 1965), p. 61.

21. Veysey, *Emergence of the University,* pp. 61, 80, 107. Jordan was trained as an ichthyologist.

22. Starr, *Americans,* p. 308.

23. Millicent W. Shinn, "The University of California," *Overland Monthly* 20 (October 1892):85. California had seven presidents between 1868 and 1891.

24. Bernard Moses, "Notes toward an Autobiography," University Archives, Bancroft Library, University of California, Berkeley, p. 97.

25. Charles Albro Barker, *Henry George* (New York: Oxford University Press, 1955), pp. 240–43.

26. Wesley C. Mitchell, *Types of Economic Theory: From Mercantilism to Institutionalism,* ed. Joseph Dorfman (New York: Kelley, 1964), p. 230.

27. Ira B. Cross and Malcolm M. Davisson, "Economics," in Verne A. Stadtman et. al., *The Centennial Record of the University of California* (Berkeley: University of California Press, 1967), p. 84.

28. Moses, "Social Science and Its Method," *Berkeley Quarterly: A Journal of Social Science,* January 1880, p. 10.

29. This evaluation was reported by Shinn, "University of California," p. 361. Shinn was the first woman to receive a Ph.D.—in 1897—from California.

30. Six articles by Moses appeared in the *Journal of Political Economy* and

the *Quarterly Journal of Economics* in the 1890s. In addition, he was invited to teach political economy in summer sessions at the University of Chicago. In 1899 he was appointed a member of the Philippines Commission by President William McKinley and was active in the organization of the educational system there.

31. Joseph Dorfman, *The Economic Mind in American Civilization* (New York: Viking Press, 1949), 3:98.

32. Henry Hatfield, "Jessica Blanche Peixotto," in *Essays in Social Economics in Honor of Jessica Blanche Peixotto* (Berkeley: University of California Press, 1935).

33. University of California *Register,* 1890, University Archives, Bancroft Library, Berkeley.

34. Carl C. Plehn, "The Progress of Economics during the Last Thirty-five Years," Eleventh Annual Faculty Research Lecture, March 21, 1924, Bancroft Library, Berkeley.

35. As quoted in William Warren Ferrier, *Origin and Development of the University of California* (Berkeley: The Sather Gate Book Shop, 1930), p. 446.

36. Assistant Professor Carl C. Plehn, Outline for Introduction to Political Economy, Plehn Papers, Bancroft Library, ca. 1902.

37. For the reactions of Laughlin and of William Rainey Harper, Chicago's president, to the exodus of Miller and Mitchell, see Chapter 10, herein.

38. Joseph Dorfman, "The Background of Institutional Economics," in Dorfman et. al., *Institutional Economics: Veblen, Commons, and Mitchell Reconsidered* (Berkeley: University of California Press, 1963), p. 6.

39. Wesley C. Mitchell, *Business Cycles* (Berkeley: University of California Press, 1913).

40. Joseph Dorfman, "Wesley C. Mitchell," *The National Cyclopedia of American Biography* (New York: James T. White, 1958).

41. M. E. Cookingham, "Economists and Social Reform: Berkeley, 1906–1961," *History of Political Economy,* 19 (Spring, 1987), 47–65.

42. Delmar Gross Cooke, "An American Idyll," *University of California Chronicle* 22 (1920):99–100.

43. Cross named one of his sons Carleton Parker Cross.

44. His writings included "The California Casual and His Revolt," *Quarterly Journal of Economics,* November 1915, and *The Casual Laborer and Other Essays* (1920).

45. Over the course of his career, he mediated thirty-two strikes, served on two arbitration boards, and conducted three cost-of-living studies for the government. See Cornelia Stratton Parker, *An American Idyll: The Life of Carleton H. Parker* (Boston: Atlantic Monthly Press, 1923).

46. Wheeler, however, fought hard to keep his rising stars at Berkeley. In the academic year 1908–9, Mitchell was being wooed by Laughlin to return to Chicago. Wheeler matched Chicago's salary offer and topped it in status. Mitchell was advanced to the rank of full professor at the University of California at the age of thirty-five. Lucy Sprague Mitchell, *Two Lives: The Story*

of Wesley Clair Mitchell and Myself (New York: Simon and Schuster, 1953), pp. 161, 173–75.

47. Veysey, *Emergence of the University*, p. 406.
48. Jordan to Jane Stanford, quoted in Elliott, *Stanford University*, p. 52.
49. Elliott, *Stanford University*, pp. 61–62.
50. Anna Haddow, *Political Science in American Colleges and Universities, 1636–1900* (New York: Appleton-Century, 1939), p. 220.
51. Elliott later authored the official history of Stanford's early years.
52. Stanford University *Register*, 1892–93, Stanford University Archives.
53. In "Some Experiments on Behalf of the Unemployed," *Quarterly Journal of Economics*, October 1890, pp. 1–23, and *American Charities*, Warner presented his analysis of workhouses in Europe as a means of dealing with poverty and proposed some socioeconomic projects that still needed to be carried out.
54. Elliott, *Stanford University*, p. 117.
55. Jordan quotation, ibid., p. 331.
56. Stanford University *Register*, 1893–94, p. 74.
57. Stanford University *Register*, 1896–97, p. 86.
58. Ross had previously annoyed Mrs. Stanford with his vocal support for Eugene Debs in the Pullman strike in 1894.
59. Elliott, *Stanford University*, p. 338.
60. Julian Weinberg, *Edward Alsworth Ross and the Sociology of Progressivism*, (Madison: University of Wisconsin Press, 1972), pp. 39–40.
61. Ibid., p. 340.
62. Jane Stanford to Jordan, May 9, 1900, as quoted in Jane Lathrop Stanford, Address on the Right of Free Speech to the Board of Trustees of the Leland Stanford Junior University, April 23, 1903, Stanford University, 1903, pp. 9–10.
63. Elliott, *Stanford University*, pp. 347–53.
64. For further discussion of this episode, see Veysey, *Emergence of the University*, pp. 397–412; Edward Alsworth Ross, *Seventy Years of It: An Autobiography* (New York: Appleton-Century, 1936), pp. 64–86.
65. The railroad was also known for seeking special treatment from communities such as Los Angeles by threatening to bypass them.
66. Cleland, *Wilderness to Empire*, p. 175.
67. James C. Mohr, "Academic Turmoil and Public Opinion: The Ross Case at Stanford," *California Historical Review*, 1970, pp. 55–60; Mary O. Furner, *Advocacy and Objectivity: A Crisis in the Professionalization of American Social Science, 1865–1905* (Lexington: University Press of Kentucky, 1975), pp. 229–59.
68. Jordan to Fetter, May 26, 1900, Fetter Manuscripts, Lilly Library, Indiana University.
69. Jordan to Fetter, November 16, 1900, Fetter Manuscripts.
70. Warren Samuels, "The Resignation of Frank A. Fetter from Stanford University," *History of Economics Society Bulletin*, Winter 1985, pp. 16–25.

71. Fetter to Jordan, December 20, 1900, Fetter Manuscripts.

72. Fetter to Jordan, January 29, 1901, Fetter Manuscripts.

73. Jordan to Fetter, February 5, 1901, Fetter Manuscripts.

74. "Dr. Fetter Will Leave Stanford," *San Francisco Chronicle,* March 20, 1901.

75. It is interesting to note that Jordan makes no mention of the "Ross incident" in his autobiography, *The Days of a Man.*

76. Furner, *Advocacy and Objectivity,* p. 254.

77. Cross studied at Wisconsin under both Ely and Commons. Ira Cross, "Portrait of an Economics Professor," Oral History, Bancroft Library, Berkeley, p. 13.

78. Young to Jordan, April 14, 1906, Presidential Papers, Stanford University Archives, Green Library, Stanford University.

79. For details of Veblen's circumstances at this time, see Chapter 10, herein.

80. Veblen to Jordan, April 9, 1906, Presidential Papers.

81. Veblen to Jordan, April 16, 1906, Presidential Papers.

82. Joseph Dorfman, *Thorstein Veblen and His America* (New York: Viking Press, 1966), p. 268; Fourth Annual Report of the President of the University, 1907, p. 34.

83. Dorfman, *Veblen,* p. 269.

84. Cross was one of Veblen's teaching assistants, and Duffus was a housekeeper for him. Cross, "Portrait"; R. L. Duffus, *The Innocents at Cedro* (New York: Macmillan, 1944).

85. Cross, "Portrait," p. 20.

86. Dorfman, *Veblen,* p. 254, and correspondence between Jordan and Mrs. Veblen in 1909, Stanford University Archives.

87. Jordan to Henry P. Judson, October 6, 1909, Presidents' Papers, University of Chicago Archives.

88. Veblen subsequently found academic employment at the University of Missouri and at the New School for Social Research in New York.

89. Young later taught at Cornell and at Harvard and became the first American to hold a professorial chair in Britain when he went to the London School of Economics in 1927.

90. Charles P. Blitch, "Allyn A. Young: A Curious Case of Professional Neglect," *History of Political Economy* 15 (Spring 1983), p. 4.

91. Cross, "Portrait," p. 14.

92. Cookingham, "Economists and Social Reform."

CHAPTER 12   MASSACHUSETTS INSTITUTE OF TECHNOLOGY

1. William Barton Rogers, "A Plan for a Polytechnic School in Boston" (1846), reprinted in Samuel C. Prescott, *When M.I.T. Was "Boston Tech": 1861–1916* (Cambridge, Mass.: Technology Press, 1954), pp. 335, 336.

2. Prescott, *When MIT Was Boston Tech,* pp. 7–8.

3. Ibid., pp. 15–16.

4. Ibid., p. 22.

5. James Phinney Munroe, *A Life of Francis Amasa Walker* (New York: Holt, 1923), p. 211.

6. Ibid., p. 213.

7. Prescott, *When MIT Was Boston Tech*, pp. 27–32.

8. Ibid., pp. 32–45. See also Munroe, *Life of Walker*, pp. 211–13.

9. Prescott, *When MIT Was Boston Tech*, pp. 50–51.

10. *Catalogue of the Massachusetts Institute of Technology, 1865–66*, p. 2.

11. "Course XXI: A History," in Travis R. Merritt, ed., *Course XXI Survey and Register, 1958–1983*, (Cambridge, Mass.: Humanities Undergraduate Office, MIT, 1984), pp. 10–11.

12. Although the Institute's early planning documents made no reference to the training of women, Eliot had from the outset welcomed several to his evening classes in chemical practice. Early in 1867, one of these students sought permission to attend regular day classes in chemistry, and her letter was sent by the Committee on Instruction to Rogers with the query, "Can there be any objection to ladies entering as special students except possibly want of room in the laboratory?" There being none, the president promptly announced a plan for special instruction in afternoon and evening classes for students unable to attend day classes and made clear that when it was organized the faculty would gladly receive both men and women as students. The first woman admitted was the estimable Ellen H. Swallow, a graduate of Vassar, who became a special student in chemistry in 1871. Within two years, she had completed all the requirements for the institute's S.B. degree and became the school's first woman graduate in 1873. Three years later, Swallow (now Mrs. Robert H. Richards) was appointed director of the new Women's Laboratory at MIT, an institutional home for more than a hundred special students in chemistry, mineralogy, and natural history, some of whom later received the regular bachelor's degree. The laboratory's success was such that it was abolished in 1883 in favor of the regular admission of qualified women to all of the Institute's instructional programs on the same basis as men. For her part, Ellen Richards taught chemistry at the Institute continuously from 1873 until her death in 1911. Prescott, *When MIT Was Boston Tech*, pp. 53–55, 99.

13. The institute's own rather idiosyncratic system of classification will be used throughout the remainder of this essay: the term "subject" refers to a single, semester-long course in a specific area, and the proper noun "Course" is reserved for a major program or field of concentration in a particular discipline. Thus, for example, students enrolled in the Course in Physics would be expected to take individual subjects in mechanics and calculus.

14. *Catalogue, 1865–66*, p. 3.

15. "Course XXI: A History," pp. 8–9, 11.

16. By 1876 nine of the Institute's 170 graduates to date had taken their degrees in Course IX. *President's Report for the Year Ending September 30, 1876, Massachusetts Institute of Technology*, p. vi.

17. H. C. Spaulding, "William Parsons Atkinson: A Student's Tribute," *Technique* (the MIT student yearbook), 1892, p. 78.

18. *Catalogue, 1873–74.*

19. *President's Report for 1872,* pp. 82–83.

20. *President's Report for 1873,* p. 9. Howison's own commitment to a scientific rather than normative conception of political economy is suggested by the first of the questions he composed for that year's examination in the subject: "Show how the action of the three elements—Desire, Labor, and Wealth—renders the realm of Political Economy an ever expanding one, and how it is that they render Political Economy a *positive* science" (ibid.; italics in original).

21. Political economy, he wrote in 1877, "is another of those studies, some knowledge of which is a necessary foundation to all profitable reading of History, and it seems almost an absurdity that in a practical school like ours some attention to this, one of the most important of all practical subjects, should not be required of all students." *President's Report for 1877,* p. 38.

22. Prescott, *When MIT Was Boston Tech,* p. 101.

23. Ibid., pp. 69–70.

24. Ibid., p. 72.

25. Ibid., p. 79.

26. Ibid., p. 90.

27. Ibid., pp. 101–2.

28. Munroe, *Life of Walker,* pp. 225–26.

29. Ibid., p. 382.

30. Prescott, *When MIT Was Boston Tech,* pp. 108–11.

31. Bernard Newton, *The Economics of Francis Amasa Walker: American Economics in Transition* (New York: Augustus Kelley, 1968), pp. 2, 5–7; Munroe, *Life of Walker,* pp. 101–9.

32. Newton, *Economics of Walker,* p. 20.

33. Ibid., pp. 137–41; Joseph Dorfman, *The Economic Mind in American Civilization* 3 : 102. (New York: Viking Press, 1949).

34. Munroe, *Life of Walker,* p. 140; see also Chapter 6, herein.

35. Munroe, *Life of Walker,* p. 150.

36. Quoted in Newton, *Economics of Walker,* p. 23.

37. Dorfman, *Economic Mind,* p. 102.

38. Prescott, *When MIT Was Boston Tech,* pp. 112–13.

39. Newton, *Economics of Walker,* p. 45; Dorfman, *Economic Mind,* p. 108.

40. T. W. Hutchison, *A Review of Economic Doctrines, 1870–1929* (Oxford: Clarendon Press, 1953), p. 320.

41. Francis A. Walker, *Political Economy,* 2nd ed. (New York: Holt, 1884), p. 228.

42. Newton, *Economics of Walker,* p. 154.

43. Munroe, *Life of Walker,* pp. 146–47.

44. See Chapter 6, herein.

45. Munroe, *Life of Walker,* pp. 205–9, 216–18.

46. By 1894 Walker could proudly write: "It has been stated that not less than one hundred colleges and universities in the United States are to-day offering a technical instruction. There is now not a state in the Union without an institution in which more or less of a course in engineering is laid out. Some of these are classical institutions of long standing and high repute, which are as rapidly as possible transforming themselves to meet the wants of the age. If, indeed, 'imitation is the sincerest form of flattery,' those who originated the earlier schools of science and technology have reason to pray that their heads may not be turned, as one classical college after another throws overboard studies and exercises which thirty years ago were declared to be absolutely essential to mental discipline and culture, without which no one could become a thoroughly educated and cultivated man, to make room for studies and exercises which, even down to recent days, have been stigmatized as interested, mercenary, and of a base flavor. Certainly [those who] supported President Rogers and Dr. Jacob Bigelow in the demand for an educational system better adapted to the wants of modern life than the mediaeval and monastic culture then alone offered to the aspiring student, have reason to rejoice that the battle of the New Education is won." *President's Report for 1894*, p. 7.

47. *President's Report for 1883*, pp. 21–24.

48. Prescott, *When MIT Was Boston Tech*, pp. 113–50; Munroe, *Life of Walker*, pp. 218–49.

49. *Catalogue, 1881–82*, p. 7.

50. On Walker's attitudes toward entrepreneurship, see Newton, *Economics of Walker*, pp. 32–37, 163–64. As individuals operating successfully in the practical world of commerce and industry, the Institute's graduates participated directly and effectively in the organizational revolution of their day. True to Rogers's vision, the vast majority of them held engineering positions that brought them into close contact with the managerial side of their enterprises, and a sizable proportion of these became entrepreneurs or business administrators themselves, including Alfred P. Sloan, Gerard Swope, and Roger Babson. Inclined by their training to think in terms of clearly defined objectives and sensitive to material and economic constraints, they turned their analytic powers not just to designing bridges or machines but, where the occasion arose, to designing and constructing the companies that would build them, too. For them, as for many other thoughtful but practically oriented minds of the period, the appropriate metaphor for the corporation was mechanical, a machine whose operation reflects the purposes of its human designer and whose parts are constrained to move in concert at the behest of a single will. It is thus hardly surprising that the nascent science of industrial management looked for inspiration and prestige to the discipline of engineering and that its proponents drew the analogies that followed from this conception of administrative theory; if the task of the engineer was to manipulate objects according to the laws of physical science so as to further the interests of men, the task of the manager was to manipulate men

according to the laws of social science so as to further the interests of the firm. On the relationship between management science and engineering during this period, cf. Robert B. Reich, *The Next American Frontier* (New York: Times Books, 1983), pp. 47–82.

51. Walker to Richard T. Ely, April 30, 1884, quoted in A. W. Coats, "The First Two Decades of the American Economic Association," *American Economic Review* 50 (September 1960):558.

52. Ibid., pp. 555–63.

53. Joseph Dorfman, "The Role of the German Historical School in American Economic Thought," *American Economic Review* 45, Papers and Proceedings (May 1955):17.

54. Ibid., p. 19.

55. Ibid., p. 23.

56. Ibid., p. 21.

57. Dorfman, *Economic Mind*, p. 107.

58. Thus, wrote Ely in 1910, referring to Walker's unanimous election to the presidency of the AEA in 1885, "He was not selected because we necessarily agreed with his views, but because we looked upon him as a champion and emancipator"; quoted in Newton, *Economics of Walker*, p. 13.

59. Walker, *Political Economy*, p. 16.

60. Quoted in Newton, *Economics of Walker*, p. 19.

61. In an 1893 article for the *Atlantic Monthly,* Walker clearly had in mind the inferior position occupied at Yale by the Sheffield School when he wrote that "young men do not greatly care to go to schools where they are not respected equally with the best; where all the praise and all the prizes go to others; where the stained fingers and rough clothes of the laboratory mark them as belonging to a class less distinguished than students of classics or philosophy"; quoted in Munroe, *Life of Walker,* p. 231.

62. Ibid., p. 343.

63. "Now, this [competition] may appear a very unamiable thing; yet, rightly viewed, perfect competition would be seen to be the order of the economic universe, as truly as gravity is the order of the physical universe, and to be not less harmonious and beneficent in its operation." Walker, *Political Economy,* p. 228. But "[g]overnment will never accomplish more than a part of the good it intends; and it will always, by its intervention, do a mischief which it does not intend." Francis A. Walker, "Socialism," *Scribner's Magazine* 1 (January 1887):116, quoted in Munroe, *Life of Walker,* p. 225.

64. Walker, *Political Economy,* pp. 255–56; italics in original. To those who argued that the trusts were a natural and praiseworthy product of evolution, Walker remarked caustically that he supposed that the modern train robber was merely the normal evolution of the old-fashioned highwayman. "Some evolution," he went on, "is worthy of only condemnation. Some evolutionists ought to be hanged" (p. 256).

65. Ibid., pp. 258–59.

66. Newton, *Economics of Walker*, p. 150.

67. Cf. Robert H. Wiebe, *The Search for Order, 1877–1920* (New York: Hill and Wang, 1967), pp. 133–63 ("A Revolution in Values").

68. Frank Tariello, Jr., *The Reconstruction of American Political Ideology, 1865–1917* (Charlottesville: University of Virginia Press, 1982). See also Wiebe, *Search for Order*, pp. 140–48.

69. Newton, *Economics of Walker*, pp. 143–50.

70. Francis A. Walker, "Restriction of Immigration," *Atlantic Monthly* 77 (June 1896): 822–29; quoted in Munroe, *Life of Walker*, pp. 301–2. The following year, he was even more explicit: "We must strain out of the blood of the race more of the taint inherited from a bad and vicious pool before we can eliminate poverty, much less pauperism, from our social life. The scientific treatment which is applied to physical disease must be extended to mental and moral disease, and a wholesome surgery and cautery must be enforced by the whole power of the State for the good of all." Francis A. Walker, "The Causes of Poverty," *Century Magazine* 55 (December 1897): 210–16; quoted in Munroe, *Life of Walker*, pp. 304–5.

71. The book's dedication was "To the Seminary of the Department of History, Politics, and Economics at Johns Hopkins University, of which the author was a member from 1883 to 1886. Under the guidance of Adams, Ely, and Jameson, we read and learned. The first has gone, leaving affectionate memories and organized activities of permanent usefulness; the others are still doing their work in a spirit of broad-minded sympathy and fine scholarship." Davis R. Dewey, *Financial History of the United States*, 12th ed. (New York: Longmans, Green, 1934), p.v. In 1904 the book was awarded the John Marshall Prize by Johns Hopkins University.

72. Biographical Sketch of Davis Rich Dewey, MIT Archives, Collection MC70, p. 5.

73. Dewey was promoted to associate professor in 1889 and to professor in 1892. Like Walker before him, Dewey was also active in the American Statistical Association, serving as its secretary from 1886 to 1906 and helping to edit its journal as well. Ibid., p. 3.

74. *Catalogue, 1888–89*, pp. 54–55.

75. *Catalogue, 1891–92*, pp. 70–73.

76. Ibid., pp. 46, 71. Dewey had become chairman of the Department of General Studies upon Atkinson's retirement in 1889.

77. *President's Report for 1895*, p. 27; Edwin R. A. Seligman, "Economics in the United States: An Historical Sketch," in *Essays in Economics* (New York: Macmillan, 1925), p. 155.

78. *Catalogue, 1897–98*.

79. Prescott, *When MIT Was Boston Tech*, pp. 164–66.

80. Ibid., pp. 193–203.

81. Dewey to Richards, October 3, 1905, MIT Archives, Collection M70, box 4, folder 43.

82. *Catalogue, 1907–8*, p. 60.

83. *President's Report for 1907*, pp. 20–21.
84. *President's Report for 1903*, p. 27.
85. *Catalogue, 1906–7*.
86. *President's Report for 1908*.
87. *Catalogue, 1906–7*. Dewey also taught a required subject in Vital and Sanitary Statistics for biology majors.
88. *President's Report for 1914*, pp. 17–18.
89. *Catalogue, 1914–15*, p. 128.
90. Thus, among other things, students considered "the organization of the executive force, departmental functions, factory efficiency, standardization of goods, stock keeping, routing of orders, management of labor, efficiency methods, marketing of goods, publicity and advertising, credit department, insurance, and business ethics." Ibid.
91. Cf. n. 50, above.

CHAPTER 13   UNIVERSITY OF WISCONSIN

1. As quoted in Laurence R. Veysey, *The Emergence of the American University* (Chicago: University of Chicago Press, 1965), p. 104.
2. As quoted in Merle Curti and Vernon Carstensen, *The University of Wisconsin: A History, 1848–1925* (Madison: University of Wisconsin Press, 1949), 1:6.
3. Ibid., pp. 24–25.
4. Three colleges in the state predated the University of Wisconsin: Carroll, founded in 1840 by the United Presbyterian Church; Beloit, founded in 1846 by Congregational and Presbyterian interests; and Lawrence, begun in 1847 as a nonsectarian establishment. A fourth, Ripon, began in 1850 as a private, nonsectarian college. By 1856 Lawrence had half again as many students as the University of Wisconsin, even when the large number of "preparatory" students were counted among the enrollees in the latter. Ibid., p. 185.
5. Ibid., p. 73.
6. The first chancellor—John H. Lathrop, who served from 1848 to 1858—also held the title of Professor of Ethics, Civil Polity, and Political Economy. Presidents Paul A. Chadbourne (1867–70), John H. Twombly (1871–74), and John Bascom (1874–87) held concurrently the chair of Mental and Moral Philosophy. *General Catalogue of the Officers and Graduates of the University of Wisconsin, 1849–1902.*
7. As quoted in Curti and Carstensen, *University of Wisconsin*, 1:97–98.
8. Ibid., pp. 117, 374.
9. In its first quarter-century, friction between the Board of Regents and the university's senior administrators was endemic. In the eyes of much of the wider public, the situation at the University of Wisconsin was unstable. This reputation no doubt contributed to the decision of Daniel Coit Gilman—later president of the University of California and of the Johns Hopkins Uni-

versity—to decline an invitation to serve as Wisconsin's president in 1867 and to a similar decision on the part of J. Lewis Diman, professor of history and political economy at Brown, in 1871.

10. Curti and Carstensen, *University of Wisconsin*, 1:217.

11. John Bascom, *Political Economy Designed as a Text-Book for Colleges* (Andover, Mass.: Draper, 1859).

12. John Bascom, *Ethics; or, Science of Duty* (New York: Putnam, 1880), pp. 296–97.

13. Ibid., p. 311.

14. Joseph Dorfman, *The Economic Mind in American Civilization* (New York: Viking Press, 1949), 3:178–79.

15. Bascom to Richard T. Ely, as quoted in Curti and Carstensen, *University of Wisconsin*, 1:289.

16. Bascom, *Sociology* (New York: Putnam, 1898), pp. 67, 69, 146.

17. Bascom, Baccalaureate Address, 1887, as quoted in Curti and Carstensen, *University of Wisconsin*, 1:287.

18. Charles R. Van Hise, *Memorial Service in Honor of John Bascom,* as quoted in ibid., pp. 280–81.

19. In the mid-1880s, the University of Michigan enrolled nearly 1,200 students, and the University of Iowa catered to 479. Wisconsin's enrollment at that time was 387. Curti and Carstensen, *University of Wisconsin*, p. 326.

20. The subject matter of extension courses (of six lectures each) then included American history, English literature, Scandinavian literature, economics, antiquities of India and Iran, bacteriology, physiology of plants, electricity, and landscape geology. Ibid., p. 725.

21. Ibid., p. 345.

22. Ibid., p. 631.

23. Ray Allen Billington, *Frederick Jackson Turner: Historian, Scholar, Teacher* (New York: Oxford University Press, 1973), pp. 80, 88.

24. For background on Ely's circumstances at this time, see Chapters 8 and 10, herein.

25. Turner to Ely, November 25, 1891, Ely Papers, Wisconsin State Historical Society, Madison.

26. Billington, *Frederick Jackson Turner*, pp. 90–91.

27. Chamberlin described Ely as follows: "He is one of the foremost economists in the country. . . . Probably no one among the younger generation of economists is more widely or favorably known. His employment would direct attention to the development of the University in a most pointed and effective way, and would aid greatly in giving it recognition as a leading institution." Chamberlin to Regent Clark et al., March 5, 1892, as quoted in Curti and Carstensen, *University of Wisconsin*, 1:619.

28. Ely to Albert Shaw, January 25, 1892, as quoted in Richard T. Ely, *Ground under Our Feet* (New York: Macmillan, 1938), pp. 180–81.

29. *Catalogue, 1892–93.*

30. See Benjamin G. Rader, *The Academic Mind and Reform: The Influence*

of Richard T. Ely in American Life (Lexington: University Press of Kentucky, 1966), pp. 106–29.

31. Ely reprinted the text of Wells's letter in his autobiography; see *Ground under Our Feet,* pp. 219–20.

32. Edward W. Bemis, an Ely protégé who was then being forced out of the University of Chicago, found his mentor's position on this point disheartening, observing that he was "sorry only that you seemed to show a vigor of denial as to entertaining a walking delegate or counseling strikers as if either were wrong, instead of under certain circumstances a *duty.*" Bemis to Ely, October 4, 1894, as quoted in Rader, *Academic Mind,* p. 143.

33. Report of the Board of Regents, University of Wisconsin, September 18, 1894, as quoted in Curti and Carstensen, *University of Wisconsin,* 1 : 525. President Adams is thought to have been the author of this language. The willingness of the regents to endorse it may, however, have been inspired more by a desire of the board's majority to dissociate itself from Wells (whom many had come to regard as an embarrassment to their membership) than by a desire to assert commitment to a general principle. Ths interpretation has been suggested by Walter P. Metzger, "The Age of the University," in Richard Hofstadter and Walter P. Metzger, *The Development of Academic Freedom in the United States* (New York: Columbia University Press, 1955), pp. 426–36.

34. Curti and Carstensen, *University of Wisconsin,* 1 : 641; Archives of the Department of Economics, University of Wisconsin. The university awarded its first Ph.D. in 1892 to Charles R. Van Hise in geology.

35. Adams, Reports to the Regents, January 21, 1896, as quoted in Curti and Carstensen, *University of Wisconsin,* 1 : 641.

36. Billington, *Frederick Jackson Turner,* pp. 155–56.

37. William A. Scott, "Training for Business at the University of Wisconsin," *Journal of Political Economy,* February 1913, p. 130.

38. Curti and Carstensen, *University of Wisconsin,* 1 : 643–45.

39. Ibid., 2 : 29–30.

40. In 1902 Ely actively sought an appointment in Washington as assistant secretary of the Treasury. Although President Theodore Roosevelt thought well of this idea, Ely mismanaged his attempt to get the political endorsements needed to push such an appointment through. Rader, *Academic Mind,* pp. 162–64.

41. In his capacity as president of the American Economic Association, Ely was instrumental in the creation of a committee to investigate the dismissal of his former Johns Hopkins student Edward A. Ross by Stanford University. For additional background on this episode, see Chapter 11, herein.

42. John Bates Clark of Columbia and Albert Shaw, editor of the *Review of Reviews* and a former Ely student at Johns Hopkins, served on the advisory board for the bureau.

43. Dorfman, *Economic Mind,* 3 : 277.

44. Ultimately, one of the more generous contributors to the research work of the bureau was Henry W. Farnam, Yale's in-house philanthropist, who had

certainly not been a fan of the Elyite approach to economics in the early 1890s. In 1906 Farnam, Ely, and Commons joined forces to establish an American Association for Labor Legislation. Commons reported a conversation at that time in which Farnam remarked: "Curious, isn't it, that you, a radical, and I, a conservative, find ourselves working together." As quoted in John R. Commons, *Myself* (Madison: University of Wisconsin Press, 1964), p. 139. For a discussion of Farnam's support for the promotion of economic research in other settings, see Chapter 6, herein.

45. When moving to Syracuse in 1895, Commons thought it prudent to tell its chancellor "the whole truth." As he later wrote: "I told him I was a socialist, a single taxer, a free-silverite, a municipal ownerist, a member of the Congregational Church. He answered to the effect: I do not care what you are if you are not an 'obnoxious socialist.'" Ibid., p. 53.

46. In his autobiography, Commons observed that his experience at Syracuse had led him to conclude that "it was not religion, it was capitalism, that governed Christian colleges." Ibid., p. 58.

47. Lafayette G. Harter, Jr., *John R. Commons: His Assault on Laissez-Faire* (Corvallis: Oregon State University Press, 1962), pp. 23–24.

48. Mark Perlman, *Labor Union Theories in America: Background and Development* (Evanston, Ill., and White Plains, N.Y.: Row, Peterson, 1958), p. 35.

49. Commons, *Myself*, pp. 127–28.

50. Ibid., p. 156.

51. Rader, *Academic Mind*, p. 176.

52. Ibid., pp. 193–94.

53. See Chapter 11, herein, for an account of Ross's difficulties on the West Coast.

54. Young wrote the sections on value and distribution and on money and banking; Lorenz (who therein presented the "curve" that bears his name to depict inequalities in the income distribution) covered the statistical sections; Adams wrote the chapters on labor and public finance; Ely continued to cover the historical materials.

55. As quoted in Harold L. Miller, "The American Bureau of Industrial Research and the Origins of the 'Wisconsin School' of Labor History," *Labor History*, Spring 1984, p. 180.

56. Rader, *Academic Mind*, p. 168.

57. Lincoln Steffens, "Sending a State to College," *American Magazine*, February 1909, as quoted in Veysey, *Emergence of the University*. It was through Lincoln Steffens's influence that the "sifting and winnowing" statement was put on a plaque and attached to Bascom Hall.

58. Although a geologist by training, Van Hise was totally sympathetic to this program and added his own voice to the discussion of Progressive economics with the publication of a book entitled *Concentration and Control: A Solution of the Trust Problem in the United States* in 1912.

59. Chester L. Jones, "Tendencies in Economic Legislation in Wisconsin," *Journal of Political Economy*, October 1914, pp. 756–74.

60. La Follette left the governorship in 1907 to take a seat in the United States Senate.
61. Curti and Carstensen, *University of Wisconsin*, 2:88.
62. Charles McCarthy, *The Wisconsin Idea* (New York: Macmillan, 1912), pp. 313–17.
63. Frederic C. Howe, *Wisconsin: An Experiment in Democracy* (New York: Scribner, 1912), p. 39.
64. McCarthy, *Wisconsin Idea*, p. 138.
65. Ibid., p. 138.
66. Ibid., p. 20.
67. Ibid., p. 28.
68. Ibid., p. 30.
69. Ely, *Property and Contract in their Relations to the Distribution of Wealth* (New York: Macmillan, 1914), 1:41.
70. Commons, *Myself*, p. 106.
71. Curti and Carstensen, *University of Wisconsin*, 2:101.
72. Ibid., p. 72.

CHAPTER 14   PROFESSIONALIZATION OF
AMERICAN ECONOMICS

1. William J. Goode, "Encroachment, Charlatanism, and the Emerging Professions: Psychology, Sociology, Medicine," *American Sociological Review* 25 (1960):902.
2. F. W. Taussig wrote to H. C. Adams, July 4, 1886, "We must look to the Germans for suggestions, but must work out our salvation in our own way—a fact which some of our friends are apt to overlook." Adams Papers, Michigan Historical Collections, University of Michigan; quoted in Mary O. Furner, *Advocacy and Objectivity: A Crisis in the Professionalization of American Social Science, 1865–1905* (Lexington: University Press of Kentucky, 1975), p. 91.
3. Daniel Coit Gilman, *University Problems in the United States* (New York: Century Publishing Co., 1898), p. 19. Gilman explicitly put the promotion of useful knowledge before pure research. It is significant that the ill-fated early president of the University of Michigan, Henry P. Tappan, "had an almost religious faith in the cultivation of intellect for its own sake." Cf. Richard Storr, *The Beginnings of Graduate Education in America* (Chicago: University of Chicago Press, 1953), p. 131.
4. Thorstein Veblen, *The Higher Learning in America: A Memorandum on the Conduct of Universities by Businessmen* (New York: Huebsch, 1918).
5. John Dewey, *School and Society* (Chicago: University of Chicago Press, 1922), p. 25. Originally published in 1899.
6. J. A. Woodburn, *A History of Indiana University, 1820–1907* (Bloomington: Indiana University Press, 1949), 2:995. According to Lotus D. Coffman, president of the University of Minnesota, "The State Universities hold

that there is no intellectual service too undignified for them to perform. They maintain that every time they lift the intellectual level of any class or group, they enhance the intellectual opportunities of every other class or group." *The State University* (Minneapolis: University of Minnesota Press, 1934), pp. 205–6.

7. Alexandra Oleson and John Voss, eds., *The Organization of Knowledge in Modern America, 1860–1920,* (Baltimore: Johns Hopkins University Press, 1979), Introduction, pp. xviii–xix.

8. Ibid., p. xix.

9. George P. Schmidt, *The Liberal Arts College: A Chapter in American Cultural History* (New Brunswick, N.J.: Rutgers University Press, 1957), p. 182. *The Historical Statistics of the United States* provide a broad index of the trend toward concentration in higher education during the same period. Whereas the number of colleges and universities increased by 170 percent, the number of degrees awarded grew by 450 percent, almost twice as rapidly as the total population.

10. Bernard Berelson, *Graduate Education in the United States* (New York: McGraw-Hill, 1960), pp. 14, 15. See also Storr, *Beginnings,* passim. The other institutions were Catholic University, Clark, Cornell, Michigan, Pennsylvania, Princeton, Wisconsin, and Yale.

11. David Madsen, *The National University: Enduring Dream of the USA* (Detroit: Wayne State University Press, 1966).

12. Ibid., p. 76.

13. John B. Parrish, "The Rise of Economics as an Academic Discipline: The Formative Years to 1900," *Southern Economic Journal* 34 (July 1967): 11. I have drawn heavily on this valuable article, which contains much more relevant information than can be included herein.

14. J. Laurence Laughlin, "Courses of Study in Political Economy in the United States in 1876 and 1892–3," *Journal of Political Economy* 1 (December 1892): App. 1, pp. 143–51. A somewhat similar estimate for the "six or eight leading American institutions" was provided in Charles F. Dunbar, "The Academic Study of Political Economy," *Quarterly Journal of Economics* 5 (July 1891): 400.

15. Parrish, "Rise of Economics," pp. 7, 9. At a lower level, political economy was also taught in many of the commercial and business colleges, which increased in number from 60 in 1871 to 222 in 1889. The annual reports of the United States commissioner of education contain detailed data on these and related matters.

16. Ibid., p. 10.

17. These discussions appear in the reports of the AEA's annual meetings and in the *Journal of Political Economy.*

18. Parrish, "Rise of Economics," pp. 10–11.

19. John Higham, "The Matrix of Specialization," in Oleson and Voss, *Organization of Knowledge,* p. 12.

20. Ibid. For a valuable account of the development of a department at a uni-

versity not covered in this volume, see Marjorie C. Brazer, "The Economics Department of the University of Michigan: A Centennial Retrospective," in Saul H. Hymans, ed., *Economics and the World around It* (Ann Arbor: University of Michigan Press, 1982), pp. 133–275. As the author remarks, "An academic department is a unique institution. It provides a structure for the association of scholars concerned with a definite body of knowledge and the setting in which they transmit their discipline to students. Yet each member functions autonomously in his teaching and in his research. The department is, in principle, merely an administrative convenience. In practice it is much more than that. Participation in the group itself generates an atmosphere of intellectual and social interchange that, with the passage of time, stamps a university department with a distinctive personality" (p. 133).

21. Higham, "Matrix of Specialization," p. 11.

22. Parrish, "Rise of Economics," p. 11.

23. On this matter, see A. W. Coats, "The American Economic Association's Publications," *Journal of Economic Literature* 7 (March 1969).

24. J. Laurence Laughlin of Chicago should be added to the list if the concept of "early membership" in the AEA can be stretched to 1904. As indicated below, prior to that time he refused to join. A valuable, though far from complete account is provided in Robert L. Church, "Economists as Experts: The Rise of an Academic Profession in the United States, 1870–1920," in Lawrence Stone, ed., *The University in Society*, vol. 2: *Europe, Scotland, the United States from the Sixteenth to the Twentieth Century* (Princeton, N.J.: Princeton University Press, 1974), pp. 571–609.

25. As Walter Metzger has observed, though the moral philosophy course provided "dessert for seniors, to be taken only after the less appetizing studies of Greek verbs, syllogistic logic, and English grammar," and a rare opportunity for observations on the burning issues of the day, the assumption that most students were "morally deficient or immature . . . intellectually innocent and impressionable . . . gullible and perverse" discouraged any critical spirit of inquiry. It appears that "the teacher *qua* teacher was far less willing to engage in controversy than the teacher *qua* citizen, and that this was in part related to the college's educational norms." An additional factor was that the president, who usually taught moral philosophy, was almost invariably a minister. Richard Hofstadter and Walter P. Metzger, *The Development of Academic Freedom in the United States* (New York: Columbia University Press, 1955), pp. 280–82. Metzger summarizes the educational ideals of the old regime as "traditionalism, paternalism, doctrinal moralism, and sectarianism," which combined to depress the demand for freedom of instruction and inquiry (p. 303).

26. Cf. Thomas Le Duc, *Piety and Intellect at Amherst College* (New York: Columbia University Press, 1946), chaps. 2–4. For the general context, see John S. Brubacher and Willis Rudy, *Higher Education in Transition: A History of American Colleges and Universities, 1626–1976* (New York: Harper and Row, 1976), chap. 14.

27. Hadley claimed that the German university idea of a group of professional schools "is a good one intellectually but a bad one morally." Cf. "Education in Germany," *The Youth's Companion,* January 6, 1910, p. 3. Of course, some critics argued that the old-time college did as little for character as for the intellect. Thus, David Starr Jordan, president of the University of Indiana and later Stanford, declared that "if your college pretends to stand *in loco parentis* with a rod in hand and spy-glasses on its nose, it will not do much for moral training. If your professors are detective officers, and your president a chief of police, the students will keep them always busy." Cited in J. A. Woodburn, *A History of Indiana University, 1820–1902* (Bloomington: Indiana University Press, 1940), 1 : 385. For a more typical midtwentieth century secular view, see Robert McIver, *Academic Freedom in Our Time* (New York: Columbia University Press, 1955), who argues that when educators claim to place "character building" or the "propagation of Christian principles" first "there is always an implicit or explicit rejection of the creed of the scholar, the creed by which alone a university lives. The university is not the church or a missionary society. It is sheer confusion to ask it to do the work of either of these" (p. 14).

28. For references to the Lowell Scientific School at Harvard and the Sheffield Scientific School at Yale, see Chapters 5 and 6, herein. In 1852 Dartmouth founded the Chandler Scientific School, and Brown organized a Department of Practical Science. In 1855 Pennsylvania created a Department of Mines, Arts, and Manufactures. Rensselaer Polytechnic Institute, the first distinct and separate technical school in the United States, was also "the first institution to offer the degree of bachelor of arts to students who had completed a course of study in the natural, mental, and social sciences." The curriculum included political economy; Palmer C. Ricketts, ed., *The Centennial Celebration of Rensselaer Polytechnic Institute* (Troy, N.Y.: Board of Trustees, 1925), p. 129. A new trend was started by the founding of the Massachussets Institute of Technology in 1865. Cf. Chapter 12, herein.

29. Brubacher and Rudy, *Higher Education,* chap. 6, provides a general account of this process.

30. There is a large literature of biographies and reminiscences, and there are many scholarly analyses of this experience. For a useful summary, see Jurgen Herbst, *The German Historical School in American Scholarship: A Study in the Transfer of Culture* (Ithaca, N.Y.: Cornell University Press, 1965), esp. chap. 1; chap. 6 deals specifically with political economy and sociology.

31. According to Fritz Ringer, "the German professor held a particularly eminent place in his society. He not only controlled admission to the civil service and the academic professions generally; he also created and perpetuated the ideology of the intellectual elite, the symbols and instruments of its cultural leadership." His position resulted from "Germany's distinctive road to modernity. Late industrialization combined with the survival of aristocratic dominance and of the bureaucratic monarchy to create a middle class oriented less toward industry and commerce than toward government and

the liberal professions." Ringer, "The German Academic Community," in Oleson and Voss, *Organization of Knowledge,* pp. 410–11. Needless to say, the status of the professoriat in the United States in the 1870s and 1880s was very different, as the returning students were to discover, sometimes to their chagrin, as their high aspirations clashed with academic and social realities.

32. By the turn of the century the German professoriat was beginning to experience a sense of crisis as the growth of specialization undermined its former authority and "spiritual guardianship of the nation." Ibid., p. 426. For a more general account, see Fritz Ringer, *The Decline of the German Mandarins: The German Academic Community, 1890–1933* (Cambridge, Mass.: Harvard University Press, 1969). According to John B. Parrish, "the era of German study reached its peak in 1890–94." Parrish, "Rise of Economics," p. 5.

33. Joseph Dorfman, "The Role of the German Historical School in American Economic Thought," *American Economic Review* 45 (May 1955):17–28.

34. There are several, not entirely consistent, accounts of the events leading up to the Saratoga Springs meeting. See, especially, Richard T. Ely's "Report of the Organization of the American Economic Association," *Publications of the AEA, First Series,* 1 (March 1887):5–46; idem, "The American Economic Association, 1885–1909," *Publications of the AEA, Papers, Third Series* 11 (April 1910):47–93; idem, "The Founding and Early History of the American Economic Association," *American Economic Review* 26 (March 1936):141–50; and his autobiography, *Ground under Our Feet* (New York: Macmillan, 1938), pp. 121–64. For a revealing interpretation of Ely's role, based on contemporary sources, see Daniel M. Fox, *The Discovery of Abundance: Simon N. Patten and the Transformation of Social Theory* (Ithaca, N.Y.: Cornell University Press, 1967). esp. pp. 36ff. Also Joseph Dorfman, *The Economic Mind in American Civilization* (New York: Viking Press, 1949), vol. 3, chap. 9; A. W. Coats, "The First Two Decades of the American Economic Association," *American Economic Review* 50 (September 1960):555–75; Benjamin Rader, *The Academic Mind and Reform: The Influence of Richard T. Ely in American Life* (Lexington: University Press of Kentucky, 1966).

35. The next two paragraphs are based largely on Thomas L. Haskell, *The Emergence of Professional Social Science: The American Social Science Association and the Nineteenth Century Crisis of Authority* (Urbana: University of Illinois Press, 1977). Limitations of space preclude consideration of his fascinating but overambitious attempt to add an epistemological level to his general intellectual, sociological, and historical analysis, arguing that "as society became increasingly interdependent, the conditions of adequate explanation changed. . . . The main point of cleavage between the professional theorists and the declining amateur theorists . . . is the recognition of, or the failure to recognize, the objective fact of social interdependence" (p. 15). An older study of the ASSA, by Luther Lee Bernard and Jessie Bernard, *Origins of American Sociology: The Social Science Movement in the United States* (New York: Crowell, 1943), is still valuable.

36. Haskell, *Emergence*, p. 172.
37. For the relevant context, see Chapter 8, herein; also Hugh Hawkins, *Pioneer: A History of the Johns Hopkins University, 1874–1889* (Ithaca, N.Y.: Cornell University Press, 1960); and Ely, *Ground under Our Feet.*
38. Haskell, *Emergence*, p. 160; he devotes an entire chapter to the merger episode. John Higham, with Leonard Krieger and Felix Gilbert, *History: The Development of Historical Studies in the United States* (Englewood Cliffs, N.J.: Prentice-Hall, 1965), pp. 8–9.
39. This is the central theme of Mary O. Furner's excellent study, *Advocacy and Objectivity.*
40. John Higham, *History: Professional Scholarship in America* (New York: Harper Torchbooks, 1965), p. 20. The inadequacy of Arthur S. Link's account of "The American Historical Association, 1884–1894: Retrospect and Prospect," *American Historical Review* 90 (February 1985): 11–17, is clear from an examination of Haskell, *Emergence*, pp. 168–77.
41. Ely, "Report of the Organization of the AEA," p. 19. The committee consisted of H. C. Adams (chairman), Ely (secretary), J. B. Clark (Carleton College), Alexander Johnson (Princeton), and Washington Gladden (a leading Social Gospel minister). There was also a committee on organization consisting of E. J. James (Pennsylvania), H. B. Adams (Johns Hopkins), and E. B. Andrews (p. 29). Mary Furner, *Advocacy and Objectivity,* confuses the two Adamses, on p. 75.
42. Ely, "Report of the Organization of the AEA," pp. 6, 7, 19.
43. Ibid., p. 19. Ely, *Ground under Our Feet,* p. 154.
44. The articles were subsequently reprinted as Richard T. Ely et. al., *Science Economic Discussion* (New York: Science, 1886). There is a useful summary in Furner, *Advocacy and Objectivity,* pp. 92–106.
45. The year before the AEA was launched Ely had published an aggressive attack on orthodoxy in his "Past and Present of Political Economy," *Johns Hopkins Studies in Historical and Political Science* 2 (March 1884): 137–202. Furner, *Advocacy and Objectivity,* comments that "Ely's analysis was a study in exaggerated opposites" (p. 60). Compare Simon Newcomb, "The Two Schools of Political Economy," *Princeton Review* 14 (November 1884): 291–301. Furner's valuable study of this debate and the broader professionalization issue is unfortunately marred by occasional overdramatization. For example, the "battle between the schools" became "an academic free-for-all of classic proportions" (p. 63). "The economists' controversy . . . robbed the rapidly changing society of a source of stability and understanding" (p. 59), and after the formation of the AEA the "economists experimented almost feverishly with various ways of perceiving their professional obligations and defining their prerogatives—so feverishly, in fact, that their behavior often seemed contradictory" (p. 81).
46. Ely, "Report of the Organization of the AEA," pp. 7, 20. It is worth noting that the James–Patten prospectus had not specifically mentioned laissez-faire, although its central thrust was unequivocally against that doctrine. There was a revealing description of the older generation by a young conser-

vative, Arthur T. Hadley, in his presidential address to the AEA. He called them "commanding men," who regarded economics as a body of concrete propositions from which definite, explicit policy conclusions could be drawn, and preferred their position to the more cautious and vague approach of the younger generation. In place of a "presumptuous claim to knowledge," the new political economy "substitutes either controversies or confessions of ignorance." "The Relation between Economics and Ethics," reprinted in Hadley, *The Education of the American Citizen* (New York: Scribner's, 1901), p. 70.

47. For a brief general survey, see A. W. Coats, "The American Economic Association amd the Economics Profession," *Journal of Economic Literature* 23 (December 1985): 1697–1727.

48. Furner, *Advocacy and Objectivity*, p. 24.

49. The constitution of the society is reprinted in Ely, *Ground under Our Feet*, pp. 296–99, and in "The American Economic Association," pp. 50–53. As a rough indication of comparative length, the society's constitution amounted to 151 lines of small print; the platform claimed 27 lines, and the Statement of Principles 16 lines of larger print.

50. For a broad survey of this movement, see Sidney Fine, *Laissez Faire and the General-Welfare State: A Study of Conflict in American Thought* (Ann Arbor: University of Michigan Press, 1956).

51. Ely, "Report of the Organization of the AEA," pp. 6–7, 23, 35–36.

52. See Newcomb's review of Ely's *Outlines of Economics* in the *Journal of Political Economy* 3 (December 1894): 106–11. One speaker at the inaugural meeting objected to the word "Church," on the grounds that "there is no Church in this country, only a group of religious societies." Ely, "Report of the Organization of the AEA," pp. 23, 24.

53. Cf. J. R. Everett, *Religion in Economics: A Study of John Bates Clark, Richard T. Ely, and Simon N. Patten,* (New York: King's Crown Press, 1946). Also see A. W. Coats, "Henry Carter Adams: A Case Study in the Emergence of the Social Sciences in the United States, 1850–1900," *Journal of American Studies* 2 (October 1968): 177–97; and Richard Allen Swanson, "Edmund J. James, 1855–1925: A 'Conservative Progressive' in American Higher Education" (Ph.D. diss., University of Illinois, 1966), esp. pp. 5–7. In his introduction, Everett notes that the interpenetration of science and religion was much more noticeable in the United States at this time than in Germany. There is a good general account in Fine, *Laissez Faire,* chap. 6; see also his chap. 7, "The New Political Economy." For the close similarities between the James–Patten constitution and Lyman Abbott's reform proposals, see Fine, pp. 182–83; also Josiah Strong's description of the new school as "a Christian school of political economy" (p. 201). Robert M. Crunden, *Ministers of Reform: The Progressives' Achievement in American Civilization, 1889–1920* (New York: Basic Books, 1982), emphasizes the progressives' belief in the need for spiritual reformation. His study demonstrates the links between the emerging social sciences and broader cultural trends in the period. Furner's estimate of the number of ministers who joined

the AEA differs slightly from Fine's. She also notes that only thirteen ASSA members joined the AEA, half of whom were young professional economists who had only recently joined the older body (*Advocacy and Objectivity*, p. 75). In his autobiography Ely especially recalled the strong support he received from the historians C. K. Adams, H. B. Adams, and A. D. White, who "because they were not bound and limited by the traditions of the old classical economists, . . . were more open-minded than the economists" (*Ground under Our Feet*, p. 179).

54. For example, Adams wrote in his personal diary: "I am a socialist—to tell the truth—with the very characteristic exception of questioning their plan of reconstruction" (December 7, 1878), and to his mother he wrote: "Do you want to know what I am? I am a socialist of the general Philosophy of Karl Marx. . . . I do not think he has the true method of work and agitation but his criticisms upon our present society are just and true" (November 7, 1883). Later he became more conservative. For the context, see Coats, "Henry Carter Adams." In a review of Ely's *Labor Movement in America*, H. W. Farnam observed dryly: "Dr. Ely says—and he ought to know—that he is no socialist. Yet much that he says sounds so much like what a good many of the socialists say, that he ought not to complain, if people occasionally mistake him for one." *Political Science Quarterly* 1 (December 1886): 686. As Crunden argues, in *Ministers of Reform*, pp. 12–13: "as with so many progressives, the mental habits and world view of childhood persisted into the new professions of adulthood and Ely remained an evangelist and missionary to those unconverted to his economic, sociological, and political doctrines. . . . [In his work] the common distinctions often made between progressivism, populism, and socialism no longer seem meaningful."

55. Ely identified socialism and the state with Christianity. The state, he argued, "is religious in its essence"; "God works through the State in carrying out His purposes more universally than through any other institution." Fine, *Laissez Faire*, pp. 180–81. He informed the working class that "Christ and all Christly people are with you," and his mild criticisms of organized labor were overshadowed by his exaggerated commendation of the Knights of Labor. Cf. Rader, *Academic Mind*, chap. 3. In response to Ely's request for comments on his work, J. B. Clark, a mild-mannered man, asked: "Does this passage justify the accusation brought against us of confusing the boundaries of economics and ethics? . . . is political economy ever hortatory?" And again: "Is not the rhetoric of restrained statement, if not understatement, better?" H. C. Adams wrote: "The political economy of Mill does not 'glorify selfishness.' The expression is unscientific. A good deal of this part of your paper seems to me to be polemic rather than critical." Ely Papers, vol. 18, Miscellaneous Scrap Books, November 1887, Wisconsin State Historical Society, Madison. See also quotations in Furner, *Advocacy and Objectivity*, pp. 91–92, 119–20.

56. Ely, "Report of the Organization of the AEA," p. 28. Ely, *Ground under Our Feet*, pp. 141–42.

57. Joseph A. Schumpeter, *History of Economic Analysis* (New York: Oxford

University Press, 1954), pp. 756, 800–3. Eventually 188 volumes of Verein reports were published. It is worth noting that the Verein originally demanded a pledge from its adherents but subsequently changed that policy. For contemporary accounts of the organization, see John G. Gray, "The Verein für Sozialpolitik," *Annals of the American Academy* 1 (October 1890): 515–20; Eugen von Philippovich, "The Verein für Sozialpolitik," *Quarterly Journal of Economics* 5 (January 1891): 220–37. At the inaugural meeting, AEA standing committees on the following topics were established: Labor, Transportation, Trade, Public Finance, Exchange, General Questions of Economic Theory, and Statistics.

58. The Executive Committee consisted of the president, vice-presidents, secretary, treasurer.

59. For an account of this organization, see A. W. Coats, "The Political Economy Club: A Neglected Episode in American Economic Thought," *American Economic Review* 51 (September 1961): 624–37.

60. Walker to Ely, April 8, 1884, Ely Papers.

61. A safeguard was provided by the election of a substantial number of members to the Association's Council.

62. Cf. the references in note 34, above.

63. Cf. Edward W. Bemis, September 29, 1886, Ely Papers. Laughlin to E. R. A. Seligman, July 11, 1890, Edwin R. A. Seligman Papers, Columbia University Special Collections.

64. Walker to Ely, April 30, 1884; quoted in Ely, "The American Economic Association," p. 78. F. A. Walker, "Recent Progress of Political Economy in the United States," *Publications of the American Economic Association,* Proceedings, First Series 4 (July 1889): 254. In 1887 Walker offered to resign the presidency if it would serve the cause of unity. The following year he favored dropping the Statement of Principles, which he had never liked, and in 1892 he counseled caution when Ely threatened to cause a public scandal over the Chautauqua decision. Cf. Coats, "First Two Decades," pp. 559, 564, 565.

65. Taussig to Seligman, March 17, 1892, Seligman Papers.

66. Cf. Coats, "American Economic Association's Publications."

67. For an interpretation of the general differences between eastern colleges and midwestern state universities, see, e.g., Norman Forester, *The American State University: Its Relation to Democracy* (Chapel Hill: University of North Carolina Press, 1937), esp. pp. 21–27; H. W. Odum, "The Social Sciences," in *A State University Surveys the Humanities,* ed. L. C. MacKinney, N. B. Adams, H. K. Russell (Chapel Hill: University of North Carolina Press, 1945), pp. 108–17; and Brubacher and Rudy, *Higher Education,* pp. 153–73.

68. A revealing example of local sensitivity to specific issues is contained in a letter from President Jesse of the University of Missouri to Ely in 1891 concerning the new chair of history and political economy. The curators, he said, "personally . . . would take a Democrat, or a Republican, gold or silver

man; but they are afraid that the man himself would have a hard time at the hands of the press and the University [would suffer] next winter before the Legislature unless he were something of a Democrat and favored some coinage of silver. . . . A *moderate* Democrat, who favored gradual revision of the tariff in the direction of free trade, and a limited coinage of silver—at least until international agreement confirm or forbid—would about fill our political want. Such a man would please nobody violently, nor displease any grievously. But such a man, with fine ability and good attainments, has not yet been found." Quoted in Dorfman, *Economic Mind,* 3 : 239–40; italics in original. Also see Dorfman's account of the dramatic saga of economist Thomas Will and the Populists at Kansas State Agricultural College in the same decade.

69. For a more detailed treatment of these matters, see Furner, *Advocacy and Objectivity,* esp. chaps. 5 and 6; Coats, "First Two Decades," pp. 557–67; Dorfman, *Economic Mind,* vol. 3, chap. 9.

70. See, e.g., Haskell, *Emergence,* and Burton J. Bledstein, *The Culture of Professionalism: The Middle Class and the Development of Higher Education in America* (New York: Norton, 1976).

71. Cf. Chapter 13, herein; also, Hofstadter and Metzger, *Development of Academic Freedom,* pp. 426ff., and Furner, *Advocacy and Objectivity,* pp. 147–58. For further details on the matters in this and the next two paragraphs, see Furner, chap. 11, and Coats, "First Two Decades," pp. 567–70.

72. H. C. Adams to J. W. Jenks, January 7, 1895, in American Economic Association Papers, Northwestern University. John R. Commons, a former student of Ely at Johns Hopkins, was then teaching at the University of Indiana. For evidence of the variety of motives at work, see Coats, "First Two Decades," p. 568.

73. Knight to H. C. Adams, January 8, 1895, in AEA Papers; italics in original. The officers of the new Political Science Association were: president, Jesse Macy, president of Grinnell College, Iowa, a friend of Ely; vice-presidents, A. W. Small (Chicago, sociology), C. H. Haskins (Wisconsin, history), Adams (Michigan, economics), and J. Woodburn (Indiana, political science); treasurer, F. W. Blackmar (Kansas, economics); secretary, G. W. Knight (Ohio State, economics).

74. Commons to Adams, April 6, 1895, AEA Papers. The selection committee consisted of Taussig (Harvard), chairman; Farnam (Yale); R. D. Falkner (Pennsylvania); Ross (Stanford); and W. A. Scott (Wisconsin). Furner's comment that Adams "seized the opportunity to consolidate his influence in the national association" (*Advocacy and Objectivity,* p. 264) is a typical example of her tendency to impute strategic self-interested motives to individuals. Though probably true of Ely, such behavior was not in character in Adams's case. He was simply concerned to build a bridge between the westerners, of whom he was one, and the AEA.

75. Dorfman, *Economic Mind,* 3 : 228.

76. Adams to Mrs. E. D. Adams, October 18 and November 7, 1896, Adams Papers.

77. On another occasion, referring to the Progressives, White said that populism had "shaved its whiskers, washed its shirt, put on a derby, and moved up into the middle of the class—the upper middle class." Quoted in Russell B. Nye, *Midwestern Progressive Politics: A Historical Study of Its Origins and Development* (East Lansing: Michigan State College Press, 1959).

78. W. J. Ashley, "On the Study of Economic History," *Quarterly Journal of Economics* 7 (January 1893):115; cf. J. L. Laughlin, "The Study of Political Economy in the United States," *Journal of Political Economy* 1 (December 1892), and Dunbar, "Academic Study of Political Economy," pp. 402–3.

79. Laughlin, "Study of Political Economy," p. 9; Ashley, "Study of Economic History," pp. 118, 123; and Ashley to Seligman, August 21, 1897, Seligman Papers. As early as 1881 William Graham Sumner had argued that, despite the excesses of the movement, "the rise of a school of 'historical' economists is itself a sign of a struggle towards a positive and scientific study of political economy, in its due relations to other social sciences . . . the essential elements of political economy also include whatever is sound in the 'historical school,' and finishes whatever that school is apparently seeking after." "Sociology," *Princeton Review* 57 (1881):313–15.

80. Powers to Ely, December 31, 1899, Ely Papers. By 1902 F. H. Giddings, a former vice-president, was commenting on the program: "I'd like to see the d——d indolent old Economic Association get downright mad over something, and the tariff is just the thing." Giddings to Seligman, undated, AEA Papers. Giddings, a Columbia sociologist, was no radical.

81. Membership fell from 781 in 1893 to 661 in 1894 and rose thereafter to 685 by 1898 and 745 by late 1899. See F. B. Hawley to J. W. Jenks, November 5, 1894, and Seligman to W. Willcox, February 15, 1899, American Economic Association Papers. Other letters of 1899 refer to the "crisis" and the need for "careful attention and nursing."

82. Cf. Hofstadter and Metzger, *Development of Academic Freedom*, chap. 9; Furner, *Advocacy and Objectivity*, chaps. 6–10.

83. Sumner, "Sociology," p. 311. For a general background treatment, see Fine, *Laissez Faire*, passim.

84. Lester Ward, "The Scientific Basis of Positive Political Economy, I," *International Review* 12 (1882):363; "The Psychologic Basis of Social Economics," *American Academy of Political and Social Sciences Proceedings*, no. 77 (1893):81. Writing to Ely, Ward commented: "Your teachings are, as it were the flower, or rather the fruit, of the tree, of which my Dynamic Sociology is the root." Ward to Ely, November 23, 1887, Ely Papers. H. C. Adams drew on Ward's ideas, protesting "There must be, for organisms of an advanced development, a higher law than the struggle for individual existence." *Relation of the State to Industrial Action*, ed. J. Dorfman (New York: Columbia University Press, 1954), p. 73. For general background, see R. Hofstadter, *Social Darwinism in American Thought* (Boston: Beacon, 1955); Eric F.

Goldman, *Rendezvous with Destiny* (New York: Knopf, 1953), esp. chap. 5, for the distinction between conservative and reform Social Darwinism.

85. H. H. Powers to Ely, October 4, 1894, Ely Papers.

86. Walter Metzger, "The German Contribution to the American Theory of Academic Freedom," *Bulletin of the American Association of University Professors* 41 (1955): 214–30; also, Hofstadter and Metzger, *Development of Academic Freedom*, pp. 383 ff. When Ely was "tried" at Wisconsin, the regents steadfastly refused to accept responsibility for his writings and concentrated attention mainly on his teachings. Cf. Merle Curti and Vernon Carstensen, *The University of Wisconsin: A History, 1848–1925* (Madison: University of Wisconsin Press, 1949), 1:520–25. In his classic report on academic freedom, President Lowell of Harvard insisted: "If a university or college censors what professors may say, if it restrains them from uttering something it does not approve, it thereby assumes responsibility for that which it permits them to say." Quoted in Hofstadter and Metzger, *Development of Academic Freedom*, p. 503. President Jordan's difficulties at Stanford arose partly because he was in too weak a position to adhere to this distinction. Though he conceded that each professor "as a private citizen is perfectly free to take any stand in politics he may choose," he added that "an institution like ours has a right to expect its members not to compromise its dignity. As it cannot escape some degree of responsibility for the public acts of its members . . ." Orrin L. Elliott, *Stanford University: The First Twenty-Five Years* (Stanford, Calif.: Stanford University Press, 1937), pp. 336, 337–38. This largely explains why American academics attached so much importance to the "scholarly virtues of tact, moderation, caution, diplomacy, decorum, etc."

87. From Eliot's inaugural address of 1869, reprinted in his *Educational Reform* (New York: Century, 1898), pp. 7–8. John Dewey made a similar observation in an article on "Academic Freedom," *Educational Review* 23 (1902): 12–13.

88. Furner, *Advocacy and Objectivity*, pp. 3, 228. For an account of the hierarchy of institutions, see Edward Shils, "The Order of Learning in the United States: The Ascendancy of the University," in Oleson and Voss, *Organization of Knowledge*, pp. 19–47. See also Metzger, "German Contribution," pp. 489 ff.; Furner, *Advocacy and Objectivity*, chap. 10.

89. Furner, *Advocacy and Objectivity*, pp. 257–58; sentence order reversed.

90. Hadley, "Economic Theory and Political Morality," reprinted in *The Education of the American Citizen*, pp. 86, 87.

91. John R. Commons, "Economic Theory and Political Morality: Discussion," *Publications of the AEA*, 3rd ser. 1 (1900): 62–88, 287–88. The other discussants were Seligman, Edward Bemis, Richmond Mayo-Smith, and Powers. For a somewhat different, more dramatic, account of this episode see Furner, *Advocacy and Objectivity*, pp. 273–75.

92. See Veblen's essays, "The Preconceptions of Economic Science," *Quarterly Journal of Economics* 13 (January 1899 and July 1899) and 14 (February 1900).

93. The conflict of regional attitudes cut both ways. According to Jordan, recalling his period as president of the University of Indiana, "among my own early selections were a few young teachers from seaboard universities, but most of them failed to adapt themselves, appearing to feel that coming so far west was a form of banishment. Indeed, as a whole, they seemed more eager to get back to the East than to build up a reputation in Indiana"; quoted in Woodburn, *History of Indiana University*, 1:376. Somewhat similar attitudes were evident among the economists when Ely proposed Chautauqua as the site of the 1892 AEA annual meeting. There was, however, some justification for the reluctance to move west as revealed in L. Esarey, *A History of Indiana* (Indianapolis: W. K. Stewart, 1918), 2:993–94: "The college professor and college learning . . . was a great joke to most Indianians before 1880. A professor, if honest and able, was an object of pity, because he had not undertaken some public service where his efforts would have been appreciated. He was generally condemned for wasting in useless pursuits endowments that might have been put to profitable use. If a professor were dishonest he was drummed out of the community just like an immoral preacher. Lapses that would not have excited neighborhood gossip were magnified into State scandal if done by a professor." The psychologist G. Stanley Hall even contended that there were discernible differences between the representative type of scholar in different areas. Hall, *Life and Confessions of a Psychologist* (New York: Appleton, 1923), p. 564.

94. The *Springfield Republican*, May 21, 1889. The article concluded that "since the Kansas legislature by resolution condemned the use of the terms 'dean,' 'regent,' and all other terms, practices, and teachings in the state University smacking of 'English,' and English free trade notions, we have had no more sorrowful exhibition of how a reputable cause can be made ridiculous by parrot-pated friends than is afforded by this attack on Professor Adams." Adams's Scrapbook, Adams Papers. Seligman to Adams, May 25, 1889, Adams Papers. Adams to C. O. Pauley, Cornell College, Iowa, February 28, 1899, Adams Papers. (This letter may not have been dispatched.) Even before his dismissal from Cornell University, Adams had been a firm believer in state control of higher education. See Adams to J. B. Angell, March 25, 1886, Angell Papers, University of Michigan Historical Collections. Part of the splendid correspondence between Adams and Angell, when the former's appointment at Michigan was under consideration, has been reprinted in Joseph Dorfman, ed., *Two Essays by Henry Carter Adams* (New York: Columbia University Press, 1969). It contains a frank discussion of the relationships between the academic community and the public.

95. After Ross's dismissal from Stanford, Albion Small, the Chicago sociologist, invited him to give some lectures at the university, explaining to President Harper: "I am convinced that Ross deserved everything he got . . . [but] I still think that we are missing a chance to queer the popular ideas about universities if we omit to engage Ross for the Summer Quarter. Nothing

that he could say could hurt us; but on the other hand his engagement would spike the guns of the people who are bound to claim that the 'proprietary institutions' are afraid of the things that such men may say." Small to Harper, January 3, 1901, A. W. Small file, University of Chicago Library. In 1894, after Ely's "trial," the University of Wisconsin regents issued their famous manifesto: "Whatever may be the limitations which trammel inquiry elsewhere we believe the great state University of Wisconsin should ever encourage that continual and fearless sifting and winnowing by which alone the truth can be found." Curti and Carstensen, *University of Wisconsin*, 1:524–25. Ironically, when the class of 1910 sought to place a tablet bearing these words in a prominent position on the campus, its request was denied. See F. C. Howe, *Wisconsin: An Experiment in Democracy* (New York: Scribner, 1912), p. 31. The tablet was subsequently placed. By 1905 Eliot could write that "the dismissal of professors is generally regarded by the public as evidence of an institution's inexperience, or some temporary intrusion of forces . . . alien to the common university spirit." "Resemblances and Differences among American Universities," *Science,* 22 (1905):773.

96. Merle Curti, *The American Paradox: The Conflict of Thought and Action* (New Brunswick, N.J.: Rutgers University Press, 1956); Daniel Boorstin, *The Americans: The Colonial Experience* (Chicago: University of Chicago Press, 1958), p. 150. In 1871 an orator at the University of Vermont inquired whether it was either necessary or in accord with American principles "to have a class of professional men, who are elevated above the masses of the people by superior knowledge." E. H. Byington, "The Position and Methods of the American Scholar," *Bibliotheca Sacra* 28 (1871):445. Many such examples could be cited.

97. Jacques Barzun, *The House of Intellect* (New York: Columbia University Press, 1959), p. 8. For a general treatment, see Richard Hofstadter, *Anti-intellectualism in American Life* (New York: Knopf, 1962).

98. Higham, "Matrix of Specialization," pp. 5, 10. Higham cites four distinctively American contributions to the institutional matrix: the Ph.D., as a standardized entry requirement for the profession; the university department as a self-governing society of equals; multipurpose agencies to sponsor research; and rule by reference works. On the increasing use of economists as experts, see Church, "Economists as Experts," passim.

99. Furner, *Advocacy and Objectivity,* p. 258. Morton G. White, *Social Thought in America: The Revolt against Formalism* (Boston: Beacon Press, 1957, 1966).

Index

abolitionism, 55, 60, 65
Academy of Political Science, 197
Adams, Charles Kendall, 318, 328–329, 330
Adams, Henry Carter, 207–208, 222, 260, 281, 353, 365, 366, 372–373
Adams, Herbert Baxter, 208, 209, 212, 213, 221, 224, 246, 304, 306, 325, 354
Adams, James H., 66
Adams, John, 44
Adams, Thomas S., 333, 334, 336
Agassiz, Louis, 129
agriculture, 8, 51, 65, 83, 125, 228–229, 320
Albemarle Academy, 23, 25
Aldrich, Morton, 284
American Academy of Political and Social Science, 230–231
American Association for the Advancement of Science, 292
American Association of University Professors, 14, 370
American Bureau of Industrial Research, 331, 333, 334
American Economic Association (AEA), 117, 129, 166, 224, 236, 275, 277, 338, 370
   Bureau of Information of, 359
   Ely and, 13, 90, 107, 150, 164, 197, 213, 216–217, 230, 246, 328, 331, 352, 355–356, 358, 359, 360, 361, 362, 363, 364
   founding of, 13, 90, 93–94, 150, 197, 199, 216–217, 306–308, 310, 344, 352–361
   growth of, 362–365
   James-Patten proposal for, 352, 355, 357–358, 359, 362

   Laughlin and, 248, 261, 263, 360, 362, 367, 371
   membership of, 130, 284, 289, 359, 360–361
   Publication Series of, 348, 363
   public opinion on, 357, 361, 368–369
   regional divisions in, 363, 364–365
   Statement of Principles of, 356, 358, 360, 362
   Walker and, 216–217, 360, 361–362, 363
American Economic Review, 312, 348, 363
American Historical Association, 165, 213, 353, 354, 367
American Paradox, The (Curti), 373
American Political Economy (Bowen), 100
American Political Science Association, 354
American Social Science Association, 205, 275, 352–354, 364
American Sociological Society, 354
American Statistical Association, 367
Anderson, Robert, 18
Andrew, John, 294
Andrews, Elisha Benjamin, 13, 88–90, 91–94, 284, 359, 367, 369, 370
Andrews, John Bertram, 334
Angell, James B., 343
"Argonauts," 267
Ashley, William J., 116, 123, 124, 366
Association of American Universities (AAU), 344
Atkinson, Edward, 113
Atkinson, William Parkinson, 294, 296–297, 305, 306, 312–313

Babcock, E., 178

banking, 30, 78, 106, 108, 114
   national system of, 53, 106, 185
Bank of the United States, 53
Banks, Nathaniel, 293
Baptists, 21, 56, 72–73, 242
Bard, Samuel, 177
Barnard, Frederick A., 172, 176, 188,
   189, 190, 193
Barnard College, 199
Barnett, George E., 224
Barnwell, Robert, 68
Barnwell, R. W., Jr., 67
Barzun, Jacques, 373
Bascom, John, 321–324, 334
Bastable, Charles, 313
Bastiat, Frédéric, 95
Bateman, Clifford, 191, 194
Bates, Helen Page, 330
Beardsley, Charles, 114
Becker, Carl, 369
Bemis, Edward W., 249–250, 251–255,
   257, 259, 261, 263, 264
Bentham, Jeremy, 44, 58
Berkeley Quarterly: A Journal of Social
   Science, 275
Betts, William, 176
Biddle, Nicholas, 53, 59
Bierce, Ambrose, 284
bimetallism, 91, 93, 149, 153, 313
Blanqui, Jérôme, 69
Blum, Solomon, 278, 279, 288
Bôcher, Ferdinand, 294
Böhm-Bawerk, Eugen von, 116, 118
Boorstin, Daniel, 373
Bourbon Redeemers, 68, 69
Bowen, Francis, 9, 96–100, 101, 105,
   120, 127, 129, 227
Bowles, Samuel, 301
Bracken, John, 32
Brandeis, Louis D., 314
Bronson, Isaac, 179
Brooks, John Graham, 121–122, 251,
   252, 255
Brown, John, 48
Brown, Nicholas, 73
Brown University:
   Committee on Advice of, 82
   curriculum of, 74, 84, 90–91
   degrees awarded by, 84, 85, 86
   economics at, 72–94

educational reform at, 81–86
elective system of, 91
enrollment of, 73, 82, 85
faculty salaries at, 84–85
finances of, 82, 87
founding of, 72–73
housing at, 83–84
religious influence on, 72–73
"Report to the Corporation" of,
   82–83
tuition for, 73
Wayland's influence on, 72–86
Bryan, William Jennings, 93, 283,
   365–366
Bullock, Charles J., 70, 125, 127, 130,
   326
Burbank, Harold H., 112
Burgess, John, 187, 188–194, 196, 199,
   201, 202
Burke, Edmund, 44
business cycles, 278
Business Cycles (Mitchell), 278
Butler, Nicholas Murray, 173, 187, 343

Cabell, Joseph, 25, 26
Cairnes, John, 105
Caldwell, William, 249
Calhoun, John C., 57
California, University of:
   Board of Regents of, 268, 269, 270,
      273
   economics at, 273–280, 288–289
   faculty of, 270, 277–279
   finances of, 269, 270, 289
   founding of, 266, 268–271
   modern curriculum at, 269
   as nontuition institution, 269
   "Political Code" for, 269–270
   Stanford University vs., 270–271, 273,
      276, 288–289
   student body of, 273
Callender, Guy S., 123–124
Calvinism, 46, 57
capital:
   accumulation of, 30, 77, 119, 180
   concentration of, 161, 162, 335
   foreign, 188
   "human," 182
   labor and, 62
   production and, 301

Cardozo, Nicholas, 49
Carey, Henry C., 8–9, 105, 110, 117, 127, 225, 227, 228, 238
Carey, Mathew, 8–9, 52
Carr, Peter, 23, 24
Carver, Thomas Nixon, 118–119, 120, 125, 126–127, 130
census, population, 301, 302, 304
Chamberlin, Thomas C., 324–325, 328
Chapters on the History of the Southern Pacific (Daggett), 279
charity, 77, 122
Chautauqua summer school, 213, 246, 253
Chicago, University of:
  Bemis affair at, 251–255, 257, 261, 262, 264
  College of Commerce and Administration of, 259
  departments of, 244, 255–256
  economics at, 241–265, 365
  Ely and, 221, 246–248
  enrollments of, 256
  Extension Division of, 243, 249, 250, 251, 252
  faculty of, 244–245, 248–250, 256
  founding of, 241–245, 362
  graduate program of, 243, 342
  Laughlin's influence on, 248, 249, 250, 251, 252–253, 255, 256, 260–262, 265, 278
  Official Bulletin of, 243
  organization of, 242–245
  private endowment of, 12, 241, 242
  student body of, 256
Church, Robert, 122, 123
Civil Liberty (Lieber), 149
Clark, F. C., 281
Clark, J. M., 200
Clark, John Bates, 116, 118, 167, 196, 199–201, 221, 223, 224, 303
Clark University, 12, 245
class conflict, 7, 371
"class consciousness," 332
Cleland, Robert, 284
Clemson, Thomas, 69
"clingers," 234–235, 236
"College Anarchist, The" (Wells), 329
College of Geneva, 22
colleges and universities:
  academic freedom in, 93–94, 101, 102, 251–255, 284, 285, 286, 329,

363, 365, 367, 369–375
  admissions examinations for, 80
  "advocacy" in, 240
  as business enterprises, 264–265
  colonial, 5
  competition among, 347–348
  curriculums of, 346, 349, 350
  degrees awarded by, 347, 348, 351
  departments of, 347
  differentiation of, 12
  enrollments of, 10–11, 343–344
  graduate work in, 343, 344, 348
  growth of, 9, 10
  intellectual trends in, 104
  land-grant, 11, 68, 268, 320, 342
  localism of, 4
  as "marginal institutions," 128
  moral teachings in, 4–5
  national, 344–345
  private endowments of, 12
  reforms of, 264–265, 322–323, 340–352
  religious influence on, 4–5, 13, 14, 19, 349
  research seminars in, 346, 351
  specialization in, 229–230, 243, 347, 374
  state sponsorship of, 5
  women in, 10, 199, 320
  see also individual colleges and universities
Columbia Studies in the Social Sciences, 199
Columbia University:
  Committee on the College Course of, 175, 176, 179
  curriculum of, 174–176, 189
  degrees awarded by, 81, 176, 192
  departments of, 169
  economics at, 169–202
  electives system at, 175–176, 186, 189, 190, 191
  enrollments of, 173
  expansion of, 172
  faculty of, 172, 176
  faculty salaries at, 172
  finances of, 172–173, 176
  founding of, 170
  Gibbs Manifesto and, 172, 175
  graduate program of, 169, 186, 189, 190, 191, 193, 195, 201–202

Columbia University (*continued*)
  Lieber at, 169, 173–174, 176,
    185–188, 189, 190, 195, 200
  modernization of, 174–176
  political science library of, 193, 194
  religious influence on, 170–171, 173
  research seminars at, 196, 197–198,
    201
  School of Political Science of,
    191–193, 201
  Scientific and Literary Course of,
    174–175
  social role of, 181
  teaching methods at, 173–174,
    177–179, 187
  trustees of, 171, 174, 175, 176, 179,
    187, 189, 191
*Commentary and Review of Montes-
  quieu's Spirit of the Laws* (Tracy), 24
Commons, John R., 331–333, 334, 337,
  338, 364, 365, 371–372
comparative advantage theory, 77, 233
competition:
  domestic, 95, 98, 210
  foreign, 8, 228–229
  free, 309–310
  theory of, 8, 95, 98, 161, 238
  unfair, 230
Compromise of 1808, 45
Compromise of 1850, 96, 266
Comte, Auguste, 39
Congregationalists, 132–133, 134, 137,
  166
Conkin, Paul, 128
Conrad, Johannes, 230, 352
Constitution, U.S., 130
consumption, 232–233
Control of Trusts, The (Clark and
  Clark), 200
Conversations on Political Economy
  (Marcet), 49
Cook, Howard H., 127
Cooley, Thomas L., 208
Cooper, Thomas, 7–8, 23, 25–26, 60
  economic views of, 42–43, 50–58
  Jefferson and, 42, 44, 46–47, 49, 52
  political views of, 52–53, 56–57
  religious views of, 44, 46, 47, 48–49,
    56, 57, 58, 64

  at South Carolina College, 42–58,
    70–71, 185
  as teacher, 48–49, 63
Cornell University, 12
corn laws, 30
corporations, 316–317
cotton prices, 54–55, 65
Crafts, James Mason, 315
credit, 108
Cross, Ira, 279, 286, 287, 288
Cummings, Edward, 122, 123, 124
Cummings, John, 122–123, 262
currency, 75, 106, 257
Currier, Charles F. A., 313, 315
Curti, Merle, 373

Dabney, Richard Heath, 38–39
Dabney, Robert Lewis, 32
Daggett, Stuart, 279
Dartmouth College, 6
Davenport, Herbert, 262
Davis, Noah Knowles, 38, 39
Davis, R. Means, 69
Day, Edmund E., 125
Debs, Eugene, 252
deism, 45, 54, 56
democracy, 181, 235, 372–373, 374
Democratic party, 329
deposits, bank, 106, 108
depressions, economic, 106
Detroit Tribune, 372
Development of English Thought, The
  (Patten), 234–236
Devine, Edward T., 237
Dew, Thomas Roderick, 8, 15, 30,
  34–37, 38, 40–41, 52, 59
Dewey, Davis Rich, 311–313, 314, 315,
  316–317
Dewey, John, 341
Dewey, Melvil, 193, 194
Dewsnup, E. R., 263
Dexter, Franklin B., 155
*Digest of the Laws, Customs, Manners,
  and Institutions of the Ancient and
  Modern Nations* (Dew), 34
Diman, J. Lewis, 87–88, 208
displacement principle, 311
distribution, land, 51–52, 62
Distribution of Wealth, The (Clark), 200

distribution theory, 302–303
Documentary History of American Industrial Society, The, 334
Dorfman, Joseph, 180, 183, 197, 275, 306, 322, 365
dormitories, 80, 83–84
Doten, Carroll W., 316
Drayton, William, 59–60
DuBois, W. E. B., 131
Duffus, Robert, 287
Dunbar, Charles Francis, 11, 12, 70, 96, 100, 103, 124, 360, 362, 363
  economic views of, 104–110, 123
  influence of, 113, 114, 126–127, 131
Du Pont de Nemours, Pierre Samuel, 22–23
Durand, Dana, 283
Dwight, Timothy, 135, 136, 137, 139

Ecole Libre des Sciences Politiques, 191
"Economical Science in America" (McVickar), 184
"Economic Basis of Irish Emigration, The" (Cook), 127
Economic Basis of Protection, The (Patten), 231
"Economic Interpretation of History, The" (Seligman), 197, 198
economics:
  agricultural, 8, 51, 65, 83, 125, 228–229, 320
  American contribution to, 6, 11–12, 76, 105, 184, 265, 349–350
  antiintellectualism and, 373–374
  applied, 165–166
  of banking, 30, 53, 78, 106, 108, 114, 185
  British, 3–4, 6–7, 11–12, 215, 301, 307
  business and, 129, 262, 264, 278, 309, 317, 331
  classical, 6–8, 11–12, 50, 106, 118, 179, 180, 182, 183, 195, 228, 231–232, 261, 275, 301, 306, 308
  as "dangerous science," 3
  deductive method of, 219, 308
  educational role of, 368–375
  French, 8
  German historical, 13, 88, 94,
    106–107, 109, 116, 129, 194, 195, 200, 210, 214, 230, 232, 274, 275, 301, 304, 306–313, 352, 356, 359
  inductive method of, 123, 194, 307, 308, 312
  institutionalization of, 3, 102, 128–131, 278, 332, 340–375
  journals of, 96, 113–117, 164–166, 250–251, 348, 362–363
  laissez-faire, 13, 52, 89, 98, 99, 149, 162, 210, 303, 306, 309, 310, 321, 356, 358, 360, 362, 368
  laws of, 75, 76, 90, 97, 215, 218, 232, 307
  legislation and, 14, 335–336
  "liberal system" of, 181–182, 184
  Methodenstreit of, 13–14, 107, 214, 366
  as "modern" subject, 3, 5–6, 9–10, 12
  monetary policy and, 30, 53, 75, 92, 106, 108, 114, 150, 257, 259
  morality and, 29, 92, 99, 181, 218–219, 359
  national influence of, 113, 261–262
  "national system" of, 8–9, 352
  neoclassical, 234
  in nineteenth century, 3–14
  origins of, 3–10, 14, 48
  political applications of, 107–108, 365–366
  pre-Civil War context of, 3–10
  professionalization of, 340–375
  quantitative analysis in, 160, 161, 213–220
  rationality and, 235–236
  "real-world" issues of, 14
  regionalism in, 9, 363, 364–365
  religion and, 74–75, 89
  as science, 107–108, 257, 258, 265, 300, 301, 313–314, 356, 364, 367, 369–370, 371–372
  secularization of, 7
  social context of, 97–98, 126, 129–130, 210–211, 218–220, 310–311, 353, 356–357, 363–364, 368–369, 371, 373
  statistics and, 301, 302, 307, 356, 359
  texts for, 5, 6, 13, 27, 31, 49–50, 69, 70, 95, 275

economics (*continued*)
  types of, 13
  in university curriculum, 3, 5-10,
    11–13, 327
education:
  agricultural, 320
  classical, 73, 75, 83
  European models for, 3–5, 22, 202,
    340–341, 349
  German methods of, 11, 111, 129,
    138, 174, 177, 186, 229, 337, 338,
    341, 345, 346, 347, 351–352, 369
  as "industry," 78–79
  market for, 79–81, 83
  modern, 73–74
  practical, 11, 78, 83, 319, 324–325,
    331, 333, 341–342
  private vs. public sphere of, 6, 79–81
  reform of, 12–13, 73, 147, 264–265,
    340, 341, 343, 344–345, 350
  specialization in, 131
  in U.S., 340–352
  value of, 79
Elements of Political Economy (Laughlin), 13
Elements of Political Economy (Perry),
  69, 87, 149
Elements of Political Economy (Wayland), 7, 68, 74, 75, 87, 143, 188
Eliot, Charles W.:
  as educational reformer, 340, 343,
    344–345, 350, 369
  as president of Harvard, 95–96,
    100–103, 112, 113, 117, 120–121,
    131, 273, 294, 298, 299, 315
Elliott, Orrin Leslie, 281
Ely, Richard T., 284, 286
  American Economic Association and,
    13, 90, 107, 150, 164, 197, 213,
    216–217, 230, 246, 328, 331, 352,
    355–356, 358, 359, 360, 361, 362,
    363, 364
  in Bemis affair, 253–255
  economic views of, 13, 113, 210–211,
    306–107
  educational views of, 337
  Gilman and, 215, 216, 217–218, 220,
    221–222, 247
  at Johns Hopkins, 209–220,
    221–222, 224, 281, 306, 325

Newcomb vs., 213–220, 223, 356,
  358, 360
  political views of, 210–211, 218–220,
    322, 329, 369
  University of Chicago's offer to, 221,
    246–248
  at University of Wisconsin, 325–330,
    331, 333, 334, 337, 338
Emery, Henry Crosby, 167
Encyclopaedia Americana, 58, 66, 185
Encyclopaedia Britannica, 180
Encyclopaedia of the Social Sciences, 197
Engels, Friedrich, 196
Episcopalians, 21, 46, 137, 173
equilibriums, market, 234
Essay on the Interest of Money (Dew),
  35
Essays on Property and Labour (Lieber),
  61
*Essay upon the Principles of Political
Economy* (McVickar), 180, 183
Essentials of Economic Theory, The
  (Clark), 200
Essentials of Socialism, The (Cross), 288
exchange, equation of, 257
exchange values, 75

Farnam, Henry W., 154–156, 157, 158,
  160, 164, 166, 168, 360
Fawcett, Henry, 87, 229
Fawcett, Millicent, 188
Fetter, Frank R., 70, 283, 284, 285–286,
  288
Financial History of the United States
  (Dewey), 312
Fish, Hamilton, 171, 186, 187, 191
Fisher, Irving, 160, 163, 165, 166–167
Franklin, Benjamin, 184, 225
Free Banking Act of New York, 185
free trade, 7, 30, 35, 50, 52, 56, 60, 61,
  62, 63, 64, 75, 77, 87–88, 99, 100,
  150, 227, 228, 229, 233, 234,
  349–350, 372
Fugitive Slave Law, 96
fundamentalism, Protestant, 55–56
Furner, Mary, 240, 356, 370, 375

Gammell, William, 84, 86–87
Gardner, Henry B., 90–91, 94
Garfield, James A., 301, 304

Gay, Edwin F., 124–125, 130
general equilibrium theory, 303
General Theory (Keynes), 130
George, Henry, 93, 110, 196, 197, 269, 274
Gibbs, Wolcott, 171, 172, 175
Giddings, Franklin H., 196, 199, 201
Gide, Charles, 69
Gilman, Daniel Coit, 141–143, 153, 168, 269–270, 302
    Ely and, 215, 216, 217–218, 220, 221–222, 247
    as president of Johns Hopkins, 203, 205–208, 210, 211, 212, 223, 224, 244, 306, 341, 343, 354
Gold, Prices, and Wages under the Greenback Standard (Mitchell), 278
gold rush, 266–267
gold standard, 92, 257, 365–366
Goode, William J., 340
governments:
    economic role of, 30, 31, 45, 51, 61, 75, 89, 179, 185, 303, 357, 371
    intervention by, 8, 13, 77–78, 103, 129–130, 149, 162, 184–185, 230, 275, 307, 310–311
Grant, Ulysses S., 303
grants, financial, 80
Gray, John, 116
"Great Britain and Her American Colonies" (McVickar), 184

Hadley, Arthur T., 113, 360, 367, 371, 372
    as economics professor, 154, 156–157, 158, 160–163, 164, 165
    as president of Yale, 166–168, 349
Halsey, John J., 286
Hamilton, Alexander, 27, 108, 184
"harmony of interests" doctrine, 183–184
Harper, William Rainey, 241–245, 252, 254, 257, 259, 260, 262, 263–264, 265, 343
Harrison, Charles H., 237
Harriss, W., 170
Harvard University:
    curriculum of, 96, 103–104
    economics at, 95–131
    electives system at, 12, 101, 102, 103,

111, 144, 146, 350
    Eliot as president of, 95–96, 100–103, 112, 113, 117, 120–121, 131, 273, 294, 298, 299, 315
    enrollments of, 10, 96, 104, 109, 121
    faculty of, 101, 102, 112, 120–125
    graduate program of, 113, 125–126
    Lawrence Scientific School of, 102, 202, 290, 298
    Massachusetts Institute of Technology vs., 294, 298, 299, 304, 315
    modernization of, 95–96, 100–103
    state sponsorship of, 5
    teaching methods at, 110–112, 126, 130–131
    as university, 95–96, 342
    visiting committee for, 125–126
Harvey, William H. "Coin," 257
Hatfield, Henry Rand, 277–278
Hawkins, Hugh, 102
Henley, S., 16–17
Henry, Robert, 47, 48, 49, 59
Herbst, Jurgen, 129
Herzog, F. B., 192
Higham, John, 346, 347, 354
Higher Learning in America, The (Veblen), 264–265
Hints on Banking (McVickar), 179, 185
historical materialism, 197
History of Bimetallism in the United States (Laughlin), 113
History of Political Economy (Blanqui), 69
Hobson, John A., 260
Hollander, Jacob, 224
Holman, Silas, 304
Holmes, George Frederick, 37, 38, 39
Holst, Hermann von, 208
Hopkins, Johns, 203
Howard, Burt Estes, 285, 286
Howison, George H., 297
Hughitt, Marvin, 252
hydro-static mechanisms, 160

Illustrations of Political Economy (Martineau), 143
immigration, 283, 311
income distribution, 116, 180, 183
individualism, 102, 321

Industrial Workers of the World (IWW), 279
industry:
  agriculture vs., 228–229
  concentration of, 92
  development of, 99–100, 117
  "infant," 30, 35
  specialization of, 228
"infant-industry" argument, 30, 35
inflation, 53
Ingram, John Kells, 307
inheritance tax, 197
Institutes of Economics (Andrews), 13, 88–89
"institutionalized individualism," 102
Interest Made Equity (McVickar), 180
interest rates, 34
Introduction to English Economic History and Theory, An (Ashley), 123
Introduction to Political Economy, An (Ely), 13, 331
Introduction to Public Finance (Plehn), 277
Introduction to the Study of Economics (Bullock), 70
Introduction to the Study of International Law (Woolsey), 143
Introductory Lecture (McVickar), 181–182
"invisible hand," 7, 75, 89, 129

Jackson, Andrew, 53, 78
James, Edmund J., 230–231, 235, 237, 238, 239–240, 255
  American Economic Association and, 352, 355, 357–358, 359, 362
James, William, 129
Jefferson, Thomas, 5, 15, 16, 37, 42
  Cooper and, 42, 44, 46–47, 49, 52
  economic views of, 24, 28
  educational views of, 20–21, 31, 344
  as governor, 17
  University of Virginia planned by, 15, 20–28, 31, 40, 41, 318
Jenks, Jeremiah, 281
Jevons, W. S., 229
Johns Hopkins University:
  economics at, 203–224
  Ely at, 209–220, 221–222, 224, 281, 306, 325
  faculty of, 205–213, 222–224
  fellowship program of, 204–205
  finances of, 203, 220–221
  founding of, 203–205
  Gilman as president of, 203, 205–208, 210, 211, 212, 223, 224, 244, 306, 341, 343, 354
  graduate schools of, 11, 12, 153, 201, 204, 207, 212–213, 221, 243, 342, 344, 354, 362
  practical education at, 11, 341
  publication series of, 113
  research seminars at, 212
Jones, Edward D., 330
Jones, Hugh, 16
Jordan, David Starr, 272, 280, 281, 283–284, 285, 287–288, 289
Journal of Political Economy, 165, 250–251, 255, 258–259, 261, 263, 287, 328, 345, 362

Kansas-Nebraska Act (1854), 78
Kathedersozialisten, 357
Keynes, John Maynard, 3, 130
King, Charles, 171, 175, 186
King, Clyde, 237
Kinley, David, 251, 327, 330
Knies, Karl, 199, 209
Knight, G. W., 365
Knights of Labor, 322

labor:
  capital and, 62
  child, 239
  division of, 30, 98, 180, 228–229, 340
  productive vs. unproductive, 7, 30, 75–76, 182
  value and, 51, 61–62, 75, 183
Labor Movement in America (Ely), 322, 331
"labor question," 219–220
La Follette, Robert M., 323, 335, 337, 338
land:
  marginal, 30
  rents from, 6, 29–30, 36, 51–52, 62, 76, 95, 183, 234, 302
landlords, 233–234
Laughlin, J. Laurence, 13, 69, 109, 110–111, 112–113, 127, 276

American Economic Association and,
248, 261, 263, 360, 362, 367, 371
in Bemis affair, 251, 252–253
economic views of, 257–258, 259,
261
at University of Chicago, 248, 249,
250, 251, 252–253, 255, 256,
260–262, 265, 278
Veblen and, 263, 264
Laws of Wages, Profits, and Rent, Investigated, The (Tucker), 29
"lecture-and-examination" method, 63
*Lectures on the Elements of Political
Economy* (Cooper), 7–8, 49–50, 52,
53, 60
Lectures on the Restrictive System (Dew),
34–35, 36, 51
Leslie, Cliffe, 12, 108
Levermore, Charles H., 216, 313
Lewis, William Draper, 237
liberalism, 322
Lieber, Francis, 43, 50, 149
academic career of, 58–59, 64–66
at Columbia University, 169,
173–174, 176, 185–188, 189, 190,
195, 200
economic views of, 60–62, 143,
186–188
political views of, 60, 61, 63–64,
66–67
at South Carolina College, 58–67,
70–71
as teacher, 63
Lincoln, Abraham, 268
List, Friedrich, 9, 52
Locke, John, 18, 44
Lomax, John Tayloe, 27, 29
Longstreet, Augustus, 67
Lorenz, Max, 334
Low, Seth, 193, 199
Lowell, Abbot Lawrence, 111–112
Lowell, Francis Cabot, 292–293
Lowell, John Amory, 292
Lowell Institute, 292
Luddites, 75

McCarthy, Charles, 335, 336, 337
McCay, Charles, 66, 67
McClellan, George B., 268
McCrea, Roswell, 237

McCulloch, J. R., 49, 75, 180, 182, 183
McCulloh, Richard, 171
McCutchen, George, 69–70
McGuffey, William Holmes, 38, 39
McKinley, William, 93
Maclaurin, Richard Cockburn, 316, 317
McLean, Simon James, 286
Macvane, Silas Marcus, 108–109, 116,
118
McVickar, John, 49, 169, 171, 172, 173,
175
economic views of, 179–185
as teacher, 177–179, 187, 189, 195,
200
Madison, James (bishop), 15, 17–20, 38,
40
Madison, James (president), 25, 27, 344
Malthus, Thomas Robert, 7, 17, 29–30,
31, 51, 77, 95, 120
"mandarinism," 147
"Manifestations of the Beneficence of Divine Providence towards America"
(Madison), 19
*Manual for Political Economy for
Schools and Colleges* (Rogers), 188,
194
Manual of Political Economy, A
(Cooper), 50
Manual of Political Ethics (Lieber), 61
Marcet, Jane, 49, 53
marginal analysis, 116–117, 120, 234,
303
marginal utility doctrine, 160–161, 200,
232
market dynamics, 30, 238
Marshall, Alfred, 117, 163, 195, 308,
366
Marshall, John, 27
Martineau, Harriet, 143
Marx, Karl, 131, 156, 196, 197, 332
Mason, John M., 170
Massachusetts Institute of Technology
(MIT):
Course IX at, 295–297, 305–306,
313, 314, 315–316
economics at, 290
engineering studies at, 293–295
faculty of, 299, 314–315
finances of, 297, 299
founding of, 290–296

MIT (*continued*)
  Harvard vs., 294, 298, 299, 304, 315
  President's Reports of, 304, 308, 314
  scientific instruction at, 291, 293,
    304–305
  student body of, 305
  Walker's influence on, 299–315
materialism, 50, 54, 186, 197, 343
Maxcy, Jonathan, 47, 48
Mayo-Smith, Richmond, 188, 191,
  194–197, 198, 200, 201
Meade, William, 19
mercantilist system, 30, 180, 186, 188
Messer, Asa, 73
metaphysics, 48–49, 59
Methodists, 56
Metzger, Walter, 369
Meyer, Balthasar H., 336
Meyer, Hugo R., 262
microeconomic theory, 232
Miles, William P., 68–69
Mill, John Stuart, 13, 58, 68, 87, 97,
  105, 107, 108, 109, 110, 111, 112,
  149, 160, 195, 234, 248, 261, 300,
  321
Miller, Adolph C., 249, 256, 258, 260,
  262, 263, 273, 276, 277, 280, 285
Miller, Samuel, 18
Millis, Harry A., 286, 288
Mitchell, Wesley C., 256, 260, 262, 263,
  277–278, 280
Modern Distributive Process, The, (Giddings and Clark), 199
monetary policy, 30, 53, 75, 92, 106,
  108, 114, 150, 257, 259
money supply, 257
monometallism, 92, 248
monopolies, 108, 151, 162, 254, 328,
  335
Montesquieu, Charles de Secondat,
  Baron de La Brède et de, 134
Montgomery, Benjamin R., 48
moral philosophy, 48, 95, 120, 127,
  128–129, 234
Morrill Act (1862), 11, 268, 320, 342
Morrison, Robert J., 37
Moses, Bernard, 273–276
"mugwumps," 231, 235, 236

Nairne, Charles Murray, 174, 176, 186,
  188
Nation, 214, 329
National Academy of Science, 194
National Bank and Subtreasury, U.S., 36
National Civic Federation, 332
nationalism, 65, 311
National Municipal League, 231
"national system" doctrine, 9, 362
National Teachers' Association, 344
natural laws, 200
natural philosophy, 19
Nearing, Scott, 237, 238–239
Newcomb, Simon, 209, 213–220, 223,
  356, 358, 360
"Newcomb on Mathematical Economy,"
  216
New Princeton Review, 198
New Republican party, 225
"new statesmanship," 188
New York Times, 301
New York University, 174, 177
New York World, 254
Niles, William, 315
North Carolina, University of, 5
Northwest Ordinance (1787), 318
Norton, John Pitkin, 139–140
"Notes on Fallacies of American Protec-
  tionists" (Lieber), 61, 187–188
nullification crisis, 55

"Objects and Plan for an Institute of
  Technology," 294
Ogden, Gouverneur, 171, 191
On Civil Liberty and Self-government
  (Lieber), 61, 64
"On the Possibility of Applying Mathe-
  matics to Political Economy"
  (Newcomb), 215–216
On the Proposed Alteration of the Tariff
  (Cooper), 50
"opportunity costs," 79
"Our Colleges Before the Country"
  (Sumner), 147
Outlines of Economics (Ely), 333
Outlines of Political Economy
  (McVickar), 179, 180, 182–185
Owen, Robert, 196

Page, Thomas Walker, 38
Paine, Thomas, 18, 44
Paley, William, 48, 134
Palmer, John M., 366
Parker, Carleton, 278, 279
Parkinson, John B., 324, 325, 328
Parsons, Talcott, 102
Past and Present of Political Economy, The (Ely), 214–215
Patten, Simon Nelson:
  American Economic Association and, 352, 355, 357–358, 359, 362
  economic views of, 231–236, 352
  influence of, 236–240, 327
Peabody, Francis, 126, 129
Peixotto, Jessica, 275, 278, 288
Pelham, Charles, 67
Pennsylvania, University of:
  classical curriculum of, 226
  economics at, 225–240
  expansion of, 229–232
  founding of, 225–226
  graduate program of, 236
  "national system" doctrine and, 9, 362
  Patten's influence on, 236–240
  Philadelphia business community and, 225, 226–227, 229, 238
  protectionism as issue at, 225, 226–229, 231, 238
  religious influence on, 225–226
  research seminars at, 236
  trustees of, 226, 238–239
  Wharton School of, 227, 228, 229, 230, 232, 237–238, 324
Perry, Arthur L., 13, 69, 87, 149
philanthropy, 343
Philosophy of Wealth, The (Clark), 200
"Plan for a Polytechnic School in Boston, A" (Rogers), 292
Plato, 122
Platt, Gerald, 102
Plehn, Carl Copping, 276–277
"Political Economy" (McCulloch), 180
Political Economy (Walker), 272, 281, 302
Political Economy for Beginners (Fawcett), 188
Political Economy Club, 112, 150, 209, 360, 361

Political Essays (Cooper), 50
political philosophy, 61
Political Science Association, 364–365
Political Science Quarterly, 114, 165, 197, 198–199
population:
  census of, 301, 302, 304
  growth of, 7, 29–30, 31, 36, 51, 77, 95, 128–129
Populist movement, 131, 257, 365–366
Porter, Noah, 143–145, 147, 148
poverty, 77
Powers, H. H., 367
Presbyterians, 21, 25, 46, 56, 60
Present State of Virginia, The (Jones), 16
prices:
  control of, 325
  "fair," 162
  levels of, 257
  market, 116, 180, 183, 234
  natural, 183
price-specie flow, 53
Priestley, Joseph, 21–22, 42, 44
Princeton Review, 215
Principles of Economics (Fetter), 70
Principles of Economics (Marshall), 163, 195, 366
Principles of Economics (Taussig), 126
Principles of Inland Transportation (Daggett), 279
Principles of Moral and Political Philosophy (Paley), 48, 134
Principles of Political Economy (Gide), 69
Principles of Political Economy (Mill), 13, 69, 87, 97, 149, 195, 248
Principles of Political Economy (Newcomb), 214, 217
Principles of Political Economy, The (Bowen), 97–98
Principles of Social Science (Carey), 127
Pritchett, Henry Smith, 315–316
prizes, academic, 81
Problem of Monopoly, The (Clark), 200
Problems of Political Economy (Sumner), 13
Problems of Today (Ely), 13
product differentiation, 8
production costs, 161–162, 301

productivity, 80, 228, 233
profits, wages and, 183–184
Progress and Poverty (George), 274
Progressive movement, 103, 237–238,
    239, 240, 310, 311, 318, 323,
    334–337, 366
Prohibition movement, 322
property, private, 75
protectionism, 9, 34, 35, 52, 92,
    99–100, 115–116, 149, 187–188,
    349–350, 362, 372
    as issue at University of Pennsylvania,
    225, 226–229, 231, 238
public finance, 62, 127, 197
Public Finance (Bastable), 313
Pullman strike, 252, 257, 329
Puritans, 235

quantity theory, 257
Quarterly Journal of Economics, 96,
    113–117, 118, 119, 123, 165, 198,
    334, 362

Radical Republican party, 62, 68
Railroad Transportation (Hadley), 157
Railroad Transportation Question, The
    (Herzog), 192
railway industry, 161, 252–253,
    262–263
Raymond, George, 9
Reconstruction era, 37–38, 39, 62,
    67–68
"Relation of the Economist to the Public,
    The" (Newcomb), 223
Rensselaer Institute, 293
rents, land, 6, 29–30, 36, 51–52, 62,
    76, 95, 183, 234, 302
"Report on a Course of Liberal Educa-
    tion," 138
Republican party, 62, 68, 225, 231,
    337–338
returns, diminishing, 228, 232
*Review and Commentary upon Montes-
    quieu* (Tracy), 33
*Review of the Debates in the Virginia
    Legislature* (Dew), 34
Ricardo, David, 6–7, 30, 31, 35, 36,
    51–52, 54, 61, 63, 76, 95, 131, 180,
    183, 184, 226, 228, 232–234, 235,
    302, 358

Rice, Isaac, 193
Richards, Robert H., 315
Rights of Man (Paine), 18
Ringer, Fritz, 128
Ripley, William Z., 125, 314, 315, 316
Roberts, T. N., 68
Rockefeller, John D., 241, 242
Rockfish Gap Commission, 25–26
Rogers, Henry, 291, 292, 293
Rogers, J. E. T., 188, 194
Rogers, William Barton, 290–296,
    297–298, 299, 304
Roosevelt, Franklin D., 131
Rosengarten, Joseph, 239
Ross, Edward Alsworth, 281, 282–284,
    285, 286, 289, 333, 363, 367
Rousseau, Jean Jacques, 18, 33, 44
Ruggles, Samuel B., 171–172, 185–186,
    187, 189, 190, 191, 194
Runkle, John D., 294, 297–298, 299

San Francisco Chronicle, 285–286
Say, Jean-Baptiste, 6, 26, 29, 30, 31, 50,
    60–61, 63, 67, 68, 74, 75, 187
"Saybrook Confession of Faith," 134,
    137
scale economies, 31
School and Society (Dewey), 341
Schwab, John C., 149, 154, 157–158,
    160, 163, 164, 165
Science, 218, 356, 360, 367
Science of Wealth, The (Walker), 13, 87,
    143, 152, 297, 301
Scott, William A., 326, 327
Sears, Barnas, 86
secessionists, 56–57, 59, 61, 62, 63–64,
    66
Sedgwick, William T., 304
Seelye, Julius H., 189
Seligman, Edwin R. A., 93, 164,
    196–198, 200, 201, 372
"sensualists," 235, 236
services sector, 75
Shaw, Albert, 217, 220, 246, 327, 328
Shaw, George Bernard, 114
Shaw, William B., 116, 117
Sherwood, Sidney, 222–223, 224
Silliman, Benjamin, 59, 136–137, 138
silver standard, 92, 93, 257, 283,
    365–366

slavery, 7–8, 15, 30, 31, 34, 35, 40–41,
    52–53, 55, 58, 60, 62, 63, 64, 66–67,
    78, 189, 318–319
Sloan, Alfred P., 317
Small, Albion, 250, 253, 255
Small, William, 16
Smith, Adam, 5, 15, 18–20, 33, 51, 52,
    54, 62, 75, 95, 97, 128, 129, 180, 182,
    188, 228, 234, 349, 350
Smith, John Augustine, 33–34
Smith, Mary Roberts, 286
Smith, Munroe, 176, 191, 194, 198
Social Darwinism, 104, 129, 148–149,
    160, 162, 368
social effective utility, 200
social ethics, 126
Social Gospel movement, 358
socialism, 88, 89, 92–93, 149, 162, 201,
    218, 283, 322, 328, 357, 358–359
Social Science and National Economy
    (Thompson), 227–228
"social technologies," 310
sociology, 199
"Some Lessons of the Strike," 252
"sound money," 257, 259
South Carolina College:
    academic freedom at, 71
    Board of Visitors of, 46
    Cooper's influence on, 42–58, 70–71,
        185
    economics at, 25–26, 42–71
    enrollments of, 57–58
    faculty salaries at, 43
    finances of, 43, 44–45, 46, 54–55
    founding of, 43, 45
    Lieber's influence on, 58–67, 70–71
    low-country aristocratic support for,
        46, 56, 69
    in Reconstruction era, 67–68
    religious influence on, 45, 46, 47,
        48–49, 55–56, 57, 59, 64
    as southern institution, 46, 54–55, 64,
        67
    state funding of, 45, 46
    student body of, 48–49
    trustees of, 47, 59, 65, 66
Southern Pacific railroad, 284
Spencer, Herbert, 148, 149
Spirit of the Laws (Montesquieu), 134
Sprague, O. M. W., 125

Springfield Republican, 301, 372
"stalwarts," 235, 236, 338
Stanford, Jane, 272, 281, 283–284, 289
Stanford, Leland, 271–272, 280, 284
Stanford University:
    economics at, 280–289
    faculty of, 273, 280, 285–286
    finances of, 12, 269, 270, 271–272,
        280, 289
    founding of, 271–273
    as nontuition institution, 272
    private endowment of, 12, 271–272,
        280
    Ross incident at, 283–284, 285, 286,
        289
    student body of, 273
    University of California vs., 270–271,
        273, 276, 288–289
states' rights, 56–57, 63–64
Statistical Atlas (1874), 301
statistics, 301, 302, 307, 356, 359
Steffens, Lincoln, 335
Stewart, Dugald, 22
Stiles, Ezra, 134, 136
Stotesbury, Edward, 239
Strong, George, 171, 187
Study of Sociology (Spencer), 148
Sumner, Helen Laura, 334
Sumner, William Graham, 13, 143
    as administrator, 152, 153, 154, 157,
        158, 159, 164, 168
    as economist, 145–151, 179, 303,
        360, 362, 368
sumptuary laws, 31
supply and demand, 51, 61–62, 118,
    128, 183
Sur l'éducation nationale dans les Etats-
    Unis d'Amerique (Du Pont), 22
Swain, George F., 304
Swope, Gerard, 317
Syllabus (Smith), 33–34

tariffs, 8–9, 30, 52, 55, 56, 92, 99, 108,
    115–116, 127, 131, 180, 233, 238
Taussig, Frank William, 281, 360, 362
    economic views of, 109, 110–112,
        119–120, 123, 128, 129–130
    educational views of, 103, 110–112,
        131

Taussig, Frank William (*continued*)
  influence of, 113, 114, 117, 124,
    126–127, 131
taxation, 93, 185, 197
Thayer, John E., 113
Theory of Business Enterprise (Veblen),
  262, 287
Theory and History of Banking (Dunbar), 70
Theory of the Leisure Class, The
  (Veblen), 258, 287
Theory of Money and Banks Investigated
  (Tucker), 29
Theory of the Leisure Class, The
  (Veblen), 258, 287
Thompson, Robert Ellis, 227–228,
  229–230, 231, 239
Thornwell, James, 64, 66
Thoughts on the Present Collegiate System in the United States (Wayland),
  78–81
Tillman, "Pitchfork Ben," 69
Tracy, Antoine Destutt de, 15, 22, 24, 27
trade, international, 53, 228
Treaties on Political Economy (Say), 6,
  60–61, 63, 68, 187
Treatise on Political Economy (Tracy),
  15, 24, 27
trusts, 151, 309
Tucker, Beverley, 37
Tucker, George, 15, 27, 28–32, 38, 39,
  41
Turner, Frederick Jackson, 325, 330
Tyler, Lyon G., 38

unemployment, 75
Unionists, 57, 59, 60, 62, 66
unions, labor, 93, 219–220, 279,
  309–310, 322, 329, 332, 333
Unitarians, 46, 73, 101
unit costs, 161
universities, *see* colleges and universities
usury laws, 30, 33
utilitarianism, 50, 321
utilities, public, 117, 283
utility, 233

value:
  labor and, 51, 61–62, 75, 183
  theory of, 116–117, 128

Van Hise, Charles R., 323, 334, 336, 338
Veblen, Thorstein, 116, 117, 199, 288
  economic views of, 258, 262, 287, 372
  educational reform as viewed by,
    264–265, 341, 343
  Laughlin and, 263, 264
  at Stanford University, 286–287
  as teacher, 256–257, 262
  at University of Chicago, 249,
    256–257, 258, 262, 263–265
  unorthodox life-style of, 263,
    287–288
Verein für Sozialpolitik, 230, 307, 352,
  355, 357, 359
Vethake, Henry, 226, 238
Veysey, Laurence, 280–281
Virginia, University of:
  Board of Visitors of, 25, 26
  economics at, 15–16, 20–32, 37,
    38–40, 41
  electives system at, 6
  enrollments of, 10
  founding of, 23, 25–28
  funding of, 23–24, 39–40
  Jefferson's plans for, 15, 20–28, 31,
    40, 41, 318
  lecture system of, 31
  Literary Fund for, 23–24, 25
  modern curriculum of, 5–6, 21–22,
    26–27
  in Reconstruction era, 39
  student body of, 28, 39
  Tucker's influence on, 28–32

Wadsworth, James, 179
wages, 62, 183–184
Wages and Capital (Taussig), 119–120
wages-fund issue, 111, 116, 117–120,
  131, 302
Wages Question, The (Walker), 302
Wagner, Adolph, 156
Walker, Amasa, 13, 87, 143, 152, 297,
  300–301
Walker, Francis Amasa, 13, 116, 118,
  143, 272, 281
  economic views of, 302–303,
    307–312
  as lecturer at Johns Hopkins, 206, 224,
    303–304
  as president of American Economic As-

sociation, 216–217, 360, 361–362,
363
as president of Massachusetts Institute
of Technology, 299–315
at Yale, 151–153, 155, 168, 206–207,
208, 302–304, 305
Wanderjahren, 350–351
Ward, Lester, 368
Warner, Amos G., 246, 281–282, 284,
327, 328
Washington, George, 344
Washington, Henry Augustine, 37
Wayland, Francis, 7, 68, 87, 143, 188
at Brown University, 72–86
economic views of, 74–78, 94
as educational reformer, 73–74,
78–88, 265
political views of, 77–78
religious views of, 74–75
wealth:
labor and, 98, 228
national, 183
natural, 105
production of, 179
theory of, 29, 75
Wealth of Nations, The (Smith), 5, 15,
18–20, 33, 97
Webb, Sidney, 113–114
Wells, David A., 125, 301
Wells, Oliver E., 329
Wharton, Joseph, 227, 231, 234
Wheeler, Benjamin Ide, 273, 277, 289
Whitaker, Albert Conser, 286, 288
White, Andrew D., 209, 210, 343
Wildman, Murray Shipley, 288
William and Mary, College of:
curriculum of, 32–33
Dew's lectures at, 34–37
early history of, 16–17
economics at, 5, 15–20, 32–38,
40–41
educational reforms at, 21
enrollments of, 37
founding of, 16
Normal School for Men of, 38
in Reconstruction era, 37–38
in Revolutionary War, 17
teaching methods at, 18–19
textbooks used by, 32, 33

Wilson, Woodrow, 310
Wines, F. W., 327
Wisconsin, University of:
"bill factory" at, 335–336
Board of Regents of, 319, 323,
324–325, 328, 329, 330
coeducation at, 320
curriculum of, 319–320, 323–325,
331
economics at, 318–339
educational reform at, 318, 322–324
Ely at, 325–330, 331, 333, 334, 337,
338
enrollments of, 320, 329–330
extension courses offered by, 324, 328,
334
faculty of, 327–328, 330
finances of, 319, 338
founding of, 319–320
graduate program of, 324, 325, 328,
330
institutionalism at, 332
research published by, 334–335
research seminars at, 327
student body of, 319, 320, 325, 333
"Wisconsin Idea" of, 318, 334–339
Wisconsin's relations with, 334–338
women's rights, 322
Wood, Stuart, 117, 127
Woolsey, Theodore, 143
working conditions, 274, 275, 276, 278
workingmen's compensation, 335
Wythe, George, 17

Yale, Elihu, 132
Yale Review, 164–166
Yale University:
academic freedom at, 148
classical curriculum of, 6, 12,
132–137, 138, 142, 144, 158
conservatism of, 135, 136, 168, 342,
349
degrees awarded by, 141, 152, 158,
159
departments of, 136, 140, 162–163
economics at, 132–168
educational reform at, 135, 137–139,
141–142, 144–147, 166–168
enrollments of, 10, 153, 159

Yale University (*continued*)
faculty of, 134, 150
graduate program of, 152–153, 163
modernization of, 134–135, 139, 144, 167–168
optionals system at, 146–147, 154, 158
religious influence on, 132–133, 134, 137, 166
research seminars at, 158
Sheffield Scientific School of, 139–143, 144, 151, 155, 158, 168, 202, 204, 269, 290, 302, 303–304
state funding of, 5, 132, 135, 138
student body of, 133–134, 140, 163
Walker at, 151–153, 155, 168, 206–207, 208, 302–304, 305
Young, Allyn A., 127, 286, 288, 333–334
Young Yale movement, 144–145

Contributors

Richard P. Adelstein is Associate Professor of Economics, Wesleyan University.

William J. Barber is Andrews Professor of Economics, Wesleyan University.

Michael D. Bordo is Professor of Economics, University of South Carolina.

A. W. Coats is Research Professor of Economics, Duke University, and Emeritus Professor of Economic and Social History, University of Nottingham.

Mary E. Cookingham is Associate Professor of Economics, Michigan State University.

John P. Henderson is Professor of Economics, Michigan State University.

Byrd L. Jones is Professor of Education, University of Massachusetts, Amherst.

William H. Phillips is Associate Professor of Economics, University of South Carolina.

Franek Rozwadowski is Assistant Professor of Economics, Wesleyan University.

Steven A. Sass is Research Associate, Pension Research Council, The Wharton School, University of Pennsylvania, and Adjunct Lecturer, The Heller School, Brandeis University.

John K. Whitaker is Paul Goodloe McIntyre Professor of Economics, University of Virginia.

About the Book

Breaking the Academic Mould was composed in Sabon by G & S Typesetters of Austin, Texas, and printed and bound by McNaughton & Gunn of Ann Arbor, Michigan. The design is by Kachergis Book Design & Production, Inc. of Pittsboro, North Carolina.

Wesleyan University Press, 1988